The Presence of Others

Voices and Images
That Call for Response

FIFTH EDITION

The Presence of Others

Voices and Images
That Call for Response

ANDREA A. LUNSFORD
Stanford University

JOHN J. RUSZKIEWICZ
The University of Texas at Austin

BEDFORD/ST. MARTIN'S
Boston ◆ New York

For Bedford/St. Martin's

Developmental Editor: Carolyn Lengel
Production Editor: Bernard Onken
Production Supervisor: Sarah Ulicny
Senior Marketing Manager: Karita dos Santos
Art Director: Lucy Krikorian
Copy Editor: Diana Puglisi George
Indexer: Kirsten Kite
Photo Research: Linda Finigan
Cover Design: Donna Dennison
Composition: ICC Macmillan Inc.
Printing and Binding: R.R. Donnelley & Sons Company

President: Joan E. Feinberg
Editorial Director: Denise B. Wydra
Editor in Chief: Karen S. Henry
Director of Development: Erica T. Appel
Director of Marketing: Karen Melton Soeltz
Director of Editing, Design, and Production: Marcia Cohen
Managing Editor: Shuli Traub

Library of Congress Control Number: 2007905817

Manufactured in the United States of America.

2   1   0   9   8   7
f   e   d   c   b   a

For information, write: Bedford/St. Martin's, 75 Arlington Street, Boston, MA 02116   (617-399-4000)

ISBN-10: 0-312-46439-8
ISBN-13: 978-0-312-46439-4

Acknowledgments

Acknowledgments and copyrights appear at the back of the book on pages 691–94, which constitute an extension of the copyright page.

It is a violation of the law to reproduce these selections by any means whatsoever without the written permission of the copyright holder.

Preface

"For excellence," writes philosopher Hannah Arendt, "the presence of others is always required." Not genius, she tells us, not divine inspiration, not even good old-fashioned hard work, but *others*. In choosing a title for this text, we thought of Arendt's statement, because this book aims to lead students toward excellence in reading and writing, toward excellence in thinking through difficult ideas and topics, and toward excellence in articulating their own positions on issues and providing good reasons for supporting those positions, always in relation to other people's thoughts, words, and images.

Given these aims, we have been delighted at the response from those using the first four editions of *The Presence of Others*: teachers and students report that they have indeed been spurred to react to the many perspectives presented in the text, saying "yes" to some, and "no" or even "maybe" to others. They have been moved to think hard about these differing viewpoints and about their own positions. Equally important, they tell us that the multiple — and often competing — voices and views in this text call out for response, leading from reading and thinking to writing and often back again.

Two of the voices calling out for response in this book belong to us, the editors, Andrea Lunsford and John Ruszkiewicz. Longtime friends, we take very different views on most issues, and we make many of those views and opinions known in *The Presence of Others*. But disagreement, conflict, and agonism are not guiding principles of this book. It is not a tennis match of ideas, one that will yield winners and losers. Rather, we are interested in how we all come to know and to take stances on various issues, how we can nurture productive exchanges of ideas. These are the kinds of open discussions the readings from *The Presence of Others* have generated in our own classes.

So we invite readers to join the conversation yet again: to question, challenge, and delight in many points of view, including our own. For this fifth edition, we've tried our best to provide a balanced set of readings that represent widely varying opinions on the ideas and topics that shape our times — ranging from education to ethics, from science and technology to the world of business and labor. Many of these provocative readings will likely surprise anyone who believes that attitudes can be predicted by labels as equivocal as "liberal" or "conservative" — just as we have been surprised by the complex positions students have taken in our classes.

The Presence of Others thus aims to open and sustain animated conversation among more than seventy readings; the editors, students, and professionals whose commentaries accompany some readings; and the teachers and students who we hope will put forth their own ideas and responses. To encourage this engagement, we offer a variety of pedagogical features.

NOTABLE FEATURES

A *balance of viewpoints* gives every student ideas to support and to dispute. Readings represent many genres as well — op-ed pieces, speeches, letters, short fiction, poems, memoirs, reports, satires, mission statements, Web documents, photographs, and comics, as well as essays and articles — and they take a wide range of varying and sometimes opposing perspectives. In Chapter 6 on identities, for instance, Dave Barry and Maxine Hong Kingston rub conversational shoulders with Zora Neale Hurston, Andrew Sullivan, and Lynda Barry. Cross-references throughout lead readers back and forth among the readings, drawing them deeper into the discussion.

The *editorial apparatus* encourages students to join the conversation as well. Headnotes to each reading provide background information and offer some explanation for our editorial choices. Because these introductions often offer our own strong opinions about the selection, each one is signed with our respective initials. The selections are followed by sequences of questions that ask students to challenge the text (and sometimes the headnote), to make connections with other readings, and to join the conversation by writing. One or more of the questions in each reading is designed for group work, which we hope will encourage further dialogue and make the presence of others evident right there in the classroom.

An *annotated reading* in each chapter includes commentary by the editors and student commentators, demonstrating how to ask critical questions and read with a critical eye.

A *consistent emphasis on reading images and visual rhetoric* throughout *The Presence of Others* helps students to consider how images achieve their power and how written and visual texts work together. The visual text that opens each thematic chapter is accompanied by questions to help students read images critically. A few selections are accompanied by their original illustration(s), enabling students to consider how written and visual texts work together. The fifth edition includes over thirty visual texts, some in full color, for students to respond to and analyze.

Chapters 1 and 2 provide strategies on *reading and thinking critically* and on *moving from reading to writing*. In addition, guidelines for writing a critical response essay and two sample student essays appear in Chapter 2, showing students how they might respond in writing to what they have read.

Readings from online sources and *material on the challenges of reading and writing online* in the introductory chapters guide students in thinking critically about how texts and rhetorical strategies differ between online and print media.

A companion Web site, **bedfordstmartins.com/presenceofothers**, offers students the best and most current Internet links for further research on the ideas presented in *The Presence of Others*. The accompanying *Guide for Teachers*, written by Melissa Goldthwaite and revised by Sharan Daniel and, for the fifth edition, by John Kinkade, provides detailed advice for teaching this book, including commentary on each selection, sequenced reading and writing assignments, and a selection of essays and articles regarding current controversies over the college curriculum.

NEW TO THIS EDITION

- **New commentaries — two in each chapter — by professionals in various fields and academics in disciplines other than English** help readers appreciate how complex and multidimensional almost every issue and argument can be. Commentaries from a psychologist, a filmmaker, a physician, a labor lawyer, and a biology teacher, and from professors of economics, sociology, education, psychology, public health, history, and art history, suggest the wide variety of approaches to reading, writing, and thinking about issues that can be useful in academic and professional life.

- **Thirty-two fresh, new readings** offer a diverse collection of views and authors on the thought-provoking topics that shape our world. Among the authors and topics newly represented are Christina Hoff Sommers and Katha Pollitt on the problems of boys in American culture; Denise Grady on treating those injured in war; Sherman Alexie on Sacagawea; and John Leo on freedom of speech on U.S. campuses.

- **A refocused chapter on "Business and Labor"** broadens the perspective on working life in the United States. The chapter examines conditions of the workplace, focusing on issues of equity and safety (it includes a full chapter from Eric Schlosser's *Fast Food Nation*) — but it also considers that the business of America remains business, often to our benefit.

- **A new full-color photo essay, Dulce Pinzón's "The Real Story of the Superheroes,"** features Mexican immigrants going about their everyday work with one twist: they are dressed in superhero garb. Pinzón's images, which challenge the traditional American cultural icon of the comic-book superhero, are accompanied by questions that ask readers to examine, evaluate, and even challenge reigning myths about heroes, about superheroes, and about immigrants and the roles they play in the United States.

ACKNOWLEDGMENTS

This anthology has changed considerably in the fourteen years since we first began exploring its possibilities, primarily because of the presence of many, many others whose perspectives and voices echo in these pages. Of great importance have been the extensive support and ongoing spirited conversation we have received from the Bedford/St. Martin's staff, and particularly from editor Carolyn Lengel, who shouldered much of the burden of this new edition. We deeply appreciate her skill, organization, and creativity. We also thank managing editor Shuli Traub and project editor Bernard Onken, who managed this project with aplomb. For this edition, we are especially grateful for the insights and extensive legwork of photo researcher Linda Finigan.

In addition to these friends at Bedford/St. Martin's, we are indebted to many colleagues: to Professor John Kinkade of Centre College, who assisted in searching for the best possible readings, in writing the accompanying apparatus, and in updating and revising the *Guide for Teachers* for the fifth edition; to Sharan Daniel, who revised the *Guide for Teachers* in the fourth edition; and to Melissa A. Goldthwaite of Saint Joseph's University, who prepared earlier editions of the *Guide for Teachers*. This manual we believe to be thoroughly informed by contemporary writing and reading theories as well as by the authors' practical experience from having taught the materials in the text.

We are particularly grateful to the students who agreed to add their voices to this text: John Erik Metcalf and Joshua G. Rushing from the University of Texas at Austin, and Lindsay Schauer and Beatrice Kim from Stanford University. And we salute as well the many other students who have taught us over the years how to be better classroom colleagues. In many subtle ways, their voices are everywhere present in this text.

For their help in finding respondents from other disciplines and professions, we also want to express our thanks to Ester Bloom, Stephanie Butler, Heidi Hood, Nancy Perry, and Sara Wise from Bedford/St. Martin's and to Sharon Balbos, Kevin Feyen, Erik Gilg, and Mimi Melek from Worth Publishers. And particular gratitude goes to the respondents themselves: Robert C. Bulman, Marjorie Butler, Treena Crochet, Rosemary Thomas Cunningham, Lisa D. Galynker, Michelle Gittler, Kareem J. Johnson, Russell Kirby, Donna Light-Donovan, Timothy J. Shannon, Bonnie S. Sunstein, and Jan Weber. Their unique perspectives, thoughtful insights, and fine writing have added much to the scope of the book.

Finally, we have been instructed and guided by extraordinarily astute reviewers, with whom we have been in conversation throughout this project. We thank Judith Angona, Ocean County Community College; Susan H. Aylsworth, California State University, Chico; Mary McAleer Balkun, Seton Hall University; Alan Bart Cameron, Bronx Community College of The City University of New York; Amy A. Childers, North Georgia College & State University; Deborah Coxwell-Teague, Florida State University; Stacy

M. Clanton, Southern Arkansas University; Dennis Daniels, University of Michigan–Dearborn; Kevin Davis, East Central University; Chidsey Dickson, Christopher Newport University; Michelle Dowd, Chaffey College; Mara Fagin, Modesto Junior College; Deborah Fleming, Ashland University; Debra Fletcher, University of Michigan–Dearborn; Todd Fox, California State University, Long Beach; Richard Frohock, Oklahoma State University; Megan Fulwiler, The College of Saint Rose; Philip Gaines, Montana State University; Susan Gerson, Fairleigh Dickinson University; Kevin Gibley, Indiana University–South Bend; Michael Goins, Cy-Fair College; Gary R. Hafer, Lycoming College; Tracy Hudson, Winthrop University; Mary G. Jackson, St. Mary's University; Mary Kasimer, St. Cloud Technical College; Dennis Keen, Spokane Community College; Marsha B. Kruger, University of Nebraska at Omaha; John Larkin, Castleton State; Gary M. Levine, Ashland University; Theresa Madden, Howard Community College; Renee H. Major, Louisiana State University; Bobby L. Matthews, Louisiana State University; Vickie Melograno, Atlantic Cape Community College; Linda F. Mercer, University of Cincinnati; Daniel Melzer, Florida State University; Linda Trinh Moser, Missouri State University; Jamili Omar, Cy-Fair College; Marisa Anne Pagnattaro, University of Georgia; Kris Peleg, Century College; Melissa Simko Sanders, University of Cincinnati; Julie Sanford, Roosevelt University; Melissa Scully, St. Mary's University; Tracey Teets Schwarze, Christopher Newport University; Mary Ann Duncan Simmons, University of North Carolina–Wilmington; Shelina Shariff, Northern Kentucky University; Katherine S. Taylor, Front Range Community College; Linda Tucker, Southern Arkansas University; Leonard King Vandegrift IV, California State Polytechnic–Pomona; Lisa Wilde, Howard Community College; and John M. Yozzo, East Central University.

Andrea A. Lunsford
John J. Ruszkiewicz

Contents

"If then a practical end must be assigned to a University course, I say it is that of training good members of society."

"Our graduates will have an understanding of interdependence and global competence, distinctive technical and educational skills, the experience and abilities to contribute to California's high-quality work force, the critical thinking abilities to be productive citizens, and the social responsibility and skills to be community builders."

"The American tradition, in learning as well as jazz and activism, is improvisatory. There are as many ways to become an educated American as there are Americans."

"[O]ne of the most important conversations in the history of education is about 'the key of life': how does learning work inside school? How does it work outside of school? Is there a connection? Is it nature or nurture that makes us grow? And whatever the proportions of each, how does a school allow for both?"

"What does a woman need to know to become a self-conscious, self-defining human being?"

"Science, or knowledge production more generally, has always had deep connections to the general political economy of its time. . . . Thus, we cannot argue for some untainted 'ivory tower' or 'golden age' of institutional independence. We need instead to articulate the values and goals that should direct a wide range of commercial ventures on campus."

"If the canon itself is the answer to our educational inequities, why has it historically invited few and denied many?"

"Research on 'stereotype threat' has demonstrated that subtly reminding people of negative stereotypes about their group can adversely affect their cognitive performance.... [T]he effects occur even if participants do not endorse the stereotype. Simply being aware of the stereotype and having it mentally activated is enough to cause significant cognitive and behavioral consequences."

"We real cool. We
left school. . . ."

"I have tried to make clear that it is wrong to use immoral means to attain moral ends. But now I must affirm that it is just as wrong, or perhaps even more so, to use moral means to preserve immoral ends."

"We, the People of the United States, who a little over two hundred years ago ordained and established the Constitution, have a serious problem: too many of us nowadays neither mean what we say nor say what we mean."

"All over the world most women who can't have children must simply accept the fact and adopt, or find other roles in society. But especially here in the United States wealth can enable such couples to have a child of their own and to determine how closely that child will resemble the one they might have had — or the one they dream of having."

"Cheating *is* an answer. . . . It might not be a good answer, but none the less it is an answer."

". . . [M]orality is an artifact of human culture, devised to help us negotiate social relations. It's very good for that. But just as we recognize that nature doesn't provide an adequate guide for human social conduct, isn't it anthropocentric to assume that our moral system offers an adequate guide for nature?"

"I went back to college to become a labor lawyer precisely to fight for the rights of workers on the job. I never forgot the lessons from the line: that people from all over the world come here to work and feed their families, that workers deserve to be treated with dignity, that bodies can be pushed and pushed and pushed for more production until they break, and that most injuries are caused by poor safety conditions or poor training and are preventable."

"Ever since Merck announced . . . that the pain reliever Vioxx could be linked to an increased risk of strokes or heart attacks, ads from lawyers trolling for potential plaintiffs ('Hire a Texas Vioxx lawyer,' 'Vioxx injury claims') have become ubiquitous on the Internet and cable television."

"If we take the perspective that pharmaceutical companies are developers of a high-risk product, we can understand their high prices and high profit margins. However, their aggressive marketing strategy, which aims to circumvent the cautionary judgment of medical professionals, makes us more willing to extract penalties for problems that emerge."

"The children toddling through the Chandler mall hugging their soft Build-A-Bear animals are no less delighted because kids can also build a bear in Memphis or St. Louis."

"Given the option of getting another 1,800% richer in exchange for another 0.7 degrees Celsius warmer, I'd take the heat in a heartbeat."

"The work of the world is as common as mud."

Profiles of the Editors
and Student Commentators

Throughout *The Presence of Others*, you will read the comments of the editors who chose the selections and wrote the introductions. You will also meet four student editors — two from The University of Texas at Austin and two from Stanford University — and learn their opinions. To give perspective to their sometimes strong, sometimes controversial remarks, we include the following brief self-portraits of Andrea A. Lunsford (A.L.), John J. Ruszkiewicz (J.R.), Joshua G. Rushing (J.G.R.), Beatrice Kim (B.K.), Lindsay Schauer (L.S.), and John Erik Metcalf (J.E.M.). Use these biographies to help you read particular introductions and commentaries with more awareness of the editors' experiences, sensitivities, and blind spots. Think, too, about how your own ideas and beliefs have been shaped by your upbringing, communities, and education.

ANDREA ABERNETHY LUNSFORD   I was born in Oklahoma and have lived in Maryland, Florida, Texas, Washington, Ohio, British Columbia, and California. Yet when I think of "home" I think of the soft rolling foothills of the Smoky Mountains in eastern Tennessee. The hills there are full of Cunninghams, and my granny, Rosa Mae Iowa Brewer Cunningham, and her husband, William Franklin, seemed to know all of them. Like many people in this region, my mother's folks claimed Scottish descent. Indeed, when I later traveled to Scotland, I discovered that many of the songs we sang on my grandparents' big porch were Scottish.

The only one of her large family to enjoy postsecondary education, my Mama graduated with training in teaching and in French from Maryville College in Tennessee. An uncle helped pay her way to school, and it was on a visit to see him that she met my father, another Scottish descendant, Gordon Grady Abernethy. His college education cut short by World War II, Dad gave up his goal of following his father into dentistry and instead took examinations to become a certified public accountant. In hard times, he and my mother left Oklahoma and settled near her family, where Dad got a job with a defense contractor at Oak Ridge. Mama taught briefly and then stayed home with me and, later, with my two sisters and brother. I played in a special playhouse I built in the woods, spent weekends with my grandparents and dozens of Cunningham cousins, and alternated attending my grandparents' Baptist church (where they baptized my cousins by plunging them into a river) and my parents' Presbyterian church, where baptisms seemed like a snap. On occasional Sundays, I got to visit a sister church whose congregation was black, where the music was mesmerizing, and where I first began to recognize this country's legacy of segregation and racism. My family, I learned, was proud to have fought for the North, although supporting the Union's cause did not exempt them — or me — from that legacy.

We read a lot in Sunday School and at Summer Bible School, and at home as well. There I had the luxury of receiving books as gifts, especially from my father's sister, and of being read to often: *Gulliver's Travels* as it appeared in *The Book of Knowledge* (our family's one encyclopedia), "Joseph and His Coat of Many Colors" from Hurlbut's *Stories of the Bible*, Tigger and Roo and Christopher Robin from A. A. Milne, and poems from *A Child's Garden of Verses* are among my earliest memories of texts that grew, over the years, into an animated chorus of voices I still carry with me. Later, I read all of the Nancy Drew, Hardy Boys, and Cherry Ames Senior Nurse series, to be regularly punished for reading in school when I should have been doing something else. Like many young women, I was often "lost in a book," living in a world of heroines and heroes and happy endings. Only slowly and painfully did I come to question the master plot most of these stories reproduced, to realize that endings are never altogether happy and that the roles I play in my own story have been in some important senses scripted by systems beyond my control.

My father wanted me to begin secretarial work after high school, but when I won a small scholarship and got a student job, he and my mother agreed to help me attend our state school, the University of Florida. I graduated with honors but was encouraged by my (male) advisor not to pursue graduate school but rather to "go home and have babies." Instead, I became a teacher, a reasonable job for a woman to aspire to in 1965. Probably no memory from these college years is more vivid to me than the assassination of President John F. Kennedy, though I have many rival memories — police mowing down demonstrators with rushing water from fire hoses (and worse); the Selma bombings; Rosa Parks defying orders to sit in the back of the bus; the violent attempts to block James Meredith's enrollment at the University of Mississippi; Martin Luther King Jr. on the steps of the Lincoln Memorial. These images come together for me in the nightmare series of assassinations: John Kennedy, Malcolm X, Martin Luther King Jr., Robert Kennedy. Like so many others of my generation, these life-changing events intensified my engagement with civil rights, feminism, and activism for social justice, commitments I took with me when, after seven years of teaching, I gathered my courage to apply to graduate school and pursue a Ph.D. The events of the 1960s also helped reaffirm my commitment to a career in education and led me to the concerns that have occupied me ever since: What can I know and learn from and through my relationships with others? What are the rights — and responsibilities — of teaching? What is the connection between teaching and learning? What does it mean to be fully literate in an information age?

I pursued these questions in graduate school at Ohio State and beyond, all the while trying to live through two marriages and the loss of my granny; of both my parents; of my brother, Gordon Abernethy; of a much-loved aunt, Elizabeth McKinsey; and, most recently, of my sister Kerry Abernethy. Such experiences have led me to think hard not only about the burdens and hard sorrows every human life entails but also about the privileges my status as a white, relatively middle-class woman has afforded me. These privileges are considerable, and I do not wish to forget them. In addition, I have enjoyed the support of a vital network of women friends and colleagues. Thanks in large measure to them, I am now a professor in a large research university, can savor the time I can spend with those I love (especially Lisa Ede, my sisters Ellen and Liz, and their children), and am somewhat able to indulge my desire to experience as much of the world as possible. I even have season tickets to basketball and football games (no mean feat these days). These relationships — and my very special relationship with my students — have added to the chorus of animated voices I carry with me always.

These and other formative relationships and experiences have helped me learn a lesson that informs my teaching, my life, and my work on this book: that where you stand influences in great measure what you can see. My college advisor, standing as he did in an all-white male professoriate, couldn't quite "see" a young woman joining this elite group, even as a student. My parents, standing as they did in a lower-middle-class, single-income family with vivid memories of the Depression, couldn't easily "see" beyond the desire for their oldest daughter to get a good, steady job as soon as possible. And I, standing where I do now, am not able to "see" through my students' eyes, to experience the world as they experience it.

Keeping this point in mind leads me to two acts that are by now habitual: examining where I stand, with all that implies about inevitable partial vision and perspective; and asking myself where others stand as well. So I came to this textbook project with John, my friend of almost thirty years now, with at least one specific agenda item: to look as carefully and respectfully as I could at his perspective, at where he stands, and to do the same thing for myself and for every voice included in this text. Such acts are necessary, I believe, before I can say that my opinions are fully considered. My view will always be heavily informed by where I stand. But insofar as I am able to entertain other points of view, I have a chance to understand my own better and to broaden my point of view as well.

JOHN J. RUSZKIEWICZ   My grandparents never spoke much about their reasons for emigrating from eastern Europe early in the twentieth century; their grounds for starting new lives in the United States must have seemed self-evident. Like the immigrants welcomed by Emma Lazarus's poem "The New Colossus," they abandoned those "old countries" willingly. They rarely talked to me about the places they left behind because there were few fond memories.

So I'm a second-generation American with roots in, but no strong ties to, Slovakia, Poland, and Ukraine.

My father and mother were both born in rural Pennsylvania, my dad with five brothers and sisters, my mom with seven — eight if you count the infant boy who died of measles. Both my grandfathers mined coal in western Pennsylvania, as did several uncles — a difficult and dangerous living. After World War II, my parents moved to Cleveland, where jobs were more plentiful then, and my father began a thirty-year stretch on the loading dock at Carling's Brewery. I did my share of manual labor, too, for a short time working in a tool-and-die factory, even paying dues to the Teamsters.

But my blue-collar stints were merely summer jobs between college semesters. Education would be my generation's ticket to the American dream. My parents never allowed my brother (who became a physician) or me to think we had any choice but college. We attended parochial schools, where headstrong nuns and priests introduced us to learning, personal responsibility, and culture. (By eighth grade, students at St. Benedict's elementary school could sing three high Masses and two Requiems, one of those services in Gregorian chant. We knew what most of the Latin words meant, too.) As grade-schoolers, we had homework — hours of it — every night. High school was the same, only tougher. I didn't have a free period in high school until the semester I graduated — and I'm still grateful for that rigor.

The ethnic neighborhood in Cleveland where I grew up in the 1950s is now considered inner-city. It was very much *in the city* when I lived there too, but a nine- or ten-year-old could safely trudge to church alone at 6:00 A.M. to serve Mass or ride the rapid transit downtown to see a baseball game. I did so, often. In the long, hot summer of 1966, however, Cleveland erupted in racial riots. From my front porch, I could see fires burning.

Politically, I come from a family of Democrats — my gregarious mother, far more interested in people than issues, was a party worker in Cleveland's 29th Ward. One of my first political memories is watching John F. Kennedy parade down Euclid Avenue in 1960 during his presidential campaign. But frankly, I was more interested in the new Chrysler convertible ferrying the portly governor of Ohio. I have retained my fondness for old Chryslers — and just about anything with four wheels.

The first president I voted for was George McGovern, but what could you expect from a kid who spent high school listening to Bob Dylan and who went to college in the sixties? Nevertheless, it was during an antiwar rally at St. Vincent College in Latrobe, Pennsylvania, that my drift to the political right began. I had read enough about the history of Vietnam to know that the communist Viet Cong were no angels, but the people at that demonstration spoke as if they were. A professor of physics delivered an impassioned anti-American speech filled with what I knew to be falsehoods, but no one seemed to care. That moment resonates, even after all these years.

Despite the activist times, my college days remained focused on academic subjects — philosophy, history, literature, and cinema. St. Vincent's was small enough to nurture easy commerce among disciplines, so I knew faculty from every field, and my roommates were all science majors with views of the world different from my own. Debate was intense, frequent, and good-natured. Emotionally I leaned left, but intellectually I found, time and again, that conservative writers described the world more accurately for me. I think they still do — though I am less confident than I was four or five years ago.

National politics didn't matter much in graduate school at Ohio State in the mid 1970s — though I was the only Ph.D. candidate in English who would admit to voting for Gerald Ford. My interests then were mainly Beowulf, Shakespeare, and rhetoric. I met my coeditor, Andrea Lunsford, during our first term at Ohio State in an Old English class; we graduated on the same day five years later. She inspired me to think seriously about teaching as well as scholarship, and I remain in her debt for that insight.

Today, I consider myself an academic and political conservative. Where I work, that makes me a member of the counterculture more than ever now, a role that I admit is growing tiresome. Unfortunately, there still aren't many conservatives among humanities professors in American universities. That's a shame because the academy would be a richer place were it more genuinely diverse.

Like any good conservative, I prefer to keep my life simple — I could be content with a good truck, a sensible dog, and a capable racquetball partner (though I play *much* less than I used to). But for the past twenty-five years, I've been teaching at the University of Texas at Austin, where life is rarely dull or simple. If in the past I've been embroiled in controversies over political correctness, today my campus concerns are chiefly in seeing that our new major in Rhetoric and Writing prospers.

It's about classroom matters that my coeditor Andrea and I are most likely to agree — since our political stands differ by about 180 degrees. So when I first proposed an anthology for writing classes that would broaden the range of readings available to students and make the political persuasion of the editors a part of the package, Andrea agreed to the project. She said it embodied the feminist concept of "situated knowledge." Well, sure, if that makes her happy. I'm no theorist. I'm just glad to have the ongoing privilege and distinct pleasure of working with my good friend and political other.

JOSHUA G. RUSHING Although I was made in Japan (conceived on a parental vacation), I cannot claim to be anything other than a pure Texan — as well as a father, husband, former college student, and full-time Marine. During my time in the Corps, almost a decade now, I have been fortunate to be granted extended visits to exotic locations such as Europe, the Middle East, and the Arctic Circle. In addition to getting to see the world outside the United States, I have enjoyed my long stay in coastal North Carolina, where I was stationed for almost four years, and my time in New Orleans and Los Angeles. But no matter where I am, in my soul a neon Lone Star perpetually flashes to the rhythm of a Willie Nelson tune.

That I refer to my "soul" seems strange, considering my pragmatic agnosticism. Having previously staked claims on both sides of the divine fence (for which I wish there were a saddle), I have been forced between a rock (the lack of empirical evidence for the existence of God, hence the need for faith) and a hard place (the same void of conclusive proof that there is not a God, hence the same need for faith).

I tend to be no more polar in politics than I am in religion. My centrist beliefs might make it seem as though I lead a fairly dull life when it comes to opinions, but on the contrary, I have found that practicing the fine and delicate art of fence-riding allows me to take sides in more arguments than William F. Buckley Jr. My niche affords me the freedom to play the incessant devil's advocate. One would be hard pressed to find an issue on which I could not disagree with people — no matter what side of the argument they're on. Having said that, I must admit that the inevitable responsibilities of life have been swaying me from my well-worn tracks down the middle. As I grow older, my political views are starting to lean to the right — a predictable trend that, in my experience, affects most people.

Glancing to the future, I still wonder what I will be after my stint in the Marines. I have no clue and, truthfully, not even a desire for a particular profession. I have always been envious of peers who have known since they were four that they wanted to be doctors and at my age are now graduating from medical school. My strongest hopes are to be a good father and husband; besides that I think I will abide by the old Scottish proverb: "Be happy while you're living for you're a long while dead."   *[1999]*

BEATRICE KIM   "I am a Korean with a southern accent. At least that's what my friends from Washington would say. Of course, my friends in the Rio Grande Valley would argue that I am a Korean who speaks Spanish with a gringo accent. And my family would argue that I am a Korean who speaks Korean with an American accent. So I am a Korean southerner with a southern accent for English, a gringo accent for Spanish, and an American accent for Korean. I suppose I'm just a person who talks funny."

The preceding paragraph was the opening to my Stanford application essay. I began with this paragraph because it demonstrates the gift I've received from living in so many diverse cultural places. I was born in Michigan; lived in Mississippi when the miscegenation laws were still in effect; spent my elementary years in Walla Walla, Washington, where the population was 99.9 percent white; lived in McAllen, Texas, where the population was 70 percent Mexican; and now I find myself in Stanford, California, a beautiful concoction of browns, yellows, whites, blacks, and everything in between.

Growing up throughout the United States, I have experienced prejudice as a member of both a minority race and a minority gender. As a youngster,

I heard the constant singsong taunts of children singing, "My mom is Chinese, my dad is Japanese . . .," with the corresponding hand movements of stretching the eyelids up and down. And because I grew up in a traditional Korean family, ruled by the patriarchic customs of Asian culture, my "role" as a woman has been pressed upon me time and time again. "Girls don't do that" is a directive that I have been subjected to not only by my family but also by close friends who unknowingly conform to society's "laws" of gender bias. All of us, I believe — men as well as women — are hurt by such limiting ideas.

Still, the wonderful friends of different ethnicities and genders that I encounter every day have helped me put my negative experiences in perspective and have reenforced my faith in people. Because of my experiences both old and new, I feel that I will always be sincerely empathetic to the cause of spreading knowledge and encouraging tolerance in others.

As I wrap up my undergraduate college career — I am currently a junior with a Communication major and a Creative Writing minor — I am uncertain of what life after college holds for me. But I am sure of one thing: my strong love for God, family, and friends and my diverse experiences from my past and at Stanford will carry me through.   *[2003]*

LINDSAY SCHAUER   Having grown up in Oregon and attended college in California, with my family strung out along the left side of the nation from Los Angeles all the way up to Seattle, I consider myself a West Coast girl through and through. I love the mountains, green open spaces, and winding coastlines I have always called home, and I relish the laid-back attitude (and liberal ideas) typically associated with this beachy side of the continent. My travels around the world have made me especially appreciate this incredible area of the globe.

After graduating from high school in Eugene, Oregon, I set off as an eager 18-year-old to complete a year as a Rotary International Exchange Student in Thailand. I thought my open mind and language skills — I'd been learning French in school since the first grade — would have prepared me well to take on a new foreign language and drastically different culture, but the year proved exceptionally difficult. For the first time in my life, I experienced what it was like to be completely illiterate in a society. For months, I couldn't read the street signs around me, speak to new friends I wanted to meet, or understand which bathroom was for women and which for men. I had never quite grasped the importance of reading and writing skills — I was paralyzed without them.`

On top of the language difficulties, I was also the only Caucasian student living in my rural town in northeastern Thailand. Having come from the West Coast, where I had always fit in, I found that life as a drastic minority in Thailand gave me an experience that many middle-class white Americans like myself never have. It shaped my political views and my perspective on my own country, lending me a compassion for immigrants and minorities in our country.

After a year in Thailand I attended the University of Colorado for a year before deciding that I wanted to be back on — you guessed it — the West

Coast. I landed at Stanford in my sophomore year, where I studied English, pursuing my passion for literacy and writing, and graduated in 2007.

My two academic loves have always been education and journalism. I am profoundly grateful for experiences with tutoring, summer camp counseling, and mentoring high school students. The students I have met in the broader community around Stanford, notably East Palo Alto, have inspired in me a passion for social justice and an interest in promoting equality in education. My dream is to be able to write about those issues for a few years, gaining experience as a journalist with a magazine or small publication in California, and then, when I've gained a little more life experience, go into teaching. And of course, you'll likely be able to find me pursuing these dreams in one of the splendid West Coast states.   *[2007]*

JOHN ERIK METCALF   In my childhood, empathy and critical thinking — though we never called them that — were the name of the game. Phrases like these punctuated my upbringing: "Put yourself in their shoes!" "Do you *understand* why you shouldn't do that?" "Remember the Golden Rule. . . ." An only child, I grew up in the hill country north of San Antonio, Texas. I was homeschooled until eighth grade, when I choose to enroll in public school.

My parents, moderate conservatives, both work primarily from home — teaching me there was a natural fit. Their approach was similar to the Montessori Method. I'd focus on one subject as long as I wished, sometimes for weeks; when I lost interest I'd move to another. Our computers — the first was a Tandy 1000 — were incorporated into many of my lessons. I'd recode them, then "test 'em out."

Public school was interesting. I learned about cliques for the first time and that I wasn't wired for standardized testing. While it was far from the most productive time in my life, I learned how to navigate among my contemporaries. In high school I began looking at school as a game; to thrive I had to understand the game better than the other players.

I bounced around a lot my first few years at The University of Texas, looking for a degree with the right curriculum and meta-framework. Starting in economics, then computer science, then business, I ended with a B.S. in advertising. Blending elements of creativity, synthetic thinking, and sociology, this degree plan was an ideal fit for my thought process.

In 2003, after my sophomore year, I started a consulting company. Helping small businesses and nonprofits use technology to create an efficient work environment is what I do best. Economically and collaboratively, open source and Web 2.0 applications are transforming the workplace. I love being the one to make it happen.

Today, I prefer to spend my days following the latest social entrepreneurs, Internet trends, and Austin bike trails. I will continue to follow the example my parents have set for me and apply the concepts they have instilled in me to new facets of experience.   *[2007]*

The Presence of Others

Voices and Images
That Call for Response

On Reading
and Thinking Critically

Introduction

THIS IS A BOOK for and about reading. Its pages contain voices joined in conversation and debate over issues important to all of us: What, how, and under what circumstances should we learn and become educated? Who are we as individuals and as members of various groups and cultures? What do we believe and why? How do the media try to influence us? Why and how do we work? In the conversations surrounding these and other issues, the editors of this book (and other teachers and students) have joined the dialogue; you will find our reasons for choosing particular selections and our thoughts about these selections running throughout this text. The primary aim of the book, however, is to invite *you* to join this conversation, to add your voice to the discussion in these pages. Doing so invites you to assume the perspective of a *critical reader*.

• • •

WHAT IS CRITICAL READING?

If you've been wondering what critical reading is, you're already demonstrating one of the hallmarks of a critical reader: an inquisitive attitude, one that probes for definitions, explanations, assumptions, and proofs. Perhaps we can further clarify what we mean by critical reading by focusing on two everyday uses of the word *critical*. In its most common usage, *critical* means acting like a critic, as in "many voters have been highly critical of current American foreign policy," or "some members of the African American community have been critical of what they see as Terry McMillan's negative treatment of men in her novels." In this sense of the word, *critical* suggests that you have explored an issue and are ready to evaluate it, to see whether and how it meets your standards.

But *critical* is also used to denote something of special importance, as in "critical care unit" or "a critical point in negotiations." In this sense of the word, *critical* suggests that you attach importance to what you are examining and to your own critical responses to it. For the purposes of this book, then, **critical readers are those who bring all their powers to bear on understanding, analyzing, and evaluating some important question, issue, or perspective contained in a text**. That "text" will usually take the form of words on a page or screen, but it might also involve other media — images, film clips, audio clips — all working together to make a point. So, whether reading a book, digesting an online editorial, or viewing a documentary, critical readers do not accept things blindly or at face value. Instead, they examine texts and issues from many perspectives, saying both *yes* and *no* to them until they are ready to take their own stances.

Saying *Yes, No,* and *Maybe*

The chapters of this book will offer you many chances to practice saying *yes* and *no* — and sometimes *maybe* — to ideas. For example, as you examine the selections in Chapter 3, Education, you will encounter widely varying perspectives on higher education and many different questions about its nature and purpose. As you read Adrienne Rich's "What Does a Woman Need to Know?" Rich's arguments may at first seem perfectly reasonable, and you may say *yes* to her ideas. But then you may begin to wonder about them and find yourself thinking, *maybe*, or perhaps even *no*, especially when you realize that her essay was written decades ago. Are Rich's ideas about education appropriate today, and do they respond to the problems women need to confront? Are the charges she brings both fair and accurate? All of these acts — saying *yes, maybe*, and/or *no* — are necessary for critical reading, for the kind of reading that is open to new ideas but that insists on thinking them through from every perspective.

Critical reading is not a skill limited to college English classes. It is what you do when you understand the terms of a contract you are about to sign, decide which of several automobile financing plans will work best for you, master the material necessary to do well on an important examination, evaluate the arguments for or against a political proposal or candidate, or compare doctors' opinions about whether you should undergo surgery. It is the kind of reading Mortimer Adler is talking about when he says, "When [people] are in love and are reading a love letter, they read for all they are worth. They read every word three ways; they read between the lines and in the margins; they read the whole in terms of the parts, and each part in terms of the whole."

WHY BECOME A CRITICAL READER?

Given our definition of critical reading, the answer to this question is probably already obvious to you. Critical readers are the players in this world. They find themselves 'in on' the conversation surrounding any issue. They are the people

This parody advertisement, taken from adbusters.org, uses sheep to suggest that advertising manipulates public opinion.

others turn to for advice or counsel because they resist ready-made or hand-me-down opinions. Much in our society makes such critical reading difficult; we are, after all, inundated with canned opinions and images on television and in other mass media as well as in religious, political, and even educational institutions. In fact, so many forces are trying to make up our minds for us that many people question whether we control language at all, rather than the other way around.

You can probably think of many instances in which language seems to be "in control." When you go to a movie, for instance, you notice how commercials entice you to buy grotesquely overpriced popcorn and soda. Or you may be aware that educational labels like *honors* or *remedial* have dramatically affected your life. Many studies suggest that we tend to live up (or down) to such labels — for better or worse. This fact of modern life led one language theorist to say that the words we try to control are already "half-way in someone else's mouth," meaning that the expressions we use are already so weighed down with societal meanings that it is hard not to accept those meanings. That is, it's hard for any one person to resist the lure of advertising or to reject the power of educational or social labels.

To some extent, this theory rings true: we do not absolutely control the language we use or read. But to accept such a position totally is to give up on trying to make your voice heard or to bring about any change. Why become a critical reader, then? To resist being controlled by other people's language, to exert some control of your own, to test your wits, to define your own perspective on any issue, to contribute to the thoughts and actions related to those issues. **You become a critical reader, in short, to get involved in the conversation and to make your voice count.**

ARE YOU A CRITICAL READER?

Our guess is that you are already a critical reader when you need to be. You may want to take stock of your general reading habits, however. When you are reading important material — whether print or digital — you will probably want to follow these "best practices."

Pay close attention to the text.

- Read carefully, with or without skimming the text first.
- "Talk back" to the text as you read, noting what does and doesn't make sense. Ask questions.
- Take notes.
- Summarize the main points of the reading.

Think critically about the writer.

- Ask yourself why the writer takes the position he or she does. What are the writer's interests in creating the piece?
- Consider the writer's credentials. Is he or she a recognized authority? How can you tell?
- Ask what larger social, political, economic, or other conditions may have influenced the creation of this piece of writing.

Think critically about the source.

- Consider who is responsible for publishing the document (in print or electronically). Do you trust this source?
- Ask what the goal of publication might be. Does the writing aim to inform, to persuade readers to take action, to sell something, or to do something else?
- Notice when the piece of writing was published (whether in print or online) or most recently updated. Is it current? A classic? Outdated?
- Check the bibliography, notes, references, and/or links. What do these references and recommendations tell you about the credibility of the writing?
- Consider how the format — including use of visuals, graphics, color, layout, and so forth — affects the message.

Take stock of your own perspective.

- Consider what in your experience and background leads you to agree with or like (or disagree with or dislike) this piece of writing.
- Compare what you are reading with other things you have heard or read about the subject.
- Imagine other ways of looking at the subjects or ideas presented.

Examining Your Reading Habits   If you usually follow most of the guidelines in the preceding list, you are already reading with a critical eye, and you will understand what we mean when we say reading is a partnership: the text in front of you has words and images set down, but you are the one who realizes the ideas in those words and images, tests them against what you know, and puts them to use in your life.

Take five or ten minutes to write or draw a description of yourself as a reader. How do you usually approach a text that you want or need to understand? Do you usually practice critical reading habits? Why, or why not? Bring your description to class for discussion. Compare your description with those of two or three other students in your class, noting the ways in which your reading strategies are similar and/or different.

HOW CAN YOU BECOME A MORE CRITICAL READER?

If you have compared the way you read to how your friends and classmates do, you have probably noticed some differences. Indeed, habits of reading vary widely, and even highly skilled readers differ in their approaches. Moreover, what works for your friends or expert readers may not work for you. That's because your reading strategies are connected to who you are — to your gender, age, cultural background, life experiences, prior reading experiences, even your eyesight. In addition, you probably read differently depending on your purpose and situation: you might just skim the ingredients listed on a food package to check that the food doesn't contain too much fat, whereas you might linger over the directions for operating a digital camera to make sure that you can make the equipment do what you want it to do.

Thus, part of your job as a critical reader is to appreciate your own preferred strategies. You need to recognize the strengths and weaknesses of your reading strategies and to build on your strengths. To help you, we can offer some general guidelines. You can experiment with them to develop a personal blueprint for effective critical reading. We hope that these guidelines will help you when you tackle difficult reading material or material for which you have almost no background. In the annotated essays in Chapters 3 through 8 of this book, you will find examples of most of these strategies, written in the margins as our responses to those essays.

Previewing

- Determine your purpose for reading. Is it to gather information for a writing assignment? To determine whether a source will be useful for a research project? To study for an examination? To prepare for class discussion? To determine your own stance toward a topic — and what in your experience and background leads you to take that stance?

- Consider the title and subtitle, if there is one. What do they tell you about what is to come? If you are reading online, what does the home page or site tell you about its content or links?

- Think about what you already know about the subject. What opinions do you hold on this subject? What assumptions do you bring to the subject? If you find yourself reacting very favorably or unfavorably to the subject, ask where that reaction is coming from: what has influenced you to respond in that way?

- What major topics do you anticipate? What do you hope to learn? What other things about this topic have you read?

- What do you know about the author(s)? What expertise does he or she have in the subject? What particular perspective on the subject might he or she hold? If an author isn't identified, why is that? Does the piece represent the opinion or work of a group or institution? What can you discover about that group or institution?

- What does the headnote or opening of the reading tell you?

- Look at how the text is structured. Are there subdivisions? Read over any headings. Skim the opening sentences of each paragraph. For a Web site, check to see if there is a site map, or explore the architecture of the site: does it offer a sequence of pages, a hierarchy of materials, or a ring of connected items?

- Decide what you think the main point or theme of the text will be. Does the material lead to one specific point or encourage you to construct your own meanings?

- Check to see if the conclusion contains a summary of the main point or a statement of its significance — or look for an abstract of the text that gives a comparable synopsis. Previewing either of these elements can help you read more efficiently and critically.

Annotating

- Read carefully, marking places that are confusing or that you want to reread.

- Identify key points or arguments, important terms, recurring images, and interesting ideas, either by underlining them in the text or by making notes in the margin.
- Note any statements you question or disagree with and any counterevidence or counterarguments that occur to you.
- Note any sources used in the text.

Summarizing

- Summarize the main points. Do they match your expectations? Why, or why not?
- Jot down any points you want to remember, questions you want to raise, and ideas for how you may use this material.

Analyzing

- Identify evidence that supports the main argument or illustrates the main point. Is it sufficient to convince you? Is there any evidence that seems to contradict the author's point?
- Identify the writer's underlying assumptions about the subject, where he or she is "coming from" on this issue.
- Ask what may have led the author to this position.
- Consider how the writer's stance affects his or her presentation of the material or argument.
- Describe the writer's tone. Is it cautious? Angry? Insulting? Serious or amusing? How is the tone created, and what effects does it strive to achieve?
- Question the sources used. Ask yourself whether each source is relevant to the topic, whether it is timely, whether it carries sufficient expertise, and whether its perspective or position on the subject is different from yours or from others' you know and respect. If so, why?
- Think of other points of view on this topic, perhaps from other things you have read or seen. Is the author's perspective the most persuasive? Why, or why not?
- Examine the way the writer presents information or data. Read any accompanying tables and charts carefully. Look at any photographs or drawings that are part of the text. How do these visual elements expand or illuminate the points the writer seeks to make?

Rereading

- Reread quickly to be sure you have understood the reading.
- Identify the author's purpose(s). Were those purposes accomplished?
- Determine whether the questions you had during the first reading have been answered.

Responding

- What one question would you like to ask the writer? How do you think the writer might respond?
- Think about the reading as a whole. What did you like best about it? What puzzled or irritated you? What caused you to like or dislike the piece? Were your expectations met? If not, why not? What more would you like to know about the subject? Remember to explore the reasons for your reaction to the reading: what influences may have led to that response?
- Note what you have learned about effective writing from this reading.
- If you keep a reading log, record these notes there.

Examining Your Critical Literacy   To practice reading a text critically, turn to one of the texts in this book that is *not* annotated and analyze the piece using the guidelines for thinking and reading critically. For an example of one student's critical response to a reading, see pp. 41–46.

HOW CAN YOU READ VISUAL TEXTS CRITICALLY?

Today, images crowd in from all directions, not only from television, video, film, and the Web, but from traditional print texts as well — from the graphs and charts in a financial report to the daily newspaper to the textbook you hold in your hand. And as we have indicated throughout this chapter, far from being mere decoration, these images carry part or most of the message readers are intended to receive. As a result, critical readers pay very careful attention to the visuals in any text they read, understanding that these have a significant impact on how readers interpret and respond to those texts. If a picture *is* sometimes worth a thousand words, it pays to spend some time thinking about what makes that picture so valuable.

Some visual texts in and of themselves appear to embody ideas or arguments. Consider the now-famous electoral map from the U.S. presidential election of 2000; it purports to show a nation sharply divided both politically and geographically. Of course, the image glosses over the fact that many states were close calls and had nearly the same numbers of voters for each candidate — but the winner-take-all electoral college system gives the map the appearance that the country contains solid blocs of Republican and Democratic voters. Studying the map on p. 9, you could make many deductions about political and

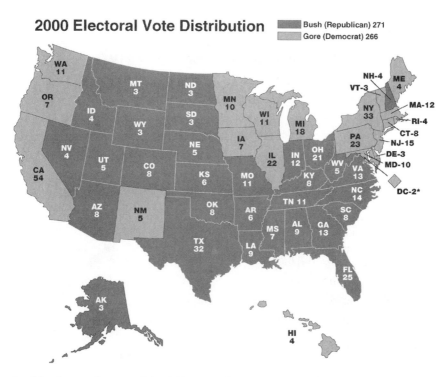

2000 Electoral Vote Distribution
- Bush (Republican) 271
- Gore (Democrat) 266

In this electoral map of the 2000 presidential election, created by the Federal Election Commission, states Al Gore won are in gray, and states George W. Bush won are in black.

social trends in the country. And that, in fact, is what David Brooks does in "One Nation, Slightly Divisible," an essay we have included in this anthology because it is an extended critical reading of a visual text. Still, it is important to remember that the electoral map itself was not created to embody any particular political or social trends. It simply reported the final distribution of each state's electoral votes.

Other images, however, are more deliberately crafted to influence you. Such images demand especially careful and critical reading so that you can appreciate both the arguments they offer and how such arguments are made. Just as important, you have to understand the context in which images operate, asking the same questions about authors, audience, and purpose that you would raise for a written piece. Consider, for example, the analytical techniques you would use with the public service announcement from the Ad Council on p. 10. The image depicts common food items found in many household cupboards, but the cans and jars with their familiar shapes and labels take on an ominous significance when the meaning of the words sinks in. What makes this an effective visual?

The following questions can help you shape your critical reading of visual texts — whether they stand on their own, as in a photograph or painting, or are combined with print — beginning with those you find throughout this book.

For Charts, Graphs, and Tables

1. What information does the chart, graph, or table convey?

2. Does it present numbers or statistics? How does the visual representation affect your understanding of the information? Does it emphasize or downplay, or even exaggerate or understate, anything?

3. Does it illustrate a trend or change? If so, does it emphasize the change fairly or not?

4. Does it highlight anything (a particular year? a topic?) to attract your attention?

For Photographs, Drawings, and Advertisements

1. Why was the visual created? What does its main meaning or message seem to be? How does the visual make you notice and perhaps remember this message?

2. What in the visual is your eye drawn to, and why?

3. What is in the foreground? In the background? What is in focus or out of focus? Is the most important part of the visual blended into the rest, or is it contrasted somehow? What details are included or emphasized? What is omitted or de-emphasized, and why?

4. What is placed high in the visual? What is placed low? To the left? To the right? What is the effect of such placement?

5. How are light and color used? How do they affect your reading of the visual?

6. Is anything in the visual repeated, intensified, or exaggerated? Look for anything that is made to seem "supernormal" or idealized (by airbrushing or computer manipulation, for example). What effect does the exaggeration or repetition have on you as a reader?

7. Is anything downplayed? Ambiguous? Confusing or distracting? If so, what effect does this have on your reading of the visual? Does any ambiguity call on you as a reader to fill in some gaps? If so, to what effect?

8. What values or ideals does the visual convey or allude to? Family values? The good life? Harmony? Success? Beauty? Power? Pleasure? Sex appeal? Youth? Wisdom? Adventure? Is the visual text reinforcing or questioning these values? How does it do so?

9. Does the visual include positive or negative imagery or show people that carry very positive — or very negative — associations? If so, how does this imagery affect your response? (Think of ads that use celebrities to make readers notice — and buy! — the product.)

10. Does the visual use humor? If so, how does the humor affect your reaction?

11. How does the visual relate to any written text that accompanies it? Do the two reinforce each other, or does one undermine the other?

HOW CAN YOU READ ONLINE TEXTS CRITICALLY?

The texts you encounter online, especially pages on the Web, require new reading skills because they combine many different elements — including headlines, groups of words, static images, moving images, sounds, and even film clips. Chances are you barely think about how different the conventions for reading online are from the conventions for reading print, from scrolling pages (rather than turning them) to clicking items to move to new places. But you need to do more than just explore online texts; you need to appreciate how they work to attract and direct your attention.

In many cases, the visual and, to a lesser extent, aural items on a Web page are designed to encourage you to select specific menus or links. But commercial pages usually offer many more options than you need just to keep you browsing and looking. Web pages may be interrupted by pop-up advertisements designed to get you to move to more sites. The visual clutter of many commercial pages, especially those for some Web search engines (Google is a welcome exception), may even surprise you. The box for typing in a search term is often obscured by blinking images and clusters of links, all competing for your attention and, often, your money.

So you have to learn to filter out the clutter on electronic pages and evaluate their overall design to determine what information is being offered to you and in what order. The way that information is presented usually tells you what the site designers or sponsors value. They may use colors or images to highlight ideas they want you to encounter and bury less important material deep in a site or omit it entirely.

You should be especially careful with online texts that fail to identify themselves clearly. Look for information about identity, authorship, sponsorship, and currency. If an online text resists even your basic attempts to read it critically, you should perhaps move on to another. There are likely to be dozens of additional choices, whatever subject you are exploring.

1. How does the text combine visual and written material? Which dominates, and to what effect?

2. What perspective is represented in text? What group or individual is responsible for the information provided? What is the credibility or reputation of the author or sponsor? Is the text sponsored by or linked to a commercial enterprise? For Web sites, be sure to check out the domain name: *.com* indicates a commercial site; *.edu* indicates a site sponsored by

an educational institution; *.org* indicates a nonprofit organization; and *.gov* indicates a government site. Is there an email address you can use to contact those responsible for the text?

3. Does the text include links to other online texts? If so, what do the links tell you about the credibility and usefulness of the text you are reading?

4. How current is the text? When was it last updated?

5. How easy is it to find information in this text? Does it have a search function and/or a site map that will help you read it?

WHAT DOES READING HAVE TO DO WITH WRITING?

In one sense, critical reading *is* writing. That is, as you read carefully, asking questions and talking back to a text, you inevitably create your own version of the text. Even if that interpretation is not written down on paper, it is "written" in your mind, composed and put into words you can understand and remember. And if you add some of your own ideas — or those you and classmates develop together — to what you read, you can build a new work altogether, one you might later write down.

As our society uses electronic texts more often, reading and writing will almost certainly become even more intertwined. The "reader" of interactive fiction or a hypertext, for instance, may write part of the text. Those on electronic bulletin boards or Web logs may write their own ideas and responses into what they are reading on the screen, something first written by another reader.

But critical reading is also closely related to your own writing because it enables you to assess what you have written, to say *yes* and *no* and *maybe* to your own ideas — to evaluate the logic of your prose, the effectiveness of your word choices, the degree to which you have gotten your points across. In short, you can apply these same reading strategies to your own writing, to see your own words with a critical eye. Thus, reading critically and writing effectively become reciprocal activities, strengthening each other as you learn to use language more powerfully.

Because we are convinced that reading and writing are closely related, we want this text to offer you many opportunities for moving back and forth from reading to writing to reading. We will, in fact, invite you to experiment with a number of kinds of writing as you read your way into the conversations taking place in the chapters that follow. We turn now, therefore, to Chapter 2, From Reading to Writing, for an overview of the writing practices this book invites you to experience.

From Reading to Writing   2

Introduction

NO ONE CAN PREDICT how you will respond to what you read, but the act of reading does often lead to action. Maybe reading a pamphlet handed to you on campus will convince you to vote for a student government candidate. Or a slick brochure arriving in the mail could lead you to buy apartment insurance — or to complain about false advertising to a state regulatory agency. Gaudy graphics on a Web page might entice you to click for more information, or maybe all that design clutter offends you so much that you remove the annoying site from your "favorites" list. A dull book could make you reconsider your major; a great book might change your life.

One action that reading often provokes is writing, which can preserve and extend your ideas. When you write about what you have read, you enter a conversation someone else has started, contribute your own ideas to it, and invite still others to join you. Sometimes these conversations will be simple and immediate, as when you respond quickly to email or IM requests from people you know well. At other times, your reading and writing will bridge wider gaps, perhaps even between different cultures or eras, and then you'll need to respond much more deliberately.

• • •

WRITING TO LEARN

Most classes in college will require some written work. Although these tasks may seem too routine to think of as actual "writing," don't underestimate them. Writing of almost any kind can fix ideas in your mind and stimulate your thinking. Following are some types of college writing that may help you learn better: class notes, lab notes, reading notes and annotations, listserv messages, comments on other students' writing, research log entries, abstracts of articles, summaries, outlines, annotated bibliographies, essay examinations, and class presentations. Consider such writing assignments as opportunities to learn.

LEARNING TO WRITE EFFECTIVELY

In many of your college courses, instructors will ask you to prepare formal essays or other extended pieces of writing related to what you read, hear, or learn. The following guidelines are designed to help you respond effectively to such assignments.

Considering the Assignment

Find out as much as you can about an assignment before starting to write.

- Analyze a writing project carefully. Look for key words in the assignment, such as *analyze, summarize, compare, contrast, illustrate, argue, defend, refute, persuade, respond,* and so on.
- If you don't understand an assignment, ask your instructor for clarification.
- Pay attention to limits on length and time. The length of an assignment will influence the focus and thesis of any essay. In general, the shorter the piece, the narrower its focus will need to be.
- Note whether you are asked to use a particular format (a lab report, for example, or a memo) and whether you are expected to include any visuals in your writing.
- Plan your time to allow for all necessary reading, thinking, drafting, and editing.

Considering Purpose and Audience

Beyond what the assignment itself dictates, consider the larger purpose of the writing. In all your school writing, one purpose will be to demonstrate that you have done a fine job of responding to the assignment, but beyond that very large-scale purpose lie additional purposes. An assignment that asks you to prepare a report suggests that your purpose will be to inform, while an assignment that asks you to prepare an editorial column will call for a clear argumentative position. How will your writing accomplish your purposes successfully? Your responses to that question will help determine the form, organization, tone, style, and length of your writing. Here are some other questions to help you think about purpose:

- Does the assignment itself specify a purpose?
- What does your instructor expect you to do in this assignment? What do you need to do to meet those expectations?
- How do you want readers to react to your writing? Do you want them to be entertained? Should they learn something? Should they be moved to action?
- Where might you like to have this piece read? Will it appear in print or online?

Consider also who will read your piece. The primary audience for your college writing may be instructors, but *they* may have in mind some other specific audience — your classmates, for example, or the general public. Following are some questions that can help identify key characteristics of your audience:

- Do your readers belong to some identifiable group: college students, Democrats, women, parents, sociologists?
- What is your relationship to your readers? Is it friend to friend? Employee to employer? Citizen to community? Some other relationship?
- How would you characterize your readers? What assumptions can you legitimately make about your audience members? What values and principles do you hold in common with them? What differences are there between you? What attitudes might disturb or offend them?
- Are your readers likely to know more or less than you do about your subject? What background information do you need to provide?
- What languages and varieties of English do your audience members know and use? What special language, if any, might they expect you to use?
- Are your readers likely to be engaged by your subject, or do you have to win their attention?
- Are your readers likely to be favorable, neutral, or hostile to your positions?
- Should you use simple, general language, or technical language?
- Should you use images or other forms of illustration? Would adding sound and/or video clips be appropriate to your purpose and readers?
- Are you addressing more than one audience? If so, do any of the audiences seem incompatible?
- Is your writing going online, where it can be read by the general public? If so, take special care to examine how — and if — such distant readers will understand your arguments, references, allusions, and so on.

Generating Ideas and Making Plans

You don't need to know what you are going to say before you begin writing. Even so, all writers must start somewhere. You may find the following techniques helpful in discovering ideas:

- Take a quick written inventory of everything you know about your subject, followed by a list of what you think you'll need to research.
- Read any assigned material carefully, annotating key information, summarizing main points, and noting connections among readings.
- Try specific techniques for developing ideas, such as freewriting, brainstorming, or journal writing. (Consult a writing handbook for more about these techniques.)

- Get more information — from your library's databases, from the Web, from professional organizations, from friends or instructors, and so on.
- Do field research. Conduct a survey or some interviews — or carry out a detailed and careful observation of some phenomenon.
- Get involved in discussions about your subject. Talk to people. Listen to their ideas and opinions. Read a newsgroup or join a listserv.
- Draw on your personal experiences, especially when dealing with social, cultural, and political issues. *Your* experience counts.

Once you have ideas, sketch out a plan — a scheme to make a project manageable. Here are some ways of working out a plan:

- Fix on a tentative thesis statement, claim, or main point you want to prove, defend, or illustrate. Think of it as a commitment to your readers.
- Prepare a scratch outline by listing the major ideas you want to cover and then arranging them in an order that makes sense to you. If you have access to brainstorming software, take advantage of it.
- Construct a formal outline if you find such devices useful.
- Try a "zero draft" — a quick, discardable version of an essay to help you focus on the major issues.

DRAFTING

Drafting is the point in the writing process when you commit your words and thoughts to the page or screen. The "cold swimming hole" approach works best for some writers: just plunge in and start writing. After all, you can't do much as a writer until you produce some words. In case you don't much like cold water, however, here's some other advice for getting started on a first draft:

- Make a commitment to begin writing. Sometimes just getting started is the hardest part of writing, so setting a date and time for beginning can be important.
- Control your expectations. No one expects a first draft to be perfect. In fact, no one expects a final draft to be the last word on any subject. So take it easy.
- Skip the introduction if you find yourself stuck on the opening sentences. Start somewhere else, perhaps with an idea you are especially eager to develop. Then write another portion of the essay, and then another. You can put all the parts together later.
- If you are working on a computer, set up a folder or file for your essay, choosing a clear and relevant file name, and save your document often.
- Have all your information close at hand and arranged according to when you will need it.

- Set some reasonable goals, especially for longer projects. Commit your-self to writing for at least thirty minutes, or until you have at least one or two pages, before getting up from your desk.
- Stop writing at a place where you know exactly what should come next. That way, beginning again will be easier. Reward yourself when you meet your goal.
- Try a quick draft: sketch out the full essay without stopping.

Getting — and Giving — Feedback

Seek responses from other readers. Within whatever guidelines your instructor establishes, ask classmates, friends, or any potential readers to read and react to your drafts. Here are some guidelines for your readers to use in reviewing your draft (and for you to use in responding to others'):

- Begin by describing what you think the draft is saying. That description might prove enlightening to the author. Go on to paraphrase the thesis as a promise: *In this paper, the writer promises to* _____. Then see whether the draft fulfills that promise.
- Decide whether the draft carries out the assignment and, if not, what the writer can do to better fulfill it.
- List the major points in order. Then decide which points, if any, need to be explained more or less fully. Should any be eliminated? Are any confusing or boring? How well are the major points supported by evidence, examples, details, and so on?
- Consider how visuals — photographs, charts, graphs, maps, screen shots, and so on — are used to support the major ideas. How well are visuals integrated into the text? Are they introduced, commented on, and clearly labeled?
- Point out any word, phrase, or sentence that is confusing or unclear.
- Describe what is most memorable in the draft.
- List the strengths of the draft. How can they be enhanced?
- List the weaknesses. How might they be eliminated or minimized?
- Suggest specific revisions. What more do you as a reader want or need to know? Which other arguments or ideas should be considered?

Revising

Respond to comments on a first draft by looking at the entire assignment anew. Reshape the essay as much as necessary to serve your purpose, your subject matter, and your readers. Here are some specific suggestions for revising:

- To gain perspective, put a printed draft aside for a day or two.

- Be as tough minded as you can about the condition of a draft. Discard whole paragraphs or pages when they simply don't work. Don't just tinker or look for the easiest way of salvaging weak material. You may need a new thesis or a completely different structure.
- Consider very carefully any responses you've received — but don't overreact to criticism.
- Consider alternative plans for organization. Be flexible.
- Consider the overall strategy of the essay. Might a different point of view or tone make it more effective?
- Review your thesis or main idea. Is the thesis fully explained and supported?
- Reconsider whether you know enough about your subject to write about it with authority. If not, go back to your sources or do more reading.
- Pay attention to transitions. You can help your readers with a few careful phrases that point to where you're going — or where you've been.
- Pay attention to visual details — to any images you are using and the design of the text. Test them with readers to make sure they are appropriate and effective.

Editing

Once you've revised your draft, it's time to edit your work by paying close attention to the structure of paragraphs, the shape of sentences, the choice of words, the presentation of visuals, and the conventions of punctuation and mechanics.

- Reconsider openings and closings. In academic writing, introductions should capture the reader's attention and identify key points, while conclusions should summarize ideas and draw implications.
- Read your draft aloud, paying attention to the length, variety, rhythm, and coherence of sentences.
- Look for wordiness. Stylistically, nothing hurts an essay more than empty phrases.
- Take advantage of your word processor. In addition to making sure you've run the spell checker, search for words you often confuse — *their* for *there*, for example — and double-check to make sure that each usage is correct.
- Proofread carefully for mistakes your spell checker cannot catch, such as misspelled names.
- Consider your vocabulary for appropriateness. Is it appropriate to use contractions or slang or dialect? Do any technical terms need defining?

- Check any documentation of sources for the correct form. Do you quote, paraphrase, and summarize appropriately? Do you weave quotations smoothly into your own text? Do your Web links make sense?

- Check for problems of grammar and usage, particularly for any types of errors that have caused you problems in the past.

- For detailed examples and answers to questions of grammar, usage, and style, check a handbook.

- Find a suitable title for your print or online document. For most academic work, titles should provide clear descriptions of the contents.

Preparing the Final Version

When you are satisfied with your revised and edited draft, assemble and check your final version.

- Review the assignment to be sure you have met all requirements of form. Does your instructor want a title page? An outline? A Works Cited page?

- Be sure your name appears in the proper place(s).

- Paginate and clip printed pages together. (Do not staple them.)

- Proofread one last time for typographical errors, spelling errors, and other slips. Run your spell checker for a final check.

- Make sure the final printed text or electronic document is presented professionally.

AN ALPHABETICAL CATALOG OF THE WRITING ASSIGNMENTS IN THIS BOOK

Throughout *The Presence of Others* we invite you to respond to the readings we've selected, to join in conversation with all the people who've collaborated to write this book — writers, editors, reviewers, and students. Following is an alphabetical catalog of guidelines to the writing assignments you may be asked to do as you use this book. As you read and use these guidelines, remember that a *text* can be an article, a visual, a Web site — anything that you "read."

Analysis

Analytical writing puts ideas under scrutiny. To analyze a print, visual, or electronic text is to question the validity of arguments, the accuracy of facts, the logical relationship of ideas, the fairness of conclusions, and the assumptions underlying them. Here are some suggestions for analyzing a text:

- Identify exactly what you want to analyze, whether a single paragraph or a full work.

- Note any preconceptions or assumptions you bring to the topic of your analysis. Think about how they may affect your analysis.

- Mark the text you are analyzing thoroughly, including any visuals. Annotate in the margins, highlight key quotations, and circle terms or features you think are especially important.

- Divide the text into its main ideas, and look at each one carefully. What support and details exist for each idea?

- Look for connections between and among ideas. Are these connections clear and logical to you? Do you see the point of intriguing juxtapositions of ideas or visuals?

- Try to think of opposing points of view or alternative perspectives on the topic. Does the writer consider them fairly?

For an example of analysis, see the essay by Adrienne Rich (p. 74).

Rhetorical Analysis   In its simplest form, a rhetorical analysis explores two basic questions: What is the writer's purpose? How is that purpose presented to an intended audience? Answers to these important questions help readers appreciate the options that writers face and the possible reasons behind particular choices of language, image, genre, and so on. A rhetorical analysis does not focus on what a text means but rather looks at the particular strategies a writer uses to get across that meaning and gauges their success. A rhetorical analysis can also consider how a writer's cultural, economic, social, or political contexts affect the reading and writing of the text. Here are tips for examining a text rhetorically:

- Try to define the major purpose of the text, but understand that it may be composed for more than one reason. Identify these multiple purposes when you can, pointing out in your analysis where they may conflict. When possible, show where such conflicts may have affected the writer's choice of arguments, evidence, vocabulary, examples, visual elements, and so on.

- Try to identify a primary audience and describe its expectations. What do members of the primary audience know about the subject, and what do they need to know? How does the text address their expectations or needs?

- Identify any secondary audiences. How do their needs differ from those of the primary audience?

- Explore the author's attitude toward the topic or issue — is it favorable or unfavorable? Mocking or satirical? Judgmental or neutral? What is the author's stake in the subject?

- Explore the relationship of the author to the audience. Does he or she maintain a position of distance and authority or seek to "come close to" readers?
- Explain how the text uses rhetorical strategies, including choice of evidence and detail, the author's tone and voice, the vocabulary choices, and the kinds of sentences.

For an example of a rhetorical analysis, see the essay by David Brooks (p. 525).

Critical Analysis A critical analysis may examine many of the same issues as a rhetorical analysis. But a critical analysis usually makes more value judgments about the integrity of a text — its power and its reach.

A critical analysis looks carefully at the logic of a text, identifying its claims and assessing the premises and evidence that support those claims. Critical analysis seeks to answer questions such as these: Does the author make a coherent claim? Are the assumptions behind the claim defensible? Are the connections among assumptions, claims, and evidence logical? Is the evidence presented sufficient and reliable? Is the text fair, or is the author biased in a way that undermines the credibility of the piece?

A critical analysis also looks at the *success* of a text — at how persuasive it is, how well it makes emotional or ethical appeals, how successfully it moves or delights readers. Here are some tips for examining a text critically:

- Understand the intended audience(s) and purpose(s). Consider the work's historical, social, and political contexts in some detail.
- Identify the claims, both stated and implied.
- Identify the premises behind the claims, and determine how those assumptions would be received by the intended reader(s).
- Examine the evidence for each claim. What are the sources of information? Study any statistics and how they are used. Consider the sources and reliability of polls and surveys.
- Explore the logic of the argument. Does the writer use any logical fallacies? Consider, too, the rhetorical force of the evidence. Is it sufficient? Overwhelming?
- Consider the way the writer presents himself or herself. Does the author make a persuasive, appealing case? Is he or she appropriately engaged in or deliberately removed from the text?
- If visuals are included, do they fairly and appropriately support the author's points?
- Consider the way the text makes its overall appeal. Is the format appropriate to its audience? Is it appropriately serious? Humorous? Academic? Colloquial?

For an example of critical analysis, see the essay by Michael Pollan (p. 204).

Argument

Among a writer's toughest jobs is making a persuasive argument, one that moves readers to reaffirm a commitment — or to consider changing their minds or taking action. Almost all the readings and visuals in this book contain arguments. As you work at reading these texts, you may want to construct arguments of your own. Here are some suggestions for writing an effective academic argument:

- Develop a clear, carefully limited thesis to defend. This thesis will often evolve gradually as you learn about your subject.

- Find some good reasons for your audience to agree with the thesis. Support all statements with specific and appropriate evidence, including visuals if appropriate.

- Show that any evidence you have gathered is fair, appropriate, and accurate; that your various arguments support one another; and that they outweigh possible counterarguments.

- When building an argument from something you've read, regard the text and everything connected with it — the language and style of the writer, his or her background and reputation, the time and place of publication, the reputation of the publisher, visuals that accompany the written text, and so on — as potential evidence. When appropriate, quote from a piece of evidence carefully to demonstrate the points you are making. Bring the writer's voice into the conversation, but don't let his or her words be a substitute for what you have to say.

- Appeal to the readers you are trying to convince by connecting your argument to subjects they are likely to know and care about. An effective argument stimulates thinking and conversation. It doesn't close off discussion or create enemies.

For examples of effective arguments, see the essays by Barbara Dafoe Whitehead (p. 224) and J. Michael Bishop (p. 304).

Brainstorming

Brainstorming is an activity that can jump-start your thinking. It consists simply of putting down ideas — about a reading, a writing topic, a problem to solve, whatever — just as they come to mind. Although you can certainly brainstorm alone, brainstorming often works better in a group because you can bounce your ideas off other people. If you are working with a group, assign one person to jot down notes.

You can brainstorm either as you read or immediately afterward. Here are some specific tips for brainstorming:

- List your thoughts as they occur. Put down whatever comes to mind; let your ideas flow. Prune and reorder ideas *later.*

- Don't judge the quality of your brainstorming prematurely. Record your intuitions. Give yourself slack to explore ideas — even silly or outlandish ones.
- Once you've written all your thoughts down, look for connections among them. What conclusions can you draw about your position on the subject by looking at these connections?

Comparison and Contrast

Strictly speaking, when you compare things, you are looking for similarities; when you contrast them, you are pointing out differences. Here are some suggestions for comparing and contrasting:

- Break your subject into parts or aspects that can be studied profitably. As the old saying goes, you don't want to compare apples and oranges.
- Pursue your comparison or contrast analysis systematically, point by point, using visuals as well as words if they are appropriate. Group the comparisons or contrasts purposefully so that they make or support a point about your subject.
- Use appropriate transitional words and phrases. Readers can easily get lost if you jump from one point of comparison or contrast to another without providing the necessary bridges.
- Be fair. Even when you are inclined to favor one side over another, be sure to consider the other side fairly.

The selection by Andrew Sullivan (p. 381) provides examples of comparing and contrasting.

Definition

When asked to define a word or concept in a paragraph, you're usually expected to write an extended explanation of the term, accompanied by illustrations and examples. Terms can also be defined through descriptions of their components, descriptions of processes (how something works), or any appropriate combination of these methods. Here are some suggestions for defining:

- To define a term, place it within a larger category and then list features or characteristics that distinguish it from other items in that category: "A skyscraper is a building of unusual height."
- Then expand the simple definition by providing additional distinguishing details: "A skyscraper is a building of unusual height, most often supported by a steel skeleton and having many stories. The earliest skyscrapers appeared in American cities, especially Chicago and New York, late in the nineteenth century. The height of buildings was confined at first by

construction techniques that required massive masonry walls and by the limits of elevator technology. The invention of steel skeletons that supported both floors and walls and the development of high-speed elevators made much taller buildings possible. Among the most famous skyscrapers are the Empire State Building in New York and the Sears Tower in Chicago."

- In most cases, try to keep the tone of a formal definition factual and impersonal. An extended definition, however, can be composed in many different registers, from the serious to the satiric.

Differences over definitions often give rise to the disagreements that people have about important political and social issues. Therefore, always be sensitive to the key words in a text. Quite often, while you and other readers agree on the core meanings of such important terms (their denotations), you may not share the feelings, images, and associations that these words evoke (their connotations). For examples of definition, see the essay by Dave Barry (p. 405).

Description

A description provides a snapshot of something — explaining what it looks like at a particular moment. You can describe things through words or visuals.

- Consider your perspective on the item you want to describe. From what angle are you observing it? Share this point of view with readers.
- Spend some quiet time observing what you plan to describe very carefully.
- Record the most distinctive features and details, those that will enable readers to visualize what you are describing. In most types of writing, your goal is to convey an accurate *impression* of what you have seen, be it person, thing, or even idea.
- Written descriptions depend heavily on modifiers — words that convey concrete, sensory details by specifying shape, size, color, smell, and so on. Modifiers should be chosen very deliberately — and used sparingly.

For an effective example of description, see the selection by Eric Schlosser (p. 654).

Dialogue

A dialogue is a conversation between two or more people — as in an interview, where ideas and opinions are exchanged, or in fiction or nonfiction writing, where a conversation is reproduced or imagined. To write such a conversation, you need to know something about the way the participants think, how they view the world, even the way they speak. Writing a fictional dialogue thus requires — and allows — imaginative role playing. Here are some suggestions for creating one:

- Try to put yourself within the minds of the characters, and consider how they might respond to each other. Look closely at the typical attitudes, interests, habits, and expressions used by your characters. Try to reproduce them.
- It's not enough just to have characters "talk"; you have to decide on a subject for them to talk about. The liveliest dialogues usually feature some exchange of ideas or opinions.
- Set the dialogue in a particular place and time.
- A dialogue can be a stimulating way to respond to a reading. Imagine a dialogue among yourself and some friends on the reading — or place yourself in conversation with the writer. What would you like to say to Jessica Cohen (p. 190) or Mary Shelley (p. 285)? What might they say to you?

Evaluation

Writing an evaluation involves making and justifying judgments. First, you need to determine the appropriate criteria for the evaluation. Obviously, you wouldn't use the same standards in evaluating an elementary school play that you would in reviewing one produced by the Yale Repertory Theater. In most reviews, it is best to take a clear position. Don't make your evaluation so subtle that no one can tell what your stance is. Here are some suggestions for writing an evaluation:

- Determine the appropriate criteria for the evaluation. Sometimes these standards will be obvious or given. In other cases, you will have to establish and define them. Readers will want to know why you are applying certain measures so that they can determine whether to trust your opinions.
- Measure your subject according to these standards.
- Base your evaluation on clear and sufficient evidence. A good evaluation is based on tangible facts and compelling arguments.
- Let readers see how you arrived at your judgment. For example, if you are raising doubts about the competence of an author, make clear what led you to that conclusion. If you are evaluating something visual, include illustrations if possible.
- Arrange your arguments in logical order — perhaps in order of increasing importance. Sometimes you can bolster your argument by comparing and contrasting your subject with objects or ideas already familiar to your readers.

For an example of evaluation, see the selection by Malcolm Gladwell (p. 238).

Exploration

The point of exploratory writing is to examine subjects imaginatively, so such pieces are often more tentative than reports or more purely argumentative writing. Exploratory essays allow you to take risks, to jump into controversies too complex to be resolved easily. So when you want to explore an issue in writing, try to go beyond predictable and safe positions. Following are some strategies for doing so:

- Read a series of provocative articles from various perspectives. Talk with friends or classmates. Reach for dialogue, discussion, and debate.

- Be prepared for multiple drafts. Your best ideas are likely to emerge during the composing process.

- Be open to alternative views and voices, especially those that are heard less frequently. Bring other writers into the discussion.

- As the essay evolves, show it to interested readers and ask for their frank responses. Incorporate questions, debates, or other material into the discussion. Dialogue can be a particularly stimulating technique for exploration.

- Don't expect to wrap up this kind of writing with a neat bow. Be prepared for gaps and gaffes. Exploratory writing often produces more questions than answers.

For examples of exploratory writing, see the essays by Jane Mayer (p. 252) and Zora Neale Hurston (p. 416).

Freewriting

Freewriting is a technique for generating ideas. When you freewrite about something, you follow ideas to see where they lead. Freewriting in response to an essay might be prompted by particular words, phrases, passages, or images that you have highlighted while reading. It can also be useful for exploring connections between two or three different selections. Here are some specific tips for freewriting:

- One way to get started is by answering a question — for instance, "What does this topic make me think of?" or "When I think of this topic, what do I feel?"

- Write nonstop for a fixed period of time — five or ten minutes, perhaps. Don't stop during that time; the point is to generate as much material as you can.

- If you can't think of anything to write, put down a nonsense phrase or repeat a key word just to keep moving.

- Don't stop to question or correct your work while freewriting. Forget about style and correctness. Get the intellectual juices flowing.

- After freewriting, read the words you have produced to recover the ideas you may have generated. If you have come up with observations worthy of more exploration, make those ideas the focus of more freewriting.

Interview

We routinely ask people questions to satisfy our curiosity, but to turn a conversation with an interesting and knowledgeable person into a useful interview, you need to do your homework. The first step is to decide whom you wish to interview — and you don't have to limit yourself to experts. Friends and classmates have knowledge and opinions you might tap by interviewing them. Think of an interview as a high-powered conversation, a new way to learn. Here are some suggestions for arranging, conducting, and recording an interview:

- Determine the purpose of your interview, and make sure it relates closely to your topic.

- Call or write ahead for an appointment, and specify how long the interview will take. If you want to record the session, ask for permission to do so.

- Prepare your questions in advance, perhaps brainstorming a preliminary list, then augmenting it with who-what-where-when-why-how items. Arrange your queries in a sensible order, perhaps beginning with more factual questions and then moving to more complex questions of opinion.

- Prepare some open-ended questions — the kind that can't be answered in a word or phrase. Give yourself leeway to take the conversation down any paths that open up spontaneously.

- Try out your questions on one or two people to make sure they are clear and understandable. If not, revise.

- Get any equipment you need ready beforehand — from your pen to your tape recorder, laptop, and so on — and make sure the recording device you plan to use is working properly before you begin the interview.

- Be on time!

- Record your subject's responses carefully, later double-checking with him or her any direct quotations you might want to use. Even if you are taping, take notes.

- Record time, date, place, and other pertinent information about the conversation for your records.

- After an interview, summarize the information briefly in your own words.

- Remember to follow up with a thank-you note or email.

Letter to the Editor

A familiar kind of persuasive writing is the letter to the editor, in which writers explain why they agree or disagree with something they've read. Such letters are typically composed in response to positions taken by newspapers, magazines, or journals. In most cases, letters to the editor are spirited arguments, somewhat personal, and carefully targeted.

Letters to the editor follow the conventions of business letters and should be dated and signed. Here are some suggestions for writing one:

- Think about who reads the periodical to which the letter will be sent. Because such a letter is intended for publication, it is usually written more to win the support of other readers than to influence editors or publishers.

- Identify your target article within the first line or two. Let readers know exactly what piece provoked your ire or admiration.

- Make your case quickly. Since space for letters is very limited in most publications, expect to make only one or two points. Execute them powerfully and memorably, using the best examples and reasons you can.

- When appropriate, use irony, satire, or humor.

Narration

Whereas descriptions usually refer to stationary things, narratives depict motion, whether it be the action of a single person or the unfurling of a complex historical event, such as a war or social movement. When you narrate, you usually tell a story of some kind. But a narrative may also explain *how something occurred* (analyzing a process) or *why something happened* (tracing cause and effect). Here are some suggestions for narrating:

- Place the events you are discussing in a meaningful order, usually chronological — first this happened, then this, then this, and so on.

- Provide necessary background information by answering the questions who, what, where, when, why, and how the events occurred.

- Most narratives call for some description. Flesh out any characters and describe any scenic details necessary to the narrative. Consider using appropriate images.

- Use transitional phrases (*then, next, on the following day*) or series (*in the spring, during the summer, later in the year*) to keep the sequence of the narrative clear. Remember, however, that the sequence doesn't always have to be chronological (you've certainly seen flashbacks in movies).

For examples of narration, see the selections by Mary Shelley (p. 285) and Maxine Hong Kingston (p. 394).

Online Forum or Listserv

In some courses, you may be expected to write about a topic or reading in an online forum or on a listserv. In a topic forum, you typically respond to a prompt on a Web page and read what your classmates have to say there; postings to and from a listserv are exchanged as email messages. Whichever technology is used, electronic discussions provide instantaneous communication and rapid response — which are both their strength and their weakness. But you can learn to write effectively in these environments with just a little practice.

- If you are the first to post a response to a prompt from an instructor or classmate, address the question directly and thoughtfully; you may be setting the tone for an entire discussion.

- When you join a discussion already in progress, get a feel for the conversation before posting a message. Pay attention to both the content and the tone of the forum. Let your message suggest that you have given due consideration to the thoughts of others who have already contributed to the discussion. Avoid the temptation to fire off just a few quick words in response to a classmate's posting. No one wants to open a message that says simply *You're wrong!* or *I agree.*

- Be sure your message places your ideas in context. Quite often, you'll be responding to a specific question or to messages others have already sent. So sometimes it helps to repeat portions of previous messages in your posting, but don't copy long strings of text. Such repetition may clutter your own message and even make it hard to find.

- Consider how the title of your posting might convey both your context and your point. In most forums, the responses to an original posting will be linked by the familiar abbreviation *Re*, which means "with reference to." You can keep a string of responses going, but vary the title of your message slightly to indicate your own slant.

  Newman's THE IDEA OF A UNIVERSITY
  Re: Newman's THE IDEA OF A UNIVERSITY — Still relevant?
  Re: Newman's THE IDEA OF A UNIVERSITY — Old-fashioned
  Re: Newman's THE IDEA OF A UNIVERSITY — Makes sense!

- Remember to consider differences your group may have, not only in terms of computer compatibility but also in terms of accessibility. Will everyone in your group be able to read what you have posted with ease?

- Edit your posting before you send it. Online communications tend to be less formal than other kinds of writing. But show respect for your classmates by editing messages before you send them into the public square. Remember that you won't be able to recall or correct your blunders once you hit "send."

Parody

Your appreciation of a written work can't be tested better than by parody. A *parody* is an imitation of an author, a work, or an attitude written with a humorous and sometimes critical edge. Parody succeeds when readers recognize both your target and your criticism; they should laugh at the wit in your mimicking something they too have experienced.

When you write a parody, you are in certain ways collaborating with other writers. You will necessarily learn much about the way they think and use language. Here are some suggestions for writing a parody:

- Choose a distinctive idea or work to parody. The more recognizable an attitude or famous a work is, the easier it will be to poke fun at. But even the most vapid work can be mocked for its dullness.

- Look for familiar subjects, motifs, images, or opinions, and distort them enough to be funny but not so much that the original idea becomes unrecognizable.

- When parodying a well-known work or writer, try shifting from a serious theme to a frivolous one; for example, imagine a pompous opera critic reviewing an Eminem video.

- Pinpoint the habits of language ordinarily used to discuss your subject — typical sentence openers, preferred jargon, distinctive patterns of repetition, favorite sentence patterns, unusual punctuation. Then exaggerate those habits.

- Don't make your parody too long. Parody is a form of wit, and brevity is its soul.

- Above all, have fun. When a parody ceases being funny, it becomes simply tedious imitation.

For an example of parody, see Bobby Henderson's "Church of the Flying Spaghetti Monster's Open Letter to the Kansas School Board" (p. 348).

Position Paper

A position paper is a short (often one-page or one-screen) argument that can sometimes be exploratory. In it, you will usually present a thesis — a statement that needs to be proved or defended. But such a paper is often assigned to jump-start discussions or to get various points of view on the table, so feel free to take risks and examine new approaches. A position paper need not have the gloss of a polished argument, and its language can be livelier than that of more formal academic arguments. It should stimulate your readers — often your classmates — to respond actively to your ideas. Here are some suggestions for writing a position paper:

- Begin by taking a stand on a subject. Find a statement you can defend reasonably well.

- Support your thesis with various kinds of evidence — arguments, examples, statistics, illustrations, expert opinions, and so on.
- If the position paper is very brief, suggest the direction a fuller argument might take.
- Write an open-ended conclusion, qualifying your original thesis or pointing to avenues for further study.

For an example of a position paper, see the reading selection by John Yoo (p. 275).

Proposal

Proposals identify a problem and suggest action that will remedy the problem. You need to convince readers first that a problem exists and is serious, then that your solution is a feasible remedy. Often you will try as well to inspire your readers to take some action.

- To demonstrate that the problem exists, give examples and cite evidence such as statistics or the testimony of experts. Use photographs or other visuals if appropriate.
- Consider your audience. Are readers likely to be aware of the problem? Try to connect the problem to concerns they might have.
- To convince readers to accept your solution, you need to show that it is feasible — and that it is better than other solutions that might reasonably be proposed. Again, visuals may help here.

For an example of an essay that proposes a solution, see the selection by Adrienne Rich (p. 74).

Reading Log

Many writers use reading logs to record their feelings and detailed impressions about what they're reading and thinking. Your instructor may ask you to keep one and turn it in as part of your work for a course. You may decide to keep such a log in a notebook or on your computer. For a computer reading log, make sure to set up a special folder or file for it, label it clearly, and then save each entry with an identifiable title. Here are some suggestions for keeping a reading log:

- If you want to remember what you've read, take time to summarize the text or list its main ideas. You may want to keep a double-entry log — one set of pages reserved for summaries, paraphrases, and quotations, and another set of pages reserved for your reactions and responses to what you are reading.

- Write out your immediate reactions to the text. These may include memorable lines; things that made you angry, sad, puzzled, or delighted; or things that you want to know more about. Later, in a more extended comment, summarize your thoughts about the text. Reflect on what in the piece and in your experience may have shaped your reactions.

- Make some notes about the author's perspective, where he or she seems to be coming from, noting places in the text that provide clues to the perspective.

- Write in an informal, exploratory style, almost as if you were talking to yourself.

- Date your entries and be sure to identify the text.

- Look at your commentary in the context of your notes on other readings. Do you see any useful or interesting connections?

For examples of writing that is similar to reading log entries, see the editors' responses to John Leo's essay (p. 592).

Report

Doing a report is one of the most common academic assignments. Reports are explanations that transfer information from writers to readers. That information may come directly from the writers' minds or from other sources of information — from traditional libraries to field research to computer networks.

- Focus a report on a thesis, a clear statement of purpose. The thesis is the main point or controlling idea of a piece of writing. A thesis statement makes a promise to readers, telling them what to expect, and it limits the subject matter and scope of your report.

- Acknowledge any sources you use.

- Define any terms your readers are unlikely to know.

- Arrange information according to a plan your readers can easily follow. For example, a report on the major events of the cold war could follow a chronological organization: first, second, third. A report on the cold war policies of Joseph Stalin and Harry Truman might use a structure comparing and contrasting the two leaders.

- Use visuals if they will help readers follow your points.

- Conclude by summarizing your work and exploring its implications.

- Give the report a concise, factual, and descriptive title.

For an example of a report, see the selection by Mark Clayton (p. 198).

WORKING WITH SOURCES

Much of your college writing will involve the use of source materials. Following are guidelines for evaluating, quoting, paraphrasing, and summarizing sources.

Evaluating Sources

Not all sources are equally authoritative or useful. Here are some general tips for evaluating sources; consult your instructor, librarian, or writing handbook for further advice.

- Note whether a source is a primary or secondary one.
- Learn the differences between scholarly and trade books, and choose sources appropriate to your work. The claims in scholarly books are systematically documented and carefully reviewed; trade books may be just as factual and reliable, but they typically lack formal documentation.
- Understand the differences between scholarly journals and popular magazines. Both may serve your research needs, but in different ways. Journals written for specialists will often be highly technical and, consequently, difficult for people outside a profession to read; popular magazines serve wider audiences and present more accessible — if less authoritative — information.
- Take advantage of the databases that are available through your library. Most college libraries pay for subscriptions to the most reliable and credible databases, such as LexisNexis, thus giving you free access to them.
- Understand the limits of commercial online sources. Web sites, for example, vary enormously in quality, from those carefully maintained by institutions and professional organizations to playful home pages posted by individuals. Be especially careful with sites associated with familiar figures or institutions but not actually maintained or authorized by them.

Quoting

Quoting involves noting a source's *exact words.* In working with the selections in this book, you will have many opportunities to use direct quotation. Many of the headnotes that introduce each reading show examples of direct quotation.

- Copy quotations *carefully*, with punctuation, capitalization, and spelling exactly as in the original.
- Use ellipses to indicate any omitted words.

- Bracket any words you need to add to the quotation.
- Enclose the quotation in quotation marks.

Paraphrasing

A paraphrase accurately states all the relevant information from a passage *in your own words and phrasing*, without any additional comment or elaboration. Use paraphrases when you want to cite ideas from a source but have no need to quote exact words.

- Include the main points and some important details from the original, in the same order in which they are presented in the source.
- Use your own words and sentence structures. If you want to include especially memorable language from the original, enclose it in quotation marks.
- Leave out your own comments and reactions.
- Recheck the paraphrase against the original to be sure that the words and structures are your own and that they express the author's meaning accurately.

Summarizing

A summary concisely restates key ideas *in your own words*. Sometimes you may need to summarize something in a sentence or two: "In *The Culture of Disbelief*, Stephen L. Carter argues that American culture pressures people with strong religious beliefs not to act on their principles." Often a more detailed synopsis is necessary. Preparing such a summary takes some planning. Here are some suggestions:

- Outline the text you are summarizing. Identify its main points, supoints, and key bits of supporting evidence.
- Flesh out the outline with necessary details, taking care to show the connections between key ideas.
- Check that your concise version of a longer work can stand on its own. Remember that your readers may not have access to the original piece, so all references need to be clear.
- Double-check against the piece you are summarizing to make sure the wording in your summary is your own.

For an example of summary, see portions of Barbara Dafoe Whitehead's essay (p. 224).

Deciding Whether to Quote, Paraphrase, or Summarize

- *Quote*

    Wording that expresses a point so perfectly that you cannot improve or shorten it without weakening the meaning you need

    Authors' opinions you wish to emphasize

    Respected authorities whose opinions support your own ideas

    Authors whose opinions challenge or vary from others in the field

- *Paraphrase*

    Passages that you do not wish to quote but whose details you wish to note *fully*

- *Summarize*

    Long passages whose *main points* you wish to record *selectively*

Integrating Sources into Your Writing

Integrate quotations, paraphrases, and summaries into your own writing carefully, often by using a signal phrase such as *he said* or *she remarks.* Choose the verbs you use to introduce source material carefully; be sure they express your thoughts accurately. Notice, for instance, the difference between saying someone "said," "claimed," or "asserted."

In the following sentence, "As Richard deCordova notes in a memorable phrase, the studios wanted to convince millions of moviegoers that 'the real hero behaved just like the reel hero'" (Gallager 2), the signal verb *notes* makes it clear that the quotation is by deCordova and that the author agrees with it: if the author had wanted to indicate that deCordova's point is more open to disagreement or that other authorities might disagree with it, she would have chosen a different verb such as *claims* or *asserts.* For effective integration of sources, see the many quotations in Robert D. King's essay (p. 434).

Integrating Visuals into Your Writing

Remember that any visuals you use need to be as carefully integrated into your text as quotations, paraphrases, or summaries. In addition, make sure that you introduce each visual and comment on it in some way. Finally, label (as figures or tables) and number (Fig. 1, Fig. 2, and so on) all visuals, provide a caption (see Fig. 2.1 on p. 38), and cite the source in your list of works cited. Even if you create a visual (such as a bar graph) by using information from a source (such as the Gallup Poll), you must cite that source (again, see Fig. 2.1). If you use a photograph you took yourself, cite that as well.

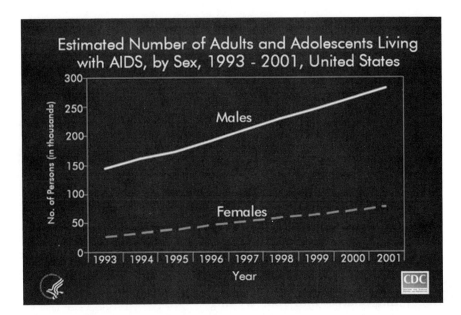

Fig. 2.1   Estimated U.S. AIDS Cases by Sex, 1993–2001. Source: Centers for Disease Control and Prevention (CDC).

Acknowledging Sources

When quoting, paraphrasing, or summarizing sources in formal essays, reports, or research projects, be sure to acknowledge all sources according to the conventions required by your field or instructor. It is especially important to avoid cutting and pasting anything from an online source into your own text without full citation.

Plagiarism, using the words of others without citation, has been much in the news in the last few years, with at least two distinguished historians accused of using the work of others without acknowledgment and online companies such as turnitin.com springing up to try to ferret out cheaters. So it's well worth taking extra care to make sure you have not been careless or sloppy in your use of sources.

WORKING WITH OTHERS

The title for this book recalls a remark by philosopher Hannah Arendt that "for excellence, the presence of others is always required." Nowhere is Arendt's observation more accurate than in the college community. Your college coursework will call on you to read, write, and research a vast amount of material. But you will not — or need not — do all that reading, writing, and researching alone. Instead, you can be part of a broad conversation that includes all the texts you read; all the writing you produce; all the discussions you have with teachers, friends, family members, and classmates; all the observations and interviews you conduct. Throughout this book, we draw on Arendt's concept — from our title to the way we group readings in conversation with one another to the commentaries or selections by teachers and professionals to the many collaborative assignments.

Collaboration can play an important part in all the writing you do, first if you talk with others about your topic and your plans for approaching it, then if you seek responses to your draft and gather suggestions for improving it. In much the same way, reading can be done "with others" — first by entering into mental conversation with the author and with the social and historical forces at work shaping the author's text, then by comparing your understanding of the text with that of other readers and using points of agreement or disagreement as the basis for further analysis.

As you read this book, the most immediate and valuable of your collaborators may be your classmates. Indeed, you can learn a great deal by listening carefully both to them and to your instructor. You can profit even more by talking over issues with them, by comparing notes and ideas with them, and by using them as a first and very important audience for your writing. They will inevitably offer you new perspectives, new ways of seeing and knowing. Here are some guidelines for effective collaboration:

- Once you establish a group, trade contact information and schedules, and set a time to meet.

- Set an agenda for each meeting. If you intend to study or compare certain readings, be sure everyone knows in advance and brings the essay or book to the meeting. Perhaps begin by brainstorming major questions group members have about the reading.

- Use the group to work through difficult readings. If a reading is especially long, have each member take one section to explain and "teach" to the others.

- If you need to prepare a presentation or report as a group, decide on a fair and effective means of dividing the task. Assign each group member specific duties. Arrange for a time to meet when those individual duties will have been accomplished. At the meeting, work to review the various parts and put them together. Decide on any visual aids or handouts in advance, and prepare them carefully. Finally, *practice the presentation.* Everyone will benefit from a dress rehearsal. If it's possible to get someone to videotape the rehearsal, do so; you'll learn a great deal from watching yourself do an actual presentation.

- Most important, listen to every member of the group carefully and respectfully; everyone's ideas must be taken into consideration. If conflict arises — and in any lively and healthy collaboration, it will — explore all areas of the conflict openly and fairly before seeking a resolution.

- At each meeting, take time to assess the effectiveness of the group. Consider these questions: What has the group accomplished so far? How has the group been most helpful? How has it been least helpful? What have you personally contributed? What has each of the others contributed? How can all members make the group more effective?

TWO STUDENT SAMPLE ESSAYS

We have outlined in this chapter some of the ways you may be asked to respond to selected readings in your writing classes. Following are two examples by students of common assignments.

The first, on p. 41, is a critical response essay (guidelines for writing a critical analysis begin on p. 23). Jennifer E. Smith responds to the selection in the book by J. Michael Bishop, "Enemies of Promise" (p. 304). She was not asked to use additional sources, so her works cited page lists only the essay from this anthology.

The second is a comparison and contrast essay using two essays in this anthology as well as additional sources. (For guidelines on writing comparison and contrast, see p. 25; for guidelines on working with sources, see p. 35.) In the essay that begins on p. 44, Rudy Rubio compares John Tierney's "Male Pride and Female Prejudice" (p. 130) with Katha Pollitt's "Girls against Boys?" (p. 139). His works cited page includes these sources as well as the additional research he includes in his paper.

JENNIFER E. SMITH
Questioning the Promises of Science

It is overwhelming to think of the number of questions that science seeks to answer. Science tries to explain how every aspect of the universe works; it is indeed a broad topic. For this reason, as J. Michael Bishop concludes in his essay "Enemies of Promise," educating the public about the advancements, or even general knowledge, of science is difficult. Thus, Bishop points out, the scientific ignorance of the public leads to a fear of science: "[r]esistance to science is born of fear" (308). Though Bishop, on behalf of the scientific community, takes responsibility for neglecting public scientific education, he seems to accuse all those who question science of suffering from ignorance. Though I agree with Bishop's point about the lack of education in the sciences, I disagree with his approach. Bishop does not prove his point well in "Enemies of Promise"; he does not offer sufficient counterarguments to his postmodern detractors, nor does he offer any solutions to the problems with education, which he claims are the cause of postmodern critiques.

Bishop begins "Enemies of Promise" by marveling over the "fruits of scientific inquiry" (304) and questioning why "science today is increasingly mistrusted and under attack" (304). Throughout the essay, Bishop seems too proud of the scientific field to admit that current scientific methods are less than perfect. Even in the age of computer technology, scientists, *humans*, still perform the research. When humans are involved, there will always be some degree of bias; business and politics will have their influence. Though these biases may be minimal and are usually unintended, they still exist; science is not immune to human nature. Bishop does not recognize this and angrily dismisses the postmodern view, which calls science on its biases, as "arrant nonsense" (305). The postmodern view may be an exaggerated response to the frustration associated with the politics of science, but these critics do raise some valid points and should not be dismissed. It is ironic that the scientific community, which was born out of questioning that which was assumed to be known, is now angered when its own knowledge is questioned. Bishop shows this anger throughout the essay when he responds to his critics. He refers to postmodernism as "either a strategy for advancement in parochial precincts . . . or a display of ignorance" (305). Instead of debating Václav Havel's remarks on science, Bishop accuses him of using "angry words" whose "precise meaning is elusive" (305). Bishop also refers to all questioners of science as a "chorus of criticism and doubt" (305).

While his easy dismissal of some critics is troubling, Bishop does offer a good response to the criticisms of Brown and Lamm. Brown is frustrated by the "'knowledge paradox,'" which Bishop paraphrases as "an expansion of fundamental knowledge accompanied by an increase in social problems" (305). Lamm no longer believes "that biomedical research contributes to the improvement of human health" (305–6) because of the lack of access in the United States to these health care advancements as well as the abundance of social diseases in today's society. Bishop points out that Brown and Lamm are placing blame on science for "the failures of individuals or society to use the knowledge that science has provided" (306). He also notes that critics often expect too much, too soon, from science and fail to realize that scientific study is dependent on feasibility and that results are often unpredictable.

Bishop continues "Enemies of Promise" by noting the stereotypes that the public has about scientists themselves and how these stereotypes contribute to the general mistrust of science. According to him, the public has "exaggerated expectations about what science can accomplish" (307) because of the rapid successes of science in the past. Bishop then attacks the 1992 film *Lorenzo's Oil*, equating it with some sort of anti-science propaganda. The movie does portray scientists according to common stereotypes; as Bishop points out, it shows them as "insensitive, close-minded, and self-serving" (307). However, Bishop does little to disprove this stereotype; in fact, throughout the essay he shows signs of possessing all of these characteristics. He is obviously close-minded in response to his critics, especially postmodernists. He seems insensitive in his discussion of the true life story behind *Lorenzo's Oil* and in the way he discusses other people's scientific ignorance. Though Bishop is not obviously "self-serving," he does seem overly proud of his role as a scientist and of the role of science in general. Describing our age as one "of scientific triumph," he sees science as "one of the great, ennobling tasks of humankind" (305) and biomedical research as "one of the great triumphs of human endeavor" (307).

Bishop begins his conclusion to "Enemies of Promise" well with his discussion of the difficulties in educating people about science. He admits how far behind the United States is in the process and notes that most scientists specialize and are often ignorant about fields of science outside their own. Bishop correctly places blame for this lack of education with the scientific community. However, as soon as he notes this problem, instead of offering a solution, he returns to praising science with flowery language: "We of science have begun the quest well, by building a method of ever-increasing power, a method that can illuminate all that is in the natural world" (309). The concluding paragraph is consistent with the rest of the essay in that it focuses too much on building up science as the quintessence of human reason rather than addressing the real problems of educating others about science.

5

Bishop's pride seems to have prevented him from providing a proper focus in his essay. For his argument to be a convincing one, the focus should have been directed toward the education problem. Bishop concludes that those who question science do so out of ignorance, yet he offers no suggestions for how to diminish this ignorance. Instead, the whole essay seems to focus on asserting how great science is, not with evidence but with catchy phrases. As a result, this essay seems to support the stereotypes that the public has about scientists and their egocentricity.

WORKS CITED

Bishop, J. Michael. "Enemies of Promise." *The Presence of Others*. 5th ed. Ed. Andrea A. Lunsford and John J. Ruszkiewicz. Boston: Bedford/ St. Martin's, 2008. 304–309.

RUDY RUBIO
The Gender Education Gap

In "Male Pride and Female Prejudice," John Tierney urges his readers to recognize a very particular problem: since women are now attending college in greater numbers than men, both men and women will have increased difficulty finding spouses in the future. In "Girls Against Boys?," however, Katha Pollitt responds with firm support for the advances women have made in education and returns the argument where she believes it belongs, to the question of boys' educational problems.

Tierney makes it clear that he is not searching for the answer to an "academic question" but is concerned with the future of available marriage prospects, which effectively directs the reader's attention away from the actual problem of gender inequality in education. He begins his article with a question regarding a dearth of educated men for a new generation of educated women: "When there are three women for every two men graduating from college, whom will the third woman marry?" (Tierney 130). Despite the undercurrent of concern about educational inequality, the question does not help the reader better understand social issues surrounding gender. Tierney claims that "college-educated women and high-school educated men will have a harder time finding partners as long as educators keep ignoring the gender gap that starts long before college," indicating that his intention is to draw attention to the inequality in education that leads to future inequality for marriage-seeking adults (132). But the issue of marriage remains paramount in his article, leading readers to focus on the dangers to marriage rather than to education. If Tierney truly hopes to engage his reader in the issue of social inequality, especially concerning gender, then marriage may not be the best lens through which to examine the issue.

Furthermore, in spite of its apparent concern for women facing a single life, Tierney's article emphasizes the male perspective, reflecting the continuation of men's dominant role in society. He cites research from the National Survey of Families and Households that indicates that "the average single man under 35 said he was quite willing to marry someone earning much more than he did. He wasn't as interested in marrying someone making much less than he did, and he was especially reluctant to marry a woman who was unlikely to hold a steady job" (Tierney 131). He remarks that he is unable to think of a friend "who refused to date a women because she made more money than he did" and says he has never heard "guys insult a man ... for making less than his wife" and then immediately claims that "the only snide comments I've heard have come from women talking about their friends' husbands," suggesting that men are more enlightened about gender roles than today's women (Tierney 131).

This is not the only evidence that Tierney portrays the marriage "problem" as a battle between the sexes. According to Tierney, men seem to be approaching marriage in good faith while women's commitment to this institution is capricious at best, especially those who earn more than their spouses. Tierney cites researcher Steven Nock, who argues that "women with higher incomes seem less tolerant of their husbands' shortcomings" and are therefore "more likely to initiate divorce," views he accepts without counterargument from a female perspective of any sort (Tierney 131). While it is true that women initiate a majority of divorces, the National Marriage Project at Rutgers University argues that "the higher rate of women initiators is probably due to the fact that men are more likely to be 'badly behaved' . . . [including having] problems with drinking, drug abuse, and infidelity" ("Top Ten"). Tierney never questions whether there might be alternative reasons for the high divorce rate, at least on the part of women.

It isn't as if divorce benefits educated women. Findings presented by Professors Atlee Stroup and Gene Pollock of the College of Wooster show that the standard of living for women at every income level actually decreases substantially after a divorce when compared to that of men at comparable levels (Stroup and Pollack 40). Stroup and Pollack do note that an individual's "education and ability to compete in the labor market are associated with higher levels of adjustment" after a divorce (40). But even if Tierney is right that professional women generally marry professional men, women still suffer a lower standard of living after divorce than do men — professional women's standards decrease by 12 percent compared to an 8 percent decline for professional men (Stroup and Pollack 47).

Pollitt's response to Tierney is rooted in issues of equality between men and women, both in education and in careers. She agrees with Tierney on the existence of a gender gap in education, even citing the same figures he uses: female undergraduates today comprise 57 percent of the total, with the ratio "projected to reach 60/40 in the next few years" (Pollitt 140). Noting that her own college had a ratio of "four male students for every female one," she differs from Tierney in seeing this increasing percentage of women in college as a positive change — and she also points out that both men and women "are much more likely to go to college than forty years ago" (Pollitt 140).

Pollitt takes a very different critical perspective on gender roles than does Tierney, pointing out that "[i]f the mating game worked fine when women were ignorant and helpless and breaks down when they smarten up, that certainly tells us something about marriage" (Pollitt 141). She also raises the question of whether women need college more than men do because of ongoing gender bias in the workforce. She asserts that students go to college "to get credentials for employment and, because of the sexist nature of the labor market, women need those credentials more than men" (Pollitt 141). Some people dispute the claim that sexism is to blame for women's lower pay overall. John G. Roberts Jr., currently the Chief Justice of the U.S. Supreme Court, referred dismissively to a "purported gender gap" in writings during the Reagan Administration (Goldstein, Smith, and Becker), while others argue that financial disparities in pay exist not because of hidden sexism but because women more often accept lower-paying positions (Viall). However, according to a report produced in 2007 by the American Association of University Women, even if one assumes that the playing field for men and women in the workforce is level — that is, that males and females in the same field, such as engineering or teaching, are given equal opportunities to succeed — several factors still prevent women from earning as much as men. Taking time off to care for children and the fact that in the U.S. workplace, "those who fail to work long hours are off the 'fast track' — probably for good" prevent the gap from closing and income equality from being reached (Dey and Hill 7).

In sum, by cloaking his argument for increased recognition of the gender gap in education with his concern for marriage, Tierney misdirects his readers. As Pollitt shows, we must understand the underlying problems before deciding on the appropriate methods for alleviating inequality.

Works Cited

Dey, Jude G., and Catherine Hill. *Behind the Pay Gap.* 2007. Washington D.C.: American Association of University Women Educational Foundation. 1 May 2007 <http://www.aauw.org/research/behindPayGap.cfm>.

Goldstein, Amy, R. Jeffrey Smith, and Jo Becker. "Roberts Resisted Women's Rights." *Washington Post Online* 19 Aug. 2005. 1 May 2007 <http://www.washingtonpost.com/wp-dyn/content/article/2005/08/18/AR2005081802041.html>.

Lunsford, Andrea A., and John J. Ruszkiewicz, eds. *The Presence of Others.* 5th ed. Boston: Bedford/St. Martin's, 2008.

Pollitt, Katha. "Girls Against Boys?" *The Nation* 30 January 2006. Rpt. in Lunsford and Ruszkiewicz 139–41.

Stroup, Atlee L., and Gene E. Pollack. "Economic Consequences of Marital Dissolution." *Journal of Divorce and Remarriage* 22 (1994): 37–54.

Tierney, John. "Male Pride and Female Prejudice." *New York Times* 3 January 2006. Rpt. in Lunsford and Ruszkiewicz 130–32.

"Top Ten Myths of Divorce." *National Marriage Project.* Ed. David Popenoe and Barbara Dafoe Whitehead. Rutgers University. 2002. 5 May 2007 <http://marriage.rutgers.edu>.

Viall, Nate. "Gender Pay Differences: Mind the Gap; It's Not There." *Des Moines Register* 14 May 2007. 03 June 2007 <http://desmoinesregister.com/apps/pbcs.dll/article?AID=/20070514/OPINION01/705140302>.

The photo on the preceding page shows a student in the stands during a Georgia Tech game. Who is the audience for his poster — His parents? Television viewers? Someone else? ■ Do you empathize with this student? Which details of this photograph influence the way you feel about his message? ■ Consider what "a good education" means to you. Is it possible to get one without financial resources? Why or why not? ■ Has your college experience so far been worth the money? Explain.

Education   3

Y OU MAY BE SURPRISED to learn that until fairly recently in the United States most people either did not have the resources to attend college or were excluded from the majority of colleges for other reasons (such as race or gender). Today, however, nearly half of all high school graduates extend their education at a two-year or four-year college or university. And many older individuals who had never pursued higher education or had left college for some reason are now returning to the classroom. More and more people are attending college these days — but what kind of education are they receiving?

In fact, questions about the purpose of education have been under scrutiny at least since Socrates was put on trial in 399 B.C. on charges of corrupting the youth of Athens by his teaching of philosophy. But no one seems to agree these days in the United States, any more than in ancient Greece, about what the role of higher education should be. Who should be encouraged to attend colleges and universities — and who should not be? Should education be a mechanism for advancing the welfare of the nation — augmenting its productivity, management skills, and technology and preserving the quality of its workforce? Should it be an instrument of social change — teaching ideas of social justice, adjusting to new demographics in the population it serves, and providing the rationale for radical reforms of the economic order? Should it exist primarily to stimulate the intellect and the imagination of students? Or should schooling serve other or multiple purposes?

In this chapter, we have selected readings that bring different perspectives — and offer very different answers — to these central questions about the purposes of higher education. We hope these readings will lead you to consider such questions yourself, to think hard and long about what higher education is for and what it *should* be for in the future. Before you begin reading, however, you may want to think over some of the issues raised in this chapter. Here are some questions to get you started thinking:

- What are your reasons for coming to college? Do you think your reasons correspond to your college's or university's goals for its students?

- In what ways was your decision to attend college shaped or influenced by factors outside your control?

- What should be the goals of higher education? If you were president of your college or university, what would you list as the school's aims? What would be your top priorities?

• • •

JOHN HENRY NEWMAN
The Idea of a University

JOHN HENRY NEWMAN's The Idea of a University *is among the most famous attempts to define a liberal arts education. Originally written in 1852 in response to a papal proposal for a Roman Catholic university in Ireland,* The Idea of a University *served as an intellectual manifesto for Catholics, who had long been an oppressed minority in the British Isles. Full emancipation occurred for them only in 1829; prior to that date, Catholics had been denied political rights in England and Ireland as well as admission to the great British universities, Oxford and Cambridge.*

Newman (1801–90), a well-known Anglican priest who had converted to the Roman church, wrote The Idea of a University *to explore what a Catholic university would be like — how it might merge religious and secular concerns. He was also responding to a world growing ever more secular in its interests, more scientific in its methods, more utilitarian in its philosophy. Revolutions in technology and industrial organization seemed to be reshaping every human endeavor, including the university.*

Newman had reservations about these changes, many of which we take for granted today, such as the division of universities into various "schools" (arts, sciences, professional schools), the selection by students of their own programs of study, and the establishment of areas of specialization (what we would call majors*). His aim in this essay is to defend the value of learning for its own sake.*

The Idea of a University *is an example of deliberative rhetoric: Newman is both recommending and defending the proposal for a Catholic university. He faces both an entrenched Anglican tradition and a scholarly community leaning in the direction of what is today called* secular humanism. *The following excerpts from this book-length work do not focus on religious issues, however. Instead, they explain several of Newman's goals for the liberal arts university.*

—J.R.

DISCOURSE V
KNOWLEDGE ITS OWN END

1

I have said that all branches of knowledge are connected together, because the subject-matter of knowledge is intimately united in itself, as being the acts and the work of the Creator. Hence it is that the Sciences, into which our knowledge may be said to be cast, have multiplied bearings one on another, and an internal sympathy, and admit, or rather demand, comparison and adjustment. They complete, correct, balance each other. This consideration, if well-founded, must be taken into account, not only as regards the attainment of

51

truth, which is their common end, but as regards the influence which they exercise upon those whose education consists in the study of them. I have said already, that to give undue prominence to one is to be unjust to another; to neglect or supersede these is to divert those from their proper object. It is to unsettle the boundary lines between science and science, to disturb their action, to destroy the harmony which binds them together. Such a proceeding will have a corresponding effect when introduced into a place of education. There is no science but tells a different tale, when viewed as a portion of a whole, from what it is likely to suggest when taken by itself, without the safeguard, as I may call it, of others.

Let me make use of an illustration. In the combination of colors, very different effects are produced by a difference in their selection and juxtaposition; red, green, and white, change their shades, according to the contrast to which they are submitted. And, in like manner, the drift and meaning of a branch of knowledge varies with the company in which it is introduced to the student. If his reading is confined simply to one subject, however such division of labor may favor the advancement of a particular pursuit, a point into which I do not here enter, certainly it has a tendency to contract his mind. If it is incorporated with others, it depends on those others as to the kind of influence which it exerts upon him. Thus the Classics, which in England are the means of refining the taste, have in France subserved the spread of revolutionary and deistical doctrines. In Metaphysics, again, *Butler's Analogy of Religion** which has had so much to do with the conversion to the Catholic faith of members of the University of Oxford, appeared to Pitt* and others, who had received a different training, to operate only in the direction of infidelity. And so again, Watson, Bishop of Llandaff,* as I think he tells us in the narrative of his life, felt the science of Mathematics to indispose the mind to religious belief, while others see in its investigations the best parallel, and thereby defense, of the Christian Mysteries. In like manner, I suppose, Arcesilas* would not have handled logic as Aristotle, nor Aristotle have criticized poets as Plato; yet reasoning and poetry are subject to scientific rules.

It is a great point then to enlarge the range of studies which a University professes, even for the sake of the students; and, though they cannot pursue every subject which is open to them, they will be the gainers by living among those and under those who represent the whole circle. This I conceive to be the advantage of a seat of universal learning, considered as a place of education. An assemblage of learned men, zealous for their own sciences, and rivals of each other, are brought, by familiar intercourse and for the sake of intellectual

---

Butler's Analogy of Religion: a defense of Christian revelation (1736) by Joseph Butler (1692–1752)

Pitt: William Pitt (1708–78), British parliamentarian and orator

Watson, Bishop of Llandaff: Richard Watson (1737–1816), a professor of chemistry and divinity

Arcesilas: Greek philosopher (c. 316–241 B.C.) who advocated rational skepticism

peace, to adjust together the claims and relations of their respective subjects of investigation. They learn to respect, to consult, to aid each other. Thus is created a pure and clear atmosphere of thought, which the student also breathes, though in his own case he only pursues a few sciences out of the multitude. He profits by an intellectual tradition, which is independent of particular teachers, which guides him in his choice of subjects, and duly interprets for him those which he chooses. He apprehends the great outlines of knowledge, the principles on which it rests, the scale of its parts, its lights and its shades, its great points and its little, as he otherwise cannot apprehend them. Hence it is that his education is called "Liberal." A habit of mind is formed which lasts through life, of which the attributes are, freedom, equitableness, calmness, moderation, and wisdom; or what in a former Discourse I have ventured to call a philosophical habit. This then I would assign as the special fruit of the education furnished at a University, as contrasted with other places of teaching or modes of teaching. This is the main purpose of a University in its treatment of its students.

And now the question is asked me, What is the *use* of it? and my answer will constitute the main subject of the Discourses which are to follow.

ع ع ع

Discourse VII
Knowledge Viewed in Relation to Professional Skill

10

But I must bring these extracts to an end. Today I have confined myself   5
to saying that that training of the intellect, which is best for the individual himself, best enables him to discharge his duties to society. The Philosopher, indeed, and the man of the world differ in their very notion, but the methods, by which they are respectively formed, are pretty much the same. The Philosopher has the same command of matters of thought, which the true citizen and gentleman has of matters of business and conduct. If then a practical end must be assigned to a University course, I say it is that of training good members of society. Its art is the art of social life, and its end is fitness for the world. It neither confines its views to particular professions on the one hand, nor creates heroes or inspires genius on the other. Works indeed of genius fall under no art; heroic minds come under no rule; a University is not a birthplace of poets or of immortal authors, of founders of schools, leaders of colonies, or conquerors of nations. It does not promise a generation of Aristotles or Newtons, of Napoleons or Washingtons, of Raphaels or Shakespeares, though such miracles of nature it has before now contained within its precincts. Nor is it content on the other hand with forming the critic or the experimentalist, the economist or the engineer, though such too it includes within its scope. But a University

Importance for Knowledge to Knowledge

training is the great ordinary means to a great but ordinary end; it aims at raising the intellectual tone of society, at cultivating the public mind, at purifying the national taste, at supplying true principles to popular enthusiasm and fixed aims to popular aspiration, at giving enlargement and sobriety to the ideas of the age, at facilitating the exercise of political power, and refining the intercourse of private life. It is the education which gives a man a clear conscious view of his own opinions and judgments, a truth in developing them, an eloquence in expressing them, and a force in urging them. It teaches him to see things as they are, to go right to the point, to disentangle a skein of thought, to detect what is sophistical, and to discard what is irrelevant. It prepares him to fill any post with credit, and to master any subject with facility. It shows him how to accommodate himself to others, how to throw himself into their state of mind, how to bring before them his own, how to influence them, how to come to an understanding with them, how to bear with them. He is at home in any society, he has common ground with every class; he knows when to speak and when to be silent; he is able to converse, he is able to listen; he can ask a question pertinently, and gain a lesson seasonably, when he has nothing to impart himself; he is ever ready, yet never in the way; he is a pleasant companion, and a comrade you can depend upon; he knows when to be serious and when to trifle, and he has a sure tact which enables him to trifle with gracefulness and to be serious with effect. He has the repose of a mind which lives in itself, while it lives in the world, and which has resources for its happiness at home when it cannot go abroad. He has a gift which serves him in public, and supports him in retirement, without which good fortune is but vulgar, and with which failure and disappointment have a charm. The art which tends to make a man all this, is in the object which it pursues as useful as the art of wealth or the art of health, though it is less susceptible of method, and less tangible, less certain, less complete in its result.

QUESTIONING THE TEXT

1. Examine the goals Newman explicitly provides for the university in the passage from Discourse VII. Do these goals still seem relevant today? Why, or why not? If you keep a reading log, answer this question there.

2. As you reread Newman's essay, record your reactions to his style in the margins. Does it feel stuffy or solemn? Does it move you or impress you? When you are finished, draw some conclusions from your comments.

3. The introduction emphasizes that Newman's *The Idea of a University* was written in response to changes occurring in the United Kingdom in the nineteenth century. Do any of these changes seem relevant to events in the United States in the twenty-first century?

MAKING CONNECTIONS

4. Would Mike Rose or the students he describes in "Lives on the Boundary" (p. 90) fit into the university Newman describes? Write a two- to three-page essay exploring this issue.

5. Compare Newman's ideas about knowledge for its own sake and the more politically driven ideas about the purpose and effects of education in articles by John Tierney (p. 130) and Katha Pollitt (p. 139). How do you think Newman would respond to an article such as Sokolove's, which focuses on the role of sports in the modern university (p. 104)? In a discussion with a group of classmates, analyze how the arguments about the role of the university have changed in the century and a half since Newman was writing.

JOINING THE CONVERSATION

6. Can Newman's concept of *liberal arts* survive in our world today? Does it deserve to? Why, or why not? Write a position paper on this subject.

7. For a national newsmagazine, write an evaluation of American higher education as you imagine Newman might regard it if he were living today. What might he admire? What would he criticize?

8. With a group of classmates, discuss the usefulness of the education you have had in high school and college. Which courses of study seem to have the most direct application to daily life? Which, if any, seem designed primarily as learning for its own sake?

THE UNIVERSITY OF MINNESOTA;
MOREHOUSE COLLEGE;
BEREA COLLEGE;
THE EVERGREEN STATE COLLEGE;
CALIFORNIA STATE UNIVERSITY,
MONTEREY BAY; and
THOMAS AQUINAS COLLEGE
Mission Statements

If John Henry Newman had been able to build a Web site for his ideal university, what might it have looked like, and how would it have represented his goals for the institution? These are questions we had in mind as we set out to browse contemporary college and university Web sites, much as you may have done as you began thinking about which schools you might prefer or be able to attend. Of special interest to us are the ways in which various institutions describe their goals on their Web sites, where readers' patience is often limited. So we decided to take a closer look at these representations, and to choose several for you to examine in the context of this chapter's discussion of education.

The six statements we have chosen represent different kinds of schools in different areas of the country. The University of Minnesota, in Minneapolis, is one of the country's largest research universities; it has extensive undergraduate and graduate curricula. In contrast, California State University, Monterey Bay, is a relatively new and as yet small school that focuses primarily on undergraduates. Morehouse College (in Atlanta, Georgia), Berea College (in Berea, Kentucky), The Evergreen State College (in Olympia, Washington), and Thomas Aquinas College (in Santa Paula, California) are all liberal arts colleges. Morehouse is one of the country's most distinguished historically black colleges and admits only male students; Berea College, founded by abolitionists, is a Christian college committed to serving the Appalachian region; Evergreen State, a coeducational school, is well known for its emphasis on experimentation and innovation. And Thomas Aquinas is distinctive in its own way, with a curriculum focused on the Great Books and a Roman Catholic orientation.

You may want to visit the Web sites of these six schools to discover more about their campuses, students, faculty, and staff. Or you may decide to visit your own campus Web site, seeking out its statement of mission, vision, or belief in order to compare it to the ones offered here. Which school's mission most appeals to your own goals and values?

—A.L. and J.R.

University of Minnesota
Mission

The University of Minnesota, founded in the belief that all people are enriched by understanding, is dedicated to the advancement of learning and the search for truth; to the sharing of this knowledge through education for a diverse community; and to the application of this knowledge to benefit the people of the state, the nation, and the world. The University's mission, carried out on multiple campuses and throughout the state, is threefold:

1. **Research and Discovery**
   Generate and preserve knowledge, understanding, and creativity by conducting high-quality research, scholarship, and artistic activity that benefit students, scholars, and communities across the state, the nation, and the world.

2. **Teaching and Learning**
   Share that knowledge, understanding, and creativity by providing a broad range of educational programs in a strong and diverse community of learners and teachers, and prepare graduate, professional, and undergraduate students, as well as non-degree-seeking students interested in continuing education and lifelong learning, for active roles in a multiracial and multicultural world.

3. **Outreach and Public Service**
   Extend, apply, and exchange knowledge between the University and society by applying scholarly expertise to community problems, by helping organizations and individuals respond to their changing environments, and by making the knowledge and resources created and preserved at the University accessible to the citizens of the state, the nation, and the world.

In all of its activities, the University strives to sustain an open exchange of ideas in an environment that embodies the values of academic freedom, responsibility, integrity, and cooperation; that provides an atmosphere of mutual respect, free from racism, sexism, and other forms of prejudice and intolerance; that assists individuals, institutions, and communities in responding to a continuously changing world; that is conscious of and responsive to the needs of the many communities it is committed to serving; that creates and supports partnerships within the University, with other educational systems and institutions, and with communities to achieve common goals; and that inspires, sets high expectations for, and empowers individuals within its community.

Morehouse College
About Morehouse: Mission

Guided by a commitment to excellence, Morehouse, an historically black liberal arts college for men, assumes a special responsibility for teaching students about the history and culture of black people. The college seeks to develop men with disciplined minds, emphasizing the continuing search for truth as a liberating force.

Morehouse prepares its students for leadership and service through instructional programs and extracurricular activities that:

- develop skills in oral and written communications, analytical and critical thinking and interpersonal relationships;
- foster an understanding and appreciation of the elements and evolution of various cultures and the nature of the physical universe;
- foster understanding and appreciation of the specific knowledge and skills needed for the pursuit of professional careers and/or graduate study and;
- cultivate the personal attributes of self-confidence, tolerance, morality, ethical behavior, humility, a global perspective, and a commitment to a social justice.

Berea College
Mission: The Great Commitments of Berea College

Berea College, founded by ardent abolitionists and radical reformers, continues today as an educational institution still firmly rooted in its historic purpose "to promote the cause of Christ." Adherence to the College's scriptural foundation, "God has made of one blood all peoples of the earth," shapes the College's culture and programs so that students and staff alike can work toward both personal goals and a vision of a world shaped by Christian values, such as the power of love over hate, human dignity and equality, and peace with justice. This environment frees persons to be active learners, workers, and servers as members of the academic community and as citizens of the world. The Berea experience nurtures intellectual, physical, aesthetic, emotional, and spiritual potentials and with those the power to make meaningful commitments and translate them into action.

To achieve this purpose, Berea College commits itself

- To provide an educational opportunity primarily for students from Appalachia, black and white, who have great promise and limited economic resources.

- To provide an education of high quality with a liberal arts foundation and outlook.
- To stimulate understanding of the Christian faith and its many expressions and to emphasize the Christian ethic and the motive of service to others.
- To provide for all students through the labor program experiences for learning and serving in community, and to demonstrate that labor, mental and manual, has dignity as well as utility.
- To assert the kinship of all people and to provide interracial education with a particular emphasis on understanding and equality among blacks and whites.
- To create a democratic community dedicated to education and equality for women and men.
- To maintain a residential campus and to encourage in all members of the community a way of life characterized by plain living, pride in labor well done, zest for learning, high personal standards, and concern for the welfare of others.
- To serve the Appalachian region primarily through education but also by other appropriate services.

The Evergreen State College
Evergreen's Mission: Making Learning Happen

The Evergreen State College is a public, liberal arts college serving Washington State. Its mission is to help students realize their potential through innovative, interdisciplinary educational programs in the arts, social sciences, humanities, and natural sciences. In addition to preparing students within their academic fields, Evergreen provides graduates with the fundamental skills to communicate, to solve problems, and to work collaboratively and independently in addressing real issues and problems. This mission is based on a set of principles, described below, that guide the development of all college programs and services.

Principles that guide Evergreen's educational programs:

- Teaching is the central work of the faculty at both the undergraduate and graduate levels. Supporting student learning engages everyone at Evergreen — faculty and staff.
- Academic program offerings are interdisciplinary and collaborative, a structure that accurately reflects how people learn and work in their occupations and personal lives.
- Students are taught to be aware of what they know, how they learn, and how to apply what they know; this allows them to be responsible for their own education, both at college and throughout their lives.

- College offerings involve active participation in learning, rather than passive reception of information, and integrate theory with practical applications.

- Evergreen supports community-based learning, with research and applications focused on issues and problems found within students' communities. This principle, as well as the desire to serve diverse placebound populations, guides Evergreen's community-based programs in Tacoma and on Tribal Reservations.

- Because learning is enhanced when topics are examined from the perspectives of diverse groups and because such differences reflect the world around us, the college strives to create a rich mix in the composition of its student body, staff, and faculty, and to give serious consideration to issues of social class, age, race, ethnicity, (dis)ability, gender, religious preference, and sexual orientation.

- Faculty and staff continually review, assess and modify programs and services to fit changing needs of students and society.

- The college serves the needs of a diverse range of students including recently graduated high school students, transfer students, working adults, and students from groups that historically have not attended college.

As evidenced by these principles, an important part of Evergreen's educational mission is engagement with the community, the state, and the nation. One focus of this engagement is through the work of public service centers that both disseminate the best work of the college and bring back to the college the best ideas of the wider community.   *(2006)*

California State University, Monterey Bay
Vision Statement

California State University, Monterey Bay (CSUMB) is envisioned as a comprehensive state university which values service through high quality education. The campus will be distinctive in serving the diverse people of California, especially the working class and historically undereducated and low-income populations. It will feature an enriched living and learning environment and year-round operation. The identity of the university will be framed by substantive commitment to multilingual, multicultural, gender-equitable learning. The university will be a collaborative, intellectual community distinguished by partnerships with existing institutions both public and private, cooperative agreements which enable students, faculty, and staff to cross institutional boundaries for innovative instruction, broadly defined scholarly and creative activity, and coordinated community service.

The university will invest in preparation for the future through integrated and experimental use of technologies as resources to people, catalysts for learning, and providers of increased access and enriched quality learning. The curriculum of CSUMB will be student and society centered and of sufficient breadth and depth to meet statewide and regional needs, specifically those involving both inner-city and isolated rural populations, and needs relevant to communities in the immediate Tri-County region (Monterey, Santa Cruz, and San Benito). The programs of instruction will strive for distinction, building on regional assets in developing specialty clusters in such areas as: the sciences (marine, atmospheric, and environmental); visual and performing arts and related humanities; languages, cultures, and international studies; education; business; studies of human behavior, information, and communication, within broad curricular areas; and professional study.

The university will develop a culture of innovation in its overall conceptual design and organization, and will utilize new and varied pedagogical and instructional approaches including distance learning. Institutional programs will value and cultivate creative and productive talents of students, faculty, and staff, and seek ways to contribute to the economy of the state, the wellbeing of our communities, and the quality of life and development of its students, faculty, and service areas.

The education programs at CSUMB will:

- Integrate the sciences, the arts and humanities, liberal studies, and professional training;
- Integrate modern learning technology and pedagogy to create liberal education adequate for the contemporary world;
- Integrate work and learning, service and reflection;
- Recognize the importance of global interdependence;
- Invest in languages and cross-cultural competence;
- Emphasize those topics most central to the local area's economy and ecology, and California's long-term needs;
- Offer a multicultural, gender-equitable, intergenerational, and accessible residential learning environment.

The university will provide a new model of organizing, managing, and   5
financing higher education:

- The university will be integrated with other institutions, essentially collaborative in its orientation, and active in seeking partnerships across institutional boundaries. It will develop and implement various arrangements for sharing courses, curriculum, faculty, students, and facilities with other institutions.
- The organizational structure of the university will reflect a belief in the importance of each administrative staff and faculty member, working to integrate the university community across "staff" and "faculty" lines.

- The financial aid system will emphasize a fundamental commitment to equity and access.

- The budget and financial systems, including student fees, will provide for efficient and effective operation of the university.

- University governance will be exercised with a substantial amount of autonomy and independence within a very broad CSU systemwide policy context.

- Accountability will emphasize careful evaluation and assessment of results and outcomes.

Our vision of the goals of California State University, Monterey Bay includes: a model pluralistic academic community where all learn and teach one another in an atmosphere of mutual respect and pursuit of excellence; a faculty and staff motivated to excel in their respective fields as well as to contribute to the broadly defined university environment. Our graduates will have an understanding of interdependence and global competence, distinctive technical and educational skills, the experience and abilities to contribute to California's high quality work force, the critical thinking abilities to be productive citizens, and the social responsibility and skills to be community builders. CSUMB will dynamically link the past, present, and future by responding to historical and changing conditions, experimenting with strategies which increase access, improve quality, and lower costs through education in a distinctive CSU environment. University students and personnel will attempt analytically and creatively to meet critical state and regional needs, and to provide California with responsible and creative leadership for the global 21st century.

—September 27, 1994

Thomas Aquinas College

The College's program of Catholic liberal education is unique in American higher education.

Fundamental in the Catholic intellectual tradition is the conviction that learning means discovering and growing in the truth about reality. It is the truth that sets men free and nothing else. Since truth concerns both natural and supernatural matters, the College's program has both natural and divine wisdom as its ultimate objectives.

There are no textbooks. The prescribed, four-year interdisciplinary course of studies is based on the original works of the best, most influential authors, poets, scientists, mathematicians, philosophers, and theologians of Western civilization. In every classroom, the primary teachers are the authors of the "Great Books" from Aristotle, Homer and Euclid to St. Thomas Aquinas, T. S. Eliot and Albert Einstein.

There are no lectures. Teaching and learning demand a meeting of the minds. The course is, therefore, essentially a sustained conversation in tutorials, seminars, and laboratories guided by tutors who assist students in the work of reading, analyzing, and evaluating the great works which are central in the collected wisdom of Civilization. Classes are Socratic in method and do not exceed twenty students. Every student has daily practice in the arts of language, grammar, and rhetoric; in reading and critical analysis of texts; in mathematical demonstration; in laboratory investigation.

There are no majors, no minors, no electives, no specializations. The arts and sciences which comprise the curriculum are organized into a comprehensive whole. The College aims at providing its students with a thorough grounding in the arts of thinking and a broad and integrated vision of the whole of life and learning.

—2002, Thomas Aquinas College Board of Governors

QUESTIONING THE TEXT

1. These six statements use different phrases to introduce their missions. Four use the term "mission," with two then adding other phrases: "Making Learning Happen" in one case, "The Great Commitments" in another. Another school offers a "Vision Statement," and the last statement simply begins with the contention that its "program . . . is unique in American higher education." Think carefully about these differing terms and phrases, and spend five or ten minutes brainstorming with your classmates about the effect these choices have on readers. What differing messages do they send?

2. Are any aspects of college life as you know it absent from these mission statements? Identify some of those components and then, in a group, discuss possible explanations for the omissions.

MAKING CONNECTIONS

3. Choose another reading from this chapter and use it as the basis for inferring a "mission statement" that the author might write for his or her ideal university. Which one of the mission statements reproduced here would this inferred statement most resemble, and why?

4. In the *Slate* piece called "Morality-Based Learning" (p. 126), S. Georgia Nugent argues that colleges need to reclaim their commitment to students' moral education. Do any of these schools focus on a moral education? Do any schools *imply* a moral basis to their education without explicitly stating it?

JOINING THE CONVERSATION

5. Working with classmates, examine the mission statement of your college or university. Then draft a new mission statement that you think better reflects the goals of your school. You might focus on updating the statement or on being more realistic about what actually happens on your campus.

6. Write a parody of a college mission statement. Use the parody as a way to explore problems in education today rather than just to poke fun at an institution.

JON SPAYDE
Learning in the Key of Life

"*T*HE WHOLE WORLD'S A CLASSROOM," *says Jon Spayde, a concept he much prefers to narrower definitions of education that limit it to what takes place in school, where it is too often equated with technical competence or "training for competitiveness." Noting that* training *is often a code word for the education of poor Americans, Spayde rejects these narrow utilitarian goals in favor of enriched study of the humanities* in the context of everyday life. *This "in-the-streets definition of education" assumes that learning takes place across the span of a lifetime, not just in sixteen years of formal schooling, and that what is being learned takes root and is nurtured through connections we make in "the real world." A truly good education, Spayde argues, may well be one "carpentered out of the best combination we can make of school, salon, reading, online exploration, walking the streets, hiking in the woods, museums, poetry classes at the Y, and friendship. . . ."*

Spayde's definition of education is perhaps particularly appealing at a time when change is so swift that the shelf life of technical knowledge is six months (at best). In addition, his definition appeals to my own sense that much of our most important and lasting education has always taken place outside of — or on the periphery of — school. In this brief essay, however, Spayde is short on specifics. Although he offers several examples of "in-the-streets education," he hasn't the time or space to set forth any concrete proposals for change. As a result, I would like to hear much more about how ordinary citizens and students might take up this new definition of education in their own lives. If you would like to hear more, check out other work by Spayde, well-known interviewer, editor, and longtime contributor to the Utne Reader *(where this essay first appeared in May–June 1998).*

—A.L.

What does it mean — and more important, what *should* it mean — to be educated?

This is a surprisingly tricky and two-sided question. Masquerading as simple problem-solving, it raises a whole laundry list of philosophical conundrums: What sort of society do we want? What is the nature of humankind? How do we learn best? And — most challenging of all — what is the Good? Talking about the meaning of education inevitably leads to the question of what a culture considers most important.

Yikes! No wonder answers don't come easily in 1998, in a multiethnic, corporation-heavy democracy that dominates the globe without having much of a sense of its own soul. For our policyheads, education equals something called "training for competitiveness" (which often boils down to the mantra of "more computers, more computers"). For multiculturalists of various stripes, education has become a battle line where they must duke it out regularly with

Left to right from top: Lao Tzu   Toni Morrison   Black Elk   Anaïs Nin
Henry David Thoreau   Orson Welles   Thelonious Monk   Groucho Marx
Leo Tolstoy   Miles Davis   Jane Austen   Johann Sebastian Bach   Billie
Holiday   Jalal ad-Din ar-Rumi   Bart Simpson   Gabriel Garcia Marquez
Mohandas Gandhi   Simone de Beauvoir

incensed neo-traditionalists. Organized religion and the various "alternative spiritualities" — from 12-step groups to Buddhism, American style — contribute their own kinds of education.

Given all these pushes and pulls, is it any wonder that many of us are beginning to feel that we didn't get the whole story in school, that our educations didn't prepare us for the world we're living in today?

We didn't; we couldn't have. So what do we do about it?   5

The first thing, I firmly believe, is to take a deep, calm breath. After all, we're not the first American generation to have doubts about these matters. One of the great ages of American intellectual achievement, the period just before the Civil War, was ruled by educational misfits. Henry David Thoreau was fond of saying, "I am self-educated; that is, I attended Harvard College," and indeed Harvard in the early 19th century excelled mainly in the extent and violence of its food fights.

Don't get me wrong: Formal education is serious stuff. There is no divide in American life that hurts more than the one between those we consider well educated and those who are poorly or inadequately schooled. Talking about education is usually the closest we get to talking about class; and no wonder — education, like class, is about power. Not just the power that Harvard- and Stanford-trained elites have to dictate our workweeks, plan our communities, and fiddle with world financial markets, but the extra power that a grad school dropout who, let's say, embraces voluntary simplicity and makes $14,000 a year, has over a high school dropout single mom pulling down $18,000. That kind of power has everything to do with attitude and access: an attitude of empowerment, even entitlement, and access to tools, people, and ideas that make living — at any income level — easier, and its crises easier to bear.

That's something Earl Shorris understands. A novelist and journalist, Shorris started an Ivy League–level adult education course in humanities for low-income New Yorkers at the Roberto Clemente Family Guidance Center on the Lower East Side, which he described in his book *New American Blues* (Norton, 1997). On the first day of class, Shorris said this to the students, who were Asians, whites, blacks, and Hispanics at or near the poverty line: "You've been cheated. Rich people learn the humanities; you didn't. The humanities are a foundation for getting along in the world, for thinking, for learning to reflect on the world instead of just reacting to whatever force is turned against you. . . . Do all rich people, or people who are in the middle, know the humanities? Not a chance. But some do. And it helps. It helps to live better and enjoy life more. Will the human-ities make you rich? Absolutely. But not in terms of money. In terms of life." And the Clemente course graduates did get rich in this way. Most of them went on to further higher education, and even the hard-luck Abel Lomas (not his real name), who got mixed up in a drug bust after he graduated, dumbfounded the classics-innocent prosecutor with arguments drawn from Plato and Sophocles.

By deliberately refusing to define poor Americans as nothing more than economic units whose best hope is "training" at fly-by-night computer schools,

Shorris reminds us all that genuine education is a discourse — a dialogue — carried on within the context of the society around us, as well as with the mighty dead. School helps, but it's just the beginning of the engagement between ideas and reality — as Abel Lomas can attest.

Shorris' radical idea — more controversial even than expecting working-class students to tackle a serious college curriculum — was to emphasize the humanities, those subtle subjects that infuse our minds with great, gushing ideas but also equip us to think and to argue. As more and more colleges, goaded by demands for "global competitiveness" from government officials and business leaders, turn themselves into glorified trade schools churning out graduates with highly specialized skills but little intellectual breadth, you might think humanities would go the way of the horse and buggy.   10

"It's an enormous error to believe that technology can somehow be the content of education," says John Ralston Saul, a Canadian historian and critic with years of experience in the business world. "We insist that everyone has to learn computer technology, but when printing came in with Gutenberg and changed the production and distribution of knowledge profoundly, nobody said that everyone should learn to be a printer. Technical training is training in what is sure to be obsolete soon anyway; it's self-defeating, and it won't get you through the next 60 years of your life." Training, says Saul, is simply "learning to fit in as a passive member of a structure. And that's the worst thing for an uncertain, changing time."

Oberlin College environmental studies professor David Orr poses an even fiercer challenge to the argument that education in the 21st century should focus primarily on high-tech training. In a recent article in the British magazine *Resurgence* (No. 179), he defines something he calls "slow knowledge": It is knowledge " shaped and calibrated to fit a particular ecological and cultural context," he writes, distinguishing it from the "fast knowledge" that zips through the terminals of the information society. "It does not imply lethargy, but rather thoroughness and patience. The aim of slow knowledge is resilience, harmony, and the preservation of long-standing patterns that give our lives aesthetic, spiritual, and social meaning." Orr says that we are focusing far too much of our energy and resources on fast knowledge, ignoring all the richness and meaning slow knowledge adds to our lives. Indeed, slow knowledge is what's needed to save the planet from ecological disaster and other threats posed by technological, millennial society.

"Culturally, we just are slow learners, no matter how fast individuals can process raw data," he says. "There's a long time gap between original insights and the cultural practices that come from them. You can figure out what you *can* do pretty quickly, but the ethical understanding of what you *ought* to do comes very slowly."

Miles Harvey, a Chicago journalist who assembled a list of environmental classics for *Outside* magazine (May 1996), reminds us that much of the divisiveness in contemporary debates on education boils down to a time issue.

"The canon makers say you've only got so much time, so you have to choose between, say, Shakespeare and Toni Morrison, on the assumption that you can't get to both," he says. "Well, it is hard. The level of creativity and intellectual activity in this country would jump up if we had a four-day workweek."

But suppose we redefined this issue from the very beginning. Suppose   15
we abandoned the notion that learning is a time-consuming and obligatory filling of our heads, and replaced it with the idea, courtesy of Goethe, that "people cannot learn what they do not love" — the idea of learning as an encounter infused with eros. We always find time for what we truly love, one way or another. Suppose further that love, being an inclusive spirit, refused to choose between Shakespeare and Toni Morrison (or Tony Bennett, for that matter), and we located our bliss in the unstable relationship between the two, rattling from book to book, looking for connections and grandly unconcerned about whether we've read "enough," as long as we read what we read with love.

And we wouldn't just read. We would reflect deeply on the relationship between our everyday lives and big philosophical questions — for, as Nietzsche memorably said, "Metaphysics are in the street." The Argentine novelist Ernesto Sabato glosses him this way: "[By metaphysics Nietzsche means] those final problems of the human condition: death, loneliness, the meaning of existence, the desire for power, hope, and despair." The whole world's a classroom, and to really make it one, the first thing is to believe it is. We need to take seriously the proposition that reflection and knowledge born out of contact with the real world, an education carpentered out of the best combination we can make of school, salon, reading, online exploration, walking the streets, hiking in the woods, museums, poetry classes at the Y, and friendship, may be the best education of all — not a makeshift substitute that must apologize for itself in the shadow of academe.

One of the things I like about this in-the-streets definition of education is how classical it is. In what's still one of the best concise summaries of classical education, Elizabeth Sutton Lawrence notes in *The Growth of Modern Education* (1971), that ancient Greek education "came largely from firsthand experience, in the marketplace, in the Assembly, in the theater, and in the religious celebration; through what the Greek youth saw and heard." Socrates met and challenged his adult "pupils" in the street, at dinner parties, after festivals, not at some Athenian Princeton.

Educational reactionaries want to convince us that the Western classical tradition is a carefully honed reading list. But as the dynamic classicist and philosopher Martha Nussbaum, who teaches at the University of Chicago Law School, insists, "The very idea that we should have a list of Great Books would have horrified the ancients. If you take to heart what the classical philosophers had to say, you'll never turn them into monuments. Their goal was to enliven the mind, and they knew that to enliven the mind you need to be very alert to what is in the world around you."

To really believe this casts a new light, to say the least, on the question of what the content of our learning ought to be. In her latest book, *Cultivating Humanity: A Classical Defense of Reform in Liberal Education* (Harvard University Press, 1997), Nussbaum argues compellingly that study of the non-Western world, of women's issues, of alternative sexuality, and of minority cultures is completely in line with classical principles, in particular the Stoic ideal of the "world citizen" with a cultivated ability to put her- or himself into the minds and lives of the members of divergent groups and cultures.

And New York jazz and rock writer Gene Santoro — trained in the classics   20 and Dante studies — points out there's nothing frivolous about paying attention to popular culture: "Popular culture, and particularly popular music, is the place where the dominant culture is most heavily affected by marginal cultures. Jazz, for example, became wide enough to take in much of the range of American reality, from the African American experience to the European classical tradition to the Latin and Caribbean spirit. It's the artistic version of the American social experience, and if you care about this culture, you'll look at it." And, he adds in a Socratic vein, "Jazz can help you think. It's both disciplined and unpredictable. It gives you tradition but doesn't let you settle into preconceived notions."

Colin Greer — co-editor of *The Call to Character* and *The Plain Truth of Things*, progressive responses to William Bennett's *Book of Virtues* — suggests further ways to make the most of the relationship between books and what's going on in the streets. "You could study the moments of major change in the world," he proposes. "The end of slavery. The early struggle against child labor. Woman suffrage. The organization of labor. People have forgotten what it really took to accomplish these things: What pragmatic things were done and how people learned to be generous and decent to their opponents. It's important to know the real story of how change works, and recognize that to fall short of your highest goals is OK as long as you stick to the struggle."

You get the idea. The American tradition, in learning as well as jazz and activism, is improvisatory. There are as many ways to become an educated American as there are Americans. To fall short of your highest goals — mastering that imaginary "complete" reading list, say — is OK as long as you stick to the struggle. And the joy.

Reading across Disciplines
BONNIE S. SUNSTEIN, Education

In the liner notes for his 1976 *Songs in the Key of Life*, singer Stevie Wonder writes that "an idea is a formed thought in the subconscious. . . . I shall live the idea of a song and use its words as my sight into the unknown." His album has become a classic included on many all-time-best lists. For fans, this album is the soul of Soul. But for me, as a teacher, both the album and its songs say something about education: we learn by applying the thoughts we form in our subconscious to our surroundings in ways that our surroundings have taught us to understand them, use them, and share them with others.

I assume that Jon Spayde's essay title, "Learning in the Key of Life," is a nod to Stevie Wonder's album title. I know for certain that one of the most important conversations in the history of education is about "the key of life": how does learning work inside school? How does it work outside of school? Is there a connection? Is it nature or nurture that makes us grow? And whatever the proportions of each, how does a school allow for both?

Before the American Revolution, British philosopher John Locke borrowed ideas from Aristotle and Aquinas for his notion of the *tabula rasa*: we're all born with a "clean slate" upon which our surroundings, our families, our schools, and our experiences are written as we continue to learn through a lifetime. Since then, generations of educators and researchers have shown that we learn by linking new ideas with our prior knowledge. A college sophomore told me recently that in order to understand ideas in his philosophy course that he'd not encountered before, he related them to movies and TV shows he knew. A graduate student I know memorized a list of twenty-seven topics in Aristotle's *Rhetoric* by linking them to the baseball card collection he had as a child. Certainly, much of school is about learning *how* we learn — and linking what we don't know to what we already know.

Spayde suggests that "talking about education is usually the closest we get to talking about class" — that even in these times of political correctness, inequality continues in American education. Schools' attitudes are a reflection of people's cultural attitudes, and our culture continues to think hierarchically about learners. Even common metaphors demonstrate this: we call students "bright" or "dull," "quick" or "slow." And our "lower level" students get "technical training," "basic skills," and "remediation" while we leave the big academic ideas for the "upper level" students, the ones who are singled out to be in the company of history's great thinkers and writers.

Stevie Wonder's profile would have labeled him an "at risk" student, even at the time he was writing *Songs in the Key of Life*. He comes from a large urban family with a single mother. A premature birth caused his complete blindness from the start. But his family provided rich expectations along with musical and educational experiences, and his surroundings both in and out of school offered him many ways to learn. By the time he was thirteen, he had recorded his first album. In the liner notes to *Songs in the Key of Life*, Wonder acknowledges that his learning is both classical and "in the street" by thanking not only his teachers and schoolmates at three schools and his family and friends, but also doctors, hospital staff, publishers, theater managers, and airline and hotel workers.

Popular music, as Spayde reminds us, is the juncture at which marginal cultures influence the dominant culture. It requires rigor, artistry, the "serious stuff" of formal schooling, both the "disciplined" and the "unpredictable." It helps us think. In the improvisatory tradition of American music, artist/thinkers like Stevie Wonder combine formal schooling with other knowledge to read and write their worlds. They succeed as citizens by learning ways to link subconscious ideas with the forms of scholarship, whether they're urban or suburban, rich or poor, "bright or dull," "high or low." We should "stick to the struggle," as Spayde reminds us, and the joy that comes with learning in the key of life.

Bonnie S. Sunstein is professor of both English and education at the University of Iowa.

QUESTIONING THE TEXT

1. Spayde opens his essay with a question: "What does it mean — and more important, what *should* it mean — to be educated?" After reading the essay carefully with this question in mind, identify the answers Spayde provides. Do his answers fulfill the implicit promise he makes in the opening — to tell readers what it means to be educated? Why or why not?

2. Look carefully at the illustration that accompanies this essay. How many of the people depicted do you recognize? How many have you heard of? Does the illustrator add evidence or proof for the argument Spayde is making? Why or why not?

3. Spayde uses first-person plural forms (especially *we* and *our*) often in his essay. Why do you think Spayde made this choice? What is its effect on you as a reader? Are you included in this *we* — and why or why not?

MAKING CONNECTIONS

4. Which of the writers in this chapter would be most likely to approve of what Spayde calls "in-the-streets education"? Choose one writer who would likely *not* approve of Spayde's definition of education, and write a one-page criticism of Spayde from that writer's point of view.

5. Look back at the six college mission statements (pp. 56–63). Which mission fits best with the kind of education Spayde advocates? Which fits least well — and why?

JOINING THE CONVERSATION

6. Working with two classmates, come up with a name for a hypothetical college that will promote Spayde's vision of education. Then create a home page for that college.

7. Working on your own or with a classmate, try writing your own extended definition of what it means to be educated. (For guidelines on writing definitions, see p. 25.)

ADRIENNE RICH
What Does a Woman Need to Know?

ADRIENNE RICH (b. 1929) has been a writer and a teacher all her life. Winner of the Yale Series of Younger Poets Award in 1951 for her first volume of poems, A Change of World, *of the National Book Award for Poetry in 1974 (for* Diving into the Wreck), *and of numerous other awards, she has also written novels, plays, essays, and speeches, including the one you are about to read.*

If John Henry Newman describes the university as "an assemblage of learned men," Rich looks at college from a slightly different perspective, noting the "changing landscape of knowledge itself" and asking "what does a woman need to know?" to negotiate such a landscape. Rich's question is particularly appropriate in context, for she delivered this speech as a commencement address to the graduates of a women's college, Smith, in 1979. Speaking directly to her audience, Rich pulls no punches; she is not sanguine about the state of women's education. In fact, she finds that "there is no women's college today which is providing young women with the education they need for survival as whole persons in a world which denies women wholeness." In the face of what she sees as a fact of life in the academy, Rich argues that women should gain all the knowledge they can from their university educations and from the professions they enter. But they should also realize that what they most need to know will have to be self-taught.

Rich challenges women students to take control of their own learning experience, to find out what they need to know, and to take responsibility for seeing that they learn it. Although she does not say so directly, the substance and site of this commencement address suggest an implicit argument for attending same-sex institutions, a topic of considerable interest to the first-year college students I am teaching, more than two decades after Rich's address. I chose this speech not only because it raises the issue of all-female or all-male schools, however, but because I wish I had heard such a commencement address when I graduated from college. In the thirty-something years since my graduation day, I have come to recognize how much my own career has been influenced by the kinds of schools I attended, by the kinds of teachers I had (no women in my college experience!), and by the kinds of models I emulated (all of them male/masculine). While I still value some of those teachers and models, Rich suggests that I might profit from asking what they did not teach me — and how I might have taught myself better. —A.L.

I have been very much moved that you, the class of 1979, chose me for your commencement speaker. It is important to me to be here, in part because Smith is one of the original colleges for women, but also because she has chosen to continue identifying herself as a women's college. We are at a point in history where this fact has enormous potential, even if that potential is as yet unrealized. The possibilities for the future education of women that haunt these buildings and grounds are enormous, when we think of what an independent women's college might be: a college dedicated both to teaching women what women need to know and, by the same token, to changing the landscape of knowledge itself. The germ of those possibilities lies symbolically in The Sophia Smith Collection, an archive much in need of expansion and increase, but which by its very existence makes the statement that women's lives and work are valued here and that our foresisters, buried and diminished in male-centered scholarship, are a living presence, necessary and precious to us.

Suppose we were to ask ourselves simply: What does a woman need to know to become a self-conscious, self-defining human being? Doesn't she need a knowledge of her own history, of her much-politicized female body, of the creative genius of women of the past — the skills and crafts and techniques and visions possessed by women in other times and cultures, and how they have been rendered anonymous, censored, interrupted, devalued? Doesn't she, as one of that majority who are still denied equal rights as citizens, enslaved as sexual prey, unpaid or underpaid as workers, withheld from her own power — doesn't she need an analysis of her condition, a knowledge of the women thinkers of the past who have reflected on it, a knowledge, too, of women's world-wide individual rebellions and organized movements against economic and social injustice, and how these have been fragmented and silenced?

Doesn't she need to know how seemingly natural states of being, like heterosexuality, like motherhood, have been enforced and institutionalized to deprive her of power? Without such education, women have lived and continue to live in ignorance of our collective context, vulnerable to the projections of men's fantasies about us as they appear in art, in literature, in the sciences, in the media, in the so-called humanistic studies. I suggest that not anatomy, but enforced ignorance, has been a crucial key to our powerlessness.

There is — and I say this with sorrow — there is no women's college today which is providing young women with the education they need for survival as whole persons in a world which denies women wholeness — that knowledge which, in the words of Coleridge, "returns again as power." The existence of Women's Studies courses offers at least some kind of life line. But even Women's Studies can amount simply to compensatory history; too often they fail to challenge the intellectual and political structures that must be challenged if women as a group are ever to come into collective, nonexclusionary freedom. The belief that established science and scholarship — which have so relentlessly excluded women from their making — are "objective" and "value-free" and that feminist studies are "unscholarly," "biased," and "ideological" dies hard. Yet the fact is that all science, and all scholarship, and all art are ideological; there is no neutrality in culture. And the ideology of the education you have just spent four years acquiring in a women's college has been largely, if not entirely, the ideology of white male supremacy, a construct of male subjectivity. The silences, the empty spaces, the language itself, with its excision of the female, the methods of discourse tell us as much as the content, once we learn to watch for what is left out, to listen for the unspoken, to study the patterns of established science and scholarship with an outsider's eye. One of the dangers of a privileged education for women is that we may lose the eye of the outsider and come to believe that those patterns hold for humanity, for the universal, and that they include us.

And so I want to talk today about privilege and about tokenism and about power. Everything I can say to you on this subject comes hard-won, from the lips of a woman privileged by class and skin color, a father's favorite daughter, educated at Radcliffe, which was then casually referred to as the Harvard "Annex." Much of the first four decades of my life was spent in a continuous tension between the world the Fathers taught me to see, and had rewarded me for seeing, and the flashes of insight that came through the eye of the outsider. Gradually those flashes of insight, which at times could seem like brushes with madness, began to demand that I struggle to connect them with each other, to insist that I take them seriously. It was only when I could finally affirm the outsider's eye as the source of a legitimate and coherent vision, that I began to be able to do the work I truly wanted to do, live the kind of life I truly wanted to live, instead of carrying out the assignments I had been given as a privileged woman and a token.

For women, all privilege is relative. Some of you were not born with class or skin-color privilege; but you all have the privilege of education, even if it is an education which has largely denied you knowledge of yourselves as women. You have, to begin with, the privilege of literacy; and it is well for us to remember that, in an age of increasing illiteracy, 60 percent of the world's illiterates are women. Between 1960 and 1970, the number of illiterate men in the world rose by 8 million, while the number of illiterate women rose by 40 million.[1] And the number of illiterate women is increasing. Beyond literacy, you have the privilege of training and tools which can allow you to go beyond the content of your education and re-educate yourselves — to debrief yourselves, we might call it, of the false messages of your education in this culture, the messages telling you that women have not really cared about power or learning or creative opportunities because of a psychobiological need to serve men and produce children; that only a few atypical women have been exceptions to this rule; the messages telling you that woman's experience is neither normative nor central to human experience. You have the training and the tools to do independent research, to evaluate data, to criticize, and to express in language and visual forms what you discover. This is a privilege, yes, but only if you do not give up in exchange for it the deep knowledge of the unprivileged, the knowledge that, as a woman, you have historically been viewed and still are viewed as existing, not in your own right, but in the service of men. And only if you refuse to give up your capacity to think as a woman, even though in the graduate schools and professions to which many of you will be going you will be praised and rewarded for "thinking like a man."

---

[1]United Nations, Department of International Economic and Social Affairs, Statistical Office, *1977 Compendium of Social Statistics* (New York: United Nations, 1980).

The word *power* is highly charged for women. It has been long associated for us with the use of force, with rape, with the stockpiling of weapons, with the ruthless accrual of wealth and the hoarding of resources, with the power that acts only in its own interest, despising and exploiting the powerless — including women and children. The effects of this kind of power are all around us, even literally in the water we drink and the air we breathe, in the form of carcinogens and radioactive wastes. But for a long time now, feminists have been talking about redefining power, about that meaning of power which returns to the root — *posse, potere, pouvoir*: to be able, to have the potential, to possess and use one's energy of creation — *transforming power*. An early objection to feminism — in both the nineteenth and twentieth centuries — was that it would make women behave like men — ruthlessly, exploitatively, oppressively. In fact, radical feminism looks to a transformation of human relationships and structures in which power, instead of a thing to be hoarded by a few, would be released to and from within the many, shared in the form of knowledge, expertise, decision making, access to tools, as well as in the basic forms of food and shelter and health care and literacy. Feminists — and many nonfeminists — are, and rightly so, still concerned with what power would mean in such a society, and with the relative differences in power among and between women here and now.

Which brings me to a third meaning of power where women are concerned: the false power which masculine society offers to a few women, on condition that they use it to maintain things as they are, and that they essentially "think like men." [This is the meaning of female tokenism: that power withheld from the vast majority of women is offered to a few, so that it appears that any "truly qualified" woman can gain access to leadership, recognition, and reward; hence, that justice based on merit actually prevails] The token woman is encouraged to see herself as different from most other women, as exceptionally talented and deserving, and to separate herself from the wider female condition; and she is perceived by "ordinary" women as separate also, perhaps even as stronger than themselves.

Because you are, within the limits of all women's ultimate outsiderhood, a privileged group of women, it is extremely important for your future sanity that you understand the way tokenism functions. Its most immediate contradiction is that, while it seems to offer the individual token woman a means to realize her creativity, to influence the course of events, it also, by exacting of her certain kinds of behavior and style, acts to blur her outsider's eye, which could be her real source of power and vision. Losing her outsider's vision, she loses the insight which both binds her to other women and affirms her in herself. Tokenism essentially demands that the token deny her identification with women as a group, especially with women less privileged than she: if she is a lesbian, that she deny her relationships with individual women; that she perpetuate rules and structures and criteria and methodologies which have functioned to exclude women; that she renounce or leave undeveloped the critical perspective of her female consciousness. Women unlike herself — poor women, women of color, waitresses, secretaries, housewives in the super-market, prostitutes, old women — become invisible to her; they may represent too acutely what she has escaped or wished to flee.

President Conway tells me that ever-increasing numbers of you are going   10
on from Smith to medical and law schools. The news, on the face of it, is good: that, thanks to the feminist struggle of the past decade, more doors into these two powerful professions are open to women. I would like to believe that any profession would be better for having more women practicing it, and that any woman practicing law or medicine would use her knowledge and skill to work to transform the realm of health care and the interpretations of the law, to make them responsive to the needs of all those — women, people of color, children, the aged, the dispossessed — for whom they function today as repressive controls. I would like to believe this, but it will not happen even if 50 percent of the members of these professions are women, unless those women refuse to be made into token insiders, unless they zealously preserve the outsider's view and the outsider's consciousness.

For no woman is really an insider in the institutions fathered by masculine consciousness. When we allow ourselves to believe we are, we lose touch with parts of ourselves defined as unacceptable by that consciousness; with the vital toughness and visionary strength of the angry grandmothers, the shamanesses, the fierce marketwomen of the Ibo Women's War, the marriage-resisting women silkworkers of prerevolutionary China, the millions of widows, mid-wives, and women healers tortured and burned as witches for three centuries in Europe, the Beguines of the twelfth century, who formed independent women's orders outside the domination of the Church, the women of the Paris Com-mune who marched on Versailles, the uneducated housewives of the Women's Cooperative Guild in England who memorized poetry over the washtub and organized against their oppression as mothers, the women thinkers discredited as "strident," "shrill," "crazy," or "deviant" whose courage to be heretical, to speak their truths, we so badly need to draw upon in our own lives. I believe that every woman's soul is haunted by the spirits of earlier women who fought for their unmet needs and those of their children and their tribes and their peoples, who refused to accept the prescriptions of a male church and state, who took risks and resisted, as women today — like Inez Garcia, Yvonne Wanrow, Joan Little, Cassandra Peten — are fighting their rapists and batterers. Those spirits dwell in us, trying to speak to us. But we can choose to be deaf; and tokenism, the myth of the "special" woman, the unmothered Athena sprung from her father's brow, can deafen us to their voices.

In this decade now ending, as more women are entering the professions (though still suffering sexual harassment in the workplace, though still, if they have children, carrying two full-time jobs, though still vastly outnumbered by men in upper-level and decision-making jobs), we need most profoundly to remember that early insight of the feminist movements as it evolved in the late sixties: *that no woman is liberated until we all are liberated.* The media flood us with messages to the contrary, telling us that we live in an era when "alternate life styles" are freely accepted, when "marriage contracts" and "the new intimacy" are revolutionizing heterosexual relationships, that shared parenting and the "new fatherhood" will change the world. And we live in a society leeched upon by the "personal growth" and "human potential" industry, by the delusion that individual self-fulfillment can be found in thirteen weeks or a weekend, that the alienation and injustice experienced by women, by Black and Third World people, by the poor, in a world ruled by white males, in a society which fails to meet the most basic needs and which is slowly poisoning itself, can be mitigated or dispersed by Transcendental Meditation. Perhaps the most succinct expression of this message I have seen is the appearance of a magazine for women called *Self.* The insistence of the feminist movement, that each woman's selfhood is precious, that the feminine ethic of self-denial and self-sacrifice must give way to a true woman identification, which would affirm our connectedness with all women, is perverted into a commercially profitable and politically debilitating narcissism. It is important for each of you, toward whom many of these messages are especially directed, to discriminate clearly between "liberated life style" and feminist struggle, and to make a conscious choice.

It's a cliché of commencement speeches that the speaker ends with a peroration telling the new graduates that however badly past generations have behaved, their generation must save the world. I would rather say to you, women of the class of 1979: Try to be worthy of your foresisters, learn from your history, look for inspiration to your ancestresses. If this history has been poorly taught to you, if you do not know it, then use your educational privilege to learn it. Learn how some women of privilege have compromised the greater liberation of women, how others have risked their privileges to further it; learn how brilliant and successful women have failed to create a more just and caring society, precisely because they have tried to do so on terms that the powerful men around them would accept and tolerate. Learn to be worthy of the women of every class, culture, and historical age who did otherwise, who spoke boldly when women were jeered and physically harassed for speaking in public, who — like Anne Hutchinson, Mary Wollstonecraft, the Grimké sisters, Abby Kelley, Ida B. Wells-Barnett, Susan B. Anthony, Lillian Smith, Fannie Lou Hamer — broke taboos, who resisted slavery — their own and other people's. To become a token woman — whether you win the Nobel prize or merely get tenure at the cost of denying your sisters — is to become something less than a man indeed, since men are loyal at least to their own world view, their laws of brotherhood and male self-interest. I am not suggesting that you imitate male loyalties; with the philosopher Mary Daly, I believe that the bonding of women must be utterly different and for an utterly different end: not the misering of resources and power, but the release, in each other, of the yet unexplored resources and transformative power of women, so long despised, confined, and wasted. Get all the knowledge and skill you can in whatever professions you enter; but remember that most of your education must be self-education, in learning the things women need to know and in calling up the voices we need to hear within ourselves.

QUESTIONING THE TEXT

1. Rich says that the term *power* is "highly charged for women," and she uses it in several different senses in this essay. Look carefully at these different meanings of *power*. Which meaning fits best with your own understanding — and would you agree that *power* is "highly charged for women"?

2. Rich lists three broad areas of knowledge that, she argues, women most need. What reasons and evidence does she offer to explain why women need such knowledge?

3. How does A.L.'s reference to her own school experience affect your reading of Rich's essay, if at all? Why do you think A.L. included this information in the introduction?

MAKING CONNECTIONS

4. Do you agree with Rich that women's educational needs are different from men's? Why or why not? In "The Idea of a University" (p. 51), John Henry Newman seems to suggest that all students have the same basic needs. How might Rich respond to him on this point?

5. John Tierney's "Male Pride and Female Prejudice" (pp. 130–32) suggests that if current educational trends continue, well-educated women will have difficulty finding well-educated men to marry. How do you think Rich might respond to this concern? Write a dialogue between these two authors on the subject of what should concern women about their educations.

JOINING THE CONVERSATION

6. What, if any, changes has your school made in the last twenty-five years or so to accommodate the needs and interests of women students? Consider such factors as increased hiring of women faculty, the opening of a women's student center or a women's studies program or department, speakers on women's issues, improvements in campus safety. Write a brief editorial intended for your campus newspaper in which you reflect on the extent to which your school is "user-friendly" for women and whether women at your school can learn what they most "need to know."

7. Try your own hand at writing a brief essay answering the question "What does a woman [or man] need to know?" You may want to compare your essay with those of other classmates, noting points of agreement and disagreement — particularly among women and men.

JENNIFER L. CROISSANT
Can This Campus Be Bought?

Do you attend a Pepsi — or a Coca-Cola — school? What brand name supports your college's or university's athletic teams? What is the relationship between large corporations and your curriculum? Jennifer L. Croissant (b. 1965) asks these and other questions in the following article, which challenges readers to consider the degree to which higher education in America is being bought — and sold — by commercial interests.

   Croissant, who is an associate professor in women's studies and an assistant professor in materials science and engineering at the University of Arizona, has written extensively on social issues affecting science and technology and on science education. Editor of Degrees of Compromise: Industrial Interests and Academic Values (2001), Croissant is also active in the Pole Pilots Track and Field Club.

   This essay originally appeared in Academe, the journal of the American Association of University Professors. I chose it for inclusion because, as a college professor and researcher, I am increasingly concerned that the ideal of the university as a place devoted to free and open inquiry — without commercial constraints and the drive to make all knowledge a commodity — is in great danger today.   —A.L.

When Pepsi received the vending contract for the University of Arizona in 1998, we soda consumers at the university expected a discount, given the likely volume of purchasing among the 35,000 people on our campus. Instead, we got a price increase, and decreased shelf and fountain space in campus stores and cafeterias for competing brands. At about the same time, our athletic department developed a contract with Nike for apparel and equipment to supply our sports teams.

   An editorial in the school newspaper quipped that one of the things we promised the corporation was a tattoo across the foreheads of the incoming class. Protests against the deals ranged from placid discussions between a Students Against Sweatshops group and university president Peter Likins, to peaceful sit-ins on the lawn, to organized labor symposia and students chaining themselves to the doors of the administration building. Despite these protests, the contracts were signed. While we don't tattoo the first-year students, Nike apparel is ubiquitous, even to the extent of displacing prior contracts that varsity sports teams had had with other suppliers.

IMAGE AND ETHICS

The effects of commercial activities on university campuses are garnering increased scrutiny from both scholars and activists. Much of the research in this area, including my own, has focused on the connections among commercial activities, values, and research. We need to think critically about the way our relationships with vendors and benefactors affect students and the university image. Students are developing their identities, and that includes brand and lifestyle identities as well as the disciplinary and occupational identities that are the focus of faculty work. The obvious sites for studying the influence of commerce on academic life — the tripartite tradition of teaching, research, and service — have been pretty thoroughly covered in research on higher education. Various scholars have noted that as the distinctions between categories such as research and service or contracts and gifts have blurred, ethical expectations and rules of conduct have also lost clarity.

But other important dimensions of university activities have largely been overlooked. Student life, philanthropy, and vendor relationships are also changing because of commercialization. These features of the university, while perhaps not of central concern to faculty, are important parts of the image of an academic institution, and they are visible to students, the community, businesses, and other institutions.

Universities and their commercial activities are also part of a larger system   5
of connections and images that contribute to the legitimacy of academic institutions as producers of reliable knowledge and sites of independent discourse. When students protest subcontractor wages for service employees at Harvard, they are making a statement about the university's image and conduct.

Because of our increasing involvement with commercial activities, we need to make sure that the university does not betray its educational values and objectives. Commercial connections can help to establish an institution's relevance and, especially for public colleges and universities, a kind of accountability. Having industrial advisory committees, corporate "partners," new philanthropic ventures, vendor contracts, and fairs in the quadrangle allows a university to display an image of being connected and responsive to outside interests. But connection can also mean interference and loss of autonomy, an erosion of core academic values.

We come packaged at Arizona as part of the Pacific-10 Conference. The "Pac-10" provides a league for intercollegiate competition, as well as a reference group for comparison among many other parameters, such as library size, enrollment, and faculty salaries. The conference maintains a Web site, coordinates television revenues and scheduling, and provides for corporate sponsorship of its activities.

In the section of the conference Web site titled "corporate partner opportunities," potential partners are promised "one-stop shopping" for the attention of "260,000 students, 2 million alumni, and 42 million people living in Pac-10 states." In addition to the Internet exposure they receive on the conference Web site, corporate partners get to use conference logos for their own promotional activities, including hospitality gatherings at conference championships and advertising in conference publications and on sports television networks. Independently, the University of Arizona has its own stable of corporate partners, representing national as well as local firms. Some of the Arizona partners, such as Pepsi, are in competition with the Pac-10 partners, such as 7-Up.

STUDENT LIFE IN THE MARKETPLACE

So what do these matters have to do with faculty? Think in terms of freedom of expression. When Penn State established vendor relationships with Pepsi in the early 1990s, a policy memo was circulated, and reported in the school newspaper, prohibiting all university employees from advocating for, or otherwise representing, other beverage corporations. No such explicit policy exists at Arizona, but the disruption of coaches' prior relationships with team sponsors as a result of the umbrella Nike contract seems to point in that direction. The worst story I have heard about occurred in a high school, where a student who wore a Coca-Cola T-shirt during "Pepsi Day" was sent home.

The larger problem is that these commercial relationships seem so natural   10
to us now that it is difficult even to articulate grounds for critical thinking about corporate ties. Does it really matter to the conduct of academic affairs that our public space, "the mall," is perpetually covered with touring sideshows from Ford, Esprit, and Pepsi, as well as from craft vendors and credit-card hawkers? Those worried about student credit-card debt have protested the latter, but no one is particularly concerned about the other displays, aside from the clutter they create.

Such displays, however, point to the more subtle and important side of packaging campuses to vendors and sponsors. We, as faculty, have been lamenting the students-as-consumers model, where customer satisfaction is all too frequently taken as a surrogate for learning. The conflation of student and consumer (and citizen and consumer) is really the most insidious part of corporate relationships on campus. For many students, to be a citizen is to be a consumer, and nothing more. Freedom means freedom to purchase.

⌈Freedom of speech is elided by freedom of consumption, but no one seems to notice that the choices for consumption are extremely constrained.⌉ The most publicly visible activity near the "speaker's corner" set aside on the mall for public speaking is often the buying and selling of goods. Interesting civic activities, such as Holocaust memorial readings or rallies against relationship and sexual violence, are overwhelmed by inflatable climbing walls and Velcro-bungee games. Almost nowhere on campus, outside the academic classroom, seems exempt from commercial discourse (and classrooms, plastered in posters advertising cheap beer and Internet services, are not themselves totally exempt). This segregation makes classrooms and critiques of consumerism seem remote and irrelevant.

PHILANTHROPY AS ADVERTISING

As student life becomes increasingly commercialized, so, too, does the pattern of outside gifts to the university. The distinction between philanthropy and advertising, or philanthropy and research contracts, seems to be eroding. Posthumous and anonymous gifts from benefactors to academic institutions have often been publicized, but the fanfare surrounding large donations and capital campaigns has reached new heights. The Gates Foundation Minority Fellowship Program, for example, spends more on advertising than on the scholarships themselves. Many named chairs are now tied specifically to corporations. Seymour Papert, for example, held the LEGO chair at the Massachusetts Institute of Technology, which upon his retirement was renamed the LEGO Papert Chair. References to the chair appear in LEGO press releases and on the corporation's Web site to emphasize the educational value of LEGO toys.

Corporations are not in the business of philanthropy for its own sake. Activities such as corporate-sponsored endowed chairs must produce economic benefits for their sponsors, even if the benefits are largely intangible. Philanthropy confers a kind of legitimacy on the donor, and it provides resources and the aura of being worthy of gifts to the recipient.

But even the traditional form of individual philanthropy should be examined for the multiple benefits and costs to the giving and the receiving parties. It has long been customary for alumni to support their majors and for business schools to be named in honor of wealthy alumni who give hefty gifts. Not too many of these alumni are, however, still alive, and also embroiled in legal conflict. But now we have the Eller School of Business and Public Administration at the University of Arizona, named for regional advertising executive Karl Eller, who made a substantial donation. The Eller Enterprises are wrangling with the city of Tucson and the county over billboard and lighting regulations meant to protect the skies from light pollution and the local population from billboard blight. To what extent should we be looking our gift horses in the mouths? Is Eller's philanthropy an attempt to garner public support and perhaps influence, indirectly, city council action on billboard regulations? Does the gift help to signal the legitimacy of Eller Enterprises?

A big "gift" with no strings attached is, in theory, significantly different from a research contract with explicit performance goals. But today's donor programs, many of which are sponsored by corporations rather than anonymous individuals, may challenge the gift-contract distinction. Unlike more traditional, individual philanthropic efforts that need not obey the calculus of profit, corporations do not just give money away.

Consequently, as relationships with corporate vendors and sponsors become increasingly important, we can expect subtle accommodations to the needs of industrial and commercial interests on campus. Explicit firings for critiques of corporate activities may not become widespread, but other forms of forced acquiescence in the status quo might be expected. Will departments or units heavily dependent on the largesse of one particular sponsor tolerate criticism of that sponsor by faculty members?

The example of the relationship between the Swiss-based corporation Novartis and the Department of Plant and Microbial Biology at the University of California, Berkeley, is apt here. The multimillion dollar grant from the corporation surely enables the department to pursue an expanded research program. But it also puts subtle constraints on the scope of its program, affecting the faculty's freedom to engage in other research relationships and students' ability to determine the direction of their research. The corporation's claim to the intellectual property rights to all research from the department also affects the choices made by it. Reward structures at research institutions generally favor those who bring in external funds in contracts and grants. Although censorship is far too strong a word for the constraints on imagination that can occur in conditions of resource dependency, we can expect some accommodations.

Vendor Relations

At the same time that the way corporations and universities handle gifts and contracts is changing, institutional support services and vendor relations are also being transformed. Although some faculty members are very much involved in helping to select software packages for students or in setting the parameters for hardware purchases for their units, most faculty are clueless about such processes. These decisions are frequently based on the expectations that future employers have for graduates: Can a future project manager use Excel? Can an engineering student solve modeling equations with Matlab? Do the architecture students know Autocad? Are your students facile in some discipline-specific modeling software? Where have all the Apples gone?

An interesting cycle seems to have emerged. Expectations regarding new technologies are present either in fact, in the prospective workplaces of our students, or in the imaginations of vendors selling supplies to universities. Students are exposed to specific systems, and not necessarily informed of the alternatives. They take their training to their future work sites, perhaps influencing purchasing decisions. The expectations are then presented back to the universities by alumni, employers, and vendors, requiring institutions to purchase and maintain new technology or expensive upgrades.

In the course of a project to upgrade its student information system, the University of Arizona somehow became an Oracle campus. At the same time that we are purchasing a system from this well-established software production firm that specializes in data management, Arizona's staff is contributing to its development. It is expected that modifications to the software made by Arizona employees will fall under complex intellectual property agreements.

One of the possible capabilities of the system is an online grading function that faculty will use to keep course records. At a nearby community college, a similar system has made interim reporting of grades a requirement. So far, faculty have not discussed how the system will affect intellectual property rights, institutional policy, or workload. We have not questioned whether we may have to submit interim grades or develop grading practices compatible with the computer system, nor have we considered that software produced at the university for this project may belong to Oracle.

In a separate venture, AOL and Cisco Systems have combined forces with the university's Center for Computing and Information Technology (CCIT). The CCIT is the nonacademic unit responsible for the university's computer infrastructure, e-mail system, and software and hardware licensing. Three local high schools purchase hardware (switching equipment and cabling) at a "substantial discount," which is partly underwritten by AOL. As noted in the campus computing newsletter, the schools also pay a "yearly $500 fee to CCIT . . . although expenses are much higher than that." CCIT staff get free training in Cisco products, and the successful high school students get a Cisco Certified Network Associate certificate.

Three features of this relationship bear critical attention. First, a fair amount of money is changing hands, back and forth among schools, vendors, and the computer center. It seems that university resources subsidize the program to some extent, which would be an unusual transfer of public resources to the private sector. Second, this venture resembles distance-education initiatives in that it is largely independent of oversight by regularly appointed faculty members. CCIT employees, some of whom have Ph.D.'s, all have staff rather than faculty appointments and teach courses outside any disciplinary curricula.

The third issue has to do with providing vendor-specific training. It is   25
hard to argue against the opportunities that Cisco training might offer the students, who come from some of the more disadvantaged high schools in the area (in a region with a lot of disadvantaged schools). Their Cisco certification can give them access to job opportunities in the telecommunications and information sector. Whether such employment is meant to be in lieu of, or a precursor to, a traditional university education is unclear. In addition, the training is in a specific vendor's systems, rather than, say, in general principles of networking, which could provide wider employment horizons.

Consider that in other circumstances companies pay their employees to get advanced, firm-specific training. Under the Arizona-AOL-Cisco deal, the students are not compensated for learning a specific corporate system; instead, their schools (or the taxpayers, at least) pay for them to receive this training. In other words, a public institution is subsidizing training that corporations usually provide to their own workers. Even though this program is described as a "gift" from AOL, it seems to be a very expensive gift for the university to receive.

Especially disturbing is the dearth of program oversight and the lack of much discussion about the partnership's effectiveness and legitimacy.

LEGITIMACY

The question of legitimacy is clearly at issue in any relationship between a commercial enterprise and the university. Science, or knowledge production more generally, has always had deep connections to the general political economy of its time, whether or not it has been tied to specific industries or corporations.

Thus we cannot argue for some untainted "ivory tower" or "golden age" of institutional independence. We need instead to articulate the values and goals that should direct a wide range of commercial ventures on campus.

What seem to be in tension are the values of connection and autonomy. Discourses about connection and accountability generally strengthen the power that the various constituencies of the university (the public, students, the administration, businesses, the state) have to intervene in university life. In these discourses, it is good to be connected to the outside world, to display multiple ties to multiple audiences, to exchange resources (both money and personnel), and to demonstrate relevance. The corporatization of university life brings a new model of connectedness and accountability to the forefront as a model of legitimacy. Connection and accountability become the markers of successful campus ventures, whether in research, teaching, or service.

Discourses about autonomy are usually based on disciplinary expertise. 30
Faculty, for example, use academic-freedom arguments to preserve our control over syllabi, although at Arizona we are now required to point out that "objectionable material" may be present in certain kinds of courses. Academic institutions have, until recently, based much of their institutional legitimacy in the discourse about autonomy.

What happens to core values such as objectivity or neutrality under conditions in which business connections measure legitimacy? Biotechnology companies, for example, need the autonomy of university-based research to help maintain at least the image of objectivity in analyzing new drugs for distribution to the public. Ties that are too close undermine the public's trust that the knowledge produced is unbiased and reliable. Ties that are too loose, such as unrestricted and anonymous philanthropy, provide too few of the benefits that corporations seek.

Some of the advantages for corporate sponsors are visible and measurable: the chance to direct research and solve specific technological or scientific problems. Such benefits often accrue in traditional corporate sponsorship of research. With the new relationships, however, some of the favorable effects are intangible and more difficult to quantify and critique. Corporations gain legitimacy, visibility, and access to markets. Universities get to seem "relevant" and connected, and they gain needed cash, perhaps at the expense of independence and autonomy.

At the same time that the development office at the University of Arizona cheers large donations, others get nervous that our public institution is intensifying a cycle of dependency on corporate finances. When the law school received the gift of a large endowment, state legislators got the idea that professional programs need not be funded by the state, because wealthy benefactors and eager students can foot the bills. The benefits that corporate "partners" provide in underwriting the athletic program, or that benefactors give to departments, come to be seen as replacements for base funding for routine operating expenses, increasing our dependency on and responsiveness to corporate connections. The point is not to make an argument for pure autonomy, expecting constituencies to hand us blank checks and trust that we will produce socially optimal knowledge and well-educated students. Too much administrative bloat, too many inefficiencies, and plenty of poor performance make it hard for people to see that as a likely outcome. But complete connection, especially through identification with corporate benefactors, erodes ideas about objectivity that are important to maintaining the legitimacy of universities as sites for unfettered, and reliable, inquiry. When it becomes clear that we are indeed "Nike-Pepsi U," it will be obvious, at least to me, that we have moved too far along the autonomy-connection continuum.

QUESTIONING THE TEXT

1. In paragraph 6, Croissant warns her colleagues in higher education, "[W]e need to make sure that the university does not betray its educational values and objectives" with its commercial associations. Addressing the areas of student life, philanthropy, and vendor relations, which she claims have been overlooked in recent critiques of campus-commercial relationships, Croissant argues that these facets of university activity have an indirect impact on education through the image they present to students and others. How does she make her argument in regard to each of these three areas? What kind of evidence does she provide to support her claim that commercial relationships can have an adverse impact on an academic institution?

2. This essay opens with two examples of commercial interests encroaching upon campus life. What is the point of each example? In what other ways might Croissant have introduced the conflicts that she addresses? How would different opening strategies change the essay?

3. Croissant refrains from drawing a distinct line on the "autonomy-connection continuum" that universities should not cross. Rather, she concludes, "When it becomes clear that we are indeed 'Nike-Pepsi U,' it will be obvious, at least to me, that we have [gone] too far. . . ." (paragraph 33). Try to develop a set of criteria by which to judge what actions by a university might constitute traveling "too far" on this continuum.

MAKING CONNECTIONS

4. Croissant identifies a "tension" between "the values of connection and autonomy," between an academic institution's need to represent its various "constituencies" (paragraph 29) and its need to pursue teaching and research free of distortion from outside influences. How do her concerns complicate the knowledge for its own sake espoused by John Henry Newman (p. 51)? How might Croissant agree or disagree with Newman's idea of a university's connections to corporate or public life?

5. Croissant and Michael Sokolove (p. 104) both address the influences of nonacademic activity and commercial interests on higher education. How do their concerns differ, and how are they similar?

JOINING THE CONVERSATION

6. Croissant observes that commercial enterprises are crowding out the noncommercial exchange of ideas in central "mall" areas of many campuses. She asserts, "For many students, to be a citizen is to be a consumer, and nothing more. Freedom means freedom to purchase" (paragraph 11). Does your campus have a space dedicated to public debate? Is it also open to vendors? Do you think the marketplace of ideas on your campus is becoming too commercialized? Discuss this question with your classmates.

7. Take a tour of your campus, and note the names of buildings. For whom are the buildings named? Can you identify a connection between each building and its namesake? What do your answers suggest about commercial and philanthropic relationships at your school?

8. Croissant's concerns about the impact of commercial interests on education might also apply to other kinds of pursuits. Religious, civic, or athletic organizations, for example, can find themselves in comparable conflicts with commercial interests. Have you encountered similar conflicts in situations outside of academe? If so, how do they inform your understanding of the educational predicaments Croissant addresses?

Both have to do with the corrupted the people/education system are.

MIKE ROSE
Lives on the Boundary

As a child, Mike Rose (b. 1944) never thought of going to college. The son of Italian immigrants, he was placed in the "vocational track" in school (through a clerical error, as it turns out) and, as he says, "lived down to expectations beautifully." He was one of those who might well have been excluded from the university. In his prize-winning volume Lives on the Boundary *(1989), Rose recalls those circumstances that opened up the university to him, and he argues forcefully that education in a democracy must be truly open to all, a theme he pursues in* Possible Lives *(1996).*

In the excerpt from Lives on the Boundary *that follows, Rose describes several students he has known, considering the ways in which the "idea of a university" either includes or excludes them. In an extended discussion of what he calls the "canonical curriculum," he concludes that "books can spark dreams," but "appeals to elevated texts can also divert attention from the conditions that keep a population from realizing its dreams."*

I wanted to include this passage from Rose's book because he explicitly addresses the many calls for a university curriculum based on "Great Books," books that by definition exclude the experiences of the students Rose describes. In addition, I chose this selection because Rose is a graceful prose stylist, a gifted scholar, and a much-valued friend.

A professor of education at UCLA, Rose is also a truly extraordinary teacher. His own story, and the stories of those students whose lives he has touched, attest to the transformational power of the kind of educational experience he advocates. To "have any prayer of success" at making such experiences possible, Rose says, "we'll need many . . . blessings." We'll also need many more teachers and writers like Mike Rose. —A.L.

I have a vivid memory of sitting on the edge of my bed — I was twelve or thirteen maybe — listening with unease to a minute or so of classical music. I don't know if I found it as I was turning the dial, searching for the Johnny Otis Show or the live broadcast from Scribner's Drive-In, or if the tuner had simply drifted into another station's signal. Whatever happened, the music caught me in a disturbing way, and I sat there, letting it play. It sounded like the music I heard in church, weighted, funereal. Eerie chords echoing from another world. I leaned over, my fingers on the tuner, and, in what I remember as almost a twitch, I turned the knob away from the melody of these strange instruments. My reaction to the other high culture I encountered — *The Iliad* and Shakespeare and some schoolbook poems by Longfellow and Lowell — was similar, though less a visceral rejection and more a rejecting disinterest, a sense of irrelevance. The few Shakespearean scenes I did know — saw on television, or read or heard in grammar school — seemed snooty and put-on, kind of dumb. Not the way I wanted to talk. Not interesting to me.

There were few books in our house: a couple of thin stories read to me as a child in Pennsylvania (*The Little Boy Who Ran Away*, an *Uncle Remus* sampler), the *M* volume of the *World Book Encyclopedia* (which I found one day in the trash behind the secondhand store), and the Hollywood tabloids my mother would bring home from work. I started buying lots of Superman and Batman comic books because I loved the heroes' virtuous omnipotence — comic books, our teachers said, were bad for us — and, once I discovered them, I began checking out science fiction novels from my grammar school library. Other reading material appeared: the instructions to my chemistry set, which I half understood and only half followed, and, eventually, my astronomy books, which seemed to me to be magical rather than discursive texts. So it was that my early intrigue with literacy — my lifts and escapes with language and rhythm — came from comic books and science fiction, from the personal, non-scientific worlds I created with bits and pieces of laboratory and telescopic technology, came, as well, from the Italian stories I heard my uncles and parents tell. It came, too, from the music my radio brought me: music that wove in and out of my days, lyrics I'd repeat and repeat — "gone, gone, gone, jumpin' like a catfish on a pole" — wanting to catch that sound, seeking other emotional frontiers, other places to go. Like rocker Joe Ely, I picked up Chicago on my transistor radio.

Except for school exercises and occasional cards my mother made me write to my uncles and aunts, I wrote very little during my childhood; it wasn't until my last year in high school that Jack MacFarland* sparked an interest in writing. And though I developed into a good reader, I performed from moderately well to terribly on other sorts of school literacy tasks. From my reading I knew vocabulary words, and I did okay on spelling tests — though I never lasted all that long in spelling bees — but I got C's and D's on the ever-present requests to diagram sentences and label parts of speech. The more an assignment was related to real reading, the better I did; the more analytic, self-contained, and divorced from context, the lousier I performed. Today some teachers would say I was a concrete thinker. To be sure, the development of my ability to decode words and read sentences took place in school, but my orientation to reading — the way I conceived of it, my purpose for doing it — occurred within the tight and untraditional confines of my home. The quirks and textures of my immediate environment combined with my escapist fantasies to draw me to books. "It is what we are excited about that educates us," writes social historian Elizabeth Ewen. It is what taps our curiosity and dreams. Eventually, the books that seemed so distant, those Great Books, would work their way into my curiosity, would influence the way I framed problems and the way I wrote. But that would

---

Jack MacFarland: a man whom Rose describes as "the teacher who saved [my] life"

come much later — first with Jack MacFarland (mixed with his avant-garde countertradition), then with my teachers at Loyola and UCLA — an excitement and curiosity shaped by others and connected to others, a cultural and linguistic heritage received not from some pristine conduit, but exchanged through the heat of human relation.

A friend of mine recently suggested that education is one culture embracing another. It's interesting to think of the very different ways that metaphor plays out. Education can be a desperate, smothering embrace, an embrace that denies the needs of the other. But education can also be an encouraging, communal embrace — at its best an invitation, an opening. Several years ago, I was sitting in on a workshop conducted by the Brazilian educator Paulo Freire. It was the first hour or so and Freire, in his sophisticated, accented English, was establishing the theoretical base of his literacy pedagogy — heady stuff, a blend of Marxism, phenomenology, and European existentialism. I was two seats away from Freire; in front of me and next to him was a younger man, who, puzzled, finally interrupted the speaker to ask a question. Freire acknowledged the question and, as he began answering, he turned and quickly touched the man's forearm. Not patronizing, not mushy, a look and a tap as if to say: "You and me right now, let's go through this together." Embrace. With Jack MacFarland it was an embrace: no-nonsense and cerebral, but a relationship in which the terms of endearment were the image in a poem, a play's dialogue, the winding narrative journey of a novel.

More often than we admit, a failed education is social more than intellec-   5
tual in origin. And the challenge that has always faced American education, that it has sometimes denied and sometimes doggedly pursued, is how to create both the social and cognitive means to enable a diverse citizenry to develop their ability. It is an astounding challenge: the complex and wrenching struggle to actualize the potential not only of the privileged but, too, of those who have lived here for a long time generating a culture outside the mainstream and those who, like my mother's parents and my father, immigrated with cultural traditions of their own. This painful but generative mix of language and story can result in clash and dislocation in our communities, but it also gives rise to new speech, new stories, and once we appreciate the richness of it, new invitations to literacy.

Pico Boulevard, named for the last Mexican governor of California, runs an immense stretch west to east: from the wealth of the Santa Monica beaches to blighted Central Avenue, deep in Los Angeles. Union Street is comparatively brief, running north to south, roughly from Adams to Temple, pretty bad off all the way. Union intersects Pico east of Vermont Avenue and too far to the southwest to be touched by the big-money development that is turning downtown Los Angeles into a whirring postmodernist dreamscape. The Pico-Union District is very poor, some of its housing as unsafe as that on Skid Row, dilapidated, overcrowded, rat-infested. It used to be a working-class Mexican neighborhood, but for about ten years now it has become the concentrated locale of those fleeing the political and economic horror in Central America. Most come from El Salvador and Guatemala. One observer calls the area a gigantic refugee camp.

As you move concentrically outward from Pico-Union, you'll encounter a number of other immigrant communities: Little Tokyo and Chinatown to the northeast, Afro-Caribbean to the southwest, Koreatown to the west. Moving west, you'll find Thai and Vietnamese restaurants tucked here and there in storefronts. Filipinos, Southeast Asians, Armenians, and Iranians work in the gas stations, the shoe-repair stores, the minimarts. A lawnmower repair shop posts its sign in Korean, Spanish, and English. A Korean church announces "Jesus Loves You" in the same three languages. "The magnitude and diversity of immigration to Los Angeles since 1960," notes a report from UCLA's Graduate School of Architecture and Urban Planning, "is comparable only to the New York-bound wave of migrants around the turn of the century." It is not at all uncommon for English composition teachers at UCLA, Cal-State L.A., Long Beach State — the big urban universities and colleges — to have, in a class of twenty-five, students representing a dozen or more linguistic backgrounds: from Spanish and Cantonese and Farsi to Hindi, Portuguese, and Tagalog. Los Angeles, the new Ellis Island.

On a drive down the Santa Monica Freeway, you exit on Vermont and pass Rick's Mexican Cuisine, Hawaii Discount Furniture, The Restaurant Ecuatoriano, Froggy's Children's Wear, Seoul Autobody, and the Bar Omaha. Turn east on Pico, and as you approach Union, taking a side street here and there, you'll start seeing the murals: The Virgin of Guadalupe, Steve McQueen, a scene resembling Siqueiros's heroic workers, the Statue of Liberty, Garfield the Cat. Graffiti are everywhere. The dreaded Eighteenth Street gang — an established Mexican gang — has marked its turf in Arabic as well as Roman numerals. Newer gangs, a Salvadoran gang among them, are emerging by the violent logic of territory and migration; they have Xed out the Eighteenth Street *placas* and written their own threatening insignias in place. Statues of the Blessed Mother rest amid potted plants in overgrown front yards. There is a rich sweep of small commerce: restaurants, markets, bakeries, legal services ("Income Tax y Amnestia"), beauty salons ("Lolita's Magic Touch — Salon de Belleza — Unisex"). A Salvadoran restaurant sells teriyaki burgers. A "Discoteca Latina" advertises "great rap hits." A clothing store has a Dick Tracy sweatshirt on a half mannequin; a boy walks out wearing a blue t-shirt that announces "Life's a Beach." Culture in a Waring blender.

There are private telegram and postal services: messages sent straight to "domicilio a CentroAmerica." A video store advertises a comedy about immigration: *Ni de Aqui/Ni de Alla*, "Neither from Here nor from There." The poster displays a Central American Indian caught on a wild freeway ride: a Mexican in a sombrero is pulling one of the Indian's pigtails, Uncle Sam pulls the other, a border guard looks on, ominously suspended in air. You see a lot of street vending, from oranges and melons to deco sunglasses: rhinestones and plastic swans and lenses shaped like a heart. Posters are slapped on posters: one has rows of faces of the disappeared. Santa Claus stands on a truck bumper and waves drivers into a ninety-nine cent outlet.

Families are out shopping, men loiter outside a cafe, a group of young girls collectively count out their change. You notice, even in the kaleidoscope you pick out his figure, you notice a dark-skinned boy, perhaps Guatemalan, walking down Pico with a cape across his shoulders. His hair is piled in a four-inch rockabilly pompadour. He passes a dingy apartment building, a *pupuseria*, a body shop with no name, and turns into a storefront social services center. There is one other person in the sparse waiting room. She is thin, her gray hair pulled back in a tight bun, her black dress buttoned to her neck. She will tell you, if you ask her in Spanish, that she is waiting for her English class to begin. She might also tell you that the people here are helping her locate her son — lost in Salvadoran resettlement camps — and she thinks that if she can learn a little English, it will help her bring him to America.

The boy is here for different reasons. He has been causing trouble in school, and arrangements are being made for him to see a bilingual counselor. His name is Mario, and he immigrated with his older sister two years ago. His English is halting, unsure; he seems simultaneously rebellious and scared. His caseworker tells me that he still has flashbacks of Guatemalan terror: his older brother taken in the night by death squads, strangled, and hacked apart on the road by his house. Then she shows me his drawings, and our conversation stops. Crayon and pen on cheap paper; blue and orange cityscapes, eyes on billboards, in the windshields of cars, a severed hand at the bus stop. There are punks, beggars, piñatas walking the streets — upright cows and donkeys — skeletal homeboys, corseted girls carrying sharpened bones. "He will talk to you about these," the caseworker tells me. "They're scary, aren't they? The school doesn't know what the hell to do with him. I don't think he really knows what to do with all that's in him either."

In another part of the state, farther to the north, also rich in immigration, a teacher in a basic reading and writing program asks his students to interview one another and write a report, a capsule of a classmate's life. Caroline, a black woman in her late forties, chooses Thuy Anh, a Vietnamese woman many years her junior. Caroline asks only five questions — Thuy Anh's English is still difficult to understand — simple questions: What is your name? Where were you born? What is your education? Thuy Anh talks about her childhood in South Vietnam and her current plans in America. She is the oldest of nine children, and she received a very limited Vietnamese education, for she had to spend much of her childhood caring for her brothers and sisters. She married a serviceman, came to America, and now spends virtually all of her time pursuing a high school equivalency, struggling with textbook descriptions of the American political process, frantically trying to improve her computational skills. She is not doing very well at this. As one of her classmates observed, she might be trying too hard.

Caroline is supposed to take notes while Thuy Anh responds to her questions, and then use the notes to write her profile, maybe something like a reporter would do. But Caroline is moved to do something different. She's taken by Thuy Anh's account of watching over babies. "Mother's little helper," she thinks. And that stirs her, this woman who has never been a mother. Maybe, too, Thuy Anh's desire to do well in school, her driven eagerness, the desperation that occasionally flits across her face, maybe that moves Caroline as well. Over the next two days, Caroline strays from the assignment and writes a two-and-a-half page fiction that builds to a prose poem. She recasts Thuy Anh's childhood into an American television fantasy.

Thuy Anh is "Mother's little helper." Her five younger sisters "are happy and full of laughter . . . their little faces are bright with eyes sparkling." The little girls' names are "Hellen, Ellen, Lottie, Alice, and Olie" — American names — and they "cook and sew and make pretty doll dresses for their dolls to wear." Though the family is Buddhist, they exchange gifts at Christmas and "gather in the large living room to sing Christmas carols." Thuy Anh "went to school every day she could and studied very hard." One day, Thuy Anh was "asked to write a poem and to recite it to her classmates." And, here, Caroline embeds within her story a prose poem — which she attributes to Thuy Anh:

> My name is Thuy Anh I live near the Ocean. I see the waves boisterous and impudent bursting and splashing against the huge rocks. I see the white boats out on the blue sea. I see the fisher men rapped in heavy coats to keep their bodys warm while bringing in large fishes to sell to the merchants, Look! I see a larg white bird going on its merry way. Then I think of how great God is for he made this great sea for me to see and yet I stand on dry land and see the green and hillie side with flowers rising to the sky. How sweet and beautiful for God to have made Thuy Anh and the sea.

I interview Caroline. When she was a little girl in Arkansas, she "would get off into a room by myself and read the Scripture." The "poems in King Solomon" were her favorites. She went to a segregated school and "used to write quite a bit" at home. But she "got away from it" and some years later dropped out of high school to come west to earn a living. She's worked in a convalescent hospital for twenty years, never married, wishes she had, comes, now, back to school and is finding again her love of words. "I get lost . . . I'm right in there with my writing, and I forget all my surroundings." She is classified as a basic student — no diploma, low-level employment, poor test scores — had been taught by her grandmother that she would have to earn her living "by the sweat of my brow."

Her work in the writing course had been good up to the point of Thuy Anh's interview, better than that of many classmates, adequate, fairly free of

15

error, pretty well organized. But the interview triggered a different level of performance. Caroline's early engagement with language reemerged in a lyrical burst: an evocation of an imagined childhood, a curious overlay of one culture's fantasy over another's harsh reality. Caroline's longing reshaped a Vietnamese girlhood, creating a life neither she nor Thuy Anh ever had, an intersection of biblical rhythms and *Father Knows Best*.

Over Chin's bent head arches a trellis packed tight with dried honeysuckle and chrysanthemum, sea moss, mushrooms, and ginseng. His elbow rests on the cash register — quiet now that the customers have left. He shifts on the stool, concentrating on the writing before him: "A young children," he scribbles, and pauses. "Young children," that doesn't sound good, he thinks. He crosses out "children" and sits back. A few seconds pass. He can't think of the right way to say it, so he writes "children" again and continues: "a young children with his grandma smail . . ." "Smail." He pulls a Chinese-English dictionary from under the counter.

In front of the counter and extending down the aisle are boxes of dried fish: shark fins, mackerel, pollock. They give off a musky smell. Behind Chin are rows of cans and jars: pickled garlic, pickled ginger, sesame paste. By the door, comic books and Chinese weeklies lean dog-eared out over the thin retaining wire of a dusty wooden display. Chin has found his word: It's not *smail*, it's *smile*. "A young children with his grandma smile. . . ." He reaches in the pocket of his jeans jacket, pulls out a piece of paper, and unfolds it. There's a word copied on it he has been wanting to use. A little bell over the door jingles. An old man comes in, and Chin moves his yellow pad aside.

Chin remembers his teacher in elementary school telling him that his writing was poor, that he didn't know many words. He went to middle school for a few years but quit before completing it. Very basic English — the ABCs and simple vocabulary — was, at one point, part of his curriculum, but he lived in a little farming community, so he figured he would never use it. He did, though, pick up some letters and a few words. He immigrated to America when he was seventeen, and for the two years since has been living with his uncle in Chinatown. His uncle signed him up for English classes at the community center. He didn't like them. He did, however, start hanging out in the recreation room, playing pool and watching TV. The English on TV intrigued him. And it was then that he turned to writing. He would "try to learn to speak something" by writing it down. That was about six months ago. Now he's enrolled in a community college literacy program and has been making strong progress. He is especially taken with one tutor, a woman in her mid-thirties who encourages him to write. So he writes for her. He writes stories about his childhood in China. He sneaks time when no one is in the store or when customers are poking around, writing because he likes to bring her things, writing, too, because "sometime I think writing make my English better."

The old man puts on the counter a box of tea guaranteed to help you   20
stop smoking. Chin rings it up and thanks him. The door jingles and Chin returns to his writing, copying the word from his folded piece of paper, a word
he found in *People* magazine: "A young children with his grandma smile
gleefully."

Frank Marell, born Meraglio, my oldest uncle, learned his English as Chin
is learning his. He came to America with his mother and three sisters in
September 1921. They came to join my grandfather who had immigrated long
before. They joined, as well, the millions of Italian peasants who had flowed
through Customs with their cloth-and-paper suitcases, their strange gestural
language, and their dark, empty pockets. Frank was about to turn eight when
he immigrated, so he has faint memories of Calabria. They lived in a one-room
stone house. In the winter, the family's scrawny milk cow was brought inside.
By the door there was a small hole for a rifle barrel. Wolves came out of the
hills. He remembers the frost and burrs stinging his feet as he foraged the countryside for berries and twigs and fresh grass for the cow. *Chi esce riesce*, the saying went — "he who leaves succeeds" — and so it was that my grandfather
left when he did, eventually finding work amid the metal and steam of the
Pennsylvania Railroad.

My uncle remembers someone giving him bread on the steamship. He
remembers being very sick. Once in America, he and his family moved into the
company housing projects across from the stockyard. The house was dirty and
had gouges in the wood. Each morning his mother had to sweep the soot from
in front of the door. He remembers rats. He slept huddled with his father and
mother and sisters in the living room, for his parents had to rent out the other
rooms in order to buy clothes and shoes and food. Frank never attended school
in Italy. He was eight now and would enter school in America. America, where
eugenicists were attesting, scientifically, to the feeblemindedness of his race,
where the popular press ran articles about the immorality of these swarthy
exotics. Frank would enter school here. In many ways, you could lay his life like
a template over a current life in the Bronx, in Houston, in Pico-Union.

He remembers the embarrassment of not understanding the teacher, of
not being able to read or write. Funny clothes, oversize shoes, his hair slicked
down and parted in the middle. He would lean forward — his assigned seat,
fortunately, was in the back — and ask other Italian kids, ones with some
English, to tell him what for the love of God was going on. He had big, sad eyes,
thick hands, skin dark enough to yield the nickname Blacky. Frank remembers
other boys — Carmen Santino, a kid named Hump, Bruno Tucci — who
couldn't catch on to this new language and quit coming to school. Within six
months of his arrival, Frank would be going after class to the back room of
Pete Mastis's Dry Cleaners and Shoeshine Parlor. He cleaned and shined shoes,
learned to operate a steam press, ran deliveries. He listened to the radio, trying
to mimic the harsh complexities of English. He spread Pete Mastis's racing

forms out before him, copying words onto the margins of newsprint. He tried talking to the people whose shoes he was shining, exchanging tentative English with the broken English of Germans and Poles and other Italians.

Eventually, Frank taught his mother to sign her name. By the time he was in his teens, he was reading flyers and announcements of sales and legal documents to her. He was also her scribe, doing whatever writing she needed to have done. Frank found himself immersed in the circumstance of literacy.

With the lives of Mario and Caroline and Chin and Frank Marell as a   25
backdrop, I want to consider a current, very powerful set of proposals about literacy and culture.

There is a strong impulse in American education — curious in a country with such an ornery streak of antitraditionalism — to define achievement and excellence in terms of the acquisition of a historically validated body of knowledge, an authoritative list of books and allusions, a canon. We seek a certification of our national intelligence, indeed, our national virtue, in how diligently our children can display this central corpus of information. This need for certification tends to emerge most dramatically in our educational policy debates during times of real or imagined threat: economic hard times, political crises, sudden increases in immigration. Now is such a time, and it is reflected in a number of influential books and commission reports. E. D. Hirsch* argues that a core national vocabulary, one oriented toward the English literate tradition — Alice in Wonderland to zeitgeist — will build a knowledge base that will foster the literacy of all Americans. Diane Ravitch* and Chester Finn* call for a return to a traditional historical and literary curriculum: the valorous historical figures and the classical literature of the once-elite course of study. Allan Bloom,* Secretary of Education William Bennett, Mortimer Adler* and the Paideia Group, and a number of others have affirmed, each in their very different ways, the necessity of the Great Books: Plato and Aristotle and Sophocles, Dante and Shakespeare and Locke, Dickens and Mann and Faulkner. We can call this orientation to educational achievement the canonical orientation.

At times in our past, the call for a shoring up of or return to a canonical curriculum was explicitly elitist, was driven by a fear that the education of the select was being compromised. Today, though, the majority of the calls are

---

E. D. Hirsch: author of *Cultural Literacy: What Every American Needs to Know*, which argues for a standard national public school curriculum that would ensure that all Americans share a common cultural vocabulary

Diane Ravitch: author of *Developing National Standards in Education* and an Education Department official in the Reagan administration

Chester Finn: undersecretary of education in the Reagan administration

Allan Bloom: author of *The Closing of the American Mind* (1987)

Mortimer Adler: educator and philosopher, author of many books, including three volumes on the Paideia Proposal, an educational framework based on ancient Greek concepts

provocatively framed in the language of democracy. They assail the mediocre and grinding curriculum frequently found in remedial and vocational education. They are disdainful of the patronizing perceptions of student ability that further restrict the already restricted academic life of disadvantaged youngsters. They point out that the canon — its language, conventions, and allusions — is central to the discourse of power, and to keep it from poor kids is to assure their disenfranchisement all the more. The books of the canon, claim the proposals, the Great Books, are a window onto a common core of experience and civic ideals. There is, then, a spiritual, civic, and cognitive heritage here, and *all* our children should receive it. If we are sincere in our desire to bring Mario, Chin, the younger versions of Caroline, current incarnations of Frank Marell, and so many others who populate this book — if we truly want to bring them into our society — then we should provide them with this stable and common core. This is a forceful call. It promises a still center in a turning world.

I see great value in being challenged to think of the curriculum of the many in the terms we have traditionally reserved for the few; it is refreshing to have common assumptions about the capacities of underprepared students so boldly challenged. Many of the people we have encountered in these pages have displayed the ability to engage books and ideas thought to be beyond their grasp. There were the veterans: Willie Oates* writing, in prison, ornate sentences drawn from *The Mill on the Floss.** Sergeant Gonzalez* coming to understand poetic ambiguity in "Butch Weldy."* There was the parole aide Olga who no longer felt walled off from *Macbeth*. There were the EOP* students at UCLA, like Lucia who unpackaged *The Myth of Mental Illness* once she had an orientation and overview. And there was Frank Marell who, later in his life, would be talking excitedly to his nephew about this guy Edgar Allan Poe. Too many people are kept from the books of the canon, the Great Books, because of misjudgments about their potential. Those books eventually proved important to me, and, as best I know how, I invite my students to engage them. But once we grant the desirability of equal curricular treatment and begin to consider what this equally distributed curriculum would contain, problems arise: If the canon itself is the answer to our educational inequities, why has it historically invited few and denied many? Would the canonical orientation provide adequate guidance as to how a democratic curriculum should be constructed and how it should be taught? Would it guide us in opening up to Olga that "fancy talk" that so alienated her?

Those who study the way literature becomes canonized, how linguistic creations are included or excluded from a tradition, claim that the canonical

---

Willie Oates, Sergeant Gonzalez: students in a veterans' program that Rose worked in
The Mill on the Floss: a novel (1860) by George Eliot (1819–80)
"Butch Weldy": a poem in *Spoon River Anthology* (1915) by Edgar Lee Masters (1869–1950)
EOP: Equal Opportunity Program

curriculum students would most likely receive would not, as is claimed, offer a common core of American experience. Caroline would not find her life represented in it, nor would Mario. The canon has tended to push to the margin much of the literature of our nation: from American Indian songs and chants to immigrant fiction to working-class narratives. The institutional messages that students receive in the books they're issued and the classes they take are powerful and, as I've witnessed since my Voc. Ed. days, quickly internalized. And to revise these messages and redress past wrongs would involve more than adding some new books to the existing canon — the very reasons for linguistic and cultural exclusion would have to become a focus of study in order to make the canon act as a democratizing force. Unless this happens, the democratic intent of the reformers will be undercut by the content of the curriculum they propose.

And if we move beyond content to consider basic assumptions about   30
teaching and learning, a further problem arises, one that involves the very nature of the canonical orientation itself. The canonical orientation encourages a narrowing of focus from learning to that which must be learned: It simplifies the dynamic tension between student and text and reduces the psychological and social dimensions of instruction. The student's personal history recedes as the what of the classroom is valorized over the how. Thus it is that the encounter of student and text is often portrayed by canonists as a transmission. Information, wisdom, virtue will pass from the book to the student if the student gives the book the time it merits, carefully traces its argument or narrative or lyrical progression. Intellectual, even spiritual, growth will *necessarily* result from an encounter with Roman mythology, *Othello*, and "I heard a Fly buzz — when I died — ,"* with biographies and historical sagas and patriotic lore. Learning is stripped of confusion and discord. It is stripped, as well, of strong human connection. My own initiators to the canon — Jack MacFarland, Dr. Carothers, and the rest — knew there was more to their work than their mastery of a tradition. What mattered most, I see now, were the relationships they established with me, the guidance they provided when I felt inadequate or threatened. This mentoring was part of my entry into that solemn library of Western thought — and even with such support, there were still times of confusion, anger, and fear. It is telling, I think, that once that rich social network slid away, once I was in graduate school in intense, solitary encounter with that tradition, I abandoned it for other sources of nurturance and knowledge.

The model of learning implicit in the canonical orientation seems, at times, more religious than cognitive or social: Truth resides in the printed texts, and if they are presented by someone who knows them well and respects them, that truth will be revealed. Of all the advocates of the canon, Mortimer Adler has given most attention to pedagogy — and his Paideia books contain valuable

---

"I heard a Fly buzz — when I died — ": poem by Emily Dickinson (1830–86)

discussions of instruction, coaching, and questioning. But even here, and this is doubly true in the other manifestos, there is little acknowledgement that the material in the canon can be not only difficult but foreign, alienating, overwhelming.

We need an orientation to instruction that provides guidance on how to determine and honor the beliefs and stories, enthusiasms, and apprehensions that students reveal. How to build on them, and when they clash with our curriculum — as I saw so often in the Tutorial Center at UCLA — when they clash, how to encourage a discussion that will lead to reflection on what students bring and what they're currently confronting. Canonical lists imply canonical answers, but the manifestos offer little discussion of what to do when students fail. If students have been exposed to at least some elements of the canon before — as many have — why didn't it take? If they're encountering it for the first time and they're lost, how can we determine where they're located — and what do we do then?

Each member of a teacher's class, poor *or* advantaged, gives rise to endless decisions, day-to-day determinations about a child's reading and writing: decisions on how to tap strength, plumb confusion, foster growth. The richer your conception of learning and your understanding of its social and psychological dimensions, the more insightful and effective your judgments will be. Consider the sources of literacy we saw among the children in El Monte: shopkeepers' signs, song lyrics, auto manuals, the conventions of the Western, family stories and tales, and more. Consider Chin's sources — television and *People* magazine — and Caroline's oddly generative mix of the Bible and an American media illusion. Then there's the jarring confluence of personal horror and pop cultural flotsam that surfaces in Mario's drawings, drawings that would be a rich, if volatile, point of departure for language instruction. How would these myriad sources and manifestations be perceived and evaluated if viewed within the framework of a canonical tradition, and what guidance would the tradition provide on how to understand and develop them? The great books and central texts of the canon could quickly become a benchmark against which the expressions of student literacy would be negatively measured, a limiting band of excellence that, ironically, could have a dispiriting effect on the very thing the current proposals intend: the fostering of mass literacy.

To understand the nature and development of literacy we need to consider the social context in which it occurs — the political, economic, and cultural forces that encourage or inhibit it. The canonical orientation discourages deep analysis of the way these forces may be affecting performance. The canonists ask that schools transmit a coherent traditional knowledge to an ever-changing, frequently uprooted community. This discordance between message and audience is seldom examined. Although a ghetto child can rise on the lilt of a Homeric line — books *can* spark dreams — appeals to elevated texts can also divert attention from the conditions that keep a population from realizing its dreams. The literacy curriculum is being asked to do what our politics and our economics have failed to do: diminish differences in achievement, narrow our gaps, bring us together. Instead of analysis of the complex web of causes of poor performance, we are offered a faith in the unifying power of a body of knowledge, whose infusion will bring the rich and the poor, the longtime disaffected and the uprooted newcomers into cultural unanimity. If this vision is democratic, it is simplistically so, reductive, not an invitation for people truly to engage each other at the point where cultures and classes intersect.

I worry about the effects a canonical approach to education could have on   35 cultural dialogue and transaction — on the involvement of an abandoned underclass and on the movement of immigrants like Mario and Chin into our nation. A canonical uniformity promotes rigor and quality control; it can also squelch new thinking, diffuse the generative tension between the old and the new. It is significant that the canonical orientation is voiced with most force during times of challenge and uncertainty, for it promises the authority of tradition, the seeming stability of the past. But the authority is fictive, gained from a misreading of American cultural history. No period of that history was harmoniously stable; the invocation of a golden age is a mythologizing act. Democratic culture is, by definition, vibrant and dynamic, discomforting and unpredictable. It gives rise to apprehension; freedom is not always calming. And, yes, it can yield fragmentation, though often as not the source of fragmentation is intolerant misunderstanding of diverse traditions rather than the desire of members of those traditions to remain hermetically separate. A truly democratic vision of knowledge and social structure would honor this complexity. The vision might not be soothing, but it would provide guidance as to how to live and teach in a country made up of many cultural traditions.

We are in the middle of an extraordinary social experiment: the attempt to provide education for all members of a vast pluralistic democracy. To have any prayer of success, we'll need many conceptual blessings: A philosophy of language and literacy that affirms the diverse sources of linguistic competence and deepens our understanding of the ways class and culture blind us to the richness of those sources. A perspective on failure that lays open the logic of error. An orientation toward the interaction of poverty and ability that undercuts simple polarities, that enables us to see simultaneously the constraints poverty places on the play of mind and the actual mind at play within those constraints. We'll need a pedagogy that encourages us to step back and consider the threat of the standard classroom and that shows us, having stepped back, how to step forward to invite a student across the boundaries of that powerful room. Finally, we'll need a revised store of images of educational excellence, ones closer to egalitarian ideals — ones that embody the reward and turmoil of education in a democracy, that celebrate the plural, messy human reality of it. At heart, we'll need a guiding set of principles that do not encourage us to retreat from, but move us closer to, an understanding of the rich mix of speech and ritual and story that is America.

QUESTIONING THE TEXT

1. What do you think Rose means when he says that "a failed education is social more than intellectual in origin" (paragraph 5)? Look back to A.L.'s profile on p. 90. Does anything there suggest a time when her education failed for social — or intellectual — reasons? Describe a time when your education failed — or succeeded — largely because of social reasons. If you keep a reading log, record your answers there.

2. Rose quotes a friend who says that education can be thought of as "one culture embracing another" (paragraph 4). Give a few examples from his essay that illustrate this embrace, and then give an example from your own educational experience.

3. Why do you think Rose includes the stories of Mario, Caroline, Chin, and Frank Marell as a backdrop for his discussion about current concepts of literacy in America? What do their stories have in common? What kinds of students does he leave unmentioned?

MAKING CONNECTIONS

4. Both Mike Rose and Roland Fryer ("Acting White," p. 143) take minority achievement as one of their primary concerns. How do their approaches to the problem differ? How do they define the problem differently? Do you think that they would propose similar solutions to the problem? What points of agreement can you find, and in what ways do you think they disagree about problems or solutions?

5. Spend some time thinking about one of the students Rose describes. Then write a brief poem (using Gwendolyn Brooks as a model, perhaps; see p. 157) that characterizes that student's attitude toward school.

JOINING THE CONVERSATION

6. Try to remember a time when your relationship with someone (teacher, parent, coach, religious leader) made it easier (or harder) for you to learn what that person was trying to teach you. Write a brief description of this event for your class, concluding by summarizing those things about the person that most *helped* (or *hindered*) your learning from him or her.

7. Rose remembers that his earliest interest in literacy came from "comic books and science fiction, from the personal, nonscientific worlds I created with bits and pieces of laboratory and telescopic technology, came, as well, from the Italian stories I heard my uncles and parents tell" (paragraph 2). Brainstorm with two or three other students about your earliest out-of-school experiences with reading and writing. How were they like or unlike your experiences of reading and writing in school?

MICHAEL SOKOLOVE
Football Is a Sucker's Game

During my thirty years in academe, I have always been at schools with massive athletic departments and football teams that play in prime time, first at The Ohio State University and then at the University of Texas at Austin. So I found Michael Sokolove's "Football Is a Sucker's Game" — a lengthy essay exploring the efforts of the University of South Florida to establish an NCAA Division I-A gridiron program — compelling reading.

It is possible, I think, to be a fan of college football and still have doubts about what football programs have become in the last few decades — grossly overfunded, overproduced commercial ventures wholly disconnected from the major and even peripheral purposes of a university. Sokolove shows how schools get sucked into spiraling commitments and expenditures when school administrators, looking for an easy way to get public attention for their institutions, decide to play with the big boys of the NCAA.

What he doesn't show is how such programs lose their hold on the very students the football teams are supposed to represent. These days, ordinary undergraduates at Division I-A schools may not be able to get — or afford — decent seats at a "big" game. They've been squeezed out by alumni or businesses whose handsome contributions buy them prime real estate in a stadium enlarged every decade to cover the salaries of coaches paid like Hollywood celebrities.

Moreover, chances are most students have never taken a class with a football player or studied in the same library with one. And don't even try to make the case that football builds character or school spirit or community. Too many recent post-game victory riots undermine any notion that football, as played in Division I at least, has much to do with our better angels.

Michael Sokolove is a journalist and a writer for the New York Times Magazine, *where the following essay first appeared (in December 2002). He is also the author of* The Ticket Out: Darryl Strawberry and the Boys of Crenshaw *(2006).* —J.R.

The University of South Florida sprawls over nearly 1,500 acres in a once sparsely populated section of Tampa, close to where the city bleeds into unincorporated Hillsborough County. The campus is pancake flat and in desperate need of more trees and shade. Grass comes up in stubborn clumps through sandy soil. I can't say that I was shocked when I learned of a previous use of this parcel of land: a practice bombing range.

In many other ways, though, the University of South Florida is attractive — and useful. It has produced about 170,000 graduates in its four-decade history. It has a medical school and some well-regarded academic programs. Current enrollment stands at 39,000, and students tend to be grounded and hard-working rather than rich and entitled. (A professor told me that one challenge of his job is teaching morning classes to students who may have worked the late shift at Chili's.) What U.S.F. does not have is any kind of national profile. It has no standing. No buzz. The latest edition of the Princeton Review's *Best 345 Colleges* does not rank it low on the list — it leaves it off entirely.

University officials want U.S.F. in the guidebooks. They want fewer commuters, more out-of-state students, more residence halls and more of a "traditional" campus feel, by which they mean a campus with a soul and some spirit. It is a big job, and the burden for getting it done has fallen, largely, to Jim Leavitt.

"Sit down," he says as I enter his office one morning this fall. It's clear to me that I'm not only supposed to sit, but to do so in silence. His office is a mess. Clothes are strewn everywhere. About 50 videotapes are scattered on the floor by his desk. Leavitt himself doesn't look so great, either. His brown hair is a tousled mop, a modified crewcut gone to seed. He gives the impression of being simultaneously weary and wired.

Leavitt continues at what he was doing before I arrived, drawing with a   5
red pen on an unlined sheet of paper. At one point he reaches behind him on the floor for his Pepsi, which he drinks by the two-liter bottle. When he finally speaks again, his voice leaks out in the weak rasp of someone who does more yelling than sleeping. "I'm sorry," he says, "but I was in here late last night and I never even got to this. To be honest with you, there aren't enough hours in the day. But I've really got to get through it. It's important."

After several more minutes, when he is finally done, I walk around behind Leavitt to inspect his handiwork. On the white paper are a series of squiggles and arrows, 11 on each side of the page.

"What is it?" I inquire.

"A punt return," he says.

Football is the S.U.V. of the college campus: aggressively big, resource-guzzling, lots and lots of fun and potentially destructive of everything around it. Big-time teams award 85 scholarships and, with walk-ons, field rosters of 100 or more players. (National Football League teams make do with half that.) At the highest level, universities wage what has been called an "athletic arms race" to see who can build the most lavish facilities to attract the highest-quality players. Dollars are directed from general funds and wrestled from donors, and what does not go into cherry-wood lockers, plush carpets and million-dollar weight rooms ends up in the pockets of coaches, the most exalted of whom now make upward of $2 million a year.

The current college sports landscape is meaner than ever, more overtly   10
commercial, more winner-take-all. And just as in the rest of the economy, the gap between rich and poor is widening. College sports now consists of a class of super-behemoths — perhaps a dozen or so athletic departments with budgets of $40 million and up — and a much larger group of schools that face the choice of spending themselves into oblivion or being embarrassed on the field.

(Which may happen in any case.) It is common for lesser college football teams to play at places like Tennessee or Michigan, where average attendance exceeds 100,000, in return for "guarantees" from the host school of as much as $500,000. They are paid, in other words, to take a beating.

Any thought of becoming one of the giants and sharing in the real money is in most cases a fantasy. Universities new to Division I-A football (in addition to U.S.F., the University of Connecticut and the University of Buffalo have just stepped up to the big time) know that the first level of competition is financial. It is a dangerous game. "The mantra of the need to 'spend money to make money' can be used to justify a great deal of spending, without leading an institution to any destination other than a deeper financial hole," write James Shulman and William Bowen in *The Game of Life: College Sports and Educational Values*, their 2001 examination of the finances of college athletics.

The current college bowl season began last week and ends Jan. 3 with the national championship game, the Fiesta Bowl. This year, the cartel of teams belonging to the Bowl Championship Series — members of the six most prominent conferences plus independent Notre Dame, a total of 63 teams — will split a guaranteed payoff of at least $120 million from the Fiesta, Orange, Sugar and Rose Bowls. Teams outside the B.C.S. are eligible to play in such low-wattage affairs as the Humanitarian Bowl, the Motor City Bowl and the Continental Tire Bowl. For the privilege, they will almost certainly lose money, because the bowl payouts will not even cover travel and other expenses.

"We are receiving letters and calls from conferences that want in," Mike Tranghese, coordinator of the five-year-old B.C.S., told me. "And we have formed a presidential oversight panel to form an answer." But letting more members in would mean splitting up the money more ways. I asked Tranghese if I was missing something in assuming the B.C.S. had no incentive to cut more schools in. "If you were missing something, I would let you know," he said. "The B.C.S. consists of the major teams as determined by the marketplace. Any other system is socialism. And if we're going to have socialism, then why don't we share our endowments?"

One reason B.C.S. members do not want to share is that college sports have become so immensely expensive that even some of the biggest of the big lose money. The University of Michigan, which averages more than 110,000 fans for home football games, lost an estimated $7 million on athletics over the course of two seasons, between 1998 and 2000. Ohio State had athletic revenues of $73 million in 1999–2000 and "barely managed to break even," according to the book *Unpaid Professionals: Commercialism and Conflict in Big-time College Sports*, by Andrew Zimbalist, a Smith College economics professor. A state audit revealed that the University of Wisconsin lost $286,700 on its Rose Bowl appearance in 1998 because it took a small army, a traveling party of 832, to Pasadena.

The endemic criminal and ethical scandals of college sports are connected by a straight line to the money. Teams that do not win do not excite   15 their boosters, fill up stadiums, appear on national TV or get into postseason play, thereby endangering the revenue stream that supports the immense infrastructure. It is the desperation for cash, every bit as much as the pursuit of victory, that causes university athletic departments to overlook all kinds of rule-breaking until it splatters out into the open.

One day this fall I opened my morning sports page and, in glancing at the college football briefs, took note that it was a particularly bad day for the Big Ten. The headlines were: "Spartan Tailback Dismissed"; "Iowa Player Arrested"; "Wisconsin Back Stabbed." The Michigan State Spartans dismissed two co-captains within 10 days: the starting quarterback, who checked into rehab for a substance-abuse problem, as well as the tailback, who was accused of drunken driving and eluding arrest by dragging a police officer with his car. The next day, the head coach, Bobby Williams, with his team's record at 3–6, was fired — and sent off with a $550,000 buyout.

At tiny Gardner-Webb University in Boiling Springs, N.C. — a Baptist institution in its first season of Division I basketball — the university president resigned in the fall after acknowledging that he ordered a change in the calculation of a star basketball player's grade-point average. At Florida State University, quarterback Adrian McPherson was suspended days before his arrest for supposedly stealing a blank check, then expressed shock at the discipline meted out by the normally lenient head coach, Bobby Bowden. (When a star player was accused of theft a few years back, Bowden said, "I'm praying for a misdemeanor.") The University of Alabama at Birmingham, which started football just over a decade ago, is playing this season under a cloud. The trustees of the Alabama higher-education system have given the university two years to reverse a $7.6 million budget deficit or face being shut down. In addition, pending civil suits charge that a 15-year-old girl who enrolled at U.A.B. was sexually assaulted, repeatedly, by a large number of football and basketball players, as well as by the person who performed as the school's mascot, a dragon.

The list goes on. Ohio State's thrilling 14–9 victory over Michigan on Nov. 23 occasioned a full-scale riot by inebriated Buckeye fans who burned cars, looted businesses and caused tens of thousands of dollars in damage before 250 police officers finally restored order at 5 a.m. These sorts of things have become the background music of college sports.

Being a striving team trying to keep up in a big-time conference can be a particular kind of debacle. Rutgers University, in this regard, is Exhibit A. It belongs to the Big East, a B.C.S. football conference that also boasts powerful basketball programs. Rutgers can't compete in either sport. Its cellar-dwelling teams draw poor crowds, and the athletic department ran a deficit of about $13 million last year.

A dissident group, the Rutgers 1,000, has waged a passionate campaign   20
to get Rutgers to leave the Big East and to de-emphasize athletics. This has led, indirectly, to yet an entirely new way of throwing money away on sports. The administration tried to block publication of a Rutgers 1,000 advertisement in

an alumni magazine. Not only did Rutgers lose the ensuing court battle, but it also spent $375,000 fighting it, including court-ordered reimbursement of legal fees to the A.C.L.U., which took up the case of the Rutgers 1,000 as a free-speech issue.

"Schools get on a treadmill, and there's no getting off," says James Shulman, an author of *The Game of Life*. "They have to stay on; they have too much invested." The former Princeton basketball coach Pete Carill once said of the big-time programs: "If you want to get into the rat race, you've got to be a rat."

Another way to look at big-time college sports is as a sucker's game, one with many more losers than winners. Notre Dame, a great football team before it was a great university, is the prototype for all schools hoping to hitch a ride on the back of a popular sports team. Duke certainly has become more celebrated and academically selective in the years its basketball team has been a perennial Final Four participant. But Notre Dame and Duke are exceptions. For every Notre Dame and Duke, there are many more like Rutgers and U.A.B., schools that spend millions in a hopeless mission to reach the top.

The University of South Florida, nonetheless, wants in on the gamble and in on the perceived spoils. The new gospel there is that football is "the tip of the marketing sword." I heard the phrase from several administrators at U.S.F. Vicki Mitchell explained the concept to me. She had directed a highly successful university-wide fund-raising campaign, but in May, not long after the team jumped to Division I-A, she moved to the athletic department to raise money specifically for sports. Under Mitchell, the office devoted to sports fund-raising was ramped up from three staff members to eight, and in the first three months of this fiscal year she and her team brought in $1.6 million, just $200,000 less than the total raised in the previous 12 months. "The easiest way to build a U.S.F. brand is to build an athletic program that is known, and that means football," Mitchell said. "Maybe that's not what the university wants to be known for, but it's reality."

Nearly two decades ago, the exploits of the Boston College quarterback Doug Flutie and the success of the team were credited with increasing applications by 25 percent and transforming B.C. from a regional to a national university. The syndrome was even given a name: the Flutie effect. That's the kind of magic U.S.F. is trying to catch.

U.S.F. didn't play football at any level until 1997. Its founding president, 25
John Allen, who presided over the university from 1957 to 1970, was that rare thing in football-crazed Florida — a staunch opponent of the sport. In the 1980s, U.S.F. alumni and Tampa businessmen began pushing for football, and the U.S.F. administration began lobbying a reluctant state Board of Regents for a team. In 1993, the outgoing president, Frank Borkowski, in his final weeks at U.S.F. and with the Regents' decision on football pending, hired Lee Roy

Selmon — a former N.F.L. star and one of the most admired men in Tampa — to lead football fund-raising. That was the pivotal moment. "I was in a pretty tight box," recalls Borkowski, now chancellor at Appalachian State University. "The Regents did not want us to have a team." But to deny football would have been a slap to Selmon.

Jim Leavitt was hired in 1995, two years before the University of South Florida Bulls played their first game. From the start, the university intended to move quickly to the N.C.A.A.'s highest level and eventually challenge football factories like Florida State, the University of Florida and the University of Miami. By the time the current U.S.F. president, Judy Genshaft, arrived in 2000, the program was in full bloom. Genshaft's term has so far been marked by a thorny dispute spawned by her suspension of Sami Al-Arian, a tenured professor of computer science, over charges that he had ties to terrorism. Compared to the fallout from that, football has been pure pleasure.

Genshaft, who attends the team's games and keeps a jersey in her office with her name on the back, was an undergraduate at Wisconsin and a longtime administrator at Ohio State. "I know big sports," she says, "and I love big sports. It brings more visibility, more spirit, more community engagement. Even researchers coming to us from other big universities, they are expecting sports to be part of campus life."

The rationales put forth for big-time sports are not easily proved or disproved. One example is the assumption that successful teams spur giving to the general funds of universities. "The logic is reasonable enough," Zimbalist wrote in *Unpaid Professionals.* "A school goes to the Rose Bowl or to the Final Four. Alumni feel proud and open up their pocketbooks." But Zimbalist looked at the available evidence and concluded that winning teams, at best, shake loose dollars given specifically for sports. And only for a time; when on-field fortunes reverse, or a scandal occurs, the money often dries up.

Genshaft says that U.S.F. can play football at the highest level without financial or ethical ruin. "It's a risk and it is expensive," she says. "But we've decided that football is part of who we are and where we're going."

But others see disaster as the only possible result. At Rutgers, the sports   30
program has split the campus community and spawned an angry and unusually organized opposition. "The reality of sports at this level is it can't be done right," says William C. Dowling, an English professor and one of the leaders of the Rutgers 1,000. "It's not possible, anywhere, even at the so-called best places. Look at the differences in SAT levels."

One study showed the SAT scores of football players at Division I-A schools to be 271 points lower than incoming nonathletes. "You have kids brought to campus and maybe, maybe they could be real students if they studied 60 hours a week and did nothing else," Dowling says. "But everyone knows that's not happening. It's not their fault. They've been lied to in high school, all these African-American kids who get told that playing ball is their way up in society, even though it's never been that for any other ethnic group in America. It's dishonest. It's filthy."

When Vicki Mitchell pitches U.S.F. donors, however, she sells the program as if it were in a state of grace — unsullied by scandal, at least so far, and still operating with a degree of fiscal sanity. She begins by painting a picture of what life is like at the really big football powers. To secure a season ticket at one of those schools in a desirable part of the stadium, if that's even possible, can set a donor back tens of thousands of dollars. "I'll say to someone: 'You're a sports fan. You need to get on board, because everyone knows what it costs at those other places. Our aspirations are no less, but we're not there yet. We're young. We're fun. We're a growth stock. Get in now while it's still affordable.'"

I met head coach Jim Leavitt for the first time just a few days before the biggest home game in the history of University of South Florida football. The opponent, Southern Mississippi, was the strongest team ever to visit U.S.F. and a favorite to break its 15-game home winning streak. U.S.F. had lost an early-season road game at Oklahoma, then the second-ranked team in the nation, but outplayed the powerful Sooners for long stretches. Leavitt's team was surging in the national polls; the *New York Times* computer rankings would place it as high as 18th in the nation, ahead of such tradition-rich football powers as Tennessee, Florida State, Auburn, Clemson and Nebraska. These accomplishments, for a program playing just its sixth season, were nothing short of astounding.

As the showdown against Southern Mississippi loomed, two things obsessed Leavitt: winning the game, and money. "The kind of money we need is big, big money," he said to me not long after saying hello. He kept returning to the same point. "We have what we need for a beginning program, but we're not a beginning program anymore." Then: "I don't know what this program will look like in the future. It can be big. But you've got to have money. You've got to have facilities. If you don't, it ain't gonna happen."

Leavitt, 46, grew up in nearby St. Petersburg. He was a high-school sports   35
star, a defensive back at the University of Missouri, then an assistant coach at several universities before he came home to be the first coach of U.S.F. football.

Leavitt has won praise not just for winning, but also for doing so on the cheap. He and his nine assistant coaches work out of a complex of four trailers, in front of which Leavitt erected a split-rail fence "to make it look like the Ponderosa." Leavitt proudly told me that the couch in his office, on which he sometimes lies down for the night, is a $700 vinyl number rather than one of those $5,000 leather cruise ships to be found in the offices of so many other coaches.

This era of frugality, though, has just ended. In early November, the university unveiled drawings for a long-hoped-for training and office complex that will be as big as a football field — 104,000 square feet over two floors that will serve most of the university's men's and women's teams but will be dominated by football.

Leavitt views this as natural and right. He tells me about Oklahoma, coached by his close friend Bob Stoops, which already has "an outrageous setup, everything you can imagine," and has just raised yet another $100 million. "I imagine they'll tell you it's not for football only, and I would assume it's not," Leavitt says. "But I'm pretty sure football will get what it needs first. As it should, in my opinion."

Like many football coaches, Leavitt is no fan of Title IX regulations that mandate equal opportunity for female athletes. "Don't get me wrong," he says, "I am a big proponent of women's sports. I want us to be great at women's sports. But football should be separate from the Title IX thing, because nobody else operates like we do. We're revenue-producing."

To build the U.S.F. athletic complex will cost as much as $15 million. To furnish it — starting with $425,000 in weight-training equipment, a $65,000 hydrotherapy tub, portable X-ray machines, satellite uplinks and downlinks, trophy cases for a U.S.F. sports hall of fame in the atrium entrance — will cost up to $5 million more.   40

Despite aggressive fund-raising, private pledges for this facility have reached only $5 million, so it will be built on borrowed money. The construction bond will be backed partly by the "athletic fee" charged to students, which for those who attend full time has reached $224 a year — a fairly substantial add-on to a tuition of only $2,159.

Mitchell says the university considers students "its biggest donor," and student leaders are, in fact, courted like boosters. In October, the student government president and vice president flew on a private jet with President Genshaft to the big game at Oklahoma.

U.S.F. calculates that the football team brings in, roughly, $4 million in revenue and spends about the same amount. But as in most athletic departments, the accounting makes no attempt to measure the true resources used.

One day, I stood in a humid basement room and watched the laundry — muddy Bulls jerseys and pants, T-shirts, sweat socks, wrist- and headbands, jockstraps — from 105 football players being cleaned. Several colossal washers and dryers were fed by three athletic-department employees. They perform this task early August through late November, six days a week, 10 hours a day.

None of this — the salaries, the utility costs, the $8,000 a year just in laundry detergent — is charged against football. Nor is there any attempt to break out football's share of such costs as sports medicine, academic tutoring, strength and conditioning, insurance, field upkeep or the rest of its share of the more than $5 million in general expenses of the athletic department not assigned to a specific sport.   45

In the papers I was shown, I also could find no evidence that a $2 million fee to join Conference USA (which is not a B.C.S. conference) as a football-playing member in 2003 was accounted for in football's expense ledger. The money was borrowed from the university's general endowment, and the athletic department is paying the interest.

So when Jim Leavitt says that his football team is revenue-producing, that should not be understood as profit-generating. I would not pretend to know what football really costs at U.S.F., but it's clearly a lot more than $4 million, maybe even twice that. And another big bill is about to come due: Leavitt's next contract.

Just in case Judy Genshaft didn't know she had a hot coach on her hands who needed a big raise, she could have learned it from reading the local press. The articles began after the end of the 2001 season, when Leavitt entertained some job feelers. "U.S.F. Needs to Make Commitment to Leavitt," read a head-line in the *Tampa Tribune*. "U.S.F. said it wanted to play in the big leagues and built an impressive foundation," the columnist Joe Henderson wrote. "Now it has to finish the job, or risk that Leavitt will listen the next time someone calls."

Columns like these are the essential component of setting the market for a coach and driving up his price. An echo chamber of sports journalists, boosters, alumni, fans and national sports pundits anoints the coach a civic treasure and then campaigns that this indispensable figure must be properly rewarded lest the community risk having him stolen away. This is how it happens everywhere.

As Leavitt's Bulls piled up victory after victory this season, it got ever   50
noisier in the echo chamber. A story by the *Tampa Tribune's* U.S.F. beat man noted that Leavitt's $180,000 salary was way out of whack, that the average for Conference USA coaches was $410,000, that the coach at Houston — whose team Leavitt's slaughtered, 45–6! — could approach $1 million and that Leavitt was in fact one of the lowest-paid coaches in all of Division I-A.

A *St. Petersburg Times* columnist, Gary Shelton, celebrated Leavitt's single-mindedness — he has never purchased a CD, doesn't go to the movies, was barely aware of the Florida governor's race — and implied that the coach was too dedicated to the next game and next victory to properly focus on his own self-interest.

The drumbeat on Leavitt's behalf overlooked two things. One is that Leavitt's original contract runs through 2005, although that probably doesn't matter since college coaches are rarely held to the deals they sign. The other unaddressed question was more significant: how would U.S.F. square its big-time ambitions with its still small-time revenues?

For all the fevered energy and earnest expectations behind U.S.F. football, attendance at home games has long been stuck between 20,000 and 30,000. The team plays way across town, at the 65,000-seat Raymond James Stadium, home of the N.F.L.'s Tampa Bay Buccaneers. "We've flatlined," says Tom Veit, associate athletic director. "We had tire-kickers in the beginning, something like 50,000 at the first game in '97, and we need to bring them back in."

Students have not been dependable fans. About 3,500 live on campus; nearly 10,000 more live in off-campus garden apartments, most of which have swimming pools and frequent keg parties. Fifty-nine percent of U.S.F. stu-dents are female, so young men, the natural college football audience, may have a particular incentive not to stray too far from home. "If you want it to be," says the student government vice president, Dave Mincberg, "it's like spring break 24/7 around here."

One function that U.S.F. football does serve is as content, cheap programming in the 500-channel universe. Under a contract with ESPN Plus, U.S.F. football (and basketball) games are constantly up on the satellite — along with dozens of other games to be pulled down by viewers with a dish and a college sports package. The ubiquity of these televised college games makes the dream of a marketing bonanza — Jim Leavitt's fightin' Bulls as the tip of the sword — all the more difficult to achieve. Instead of becoming a "brand" like the well-known sports schools, U.S.F. is more likely to blend in with its anonymous brethren in Sports Satellite World, the Northern Arizonas, Coastal Carolinas and Boise States.

But U.S.F. has set its course. It's on the treadmill. It plays Alabama next season, Penn State in 2005 and the University of Florida in 2008. It didn't schedule these games to be embarrassed. Rebuilding with a new coach would be difficult competitively and, even more so, commercially. "If we lose Jim Leavitt, from a marketing point of view, that's not a place I want to be," Veit says. "I don't want to be me at that point. He's a hometown guy. He wins. People like him."

When the local sportswriters ask Leavitt about his contract, he gives carefully bland responses. He doesn't have an agent, and it could be argued that with his fawning press, he hardly needs one. The articles clearly please him. One day he says to me: "The Tampa paper is going to have another piece coming up on my salary. But you know, I don't pay too much attention. I don't deserve anything. I'm just glad I have a job. I'm blessed.

"And I mean that. I have zero interest in leaving here. But then people say to me, 'What if you were offered $1 million to go somewhere else?' Well, then I'd probably leave. Let's be realistic."

I asked him what he thought his market value was, and he did not hesitate. "About $500,000 or $600,000," he said. "At least."

The biggest of the big-time college sporting events are intoxicating. The swirl of colors, the marching bands, the deafening roars, the over-the-top political incorrectness — Florida State's Seminole mascot riding in on horseback; a Mississippi State coach some years back, on the eve of a game against the Texas Longhorns, castrating a bull. The whole thing is a little reminiscent of what I've heard some Catholic friends of mine say: even if you're a little ambivalent about the message, the pageantry will get you every time.

In college sports, the heady mix of anticipation, adrenaline, camaraderie and school pride is the gloss over the grubby reality. Pro sports operate within some financial parameters, governed by a profit motive. College sport, by contrast, is a mad cash scramble with squishy rules. Universities run from conference to conference, chasing richer TV deals; coaches from school to school, chasing cash. It's a game of mergers and acquisitions — of running out on your partners before they run out on you.

It's understandable why universities with hundreds of millions already invested in sports can't find a way out. Far less understandable is why a school like U.S.F. would, with eyes wide open, walk in. "I felt then and still feel that U.S.F. could be a model football program," says Frank Borkowski, the former president. "One with clear policies and rules, attractive to bright students, that would not go the way of so many programs — a corrupt way."

But the whole framework of college sports, with its out-of-control spending and lax academic and ethical standards, is rotten; it's difficult to be clean within it. The "student athletes," as the N.C.A.A. insists on calling them, feel the hypocrisy. When one is caught taking the wrong thing from the wrong person — not the usual perks but actual money — what ensues is a "Casablanca"-like overabundance of shock, then a bizarre penalty phase that almost always punishes everyone but the guilty parties. Thus, when the University of Michigan finally acknowledged this fall that some members of its famed "Fab Five" basketball teams of the early 1990s may have accepted payments from a booster, the university tried to get out in front of N.C.A.A. sanctions by disqualifying this year's team — whose players were about 8 years old in the Fab Five years — from participating in the 2003 N.C.A.A. tournament.

With the greater opportunities being afforded female athletes, it should be no surprise that an outsize sense of entitlement now extends to the women. Deborah Yow, the athletic director at the University of Maryland (and one of the few women leading a big athletic department), told me about a conversation she had with an athlete who had rejected Maryland.

"We just lost a great recruit in the sport of women's lacrosse, in which we   65
have won seven national championships," Yow said. "And one of the comments that the recruit made was that the school she had chosen over us had a beautiful new lacrosse stadium with a lovely locker room, and she even described the lockers in some detail. They were wood; that was the word she kept using. And, as she said, they all had that Nike gear hanging everywhere. And I've been to that facility. And I know that what she said was true."

In theory, Yow could have been pleased to be rejected by such a spoiled child. But she does not have that luxury. Instead, she felt relieved that a planned complex to be used by Maryland's women's lacrosse team would be the equal of this other palace. "We, as athletic directors, are interested in having the best possible facilities because we have noticed along the way that recruits are interested in this, that it does matter," she says.

College sport could not survive if it were viewed only as mass entertainment. On another level, it serves as a salvation story. The enterprise rests mostly on a narrative of young men pulled from hopeless situations, installed at universities, schooled in values by coaches and sent off into the world as productive citizens.

No one is better suited to tell the story than Lee Roy Selmon. The youngest of nine children in Eufala, Okla., he excelled in athletics and earned a football scholarship, as did two of his brothers, to the University of Oklahoma.

Lee Roy Selmon became the first-ever draft pick of the new Tampa Bay Buccaneers, an N.F.L. Hall of Famer, then a Tampa banker. The Lee Roy Selmon Expressway is one of the city's major thoroughfares.

To Selmon, who became U.S.F.'s athletic director a year and a half ago, college sports is a giant scholarship program for needy children. Of football's 100-player rosters, he says, "The more people here, the more people getting an education, the better. It's about generations — about student athletes developing abilities, being citizens, having families and being able to nurture their children."

One evening, I visited with some U.S.F. football players at their manda-   70
tory study hall, which takes place inside a wide-open rectangular room as big as a good-size banquet hall. Their monitor, Vik Bhide, a trim engineering student, sat just inside the front door, paging through a book called *The Dimensions of Parking*. The players clustered at round tables, reading textbooks or writing. Most had started their day very early and had already attended classes, lifted weights, endured a three-hour practice and gone to meetings in which they watched game film with coaches.

I took a walk through the room and peeked at the players' coursework. John Miller, a freshman offensive lineman, was studying vocabulary words from a textbook. On his list were "burgeoning," "inflection," "emanate," "insidious" and "obscenity." "It's a lot of hard words," he said. "But they're good for you."

Vince Brewer, a junior running back, was about to start an informative speech, which he thought he'd write on the subject of what causes a player to pass out during practice. "We get told a lot about dehydration, and the professor said to pick something you know a lot about." Chris Carothers, a massive offensive lineman, told me bluntly that he does not much like school, "but as a football player, it's something you've got to do."

In all of my interactions with U.S.F. football players, I was struck at how mannerly they were. Nearly all are from Florida, many from small towns, and in a classically Southern way, they are yes-sir, no-sir types. Maybe because U.S.F. has not yet reached its ambitions and neither the team nor its players are widely famous — not even on their own campus — there wasn't a lot of swagger.

"My mom and dad had me when they were in 11th grade," Marquel Blackwell, the Bulls' star quarterback, said. "I was raised, basically, by my two grandmothers. The main thing they taught me was how to respect other people."

Not a whole lot of trouble has attached to Jim Leavitt's boys in the six   75
years of U.S.F. football, nothing of the sort that occurs at some places and serves to indict a whole program. There have been some scuffles, as well as a gunplay accident in which a player was wounded.

"We encourage the players to be as much a part of normal campus life as possible," said Phyllis LaBaw, the associate athletic director for academic support. But no one pretends that they really are much like the typical U.S.F. student.

Nearly 70 percent of the U.S.F. football team is black on a campus that is otherwise 70 percent white. (Only 11 percent of U.S.F. students are black; the rest of the minority population is Hispanic and Asian and Native American.) The football players tend to be poorer than other students and more in need of academic help.

To be a football player at U.S.F., or an athlete of any kind, is like taking your mother to school with you — or several mothers. Academic counselors meet with athletes at least weekly. They sometimes follow them right to the door of a classroom, which in the trade is known as "eyeballing" a player to class. Where a lot of players are grouped in one class, tutors sometimes sit in and take notes. Counselors communicate directly with professors. "We don't ever ask for favors," LaBaw said. "But professors do provide us with information, which is vital."

Football players who miss a class or a mandatory study session get "run" by coaches — meaning they must show up on the practice field at 6 a.m. to be put through a series of sprints by a coach who is not happy to be there at that hour. "It is very punitive," LaBaw said.

LaBaw's department employs four full-time counselors and about 40 tutors and has an annual budget of $400,000. The staff serves all 450 intercollegiate athletes at U.S.F., so the 105 football players are less than a quarter of the clients — but as is the case with so much else, football sucks up more resources than its raw numbers would indicate. "They need more help," LaBaw said of the footballers, "but what we're doing works. Last year our football players had a mean G.P.A. of 2.52, which if we were already in Conference USA would have been the best in the conference — including Army."

LaBaw is part den mother, part drill sergeant — loving and supportive or confrontational and blunt, depending on the needs of the moment. Under her desk, she keeps a big box; when the season began, it had 5,000 condoms in it, all different colors. She hands them out like lollipops along with however much sex education she can blurt out.

Her effort, while well intentioned, is a version of closing the barn door after the horses have run out. Of the 105 players on U.S.F.'s football team — most of them between 18 and 23 years old — about 30 are fathers and many have produced multiple children. "I would say there's a total of 60 children from this team, and that's a conservative estimate," said LaBaw. "It's amazing how quickly it occurs, usually in the first year. Or they come to school already fathers."

What this means is that the recipients of Lee Roy Selmon's scholarship program for needy young men are recreating the need that many of them came from — children living in poverty, without fathers at home. With their five hours per day of football-related activity on top of class and studying, the fathers have no time even to change a diaper, let alone work to financially support their children. Most of the children live with their mothers or aunts or grandmothers. Some who are nearby spend the day at the university's day-care center, yet another cost of college football since the service is offered virtually free to U.S.F. students.

In DeAndrew Rubin's portrait in the U.S.F. football media guide, it says that his father drowned when he was 11 months old. It adds, "Father had given him a teddy bear for his first Christmas in 1978, and he places it in his locker during every game."

Rubin, 24, has two children, 3 years old and 10 months, and is engaged to their mother, his girlfriend since high school. They live just 30 minutes away in St. Petersburg. "I see them as often as I can, so if I would pass, they would remember me," he said. "I can't help that much financially, but emotionally I want to be there for them."

Unlike several other U.S.F. fathers who said they planned to make the N.F.L., Rubin is considered a prospect, although no sure thing. "It would be good for our situation," he said. "I don't want to have to work a 9-to-5; I guess nobody really does."

LaBaw spends a lot of time talking to the players. "Those who are fathers, there's a comfort aspect — having children is an opportunity to be surrounded by more love. Which is what they've always had, from grandmothers and aunts and cousins. But there is also this trophy aspect. It's let me show you the pictures, or the multiple pictures."

Football is at the center of Jim Leavitt's world, so he is not one to question the time or money devoted to it. He does not seem to have a great deal of interest in the nonfootball world. Leavitt makes appearances on campus and in the community, often related to fund-raising, but several people told me he can be brusque. If he says he has 20 minutes to give, then he's normally out the door in 20 minutes. There is always a practice to conduct or a football tape to be watched. He watches game tapes, and tapes of practices. "I sit and watch film all day long," he says. "I'm a recluse."

Because football is so central to him, he assumes his team's success is widely known and that it translates into other realms — he believes, without a doubt, in the concept of football as tip of the marketing sword. "We've had guys drafted into the N.F.L.," he says. "We have two guys with Super Bowl rings. How much does the university spend for that? What's it worth? That's worldwide publicity for the University of South Florida, right?"

I asked Leavitt if his long football hours left him much time with his 7-year-old daughter. "Quality time," he said, then repeated it as if trying to convince himself. "Quality time. It's got to be quality time."

There is one slice of humanity that Leavitt connects with — his players. "That's why I'm in this," he says. "The players. The relationships I have with those young men and the ability to make a difference in their lives. My mission is to help young people in every aspect of life. If I lose sight of that, I'll get out of coaching. The other reason I coach is for that moment when you are victorious. That's hard to create in any other part of life. You feel such contentment. That moment is so powerful." At halftime of U.S.F.'s season finale against Houston, Leavitt grew so agitated that he excitedly head-butted several of his helmeted players and came away bloody.

Beyond the field, Leavitt had reason to believe he had made a difference. His players respond to him as an authority figure and as a friend. They have absorbed his laser focus. They play football. They go to class and mandatory study hall. When the season is over, they lift weights and run. Marquel Blackwell, the quarterback, told me that more established programs like Florida and Nebraska showed interest in him but wanted to switch his position. Of Leavitt, he says: "He believed in me, and I believe in him back. I've given my heart to that man."

On the night of the big game, with U.S.F.'s home winning streak on the line against Southern Mississippi, President Genshaft played host to a couple of dozen guests in a luxury box at Raymond James Stadium — a crowd that included Florida's lieutenant governor and an assortment of local business types and politicos. Mike Griffin, the student government president, was in the box, too, wearing a "Bulls for Jeb" campaign button.

Because of Selmon's icon status, his box is the more coveted invitation, and Vicki Mitchell and her staff put together his list for maximum impact. They had targeted a wealthy U.S.F. graduate and Los Angeles lawyer as a potential big donor, but he had become critical of the athletic program on chat rooms devoted to U.S.F. sports. (Fund-raisers monitor such things.) Selmon called the lawyer during a trip to Los Angeles, just to warm him up, then invited him to fly in and sit in his box for the game. The lawyer accepted and showed up at the game with a friend who wore a muscle shirt. But both men fidgeted and looked impatient, then bolted at halftime.

The large-framed woman sitting in a corner of the box paid much more   95
interest and stayed to the end. Selmon spent time visiting with her, at one point positioning himself on one knee in the aisle next to her. She was another potentially deep-pocketed donor: Lucille Harrison, a Florida resident and Shaquille O'Neal's mother.

U.S.F. beat the odds. It preserved its home winning streak in a stirring game decided on the last play, a missed Southern Mississippi field-goal attempt. By season's end, Leavitt's long hours had paid off beyond what any football prognosticator could have predicted. The Bulls finished the season with a record of 9–2, including a dismantling of Bowling Green, then ranked 25th in the nation. A bid to a minor bowl, the money-losing kind, looked possible, but the bowls snubbed U.S.F. in favor of teams with lesser records but bigger names. Leavitt immediately surfaced as a possibility to fill open coaching jobs at marquee schools, including Alabama and Michigan State. The new program was at a crossroads. Was it going to ante up for its coach, and his assistants too, which could easily add an instant $500,000 or more to the annual football budget? Or would it start all over with someone new?

As the field goal flew wide in the Southern Miss game, one of Selmon's guests, an alum and successful stockbroker, jumped out of his seat, threw his arms around the U.S.F. athletic director and got right to the point. "We've got to keep this man!" he shouted, referring to Leavitt. "Let's raise this man some money and keep him here!"

On Dec. 12, the University of South Florida ripped up Jim Leavitt's contract and signed him to a new five-year deal that more than doubled his salary. If he keeps winning, he probably won't make it to the final year of this contract, either, when he's scheduled to make nearly $700,000. U.S.F. will have to pay more to keep him, or other programs will come looking to steal him away. That's how it is when you decide to play with the big boys. The bills just keep on getting bigger.

QUESTIONING THE TEXT

1. Is this article more about college football, big-time college sports in general, football at the University of South Florida, or another subject? Why do you think the editors included this article in a chapter on education?

2. As a feature article published in the *New York Times Magazine*, this piece is arguably of a different genre than the other prose selections in this chapter. As a journalist, Sokolove probably saw himself as writing a *report* on college football rather than making an *argument* about it. Do you think he does make an argument? Does the article have a thesis? If so, what is it, and how does Sokolove support it?

3. What does the opening description of the University of South Florida campus have to do with the rest of the article? What details in this description stand out, and how do they prepare you for information that follows? What other descriptive details does Sokolove provide throughout the article, and what points do they seem to make or emphasize?

MAKING CONNECTIONS

4. How do you think Adrienne Rich (p. 74) would react to this article? Would she agree or disagree with the perspective offered by Sokolove? Rich asserts, "[N]o woman is really an insider in the institutions fathered by masculine consciousness. When we allow ourselves to believe we are, we lose touch with parts of ourselves defined as unacceptable by that consciousness. . . ." (paragraph 11). What evidence does Sokolove provide that would support or rebut this claim?

5. Sokolove quotes U.S.F. Athletic Director Lee Roy Selmon as saying, "The more people here [in the football program], the more people getting

an education, the better. It's about generations — about student athletes developing abilities, being citizens, having families and being able to nurture their children" (paragraph 69). Does this view of a big-football program's role at a public university answer the criticisms raised by Sokolove elsewhere in the article? Do you think Mike Rose (p. 90) would agree with Selmon's claims about the educational opportunity that college football affords its players? Why, or why not?

6. Sokolove suggests that players on the team at a big-football school encounter a different educational experience than do other students at the same school. Do you think these players' college education might in any way qualify as "in-the-streets" learning, as described by Jon Spayde (p. 65)? How so, or how not?

JOINING THE CONVERSATION

7. How is the situation at your school similar to or different from the one described by Sokolove, or by J.R. in his introduction to the article? Does your school have a football program? J.R. asserts that at the big-football schools, "ordinary undergraduates" get "squeezed out" of the stands "by alumni or businesses whose handsome contributions buy them prime real estate in a stadium enlarged every decade to cover the salaries of coaches paid like Hollywood celebrities." Is this the case at your school? Can you imagine it happening? What do you think of this claim? Write your response individually, and then discuss the questions among athletes and nonathletes in your class.

8. Sokolove mentions the five hours that football consumes in each player's day at the University of South Florida. Freewrite about the kinds of activities that compete with your study time. Do the various demands on your time enable you to empathize with the football players' situations, or not? Explain.

ALISON GOPNIK, K. ANTHONY APPIAH, AND S. GEORGIA NUGENT
Slate's College Makeover

"*WHAT SHOULD STUDENTS BE STUDYING in college?*" *is the question* Slate *magazine posed to a group of prominent scholars and teachers in 2005. Not surprisingly, no general consensus emerged from these responses, which is one reason I wanted to include some of them in this textbook.*

The first is "Let Them Solve Problems" by Alison Gopnik (b. 1955), a cognitive scientist and professor of psychology at the University of California, Berkeley. Gopnik, whose books include How Babies Think: The Science of Childhood, *and* Words, Thoughts, and Theories, *points out the great discrepancy between what we know about how people learn (from close observation, active investigation, and guided apprenticeship) and how we teach (the professor lecturing while the students silently take notes). Urging academics to give up this "medieval form of learning," Gopnik suggests that college professors introduce students to the problems the faculty members are working on and invite students to join in as co-researchers. Gopnik admits that beginning students wouldn't offer much help and that years of such a curriculum wouldn't teach everything she might wish. But, she concludes, students would at least know "the most important thing. They would know how science and scholarship work."*

K. Anthony Appiah (b. 1954), the Laurance S. Rockefeller University Professor of Philosophy at Princeton, has a very different take on the question Slate *asked. In "Learn Statistics. Go Abroad," he notes that he's generally against requirements, preferring instead that students put together their own programs. But as it turns out he does have two concrete suggestions: make sure that all students understand how math and statistics "can be used and abused" and that they get beyond parochialism by broadening their horizons and their attitudes through study abroad.*

The third voice here is that of S. Georgia Nugent, president of Kenyon College and the first woman to hold that position. In "Morality-Based Learning," she argues that the aims of higher education have stayed consistent over thousands of years: to teach critical reading, cogent writing, and moral development. Today, she says, college professors agree on the first two but are less sure about the third. Nugent calls for colleges to provide a wide range of courses — from Greek tragedy to organic chemistry — that would focus on the "Big Questions: Why am I here? What is asked of me? What is the good?" Answering such questions, Nugent insists, must be at the heart of college education.

These are three very different answers to the question, "What should students be studying in college?" My own answer would take something from each of these essays (opportunities for students to be active researchers, to travel and learn from other languages and cultures, and to take a capstone course in which they would reflect on what they have learned about Big Questions and to assess what they still need to know). But I would also offer students a chance to work collaboratively, often in teams, throughout their college years, and to find multiple opportunities not only for producing knowledge but for delivering it in a range of genres and formats to a wide range of audiences. In my view, exploring, presenting, explaining, and defending your ideas is the best way to develop a strong intellect and a moral compass to direct that intellect. What is your answer? What should students be studying in college today?

—A.L.

Alison Gopnik
Let Them Solve Problems

I wonder whether the type of learning Gopnik advocates would work well with all subject matters. How does one treat history or literature as an experimental phenomenon?
—J.R.

I'm a cognitive scientist who is also a university professor. There is a staggering contrast between what I know about learning from the lab and the way I teach in the classroom. I know that human beings are designed to learn as part of their deepest evolutionary inheritance. I know that children, and even adults, learn about the everyday world around them in much the way the scientists learn. I even know something about the procedures that allow children and scientists to learn so much. They include close observation of real phenomena, active experimental investigation, and a process of guided apprenticeship. Children, and novice scientists, carefully try to imitate their mentors, and their mentors carefully watch and correct them.

As a writing teacher, I sometimes forget how much college learning still takes place in large lecture classes. Yet I also recall learning a great deal from teachers who spoke passionately about their subjects.
—J.R.

The last decades have seen a major effort to engage undergraduates in research — even in their first year of college. It is not exclusively scientific or lab research to be sure, but research nonetheless; I wonder why she doesn't mention this trend?
—A.L.

Almost none of this happens in the average university classroom, including mine. In lecture classes, the teacher talks and the students write down what the teacher says. In seminars, the students write down what other students say. This is, literally, a medieval form of learning, and it's no coincidence that modern science only began to take off when it abandoned it — at first divorcing itself from universities in the process.

When did sciences "divorce" from universities? I'd like an example here.
—L.S.

This is particularly ironic because modern universities have become the home of science and scholarship. And yet, notoriously, research is divorced from teaching. Faculty immersed in research think teaching is a distracting chore, and students are increasingly taught by academic lumpenproletariat adjuncts who don't do research. Students only get to

And yet the lecture model — the sage on the stage — continues to prevail across the university. She doesn't note, however, the degree to which students expect and even demand that model. —A.L.

do real research themselves in graduate school. What would French cooking be like if aspiring chefs never cracked an egg till after they had listened to four years of lectures about egg-cracking?

Why not make all teaching like graduate teaching (or, for that matter, the best preschool teaching)? Let freshmen students select five different areas of study — with no disciplines overlapping. Tell them about the unsolved problems that the professor is actively working on — analyzing that Jane Austen text, deciphering that Assyrian inscription, working out the economics of slavery in that small town, discovering a particular virus genome. Post the layman's abstract in the professor's latest grant proposal in the catalog. Let students choose a problem to work on.

All but the most technical areas of research can be translated into terms that a student can understand. Nowadays almost every professor has had the experience of explaining what they do to a lay audience — and if they haven't they should learn how. Give students articles about the problem to read as background — there are a plethora of popular science journals that deliberately appeal to broad audiences — instead of making them plow through a homogenized textbook with a sentence per study. Instead of zoning out in lecture halls, make them sit in on lab meetings, run the simple bits of experiments, find documents in the archives, hang out with the graduate students in the bar.

5

In subsequent years let them specialize more and take a more active hand in research. They might not help too much at first — everyone who has taught someone else to cook knows that — but the extra hours would be more productive for everyone than the ones we spend now translating professorial PowerPoint into student notes. At the end of the four years students wouldn't know everything that science and scholarship can teach, but they would know the most important thing. They would know how science and scholarship work.

K. Anthony Appiah
Learn Statistics. Go Abroad.

Nobody's ever going to put me in charge of designing the general education requirements of a major university, with or without a magic wand. Thank God. I've been on committees at a couple of great universities charged with the task and, putting aside the political difficulties (which I guess you can do, if you have a magic wand) you come to see it's one of those problems you can't solve, only manage. Here's the basic dilemma: If you say that a general education should teach you all the stuff worth knowing, there's far too much to fit around a major in a four-year education. If you say, on the other hand, that it should teach you only the essentials, there's too little. You can live a perfectly decent life with what you have to know just to get out of high school; indeed, many people do.

I've lived through three waves of general education reform in my career — and expect to see more. —A.L.

There is a middle ground between knowing everything worth knowing and getting only the essentials. —L.S.

In any case, whatever you think is good for them, some students will resist it, and others will find their way to a great education without a requirement in sight. So my general attitude to college education, I'm afraid, is let a hundred flowers bloom. Let people try core programs of different sorts and distribution requirements with categories as exotic as they like. Heck, let them try allowing students to put together a general education out of any courses they like. But since we've been offered a magic wand, there are two things that I'd want to urge most colleges to think about as ways of strengthening the liberal part of liberal education: the part, that is, that's supposed to prepare you for life as a free person.

I'd be more open to this argument if he gave an example of a school where such openness ("allowing students to put together a general education out of any courses they like") works well. —A.L.

If we can't define the criteria of a good general education — what mature men and women should hold in common — then perhaps we should offer professional education for students ready for it: teach aspiring engineers to be engineers, lawyers to be lawyers, pharmacists to be pharmacists. Let the rest work for a while — until they know what they want to do with their lives and education. It will save everyone a lot of money to boot. —J.R.

I start with two problems. One is most evident with humanities majors: Many of them don't know how to evaluate mathematical models or statistical arguments. And I think that makes you incompetent to participate in many discussions of public policy. So I favor making sure that someone teaches a bunch of really exciting courses, aimed at nonmajors in the natural and social sciences, which display how mathematical modeling and statistical techniques can be used and abused in science and in discussions of

This claim goes both ways. Many science students graduate knowing little about literature, for example. —L.S.

public policy. If there are enough of them and they're good enough, one or two required courses in this area won't seem like a chore to students. And even those who grouse will probably be grateful later. Learn Bayes' Theorem, it won't kill you.

The second problem is one that you can find in almost every major, though it's less common among those doing foreign-language majors of area studies. It is an astonishing parochialism. (This is, for obvious reasons, less common among students from abroad.) Too many of our students haven't the faintest idea what life is like anywhere outside the class and the community — let alone the country — they grew up in. Language requirements — that you should leave college with one more language than you entered with, say — can help here. And so, no doubt, can courses on other places, peoples, and times.

But parochialism isn't a matter of not knowing a bunch of cultural snippets about peoples everywhere. It's an attitude. And the fellow from Des Moines or San Francisco who spends a semester at Tallinn or Johannesburg or Berlin or even Canberra at least acquires the basic Another Country insight: They do things differently there. (The University of Tallinn will be a bit of a stretch for most students, true: They teach mostly in Estonian or Russian and use Finnish, Russian, and English textbooks. Try the Tallinn Institute of Technology, whose Web site claims that it "is the only public university in Estonia which offeres degree programs fully in English language." One thing they do differently there, it appears, is English.) So why not just reinvigorate an old tradition — the Junior Year Abroad — which, at too many campuses, has fallen into desuetude. We could take a leaf from the EU's strikingly successful Erasmus program, which makes it easy for college students to spend a semester or two at an accredited university in another country. If you want to improve the general education you're offering, in short, encourage your students to try somebody else's.

I agree that students need to be able to evaluate arguments based on statistics and that they benefit from studying about and living in different cultures. But I'd want my college graduate to know a few other things as well! —A.L.

10

Who can object to a semester abroad — except that it seems like yet another evasion of the question Appiah raises: what should students be learning in college? Sending undergraduates to France may relieve parochialism. But why should students pay a middle- 15 *man? They can travel pretty regally on their own for the average cost of a year in college.* —J.R.

S. Georgia Nugent
Morality-Based Learning

What is the knowledge most worth having? In the Western tradition, sages have asked this question since the era of the Egyptian Middle Kingdom, about 2000 B.C. One Egyptian magistrate declares, "It is to writings that you must set your mind. . . . There is nothing that surpasses writings! They are a boat upon the water. . . . I shall make you love books more than your mother." A thousand years later, a second Egyptian scribe provides a succinct curriculum: "Write with your hand, recite with your mouth, and converse with those more knowledgeable than you."

The answers offered by Western thinkers from Socrates to Benjamin Franklin have been remarkably consistent over the years: The aim of education is to teach reading (analytical interpretation), writing (clear and persuasive communication), and the moral development of character. As Franklin put it, "The Idea of what is true Merit should also be often presented to Youth . . . as consisting in an Inclination join'd with an Ability to serve Mankind . . . which Ability . . . should indeed be the great Aim and End of all Learning."

This clarity, however, does not at first glance characterize the history of the American college curriculum. When America's great universities were founded in the 18th century, the privileged young men who attended them marched through a common curriculum. Often, the undergraduate career culminated in a "capstone" course in metaphysics, taught by the college's president.

Today, a small liberal arts college like Kenyon — of which I am president — offers study in more than 30 academic departments and 10 interdisciplinary programs, mounting almost 400 courses each semester. Other sectors of higher education offer courses ranging from "turf management" to "the behavior of consumers." This proliferation of courses mirrors the explosion of knowledge in our era, which has generated professions and entire fields of thought

---

I wonder about the Eastern tradition — she doesn't say anything about those sages. —A.L.

I would use "ethical" rather than "moral" here, which would then capture the ancient Greek emphasis on balancing logical, emotional, and ethical appeals in writing and speaking. —A.L.

Here she builds her own ethos or credibility by letting us know that she is the president of a prestigious college. —A.L.

The aims discussed here still define a core of education, but shouldn't students be well along that path by the time they reach college? Of course most aren't, but college should be the place where students move toward specific knowledge in well-defined fields. —J.R.

Do employers take interdisciplinary programs seriously? They almost always look better in a catalog than on a diploma. Dual majors, I think, make better sense. —J.R.

15

(nanosciences, financial derivatives, videography) that simply didn't exist in past decades.

Does the expansion of the curriculum mean that the fundamentals have been lost sight of? I suspect not. Last year, a national survey found that 99 percent of faculty said "the ability to think critically" was crucial to a college education; 90 percent said "the ability to write effectively."

Does she mean "moral develop-ment" in the reli-gious sense? It's unclear. —L.S.

But what of the emphasis on moral development? On the same national survey of faculty, only 69 percent identified "developing moral character" as the most important aspect of a college education, and only 39 percent chose "enhancing spiritual development." When I have asked my faculty colleagues their views, they say they are too "modest" to assert the ability to develop moral character and too wary, in today's political climate, to meddle in students' spiritual development. Perhaps it's time for me and my fellow presidents to draft the syllabus for that capstone course in metaphysics with which the presidents used to send their graduates off into the world.

What would be the syllabus for such a course? My response — not at all flippant — would be: It doesn't matter. What I'm talking about is not a required reading list; rather it is an experience of understanding and growth that might take a myriad of forms. The goal is not mastery of a subject by maturity as an adult — attaining a degree of self-understanding, an appreciation for the limits of the human condition, empathy for others, and a sense of responsibility for civil society. For me, as a classicist, the syllabus would probably focus on the Homeric epics and Greek tragedy. These texts have, to my mind, almost unparalleled power to anchor us in the world and confront us with both our wrenching limitations and our soaring possibilities as human beings. But for another colleague, the entire syllabus would be Melville's *Moby-Dick*; for another, such a course would consist of teaching his students to construct a scientific instrument by hand; for a fourth, the course might be organic chemistry taught inductively through group discussion. What matters is not the subject but the sensibility. In fact, each of these hypothetical courses is one I have known a fine

Just what a student at Kenyon would want to hear: the syllabus of the cap-stone course doesn't matter. It can take "myriad forms" so long as it teaches understanding, em-pathy, and responsi-bility. You can get such training in the Boy Scouts for a lot less money. —J.R.

faculty member to teach, in a way that offered not information "to pass the exam" but the wisdom of a life-changing experience.

Reintroducing the ethical dimension into American higher education is not, I believe, a matter of specifying certain readings (à la E.D. Hirsch or William Bennett). Nor is it, finally, something to be left to "capstone" courses taught by college presidents. Rather, a recommitment to the moral dimension of higher education requires all of us who are teachers to refocus our sights on the Big Questions: Why am I here? What is asked of me? What is the good? In another national survey taken last year, a substantial majority of undergraduate students said that what they expect from college is guidance in defining their life's values. In this, it seems to me, today's students join that long line of sages who have understood that the education that most matters must touch the soul.

QUESTIONING THE TEXT

1. All three of these authors refer to their own experience — as a scientist, as someone who has served on curriculum committees at great universities, and as a college president and classicist — in answering the question of what college students should study. What kind of authority does each author claim? How does each author's identity affect your reception of the suggestions?

2. Which article do you think makes the most compelling suggestion for improving education? Analyze what makes it most effective — is it the idea being proposed? The quality of the reasoning? The authority of the writer?

MAKING CONNECTIONS

3. Compare these suggestions about how to change undergraduate education to two or three of the mission statements (pp. 56–63). Do you think that these suggestions fit with the goals of the colleges that you selected? What overlap do you see between the missions of the colleges and the statements of how to improve college education? What significant differences do you see?

4. In what ways do these suggestions align with John Henry Newman's statement about the value of the liberal arts in "The Idea of a University" (p. 51)? Do these pieces dramatically change Newman's conception of a good university? Do they complement it?

JOINING THE CONVERSATION

5. As noted in question 1, all of these authors include references to their own place in the university, and Appiah writes "Thank God" after noting that no one will actually give him a magic wand to decide what the core college curriculum should be. Who bears the most responsibility for designing a core curriculum — faculty? Administration? Students themselves? Find out what you can about how curriculum decisions are made at your school, and write an essay assessing the appropriateness of the process. Do you think that all interested parties are fairly represented?

6. Probably the most controversial of these three articles is S. Georgia Nugent's call for "morality-based learning." Has your college experience so far helped you develop your moral or ethical sense? To what degree is moral development one of the goals of your college education? Write an essay in which you discuss what role your college or university should play in your moral or ethical education and whether you feel that role is being fulfilled appropriately by your school.

JOHN TIERNEY
Male Pride and Female Prejudice

JOHN TIERNEY (b. 1953), a self-described libertarian and former op-ed columnist for the New York Times, *where this piece appeared in 2006, is concerned that women may pay a price if, as a result of their escalating dominance in college enrollment, they later find themselves with fewer suitable marriage prospects. Is this really a matter for deep concern? That fewer and fewer men are attending college is a problem only if policies currently in place are actively discouraging men from pursuing higher education — one of the surest routes to a career and income. That* could *be the case.*

But maybe we have oversold the need for college? Charles Murray and others have argued that many of the most successful entrepreneurs of our era — people like Michael Dell and Bill Gates — have done quite well, thank you, without a sheepskin. And given the cafeteria-style curricula in many colleges and universities, many students, in the liberal arts especially, leave school without any marketable skills. Their training and much of their practical education will occur on the job.

Certainly, there's still prestige in a college diploma, and the four or five years spent earning a degree remain a right of passage for people who take no academic break after high school. But how many more English, psychology, and film studies majors do we really need? Does every man and woman have to seek a diploma? We pay good money — great money — to carpenters, electricians, plumbers, mechanics, and computer technicians without giving due credit to their indispensable contributions to society. As college curricula become more and more clogged with soft offerings, we shouldn't be surprised if lots of sensible men reconsider their options. And I'd guess that a lot of women might prefer a husband who can build a house to one who can buy one.

The back deck on my house was crafted by a nineteen-year-old guy thinking maybe he should be in college. It's such a splendid piece of work that I hope he's still building decks.

— J.R.

When there are three women for every two men graduating from college, whom will the third woman marry?

This is not an academic question. Women, who were a minority on campuses a quarter-century ago, today make up 57 percent of undergraduates, and the gender gap is projected to reach a 60–40 ratio within a few years. So more women, especially black and Hispanic women, will be in a position to get better-paying, more prestigious jobs than their husbands, which makes for a tricky variation of *Pride and Prejudice.*

It's still a universal truth, as Jane Austen wrote, that a man with a fortune has good marriage prospects. It's not so universal for a woman with a fortune, because pride makes some men determined to be the chief breadwinner. But these traditionalists seem to be a dwindling minority as men have come to appreciate the value of a wife's paycheck.

A woman's earning power, while hardly the first thing that men look for, has become a bigger draw, as shown in surveys of college students over the decades. In 1996, for the first time, college men rated a potential mate's financial prospects as more important than her skills as a cook or a housekeeper.

In the National Survey of Families and Households conducted during the early 1990s, the average single man under 35 said he was quite willing to marry someone earning much more than he did. He wasn't as interested in marrying someone making much less than he did, and he was especially reluctant to marry a woman who was unlikely to hold a steady job.

Those findings jibe with what I've seen. I can't think of any friend who refused to date a woman because she made more money than he did. When friends have married women with bigger paychecks, the only financial complaints I've heard from them have come when a wife later decided to pursue a more meaningful — i.e., less lucrative — career.

Nor can I recall hearing guys insult a man, to his face or behind his back, for making less than his wife. The only snide comments I've heard have come from women talking about their friends' husbands. I've heard just a couple of hardened Manhattanites do that, but I wouldn't dismiss them as isolated reactionaries because you can see this prejudice in that national survey of singles under 35.

The women surveyed were less willing to marry down — marry someone with much lower earnings or less education — than the men were to marry up. And, in line with Jane Austen, the women were also more determined to marry up than the men were.

You may think that women's attitudes are changing as they get more college degrees and financial independence. A women who's an executive can afford to marry a struggling musician. But that doesn't necessarily mean she wants to. Studies by David Buss of the University of Texas and others have shown that women with higher incomes, far from relaxing their standards, put more emphasis on a mate's financial resources.

And once they're married, women with higher incomes seem less tolerant of their husbands' shortcomings. Steven Nock of the University of Virginia has found that marriages in which the wife and husband earn roughly the same are more likely to fail than other marriages. That situation doesn't affect the husband's commitment to the marriage, Nock concludes, but it weakens the wife's and makes her more likely to initiate divorce.

It's understandable that women with good paychecks have higher standards for their partners, since their superior intelligence, education and income give them what Buss calls high "mate value." They know they're catches and want to find someone with equal mate value — someone like Mr. Darcy instead of a dullard like the cleric spurned by Elizabeth Bennet.

"Of course, some women marry for love and find a man's resources irrelevant," Buss says. "It's just that the men women tend to fall in love with, on average, happen to have more resources."

5

10

Which means that, on average, college-educated women and high-school-educated men will have a harder time finding partners as long as educators keep ignoring the gender gap that starts long before college. Advocates for women have been so effective politically that high schools and colleges are still focusing on supposed discrimination against women: the shortage of women in science classes and on sports teams rather than the shortage of men, period. You could think of this as a victory for women's rights, but many of the victors will end up celebrating alone.

QUESTIONING THE TEXT

1. Tierney begins and ends his article by suggesting that the smaller population of male college students will lead to a problem — too few male partners for women. Does Tierney identify anyone as particularly responsible for this situation? What solutions does the article imply? What solutions does J.R. imply in his note preceding the article? Do you agree that this is a problem people should be concerned about?

2. Tierney quotes the researcher David Buss saying that "the men women tend to fall in love with, on average, happen to have more resources." How would you evaluate the tone of that statement? Is economic analysis a good research tool for thinking about marriage? The term "mate value" that Tierney borrows from Buss (paragraph 11) derives from the study of economics. How else might you think about defining "mate value" besides intelligence, education, and income?

MAKING CONNECTIONS

3. Tierney and Katha Pollitt, who responds directly to this article in "Girls against Boys?" (p. 139), both make reference to personal anecdotes and experience in arguing for larger trends. How effective do you find these moments? Is it reasonable for them to assert that their own experiences can represent a larger trend? Does one author make more persuasive use of personal experience than the other?

4. Compare Tierney's conception of how a college education prepares one for the world to how John Henry Newman ("The Idea of a University," p. 51) argues that a college education prepares one for life.

JOINING THE CONVERSATION

5. Tierney's article suggests that education and income level are significant factors in marriage choices. Write an essay in which you explain your views on the most important elements of a decision to marry.

CHRISTINA HOFF SOMMERS
The War against Boys

SOME CLAIMS EVOLVE, OVER TIME, INTO MANTRAS *of political argument, like the statistic that, on average, women earn 75 cents for every dollar earned by men. It doesn't matter that the number doesn't necessarily prove inequity or account for the vastly different career paths taken by men or women. The phrase has become a dependable rhetorical meme — a trump card to clinch the case and justify a demand for equity.*

But many other statistics get swept under the rug — such as the fact that boys aged 12 to 19 are four times more likely to commit suicide than young women or that they are 40 percent more likely to be the victim of violent crimes. One would think that numbers like these might generate more concern than, for example, the attention given to the body images of young girls. But we see and read story after story about the latter, silence about the former.

And when someone like Christina Hoff Sommers does draw attention to the inequitable treatment of boys in education, she is dismissed as unfair, uncollegial or, worse yet, conservative. Some critics even resort to urging boys just to pull themselves up by their bootstraps, behave better, and learn to succeed in school environments hostile to their ways of knowing and learning. No one tells the young women in engineering or math to work harder to compete better with the men who still dominate these courses in college. Instead, support programs are created and public relations campaigns funded to attract women into the sciences and then to mentor them toward success. Don't hold your breath to see similar efforts to make men feel welcome in colleges of education (where minority men in particular are desperately needed for careers in elementary and secondary education) or to increase male interest in English or sociology or psychology. Nor should you expect much attention to the well-being of young men electing to choose nonacademic careers — at least not until someone needs a mechanic, plumber, electrician, or mason. As Sommers points out, lots of boys are getting left by the wayside while feminists demand privileges for girls already thriving academically by almost every statistical measure.

Below is an excerpt from Sommers's article, which appeared in the Atlantic Monthly *in May 2000 and is excerpted from her book of the same name. After reading it, you may want to do some research at your school, paying attention to differences (if any) in the treatment and attention given to men and women academically and institutionally. Just for fun: look for men on your campus Web site. It can be like searching for Waldo.*

—J.R.

It's a bad time to be a boy in America. The triumphant victory of the U.S. women's soccer team at the World Cup last summer has come to symbolize the spirit of American girls. The shooting at Columbine High last spring might be said to symbolize the spirit of American boys.

That boys are in disrepute is not accidental. For many years women's groups have complained that boys benefit from a school system that favors them and is biased against girls. "Schools shortchange girls," declares the American Association of University Women. Girls are "undergoing a kind of psychological foot-binding," two prominent educational psychologists say. A stream of books and pamphlets cite research showing not only that boys are classroom favorites but also that they are given to schoolyard violence and sexual harassment.

In the view that has prevailed in American education over the past decade, boys are resented, both as the unfairly privileged sex and as obstacles on the path to gender justice for girls. This perspective is promoted in schools of education, and many a teacher now feels that girls need and deserve special indemnifying consideration. "It is really clear that boys are Number One in this society and in most of the world," says Patricia O'Reilly, a professor of education and the director of the Gender Equity Center at the University of Cincinnati.

The idea that schools and society grind girls down has given rise to an array of laws and policies intended to curtail the advantage boys have and to redress the harm done to girls. That girls are treated as the second sex in school and consequently suffer, that boys are accorded privileges and consequently benefit — these are things everyone is presumed to know. But they are not true.

The research commonly cited to support claims of male privilege and   5
male sinfulness is riddled with errors. Almost none of it has been published in peer-reviewed professional journals. Some of the data turn out to be mysteriously missing. A review of the facts shows boys, not girls, on the weak side of an education gender gap. The typical boy is a year and a half behind the typical girl in reading and writing; he is less committed to school and less likely to go to college. In 1997 college full-time enrollments were 45 percent male and 55 percent female. The Department of Education predicts that the proportion of boys in college classes will continue to shrink.

Data from the U.S. Department of Education and from several recent university studies show that far from being shy and demoralized, today's girls outshine boys. They get better grades. They have higher educational aspirations. They follow more rigorous academic programs and participate in advanced-placement classes at higher rates. According to the National Center for Education Statistics, slightly more girls than boys enroll in high-level math and science courses. Girls, allegedly timorous and lacking in confidence, now outnumber boys in student government, in honor societies, on school newspapers, and in debating clubs. Only in sports are boys ahead, and women's groups are targeting the sports gap with a vengeance. Girls read more books. They outperform boys on tests for artistic and musical ability. More girls than boys study abroad. More join the Peace Corps. At the same time, more boys than girls are suspended from school. More are held back and more drop out. Boys are three times as likely to receive a diagnosis of attention-deficit hyperactivity disorder. More boys than girls are involved in crime, alcohol, and drugs. Girls attempt suicide more often than boys, but it is boys who more often succeed. In 1997, a typical year, 4,483 young people aged five to twenty-four committed suicide: 701 females and 3,782 males.

In the technical language of education experts, girls are academically more "engaged." Last year an article in The *CQ Researcher* about male an female academic achievement described a common parental observation: "Daughters want to please their teachers by spending extra time on projects, doing extra credit, making homework as neat as possible. Sons rush through homework assignments and run outside to play, unconcerned about how the teacher will regard the sloppy work."

School engagement is a critical measure of student success. The U.S. Department of Education gauges student commitment by the following criteria: "How much time do students devote to homework each night?" and "Do students come to class prepared and ready to learn? (Do they bring books and pencils? Have they completed their homework?)" According to surveys of fourth, eighth, and twelfth graders, girls consistently do more homework than boys. By the twelfth grade boys are four times as likely as girls not to do homework. Similarly, more boys than girls report that they "usually" or "often" come to school without supplies or without having done their homework.

The performance gap between boys and girls in high school leads directly to the growing gap between male and female admissions to college. The Department of Education reports that in 1996 there were 8.4 million women but only 6.7 million men enrolled in college. It predicts that women will hold on to and increase their lead well into the next decade, and that by 2007 the numbers will be 9.2 million women and 6.9 million men.

DECONSTRUCTING THE TEST-SCORE GAP

Feminists cannot deny that girls get better grades, are more engaged aca-   10
demically, and are now the majority sex in higher education. They argue, however, that these advantages are hardly decisive. Boys, they point out, get higher scores than girls on almost every significant standardized test — especially the Scholastic Assessment Test and law school, medical school, and graduate school admissions tests.

In 1996 I wrote an article for *Education Week* about the many ways in which girl students were moving ahead of boys. Seizing on the test-score data that suggest boys are doing better than girls, David Sadker, a professor of education at American University and a co-author with his wife, Myra, of *Failing at Fairness: How America's Schools Cheat Girls* (1994), wrote, "If females are soaring in school, as Christina Hoff Sommers writes, then these tests are blind to their flight." On the 1998 SAT boys were thirty-five points (out of 800) ahead of girls in math and seven points ahead in English. These results seem to run counter to all other measurements of achievement in school. In almost all other areas boys lag behind girls. Why do they test better? Is Sadker right in suggesting that this is a manifestation of boys' privileged status?

The answer is no. A careful look at the pool of students who take the SAT and similar tests shows that the girls' lower scores have little or nothing to do with bias or unfairness. Indeed, the scores do not even signify lower achievement by girls. First of all, according to *College Bound Seniors*, an annual report on standardized-test takers published by the College Board, many more "at risk" girls than "at risk" boys take the SAT — girls from lower-income homes or with parents who never graduated from high school or never attended college. "These characteristics," the report says, "are associated with lower than average SAT scores." Instead of wrongly using SAT scores as evidence of bias against girls, scholars should be concerned about the boys who never show up for the tests they need if they are to move on to higher education.

Another factor skews test results so that they appear to favor boys. Nancy Cole, the president of the Educational Testing Service, calls it the "spread" phenomenon. Scores on almost any intelligence or achievement test are most spread out for boys than for girls — boys include more prodigies and more students of marginal ability. Or, as the political scientist James Q. Wilson once put it, "There are more male geniuses and more male idiots."

Boys also dominate dropout lists, failure lists, and learning-disability lists. Students in these groups rarely take college admissions tests. On the other hand, the exceptional boys who take school seriously show up in disproportionately high numbers for standardized tests. Gender-equity activists like Sadker ought to apply their logic consistently: if the shortage of girls at the high end of the ability distribution is evidence of unfairness to girls, then the excess of boys at the low end should be deemed evidence of unfairness to boys.

Suppose we were to turn our attention away from the highly motivated, self-selected two fifths of high school students who take the SAT and consider instead a truly representative sample of American schoolchildren. How would girls and boys then compare? Well, we have the answer. The National Assessment of Educational Progress, started in 1969 and mandated by Congress, offers the best and most comprehensive measure of achievement among students at all levels of ability. Under the NAEP program 70,000 to 100,000 students, drawn from forty-four states, are tested in reading, writing, math, and science at ages nine, thirteen, and seventeen. In 1996, seventeen-year-old boys outperformed seventeen-year-old girls by five points in math and eight points in science, whereas the girls outperformed the boys by fourteen points in reading and seventeen points in writing. In the past few years girls have been catching up in math and science while boys have continued to lag far behind in reading and writing.

In the July, 1995, issue of *Science*, Larry V. Hedges and Amy Nowell, researchers at the University of Chicago, observed that girls' deficits in math were small but not insignificant. These deficits, they noted, could adversely affect the number of women who "excel in scientific and technical occupations."

Of the deficits in boys' writing skills they wrote, "The large sex differences in writing . . . are alarming . . . The data imply that males are, on average, at a rather profound disadvantage in the performance on this basic skill." They went on to warn,

> The generally larger numbers of males who perform near the bottom of the distribution in reading comprehension and writing also have policy implications. It seems likely that individuals with such poor literacy skills will have difficulty finding employment in an increasingly information-driven economy. Thus, some intervention may be required to enable them to participate constructively.

Hedges and Nowell were describing a serious problem of national scope, but because the focus elsewhere has been on girls' deficits, few Americans know much about the problem or even suspect that it exists.

Indeed, so accepted has the myth of girls in crisis become that even teachers who work daily with male and female students tend to reflexively dismiss any challenge to the myth, or any evidence pointing to the very real crisis among boys. Three years ago Scarsdale High School, in New York, held a gender-equity workshop for faculty members. It was the standard girls-are-being-shortchanged fare, with one notable difference. A male student gave a presentation in which he pointed to evidence suggesting that girls at Scarsdale High were well ahead of boys. David Greene, a social-studies teacher, thought the student must be mistaken, but when he and some colleagues analyzed department grading patterns, they discovered that the student was right. They found little or no difference in the grades of boys and girls in advanced-placement social-studies classes. But in standard classes the girls were doing a lot better.

And Greene discovered one other thing: few wanted to hear about his startling findings. Like schools everywhere, Scarsdale High has been strongly influenced by the belief that girls are systematically deprived. That belief prevails among the school's gender-equity committee and has led the school to offer a special senior elective on gender equity. Greene has tried to broach the subject of male underperformance with his colleagues. Many of them concede that in the classes they teach, the girls seem to be doing better than the boys, but they do not see this as part of a larger pattern. After so many years of hearing about silenced, diminished girls, teachers do not take seriously the suggestion that boys are not doing as well as girls even if they see it with their own eyes in their own classrooms.

QUESTIONING THE TEXT

1. The title and the first line of this article are especially provocative. Does the argument that Sommers presents justify the title of a "war against boys"? Is it really a bad time to be a boy in America? Do these lines sound a necessary alarm, or is Sommers going overboard in making her point?

2. Sommers includes the claims and research of people who disagree with her far more than most authors might. Why does she devote so much time to those who believe differently? Does her use of figures of opposition strengthen or undermine her position? Defend your answer by explaining what you believe her strategy to be and why it does or does not work.

MAKING CONNECTIONS

3. Sommers, John Tierney (p. 130), and Katha Pollitt (p. 139) all discuss the differences in academic achievement based on gender, while Mike Rose (p. 90) and Roland Fryer (p. 143) emphasize the importance of race. To what degree is it useful for us to think about the educational achievement of students as part of identity groups? Explain your answer.

4. After reading this article, read Katha Pollitt's "Girls against Boys?" (p. 139), which mentions Sommers in passing. How do you think that Sommers would respond to Pollitt's argument? Try writing a brief article in Sommers's style responding to Pollitt's claims.

JOINING THE CONVERSATION

5. If you're in a class that involves a good deal of student discussion, carefully observe a session, noting how often each student speaks, and see if you can detect any differences between genders in terms of their participation. Also note how often one student interrupts another. (Scholars have argued that men interrupt women far more than women interrupt men.) Does your experience hold true to this pattern? Write a brief report that summarizes your observations.

6. Interview teachers from your high school or a local school about the differences in gender achievement. Have they been trained to see certain patterns? Have they witnessed any trends in their own classrooms? Write an essay in which you summarize their observations and reflect on your own experience in education. Have you seen a gender gap in your education?

KATHA POLLITT
Girls against Boys?

KATHA POLLITT (b. 1949) has been a writer and columnist for the Nation *since 1980. Some of her essays published in that journal are collected in two volumes:* Subject to Debate: Sense and Dissents on Women, Politics, and Culture *(2001) and* Virginity or Death! And Other Social and Political Issues of Our Times *(2006). Her essay on the ongoing and sometimes virulent debate known as the "culture wars" — "Why We Read: Canon to the Right of Me" — won the 1992 National Magazine Award for essays and criticism. Pollitt's work has also appeared in the* New Yorker, Harper's, Ms., Glamour, *and other prominent magazines.*

Like Pollitt, I went to college at a time when men outnumbered women, since men were accepted in far greater numbers than women. In fact, as the oldest kid in my family — and a girl to boot — I had to convince my parents that college was for me, whereas they simply assumed that my younger brother would attend. And while there's no doubt that more women have now made their ways into the coveted groves of academe, it's hard for me to wring my hands over this success. Yet that's what many critics are doing, including John Tierney and Christina Hoff Sommers, whose fears run the gamut from worrying about how all the well-educated women will find suitable partners to arguing that boys are now disadvantaged in schools that are carrying out a "war on boys."

Katha Pollitt isn't buying the "conservative spin on the education gender gap . . . that feminism has ruined school for boys." Schools, she notes, have always been about sitting still and meeting deadlines, and about reading and writing — so why have such activities suddenly become disadvantageous to boys? Nevertheless, Pollitt isn't happy about the number of young men who decide not to attend college. Perhaps it's time for parents to work harder to convince sons that higher education pays off. Just as women once learned to learn in predominantly male classrooms, maybe, Pollitt suggests, young men need to learn well in "a room full of smart women."

Are there more women than men at your school and at other colleges or universities nearby? If so, is this situation cause for concern? If you are a woman, do you feel that the larger percentage of women on campus will somehow affect your chances of finding a life partner? And if you're a man, do you feel disadvantaged by the kind of instruction you have received in school — and by the presence of more and more women in your classes and on campus? We think questions like these will yield excellent classroom debate and, we hope, some serious reflection about why you are in college and what you hope to gain from the experience.

—A.L.

I went to Radcliffe, the women's wing of Harvard, at a time when the combined undergraduate student body was fixed at four male students for every female one. I don't remember anyone worrying about the boys' social lives, or whether they would find anyone to marry — even though nationally, too, boys were more likely to go to college and to graduate than girls. When in 1975 President Derek Bok instituted equal-access admissions, nobody said, "Great idea, more marital choice for educated men!"

What a difference a few decades and a gender revolution make. Now, although both sexes are much more likely to go to college than forty years ago — the proportion of the population enrolled in college is 20 percentage points higher today than in 1960 — girls have edged ahead of boys. Today, women make up 57 percent of undergraduates, and the gap is projected to reach 60/40 in the next few years. This year, even manly Harvard admitted more girls than boys to its freshman class. So of course the big question is, Who will all those educated women marry? "Advocates for women have been so effective politically that high schools and colleges are still focusing on supposed discrimination against women," writes John Tierney in a recent *New York Times* column. "You could think of this as a victory for women's rights, but many of the victors will end up celebrating alone." If the ladies end up cuddling with their diplomas, they have only themselves — and those misguided "advocates for women" — to blame. Take that, you hyper-educated spinster, you.

The conservative spin on the education gender gap is that feminism has ruined school for boys. "Why would any self-respecting boy want to attend one of America's increasingly feminized universities?" asks George Gilder in *National Review.* "Most of these institutions have flounced through the last forty years fashioning a fluffy pink playpen of feminist studies and agitprop 'herstory,' taught amid a green goo of eco-motherism and anti-industrial phobia." Sounds like fun, but it doesn't sound much like West Texas A&M, Baylor, Loyola or the University of Alabama, where female students outnumber males in about the same proportion as they do at trendy Berkeley and Brown. Even Hillsdale College, the conservative academic mecca that became famous for rejecting federal funds rather than comply with government regulations against sex discrimination, has a student body that is 51 percent female. Other pundits — Michael Gurian, Kate O'Beirne, Christina Hoff Sommers — blame the culture of elementary school and high school: too many female teachers, too much sitting quietly, not enough sports and a feminist-friendly curriculum that forces boys to read — oh no! — books by women. Worse — books about women.

For the record, in middle school my daughter was assigned exactly one book by a woman: Zora Neale Hurston's *Their Eyes Were Watching God.* In high school she read three, *Mrs. Dalloway, Beloved* and *Uncle Tom's Cabin*, while required reading included male authors from Shakespeare and Fitzgerald and Sophocles to (I kid you not) James Michener and Richard Adams, author of *Watership Down.* Four books in seven years: Is that what we're arguing about here? Furthermore, I don't know where those pundits went to school, but education has always involved a lot of sitting, a lot of organizing, a lot of deadlines and a lot of work you didn't necessarily feel like doing. It's always been heavily verbal — in fact, today's textbooks are unbelievably dumbed down and visually hyped compared with fifty years ago. Conservatives talk as if boys should be taught in some kind of cross between boot camp and Treasure Island — but what kind of preparation for modern life would that be? As for the decline of gym and teams and band — activities that keep academically struggling kids, especially boys, coming to school — whose idea was it to cut those "frills" in the first place if not conservatives'?

If the mating game worked fine when women were ignorant and helpless 5 and breaks down when they smarten up, that certainly tells us something about marriage. But does today's dating scene really consist of women who love Woolf and men who love *Grand Theft Auto*? College may not create the intellectual divide elite pundits think it does. (Just spend some time looking at student life as revealed at www.facebook.com if you really want to get depressed about American universities.) For most students, it's more like trade school — they go to get credentials for employment and, because of the sexist nature of the labor market, women need those credentials more than men. Believe it or not, there are still stereotypically male jobs that pay well and don't require college degrees — plumbing, cabinetry, electrical work, computer repair, refrigeration, trucking, mining, restaurant cuisine. My daughter had two male school friends, good students from academically oriented families, who chose cooking school over college. Moreover, . . . sex discrimination in employment is alive and well: Maybe boys focus less on school because they think they'll come out ahead anyway. What solid, stable jobs with a future are there for women without at least some higher ed? Heather Boushey, an economist with the Center for Economic Policy and Research, noted that women students take out more loans than their male classmates, even though a B.A. does less to increase their income. The sacrifice would make sense, though, if the B.A. made the crucial difference between respectable security and a lifetime as a waitress or a file clerk.

This is not to say that boys make the right choice when they blow off school, or even that it always is a choice. People's ideas about life often lag behind reality — some boys haven't gotten the message about the decline of high-paying blue-collar work, or the unlikeliness of rap or sports stardom, the way some girls haven't gotten the message that it is foolish, just really incredibly stupid, to rely on being supported by a man. Most of them, however, have read the memo about having, if not a career exactly, career skills. Their mothers, so many of them divorced and struggling, made sure of that. As for the boys, maybe they will just have to learn to learn in a room full of smart females.

QUESTIONING THE TEXT

1. Who do you think is Pollitt's intended audience? What assumptions does she make about what her readers believe and value? Find specific textual evidence that indicates what values and ideals her readers might hold. Do you think Pollitt shares these values and ideals? How can you tell?

2. How would you describe Pollitt's tone in this article? With a classmate, brainstorm a list of adjectives that could describe her attitude toward her

subject. Next, find textual evidence that supports some of the possible descriptions you've made of Pollitt's tone. Does it change over the course of the article?

3. List all the books that you remember reading for English or literature classes over the past few years. How many assigned books were written by women? What reason does Pollitt give for including information about the genders of authors assigned in her daughter's classes? Do you agree with her reasoning?

MAKING CONNECTIONS

4. Pollitt specifically mentions John Tierney's article "Male Pride and Female Prejudice" (p. 130) as well as work by Christina Hoff Sommers (p. 133). Analyze how Pollitt uses the arguments of Tierney, Sommers, and other writers whose views she does not share. Based on your reading of Tierney and Sommers, do you think she treats the ideas of others fairly? How would you compare these authors' tones in addressing their respective audiences?

5. Both Pollitt and Christina Hoff Sommers (p. 133) stake out a position as contrarian voices speaking against a widespread agreement, but their personas still seem to be quite different. How would you compare the voices of Pollitt and Sommers? Come up with your own characterization and she if your classmates agree.

JOINING THE CONVERSATION

6. Pollitt invites her readers to "spend some time looking at student life as revealed at www.facebook.com if you really want to get depressed about American universities." Consider your own experience with Facebook or other social networking sites, or spend some time exploring such sites if you've never visited one. What picture of American college and university life do you come away with? Can you offer a positive defense of social networking sites and how they present or affect American college life?

7. If you've never read the *Nation*, the periodical in which this article first appeared, find a copy in the library, or visit its Web site (www.thenation.com) and read some of the articles from a recent issue. Analyze how the writers appeal to their audience. Can you locate specific assumptions or strategies that these writers use? Next, take a look at the *Weekly Standard* (www.theweeklystandard.com) either in the library or online. The authors in this magazine will probably hold different assumptions about their readers from those held by the writers in the *Nation*. Do they also use different strategies to persuade their readers to agree with them? Which strategies do you find persuasive and unpersuasive? Why?

ROLAND G. FRYER
Acting White

ONE OF THE YOUNGEST PEOPLE EVER *appointed to the faculty at Harvard University, economist Roland Fryer (b. 1971) has been named a "rising star" by* Fortune *and featured in* Esquire*'s "genius" issue. A graduate of the University of Texas and Pennsylvania State University, Fryer gained widespread recognition for his research on economics and the African American community and on what is often referred to as the "achievement gap" between African Americans and other (primarily white) students.*

In "Acting White," Fryer draws on a very large database assembled by the National Longitudinal Study of Adolescent Health. Using these data, Fryer concludes that "acting white" is indeed a phenomenon at work in U.S. high schools, and particularly in racially integrated public schools. But what is "acting white"? As Fryer explains it, this behavior is associated with minority kids who get good grades in school and, as a result, are less popular than white students who do well. And the costs of such behavior are steep: Fryer finds that "A Hispanic student with a 4.0 GPA is the least popular of all Hispanic students," and that "As the GPAs of black students increase beyond [3.5], they tend to have fewer and fewer friends." Recognizing that such findings are bound to be controversial, Fryer is careful to establish not only his own credentials but also the reliability of his sources and to look carefully at possible counter-explanations for his findings. Still, Fryer has plenty of critics. William Darity Jr., a professor at Duke University, puts it this way: "[Fryer's] inclination to look for an explanation based on some sort of group-based dysfunctionality is an instinct I don't have."

My own experience as a teenager was that studying hard seldom made students more popular, regardless of race. And where I teach, I see a great many remarkably talented and high-achieving students of color, who all seem to have plenty of friends. So I approached Fryer's essay with skepticism — and I still question his conclusions. Yet I find the case he makes thought-provoking enough to want to include his essay in this book. Certainly his recommendation that "society must find ways for these [minority] high achievers to thrive in settings where adverse social pressures are less intense" sounds a strong wake-up call to all teachers committed to student success.

Do Fryer's findings ring true for you and your peers? How do you feel about the relationship between high achievement and popularity? You'll find yourself asking and answering these and other questions as you read this provocative essay. —A.L.

> Go into any inner-city neighborhood, and folks will tell you that government alone can't teach kids to learn. They know that parents have to parent, that children can't achieve unless we raise their expectations and turn off the television sets and eradicate the slander that says a black youth with a book is acting white.
>
> —BARACK OBAMA, KEYNOTE ADDRESS,
> DEMOCRATIC NATIONAL CONVENTION, 2004

Acting white was once a label used by scholars, writing in obscure journals, to characterize academically inclined, but allegedly snobbish, minority students who were shunned by their peers. Now that it has entered the national consciousness — perhaps even its conscience — the term has become a slippery, contentious phrase that is used to refer to a variety of unsavory social practices and attitudes and whose meaning is open to many interpretations, especially as to who is the perpetrator, who the victim.

I cannot, in the research presented here, disentangle all the elements in the dispute, but I can sort out some of its thicker threads. I can also be precise about what I mean by acting white: a set of social interactions in which minority adolescents who get good grades in school enjoy less social popularity than white students who do well academically.

My analysis confirms that acting white is a vexing reality within a subset of American schools. It does not allow me to say whose fault this is, the studious youngster or others in his peer group. But I do find that the way schools are structured affects the incidence of the acting-white phenomenon. The evidence indicates that the social disease, whatever its cause, is most prevalent in racially integrated public schools. It's less of a problem in the private sector and in predominantly black public schools.

With findings as potentially controversial as these, one wants to be sure that they rest on the solid base. In this regard, I am fortunate that the National Longitudinal Study of Adolescent Health (Adhealth) provides information on the friendship patterns of a nationally representative sample of more than 90,000 students, from 175 schools in 80 communities, who entered grades 7 through 12 in the 1994 school year. With this database, it is possible to move beyond both the more narrowly focused ethnographic studies and the potentially misleading national studies based on self-reported indicators of popularity that have so far guided the discussion of acting white.

THE MEANING OF THE PHRASE

Though not all scholars define acting white in precisely the same way, 5 most definitions include a reference to situations where some minority adolescents ridicule their minority peers for engaging in behaviors perceived to be characteristic of whites. For example, when psychologist Angela Neal-Barnett in 1999 asked some focus-group students to identify acting-white behavior, they listed actions that ranged from speaking standard English and enrolling in an Advanced Placement or honors class to wearing clothes from the Gap or Abercrombie & Fitch (instead of Tommy Hilfiger or FUBU) and wearing shorts in winter!

Only some of these behaviors have a direct connection to academic engagement. However, as the remarks of Barack Obama, who would later win a seat in the United States Senate, suggest, it is the fact that reading a book or getting good grades might be perceived as acting white that makes the topic a matter of national concern. Indeed, negative peer-group pressure has emerged as a common explanation for the black–white achievement gap, a gap that cannot be explained away by differences in demographic characteristics alone. If minority students today deliberately underachieve in order to avoid social sanctions, that by itself could explain why the academic performance of 17-year-old African Americans, as measured by the National Assessment of Educational Progress (NAEP), has deteriorated since the late 1980s, even while that of nine-year-olds has been improving. It may also help us understand the shortage of minority students in most elite colleges and universities.

ETHNOGRAPHY VS. STATISTICS

But is this well-publicized aspect of African American peer-culture reality or urban legend? Most ethnographers who examine school life in specific locations present acting white as a pervasive fact of high-school life for black adolescents. But the only two quantitative studies that analyze data from nationally representative samples of high-school students dismiss it altogether as cultural lore. My findings confirm the existence of acting white among blacks as well as among Hispanics, but offer important qualifications about its pervasiveness.

Although they did not coin the term (its origins are obscure), it was an ethnographic study by anthropologists Signithia Fordham and John Ogbu, published in the *Urban Journal* in 1986, that did the most to bring it to the attention of their fellow academics. Their. "Capitol High," a pseudonym for a predominantly black high school in a low-income area of Washington, D.C., had what the researchers said was an "oppositional culture" in which black youth dismissed academically oriented behavior as "white."

In the late 1990s, Harvard University economist, Ron Ferguson, found much the same thing in quite another setting, an upper-class suburb of Cleveland, Ohio, called Shaker Heights. Although that city had been integrated for generations, large racial disparities in achievement persisted. When Ferguson detected an anti-intellectual culture among blacks in the local high school, Shaker Heights became virtually synonymous with the problem of acting white.

Fordham and Ogbu traced the roots of the "oppositional culture" to institutionalized racism within American society, which they contend led blacks to define academic achievement as the prerogative of whites and to invest themselves instead in alternative pursuits. Other observers, however, place the blame for acting white squarely on the shoulders of blacks. The Manhattan Institute's John McWhorter, for example, contrasts African American youth culture with that of immigrants (including blacks from the Caribbean and Africa) who "haven't sabotaged themselves through victimology." These two theories, the former blaming acting white on a racist society, the latter on self-imposed cultural sabotage, have emerged as the predominant explanations for acting white among American blacks.

10

In fact, however, shunning the academic is hardly the exclusive prerogative of contemporary African American culture. James Coleman's classic work *The Adolescent Society*, published in 1955, identified members of the sports teams and cheerleaders, not those on the honor roll, as the most popular students in public schools. . . . The former bring honor to the entire school, reasoned the University of Chicago sociologist; the later, only to themselves. Since Coleman, ethnographers have found similar tensions between self-advancement and community integration. Indeed, variants on acting white have been spotted by ethnographers among the Buraku outcasts of Japan, Italian immigrants in Boston's West End, the Maori of New Zealand, and the British working class, among others.

Even so, the question remains whether the tension that Coleman identified is more severe in some cultural contexts than others. On this topic, two sets of scholars weighed in with quantitative studies based on nationally representative surveys. Writing in 1998 in the *American Sociological Review*, James Ainsworth-Darnell of Georgia State University and Douglas Downey of Ohio State University reported that anti-intellectualism is no more severe a problem among black or Hispanic adolescents than it is among whites. Meanwhile, in a 1997 study, economists Phillip Cook of Duke and Jens Ludwig of Georgetown found that high-achieving black students are, if anything, even more popular relative to low-achieving peers than are high-achieving whites.

Of course, it is possible that the social rewards for achievement do not vary among ethnic groups in the United States. But both studies, each of which is based on data from the National Educational Longitudinal Study (NELS), have a common shortcoming in that they depend solely on a self-reported measure of personal popularity. The NELS contains a question that asks if the student "thinks others see him/her as popular." The answer choices are: very, somewhat, or not at all. Unfortunately, when students are asked to judge their own popularity, they can be expected to provide a rosier scenario than is warranted.

New Data and Methods

Fortunately, the Adhealth data I used in this study allow me to measure popularity in a more subtle way. All the students surveyed were asked to list their closest male and female friends, up to five of each sex. I first counted how often each student's name appeared on peer's lists. I then adjusted these raw counts to reflect the fact that some friends count more than others. The more frequently a peer is listed by others, the more weight I assign to showing up on his or her list.

The advantage of this research strategy is that one never has to ask a student about his or her own popularity. Students' natural tendency to brag, in this case by listing popular students as their friends, only gives us a more accurate picture of the school's most desirable friends. Students listed as a friend by many peers who are themselves popular, rise to the top of the social hierarchy. Those who are listed by only a few peers, who in turn have few admitted friends, stand out as the marginal members of the community.

Armed with an objective measure of social status, I could examine more systematically whether or not the ethnographers were correct in identifying a distinctive acting-white phenomenon within African American communities. Do high-achieving minority students have fewer, less-popular friends than lower-achieving peers? How does this compare with the experience of white students?

I first report my findings using a measure of each student's popularity within his or her own ethnic group, as that is the most direct test of the acting-white hypothesis. But as I explain below, I obtain the same set of results when I analyze the data without regard to the friends' ethnicity.

I measure student achievement with a composite of grade-point average (GPA) based on student self-reports of their most recent grades in English, math, history/social studies, and science. When comparing the popularity of high- and low-achieving students, I compare students only with students who attend the same school, ensuring that the results are not skewed by unmeasured characteristics of specific schools. Even then, I take into account a number of factors, measured by the survey, that could affect popularity differently for students from different ethnic backgrounds. These factors include parental education and occupation and participation in various school activities, such as varsity sports, student government, and cheerleading.

Finally, to subject my findings to the strongest possible test, I adjust students' popularity to reflect variation in self-reported effort in school. Recall that some types of acting-white theory say that students are penalized only for trying hard, not for achievement per se. The bright kid who can't help but get good grades is not subjected to scorn. It's the plodding rate busters with books constantly in their faces who are annoying. By adjusting for the effort students are putting into their studies, I do my best to separate the social consequences of achievement from those of effort to achieve.

New Evidence of Acting White

Even after taking into account many factors that affect student popularity, evidence remains strong that acting white is a genuine issue and worthy of Senator Obama's attention. Fig. 1, which plots the underlying relationship between popularity and achievement, shows large differences among whites, blacks, and Hispanics. At low GPAs, there is little difference among ethnic groups in the relationship between grades and popularity, and high-achieving blacks are actually more popular within their ethnic group than high-achieving whites are within theirs. But when a student achieves a 2.5 GPA (an even mix of Bs and Cs), clear differences start to emerge.

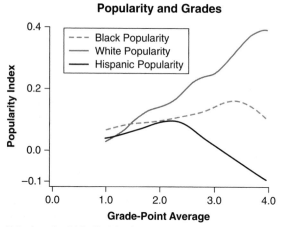

Fig. 1   Pressure to Be Average

The popularity of white students increases as their grades increase. For black and Hispanic students, there is a dropoff in popularity for those with higher GPAs.

As grades improve beyond this level, Hispanic students lose popularity at an alarming rate. Although African Americans with GPAs as high as 3.5 continue to have more friends than those with lower grades, the rate of increase is no longer as great as among white students.

The experience of black and white students diverges as GPAs climb above 3.5. As the GPAs of black students increase beyond this level, they tend to have fewer and fewer friends. A black student with a 4.0 has, on average, 1.5 fewer friends of the same ethnicity than a white student with the same GPA. Put differently, a black student with straight As is no more popular than a black student with a 2.9 GPA, but high-achieving whites are at the top of the popularity pyramid.

My findings with respect to Hispanics are even more discouraging. A Hispanic student with a 4.0 GPA is the least popular of all Hispanic students, and Hispanic-white differences among high achievers are the most extreme.

The social costs of a high GPA are most pronounced for adolescent males. Popularity begins to decrease at lower GPAs for young black men than young black women (3.25 GPA compared with a 3.5), and the rate at which males lose friends after this point is far greater. As a result, black male high achievers have notably fewer friends than do female ones. I observe a similar pattern among Hispanics, with males beginning to lose friends at lower GPAs and at a faster clip, though the male-female differences are not statistically significant.

POTENTIAL OBJECTIONS

Could high-achieving minority students be more socially isolated simply   25
because there are so few of them? The number of high-achieving minority students in the average school is fewer than the number of high-achieving white
students. To see whether this disparity could explain my findings, I adjusted the
data to eliminate the effect of differences in the number of students at each
school with similar GPAs. This adjustment, however, did little to temper the
effect of acting white.

It might also be hypothesized that high-achieving minority students are
able to cultivate friendships with students of other ethnic groups. If so, I should
obtain quite different results when I examine popularity among students of all
ethnic groups. While one finds some evidence that high-achieving students are
more popular among students of other ethnicities, the increment is not enough
to offset the decline in popularity within their own ethnic group — a predictable finding, given that black and white students have only, on average, one
friend of another ethnicity, and Hispanics just one and a half.

Indeed, when minority students reach the very highest levels of academic
performance, even the number of cross-ethnic friendships declines. Black and
Hispanic students with a GPA above 3.5 actually have fewer cross-ethnic
friendships than those with lower grades, a finding that seems particularly
troubling.

Finally, I examined whether high-achieving blacks and Hispanics can
shield themselves from the costs of acting white by taking up extracurricular
activities. There are many opportunities in schools for students to self-select
into activities, including organized sports, cheerleading, student government,
band, and the National Honor Society, that should put them in contact with
students with similar interests.

Unfortunately, when I look separately at minority students who participate in each of these activities, I find only one within which ethnic differences
are eliminated: the National Honor Society. Among students involved in every
other activity, new friends made outside the classroom do not make up for the
social penalties imposed for acting white.

A PRIVATE-SCHOOL EDGE

The patterns described thus far essentially characterize social dynamics of   30
public-school students, who constitute 94 percent of the students in the
Adhealth sample. For the small percentage of black and Hispanic students who
attend private school, however, I find no evidence of a trade-off between
popularity and achievement (see Fig. 2). Surprisingly, white private-school
students with the highest grades are not as popular as their lower-achieving
peers. The most-popular white students in private schools have a GPA of
roughly 2.0, a C average.

Popularity of Black Students in Private Schools

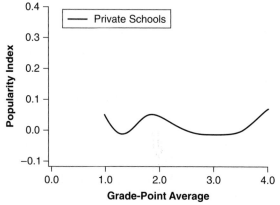

Note: A grade of 1.0 = D; 4.0 = A

SOURCE: Authors' calculations from National Longitudinal Study of Adolescent Health data

Popularity of Hispanic Students in Private Schools

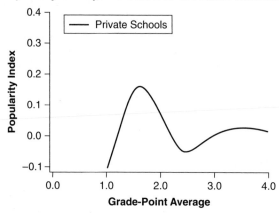

Fig. 2   The Private-School Advantage

For black and Hispanic students, the adverse effect of good grades on popularity disappears in private schools.

These data may help to explain one of the more puzzling findings in the research on the relative advantages of public and private schools. Most studies of academic achievement find little or no benefit of attending a private school for white students, but quite large benefits for African Americans. It may be that blacks attending private schools have quite a different peer group.

The Segregated School: Is It an Advantage?

I also find that acting white is unique to those schools where black students comprise less than 80 percent of the student population. In predominantly black schools, I find no evidence at all that getting good grades adversely affects students' popularity.

But perhaps this changes when school desegregation leads to cross-ethnic friendships within the school. To see how the degree of internal integration within a school affects acting-white patterns, I calculated the difference from what I would expect in the total number of cross-ethnic friends in a school based on the ethnic make-up of the student body. Schools with a greater percentage of cross-ethnic friendships than expected are considered to be internally integrated. I divide schools into two groups of equal size: those with higher and lower degrees of internal integration.

Unfortunately, internal integration only aggravates the problem. Blacks in less-integrated schools (places with fewer than expected cross-ethnic friendships) encounter less of a trade-off between popularity and achievement. In fact, the effect of acting white on popularity appears to be twice as large in the more-integrated (racially mixed) schools as in the less-integrated ones. Among the highest achievers (3.5 GPA or higher), the differences are even more stark, with the effect of acting white almost five times as great in settings with more cross-ethnic friendships than expected. Black males in such schools fare the worst, penalized seven times as harshly as my estimate of the average effect of acting white on all black students!

This finding, along with the fact that I find no evidence of acting white in predominantly black schools, adds to the evidence of a "Shaker Heights" syndrome, in which racially integrated settings only reinforce pressures to toe the ethnic line. 35

In Search of an Answer

That acting white is more prevalent in schools with more interethnic contact hardly passes the test of political correctness. It nonetheless provides a clue to what is going on. Anthropologists have long observed that social groups seek to preserve their identity, an activity that accelerates when threats to internal cohesion intensify. Within a group, the more successful individuals can be expected to enhance the power and cohesion of the group as long as their loyalty is not in question. But if the group risks losing its most successful members to outsiders, then the group will seek to prevent the outflow. Cohesive yet threatened groups — the Amish, for example — are known for limiting their children's education for fear that too much contact with the outside world risks the community's survival.

In an achievement-based society where two groups, for historical reasons, achieve at noticeably different levels, the group with lower achievement levels is at risk of losing its most successful members, especially in situations where successful individuals have opportunities to establish contacts with outsiders. Over the long run, the group faces the danger that its most successful members will no longer identify with its interests, and group identity will itself erode. To forestall such erosion, groups may try to reinforce their identity by penalizing members for differentiating themselves from the group. The penalties are likely to increase whenever the threats to group cohesion intensify.

Applying this model of behavior to minority and white students yields two important predictions: A positive relationship between academic achievement and peer-group acceptance (popularity) will erode and turn negative, whenever the group as a whole has lower levels of achievement. And that erosion will be exacerbated in contexts that foster more interethnic contact. This, of course, is exactly what I found with regard to acting white.

Understanding acting white in this way places the concept within a broader conceptual framework that transcends specific cultural contexts and lifts the topic beyond pointless ideological exchanges. There is necessarily a trade-off between doing well and rejection by your peers when you come from a traditionally low-achieving group, especially when that group comes into contact with more outsiders.

Alternative Explanations

Such a conceptualization is preferable to both of the two theories that   40
have so far dominated discussions of acting white: the notion of oppositional culture and the allegation of cultural self-sabotage.

The oppositional culture theory, developed by Fordham and Ogbu in the wake of their experiences at "Capitol High," accounts for the observed differences between blacks and whites as follows: (1) white people provide blacks with inferior schooling and treat them differently in school; (2) by imposing a job ceiling, white people fail to reward blacks adequately for their academic achievement in adult life; and (3) black Americans develop coping devices which, in turn, further limit their striving for academic success. Fordham and Ogbu suggest the problem arose partly because white Americans traditionally refused to acknowledge that black Americans were capable of intellectual achievement and partly because black Americans subsequently began to doubt their own intellectual ability, began to define academic success as white people's prerogative, and began to discourage their peers, perhaps unconsciously, from emulating white people in striving for academic success.

However plausible it sounds, the oppositional culture theory cannot explain why the acting-white problem is greatest in integrated settings. If Fordham and Ogbu were correct, the social sanctions for acting white should be most severe in places like the segregated school, where opportunities are most limited. The results of my studies, of course, point in precisely the opposite direction.

The notion that acting white is simply attributable to self-sabotage is even less persuasive. According to its proponents, black and Hispanic cultures are dysfunctional, punishing successful members of their group rather than rewarding their success. That theory is more a judgment than an explanation. A universal, it cannot explain the kinds of variations from one school setting to another that are so apparent in the data I have explored.

THE NEED FOR NEW IDENTITIES

How important are these social pressures? Although that story has yet to be fully told, in my view, the prevalence of acting white in schools with racially mixed student bodies suggests that social pressures could go a long way toward explaining the large racial and ethnic gaps in SAT scores, the underperformance of minorities in suburban schools, and the lack of adequate representation of blacks and Hispanics in elite colleges and universities.

Minority communities in the United States have yet to generate a large 45 cadre of high achievers, a situation as discouraging as the high incarceration rates among minorities who never finish high school. In fact, the two patterns may be linked. As long as distressed communities provide minorities with their identities, the social costs of breaking free will remain high. To increase the likelihood that more can do so, society must find ways for these high achievers to thrive in settings where adverse social pressures are less intense. The integrated school, by itself, apparently cannot achieve that end.

Reading across Disciplines
KAREEM J. JOHNSON, Psychology

Although most Americans believe that good fortune follows academic success, African American students have often found that seeking to do well in school carries the peril of being socially ostracized. My own reactions to Roland G. Fryer's research on "acting white," which empirically confirms this phenomenon, feel paradoxical. As a social psychologist, I am intrigued by the integration of Fryer's research with other work on the social influence of racial stereotypes. However, as an African American male who has earned a Ph.D., I find Fryer's results all too familiar.

Research in social psychology highlights the power that stereotypes hold over judgment and behavior. Many studies have been done using a technique called "priming": participants may be "primed" by being asked to think of examples and characteristics of a concept, or, at an unconscious level, by being subliminally exposed to images or words that convey the concept. Researchers have demonstrated that priming can directly influence behavior. For instance, people primed with the category "elderly" temporarily walked more slowly, acting in accord with the stereotype that elderly people are physically slow. This pattern is known as an "assimilation effect." The astonishing results of another study showed that people primed with the category "professors" answered more questions correctly in a game of Trivial Pursuit. The priming did not give them any additional knowledge, but having the category of "professors" active in their minds allowed them better access to the knowledge they already had.

One striking indication of these priming studies is that subtly activating even innocuous stereotypes can produce very real behavioral effects. The behavioral consequences of activating racial stereotypes may be significantly more dire. Studies that prime racial stereotypes (for instance, by subliminally flashing an image of an African American face) find that at an automatic, involuntary, and unconscious level it is easy to associate African Americans with negative concepts such as hostility, criminality, and poor intelligence. Most of this research is done with Caucasian participants, but when these same studies are done with African American participants, the results are largely the same. Indeed, the most severe consequences of stereotypes appear to affect the judgments and behaviors of the stereotyped target.

Research on "stereotype threat" has demonstrated that subtly reminding people of negative stereotypes about their group can adversely affect their cognitive performance. For instance, girls primed with the stereotype that boys are better at math than girls performed worse on a math test than girls who weren't primed. African Americans have been shown to perform worse on standardized tests as a result of having stereotypes primed by indicating their race before the test. The cognitive effects of stereotype threat can affect members of any group: in one study, Caucasian male engineering students performed worse on a test of quantitative ability when they believed the test was designed to determine why Asian students outperform Caucasian students in math and science. And research on assimilation effects and stereotype threat has shown that the effects occur even if participants do not endorse the stereotype. Simply being aware of the stereotype and having it mentally activated is enough to cause significant cognitive and behavioral consequences.

And this is one of the more troubling aspects of Fryer's findings: stereotypes become self-fulfilling prophecies. The stereotype that African American and Latino students do not perform as well academically as Caucasian children can have automatic, unconscious, and involuntary influences on how others evaluate these children. But knowledge of the stereotype can also impair the students' own academic performance. The results of Fryer's research reveal that the stereotypes are also self-sustaining: students who break the stereotype are punished for doing so, and as a result the stereotype gains veracity. The confirmation of the stereotype allows it to become an identifying characteristic of the group. Once it's "true" that black students don't perform as well as white students, then the black student who does perform well can no longer be authentically black.

Ironically, the social costs of "acting white" only occur in more racially integrated schools. In schools that are predominately black, high-performing students cannot lose their identity and be exiled to some opposing group. However, in the more integrated schools, the stereotypes can become part of the way dividing lines are drawn between groups. I could never argue that somehow re-segregating schools would offer any kind of solution. Instead, I believe that the solution lies in the drive of the students who choose not to be defined by the stereotypes assigned to them. I know from firsthand experience some of the social costs of "acting white." Because my grades of style of dress or manner of speaking did not conform to stereotypical expectations, I became a subtype that didn't quite fit in anywhere. As a result, I had to forge a new identity instead of fitting myself into an assigned stereotype. Although it was often difficult to feel that my identity was in some sort of limbo, I was strengthened by the knowledge that the people with the strongest identities are the ones who aren't afraid to break the mold.

Dr. Kareem J. Johnson is an assistant professor of psychology at Temple University in Philadelphia, Pennsylvania.

QUESTIONING THE TEXT

1. Fryer opens his article by citing a speech by Senator Barack Obama as evidence that the subject of "acting white" has entered the national consciousness. Having established the problem, does Fryer suggest or imply any policy that might help mitigate the phenomenon? Are there any recommendations for action that follow from his research?

2. In rhetoric, *ethos* refers to an appeal from the character of the writer or speaker — a way of talking about the author's credibility or trustworthiness. Describe Fryer's *ethos*. Do you find him trustworthy and credible? Why, or why not? Point to specific textual evidence that leads to your conclusions.

MAKING CONNECTIONS

3. Compare Fryer's use of evidence based on his statistical research with the evidence offered by John Tierney (p. 130), Christina Hoff Sommers (p. 133), and/or Katha Pollitt (p. 139). What differences do you see among these writers? What style of evidence do you find most persuasive and most accessible?

4. Compare Fryer's article to Gwendolyn Brooks's poem "We Real Cool" (p. 157). It could be argued that they deal with similar subjects, but, of course, there are vast differences between the two texts. How do the works express similar ideas about educational achievement? How do the differences between genres affect your understanding of the issue of educational achievement?

JOINING THE CONVERSATION

5. Think about your own experiences with social pressures, both in high school and college. In an essay or a personal narrative, describe a time when social pressure influenced you. Has social pressure ever pushed you to act a way you didn't want to? Has it ever encouraged you to improve or achieve in ways that you might not have done on your own?

6. Not everyone even wants to go to college, but many who do never make it. Looking back, what advice would you offer to high school students who want to go to college but aren't sure about how to approach the process? Write a letter to an imaginary high school student who asks your advice on whether pursuing college admission is a worthwhile goal and, if you think college is worthwhile, how to go about reaching the goal.

GWENDOLYN BROOKS
We Real Cool

*W*HEN *G*WENDOLYN *B*ROOKS *(b. 1917) was a little girl, her mother said, "You're going to be the first lady Paul Laurence Dunbar," a powerful and well-known black poet. Brooks met her mother's challenge and then some, becoming the first African American writer to win the Pulitzer Prize (for* Annie Allen *in 1950) and the first African American woman to be elected to the National Institute of Arts and Letters or to serve as Consultant in Poetry to the Library of Congress. A 1936 graduate of Chicago's Wilson Junior College, Brooks has received over seventy honorary degrees.*

In her most distinguished career, Brooks has drawn on the traditions of African American sermons and musical forms — especially the blues, jazz, and the spiritual — to explore the American condition and, in particular, the realities of African American life. Her brief poem "We Real Cool" depicts a group of young hookey players who have rejected — or been rejected by — their schools. This is the first poem by Brooks I ever read, and it inspired me to seek out her other poetry and prose and to be a lifelong fan of her work. It also made me think about what my life would have been like if I had "left school."

—A.L.

The Pool Players.
Seven at the Golden Shovel.

We real cool. We
Left school. We

Lurk late. We
Strike straight. We

Sing sin. We
Thin gin. We

Jazz June. We
Die soon.

IN RESPONSE

1. What message do you take away from Brooks's poem? In what ways does it speak personally to you? If you keep a reading log, answer this question there.

2. How do you think the students in the reading by Mike Rose (p. 90) might respond to the poem?

3. Brooks's poem was written in 1960, and it refers to and uses the style of an even earlier jazz tradition. Write your own contemporary version of "We Real Cool," calling on present-day styles of music and culture to do so.

Look carefully at the photograph on the preceding page, which shows Elizabeth Eckford, an African American teenager, on her way to enroll in (previously all-white) Central High School in Little Rock, Arkansas, on September 4, 1957. What first draws your attention to this photograph? ■ What story does the photo tell, both about each individual and about the group as a whole? ■ What dominant impression does it create? ■ What underlying and competing values seem to be at work in it?

Ethics   4

GEORGE JOHNSON OPENS *Fire in the Mind* (1995), a book on the relationship of faith and science, by citing a Navajo creation story:

> When all the stars were ready to be placed in the sky First Woman said, "I will use these to write the laws that are to govern mankind for all time. These laws cannot be written on the water as that is always changing its form, nor can they be written in the sand as the wind would soon erase them, but if they are written in the stars they can be read and remembered forever."

The myth gives shape to the enduring human desire for a firm ethical sense, a guide to right and wrong as immutable as the stars.

Just as persistent among nations and people is a fear of declining ethics. The Hebrew prophets in biblical times regularly denounced the sins and abominations of the Israelites. The ancient Romans had Cato the Censor to deplore their precipitous retreat from virtue. Martin Luther protested the corruption he found in the Catholic Church of the Renaissance, and his twentieth-century American namesake, Martin Luther King Jr., challenged a nation to restore its sense of justice by ending racial discrimination. Of course, reading history this way leads one to suspect that nearly every age views itself as a period of decline in need of prophets to set things right.

Some Americans, too, wonder whether their national culture can sink much lower than it already has — the news wallowing in scandal, corruption, and hate crimes, while pop culture celebrates greed, conspicuous consumption, and promiscuous sex. To many, something seems rotten in the soul of the nation.

But is that perception accurate? And, if so, how does one restore the ethical sense of a people grown too diverse and, perhaps, too worldly to look to the stars (or their equivalent) for guidance? Long-term trends are full of contradictions. There's been an increase in the rate of divorce and a surge in out-of-wedlock births, but a renewed concern for the institution of marriage and traditional families; a coarsening of social discourse, yet growing interest in manners and civility; an increase in juvenile violence, but an overall drop in crime; a steady number of abortions, but a remarkably high rate of professed religious belief; a widening rift between rich and poor, yet dwindling support for welfare programs. Trends and numbers like these, of course, can support quite different ethical interpretations — they can be read in varying ways. For instance, one writer may interpret the evident decline of the nuclear family in the United States as a threat to the country's moral core, while another regards it as welcome evidence that society is enlarging its ethical vision to accept new kinds of families. To some, the steady abortion rate represents women having the freedom to exercise choice; to others, it memorializes a new Holocaust.

In this chapter, we present authors locating their ethical assumptions in religion, philosophy, economics, and even entertainment. But this diversity of approach to questions of good and evil does not in itself necessarily signal the triumph of moral relativism — the belief that ethical choices are made on the basis of individual or local, not universal, standards. The desire for certainty transcends time and cultures, and the assertion that there is a universal moral sense continues to be heard. It is, in fact, one of the issues most under scrutiny and debate.

You might think that ethical issues are too hypothetical to win your attention. But, as this chapter demonstrates, you face practical ethical choices almost every day in school, in the workplace, and in your personal life. Moreover, we probably need not fear for the health of our society as long as debates about ethics — the kind you and your classmates might have in a dorm room or classroom — remain robust and honorable. Following are some questions to keep the debate alive:

- Do you and your friends discuss ethical issues? If so, what topics come up regularly or provoke the most discussion?

- What sorts of ethical issues affect you most directly or often? When do you find yourself most conscious of making an ethical choice?

- Do you believe people share a common ethical sense or that ethics is a matter of personal belief?

- What makes a particular belief "religious"? What do the terms *religion* and *God* mean to you? To people with views or religious convictions different from your own?

- How important is a sense of ethics to your generation? Would you characterize yourself and your peers as more or less "moral" or "ethical" than generations before or after your own?

MARTIN LUTHER KING JR.
Letter from Birmingham Jail

THE REVEREND MARTIN LUTHER KING JR. (1929–68) is remembered today for many accomplishments: his leadership of the movement for civil rights for African Americans in the 1950s and 1960s; his advocacy of nonviolent resistance to oppressive systems; his Christian ministry; his powerful and moving sermons and speeches. In King, all these elements coalesced in a figure who won the Nobel Peace Prize, changed the face of American public life, and reframed the questions any society striving to enact truly democratic principles must face. When he was assassinated in Memphis on April 4, 1968, the world lost a major spokesperson for the values of equality, freedom, and social justice — for all.

King attended Morehouse College (see p. 58 for the current Morehouse mission statement) and later received his Ph.D. in theology from Boston University. But extensive education and high intelligence did not protect him from racist forces, which eventually led to his murder and which are still present in the United States forty years after King's death. But in the face of such hostility, King's moral commitment never faltered. In August 1963, he led the March on Washington and delivered, at the foot of the Lincoln Memorial, one of his most memorable and moving speeches, "I Have a Dream," to some quarter of a million people, the largest protest demonstration in American history up to that time. The next month, King led a major protest against unfair hiring practices in Birmingham, Alabama, for which he was arrested and put in jail. While in prison, he wrote a long letter responding to local white religious leaders of several faiths, who had criticized his actions as "unwise and untimely." "Letter from Birmingham Jail," reprinted here in the revised version published in Why We Can't Wait *(1964), has emerged as a classic text on civil rights. In it, King clearly and forcefully articulates the moral principles on which his actions rest — and challenges not only the clergy of the time but all readers today to examine their own.* —A.L.

My Dear Fellow Clergymen:

While confined here in the Birmingham city jail, I came across your recent statement calling my present activities "unwise and untimely." Seldom do I pause to answer criticism of my work and ideas. If I sought to answer all the criticisms that cross my desk, my secretaries would have little time for anything other than such correspondence in the course of the day, and I would have no time for constructive work. But since I feel that you are men of genuine good will and that your criticisms are sincerely set forth, I want to try to answer your statement in what I hope will be patient and reasonable terms.

I think I should indicate why I am here in Birmingham, since you have been influenced by the view which argues against "outsiders coming in." I have the honor of serving as president of the Southern Christian Leadership Conference, an organization operating in every southern state, with headquarters in Atlanta, Georgia. We have some eighty-five affiliated organizations across the South, and one of them is the Alabama Christian Movement for Human Rights. Frequently we share staff, educational, and financial resources with our affiliates. Several months ago the affiliate here in Birmingham asked us to be on call to engage in a nonviolent direct-action program if such were deemed necessary. We readily consented, and when the hour came, we lived up to our promise. So I, along with several members of my staff, am here because I was invited here. I am here because I have organizational ties here.

But more basically, I am in Birmingham because injustice is here. Just as the prophets of the eighth century B.C. left their villages and carried their "thus saith the Lord" far beyond the boundaries of their home towns, and just as the Apostle Paul left his village of Tarsus and carried the gospel of Jesus Christ to the far corners of the Greco-Roman world, so am I compelled to carry the gospel of freedom beyond my own home town. Like Paul, I must constantly respond to the Macedonian call for aid.

Moreover, I am cognizant of the interrelatedness of all communities and states. I cannot sit idly by in Atlanta and not be concerned about what happens in Birmingham. Injustice anywhere is a threat to justice everywhere. We are caught in an inescapable network of mutuality, tied in a single garment of destiny. Whatever affects one directly, affects all indirectly. Never again can we afford to live with the narrow, provincial "outside agitator" idea. Anyone who lives inside the United States can never be considered an outsider anywhere within its bounds.

You deplore the demonstrations taking place in Birmingham. But your statement, I am sorry to say, fails to express a similar concern for the conditions that brought about the demonstrations. I am sure that none of you would want to rest content with the superficial kind of social analysis that deals merely with effects and does not grapple with underlying causes. It is unfortunate that demonstrations are taking place in Birmingham, but it is even more unfortunate that the city's white power structure left the Negro community with no alternative.

In any nonviolent campaign there are four basic steps: collection of the facts to determine whether injustices exist; negotiation; self-purification; and direct action. We have gone through all these steps in Birmingham. There can be no gainsaying the fact that racial injustice engulfs this community. Birmingham is probably the most thoroughly segregated city in the United States. Its ugly record of brutality is widely known. Negroes have experienced grossly unjust treatment in the courts. There have been more unsolved bombings of Negro homes and churches in Birmingham than in any other city in the nation. These are the hard, brutal facts of the case. On the basis of these conditions,

5

Negro leaders sought to negotiate with the city fathers. But the latter consistently refused to engage in good-faith negotiation.

Then, last September, came the opportunity to talk with leaders of Birmingham's economic community. In the course of the negotiations, certain promises were made by the merchants — for example, to remove the stores' humiliating racial signs. On the basis of these promises, the Reverend Fred Shuttlesworth and the leaders of the Alabama Christian Movement for Human Rights agreed to a moratorium on all demonstrations. As the weeks and months went by, we realized that we were the victims of a broken promise. A few signs, briefly removed, returned; the others remained.

As in so many past experiences, our hopes had been blasted, and the shadow of deep disappointment settled upon us. We had no alternative except to prepare for direct action, whereby we would present our very bodies as a means of laying our case before the conscience of the local and the national community. Mindful of the difficulties involved, we decided to undertake a process of self-purification. We began a series of workshops on nonviolence, and we repeatedly asked ourselves: "Are you able to accept blows without retaliating?" "Are you able to endure the ordeal of jail?" We decided to schedule our direct-action program for the Easter season, realizing that except for Christmas, this is the main shopping period of the year. Knowing that a strong economic-withdrawal program would be the by-product of direct action, we felt that this would be the best time to bring pressure to bear on the merchants for the needed change.

Then it occurred to us that Birmingham's mayoral election was coming up in March, and we speedily decided to postpone action until after election day. When we discovered that the Commissioner of Public Safety, Eugene "Bull" Connor, had piled up enough votes to be in the run-off, we decided again to postpone action until the day after the run-off so that the demonstrations could not be used to cloud the issues. Like many others, we wanted to see Mr. Connor defeated, and to this end we endured postponement after postponement. Having aided in this community need, we felt that our direct-action program could be delayed no longer.

You may well ask, "Why direct action? Why sit-ins, marches, and so forth? Isn't negotiation a better path?" You are quite right in calling for negotiation. Indeed, this is the very purpose of direct action. Nonviolent direct action seeks to create such a crisis and foster such a tension that a community which has constantly refused to negotiate is forced to confront the issue. It seeks so to dramatize the issue that it can no longer be ignored. My citing the creation of tension as part of the work of the nonviolent-resister may sound rather shocking. But I must confess that I am not afraid of the word "tension." I have earnestly opposed violent tension, but there is a type of constructive, nonviolent tension which is necessary for growth. Just as Socrates felt that it was necessary to create a tension in the mind so that individuals could rise from the bondage of myths and half-truths to the unfettered realm of creative analysis and objective

10

appraisal, so must we see the need for nonviolent gadflies to create the kind of tension in society that will help men rise from the dark depths of prejudice and racism to the majestic heights of understanding and brotherhood.

The purpose of our direct-action program is to create a situation so crisis-packed that it will inevitably open the door to negotiation. I therefore concur with you in your call for negotiation. Too long has our beloved Southland been bogged down in a tragic effort to live in monologue rather than dialogue.

One of the basic points in your statement is that the action that I and my associates have taken in Birmingham is untimely. Some have asked: "Why didn't you give the new city administration time to act?" The only answer that I can give to this query is that the new Birmingham administration must be prodded about as much as the outgoing one, before it will act. We are sadly mistaken if we feel that the election of Albert Boutwell as mayor will bring the millennium to Birmingham. While Mr. Boutwell is a much more gentle person than Mr. Connor, they are both segregationists, dedicated to maintenance of the status quo. I have hoped that Mr. Boutwell will be reasonable enough to see the futility of massive resistance to desegregation. But he will not see this without pressure from devotees of civil rights. My friends, I must say to you that we have not made a single gain in civil rights without determined legal and nonviolent pressure. Lamentably, it is an historical fact that privileged groups seldom give up their privileges voluntarily. Individuals may see the moral light and voluntarily give up their unjust posture; but, as Reinhold Niebuhr has reminded us, groups tend to be more immoral than individuals.

We know through painful experience that freedom is never voluntarily given by the oppressor; it must be demanded by the oppressed. Frankly, I have yet to engage in a direct-action campaign that was "well timed" in the view of those who have not suffered unduly from the disease of segregation. For years now I have heard the word "Wait!" It rings in the ear of every Negro with piercing familiarity. This "Wait" has almost always meant "Never." We must come to see, with one of our distinguished jurists, that "justice too long delayed is justice denied."

We have waited for more than 340 years for our constitutional and God-given rights. The nations of Asia and Africa are moving with jetlike speed toward gaining political independence, but we still creep at horse-and-buggy pace toward gaining a cup of coffee at a lunch counter. Perhaps it is easy for those who have never felt the stinging darts of segregation to say, "Wait." But when you have seen vicious mobs lynch your mothers and fathers at will and drown your sisters and brothers at whim; when you have seen hate-filled policemen curse, kick, and even kill your black brothers and sisters; when you see the vast majority of your twenty million Negro brothers smothering in an air-tight cage of poverty in the midst of an affluent society; when you suddenly find your tongue twisted and your speech stammering as you seek to explain to your six-year-old daughter why she can't go to the public amusement park that has just been advertised on television, and see tears welling up in her eyes when she is told that Funtown is closed to colored children, and see ominous clouds of inferiority beginning to form in her little mental sky, and see her beginning to distort her personality by developing an unconscious bitterness toward white people; when you have to concoct an answer for a five-year-old son who is ask-ing "Daddy, why do white people treat colored people so mean?"; when you take a cross-country drive and find it necessary to sleep night after night in the uncomfortable corners of your automobile because no motel will accept you; when you are humiliated day in and day out by nagging signs reading "white" and "colored"; when your first name becomes "nigger," your middle name be-comes "boy" (however old you are) and your last name becomes "John," and your wife and mother are never given the respected title "Mrs."; when you are harried by day and haunted by night by the fact that you are a Negro, living constantly at tiptoe stance, never quite knowing what to expect next, and are plagued with inner fears and outer resentments; when you are forever fighting a degenerating sense of "nobodiness" — then you will understand why we find it difficult to wait. There comes a time when the cup of endurance runs over, and men are no longer willing to be plunged into the abyss of despair. I hope, sirs, you can understand our legitimate and unavoidable impatience.

You express a great deal of anxiety over our willingness to break laws.   15
This is certainly a legitimate concern. Since we so diligently urge people to obey the Supreme Court's decision of 1954 outlawing segregation in the pub-lic schools, at first glance it may seem rather paradoxical for us consciously to break laws. One may well ask: "How can you advocate breaking some laws and obeying others?" The answer lies in the fact that there are two types of laws: just and unjust. I would be the first to advocate obeying just laws. One has not only a legal but a moral responsibility to obey just laws. Conversely, one has a moral responsibility to disobey unjust laws. I would agree with St. Augustine that "an unjust law is no law at all."

Now, what is the difference between the two? How does one determine whether a law is just or unjust? A just law is a man-made code that squares with the moral law or the law of God. An unjust law is a code that is out of harmony with the moral law. To put it in the terms of St. Thomas Aquinas: An unjust law is a human law that is not rooted in eternal law and natural law. Any law that uplifts human personality is just. Any law that degrades human personality is unjust. All segregation statutes are unjust because segregation distorts the soul and damages the personality. It gives the segregator a false sense of superiority and the segregated a false sense of inferiority. Segregation, to use the terminol-ogy of the Jewish philosopher Martin Buber, substitutes an "I–it" relationship for an "I–thou" relationship and ends up relegating persons to the status of things. Hence segregation is not only politically, economically, and sociologi-cally unsound, it is morally wrong and sinful. Paul Tillich has said that sin is sep-aration. Is not segregation an existential expression of man's tragic separation, his awful estrangement, his terrible sinfulness? Thus it is that I can urge men to obey the 1954 decision of the Supreme Court, for it is morally right; and I can urge them to disobey segregation ordinances, for they are morally wrong.

Let us consider a more concrete example of just and unjust laws. An unjust law is a code that a numerical or power majority group compels a minority group to obey but does not make binding on itself. This is *difference* made legal. By the same token, a just law is a code that a majority compels a minority to follow and that it is willing to follow itself. This is *sameness* made legal.

Let me give another explanation. A law is unjust if it is inflicted on a minority that, as a result of being denied the right to vote, had no part in enacting or devising the law. Who can say that the legislature of Alabama which set up that state's segregation laws was democratically elected? Throughout Alabama all sorts of devious methods are used to prevent Negroes from becoming registered voters, and there are some counties in which, even though Negroes constitute a majority of the population, not a single Negro is registered. Can any law enacted under such circumstances be considered democratically structured?

Sometimes a law is just on its face and unjust in its application. For instance, I have been arrested on a charge of parading without a permit. Now, there is nothing wrong in having an ordinance which requires a permit for a parade. But such an ordinance becomes unjust when it is used to maintain segregation and to deny citizens the First-Amendment privilege of peaceful assembly and protest.

I hope you are able to see the distinction I am trying to point out. In no   20
sense do I advocate evading or defying the law, as would the rabid segregationist. That would lead to anarchy. One who breaks an unjust law must do so openly, lovingly, and with a willingness to accept the penalty. I submit that an individual who breaks a law that conscience tells him is unjust, and who willingly accepts the penalty of imprisonment in order to arouse the conscience of the community over its injustice, is in reality expressing the highest respect for law.

Of course, there is nothing new about this kind of civil disobedience. It was evidenced sublimely in the refusal of Shadrach, Meshach, and Abednego to obey the laws of Nebuchadnezzar,* on the ground that a higher moral law was at stake. It was practiced superbly by the early Christians, who were willing to face hungry lions and the excruciating pain of chopping blocks rather than submit to certain unjust laws of the Roman Empire. To a degree, academic freedom is a reality today because Socrates practiced civil disobedience. In our own nation, the Boston Tea Party represented a massive act of civil disobedience.

Shadrach, Meshach, and Abednego . . . Nebuchadnezzar: In the biblical Book of Daniel, the Babylonian king Nebuchadnezzar orders the three Israelites thrown into a fiery furnace for refusing to worship a golden idol, but they emerge unharmed

We should never forget that everything Adolf Hitler did in Germany was "legal" and everything the Hungarian freedom fighters* did in Hungary was "illegal." It was "illegal" to aid and comfort a Jew in Hitler's Germany. Even so, I am sure that, had I lived in Germany at the time, I would have aided and comforted my Jewish brothers. If today I lived in a Communist country where certain principles dear to the Christian faith are suppressed, I would openly advocate disobeying that country's anti-religious laws.

I must make two honest confessions to you, my Christian and Jewish brothers. First, I must confess that over the past few years I have been gravely disappointed with the white moderate. I have almost reached the regrettable conclusion that the Negro's great stumbling block in his stride toward freedom is not the White Citizen's Counciler* or the Ku Klux Klanner, but the white moderate, who is more devoted to "order" than to justice; who prefers a negative peace which is the absence of tension to a positive peace which is the presence of justice; who constantly says, "I agree with you in the goal you seek, but I cannot agree with your methods of direct action"; who paternalistically believes he can set the timetable for another man's freedom; who lives by a mythical concept of time and who constantly advises the Negro to wait for a "more convenient season." Shallow understanding from people of good will is more frustrating than absolute misunderstanding from people of ill will. Lukewarm acceptance is much more bewildering than outright rejection.

I had hoped that the white moderate would understand that law and order exist for the purpose of establishing justice and that when they fail in this purpose they become the dangerously structured dams that block the flow of social progress. I had hoped that the white moderate would understand that the present tension in the South is a necessary phase of the transition from an obnoxious negative peace, in which the Negro passively accepted his unjust plight, to a substantive and positive peace, in which all men will respect the dignity and worth of human personality. Actually, we who engage in nonviolent direct action are not the creators of tension. We merely bring to the surface the hidden tension that is already alive. We bring it out in the open, where it can be seen and dealt with. Like a boil that can never be cured so long as it is covered up but must be opened with all its ugliness to the natural medicines of air and light, injustice must be exposed, with all the tension its exposure creates, to the light of human conscience and the air of national opinion, before it can be cured.

In your statement you assert that our actions, even though peaceful, must   25
be condemned because they precipitate violence. But is this a logical assertion?

Hungarian freedom fighters: In 1956, Hungarians revolted against the Marxist government imposed on them by the former Soviet Union

White Citizen's Counciler: member of a group organized to resist the desegregation of schools ordered by the Supreme Court's *Brown v. Board of Education* decision

Isn't this like condemning a robbed man because his possession of money precipitated the evil act of robbery? Isn't this like condemning Socrates because his unswerving commitment to truth and his philosophical inquiries precipitated the act by the misguided populace in which they made him drink hemlock? Isn't this like condemning Jesus because his unique God-consciousness and never-ceasing devotion to God's will precipitated the evil act of crucifixion? We must come to see that, as the federal courts have consistently affirmed, it is wrong to urge an individual to cease his efforts to gain his basic constitutional rights because the quest may precipitate violence. Society must protect the robbed and punish the robber.

I had also hoped that the white moderate would reject the myth concerning time in relation to the struggle for freedom. I have just received a letter from a white brother in Texas. He writes: "All Christians know that the colored people will receive equal rights eventually, but it is possible that you are in too great a religious hurry. It has taken Christianity almost two thousand years to accomplish what it has. The teachings of Christ take time to come to earth." Such an attitude stems from a tragic misconception of time, from the strangely irrational notion that there is something in the very flow of time that will inevitably cure all ills. Actually, time itself is neutral; it can be used either destructively or constructively. More and more I feel that the people of ill will have used time much more effectively than have the people of good will. We will have to repent in this generation not merely for the hateful words and actions of the bad people, but for the appalling silence of the good people. Human progress never rolls in on wheels of inevitability; it comes through the tireless efforts of men willing to be co-workers with God, and without this hard work, time itself becomes an ally of the forces of social stagnation. We must use time creatively, in the knowledge that the time is always ripe to do right. Now is the time to make real the promise of democracy and transform our pending national elegy into a creative psalm of brotherhood. Now is the time to lift our national policy from the quicksand of racial injustice to the solid rock of human dignity.

You speak of our activity in Birmingham as extreme. At first I was rather disappointed that fellow clergymen would see my nonviolent efforts as those of an extremist. I began thinking about the fact that I stand in the middle of two opposing forces in the Negro community. One is a force of complacency, made up in part of Negroes who, as a result of long years of oppression, are so drained of self-respect and a sense of "somebodiness" that they have adjusted to segregation; and in part of a few middle-class Negroes who, because of a degree of academic and economic security and because in some ways they profit by segregation, have become insensitive to the problems of the masses. The other force is one of bitterness and hatred, and it comes perilously close to advocating violence. It is expressed in the various black nationalist groups that are springing up across the nation, the largest and best-known being Elijah Muhammad's Muslim movement. Nourished by the Negro's frustration over the continued existence of racial discrimination, this movement is made up of people who have lost faith in America, who have absolutely repudiated Christianity, and who have concluded that the white man is an incorrigible "devil."

I have tried to stand between these two forces, saying that we need emulate neither the "do-nothingism" of the complacent nor the hatred and despair of the black nationalist. For there is the more excellent way of love and nonviolent protest. I am grateful to God that, through the influence of the Negro church, the way of nonviolence became an integral part of our struggle.

If this philosophy had not emerged, by now many streets of the South would, I am convinced, be flowing with blood. And I am further convinced that if our white brothers dismiss as "rabblerousers" and "outside agitators" those of us who employ nonviolent direct action, and if they refuse to support our nonviolent efforts, millions of Negroes will, out of frustration and despair, seek solace and security in Black-nationalist ideologies — a development that would inevitably lead to a frightening racial nightmare.

Oppressed people cannot remain oppressed forever. The yearning for   30
freedom eventually manifests itself, and that is what has happened to the American Negro. Something within has reminded him of his birthright of freedom, and something without has reminded him that it can be gained. Consciously or unconsciously, he has been caught up by the *Zeitgeist*, and with his black brothers of Africa and his brown and yellow brothers of Asia, South America, and the Caribbean, the United States Negro is moving with a sense of great urgency toward the promised land of racial justice. If one recognizes this vital urge that has engulfed the Negro community, one should readily understand why public demonstrations are taking place. The Negro has many pent-up resentments and latent frustrations, and he must release them. So let him march; let him make prayer pilgrimages to the city hall; let him go on freedom rides — and try to understand why he must do so. If his repressed emotions are not released in nonviolent ways, they will seek expression through violence; this is not a threat but a fact of history. So I have not said to my people, "Get rid of your discontent." Rather, I have tried to say that this normal and healthy discontent can be channeled into the creative outlet of nonviolent direct action. And now this approach is being termed extremist.

But though I was initially disappointed at being categorized as an extremist, as I continued to think about the matter I gradually gained a measure of satisfaction from the label. Was not Jesus an extremist for love: "Love your enemies, bless them that curse you, do good to them that hate you, and pray for them which despitefully use you, and persecute you." Was not Amos an extremist for justice: "Let justice roll down like waters and righteousness like an overflowing stream." Was not Paul an extremist for the Christian gospel: "I bear in my body the marks of the Lord Jesus." Was not Martin Luther an extremist: "Here I stand; I cannot do otherwise, so help me God." And John Bunyan: "I will stay in jail to the end of my days before I make a butchery of my conscience." And Abraham Lincoln: "This nation cannot survive half slave and half free." And Thomas Jefferson: "We hold these truths to be self-evident, that all men are created equal. . . ." So the question is not whether we will be extremists, but what kind of extremists we will be. Will we be extremists for hate or for love? Will we be extremists for the preservation of injustice or for the extension of justice? In that dramatic scene on Calvary's hill three men were crucified. We must never forget that all three were crucified for the same crime — the crime of extremism. Two were extremists for immorality, and thus fell below their environment. The other, Jesus Christ, was an extremist for love, truth, and goodness, and thereby rose above his environment. Perhaps the South, the nation, and the world are in dire need of creative extremists.

I had hoped that the white moderate would see this need. Perhaps I was too optimistic; perhaps I expected too much. I suppose I should have realized that few members of the oppressor race can understand the deep groans and passionate yearnings of the oppressed race, and still fewer have the vision to see that injustice must be rooted out by strong, persistent, and determined action. I am thankful, however, that some of our white brothers in the South have grasped the meaning of this social revolution and committed themselves to it. They are still all too few in quantity, but they are big in quality. Some — such as Ralph McGill, Lillian Smith, Harry Golden, James McBridge Dabbs, Anne Braden, and Sarah Patton Boyle — have written about our struggle in eloquent and prophetic terms. Others have marched with us down nameless streets of the South. They have languished in filthy, roach-infested jails, suffering the abuse and brutality of policemen who view them as "dirty nigger-lovers." Unlike so many of their moderate brothers and sisters, they have recognized the urgency of the moment and sensed the need for powerful "action" antidotes to combat the disease of segregation.

Let me take note of my other major disappointment. I have been so greatly disappointed with the white church and its leadership. Of course, there are some notable exceptions. I am not unmindful of the fact that each of you has taken some significant stands on this issue. I commend you, Reverend Stallings, for your Christian stand on this past Sunday, in welcoming Negroes to your worship service on a nonsegregated basis. I commend the Catholic leaders of this state for integrating Spring Hill College several years ago.

But despite these notable exceptions, I must honestly reiterate that I have been disappointed with the church. I do not say this as one of those negative critics who can always find something wrong with the church. I say this as a minister of the gospel, who loves the church; who was nurtured in its bosom; who has been sustained by its spiritual blessings and who will remain true to it as long as the cord of life shall lengthen.

When I was suddenly catapulted into the leadership of the bus protest in   35
Montgomery, Alabama, a few years ago, I felt we would be supported by the white church. I felt that the white ministers, priests, and rabbis of the South would be among our strongest allies. Instead, some have been outright opponents, refusing to understand the freedom movement and misrepresenting its

leaders; all too many others have been more cautious than courageous and have remained silent behind the anesthetizing security of stained glass windows.

In spite of my shattered dreams, I came to Birmingham with the hope that the white religious leadership of this community would see the justice of our cause and, with deep moral concern, would serve as the channel through which our just grievances could reach the power structure. I had hoped that each of you would understand. But again I have been disappointed.

I have heard numerous southern religious leaders admonish their worshipers to comply with a desegregation decision because it is the law, but I have longed to hear white ministers declare: "Follow this decree because integration is morally right and because the Negro is your brother." In the midst of blatant injustices inflicted upon the Negro, I have watched white churchmen stand on the sideline and mouth pious irrelevancies and sanctimonious trivialities. In the midst of a mighty struggle to rid our nation of racial and economic injustice I have heard many ministers say: "Those are social issues, with which the gospel has no real concern." And I have watched many churches commit themselves to a completely otherworldly religion which makes a strange, un-Biblical distinction between body and soul, between the sacred and the secular.

I have traveled the length and breadth of Alabama, Mississippi, and all the other southern states. On sweltering summer days and crisp autumn mornings I have looked at the South's beautiful churches with their lofty spires pointing heavenward. I have beheld the impressive outlines of her massive religious-education buildings. Over and over I have found myself asking: "What kind of people worship here? Who is their God? Where were their voices when the lips of Governor Barnett dripped with words of interposition and nullification? Where were they when Governor Wallace* gave a clarion call for defiance and hatred? Where were their voices of support when bruised and weary Negro men and women decided to rise from the dark dungeons of complacency to the bright hills of creative protest?"

Yes, these questions are still in my mind. In deep disappointment I have wept over the laxity of the church. But be assured that my tears have been tears of love. There can be no deep disappointment where there is not deep love. Yes, I love the church. How could I do otherwise? I am in the rather unique position of being the son, the grandson, and the great-grandson of preachers. Yes, I see the church as the body of Christ. But, oh! How we have blemished and scarred that body through social neglect and through fear of being nonconformists.

There was a time when the church was very powerful — in the time   40
when the early Christians rejoiced at being deemed worthy to suffer for what they believed. In those days the church was not merely a thermometer that recorded the ideas and principles of popular opinion; it was a thermostat

---

Governor Barnett . . . Governor Wallace: Ross Barnett and George Wallace were governors of Mississippi and Alabama, respectively, who resisted the racial integration of schools in their states

that transformed the mores of society. Whenever the early Christians entered a town, the people in power became disturbed and immediately sought to convict the Christians for being "disturbers of the peace" and "outside agitators." But the Christians pressed on, in the conviction that they were "a colony of heaven," called to obey God rather than man. Small in number, they were big in commitment. They were too God-intoxicated to be "astronomically intimidated." By their effort and example they brought an end to such ancient evils as infanticide and gladiatorial contests.

Things are different now. So often the contemporary church is a weak, ineffectual voice with an uncertain sound. So often it is an archdefender of the status quo. Far from being disturbed by the presence of the church, the power structure of the average community is consoled by the church's silent — and often even vocal — sanction of things as they are.

But the judgment of God is upon the church as never before. If today's church does not recapture the sacrificial spirit of the early church, it will lose its authenticity, forfeit the loyalty of millions, and be dismissed as an irrelevant social club with no meaning for the twentieth century. Every day I meet young people whose disappointment with the church has turned into outright disgust.

Perhaps I have once again been too optimistic. Is organized religion too inextricably bound to the status quo to save our nation and the world? Perhaps I must turn my faith to the inner spiritual church, the church within the church, as the true *ekklesia** and the hope of the world. But again I am thankful to God that some noble souls from the ranks of organized religion have broken loose from the paralyzing chains of conformity and joined us as active partners in the struggle for freedom. They have left their secure congregations and walked the streets of Albany, Georgia, with us. They have gone down the highways of the South on tortuous rides for freedom. Yes, they have gone to jail with us. Some have been dismissed from their churches, have lost the support of their bishops and fellow ministers. But they have acted in the faith that right defeated is stronger than evil triumphant. Their witness has been the spiritual salt that has preserved the true meaning of the gospel in these troubled times. They have carved a tunnel of hope through the dark mountain of disappointment.

I hope the church as a whole will meet the challenge of this decisive hour. But even if the church does not come to the aid of justice, I have no despair about the future. I have no fear about the outcome of our struggle in Birmingham, even if our motives are at present misunderstood. We will reach the goal of freedom in Birmingham and all over the nation, because the goal of America is freedom. Abused and scorned though we may be, our destiny is tied up with America's destiny. Before the pilgrims landed at Plymouth, we were here. Before the pen of Jefferson etched the majestic words of the Declaration

---

ekklesia: Greek word for the early Christian church

of Independence across the pages of history, we were here. For more than two centuries our forebears labored in this country without wages; they made cotton king; they built the homes of their masters while suffering gross injustice and shameful humiliation — and yet out of a bottomless vitality they continued to thrive and develop. If the inexpressible cruelties of slavery could not stop us, the opposition we now face will surely fail. We will win our freedom because the sacred heritage of our nation and the eternal will of God are embodied in our echoing demands.

Before closing I feel impelled to mention one other point in your state- 45
ment that has troubled me profoundly. You warmly commended the Birmingham police force for keeping "order" and "preventing violence." I doubt that you would have so warmly commended the police force if you had seen its dogs sinking their teeth into unarmed, nonviolent Negroes. I doubt that you would so quickly commend the policemen if you were to observe their ugly and inhumane treatment of Negroes here in the city jail; if you were to watch them push and curse old Negro women and young Negro girls; if you were to see them slap and kick old Negro men and young boys; if you were to observe them, as they did on two occasions, refuse to give us food because we wanted to sing our grace together. I cannot join you in your praise of the Birmingham police department.

It is true that the police have exercised a degree of discipline in handling the demonstrators. In this sense they have conducted themselves rather "nonviolently" in public. But for what purpose? To preserve the evil system of segregation. Over the past few years I have consistently preached that nonviolence demands that the means we use must be as pure as the ends we seek. I have tried to make clear that it is wrong to use immoral means to attain moral ends. But now I must affirm that it is just as wrong, or perhaps even more so, to use moral means to preserve immoral ends. Perhaps Mr. Connor and his policemen have been rather nonviolent in public, as was Chief Pritchett in Albany, Georgia, but they have used the moral means of nonviolence to maintain the immoral end of racial injustice. As T. S. Eliot has said, "The last temptation is the greatest treason: To do the right deed for the wrong reason."

I wish you had commended the Negro sit-inners and demonstrators of Birmingham for their sublime courage, their willingness to suffer, and their amazing discipline in the midst of great provocation. One day the South will recognize its real heroes. They will be the James Merediths,* with the noble sense of purpose that enables them to face jeering and hostile mobs, and with the agonizing loneliness that characterizes the life of the pioneer. They will be old, oppressed, battered Negro women, symbolized in a seventy-two-year-old

---

James Merediths: The U.S. Supreme Court ordered the admission of James Meredith, a black student, to the segregated University of Mississippi in 1962 despite resistance from state officials

woman in Montgomery, Alabama, who rose up with a sense of dignity and with her people decided not to ride segregated buses, and who responded with ungrammatical profundity to one who inquired about her weariness: "My feets is tired, but my soul is at rest." They will be the young high school and college students, the young ministers of the gospel and a host of their elders, courageously and nonviolently sitting in at lunch counters and willingly going to jail for conscience' sake. One day the South will know that when these disinherited children of God sat down at lunch counters, they were in reality standing up for what is best in the American dream and for the most sacred values in our Judaeo-Christian heritage, thereby bringing our nation back to those great wells of democracy which were dug deep by the founding fathers in their formulation of the Constitution and the Declaration of Independence.

Never before have I written so long a letter. I'm afraid it is much too long to take your precious time. I can assure you that it would have been much shorter if I had been writing from a comfortable desk, but what else can one do when he is alone in a narrow jail cell, other than write long letters, think long thoughts, and pray long prayers?

If I have said anything in this letter that overstates the truth and indicates an unreasonable impatience, I beg you to forgive me. If I have said anything that understates the truth and indicates my having a patience that allows me to settle for anything less than brotherhood, I beg God to forgive me.

I hope this letter finds you strong in the faith. I also hope that circumstances will soon make it possible for me to meet each of you, not as an integrationist or a civil-rights leader but as a fellow clergyman and a Christian brother. Let us all hope that the dark clouds of racial prejudice will soon pass away and the deep fog of misunderstanding will be lifted from our fear-drenched communities, and in some not too distant tomorrow the radiant stars of love and brotherhood will shine over our great nation with all their scintillating beauty.

Yours for the cause of Peace and Brotherhood,
MARTIN LUTHER KING JR.

QUESTIONING THE TEXT

1. King's letter is written to the white clergy of Birmingham, including those of Protestant, Catholic, and Jewish faiths. Look carefully at the sources King cites in his letter, and note which ones seem most likely to appeal to members of these religious groups.

2. In a number of places in his "Letter," King mentions or alludes to Socrates. Review an account of Socrates' life. What makes him a particularly appropriate and powerful example for King to use? Can you think of any risks King takes in relying on Socrates as a key figure in his argument?

3. Working with one or two classmates, identify all of the evidence King offers in his "Letter" to prove that racial injustice is immoral.

4. Is this piece of writing really a letter? What qualities and elements of it allow you to answer this question — one way or the other?

MAKING CONNECTIONS

5. King positions himself between the "'do-nothingism' of the complacent" and the "hatred and despair of the black nationalist" (paragraph 28). In "An Animal's Place," Michael Pollan (p. 204) similarly presents two stances toward nonhuman animals: "You [eat them and] look away — or you stop eating animals" (paragraph 32). He then asks, "And if you don't want to do either?" and proceeds to explore an answer. Each writer thus describes the parameters of current debate on his issue. How does this strategy influence your response to each writer and to his argument? In what kinds of rhetorical situations does this approach seem likely to work well?

6. In "The Rules about the Rules" (p. 178), Stephen L. Carter says that "[i]ntegrity . . . requires three steps: (1) *discerning* what is right and what is wrong; (2) *acting* on what you have discerned, even at personal cost; and (3) *saying openly* that you are acting on your understanding of right from wrong" (paragraph 15). Would King likely agree with Carter's description of these steps? What evidence of these three steps do you find in King's "Letter"?

JOINING THE CONVERSATION

7. Have you ever written a long letter to someone, a letter that was important to you and in which you tried hard to make a convincing case for something you believed or felt? If so, what were the features of that letter? How successful and effective was it? Take time to brainstorm about a letter you might write today. To whom would you address it? What would you argue for — or against? Where would you find support and evidence? What would be the most difficult part of writing the letter?

8. King uses a great many pronouns in his "Letter," including *you* to refer to the clergymen (there were no women clergy in Birmingham at the time) and *we* to refer to the nonviolent protesters in particular and the larger African American community in general. Working with one or two classmates, look carefully at how King uses pronouns in the reading. Then write a brief report to your class describing King's use of pronouns and explaining what effect(s) they have on readers today — and what effect(s) they may have been intended to have on the clergymen to whom the letter was addressed.

STEPHEN L. CARTER
The Rules about the Rules

*I*T IS STILL TOO EARLY *to know the long-term consequences of recent political and ethical scandals — political figures from recent Democratic and Republican administrations accused of lying to the public, taking bribes, and misbehaving with interns and pages; CEOs of major corporations convicted of misleading or bilking stockholders; writers for* the New York Times *and* WashingtonPost.com *fired for plagiarism; athletes accused of stretching or flouting the rules against performance-enhancing drugs. If little else, we have learned that Shakespeare's clown Dogberry (borrowing from scripture) has spoken truthfully: "[t]hey that touch pitch will be defiled."*

Stephen L. Carter (b. 1954), William Cromwell Nelson Professor of Law at Yale, probably isn't surprised by any of these messes, since he has for some time been detecting a wavering in the nation's ethical compass. His response, a book-length meditation, Integrity *(1996), asks its readers to consider the slippage in ethics evident everywhere in our culture — in our legal system, media, sports, businesses, and marriages. He even devotes a section to academic letters of recommendation, arguing that teachers have debased this essential part of job and professional school applications because they are unwilling to deal with students honestly.*

Integrity *is not the first book in which Carter, playing the role of public intellectual, has helped to set the agenda for a serious national discussion of issues. Earlier,* Reflections of an Affirmative Action Baby *(1991) contributed to the continuing and uneasy debate over racial preferences in academia and the workplace. Even more influential was the award-winning* The Culture of Disbelief *(1993), which, contrary to much opinion, insists that people of faith have a right to exert their influence in politics. More recently, Carter has written* Civility *(1998), a call for a more decent and polite society, and two novels,* The Emperor of Ocean Park *(2002) and* New England White *(2007).*

The selection that follows, "The Rules about the Rules," is the opening chapter of Integrity. *Omitted from the selection is a brief concluding section that summarizes the subsequent chapters of the book.* —J.R.

My first lesson in integrity came the hard way. It was 1960 or thereabouts and I was a first-grader at P.S. 129 in Harlem. The teacher had us all sitting in a circle, playing a game in which each child would take a turn donning a blindfold and then trying to identify objects by touch alone as she handed them to us. If you guessed right, you stayed in until the next round. If you guessed wrong, you were out. I survived almost to the end, amazing the entire class with my abilities. Then, to my dismay, the teacher realized what I had known, and relied upon, from the start: my blindfold was tied imperfectly and a sliver

178

of bright reality leaked in from outside. By holding the unknown object in my lap instead of out in front of me, as most of the other children did, I could see at least a corner or a side and sometimes more — but always enough to figure out what it was. So my remarkable success was due only to my ability to break the rules.

Fortunately for my own moral development, I was caught. And as a result of being caught, I suffered, in front of my classmates, a humiliating reminder of right and wrong: I had cheated at the game. Cheating was wrong. It was that simple.

I do not remember many of the details of the "public" lecture that I received from my teacher. I do remember that I was made to feel terribly ashamed; and it is good that I was made to feel that way, for I had something to be ashamed of. The moral opprobrium that accompanied that shame was sufficiently intense that it has stayed with me ever since, which is exactly how shame is supposed to work. And as I grew older, whenever I was even tempted to cheat — at a game, on homework — I would remember my teacher's stern face and the humiliation of sitting before my classmates, revealed to the world as a cheater.

That was then, this is now. Browsing recently in my local bookstore, I came across a book that boldly proclaimed, on its cover, that it contained instructions on how to *cheat* — the very word occurred in the title — at a variety of video games. My instincts tell me that this cleverly chosen title is helping the book to sell very well. For it captures precisely what is wrong with America today: we care far more about winning than about playing by the rules.

Consider just a handful of examples, drawn from headlines of the mid-1990s: the winner of the Miss Virginia pageant is stripped of her title after officials determine that her educational credentials are false; a television network is forced to apologize for using explosives to add a bit of verisimilitude to a tape purporting to show that a particular truck is unsafe; and the authors of a popular book on management are accused of using bulk purchases at key stores to manipulate the *New York Times* best-seller list. Go back a few more years and we can add in everything from a slew of Wall Street titans imprisoned for violating a bewildering variety of laws in their frantic effort to get ahead, to the women's Boston Marathon winner branded a cheater for spending part of the race on the subway. But cheating is evidently no big deal: some 70 percent of college students admit to having done it at least once.[1]

That, in a nutshell, is America's integrity dilemma: we are all full of fine talk about how desperately our society needs it, but, when push comes to shove, we would just as soon be on the winning side. A couple of years ago as I sat

5

---

[1]On cheating by college students, see Karen Thomas, "Rise in Cheating Called Response to Fall in Values," *USA Today*, August 2, 1995, p. 1A. I do not know whether the irony of the headline was intentional.

watching a televised football game with my children, trying to explain to them what was going on, I was struck by an event I had often noticed but on which I had never reflected. A player who failed to catch a ball thrown his way hit the ground, rolled over, and then jumped up, celebrating as though he had caught the pass after all. The referee was standing in a position that did not give him a good view of what had happened, was fooled by the player's pretense, and so moved the ball down the field. The player rushed back to the huddle so that his team could run another play before the officials had a chance to review the tape. (Until 1992, National Football League officials could watch a television replay and change their call, as long as the next play had not been run.) But viewers at home did have the benefit of the replay, and we saw what the referee missed: the ball lying on the ground instead of snug in the receiver's hands. The only comment from the broadcasters: "What a heads-up play!" Meaning: "Wow, what a great liar this kid is! Well done!"

Let's be very clear: that is exactly what they meant. The player set out to mislead the referee and succeeded; he helped his team to obtain an advantage in the game that it had not earned. It could not have been accidental. He knew he did not catch the ball. By jumping up and celebrating, he was trying to convey a false impression. He was trying to convince the officials that he had caught the ball. And the officials believed him. So, in any ordinary understanding of the word, he lied. And that, too, is what happens to integrity in American life: if we happen to do something wrong, we would just as soon have nobody point it out.

Now, suppose that the player had instead gone to the referee and said, "I'm sorry, sir, but I did not make the catch. Your call is wrong." Probably his coach and teammates and most of his team's fans would have been furious: he would not have been a good team player. The good team player lies to the referee, and does so in a manner that is at once blatant (because millions of viewers see it) and virtually impossible for the referee to detect. Having pulled off this trickery, the player is congratulated: he is told that he has made a heads-up play. Thus, the ethic of the game turns out to be an ethic that rewards cheating. (But I still love football.) Perhaps I should have been shocked. Yet, thinking through the implications of our celebration of a national sport that rewards cheating, I could not help but recognize that we as a nation too often lack integrity, which might be described, in a loose and colloquial way, as the courage of one's convictions. And although I do not want to claim any great burst of inspiration, it was at about that time that I decided to write this book.

TOWARD A DEFINITION

We, the People of the United States, who a little over two hundred years ago ordained and established the Constitution, have a serious problem: too many of us nowadays neither mean what we say nor say what we mean. Moreover, we hardly expect anybody else to mean what they say either.

A couple of years ago I began a university commencement address by telling the audience that I was going to talk about integrity. The crowd broke into applause. Applause! Just because they had heard the word *integrity* — that's how starved for it they were. They had no idea how I was using the word, or what I was going to say about it, or, indeed, whether I was for it or against it. But they knew they liked the idea of simply talking about it. This celebration of integrity is intriguing: we seem to carry on a passionate love affair with a word that we scarcely pause to define.

The Supreme Court likes to use such phrases as the "Constitution's structural integrity" when it strikes down actions that violate the separation of powers in the federal government.[2] Critics demand a similar form of integrity when they argue that our age has seen the corruption of language or of particular religious traditions or of the moral sense generally. Indeed, when parents demand a form of education that will help their children grow into people of integrity, the cry carries a neo-romantic image of their children becoming adults who will remain uncorrupted by the forces (whatever they are) that seem to rob so many grown-ups of . . . well, of integrity.

Very well, let us consider this word *integrity*. Integrity is like the weather: everybody talks about it but nobody knows what to do about it. Integrity is that stuff we always say we want more of. Such leadership gurus as Warren Bennis insist that it is of first importance. We want our elected representatives to have it, and political challengers always insist that their opponents lack it. We want it in our spouses, our children, our friends. We want it in our schools and our houses of worship. And in our corporations and the products they manufacture: early in 1995, one automobile company widely advertised a new car as "the first concept car with integrity." And we want it in the federal government, too, where officials all too frequently find themselves under investigation by special prosecutors. So perhaps we should say that integrity is like *good* weather, because everybody is in favor of it.

Scarcely a politician kicks off a campaign without promising to bring it to government; a few years later, more often than is healthy for our democracy, the politician slinks cravenly from office, having been lambasted by the press for lacking that self-same integrity; and then the press, in turn, is skewered for holding public figures to a measure of integrity that its own reporters, editors, producers, and, most particularly, owners could not possibly meet. And for refusing to turn that critical eye inward, the press is mocked for — what else? — a lack of integrity.

Everybody agrees that the nation needs more of it. Some say we need to return to the good old days when we had a lot more of it. Others say we as a nation have never really had enough of it. And hardly any of us stop to explain exactly what we mean by it — or how we know it is even a good thing — or

---

[2] See, for example, *Ryder v. United States*, 115 S. Ct. 2031 (1995)

why everybody needs to have the same amount of it. Indeed, the only trouble with integrity is that everybody who uses the word seems to mean something slightly different. So in a book about integrity, the place to start is surely with a definition.

When I refer to integrity, I have something very simple and very specific   15
in mind. Integrity, as I will use the term, requires three steps: (1) *discerning* what is right and what is wrong; (2) *acting* on what you have discerned, even at per-sonal cost; and (3) *saying openly* that you are acting on your understanding of right from wrong.[3] The first criterion captures the idea of integrity as requiring a degree of moral reflectiveness. The second brings in the ideal of an integral person as steadfast, which includes the sense of keeping commitments. The third reminds us that a person of integrity is unashamed of doing the right. . . . I hope that even readers who quarrel with my selection of the term *integrity* to refer to the form of commitment that I describe will come away from the book under-standing why the concept itself, whatever it may be called, is a vital one.

The word *integrity* comes from the same Latin root as *integer* and histori-cally has been understood to carry much the same sense, the sense of *wholeness*: a person of integrity, like a whole number, is a whole person, a person somehow undivided. The word conveys not so much a single-mindedness as a complete-ness; not the frenzy of a fanatic who wants to remake all the world in a single mold but the serenity of a person who is confident in the knowledge that he or she is living rightly. The person of integrity need not be a Gandhi but also can-not be a person who blows up buildings to make a point. A person of integrity lurks somewhere inside each of us: a person we feel we can trust to do right, to play by the rules, to keep commitments. Perhaps it is because we all sense the capacity for integrity within ourselves that we are able to notice and admire it even in people with whom, on many issues, we sharply disagree.

Indeed, one reason to focus on integrity as perhaps the first among the virtues that make for good character is that it is in some sense prior to everything else: the rest of what we think matters very little if we lack essential integrity, the courage of our convictions, the willingness to act and speak in behalf of what we know to be right. In an era when the American people are crying out for open discussion of morality — of right and wrong — the ideal of integrity seems a good place to begin. No matter what our politics, no matter what causes we may support, would anybody really want to be led or followed or assisted by people who *lack* integrity? People whose words we could not trust, whose motives we didn't respect, who might at any moment toss aside everything we thought we had in common and march off in some other direction?

The answer, of course, is no: we would not want leaders of that kind, even though we too often get them. The question is not only what integrity is and

---

[3]In this I am influenced to some extent by the fine discussion of integrity in Martin Benjamin's book *Splitting the Difference: Compromise and Integrity in Ethics and Politics* (Lawrence: University Press of Kansas, 1990).

why it is valuable, but how we move our institutions, and our very lives, closer to exemplifying it. In raising this question, I do not put myself forward as an exemplar of integrity, but merely as one who in daily life goes through many of the struggles that I will describe in these pages. The reader will quickly discover that I frequently use the word *we* in my analysis. The reason is that I see the journey toward a greater understanding of the role of integrity in our public and private lives as one that the reader and I are making together.

INTEGRITY AND RELIGION

The concept we are calling *integrity* has had little attention from philosophers, but has long been a central concern to the religions. Integrity, after all, is a kind of wholeness, and most religions teach that God calls us to an undivided life in accordance with divine command. In Islam, this notion is captured in the understanding that all rules, legal or moral, are guided by the *sharia*, the divine path that God directs humans to walk. In Judaism, study of the Torah and Talmud reveals the rules under which God's people are expected to live. And Christians are called by the Gospel to be "pure in heart" (Matt. 5:8), which implies an undividedness in following God's rules.

Indeed, although its antecedents may be traced to Aristotle, the basic concept of integrity was introduced to the Western tradition through the struggle of Christianity to find a guide for the well-lived life. The wholeness that the Christian tradition identified as central to life with integrity was a wholeness in obedience to God, so that the well-lived life was a life that followed God's rules. Thomas Aquinas put it this way: "[T]he virtue of obedience is more praiseworthy than other moral virtues, seeing that by obedience a person gives up his own will for God's sake, and by other moral virtues something less."[4] John Wesley, in a famous sermon, was more explicit: "[T]he nature of the covenant of grace gives you no ground, no encouragement at all, to set aside any instance or degree of obedience."[5]

But obedience to what? Traditional religions teach that integrity is found in obedience to God. Moses Maimonides put the point most simply: "Everything that you do, do for the sake of God."[6] And a Professor W. S. Tyler, preaching a sermon at Amherst College in 1857, pointed the way to generalizing the concept beyond the religious sphere: "[I]ntegrity implies implicit

20

---

[4]St. Thomas Aquinas, *The Summa Theologica*, tr. Father L. Shapcote, revised by Daniel L. Sullivan, 2d ed. (Chicago: Encyclopedia Britannica, 1990), 2a2ae, 104, 3.

[5]John Wesley, "On the Law Established through Faith," in *The Works of the Rev. John Wesley*, vol. 8 (London: Thomas Cordeaux, 1811), p. 144.

[6]Quoted in Abraham Joshua Heschel, *Maimonides: A Biography*, tr. Joachim Neugroschel (New York: Image Books, 1991), p. 203. The German edition was published in 1935.

obedience to the dictates of conscience — in other words, a heart and life habitually controlled by a sense of duty."[7]

But this is not a book about religion as such, still less about Christian doctrine. This book, rather, tries to honor our own national understanding of the word, in a tradition that is somewhat more secular but is, in its way, equally profound. My hope is to use traditional religious understandings to illuminate a concept that now has a distinct and honored place in the American ethical narrative, but to allow the narrative to tell its own story. So, although I have quoted Aquinas and will quote him again, this book is not about how Aquinas thought of integrity; it is about how we Americans think, or have thought, or should think, of it. Our demand for it illustrates that we think about it often, and a little desperately; my hope in this book is to demonstrate the value of the concept — to show *why* we think of the word with such affection — and then to examine the interplay of the integrity concept with a range of American problems and institutions.

In choosing integrity as my subject, I have tried to select an element of good character that is independent of the particular political views that one might hold; indeed, I would suspect that all of us, whatever our politics, would value, and perhaps demand, a degree of integrity in our associates, our government, and even our friends and families. So it is best that we try to reach some agreement on just what it is that we are valuing and demanding.

A good citizen, a person of integrity, I will refer to as one who leads an *integral life*. An integral life in turn requires all three steps of the definition, to which I will occasionally refer as the rules or criteria of integrity. Once this definition is understood, there are implications, from politics to marriage, from the way bosses write letters of recommendation to the way newspaper editors choose which stories to run. . . . I am, by training and persuasion, a lawyer, and so the reader should not be surprised to find many legal examples. . . ; indeed, there is even a bit of constitutional analysis. But if this is not a book about Christianity, still less is it a book about law, and certainly it is not a work of philosophy. It is, rather, a book about Americans and our society, about what we are, what we say we aspire to be, and how to bring the two closer to balance.

THE THREE STEPS

Integrity, I should explain before proceeding, is not the same as honesty, although honesty obviously is a desirable element of good character as well. From our definition, it is clear that one cannot have integrity without also displaying a measure of honesty. But one can be honest without being integral, for integrity, as I define it, demands a difficult process of discerning one's deepest understanding

25

---

[7]W. S. Tyler, *Integrity the Safeguard of Public and Private Life* (Springfield: Samuel Bowles, 1857), p. 6.

of right and wrong, and then further requires action consistent with what one has learned. It is possible to be honest without ever taking a hard look inside one's soul, to say nothing of taking any action based on what one finds. For example, a woman who believes abortion is murder may state honestly that this is what she thinks, but she does not fulfill the integrity criteria unless she also works to change abortion law. A man who believes in our national obligation to aid the homeless cannot claim to be fulfilling the criteria unless he works to obtain the aid he believes is deserved — and perhaps provides some assistance personally.

All too many of us fall down on step 1: we do not take the time to discern right from wrong. Indeed, I suspect that few of us really know just what we believe — what we value — and, often, we do not really want to know. Discernment is hard work; it takes time and emotional energy. And it is so much easier to follow the crowd. We too often look the other way when we see wrongdoing around us, quite famously in the widely unwitnessed yet very unprivate murder of Kitty Genovese* thirty years ago. We refuse to think in terms of right and wrong when we elect or reject political candidates based on what they will do for our own pocketbooks. On the campuses, too many students and not a few professors find it easier to go along with the latest trends than to risk the opprobrium of others by registering an objection. Indeed, social psychologists say that this all too human phenomenon of refusing to think independently is what leads to mob violence. But a public-spirited citizen must do a bit of soul-searching — must decide what he or she most truly and deeply believes to be right and good — before it is possible to live with integrity.

The second step is also a tough one. It is far easier to know what one believes — to know, in effect, right from wrong — than it is to do something about it. For example, one may believe that the homeless deserve charity, but never dispense it; or one may think that they are bums who should not be given a dime, yet always dig into one's pockets when confronted. We Americans have a remarkable capacity to say one thing and do another, not always out of true hypocrisy but often out of a lack of self-assurance. We see this in our politics, where nobody wants to be the one to say that the retirees who receive Social Security payments are, for the most part, receiving not a return on an investment but direct subventions from the payments being made by today's workers toward their own retirements — which, if done by a private investment firm, would be an illegal pyramid scheme. The late legal scholar Robert Cover illustrated the point quite powerfully when he examined the puzzling question of how avowedly antislavery judges in the early nineteenth century could hand down obviously proslavery decisions.[8] Equally puzzling to many political

---

Kitty Genovese: In March 1964, Genovese was stabbed to death in a New York City neighborhood while thirty-eight residents looked on, failing to come to her assistance.

[8]See Robert Cover, *Justice Accused: Antislavery and the Judicial Process* (New Haven, CT: Yale University Press, 1975).

activists is their inability to recruit support from people they know to be committed to their causes, who frequently explain that they simply do not want to get involved.

But in order to live with integrity, it is sometimes necessary to take that difficult step — to get involved — to fight openly for what one believes to be true and right and good, even when there is risk to oneself. I would not go so far as to insist that morally committed citizens living integral lives must fight their way through life, strident activists in behalf of all their beliefs; but I worry deeply about the number of us who seem happy to drift through life, activists in behalf of none of our beliefs.

This leads to the third step, which seems deceptively simple, but is often the hardest of all: the person truly living an integral life must be willing to say that he or she is acting consistently with what he or she has decided is right. When the statements of a person of integrity are the result of discernment, of hard thought, we treat them as reliable, even when they are indicators of the future — "You've got the job" or "Till death do us part." But forthrightness also matters because people of integrity are willing to tell us *why* they are doing what they are doing. So it does not promote integrity for one to cheat on taxes out of greed but to claim to be doing it as a protest; indeed, it does not promote integrity to do it as a protest unless one says openly (including to the Internal Revenue Service) that that is what one is doing. It does not promote integrity to ignore or cover up wrongdoing by a coworker or family member. And it does not promote integrity to claim to be doing the will of God when one is actually doing what one's political agenda demands.

This third step — saying publicly that we are doing what we think is right, even when others disagree — is made particularly difficult by our national desire to conform. Most of us want to fit in, to be accepted, and admitting to (or proudly proclaiming) an unpopular belief is rarely the way to gain acceptance. But if moral dissenters are unwilling to follow the example of the civil rights movement and make a proud public show of their convictions, we as a nation will never have the opportunity to be inspired by their integrity to rethink our own ideas.

This last point bears emphasis. Integrity does not always require following the rules. Sometimes — as in the civil rights movement — integrity requires *breaking* the rules. But it also requires that one be open and public about both the fact of one's dissent and the reasons for it. . . . A person who lives an integral life may sometimes reach moral conclusions that differ from those of the majority; displaying those conclusions publicly is a crucial aspect of the wholeness in which integrity consists.

Instead of a nation of public dissenters, we have become a nation experienced in misdirection — in beguiling the audience into looking in one direction while we are busy somewhere else. The media culture unfortunately rewards this, not only because a misleading sound bite is more attractive (that is, marketable) than a principled argument, but also because the media seem far more interested in tracking down hypocrisy than in reporting episodes of integrity.

Indeed, to bring the matter full circle, the media will get a healthy share of blame in this book: blame for oversimplification and for interfering with, rather than enabling, the search for right and wrong that each of us must undertake in order to live a life of integrity. But only a share of the blame. If indeed we allow the distractions of living to prevent the discernment of right and wrong so necessary to living with integrity, we should blame neither the media nor the schools nor the government nor our employers, but only ourselves. As I will explain, we as a society can and should do far more to train our children — and ourselves! — in the difficult work of sorting right from wrong and then doing the right and despising the wrong. We can try to blame other forces that interfere; but in the end, when the children grow up, they must make right choices for themselves.

CORRUPTION

If integrity has an opposite, perhaps it is corruption — the getting away with things we know to be wrong. We say that we are a nation that demands integrity, but are we really? We call ourselves a nation of laws, but millions of us cheat on our taxes. We seem not to believe in the integrity of our commitments, with half of marriages ending in divorce. We say we want integrity in our politics, and our politicians promise it endlessly. (Try searching the Nexis database for uses of the word *integrity* by politicians and commentators, and you will be inundated.) But we reward innuendo and smear and barefaced lies with our votes.

Corruption is corrosive. We believe we can do it just a little, but I wonder whether we can. Nearly all of us break small laws — I do it all the time — laws governing everything from the speed at which we may drive to when and how we may cross the street. Few of us will stop on the highway to retrieve the paper bag that the wind whips out the window of our moving car; we may not have thrown it out intentionally, but it still came from our car and it's still littering. These I shall refer to as acts of unintegrity, not an attractive neologism, but one way of avoiding the repeated use of the word *corruption*, which might be misleading. And one who engages in repeated acts of unintegrity may be said to be living an unintegral life.

Some of these acts of unintegrity can be cured by simple calls upon the virtue of consistency. It is both amusing and sad to hear liberals who have fought against the portrayal of vicious racial stereotypes in the media now saying that portrayals of sex and family life in the media affect nobody's behavior; it is just as amusing, and just as sad, to see conservatives bash the President of the United States for criticizing hateful speech on the nation's airwaves and then turn around and bash Hollywood for speech the right happens to hate. But inconsistency is the easiest example of unintegrity to spot. There are harder examples — as we shall see, there may even be some cases in which a lack of integrity is unavoidable — and I shall deal with many of them. . . .

When I began working on this book, I shared the story about the cheating football player with a few of my colleagues over lunch in the wood-paneled faculty dining room at the Yale Law School. Like me, they are lawyers, so none could be too outraged: our task in life, after all, is sometimes to defend the indefensible. They offered a bewildering array of fascinating and sophisticated arguments on why the receiver who pretended to catch the ball was doing nothing wrong. One in particular stuck in my mind. "You don't know if he was breaking the rules," one of the best and brightest of my colleagues explained, "until you know what the rules are about following the rules."

On reflection, I think my colleague was exactly right. And that, maybe better than anything else, sums up what this book is about. What are our rules about when we follow the rules? What are our rules about when we break them? Until we can answer those two questions, we will not know how much integrity we really want in our public and private lives, to say nothing of how to get it. . . .

QUESTIONING THE TEXT

1. Carter opens "The Rules about the Rules" with an anecdote from his own life that relates to the principle of integrity. In what ways does this narrative set you up for the discussion that follows? Does it make you think about the author? Does it lead you to recall times when you have acted dishonestly yourself? What does it do to make the prospect of an entire book on the subject of integrity less daunting?

2. Carter observes that "integrity is like *good* weather, because everybody is in favor of it" (paragraph 12). For the next several days, make a record of all the times you encounter the term *integrity* and the contexts in which it appears. Then compare your findings with those of your classmates. From your informal research, what conclusions, if any, can you draw about current attitudes toward integrity? When and where does the term occur most often — or has *integrity* become a word rarely spoken and written now?

MAKING CONNECTIONS

3. In Mark Clayton's article on campus plagiarism, "A Whole Lot of Cheatin' Going On" (p. 198), one student playing devil's advocate asserts that "Cheating *is* an answer. . . . It might not be a good answer, but none the less it is an answer" (paragraph 2). Can you imagine an act of

scholastic dishonesty that meets Carter's three conditions for integrity (paragraph 15)? In a group, explore this possibility.

4. Use Carter's definition of integrity to assess the actions of both Jessica Cohen and Michelle and David, the couple seeking the egg donor in "Grade A: The Market for a Yale Woman's Eggs" (p. 190). Is Carter's definition of integrity a useful measure for the quality of integrity in this situation? Why or why not?

JOINING THE CONVERSATION

5. Carter defines *integrity* (in paragraphs 25–32) by enumerating its three necessary characteristics. Try to define another moral abstraction (such as *loyalty, courage, modesty,* or *civility*) in approximately the same way, by first enumerating the steps or criteria that identify the term and then providing examples of the concept as you have defined it.

6. Most schools have documents defining *plagiarism, collusion, cheating,* and other acts of academic dishonesty. Review your institution's policies on scholastic integrity or its honor code — if it has one. Then discuss these policies with your classmates, either in face-to-face conversation or in an online forum or listserv. After the discussion, write a short essay about the integrity of academic work. Is cheating a major problem in your classes? Are there ever good reasons to cheat? Can plagiarism or collusion be defended or eliminated? Why, or why not?

7. Write a brief portrait of someone you know who might fairly be described as "a person of integrity." Use your portrait as an indirect way of defining or exploring the concept of integrity.

JESSICA COHEN
Grade A: The Market for a Yale Woman's Eggs

*W*HEN I GOT MY DECEMBER 2002 COPY *of the* Atlantic Monthly, *the title of this essay captured my attention. As a college teacher, I gravitate toward stories about higher education, though I can never remember reading one about marketing college women's eggs. As I read, I identified with the author: how utterly odd to be so actively recruited — almost wooed — and then rejected as not good enough for the apparently wealthy couple intent on buying an egg from just the right (meaning perfect) donor!*

Cohen is a 2003 graduate of Yale, where she majored in history. While at Yale she cofounded the all-female Sphincter Troupe, a group of women comedians who got together when they decided the comedy scene at Yale was a very restricted one. The essay that follows was first published in slightly different form in the Fall 2001 issue of a student publication, the New Journal; *it later won the* Atlantic Monthly's *student essay contest.*

Cohen's ambivalent feelings about the business of marketing children eventually led her to decide that "this process was something I didn't want to be a part of," even though the idea of receiving $25,000 for an egg was very attractive. Had you been in Cohen's position, what would you have decided — and why? —A.L.

Early in the spring of last year a classified ad ran for two weeks in the *Yale Daily News*: "EGG DONOR NEEDED." The couple that placed the ad was picky, and for that reason was offering $25,000 for an egg from the right donor.

As a child I had a book called *Where Did I Come From?* It offered a full biological explanation, in cartoons, to answer those awkward questions that curious tots ask. But the book is now out of date. Replacing it is, for example, *Mommy, Did I Grow in Your Tummy?: Where Some Babies Come From*, which explains the myriad ways that children of the twenty-first century may have entered their families, including egg donation, surrogacy, *in vitro* fertilization, and adoption. When conception doesn't occur in the natural way, it becomes very complicated. Once all possible parties have been accounted for — egg donor, sperm donor, surrogate mother, paying couple — as many as five people can be involved in conceiving and carrying a child. No wonder a new book is necessary.

The would-be parents' decision to advertise in the *News* — and to offer a five-figure compensation — immediately suggested that they were in the market for an egg of a certain rarefied type. Beyond their desire for an Ivy League donor, they wanted a young woman over five feet five, of Jewish heritage, athletic, with a minimum combined SAT score of 1500, and attractive. I was curious — and I fit all the criteria except the SAT score. So I e-mailed Michelle and David (not their real names) and asked for more information about the process and how much the SAT minimum really meant to them. Then I waited for a reply.

190

*"I told my parents that if grades were so important they
should have paid for a smarter egg donor."*

Donating an egg is neither simple nor painless. Following an intensive screening and selection process the donor endures a few weeks of invasive medical procedures. First the donor and the woman who will carry the child must coordinate their menstrual cycles. Typically the donor and the recipient take birth-control pills, followed by shots of a synthetic hormone such as Lupron; the combination suppresses ovulation and puts their cycles in sync. After altering her cycle the donor must enhance her egg supply with fertility drugs in the same way an infertile woman does when trying to conceive. Shots of a fertility hormone are administered for seven to eleven days, to stimulate the production of an abnormally large number of egg-containing follicles. During this time the donor must have her blood tested every other day so that doctors can monitor her hormone levels, and she must come in for periodic ultrasounds. Thirty-six hours before retrieval day a shot of hCG, human chorionic gonadotropin, is administered to prepare the eggs for release, so that they will be ready for harvest.

The actual retrieval is done while the donor is under anesthesia. The tool   5
is a needle, and the product, on average, is ten to twenty eggs. Doctors take that many because "not all eggs will be good," according to Surrogate Mothers Online, an informational Web site designed and maintained by experienced egg donors and surrogate mothers. "Some will be immature and some overripe."

Lisa, one of the hosts on Surrogate Mothers Online and an experienced egg donor, described the process as a "rewarding" experience. When she explained that once in a while something can go wrong, I braced myself for the fine print. On very rare occasions, she wrote, hyperstimulation of the ovaries can occur, and the donor must be hospitalized until the ovaries return to normal. In even rarer cases the ovaries rupture, resulting in permanent infertility or possibly even death. "I must stress that this is very rare," Lisa assured prospective donors. "I had two very wonderful experiences. . . . The second [time] I stayed awake to help the doctor count how many eggs he retrieved."

David responded to my e-mail a few hours after I'd sent it. He told me nothing about himself, and only briefly alluded to the many questions I had asked about the egg-donation process. He spent the bulk of the e-mail describing a cartoon, and then requested photos of me. The cartoon was a scene with a "couple that is just getting married, he a nerd and she a beauty," he wrote. "They are kvelling about how wonderful their offspring will be with his brains and her looks." He went on to describe the punch line: the next panel showed a nerdy-looking baby thinking empty thoughts. The following paragraph was more direct. David let me know that he and his wife were flexible on most criteria but that Michelle was "a real Nazi" about "donor looks and donor health history."

This seemed to be a commentary of some sort on the couple's situation and how plans might go awry, but the message was impossible to pin down. I thanked him for the e-mail, asked where to send my pictures, and repeated my original questions about egg donation and their criteria.

In a subsequent e-mail David promised to return my photos, so I sent him dorm-room pictures, the kind that every college student has lying around. Now they assumed a new level of importance. I would soon learn what this anonymous couple, somewhere in the United States, thought about my genetic material as displayed in these photographs.

Infertility is not a modern problem, but it has created a modern industry. 10 Ten percent of American couples are infertile, and many seek treatment from the $2-billion-a-year infertility industry. The approximately 370 fertility clinics across the United States help prospective parents to sift through their options. I sympathize with women who cannot use their own eggs to have children. The discovery must be a sober awakening for those who have always dreamed of raising a family. When would-be parents face this problem, however, their options depend greatly on their income. All over the world most women who can't have children must simply accept the fact and adopt, or find other roles in society. But especially here in the United States wealth can enable such couples to have a child of their own and to determine how closely that child will resemble the one they might have had — or the one they dream of having.

The Web site of Egg Donation, Inc., a program based in California, contains a database listing approximately 300 potential donors. In order to access the list interested parties must call the company and request the user ID and the password for the month. Once I'd given the receptionist my name and address, she told me the password: "colorful." I hung up and entered the database. Potential parents can search for a variety of features, narrowing the pool as much as they like according to ethnic origin, religion of birth, state of residence, hair color, eye color, height, and weight. I typed in the physical and religious characteristics that Michelle and David were looking for and found four potential donors. None of them had a college degree.

The standard compensation for donating an egg to Egg Donation is $3,500 to $5,000, and additional funds are offered to donors who have advanced degrees or are of Asian, African American, or Jewish descent. Couples searching for an egg at Egg Donation can be picky, but not as picky as couples advertising in the *Yale Daily News*. Should couples be able to pay a premium on an open market for their idea of the perfect egg? Maybe a modern-day Social Darwinist would say yes. Modern success is measured largely in financial terms, so why shouldn't the most successful couples, eager to pay more, have access to the most expensive eggs? Of course, as David illustrated in his first e-mail, input does not always translate perfectly into output — the donor's desirable characteristics may never actually be manifested in the child.

If couples choose not to find their eggs through an agency, they must do so independently. An Internet search turned up a few sites like Surrogate Mothers Online, where would-be donors and parents can post classified ads. More than 500 classifieds were posted on the site: a whole marketplace, an eBay for genetic material.

"Hi! My name is Kimberly," one of the ads read. "I am 24 years old, 5′11″ with blonde hair and green eyes. I previously donated eggs and the couple was blessed with BIG twin boys! The doctor told me I have perky ovaries! . . . The doctor told me I had the most perfect eggs he had ever seen." The Web site provided links to photographs of Kimberly and an e-mail address. Would-be parents on the site offered "competitive" rates, generally from $5,000 to $10,000 for donors who fit their specifications.

About a week after I sent my pictures to David and Michelle, I received   15 a third e-mail: "Got the pictures. You look perfect. I can't say this with any authority. That is my wife's department." I thought back to the first e-mail, where he'd written, "She's been known to disregard a young woman based on cheekbones, hair, nose, you name it." He then shifted the focus. "My department is the SAT scores. Can you tell me more about your academic performance? What are you taking at Yale? What high school did you attend?"

The whole thing seemed like a joke. I dutifully answered his questions, explaining that I was from a no-name high school in the Midwest, I couldn't do math or science, and my academic performance was, well, average; I couldn't help feeling a bit disconcerted by his particular interest in my SAT score.

Michelle and David now had my educational data as well as my photos. They were examining my credentials and trying to imagine their child. If I was accepted, a harvest of my eggs would be fertilized by the semen of the author of the disturbing e-mails I had received. A few embryos would be implanted;

the remaining, if there were any, would be frozen; and then I would be out of the picture forever.

The modern embryo has been frozen, stolen, aborted, researched, and delivered weeks early, along with five or six instant siblings. The summer of 2001 was full of embryo news, and the first big story was President Bush's deliberation on stem-cell research. The embryos available for genetic research include those frozen by fertility clinics for later use by couples attempting *in vitro* fertilization.

Embryos took the spotlight again when Helen Beasley, a surrogate mother from Shrewsbury, England, decided to sue a San Francisco couple for parental rights to the twin fetuses she was carrying. The couple and Beasley had agreed that they would pay her $20,000 to carry one child created from a donated egg and the father's sperm. The agreement also called for selective reduction — the abortion of any additional embryos. Beasley claimed that there had been a verbal agreement that such reduction would occur by the twelfth week. The problem arose when Beasley, who had discovered she was carrying twins, was told to abort one, but the arrangements for the reduction weren't made until the thirteenth week. Fearing for her own health and objecting to the abortion of such a highly developed fetus, she refused. At that time she was suing for the right to put the babies up for adoption. She was also seeking the remainder of the financial compensation specified in the contract. The couple did not want the children, and yet had the rights to the genetic material; Beasley was simply a vessel. The case is only one of a multitude invited by modern fertility processes. On August 15, 2001, the *New York Times* reported that the New Jersey Supreme Court had upheld a woman's rights to the embryos that she and her ex-husband had created and frozen six years before. A strange case for child-custody lawyers.

Nearly ten years ago, at the University of California at Irvine's Center for Reproductive Health, doctors took the leftover frozen embryos from previous clients and gave them without consent to other couples and to research centers. Discovery of the scam resulted in more than thirty prosecutions: a group of children had biological parents who hadn't consented to their existence and active parents who had been given stolen goods. Who can say whether throwing the embryos away would have been any better?

Even if Michelle and David liked my data, I knew I'd have a long way to go before becoming an actual donor. The application on Egg Donation's Web site is twelve pages long — longer than Yale's entrance application. The first two pages cover the basics: appearance, name, address, age, and other mundane details. After that I was asked if I'd ever filed for bankruptcy or ever had counseling, if I drank, what my goals in life were, what two of my favorite books were, what my paternal grandfather's height and weight were, what hobbies I had, what kind of relationship I would want to have with the parents and

20

child, and so forth. A few fill-in-the-blanks were thrown in at the end: "I feel strongly about____. I am sorry I did not____. In ten years I want to be____." Not even my closest friends knew all these things about me. If Egg Donation, offering about a fifth what Michelle and David were offering, wanted all this information, what might Michelle and David want?

Michelle and David were certainly trying hard. On one classified-ad site I came across a request that was strangely familiar: "Loving family seeks exceptional egg donor with 1500 SAT, great looks, good family health history, Jewish heritage and athletic. Height 5′4″–5′9″, Age 18–29. We will pay EXTREMELY well and will take care of all expenses. Hope to hear from you." The e-mail address was David and Michelle's familiar AOL account. Theirs was the most demanding classified on the site, but also the only one that offered to pay "EXTREMELY well."

I kept dreaming about all the things I could do with $25,000. I had gone into the correspondence on a whim. But soon, despite David's casual tone and the optimistic attitude of all the classifieds and information I read, I realized that this process was something I didn't want to be a part of. I understand the desire for a child who will resemble and fit in with the family. But once a couple starts choosing a few characteristics, shooting for perfection is too easy — especially if they can afford it. The money might have changed my life for a while, but it would have led to the creation of a child encumbered with too many expectations.

After I'd brooded about these matters, I received the shortest e-mail of the correspondence. The verdict on my pictures was in: "I showed the pictures to [my wife] this AM. Personally, I think you look great. She said ho-hum."

David said he might reconsider, and that he was going to keep one of my pictures. That was it. No good-bye, no thanks for my willingness to be, in effect, the biological mother of their child. I guess I didn't fit their design; my genes weren't the right material for their *chef d'oeuvre*. So I was rejected as a donor. I keep imagining the day when David and Michelle's child asks where he or she came from. David will describe how hard they both worked on the whole thing, how many pictures they looked at, and how much money they spent. The child will turn to them and say, "Ho-hum."

QUESTIONING THE TEXT

1. In this essay, Cohen recounts her experience as a respondent to an advertisement for an egg donor and also comments on that experience; the essay thus interweaves narrative and commentary. After you've read the essay once thoroughly, skim through it again and note which passages

present the narrative of Cohen's encounter and which passages comment on her experience or related issues. How does the arrangement of narrative and commentary lead you toward particular judgments about Cohen's experience, the actions of David and Michelle, or issues related to egg donation? Consider the effects that a different arrangement of the passages might have on you as a reader.

2. A.L. says that in reading this piece she "identified with" Cohen. Did you? In what ways does Cohen get you to sympathize with her, even if you have not been in the position she describes? Are there points in the text where you feel less sympathetic toward her? If so, explain why.

3. How do you think Cohen felt about her experience? Does she reveal her emotions in this essay? If so, in what words or passages? Does her writing elicit an emotional response from you as you read? If so, where and how?

MAKING CONNECTIONS

4. Consider the moral dilemmas that Cohen raises in her essay. How would you compare her concerns to those raised by Mary Shelley in the selection from *Frankenstein* presented in Chapter 5 (p. 285)?

5. Would either buying an egg or selling an egg raise an ethical dilemma, in your view? If so, which would you consider the more problematic transaction? Why? Compare Cohen's piece to Michael Pollan's "An Animal's Place" (p. 204) or consider her essay in light of the discussion of integrity in Stephen L. Carter's "The Rules about the Rules" (p. 178). How do these authors handle the issue of personal responsibility in arenas where personal and social responsibilities overlap?

JOINING THE CONVERSATION

6. Imagine yourself as a prospective parent in a position similar to that of Michelle or David in this essay: You and your partner want to have a child but are biologically prevented from doing so. Given unlimited financial means, what options would you consider seriously? What options would you refuse to consider? Reconsider the options, assuming you have *limited* financial means. What factors enter into your decision, and how do you weigh the different considerations? Compose your thoughts in an essay responding to Cohen or to Michelle and David.

7. Cohen points out that egg donation "is neither simple nor painless." Consider other donor roles that require invasive surgeries, such as the

donation of organs or bone marrow by living volunteers. How do those cases compare to the donation of an egg or of sperm? With a group of classmates, identify the different moral issues at stake in various types of human biological donor situations.

8. By Cohen's admission, the lure of $25,000 provided a strong enticement to respond to the advertisement requesting an egg donor. Have you ever been tempted by money to do something you might not otherwise consider? Conversely, have you ever donated time, services, money, or goods as a volunteer? With classmates, use your experiences to identify criteria you might use to judge whether a job, a risk, or a sacrifice of some kind is worth undertaking.

MARK CLAYTON
A Whole Lot of Cheatin' Going On

*H*AVE YOU EVER CHEATED *on a college paper or examination? If you have* not, *studies suggest you are an exception — as many as 80 percent of students admit to at least one incident of scholastic dishonesty in their careers. As the director of a major university writing program, I've had to deal with many cases of plagiarism, and they are painful experiences for instructors and students alike. When faculty members discover that a student of theirs has copied or downloaded a paper, they typically feel betrayed and angry — as if they've been violated professionally. Students themselves are, for the most part, remorseful when confronted with evidence of their cheating. But a surprising number play the sullen and resentful victim, blaming their scholastic dishonesty on unreasonable instructors, demanding (and irrelevant) curricula, or work schedules they can't quite manage.*

Many students are also simply confused by the complexities of citing sources correctly or by the confusing status of source material in electronic formats. When material moves so effortlessly from screen to the page, it's hard to recall just who owns what material and harder still to enforce the intellectual property rights of authors.

Not surprisingly, scholastic integrity is a potent topic on many campuses. When my department hosted an online forum on the subject, we quickly got more than a hundred postings, mostly from students who condemned cheating. But you can read more about this forum and concerns about academic integrity on campuses nationwide in the following selection by Mark Clayton, originally published as a feature story in the Christian Science Monitor *(January 19, 1999). Clayton (b. 1957), a writer for the* Monitor *since 1997, said in an email conversation with me that he is surprised by how casual students are about plagiarism and how unaware they often are of the serious consequences of cheating. "It might sound corny," Clayton notes, "but those [students] I interviewed said parents and educators need to make greater efforts to make clear to students that dishonesty has a real price in the real world — just as honesty has long-term rewards. After that, it's up to students."*

—J.R.

Sitting in the glow of his computer screen at 2 a.m. on Oct. 26, 1998, John Smolik, a University of Texas freshman, fires off an e-mail message to an online debate over academic cheating on the Austin campus.

Many of the 100-plus student messages argue that cheaters only hurt themselves. Not so says Mr. Smolik's missive, labeled "reality check!" "Cheating *is* an answer," he writes. "It might not be a good answer, but none the less it is an answer."

Actually, Smolik "disagrees with cheating" and was simply playing devil's advocate, he said in a recent interview. But he allows that his provocative message put forward a widely shared view. And researchers agree.

Across America, college students and college-bound high-schoolers appear to be cheating like there's no tomorrow, student surveys show.

The Center for Academic Integrity in Nashville studied 7,000 students   5 on 26 small- to medium-size college campuses in 1990, 1992, and 1995. Those studies found that nearly 80 percent admitted to cheating at least once.

"We've seen a dramatic increase in the more-explicit forms of test cheating" and illegitimate "collaboration," says Donald McCabe, associate provost at Rutgers University in Newark, who founded CAI and did its studies.

He and others blame poor role models and lack of parental guidance for the growing acceptance of cheating in colleges. Easy access to the Internet, with its vast and often hard-to-trace resources, is another factor.

Add to that a pervasive change in societal values, and students can easily be snared if they lack a strong moral compass — as well as a campus where peers and administrators take a firm stand against dishonesty.

"Nobody cheated [in the 1960s] because of the peer pressure and likelihood of being turned in," claims Johan Madson, associate provost for student affairs at Vanderbilt University in Nashville. "Students of this generation are reluctant to turn their classmates in. They feel everyone ought to have their own right to do their own thing."

The problem is hardly limited to college campuses. Critics also point to   10 widespread cheating in high school as a reason for colleges' current woes.

Who's Who among American High School Students, which lists 700,000 high-achieving students, surveyed these top performers last year and found that 80 percent said they had cheated during their academic careers. Joe Krouse, associate publisher of the listing, says it is "the highest level we've ever seen."

Mr. Krouse taps adult behavior as a factor. "Because adults and role models in society do it, some students may have used those examples to rationalize cheating," he says. In a survey conducted in 1997–98, he also found that 66 percent of the parents of these top students said cheating was "not a big deal."

COLLEGES ARE WATCHING MORE CLOSELY

Whatever the reason for cheating, its sheer volume is capturing the attention of more than a few schools. Most, chary of their images, downplay dishonesty, unwilling to air dirty laundry in public. Yet a few are confronting cheating by making it highly public — on campus, at least.

The University of Texas is the nation's largest university with about 50,000 students. It has roughly 180 academic-integrity cases pop up annually, says Kevin Price, assistant dean of students. The school is trying to raise the profile of integrity issues during orientation with skits, a 10-page handout on plagiarism, and a newsletter called the *Integrity Herald* for faculty.

Another sign of academic stirring: the Center for Academic Integrity,   15
founded in 1993, already has 175 member schools and is drafting a framework
of principles that could be applied nationwide to lower student cheating.

Schools like Stanford University, Georgetown University, the University
of Delaware, and a half-dozen others are also buffing up or introducing new
honor codes.

But Mr. Madson at Vanderbilt University says what is most needed is
for students themselves to take charge and reject the attitude that cheating can
be justified.

Students say time and workload pressure are major factors spurring
academic dishonesty, followed by parental pressure. "It's definitely what you
get assigned — and how long you have to do it — that right there determines
whether you're going to cheat," says Smolik, the University of Texas freshman.

Anne-Elyse Smith, another freshman at Texas, reasoned in an online debate that it may not be smart to cheat, but it could be educationally valuable.

"People should hold themselves accountable to a standard at which   20
they are comfortable, and get out of the education what they can," she wrote.
"If that involves looking at one answer on a quiz, I think the person is
more likely to remember that one answer since they had to resort to cheating
to obtain it."

A Little Imagination, a Lot of High Tech

Whether copying another student's homework, cheating on a test, or pla-
giarizing an essay, cheating is limited only by imagination — and technology.
Some program their calculators with formulas, but rig them to show an empty
memory if an instructor checks.

But what alarms some campus officials the most is the Internet's proven
potential for explosive growth in negative areas such as pornography — and the
possibility that plagiarism could be next. Web sites sporting names like
"Cheater.com" and "School Sucks" offer tools for rampant plagiarism at the
click of a mouse. "Download your workload" the latter site suggests, boasting
more than 1 million term-paper downloads.

Such savvy borrowing may be lost on some educators, but others, like
librarians, are catching up. "Students are finding it so easy to use these sources
that they will dump them in the middle of the papers without any attribution,"
says John Ruszkiewicz, an English professor at Texas. "What they don't realize
is how readily [professors] can tell the material isn't the student's and how easy
it is for instructors to search this material on the Web."

Anthony Krier, a reference librarian at Franklin Pierce College Library in
Rindge, N.H., is one such literary bloodhound. Last semester, he investigated
nine cases of plagiarism, three of them involving the Internet. One student had
downloaded and passed off as his own a morality essay, apparently unaware of
the irony, Mr. Krier says.

Some colleges are fighting back with explicit warnings, more detailed   25
orientations, and classes on how to cite sources — and lawsuits. Boston University
sued five online "term-paper mills" in 1997. The case was rejected by a
federal judge last month. School officials vow to refile.

Last fall, the dean of the school's College of Communication, Brent
Baker, wrote a letter to students urging them to protect their "good name" by
reviewing carefully the school's code of conduct. To drive home the point, he
attached a listing of 13 unnamed cases and the penalties — probation, suspension,
and expulsion — meted out.

Likewise, the 152 reports of academic dishonesty for 1997–98 at the University
of Southern California in Los Angeles "is higher than previous comparable
years beginning in 1991," wrote Sandra Rhoten, assistant dean in the
office of student conduct, in a letter in the campus newspaper describing
violations and sanctions assessed.

"We had a full-blown, two-year campaign [starting in 1995] to educate
people about the problem," Ms. Rhoten says in an interview. "Sometimes faculty
feel alone in this. We're reassuring them that we take this seriously too."

THE EXPECTATION OF HONESTY

Being blunt is the idea. Talking about the expectation of honesty is constant.
And along with explicit warning shots, freshmen at USC are getting
more intensive and detailed training in what constitutes plagiarism and other
forms of cheating, Rhoten says.

The school passes out brochures on plagiarism, has regular coverage in   30
the student paper on cheating cases, and has beefed up orientation courses with
training to explain subtler issues like unauthorized collaboration — the largest
area of student honor violation at USC and many other campuses, Mr. McCabe
and others say.

For instance, Lucia Brawley, a senior majoring in English at Harvard
University in Cambridge, Mass., does not believe cheating is a big problem at
her school. But when asked about the collaboration issue, she is less sure.

"With people I know in the sciences, there's so much to do and so little
time, they help each other," she says. "You go to a lecture today, I'll go next
week. You do the reading this week, I'll do it next week. It's a gray area."

Ultimately, though, it is students who will have to uphold academic
integrity themselves, many say.

The University of Virginia has a student-run honor code whose "single
sanction" for violators is expulsion. It is one of the nation's strictest. Even after
more than a century, it remains controversial on campus. Of 11 cheating cases
last semester, five resulted in expulsion. But the code has also created an atmosphere
of trust that means students can take unproctored exams. "Many of our
alumni attribute their success in life to this school's honor code," says Cabell
Vest, a graduate student who chairs UVA's honor council.

At Vanderbilt, which also has a strict code, 20 academic dishonesty cases   35
are under review, Madson says — triple the number a few years ago. But he is
confident the school is creating an atmosphere less tolerant of cheating. "You
just can't have an academic enterprise that isn't based on integrity and honesty,"
he says. "Nobody wants somebody building bridges to take shortcuts."

QUESTIONING THE TEXT

1. Clayton quotes a provost from Vanderbilt who asserts that "[n]obody
   cheated [in the 1960s] because of the peer pressure and likelihood of
   being turned in" (paragraph 9). Examine this statement in the context in
   which it is made, and then decide how you might go about testing its
   validity. What would you have to read and examine and who would you
   have to interview to confirm or refute its validity?

2. According to Clayton, one student in the online debate asserts that "it
   may not be smart to cheat, but it could be educationally valuable." Examine the student's full statement and its rationale (paragraphs 19–20). Then
   discuss the implications of the statement with your classmates in person
   or online.

MAKING CONNECTIONS

3. In "Making Peace with the Greeks" (p. 479), Susanna Ashton describes her
   methods of dealing with another kind of classroom situation — not cheating, but overly enthusiastic participation from one group of students that
   she felt intimidated or excluded others in the class. How does her solution
   to this kind of campus problem compare with the solutions colleges in
   Clayton's article are instituting to deal with cheating? Can you suggest ways
   for colleges to enlist students in the struggle against cheating, as Ashton
   enlists her students to end the problem they themselves are causing?

4. Read the college mission statements in Chapter 3 (p. 56), and imagine
   how you might present a school's position on cheating. Write a position
   statement for your institution on the issue of scholastic integrity. Imagine
   the statement as a Web page. What issues would you present? What
   visuals might you use? What links might you make?

JOINING THE CONVERSATION

5. Conduct a series of interviews on your campus to explore the issue of
   scholastic integrity within a small group you can readily identify — for

instance, your fraternity or sorority, the Young Democrats, or the club volleyball team. Use Clayton's article to prepare a list of interview questions about plagiarism, cheating, and collusion at your institution; avoid questions that can be answered by a simple yes or no. Then write a brief report summarizing what you've discovered locally about scholastic integrity. Quote freely from your interviews, but be sure to protect the interviewees' anonymity.

6. Locate a copy of your institution's policies on cheating, plagiarism, and collusion. Then write a critical analysis of these statements. Are the statements clear? Are important terms carefully defined? Do the statements provide a convincing ethical rationale for the policies announced? Do the policies account for changes as a result of electronic technology?

MICHAEL POLLAN
An Animal's Place

THROUGH THE FIVE EDITIONS OF THIS BOOK, *I have been seeking essays that raise important issues compellingly. But none of my choices so far has been as powerful an example of good argument as Michael Pollan's "An Animal's Place." It brings to the public square the argument that the welfare of animals — a back-burner issue in many minds — requires immediate attention.*

It's relatively easy to make a sentimental argument for the welfare of animals — to appeal, for example, to pet owners' devotion to their cats or dogs. The most famous probably occurs in Laurence Sterne's novel Tristram Shandy *(1759–67), when Uncle Toby spares the life of a fly:*

> *— Go — says he, one day at dinner, to an over-grown one which had buzz'd about his nose, and tormented him cruelly all dinner-time, — and which, after infinite attempts, he had caught at last, as it flew by him; . . . Go, says he, lifting up the sash, and opening his hand as he spoke, to let it escape; — go poor Devil, get thee gone, why should I hurt thee? — This world surely is wide enough to hold both thee and me.*

But it is another matter entirely to make people appreciate the disturbing moral costs involved in dining on hamburger, pork tenderloin, and chicken fajitas — or in enjoying the supple textures of leather coats, Gucci purses, or Ferragamo shoes.

Can we justify the uses we make of animals when the price they pay is lives of pointless suffering? That's the tough question Pollan poses in "An Animal's Place," understanding full well that a relatively small but active insurgency already says no *and that a largely indifferent public prefers its steaks marbled and rare.*

Pollan's essay, originally published in the New York Times Magazine *(November 10, 2002), embodies all the principles of a fair and principled rhetoric, grabbing both the mind and heart. From the very first paragraph, he conveys his own reservations about the concept of animal rights, assuring readers that he will deal with the subject fairly. Gradually, he unfolds the complexities of a substantial moral issue while avoiding sensationalism. Yet his sensible argument for change will, I think, move many readers (including habitual meat eaters) to ponder deeply what might be done to lessen the suffering of the animals we use for food and clothing. I suspect you will find "An Animal's Place" persuasive and powerful writing.*

Michael Pollan has written about environmentalism and nature for many years; his work has been published in the New York Times, Esquire, Vogue, House & Garden, *and* Harper's Magazine. *His most recent book is* The Omnivore's Dilemma: A Natural History of Four Meals *(2006).* —J.R.

The first time I opened Peter Singer's *Animal Liberation*, I was dining alone at the Palm, trying to enjoy a rib-eye steak cooked medium-rare. If this sounds like a good recipe for cognitive dissonance (if not indigestion), that was sort of the idea. Preposterous as it might seem to supporters of animal rights, what I was doing was tantamount to reading *Uncle Tom's Cabin* on a plantation in the Deep South in 1852.

Singer and the swelling ranks of his followers ask us to imagine a future in which people will look back on my meal, and this steakhouse, as relics of an equally backward age. Eating animals, wearing animals, experimenting on animals, killing animals for sport: all these practices, so resolutely normal to us, will be seen as the barbarities they are; and we will come to view "speciesism" — a neologism I had encountered before only in jokes — as a form of discrimination as indefensible as racism or anti-Semitism.

Even in 1975, when *Animal Liberation* was first published, Singer, an Australian philosopher now teaching at Princeton, was confident that he had the wind of history at his back. The recent civil rights past was prologue, as one liberation movement followed on the heels of another. Slowly but surely, the white man's circle of moral consideration was expanded to admit first blacks, then women, then homosexuals. In each case, a group once thought to be so different from the prevailing "we" as to be undeserving of civil rights was, after a struggle, admitted to the club. Now it was animals' turn.

That animal liberation is the logical next step in the forward march of moral progress is no longer the fringe idea it was back in 1975. A growing and increasingly influential movement of philosophers, ethicists, law professors and activists are convinced that the great moral struggle of our time will be for the rights of animals.

So far the movement has scored some of its biggest victories in Europe. Earlier this year, Germany became the first nation to grant animals a constitutional right: the words "and animals" were added to a provision obliging the state to respect and protect the dignity of human beings. The farming of animals for fur was recently banned in England. In several European nations, sows may no longer be confined to crates nor laying hens to "battery cages" — stacked wired cages so small the birds cannot stretch their wings. The Swiss are amending their laws to change the status of animals from "things" to "beings."

Though animals are still very much "things" in the eyes of American law, change is in the air. Thirty-seven states have recently passed laws making some forms of animal cruelty a crime, 21 of them by ballot initiative. Following protests by activists, McDonald's and Burger King forced significant improvements in the way the U.S. meat industry slaughters animals. Agribusiness and the cosmetics and apparel industries are all struggling to defuse mounting public concerns over animal welfare.

Once thought of as a left-wing concern, the movement now cuts across ideological lines. Perhaps the most eloquent recent plea on behalf of animals, a new book called *Dominion*, was written by a former speechwriter for

President Bush. And once outlandish ideas are finding their way into main-stream opinion. A recent Zogby poll found that 51 percent of Americans believe that primates are entitled to the same rights as human children.

What is going on here? A certain amount of cultural confusion, for one thing. For at the same time many people seem eager to extend the circle of our moral consideration to animals, in our factory farms and laboratories we are inflicting more suffering on more animals than at any time in history. One by one, science is dismantling our claims to uniqueness as a species, discovering that such things as culture, tool making, language and even possibly self-consciousness are not the exclusive domain of *Homo sapiens*. Yet most of the animals we kill lead lives organized very much in the spirit of Descartes, who famously claimed that animals were mere machines, incapable of thought or feeling. There's a schizoid quality to our relationship with animals, in which sentiment and brutality exist side by side. Half the dogs in America will receive Christmas presents this year, yet few of us pause to consider the miserable life of the pig — an animal easily as intelligent as a dog — that becomes the Christmas ham.

We tolerate this disconnect because the life of the pig has moved out of view. When's the last time you saw a pig? (Babe doesn't count.) Except for our pets, real animals — animals living and dying — no longer figure in our every-day lives. Meat comes from the grocery store, where it is cut and packaged to look as little like parts of animals as possible. The disappearance of animals from our lives has opened a space in which there's no reality check, either on the sentiment or the brutality. This is pretty much where we live now, with respect to animals, and it is a space in which the Peter Singers and Frank Perdues of the world can evidently thrive equally well.

Several years ago, the English critic John Berger wrote an essay, "Why   10 Look at Animals?" in which he suggested that the loss of everyday contact between ourselves and animals — and specifically the loss of eye contact — has left us deeply confused about the terms of our relationship to other species. That eye contact, always slightly uncanny, had provided a vivid daily reminder that animals were at once crucially like and unlike us; in their eyes we glimpsed something unmistakably familiar (pain, fear, tenderness) and something irre-trievably alien. Upon this paradox people built a relationship in which they felt they could both honor and eat animals without looking away. But that accommodation has pretty much broken down; nowadays, it seems, we either look away or become vegetarians. For my own part, neither option seemed especially appetizing. Which might explain how I found myself reading *Animal Liberation* in a steakhouse.

This is not something I'd recommend if you're determined to continue eating meat. Combining rigorous philosophical argument with journalistic description, *Animal Liberation* is one of those rare books that demand that you either defend the way you live or change it. Because Singer is so skilled in argument, for many readers it is easier to change. His book has converted countless thousands to vegetarianism, and it didn't take long for me to see why: within a few pages, he had succeeded in throwing me on the defensive.

Singer's argument is disarmingly simple and, if you accept its premises, difficult to refute. Take the premise of equality, which most people readily accept. Yet what do we really mean by it? People are not, as a matter of fact, equal at all — some are smarter than others, better looking, more gifted. "Equality is a moral idea," Singer points out, "not an assertion of fact." The moral idea is that everyone's interests ought to receive equal consideration, regardless of "what abilities they may possess." Fair enough; many philosophers have gone this far. But fewer have taken the next logical step. "If possessing a higher degree of intelligence does not entitle one human to use another for his or her own ends, how can it entitle humans to exploit nonhumans for the same purpose?"

This is the nub of Singer's argument, and right around here I began scribbling objections in the margin. But humans differ from animals in morally significant ways. Yes they do, Singer acknowledges, which is why we shouldn't treat pigs and children alike. Equal consideration of interests is not the same as equal treatment, he points out: children have an interest in being educated; pigs, in rooting around in the dirt. But where their interests are the same, the principle of equality demands they receive the same consideration. And the one all-important interest that we share with pigs, as with all sentient creatures, is an interest in avoiding pain.

Here Singer quotes a famous passage from Jeremy Bentham, the 18th-century utilitarian philosopher, that is the wellspring of the animal rights movement. Bentham was writing in 1789, soon after the French colonies freed black slaves, granting them fundamental rights. "The day may come," he speculates, "when the rest of the animal creation may acquire those rights." Bentham then asks what characteristic entitles any being to moral consideration. "Is it the faculty of reason or perhaps the faculty of discourse?" Obviously not, since "a full-grown horse or dog is beyond comparison a more rational, as well as a more conversable animal, than an infant." He concludes: "The question is not, Can they reason? nor, Can they talk? but, Can they suffer?"

Bentham here is playing a powerful card philosophers call the "argument   15 from marginal cases," or A.M.C. for short. It goes like this: there are humans — infants, the severely retarded, the demented — whose mental function cannot match that of a chimpanzee. Even though these people cannot reciprocate our moral attentions, we nevertheless include them in the circle of our moral consideration. So on what basis do we exclude the chimpanzee?

Because he's a chimp, I furiously scribbled in the margin, and they're human! For Singer that's not good enough. To exclude the chimp from moral consideration simply because he's not human is no different from excluding the slave simply because he's not white. In the same way we'd call that exclusion racist, the animal rightist contends that it is speciesist to discriminate against the chimpanzee solely because he's not human.

But the differences between blacks and whites are trivial compared with the differences between my son and a chimp. Singer counters by asking us to imagine a hypothetical society, that discriminates against people on the basis of something nontrivial — say, intelligence. If that scheme offends our sense of equality, then why is the fact that animals lack certain human characteristics any more just as a basis for discrimination? Either we do not owe any justice to the severely retarded, he concludes, or we do owe it to animals with higher capabilities.

This is where I put down my fork. If I believe in equality, and equality is based on interests rather than characteristics, then either I have to take the interests of the steer I'm eating into account or concede that I am a speciesist. For the time being, I decided to plead guilty as charged. I finished my steak.

But Singer had planted a troubling notion, and in the days afterward, it grew and grew, watered by the other animal rights thinkers I began reading: the philosophers Tom Regan and James Rachels; the legal theorist Steven M. Wise; the writers Joy Williams and Matthew Scully. I didn't think I minded being a speciesist, but could it be, as several of these writers suggest, that we will someday come to regard speciesism as an evil comparable to racism? Will history someday judge us as harshly as it judges the Germans who went about their ordinary lives in the shadow of Treblinka? Precisely that question was recently posed by J. M. Coetzee, the South African novelist, in a lecture delivered at Princeton; he answered it in the affirmative. If animal rightists are right, "a crime of stupefying proportions" (in Coetzee's words) is going on all around us every day, just beneath our notice.

It's an idea almost impossible to entertain seriously, much less to accept,   20
and in the weeks following my restaurant face-off between Singer and the steak, I found myself marshaling whatever mental power I could muster to try to refute it. Yet Singer and his allies managed to trump almost all my objections.

My first line of defense was obvious. Animals kill one another all the time. Why treat animals more ethically than they treat one another? (Ben Franklin tried this one long before me: during a fishing trip, he wondered, "If you eat one another, I don't see why we may not eat you." He admits, however, that the rationale didn't occur to him until the fish were in the frying pan, smelling "admirably well." The advantage of being a "reasonable creature," Franklin remarks, is that you can find a reason for whatever you want to do.) To the "they do it, too" defense, the animal rightist has a devastating reply: do you really want to base your morality on the natural order? Murder and rape are natural, too. Besides, humans don't need to kill other creatures in order to survive; animals do. (Though if my cat, Otis, is any guide, animals sometimes kill for sheer pleasure.)

This suggests another defense. Wouldn't life in the wild be worse for these farm animals? "Defenders of slavery imposed on black Africans often made a similar point," Singer retorts. "The life of freedom is to be preferred."

But domesticated animals can't survive in the wild; in fact, without us they wouldn't exist at all. Or as one 19th-century political philosopher put it,

"The pig has a stronger interest than anyone in the demand for bacon. If all the world were Jewish, there would be no pigs at all." But it turns out that this would be fine by the animal rightists: for if pigs don't exist, they can't be wronged.

Animals on factory farms have never known any other life. Singer replies that "animals feel a need to exercise, stretch their limbs or wings, groom themselves and turn around, whether or not they have ever lived in conditions that permit this." The measure of their suffering is not their prior experiences but the unremitting daily frustration of their instincts.

O.K., the suffering of animals is a legitimate problem, but the world is   25
full of problems, and surely human problems must come first! Sounds good, and
yet all the animal people are asking me to do is to stop eating meat and wearing animal furs and hides. There's no reason I can't devote myself to solving
humankind's problems while being a vegetarian who wears synthetics.

But doesn't the fact that we could choose to forgo meat for moral reasons
point to a crucial moral difference between animals and humans? As Kant
pointed out, the human being is the only moral animal, the only one even
capable of entertaining a concept of "rights." What's wrong with reserving
moral consideration for those able to reciprocate it? Right here is where you
run smack into the A.M.C.: the moral status of the retarded, the insane, the
infant and the Alzheimer's patient. Such "marginal cases," in the detestable
argot of modern moral philosophy, cannot participate in moral decision making any more than a monkey can, yet we nevertheless grant them rights.

That's right, I respond, for the simple reason that they're one of us. And
all of us have been, and will probably once again be, marginal cases ourselves.
What's more, these people have fathers and mothers, daughters and sons, which
makes our interest in their welfare deeper than our interest in the welfare of
even the most brilliant ape.

Alas, none of these arguments evade the charge of speciesism; the racist,
too, claims that it's natural to give special consideration to one's own kind. A
utilitarian like Singer would agree, however, that the feelings of relatives do
count for something. Yet the principle of equal consideration of interests demands that, given the choice between performing a painful medical experiment on a severely retarded orphan and on a normal ape, we must sacrifice the
child. Why? Because the ape has a greater capacity for pain.

Here in a nutshell is the problem with the A.M.C.: it can be used to help
the animals, but just as often it winds up hurting the marginal cases. Giving up
our speciesism will bring us to a moral cliff from which we may not be prepared to jump, even when logic is pushing us.

And yet this isn't the moral choice I am being asked to make. (Too bad; it   30
would be so much easier!) In everyday life, the choice is not between babies
and chimps but between the pork and the tofu. Even if we reject the "hard util-
itarianism" of a Peter Singer, there remains the question of whether we owe
animals that can feel pain any moral consideration, and this seems impossible to
deny. And if we do owe them moral consideration, how can we justify eating
them?

This is why killing animals for meat (and clothing) poses the most difficult animal rights challenge. In the case of animal testing, all but the most radical animal rightists are willing to balance the human benefit against the cost to
the animals. That's because the unique qualities of human consciousness carry
weight in the utilitarian calculus: human pain counts for more than that of a
mouse, since our pain is amplified by emotions like dread; similarly, our deaths
are worse than an animal's because we understand what death is in a way they

don't. So the argument over animal testing is really in the details: is this particular procedure or test really necessary to save human lives? (Very often it's not,
in which case we probably shouldn't do it.) But if humans no longer need to
eat meat or wear skins, then what exactly are we putting on the human side of
the scale to outweigh the interests of the animal?

I suspect that this is finally why the animal people managed to throw me
on the defensive. It's one thing to choose between the chimp and the retarded
child or to accept the sacrifice of all those pigs surgeons practiced on to develop
heart-bypass surgery. But what happens when the choice is between "a lifetime
of suffering for a nonhuman animal and the gastronomic preference of a human
being?" You look away — or you stop eating animals. And if you don't want
to do either? Then you have to try to determine if the animals you're eating
have really endured "a lifetime of suffering."

Whether our interest in eating animals outweighs their interest in not
being eaten (assuming for the moment that is their interest) turns on the vexed
question of animal suffering. Vexed, because it is impossible to know what really goes on in the mind of a cow or a pig or even an ape. Strictly speaking, this
is true of other humans, too, but since humans are all basically wired the same
way, we have excellent reason to assume that other people's experience of pain
feels much like our own. Can we say that about animals? Yes and no.

I have yet to find anyone who still subscribes to Descartes's belief that animals cannot feel pain because they lack a soul. The general consensus among
scientists and philosophers is that when it comes to pain, the higher animals are
wired much like we are for the same evolutionary reasons, so we should take
the writhings of the kicked dog at face value. Indeed, the very premise of a
great deal of animal testing — the reason it has value — is that animals' experience of physical and even some psychological pain closely resembles our own.
Otherwise, why would cosmetics testers drip chemicals into the eyes of rabbits
to see if they sting? Why would researchers study head trauma by traumatizing
chimpanzee heads? Why would psychologists attempt to induce depression and
"learned helplessness" in dogs by exposing them to ceaseless random patterns
of electrical shock?

That said, it can be argued that human pain differs from animal pain by an   35
order of magnitude. This qualitative difference is largely the result of our possession of language and, by virtue of language, an ability to have thoughts about
thoughts and to imagine alternatives to our current reality. The philosopher
Daniel C. Dennett suggests that we would do well to draw a distinction between
pain, which a great many animals experience, and suffering, which depends on
a degree of self-consciousness only a few animals appear to command. Suffering
in this view is not just lots of pain but pain intensified by human emotions like
loss, sadness, worry, regret, self-pity, shame, humiliation and dread.

Consider castration. No one would deny the procedure is painful to animals, yet animals appear to get over it in a way humans do not. (Some rhesus
monkeys competing for mates will bite off a rival's testicle; the very next day

the victim may be observed mating, seemingly little the worse for wear.) Surely the suffering of a man able to comprehend the full implications of castration, to anticipate the event and contemplate its aftermath, represents an agony of another order.

By the same token, however, language and all that comes with it can also make certain kinds of pain more bearable. A trip to the dentist would be a torment for an ape that couldn't be made to understand the purpose and duration of the procedure.

As humans contemplating the pain and suffering of animals, we do need to guard against projecting on to them what the same experience would feel like to us. Watching a steer force-marched up the ramp to the kill-floor door, as I have done, I need to remind myself that this is not Sean Penn in *Dead Man Walking*, that in a bovine brain the concept of nonexistence is blissfully absent. "If we fail to find suffering in the animal lives we can see," Dennett writes in *Kinds of Minds*, "we can rest assured there is no invisible suffering somewhere in their brains. If we find suffering, we will recognize it without difficulty."

Which brings us — reluctantly, necessarily — to the American factory farm, the place where all such distinctions turn to dust. It's not easy to draw lines between pain and suffering in a modern egg or confinement hog operation. These are places where the subtleties of moral philosophy and animal cognition mean less than nothing, where everything we've learned about animals at least since Darwin has been simply . . . set aside. To visit a modern CAFO (Confined Animal Feeding Operation) is to enter a world that, for all its technological sophistication, is still designed according to Cartesian principles: animals are machines incapable of feeling pain. Since no thinking person can possibly believe this any more, industrial animal agriculture depends on a suspension of disbelief on the part of the people who operate it and a willingness to avert your eyes on the part of everyone else.

From everything I've read, egg and hog operations are the worst. Beef   40
cattle in America at least still live outdoors, albeit standing ankle deep in their own waste eating a diet that makes them sick. And broiler chickens, although they do get their beaks snipped off with a hot knife to keep them from cannibalizing one another under the stress of their confinement, at least don't spend their eight-week lives in cages too small to ever stretch a wing. That fate is reserved for the American laying hen, who passes her brief span piled together with a half-dozen other hens in a wire cage whose floor a single page of this magazine could carpet. Every natural instinct of this animal is thwarted, leading to a range of behavioral "vices" that can include cannibalizing her cagemates and rubbing her body against the wire mesh until it is featherless and bleeding. Pain? Suffering? Madness? The operative suspension of disbelief depends on more neutral descriptors, like "vices" and "stress." Whatever you want to call what's going on in those cages, the 10 percent or so of hens that can't bear it and simply die is built into the cost of production. And when the output of the others begins to ebb, the hens will be "force-molted" — starved of food and

water and light for several days in order to stimulate a final bout of egg laying before their life's work is done.

Simply reciting these facts, most of which are drawn from poultry-trade magazines, makes me sound like one of those animal people, doesn't it? I don't mean to, but this is what can happen when . . . you look. It certainly wasn't my intention to ruin anyone's breakfast. But now that I probably have spoiled the eggs, I do want to say one thing about the bacon, mention a single practice (by no means the worst) in modern hog production that points to the compound madness of an impeccable industrial logic.

Piglets in confinement operations are weaned from their mothers 10 days after birth (compared with 13 weeks in nature) because they gain weight faster on their hormone- and antibiotic-fortified feed. This premature weaning leaves the pigs with a lifelong craving to suck and chew, a desire they gratify in confinement by biting the tail of the animal in front of them. A normal pig would fight off his molester, but a demoralized pig has stopped caring. "Learned helplessness" is the psychological term, and it's not uncommon in confinement operations, where tens of thousands of hogs spend their entire lives ignorant of sunshine or earth or straw, crowded together beneath a metal roof upon metal slats suspended over a manure pit. So it's not surprising that an animal as sensitive and intelligent as a pig would get depressed, and a depressed pig will allow his tail to be chewed on to the point of infection. Sick pigs, being underperforming "production units," are clubbed to death on the spot. The U.S.D.A.'s recommended solution to the problem is called "tail docking." Using a pair of pliers (and no anesthetic), most but not all of the tail is snipped off. Why the little stump? Because the whole point of the exercise is not to remove the object of tail-biting so much as to render it more sensitive. Now, a bite on the tail is so painful that even the most demoralized pig will mount a struggle to avoid it.

Much of this description is drawn from *Dominion*, Matthew Scully's recent book in which he offers a harrowing description of a North Carolina hog operation. Scully, a Christian conservative, has no patience for lefty rights talk, arguing instead that while God did give man "dominion" over animals ("Every moving thing that liveth shall be meat for you"), he also admonished us to show them mercy. "We are called to treat them with kindness, not because they have rights or power or some claim to equality but . . . because they stand unequal and powerless before us."

Scully calls the contemporary factory farm "our own worst nightmare" and, to his credit, doesn't shrink from naming the root cause of this evil: unfettered capitalism. (Perhaps this explains why he resigned from the Bush administration just before his book's publication.) A tension has always existed between the capitalist imperative to maximize efficiency and the moral imperatives of religion or community, which have historically served as a counterweight to the moral blindness of the market. This is one of "the cultural contradictions of capitalism" — the tendency of the economic impulse to erode the moral underpinnings of society. Mercy toward animals is one such casualty.

More than any other institution, the American industrial animal farm   45
offers a nightmarish glimpse of what capitalism can look like in the absence
of moral or regulatory constraint. Here in these places life itself is redefined —
as protein production — and with it suffering. That venerable word becomes
"stress," an economic problem in search of a cost-effective solution, like tail-
docking or beak-clipping or, in the industry's latest plan, by simply engineering
the "stress gene" out of pigs and chickens. "Our own worst nightmare" such a
place may well be; it is also real life for the billions of animals unlucky enough
to have been born beneath these grim steel roofs, into the brief, pitiless life of
a "production unit" in the days before the suffering gene was found.

Vegetarianism doesn't seem an unreasonable response to such an evil.
Who would want to be made complicit in the agony of these animals by eating them? You want to throw something against the walls of those infernal
sheds, whether it's the Bible, a new constitutional right or a whole platoon of
animal rightists bent on breaking in and liberating the inmates. In the shadow
of these factory farms, Coetzee's notion of a "stupefying crime" doesn't seem
far-fetched at all.

But before you swear off meat entirely, let me describe a very different
sort of animal farm. It is typical of nothing, and yet its very existence puts the
whole moral question of animal agriculture in a different light. Polyface Farm
occupies 550 acres of rolling grassland and forest in the Shenandoah Valley
of Virginia. Here, Joel Salatin and his family raise six different food animals —
cattle, pigs, chickens, rabbits, turkeys and sheep — in an intricate dance of
symbiosis designed to allow each species, in Salatin's words, "to fully express its
physiological distinctiveness."

What this means in practice is that Salatin's chickens live like chickens;
his cows, like cows; pigs, pigs. As in nature, where birds tend to follow herbi-
vores, once Salatin's cows have finished grazing a pasture, he moves them out
and tows in his "eggmobile," a portable chicken coop that houses several hundred laying hens — roughly the natural size of a flock. The hens fan out over
the pasture, eating the short grass and picking insect larvae out of the cowpats —
all the while spreading the cow manure and eliminating the farm's parasite
problem. A diet of grubs and grass makes for exceptionally tasty eggs and contented chickens, and their nitrogenous manure feeds the pasture. A few weeks
later, the chickens move out, and the sheep come in, dining on the lush new
growth, as well as on the weed species (nettles, nightshade) that the cattle and
chickens won't touch.

Meanwhile, the pigs are in the barn turning the compost. All winter long,
while the cattle were indoors, Salatin layered their manure with straw, wood
chips — and corn. By March, this steaming compost layer cake stands three feet
high, and the pigs, whose powerful snouts can sniff out and retrieve the fer-
mented corn at the bottom, get to spend a few happy weeks rooting through the
pile, aerating it as they work. All you can see of these pigs, intently nosing out
the tasty alcoholic morsels, are their upturned pink hams and corkscrew tails

churning the air. The finished compost will go to feed the grass; the grass, the cattle; the cattle, the chickens; and eventually all of these animals will feed us.

I thought a lot about vegetarianism and animal rights during the day I   50
spent on Joel Salatin's extraordinary farm. So much of what I'd read, so much of what I'd accepted, looked very different from here. To many animal rightists, even Polyface Farm is a death camp. But to look at these animals is to see this for the sentimental conceit it is. In the same way that we can probably recognize animal suffering when we see it, animal happiness is unmistakable, too, and here I was seeing it in abundance.

For any animal, happiness seems to consist in the opportunity to express its creaturely character — its essential pigness or wolfness or chickenness. Aristotle speaks of each creature's "characteristic form of life." For domesticated species, the good life, if we can call it that, cannot be achieved apart from humans — apart from our farms and, therefore, our meat eating. This, it seems to me, is where animal rightists betray a profound ignorance about the workings of nature. To think of domestication as a form of enslavement or even exploitation is to misconstrue the whole relationship, to project a human idea of power onto what is, in fact, an instance of mutualism between species. Domestication is an evolutionary, rather than a political, development. It is certainly not a regime humans imposed on animals some 10,000 years ago.

Rather, domestication happened when a small handful of especially opportunistic species discovered through Darwinian trial and error that they were more likely to survive and prosper in an alliance with humans than on their own. Humans provided the animals with food and protection, in exchange for which the animals provided the humans their milk and eggs and — yes — their flesh. Both parties were transformed by the relationship: animals grew tame and lost their ability to fend for themselves (evolution tends to edit out unneeded traits), and the humans gave up their hunter-gatherer ways for the settled life of agriculturists. (Humans changed biologically, too, evolving such new traits as a tolerance for lactose as adults.)

From the animals' point of view, the bargain with humanity has been a great success, at least until our own time. Cows, pigs, dogs, cats and chickens have thrived, while their wild ancestors have languished. (There are 10,000 wolves in North America, 50,000,000 dogs.) Nor does their loss of autonomy seem to trouble these creatures. It is wrong, the rightists say, to treat animals as "means" rather than "ends," yet the happiness of a working animal like the dog consists precisely in serving as a "means." Liberation is the last thing such a creature wants. To say of one of Joel Salatin's caged chickens that "the life of freedom is to be preferred" betrays an ignorance about chicken preferences — which on this farm are heavily focused on not getting their heads bitten off by weasels.

But haven't these chickens simply traded one predator for another — weasels for humans? True enough, and for the chickens this is probably not a bad deal. For brief as it is, the life expectancy of a farm animal would be considerably briefer in the world beyond the pasture fence or chicken coop. A sheep farmer told me that a bear will eat a lactating ewe alive, starting with her udders. "As a rule," he explained, "animals don't get 'good deaths' surrounded by their loved ones."

The very existence of predation — animals eating animals — is the cause   55 of much anguished hand-wringing in animal rights circles. "It must be admitted," Singer writes, "that the existence of carnivorous animals does pose one problem for the ethics of Animal Liberation, and that is whether we should do anything about it." Some animal rightists train their dogs and cats to become vegetarians. (Note: cats will require nutritional supplements to stay healthy.) Matthew Scully calls predation "the intrinsic evil in nature's design . . . among the hardest of all things to fathom." Really? A deep Puritan streak pervades animal rights activists, an abiding discomfort not only with our animality, but with the animals' animality too.

However it may appear to us, predation is not a matter of morality or politics; it, also, is a matter of symbiosis. Hard as the wolf may be on the deer he eats, the herd depends on him for its well-being; without predators to cull the herd, deer overrun their habitat and starve. In many places, human hunters have taken over the predator's ecological role. Chickens also depend for their continued well-being on their human predators — not individual chickens, but chickens as a species. The surest way to achieve the extinction of the chicken would be to grant chickens a "right to life."

Yet here's the rub: the animal rightist is not concerned with species, only individuals. Tom Regan, author of *The Case for Animal Rights*, bluntly asserts that because "species are not individuals . . . the rights view does not recognize the moral rights of species to anything, including survival." Singer concurs, insisting that only sentient individuals have interests. But surely a species can have interests — in its survival, say — just as a nation or community or a corporation can. The animal rights movement's exclusive concern with individual animals makes perfect sense given its roots in a culture of liberal individualism, but does it make any sense in nature?

In 1611 Juan da Goma (aka Juan the Disoriented) made accidental landfall on Wrightson Island, a six-square-mile rock in the Indian Ocean. The island's sole distinction is as the only known home of the Arcania tree and the bird that nests in it, the Wrightson giant sea sparrow. Da Goma and his crew stayed a week, much of that time spent in a failed bid to recapture the ship's escaped goat — who happened to be pregnant. Nearly four centuries later, Wrightson Island is home to 380 goats that have consumed virtually every scrap of vegetation in their reach. The youngest Arcania tree on the island is more than 300 years old, and only 52 sea sparrows remain. In the animal rights view, any one of those goats have at least as much right to life as the last Wrightson sparrow on earth, and the trees, because they are not sentient, warrant no moral consideration whatsoever. (In the mid-80s a British environmental group set out to shoot the goats, but was forced to cancel the expedition after the Mammal Liberation Front bombed its offices.)

The story of Wrightson Island (recounted by the biologist David Ehrenfeld in *Beginning Again*) suggests at the very least that a human morality based on individual rights makes for an awkward fit when applied to the natural world. This should come as no surprise: morality is an artifact of human culture, devised to help us negotiate social relations. It's very good for that. But just as we recognize that nature doesn't provide an adequate guide for human social conduct, isn't it anthropocentric to assume that our moral system offers an adequate guide for nature? We may require a different set of ethics to guide our dealings with the natural world, one as well suited to the particular needs of plants and animals and habitats (where sentience counts for little) as rights suit us humans today.

To contemplate such questions from the vantage of a farm is to appreciate just how parochial and urban an ideology animals rights really is. It could thrive only in a world where people have lost contact with the natural world, where animals no longer pose a threat to us and human mastery of nature seems absolute. "In our normal life," Singer writes, "there is no serious clash of interests between human and nonhuman animals." Such a statement assumes a decidedly urbanized "normal life," one that certainly no farmer would recognize.

60

The farmer would point out that even vegans have a "serious clash of interests" with other animals. The grain that the vegan eats is harvested with a combine that shreds field mice, while the farmer's tractor crushes woodchucks in their burrows, and his pesticides drop songbirds from the sky. Steve Davis, an animal scientist at Oregon State University, has estimated that if America were to adopt a strictly vegetarian diet, the total number of animals killed every year would actually increase, as animal pasture gave way to row crops. Davis contends that if our goal is to kill as few animals as possible, then people should eat the largest possible animal that can live on the least intensively cultivated land: grass-fed beef for everybody. It would appear that killing animals is unavoidable no matter what we choose to eat.

When I talked to Joel Salatin about the vegetarian utopia, he pointed out that it would also condemn him and his neighbors to importing their food from distant places, since the Shenandoah Valley receives too little rainfall to grow many row crops. Much the same would hold true where I live, in New England. We get plenty of rain, but the hilliness of the land has dictated an agriculture based on animals since the time of the Pilgrims. The world is full of places where the best, if not the only, way to obtain food from the land is by grazing animals on it — especially ruminants, which alone can transform grass into protein and whose presence can actually improve the health of the land.

The vegetarian utopia would make us even more dependent than we already are on an industrialized national food chain. That food chain would in turn be even more dependent than it already is on fossil fuels and chemical fertilizer, since food would need to travel farther and manure would be in short supply. Indeed, it is doubtful that you can build a more sustainable agriculture without animals to cycle nutrients and support local food production. If our concern is for the health of nature — rather than, say, the internal consistency of our moral code or the condition of our souls — then eating animals may sometimes be the most ethical thing to do.

There is, too, the fact that we humans have been eating animals as long as we have lived on this earth. Humans may not need to eat meat in order to survive, yet doing so is part of our evolutionary heritage, reflected in the design of our teeth and the structure of our digestion. Eating meat helped make us what we are, in a social and biological sense. Under the pressure of the hunt, the human brain grew in size and complexity, and around the fire where the meat was cooked, human culture first flourished. Granting rights to animals may lift us up from the brutal world of predation, but it will entail the sacrifice of part of our identity — our own animality.

Surely this is one of the odder paradoxes of animal rights doctrine. It asks us to recognize all that we share with animals and then demands that we act toward them in a most unanimalistic way. Whether or not this is a good idea, we should at least acknowledge that our desire to eat meat is not a trivial matter, no mere "gastronomic preference." We might as well call sex — also now technically unnecessary — a mere "recreational preference." Whatever else it is, our meat eating is something very deep indeed.

Are any of these good enough reasons to eat animals? I'm mindful of Ben Franklin's definition of the reasonable creature as one who can come up with reasons for whatever he wants to do. So I decided I would track down Peter Singer and ask him what he thought. In an e-mail message, I described Polyface and asked him about the implications for his position of the Good Farm — one where animals got to live according to their nature and to all appearances did not suffer.

"I agree with you that it is better for these animals to have lived and died than not to have lived at all," Singer wrote back. Since the utilitarian is concerned exclusively with the sum of happiness and suffering and the slaughter of an animal that doesn't comprehend that death need not involve suffering, the Good Farm adds to the total of animal happiness, provided you replace the slaughtered animal with a new one. However, he added, this line of thinking doesn't obviate the wrongness of killing an animal that "has a sense of its own existence over time and can have preferences for its own future." In other words, it's O.K. to eat the chicken, but he's not so sure about the pig. Yet, he wrote, "I would not be sufficiently confident of my arguments to condemn someone who purchased meat from one of these farms."

Singer went on to express serious doubts that such farms could be practical on a large scale, since the pressures of the marketplace will lead their owners to cut costs and corners at the expense of the animals. He suggested, too, that killing animals is not conducive to treating them with respect. Also, since humanely raised food will be more expensive, only the well-to-do can afford morally defensible animal protein. These are important considerations, but they don't alter my essential point: what's wrong with animal agriculture — with eating animals — is the practice, not the principle.

*the more the
you do the
less you care*
MICHAEL POLLAN / An Animal's Place   **219**

What this suggests to me is that people who care should be working not for animal rights but animal welfare — to ensure that farm animals don't suffer and that their deaths are swift and painless. In fact, the decent-life-merciful-death line is how Jeremy Bentham justified his own meat eating. Yes, the philosophical father of animal rights was himself a carnivore. In a passage rather less frequently quoted by animal rightists, Bentham defended eating animals on the grounds that "we are the better for it, and they are never the worse.... The death they suffer in our hands commonly is, and always may be, a speedier and, by that means, a less painful one than that which would await them in the inevitable course of nature."

My guess is that Bentham never looked too closely at what happens in a   70 slaughterhouse, but the argument suggests that, in theory at least, a utilitarian can justify the killing of humanely treated animals — for meat or, presumably, for clothing. (Though leather and fur pose distinct moral problems. Leather is a byproduct of raising domestic animals for food, which can be done humanely. However, furs are usually made from wild animals that die brutal deaths — usually in leg-hold traps — and since most fur species aren't domesticated, raising them on farms isn't necessarily more humane.) But whether the issue is food or fur or hunting, what should concern us is the suffering, not the killing. All of which I was feeling pretty good about — until I remembered that utilitarians can also justify killing retarded orphans. Killing just isn't the problem for them that it is for other people, including me.

During my visit to Polyface Farm, I asked Salatin where his animals were slaughtered. He does the chickens and rabbits right on the farm, and would do the cattle, pigs and sheep there too if only the U.S.D.A. would let him. Salatin showed me the open-air abattoir he built behind the farmhouse — a sort of outdoor kitchen on a concrete slab, with stainless-steel sinks, scalding tanks, a feather-plucking machine and metal cones to hold the birds upside down while they're being bled. Processing chickens is not a pleasant job, but Salatin insists on doing it himself because he's convinced he can do it more humanely and cleanly than any processing plant. He slaughters every other Saturday through the summer. Anyone's welcome to watch.

I asked Salatin how he could bring himself to kill a chicken.

"People have a soul; animals don't," he said. "It's a bedrock belief of mine." Salatin is a devout Christian. "Unlike us, animals are not created in God's image, so when they die, they just die."

The notion that only in modern times have people grown uneasy about killing animals is a flattering conceit. Taking a life is momentous, and people have been working to justify the slaughter of animals for thousands of years. Religion and especially ritual has played a crucial part in helping us reckon the moral costs. Native Americans and other hunter-gatherers would give thanks to their prey for giving up its life so the eater might live (sort of like saying grace). Many cultures have offered sacrificial animals to the gods, perhaps as a way to convince themselves that it was the gods' desires that demanded the slaughter, not their own. In ancient Greece, the priests responsible for the slaughter (priests! — now we entrust the job to minimum-wage workers) would sprinkle holy water on the sacrificial animal's brow. The beast would promptly shake its head, and this was taken as a sign of assent. Slaughter doesn't necessarily preclude respect. For all these people, it was the ceremony that allowed them to look, then to eat.

Apart from a few surviving religious practices, we no longer have any   75
rituals governing the slaughter or eating of animals, which perhaps helps to explain why we find ourselves where we do, feeling that our only choice is to either look away or give up meat. Frank Perdue is happy to serve the first customer; Peter Singer, the second.

Until my visit to Polyface Farm, I had assumed these were the only two options. But on Salatin's farm, the eye contact between people and animals whose loss John Berger mourned is still a fact of life — and of death, for neither the lives nor the deaths of these animals have been secreted behind steel walls. "Food with a face," Salatin likes to call what he's selling, a slogan that probably scares off some customers. People see very different things when they look into the eyes of a pig or a chicken or a steer — a being without a soul, a "subject of a life" entitled to rights, a link in a food chain, a vessel for pain and pleasure, a tasty lunch. But figuring out what we do think, and what we can eat, might begin with the looking.

We certainly won't philosophize our way to an answer. Salatin told me the story of a man who showed up at the farm one Saturday morning. When Salatin noticed a PETA bumper sticker on the man's car, he figured he was in for it. But the man had a different agenda. He explained that after 16 years as a vegetarian, he had decided that the only way he could ever eat meat again was if he killed the animal himself. He had come to look.

"Ten minutes later we were in the processing shed with a chicken," Salatin recalled. "He slit the bird's throat and watched it die. He saw that the animal did not look at him accusingly, didn't do a Disney double take. The animal had been treated with respect when it was alive, and he saw that it could also have a respectful death — that it wasn't being treated as a pile of protoplasm."

Salatin's open-air abattoir is a morally powerful idea. Someone slaughtering a chicken in a place where he can be watched is apt to do it scrupulously, with consideration for the animal as well as for the eater. This is going to sound quixotic, but maybe all we need to do to redeem industrial animal agriculture in this country is to pass a law requiring that the steel and concrete walls of the CAFO's and slaughterhouses be replaced with . . . glass. If there's any new "right" we need to establish, maybe it's this one: the right to look.

No doubt the sight of some of these places would turn many people into   80
vegetarians. Many others would look elsewhere for their meat, to farmers like Salatin. There are more of them than I would have imagined. Despite the relentless consolidation of the American meat industry, there has been a revival of small farms where animals still live their "characteristic form of life." I'm thinking of the ranches where cattle still spend their lives on grass, the poultry

farms where chickens still go outside and the hog farms where pigs live as they did 50 years ago — in contact with the sun, the earth and the gaze of a farmer.

For my own part, I've discovered that if you're willing to make the effort, it's entirely possible to limit the meat you eat to nonindustrial animals. I'm tempted to think that we need a new dietary category, to go with the vegan and lactovegetarian and piscatorian. I don't have a catchy name for it yet (humanocarnivore?), but this is the only sort of meat eating I feel comfortable with these days. I've become the sort of shopper who looks for labels indicating that his meat and eggs have been humanely grown (the American Humane Association's new "Free Farmed" label seems to be catching on), who visits the farms where his chicken and pork come from and who asks kinky-sounding questions about touring slaughterhouses. I've actually found a couple of small processing plants willing to let a customer onto the kill floor, including one, in Cannon Falls, Minn., with a glass abattoir.

The industrialization — and dehumanization — of American animal farming is a relatively new, evitable and local phenomenon: no other country raises and slaughters its food animals quite as intensively or as brutally as we do. Were the walls of our meat industry to become transparent, literally or even figuratively, we would not long continue to do it this way. Tail-docking and sow crates and beak-clipping would disappear overnight, and the days of slaughtering 400 head of cattle an hour would come to an end. For who could stand the sight? Yes, meat would get more expensive. We'd probably eat less of it, too, but maybe when we did eat animals, we'd eat them with the consciousness, ceremony and respect they deserve.

Reading across Professions
JAN WEBER, Filmmaker

Michael Pollan published this essay in 2002, the same year I first screened *As We Sow*, my documentary on industrialized agriculture in rural Iowa. While Pollan's focus was on the rights and welfare of animals, mine was on the rights and welfare of livestock farmers — hog farmers in particular.

Much has changed since then. For starters, consumers — or, as Pollan calls himself and other omnivores like me, "eaters" — have become more and more knowledgeable about where their food comes from, and they are making their buying decisions based not just on what the food is or how much it costs, but on how it was raised. Just five years ago, little attention was paid to the burger in the bun, or for that matter, to the lettuce, onion, pickle, or the bun itself. But now, prompted by several recent developments (the rapid growth of farmers' markets and other local food systems, the wide dissemination of food-related works by writers like Eric Schlosser and Michael Pollan, the news of disastrous food contamination cases, and the massive growth of organics — even at Wal-Mart), we eaters have begun to ask questions about everything we eat, from bok choy to pork chops: are these organic, natural, free-range, humanely raised, animal-friendly, antibiotic- and hormone-free?

But what about the farmers? Five years ago, the Iowa farmers I met and filmed were focused on survival. Small, diverse family farms were fast disappearing. Old red barns surrounded by grazing livestock, now obsolete, were being replaced by sleek new computer-operated facilities called Confined Animal Feeding Operations (CAFOs). Pig farmers, now obsolete, were being replaced by pork producers who applied assembly-line production techniques and cost-of-production analysis to the business of protein output. Desperate to keep their farms going, many small farmers opted to go under contract to powerful megacorporations that control the entire food chain "from seed to cellophane" — including the farmer. Under most contract agreements, the corporation supplies everything from the pig's genetics to the pig itself, from the feed the hogs eat to the medicines they take. Farmers, once celebrated for their independence and entrepreneurial spirit, for their mastery of animal husbandry and stewardship of the land, now get a monthly salary for following instructions.

The life cycle of a CAFO pig is maintained not by the farmer, but by corporate management with strict timetables. When the calendar hits the preappointed day, the pigs are loaded into a truck, delivered to a packing plant, and turned into ham and sausage. The farmer ends up with a lagoon full of liquid pig manure, legal and economic responsibility for any environmental damage caused by that manure, and a building to clean before the next load of pigs arrives.

If the walls of our meat industry were transparent, as Pollan posits in his essay, what would we see today? For the animals, there has been some improvement, although there is much more to do. For farmers, not much has changed. Factory farming supported by farmers under contract has never been so robust. Independent farmers have no market for their pigs and continue to go out of business in alarming numbers; they cannot pass their farms or their knowledge on to the next generation.

So what does this tell us? It tells us that unless the plight of the farmers is revealed and fixed, the plight of the animals they take care of cannot change much either. Pollan calls industrialization the "dehumanization of animal farming." I would add that it also contributes to the dehumanization of farmers. Perhaps it's time we recognize the farmer's place in the food chain, too, and treat both animals and humans with the "consciousness, ceremony and respect they deserve."

Jan Weber is a documentary filmmaker specializing in agricultural issues.

QUESTIONING THE TEXT

1. In his introduction, J.R. praises this article as the most "powerful . . . example of good argument" that he has ever selected for this book. He gives several reasons for his assessment, stating that the article "embodies all the principles of a fair and principled rhetoric, grabbing both the mind and heart" and that it "unfolds the complexities of a substantial moral issue while avoiding sensationalism." Working with a classmate, look for examples in Pollan's text that would support J.R.'s claims. Do you agree with J.R.'s assessment of the argument? Why, or why not?

2. What is Pollan's main claim? Where does he reveal this claim? Why do you think he chooses not to put this thesis in the opening paragraph?

MAKING CONNECTIONS

3. "More than any other institution, the American industrial animal farm offers a nightmarish glimpse of what capitalism can look like in the absence of moral or regulatory constraint," Pollan writes (paragraph 45). In "Grade A: The Market for a Yale Woman's Eggs" (p. 190), Jessica Cohen raises a similar issue when she asks, "Should couples be able to pay a premium on an open market for their idea of the perfect egg?" (paragraph 12). Compare the moral and economic concerns in these two arguments. Can you derive a principle that you think should guide human behavior in each of these cases?

4. Pollan suggests that "speciesism" may one day become a "form of discrimination as indefensible as racism or anti-Semitism" (paragraph 2). Use the arguments against racism presented in Martin Luther King Jr.'s "Letter from Birmingham Jail" (p. 163) to judge the validity of Pollan's analogy.

JOINING THE CONVERSATION

5. Do you or does someone you know make a living from an animal farm, or from another related business that is implicated in the animal rights conflicts Pollan raises (for example, that of a butcher, grocer, restaurateur, or leather goods merchant)? Put yourself in the position of someone whose livelihood depends on the killing of animals, and write a letter to Pollan, responding to his concerns. Can you lend further support to his argument, or do you disagree with some of his points?

6. Pollan says that he tries to limit his consumption of meat to that produced on "nonindustrial" farms (paragraph 81). Use the Internet to research other consumer boycotts related to food production. Discuss with classmates whether you would be willing to support any of these movements.

BARBARA DAFOE WHITEHEAD
The Making of a Divorce Culture

GROWING UP IN THE *1950s, I knew only one classmate whose parents were divorced. In my tight ethnic neighborhood, stable two-parent families were the rule, and divorce was something observed only occasionally on the silver screen. In fact, families breaking up seemed very much a Hollywood phenomenon. But Hollywood soon rubbed off on the rest of us.*

Within a generation, we came to accept divorce as almost normal. But normal *here simply means that divorces now happen all the time, not that the pain of separation they cause has become easier to endure, especially for children. For me, that point was made most forcefully the first time I taught selections about family life from an earlier edition of* The Presence of Others. *In class discussions, we explored all sorts of family concerns — from the changing role of fathers to conditions in nursing homes — but we had skirted one burning issue that emerged spontaneously as the theme of more than half the papers the unit produced. In draft after searing draft, my students detailed their personal and inevitably painful experiences with divorce. As we reviewed the drafts in subsequent class sessions, the writers often turned to each other for understanding and support as they recounted their feelings of hurt and betrayal. Clearly, for many students today, divorce has become a central event in their lives, shaping their views and attitudes toward family, commitment, and relationships with members of the opposite sex.*

Although it has become fashionable to talk about the normalcy of single parenthood and other nontraditional family arrangements, Barbara Dafoe Whitehead (b. 1944) argues that the willingness of American culture to accept divorce is genuinely new. A registered Democrat, Whitehead first came to public attention with an article she published in Atlantic Monthly *with the now-famous title "Dan Quayle Was Right" (April 1993). In the piece, Whitehead, wielding numerous studies and statistics, argues that then-vice president Quayle had correctly identified a major problem in American society when he attacked TV sitcom mom Murphy Brown for celebrating single parenthood. The argument of Whitehead's influential piece evolved into* The Divorce Culture *(1997), her book-length study of the causes and consequences of soaring divorce rates in America. "The Making of a Divorce Culture" is the introduction to Whitehead's book. Married and the mother of three children, Whitehead has a Ph.D. from the University of Chicago. Her most recent book is* Why There Are No Good Men Left *(2002).* —J.R.

Divorce is now part of everyday American life. It is embedded in our laws and institutions, our manners and mores, our movies and television shows, our novels and children's storybooks, and our closest and most important relationships. Indeed, divorce has become so pervasive that many people naturally assume it has seeped into the social and cultural mainstream over a long period of time. Yet this is not the case. Divorce has become an American way of life only as the result of recent and revolutionary change.

The entire history of American divorce can be divided into two periods, one evolutionary and the other revolutionary. For most of the nation's history, divorce was a rare occurrence and an insignificant feature of family and social relationships. In the first sixty years of the twentieth century, divorce became more common, but it was hardly commonplace. In 1960, the divorce rate stood at a still relatively modest level of nine per one thousand married couples. After 1960, however, the rate accelerated at a dazzling pace. It doubled in roughly a decade and continued its upward climb until the early 1980s, when it stabilized at the highest level among advanced Western societies. As a consequence of this sharp and sustained rise, divorce moved from the margins to the mainstream of American life in the space of three decades.

Ideas are important in revolutions, yet surprisingly little attention has been devoted to the ideas that gave impetus to the divorce revolution. Of the scores of books on divorce published in recent decades, most focus on its legal, demographic, economic, or (especially) psychological dimensions. Few, if any, deal fully with its intellectual origins. Yet trying to comprehend the divorce revolution and its consequences without some sense of its ideological origins, is like trying to understand the American Revolution without taking into account the thinking of John Locke, Thomas Jefferson, or Thomas Paine. This more recent revolution, like the revolution of our nation's founding, has its roots in a distinctive set of ideas and claims.

This book [*The Divorce Culture*] is about the ideas behind the divorce revolution and how these ideas have shaped a culture of divorce. The making of a divorce culture has involved three overlapping changes: first, the emergence and widespread diffusion of a historically new and distinctive set of ideas about divorce in the last third of the twentieth century; second, the migration of divorce from a minor place within a system governed by marriage to a free-standing place as a major institution governing family relationships; and third, a widespread shift in thinking about the obligations of marriage and parenthood.

Beginning in the late 1950s, Americans began to change their ideas   5 about the individual's obligations to family and society. Broadly described, this change was away from an ethic of obligation to others and toward an obligation to self. I do not mean that people suddenly abandoned all responsibilities to others, but rather that they became more acutely conscious of their responsibility to attend to their own individual needs and interests. At least as important as the moral obligation to look after others, the new thinking suggested, was the moral obligation to look after oneself.

This ethical shift had a profound impact on ideas about the nature and purpose of the family. In the American tradition, the marketplace and the public square have represented the realms of life devoted to the pursuit of individual interest, choice, and freedom, while the family has been the realm defined by voluntary commitment, duty, and self-sacrifice. With the greater emphasis on individual satisfaction in family relationships, however, family well-being became subject to a new metric. More than in the past, satisfaction in this sphere came to be based on subjective judgments about the content and quality of individual happiness rather than on such objective measures as level of income, material nurture and support, or boosting children onto a higher rung on the socioeconomic ladder. People began to judge the strength and "health" of family bonds according to their capacity to promote individual fulfillment and personal growth. As a result, the conception of the family's role and place in the society began to change. The family began to lose its separate place and distinctive identity as the realm of duty, service, and sacrifice. Once the domain of the obligated self, the family was increasingly viewed as yet another domain for the expression of the unfettered self.

These broad changes figured centrally in creating a new conception of divorce which gained influential adherents and spread broadly and swiftly throughout the society — a conception that represented a radical departure from earlier notions. Once regarded mainly as a social, legal, and family event in which there were other stakeholders, divorce now became an event closely linked to the pursuit of individual satisfactions, opportunities, and growth.

The new conception of divorce drew upon some of the oldest, and most resonant, themes in the American political tradition. The nation, after all, was founded as the result of a political divorce, and revolutionary thinkers explicitly adduced a parallel between the dissolution of marital bonds and the dissolution of political bonds. In political as well as marital relationships, they argued, bonds of obligation were established voluntarily on the basis of mutual affection and regard. Once such bonds turned cold and oppressive, peoples, like individuals, had the right to dissolve them and to form more perfect unions.

In the new conception of divorce, this strain of eighteenth-century political thought mingled with a strain of twentieth-century psychotherapeutic thought. Divorce was not only an individual right but also a psychological resource. The dissolution of marriage offered the chance to make oneself over from the inside out, to refurbish and express the inner self, and to acquire certain valuable psychological assets and competencies, such as initiative, assertiveness, and a stronger and better self-image.

The conception of divorce as both an individual right and an inner   10
experience merged with and reinforced the new ethic of obligation to the self. In family relationships, one had an obligation to be attentive to one's own feelings and to work toward improving the quality of one's inner life. This ethical imperative completed the rationale for a sense of individual entitlement to divorce. Increasingly, mainstream America saw the legal dissolution of marriage as a matter of individual choice, in which there were no other stakeholders or larger social interests. This conception of divorce strongly argued for removing the social, legal, and moral impediments to the free exercise of the individual right to divorce.

Traditionally, one major impediment to divorce was the presence of children in the family. According to well-established popular belief, dependent children had a stake in their parents' marriage and suffered hardship as a result of the dissolution of the marriage. Because children were vulnerable and dependent, parents had a moral obligation to place their children's interests in the marital partnership above their own individual satisfactions. This notion was swiftly abandoned after the 1960s. Influential voices in the society, including child-welfare professionals, claimed that the happiness of individual parents, rather than an intact marriage, was the key determinant of children's family well-being. If divorce could make one or both parents happier, then it was likely to improve the well-being of children as well.

In the following decades, the new conception of divorce spread through the law, therapy, etiquette, the social sciences, popular advice literature, and religion. Concerns that had dominated earlier thinking on divorce were now dismissed as old-fashioned and excessively moralistic. Divorce would not harm children but would lead to greater happiness for children and their single parents. It would not damage the institution of marriage but would make possible better marriages and happier individuals. Divorce would not damage the social fabric by diminishing children's life chances but would strengthen the social fabric by improving the quality of affective bonds between parents and children, whatever form the structural arrangements of their families might happen to take.

As the sense of divorce as an individual freedom and entitlement grew, the sense of concern about divorce as a social problem diminished. Earlier in the century, each time the divorce rate increased sharply, it had inspired widespread public concern and debate about the harmful impact of divorce on families and the society. But in the last third of the century, as the divorce rate rose to once unthinkable levels, public anxiety about it all but vanished. At the very moment when divorce had its most profound impact on the society, weakening the institution of marriage, revolutionizing the structure of families and reorganizing parent-child relationships, it ceased to be a source of concern or debate.

The lack of attention to divorce became particularly striking after the 1980s, as a politically polarized debate over the state of the American family took shape. On one side, conservatives pointed to abortion, illegitimacy, and homosexuality as forces destroying the family. On the other, liberals cited domestic violence, economic insecurity, and inadequate public supports as the key problems afflicting the family. But politicians on both sides had almost nothing to say about divorce. Republicans did not want to alienate their upscale constituents or their libertarian wing, both of whom tended to favor easy divorce, nor did they want to call attention to the divorces among their own leadership. Democrats did not want to anger their large constituency among women who saw easy divorce as a hard-won freedom and prerogative, nor did they wish to seem unsympathetic to single mothers. Thus, except for bipartisan calls to get tougher with deadbeat dads, both Republicans and Democrats avoided the issue of divorce and its consequences as far too politically risky.

But the failure to address divorce carried a price. It allowed the middle   15
class to view family breakdown as a "them" problem rather than an "us" problem. Divorce was not like illegitimacy or welfare dependency, many claimed. It
was a matter of individual choice, imposing few, if any, costs or consequences on
others. Thus, mainstream America could cling to the comfortable illusion that
the nation's family problems had to do with the behavior of unwed teenage
mothers or poor women on welfare rather than with the instability of marriage
and family life within its own ranks.

Nonetheless, after thirty years of persistently high levels of divorce, this
illusion, though still politically attractive, is increasingly difficult to sustain in the
face of a growing body of experience and evidence. To begin with, divorce has
indeed hurt children. It has created economic insecurity and disadvantage for
many children who would not otherwise be economically vulnerable. It has led
to more fragile and unstable family households. It has caused a mass exodus of
fathers from children's households and, all too often, from their lives. It has
reduced the levels of parental time and money invested in children. In sum, it
has changed the very nature of American childhood. Just as no patient would
have designed today's system of health care, so no child would have chosen
today's culture of divorce.

Divorce figures prominently in the altered economic fortunes of middle-
class families. Although the economic crisis of the middle class is usually
described as a problem caused by global economic changes, changing patterns in
education and earnings, and ruthless corporate downsizing, it owes more to divorce than is commonly acknowledged. Indeed, recent data suggest that marriage
may be a more important economic resource than a college degree. According to
an analysis of 1994 income patterns, the median income of married-parent
households whose heads have only a high school diploma is ten percent higher
than the median income of college-educated single-parent households.[1] Parents
who are college graduates *and* married form the new economic elite among families with children. Consequently, those who are concerned about what the
downsizing of corporations is doing to workers should also be concerned about
what the downsizing of families through divorce is doing to parents and children.

Widespread divorce depletes social capital as well. Scholars tell us that
strong and durable family and social bonds generate certain "goods" and

---

[1]An analysis of income data provided by The Northeastern University Center for Labor
Market Studies shows the following distribution by education and marital status:

Median Incomes for U.S. Families with Children, 1994

Education of Household Head	Married Couple Families	Single Parent Families
College Graduate	$71,263	$36,006
High School Graduate	$40,098	$14,698

*Based on 1994 Current Population Statistics. Families with one or more children under 18. Age of household
head: 22–62.*

services, including money, mutual assistance, information, caregiving, protection, and sponsorship. Because such bonds endure over time, they accumulate and form a pool of social capital which can be drawn down upon, when needed, over the entire course of a life. An elderly couple, married for fifty years, is likely to enjoy a substantial body of social and emotional capital, generated through their long-lasting marriage, which they can draw upon in caring for each other and for themselves as they age. Similarly, children who grow up in stable, two-parent married households are the beneficiaries of the social and emotional capital accumulated over time as a result of an enduring marriage bond. As many parents know, children continue to depend on these resources well into young adulthood. But as family bonds become increasingly fragile and vulnerable to disruption, they become less permanent and thus less capable of generating such forms of help, financial resources, and mutual support. In short, divorce consumes social capital and weakens the social fabric. At the very time that sweeping socioeconomic changes are mandating greater investment of social capital in children, widespread divorce is reducing the pool of social capital. As the new economic and social conditions raise the hurdles of child-rearing higher, divorce digs potholes in the tracks.

It should be stressed that this book is not intended as a brief against divorce as such. We must assume that divorce is necessary as a remedy for irretrievably broken marriages, especially those that are marred by severe abuse such as chronic infidelity, drug addiction, or physical violence. Nor is its argument directed against those who are divorced. It assumes that divorce is difficult, painful, and often unwanted by at least one spouse, and that divorcing couples require compassion and support from family, friends, and their religious communities. Nor should this book be taken as an appeal for a return to an earlier era of American family life. The media routinely portray the debate over the family as one between nostalgists and realists, between those who want to turn back the clock to the fifties and those who want to march bravely and resolutely forward into the new century. But this is a lazy and misguided approach, driven more by the easy availability of archival photos and footage from 1950s television sitcoms than by careful consideration of the substance of competing arguments.

More fundamentally, this approach overlooks the key issue. And that issue 20 is not how today's families might stack up against those of an earlier era; indeed, no reliable empirical data for such a comparison exist. In an age of diverse family structures, the heart of the matter is what kinds of contemporary family arrangements have the greatest capacity to promote children's well-being, and how we can ensure that more children have the advantages of growing up in such families.

In the past year or so, there has been growing recognition of the personal and social costs of three decades of widespread divorce. A public debate has finally emerged. Within this debate, there are two separate and overlapping discussions.

The first centers on a set of specific proposals that are intended to lessen the harmful impact of divorce on children: a federal system of child-support collection, tougher child-support enforcement, mandatory counseling for divorcing parents, and reform of no-fault divorce laws in the states. What is striking about this discussion is its narrow focus on public policy, particularly on changes in the system of no-fault divorce. In this, as in so many other crucial discussions involving social and moral questions, the most vocal and visible participants come from the world of government policy, electoral politics, and issue advocacy. The media, which are tongue-tied unless they can speak in the language of left-right politics, reinforce this situation. And the public is offered needlessly polarized arguments that hang on a flat yes-or-no response to this or that individual policy measure. All too often, this discussion of divorce poses what *Washington Post* columnist E. J. Dionne aptly describes as false choices.

Notably missing is a serious consideration of the broader moral assumptions and empirical claims that define our divorce culture. Divorce touches on classic questions in American public philosophy — on the nature of our most important human and social bonds, the duties and obligations imposed by bonds we voluntarily elect, the "just causes" for the dissolution of those bonds, and the differences between obligations volunteered and those that must be coerced. Without consideration of such questions, the effort to change behavior by changing a few public policies is likely to founder.

The second and complementary discussion does try to place divorce within a larger philosophical framework. Its proponents have looked at the decline in the well-being of the nation's children as the occasion to call for a collective sense of commitment by all Americans to all of America's children. They pose the challenging question: "What are Americans willing to do 'for the sake of *all* children'?" But while this is surely an important question, it addresses only half of the problem of declining commitment. The other half has to do with how we answer the question: "What are individual parents obliged to do 'for the sake of their own children'?"

Renewing a *social* ethic of commitment to children is an urgent goal, but it cannot be detached from the goal of strengthening the *individual* ethic of commitment to children. The state of one affects the standing of the other. A society that protects the rights of parents to easy, unilateral divorce, and flatly rejects the idea that parents should strive to preserve a marriage "for the sake of the children," faces a problem when it comes to the question of public sacrifice "for the sake of the children." To put it plainly, many of the ideas we have come to believe and vigorously defend about adult prerogatives and freedoms in family life are undermining the foundations of altruism and support for children.

With each passing year, the culture of divorce becomes more deeply entrenched. American children are routinely schooled in divorce. Mr. Rogers teaches toddlers about divorce. An entire children's literature is devoted to divorce. Family movies and videos for children feature divorced families. *Mrs. Doubtfire*, originally a children's book about divorce and then a hit movie, is aggressively marketed as a holiday video for kids. Of course, these books and movies are designed to help children deal with the social reality and psychological trauma of divorce. But they also carry an unmistakable message about the impermanence and unreliability of family bonds. Like romantic love, the children's storybooks say, family love comes and goes. Daddies disappear. Mommies find new boyfriends. Mommies' boyfriends leave. Grandparents go away. Even pets must be left behind.

More significantly, in a society where nearly half of all children are likely to experience parental divorce, family breakup becomes a defining event of American childhood itself. Many children today know nothing but divorce in their family lives. And although children from divorced families often say they want to avoid divorce if they marry, young adults whose parents divorced are more likely to get divorced themselves and to bear children outside of marriage than young adults from stable married-parent families.

Precisely because the culture of divorce has generational momentum, this book [*The Divorce Culture*] offers no easy optimism about the prospects for change. But neither does it counsel passive resignation or acceptance of the culture's relentless advance. What it does offer is a critique of the ideas behind current divorce trends. Its argument is directed against the ideas about divorce that have gained ascendancy, won our support, and lodged in our consciousness as "proven" and incontrovertible. It challenges the popular idea of divorce as an individual right and freedom to be exercised in the pursuit of individual goods and satisfactions, without due regard for other stakeholders in the marital partnership, especially children. This may be a fragile and inadequate response to a profoundly consequential set of changes, but it seeks the abandonment of ideas that have misled us and failed our children.

In a larger sense, this book is both an appreciation and a criticism of what is peculiarly American about divorce. Divorce has spread throughout advanced Western societies at roughly the same pace and over roughly the same period of time. Yet nowhere else has divorce been so deeply imbued with the larger themes of a nation's political traditions. Nowhere has divorce so fully reflected the spirit and susceptibilities of a people who share an extravagant faith in the power of the individual and in the power of positive thinking. Divorce in America is not unique, but what we have made of divorce is uniquely American. In exploring the cultural roots of divorce, therefore, we look at ourselves, at what is best and worst in our traditions, what is visionary and what is blind, and how the two are sometimes tragically commingled and confused.

QUESTIONING THE TEXT

1. Whitehead claims in the opening sentence that "[d]ivorce is now part of everyday American life." What evidence can you point to — from popular culture, American society, or your own experience — to support *or* refute that claim?

2. Arguing that the increasing divorce rate is due, in part, to a shift in the way marriage is viewed, Whitehead says Americans have moved from an ethic of obligation within families to an ethic of self-fulfillment. Working in a group, explore these abstractions and try to give them a more concrete shape. When does a family member act according to an ethic of obligation and when according to an ethic of self-fulfillment? How compatible are these different views of the family?

MAKING CONNECTIONS

3. Whitehead mentions a "goal of strengthening the *individual* ethic of commitment to children" as different from a "*social* ethic of commitment to children" (paragraph 25). Read Malcolm Gladwell's "The Moral Hazard Myth" (p. 238) and David Gratzer's "Where Would You Rather Be Sick?" (p. 249). How does the notion of the difference between social ethics and individual ethics matter in these readings?

4. Read "The Rules about the Rules" (p. 178), from Stephen L. Carter's book *Integrity*, paying special attention to the three criteria Carter uses to define an act of integrity. Then write an essay in which you explore when and/or whether a divorce can fit that definition.

JOINING THE CONVERSATION

5. Whitehead disputes the popular argument that children are better off when divorce "make[s] one or both parents happier" (paragraph 11), suggesting that many contemporary problems can be traced to broken families. Write an essay exploring the consequences of divorce for children. For support, draw on library materials, your personal experience, and, possibly, firsthand information gathered through interviews.

6. Whitehead largely dismisses a series of public policy proposals "intended to lessen the harmful impact of divorce on children: a federal system of child-support collection, tougher child-support enforcement, mandatory counseling for divorcing parents, and reform of no-fault divorce laws in the states" (paragraph 22). Working in a group, discuss these and other options for making divorce less devastating for children, as well as ideas for making families more stable and successful. Then write a proposal paper on your own explaining one such idea. Your proposal need not endorse Whitehead's ideas about the causes or consequences of divorce.

KAY S. HYMOWITZ
Scenes from the Exhibitionists

I*T IS BY NOW A COMMONPLACE* to say that privacy has gone the way of the dodo bird and other extinct species. We do not yet have a national identity card, but surely one is in our future. In the meantime, hackers have made health records, credit card numbers, and heaven knows what else into public information. A bit of googling will turn up information, and lots of it, on most of us (searching for "Andrea Lunsford" and "John Ruszkiewicz" turned up over 250,000 hits). Nor do many people — and especially young people — seem to care. Indeed, they are revealing information about themselves in epic proportions on MySpace, FaceBook, and all manner of blogs, so much so that potential employers have begun checking such sites to see what they can learn about the people applying for jobs. And what they find has led some companies to reject applicants — all on the basis of what they had revealed about themselves on a social networking site. The loss of privacy (in concept as well as in fact) troubles those who fear undue governmental intrusion into their lives. As MIT psychologist Sherry Turkle puts it, "Today's college students are habituated to a world of online blogging, instant messaging, and Web browsing that leaves electronic traces. Yet they have had little experience with the right to privacy. Unlike past generations of Americans, who grew up with the notion that the privacy of their mail was sacrosanct, our children are accustomed to electronic surveillance as part of their daily lives."

Kay Hymowitz (b. 1948), Senior Fellow at the Manhattan Institute and author of Ready or Not: Why Treating Children as Small Adults Endangers Their Future — and Ours *(1999) and* Liberation's Children: Parents and Kids in a Post-Marital Age *(2003), also worries about the loss of privacy as a governing concept in our society. In "Scenes from the Exhibitionists," which appeared on the editorial page of the* Wall Street Journal *in 2007, Hymowitz points the finger of blame primarily at women, saying "The fairer sex shows (and tells) too much." And she does offer a number of entertaining examples to back up her claim, from Britney Spears and Paris Hilton to D.C. sex-blogger Jessica Cutler. Rejecting the argument that acts of self-revelation are not self-indulgent exhibitionism but rather marks of bravery, showing women's determination to defy the strictures of society, Hymowitz offers as a counter-example a few women who do not bare and tell all. Susan Sontag, for instance, did not dwell on her romantic involvement with noted photographer Annie Liebovitz, in Hymowitz's view, because she did not want sexual orientation to become the primary mark of her identity.*

I am sympathetic to some of what Hymowitz says; in particular, I am troubled by the many college students I know who blithely report the most intimate details of their lives online, with little sense of the consequences those reports may entail. But I am more than a little puzzled by Hymowitz's tentative conclusion that "men have become more discreet than women." Come again? Surely Hymowitz remembers basketball star Dennis Rodman in his heyday, posing naked in a bunch of magazines? Or, more recently, Colin Ferrell's sex tapes — or the overexposed intimate lives and thoughts of

233

Tom Cruise and Mel Gibson. I could go on and on with examples of men who, like Britney, make their "own privates public." So I don't buy Hymowitz's argument when she targets women as the ones giving us a glut of exhibitionism; it seems to me as if there's plenty of guilt to go around here. But Hymowitz does raise an important issue, and her light-hearted, snappy take on it doesn't obscure what's at stake: when we lose the right — or even the desire — for privacy, we open ourselves to surveillance by Big Brother (and Big Sister) and to the kind of objectification and commodification that can threaten identity.   —A.L.

Some of my best friends are women — heck, I am a woman — but I've come to the conclusion that we've seen too much of the fairer sex. For me, the final straw came last month when Britney Spears jauntily revealed her waxed nether-regions to waiting photographers as she exited her limo. Britney's stunt made her the Internet smash of the season. But in providing America's workers with this cubicle distraction, Britney was doing a lot more than making her own privates public.

In fact, Britney was following to its logical end what has become the first rule of contemporary American girlhood: to show that you are liberated, take it off. Liberty means responsibility . . . to disrobe. Paris Hilton, Britney's BFF (Best Friend Forever), taped her sexual escapades with an ex-boyfriend, though even she was tactful enough to pretend that she hadn't meant for the video to go public. Courtney Love, Lindsay Lohan and Tara Reid have also staged their own wardrobe malfunctions. But flashing is hardly limited to celebrities. The girls-next-door who migrate to Florida during spring break happily lift their blouses and snap their thongs for the producers of *Girls Gone Wild*, who sell their DVDs to an eager public.

Nor is it just young female flashers who are driven to expose themselves to the masses. Older women, whether because of lingering traces of reticence or doubts about the camera-readiness of their intimate anatomy, use the written word to bare all. There are legions of women bloggers who write about last night's bed tricks, their underwear preferences and their menstrual cycles (yes, Virginia, there is a tamponblog.com). More sophisticated exhibitionists turn to tasteful erotic memoirs. In *A Round Heeled Woman*, Jane Juksa gives us a detailed description of her varied sexual adventures after, at age 66, she advertised for sex in the personals of the *New York Review of Books*. In *Surrender*, the ex-Balanchine dancer Toni Bentley tells of the spiritual transcendence she experienced during the 298 times she had anal sex with a former lover — making this the first transcendent sex ever to involve a calculator.

Now, this is the point at which the enlightened always begin grumbling: What's wrong with women showing that they are "sexual beings"? In this vein, the show-or-tell-all is an act of bravery, demonstrating a woman's determination to throw off society's taboos against full expression of her sexuality. "[F]emale exhibitionism is . . . an act of female power," Richard Goldstein of the *Village Voice* has written. "We should redeem the slut in ourselves and rejoice in being bad girls," Naomi Wolf once urged (but has since modified now that she has an adolescent daughter). It follows that reservations about self-exposure are a sign of anti-sex, anti-woman prudery. They may just be the first step in a long-planned, mandated return to the missionary position, female frigidity and meatloaf dinners, cooked and served by apron-clad wives.

But this Puritans-are-coming! stance, validating, as it does, someone as cracked as Paris Hilton, finally implodes. The problem with a Britney or a Bentley is not that they are floozies. It is rather that they are, paradoxical as it might seem, naïve. They underestimate the magnetic force field created by intimate sexual information and violate the logic of privacy that should be all the more compelling in a media-driven age. People in the public eye always risk becoming objectified; they are watched by hordes of strangers who have only fragmentary information about them. When that information includes details that only their Brazilian waxers should know for sure, it's inevitable that, humans being the perverse creatures that they are, all other facts of identity will fall away. Instead of becoming freer, the exhibitionist becomes an object defined primarily by a narrow sexual datum.

The writer Daphne Merkin offers the perfect cautionary tale about the dangers of giving the public Too Much Information. In 1996 Merkin published an essay in the *New Yorker* describing the erotic pleasure she found in spanking. Her sensational article hardly stalled her career; if anything it increased her name recognition. Understandably Ms. Merkin doesn't regret her essay, which she continues to believe to be "both intellectually and emotionally daring." But she kids herself when she says "I'm known more for the rigor of my thinking . . . than I am for revelations about my erotic preferences." Her article is still the major fact of her public identity; she will forever and always be Daphne Likes-To-Be-Spanked Merkin. This is not because the shocked public wants Ms. Merkin to cover herself up. It is because Ms. Merkin has invited us to know her by information that has far more power than her insights into Virginia Woolf.

It was doubtless for this reason that Susan Sontag hesitated to write about her romantic relationship with the photographer Annie Leibovitz. After her death, many accused Sontag of cowardice and hypocrisy for avoiding the L-word, but this seems an unlikely charge. A woman who braved the brutes of Kosovo, Sontag was probably less fearful of having it known that she was in love with a woman than of having it become the defining trait of her public identity; she must have dreaded being boxed in as the "lesbian writer Susan Sontag." Note that Sontag never shied from advancing a public persona on her own terms. On the contrary, that famous shock of white hair brashly announced that she was a woman with a talent for self-dramatization. But as an authority on the camera as well as on Western literature, she knew that the public gaze was always inclined to trivialize the complexities of identity.

Some people believe that it is lingering misogyny rather than naïve exhibitionism that leads the public to define women by their sexual anatomy and proclivities. Perhaps there is something to that. But the exhibitionism surely doesn't help. It seems that men, despite their reputation as braggarts, actually don't find self-exposure all that appealing. Where are the male counterparts to Britney Spears and *Girls Gone Wild*? Jessica Cutler, the D.C. sex-blogger known as Washingtonienne and a one-time congressional intern, is now being sued for $20 million by one of her gentleman callers, who for some reason preferred that his bedroom antics remain, well, in the bedroom.

In the highbrow world, Philip Roth clearly writes autobiographical novels, but it took a bitter ex-wife — the actress Claire Bloom — to rip off the fictional veil and give us the private Roth. Tom Stoppard, interviewed recently for the *New York Times Magazine* by Daphne Merkin (she once wrote an article about being spanked, by the way), hopes that his biography will be "as inaccurate as possible . . . I flinch when I see my name in the newspapers."

Why men have become more discreet than women, assuming they have,   10
is one of those cultural mysteries that is yet to be solved. But the fairer sex might want to take a lesson from Mr. Stoppard, who notes that it's not any sense of modesty that makes him reticent; rather it "has to do with not making myself available." To throw your intimate self before the public is to risk having your identity mauled by a mob of hyenas, and you will probably suffer for it. As Samuel Beckett said to Doris Lessing's lover when he heard that the novelist had used him as a model for one of her characters, "Identity is so fragile. How did you ever survive?" He peered at the man. "Or did you?"

QUESTIONING THE TEXT

1. Hymowitz ends with an anecdote about the writer Samuel Beckett asking a man on whom a fictional character had been modeled whether he had survived the experience. What do you think "survive" means in this context? Does this anecdote fit with the tone of the rest of Hymowitz's article? Why or why not?

2. In paragraph 5, Hymowitz suggests that the celebrities who expose themselves too much are naïve about the effects that too much revelation will have. Though she includes the example of noncelebrities who expose themselves in spring-break videos, most of Hymowitz's discussion of the effects of exposure seems to apply to celebrities. What about the nonfamous? Does a lack of discretion also threaten the identities of average citizens? Is so, how? If not, why not?

MAKING CONNECTIONS

3. Many of the readings in this volume depend on self-revelation for their effectiveness, even if their revelations are not as provocative as some that

Hymowitz mentions (paragraph 6). Think about some of the readings in this book that involve the revelation of intimate details (two possibilities include Michael Chorost's "My Bionic Quest for *Boléro*" (p. 291) or Jessica Cohen's "Grade A: The Market for a Yale Woman's Eggs" (p. 190). What's the difference between revealing enough about yourself to be interesting and revealing so much that you cross the line to being indiscreet? How much revelation is too much revelation?

JOINING THE CONVERSATION

4. In the last paragraphs of her article, Hymowitz notes, "Why men have become more discreet than women, assuming they have, is one of those cultural mysteries that is yet to be solved." Hymowitz's examples of discreet men, Philip Roth and Tom Stoppard, are drawn from an older generation, while most of her examples of female exhibitionists are young. Do you think that contemporary culture encourages young people today to be more exhibitionist than previous generations of youth were? Does our culture encourage women to be more exhibitionist than men? Find evidence to support your general conclusions.

5. In an exploratory essay that draws on sources in addition to Hymowitz, examine the assumptions behind some aspect of sexual behavior of your generation, whatever that generation might be. How do you think that your peers make decisions about what is right or wrong, ethical or unethical?

MALCOLM GLADWELL
The Moral Hazard Myth

Do you take your teeth — *and good dental care — pretty much for granted? If so, Malcolm Gladwell (b. 1963) has news for you. Introducing his essay on "the bad idea behind our failed health care system" with a gut-wrenching description of just how a tooth rots, Gladwell draws on interviews conducted with uninsured Americans, who point out the very bad (if unintended) consequences that occur when people are unable to afford to take care of their teeth. "If your teeth are bad," Gladwell reports, "you're not going to get a job as a receptionist, say, or a cashier. You're going to be put in the back somewhere." And you'll likely find yourself eating the kind of processed foods that may be easy on rotting or missing teeth but hard on good health.*

Gladwell asks how the richest nation on earth got into such a situation, how we can tolerate the fact that we spend far more per capita on health care than any other country in the industrialized world while still having 45 million people uninsured. The answer, Gladwell finds, is an obsession with the "moral hazard" theory, which posits that the more health coverage available to us, the more we will consume — to the point of wastefulness. Gladwell finds this theory, which is at the foundation of President George W. Bush's proposal to create a system of health savings accounts, wrongheaded at best, the final step toward an actuarial model of health care that is not a variant of universal care, as some argue, but "the very antithesis of universal health care." Gladwell compares this actuarial model to the social insurance model used when health insurance was conceived. Social insurance is the model currently in place in Canada, Germany, and Japan, and in the U.S. Medicare system, with which Americans are particularly happy.

Gladwell has spent a lot of his time and energy thinking and writing about issues related to health care, including a case study of a syphilis epidemic in Baltimore (in The Tipping Point: How Little Things Can Make a Difference *[2000]) and a study of emergency room doctors in Chicago's Cook County Hospital (in* Blink: The Power of Thinking without Thinking *[2005]) as well as the many essays he wrote as science and medicine writer at the* Washington Post. *Currently a staff writer for the* New Yorker, *Gladwell was named one of* Time Magazine's One Hundred Most Influential People of 2005. *I want to keep my eye on his work as the political season heats up: I wonder if he will write other articles that may inform the candidates' thinking about how to fix America's health care mess.*
— A.L.

1

Tooth decay begins, typically, when debris becomes trapped between the teeth and along the ridges and in the grooves of the molars. The food rots. It becomes colonized with bacteria. The bacteria feeds off sugars in the mouth and forms an acid that begins to eat away at the enamel of the teeth. Slowly, the bacteria works its way through to the dentin, the inner structure, and from there the cavity begins to blossom three-dimensionally, spreading inward and sideways. When the decay reaches the pulp tissue, the blood vessels, and the nerves that serve the tooth, the pain starts — an insistent throbbing. The tooth turns brown. It begins to lose its hard structure, to the point where a dentist can reach into a cavity with a hand instrument and scoop out the decay. At the base of the tooth, the bacteria mineralizes into tartar, which begins to irritate the gums. They become puffy and bright red and start to recede, leaving more and more of the tooth's root exposed. When the infection works its way down to the bone, the structure holding the tooth in begins to collapse altogether.

Several years ago, two Harvard researchers, Susan Starr Sered and Rushika Fernandopulle, set out to interview people without health-care coverage for a book they were writing, *Uninsured in America*. They talked to as many kinds of people as they could find, collecting stories of untreated depression and struggling single mothers and chronically injured laborers — and the most common complaint they heard was about teeth. Gina, a hairdresser in Idaho, whose husband worked as a freight manager at a chain store, had "a peculiar mannerism of keeping her mouth closed even when speaking." It turned out that she hadn't been able to afford dental care for three years, and one of her front teeth was rotting. Daniel, a construction worker, pulled out his bad teeth with pliers. Then, there was Loretta, who worked nights at a university research center in Mississippi, and was missing most of her teeth. "They'll break off after a while, and then you just grab a hold of them, and they work their way out," she explained to Sered and Fernandopulle. "It hurts so bad, because the tooth aches. Then it's a relief just to get it out of there. The hole closes up itself anyway. So it's so much better."

People without health insurance have bad teeth because, if you're paying for everything out of your own pocket, going to the dentist for a checkup seems like a luxury. It isn't, of course. The loss of teeth makes eating fresh fruits and vegetables difficult, and a diet heavy in soft, processed foods exacerbates more serious health problems, like diabetes. The pain of tooth decay leads many people to use alcohol as a salve. And those struggling to get ahead in the job market quickly find that the unsightliness of bad teeth, and the self-consciousness that results, can become a major barrier. If your teeth are bad, you're not going to get a job as a receptionist, say, or a cashier. You're going to be put in the back somewhere, far from the public eye. What Loretta, Gina, and Daniel understand, the two authors tell us, is that bad teeth have come to be seen as a marker of "poor parenting, low educational achievement and slow or faulty intellectual development." They are an outward marker of caste. "Almost every time we asked interviewees what their first priority would be if the president established universal health coverage tomorrow," Sered and Fernandopulle write, "the immediate answer was 'my teeth.'"

The U.S. health-care system, according to *Uninsured in America*, has created a group of people who increasingly look different from others and suffer in ways that others do not. The leading cause of personal bankruptcy in the United States is unpaid medical bills. Half of the uninsured owe money to hospitals, and a third are being pursued by collection agencies. Children without health insurance are less likely to receive medical attention for serious injuries, for recurrent ear infections, or for asthma. Lung-cancer patients without insurance are less likely to receive surgery, chemotherapy, or radiation treatment. Heart-attack victims without health insurance are less likely to receive angioplasty. People with pneumonia who don't have health insurance are less likely to receive X-rays or consultations. The death rate in any given year for someone without health insurance is twenty-five per cent higher than for someone with insurance. Because the uninsured are sicker than the rest of us, they can't get better jobs, and because they can't get better jobs they can't afford health insurance, and because they can't afford health insurance they get even sicker. John, the manager of a bar in Idaho, tells Sered and Fernandopulle that as a result of various workplace injuries over the years he takes eight ibuprofen, waits two hours, then takes eight more — and tries to cadge as much prescription pain medication as he can from friends. "There are times when I should've gone to the doctor, but I couldn't afford to go because I don't have insurance," he says. "Like when my back messed up, I should've gone. If I had insurance, I would've went, because I know I could get treatment, but when you can't afford it you don't go. Because the harder the hole you get into in terms of bills, then you'll never get out. So you just say, 'I can deal with the pain.'"

2

One of the great mysteries of political life in the United States is why   5
Americans are so devoted to their health-care system. Six times in the past century — during the First World War, during the Depression, during the Truman and Johnson Administrations, in the Senate in the nineteen-seventies, and during the Clinton years — efforts have been made to introduce some kind of universal health insurance, and each time the efforts have been rejected. Instead, the United States has opted for a makeshift system of increasing complexity and dysfunction. Americans spend $5,267 per capita on health care every year, almost two and half times the industrialized world's median of $2,193; the extra spending comes to hundreds of billions of dollars a year. What does that extra spending buy us? Americans have fewer doctors per capita than most Western countries. We go to the doctor less than people in other Western countries. We get admitted to the hospital less frequently than people in other Western countries. We are less satisfied with our health care than our counterparts in other countries. American life expectancy is lower than the Western average. Childhood-immunization rates in the United States are lower than average. Infant-mortality rates are in the nineteenth percentile of industrialized nations. Doctors here perform more high-end medical procedures, such as coronary angioplasties, than in other countries, but most of the wealthier Western

countries have more CT scanners than the United States does, and Switzerland, Japan, Austria, and Finland all have more MRI machines per capita. Nor is our system more efficient. The United States spends more that a thousand dollars per capita per year — or close to four hundred billion dollars — on health-care-related paperwork and administration, whereas Canada, for example, spends only about three hundred dollars per capita. And, of course, every other country in the industrialized world insures all its citizens; despite those extra hundreds of billions of dollars we spend each year, we leave forty-five million people without any insurance. A country that displays an almost ruthless commitment to efficiency and performance in every aspect of its economy — a country that switched to Japanese cars the moment they were more reliable, and to Chinese T-shirts the moment they were five cents cheaper — has loyally stuck with a health-care system that leaves its citizenry pulling out their teeth with pliers.

America's health-care mess is, in part, simply an accident of history. The fact that there have been six attempts at universal health coverage in the last century suggests that there has long been support for the idea. But politics has always got in the way. In both Europe and the United States, for example, the push for health insurance was led, in large part, by organized labor. But in Europe the unions worked through the political system, fighting for coverage for all citizens. From the start, health insurance in Europe was public and universal, and that created powerful political support for any attempt to expand benefits. In the United States, by contrast, the unions worked through the collective-bargaining system and, as a result, could win health benefits only for their own members. Health insurance here has always been private and selective, and every attempt to expand benefits has resulted in a paralyzing political battle over who would be added to insurance rolls and who ought to pay for those additions.

Policy is driven by more than politics, however. It is equally driven by ideas, and in the past few decades a particular idea has taken hold among prominent American economists which has also been a powerful impediment to the expansion of health insurance. The idea is known as "moral hazard." Health economists in other Western nations do not share this obsession. Nor do most Americans. But moral hazard has profoundly shaped the way think tanks formulate policy and the way experts argue and the way health insurers structure their plans and the way legislation and regulations have been written. The health-care mess isn't merely the unintentional result of political dysfunction, in other words. It is also the deliberate consequence of the way in which American policymakers have come to think about insurance.

"Moral hazard" is the term economists use to describe the fact that insurance can change the behavior of the person being insured. If your office gives you and your coworkers all the free Pepsi you want — if your employer, in effect, offers universal Pepsi insurance — you'll drink more Pepsi than you would have otherwise. If you have a no-deductible fire-insurance policy, you may be a little less diligent in clearing the brush away from your house. The savings-and-loan crisis of the nineteen-eighties was created, in large part, by the fact that the federal government insured savings deposits of up to a hundred thousand dollars, and so the newly deregulated S&Ls made far riskier investments than they would have otherwise. Insurance can have the paradoxical effect of producing risky and wasteful behavior. Economists spend a great deal of time thinking about such moral hazard for good reason. Insurance is an attempt to make human life safer and more secure. But, if those efforts can backfire and produce riskier behavior, providing insurance becomes a much more complicated and problematic endeavor.

In 1968, the economist Mark Pauly argued that moral hazard played an enormous role in medicine, and, as John Nyman writes in his book *The Theory of the Demand for Health Insurance*, Pauly's paper has become the "single most influential article in the health economics literature." Nyman, an economist at the University of Minnesota, says that the fear of moral hazard lies behind the thicket of co-payments and deductibles and utilization reviews which characterizes the American health-insurance system. Fear of moral hazard, Nyman writes, also explains "the general lack of enthusiasm by U.S. health economists for the expansion of health insurance coverage (for example, national health insurance or expanded Medicare benefits) in the U.S."

What Nyman is saying is that when your insurance company requires   10 that you make a twenty-dollar co-payment for a visit to the doctor, or when your plan includes an annual five-hundred-dollar or thousand-dollar deductible, it's not simply an attempt to get you to pick up a larger share of your health costs. It is an attempt to make your use of the health-care system more efficient. Making you responsible for a share of the costs, the argument runs, will reduce moral hazard: you'll no longer grab one of those free Pepsis when you aren't really thirsty. That's also why Nyman says that the notion of moral hazard is behind the "lack of enthusiasm" for expansion of health insurance. If you think of insurance as producing wasteful consumption of medical services, then the fact that there are forty-five million Americans without health insurance is no longer an immediate cause for alarm. After all, it's not as if the uninsured never go to the doctor. They spend, on average, $934 a year on medical care. A moral-hazard theorist would say that they go to the doctor when they really have to. Those of us with private insurance, by contrast, consume $2,347 worth of health care a year. If a lot of that extra $1,413 is waste, then maybe the uninsured person is the truly efficient consumer of health care.

The moral-hazard argument makes sense, however, only if we consume health care in the same way that we consume other consumer goods, and to economists like Nyman this assumption is plainly absurd. We go to the doctor grudgingly, only because we're sick. "Moral hazard is overblown," the Princeton economist Uwe Reinhardt says. "You always hear that the demand for health care is unlimited. This is just not true. People who are very well insured, who are very rich, do you see them check into the hospital because it's free? Do people really like to go to the doctor? Do they check into the hospital instead of playing golf?"

For that matter, when you have to pay for your own health care, does your consumption really become more efficient? In the late nineteen-seventies, the Rand Corporation did an extensive study on the question, randomly assigning families to health plans with co-payment levels at zero percent, twenty-five percent, fifty percent, or ninety-five percent, up to six thousand dollars. As you might expect, the more that people were asked to chip in for their health care the less care they used. The problem was that they cut back equally on both frivolous care and useful care. Poor people in the high-deductible group with hypertension, for instance, didn't do nearly as good a job of controlling their blood pressure as those in other groups, resulting in a ten percent increase in the likelihood of death. As a recent Commonwealth Fund study concluded, cost sharing is "a blunt instrument." Of course it is: how should the average consumer be expected to know beforehand what care is frivolous and what care is useful? I just went to the dermatologist to get moles checked for skin cancer. If I had had to pay a hundred percent, or even fifty percent, of the cost of the visit, I might not have gone. Would that have been a wise decision? I have no idea. But if one of those moles really is cancerous, that simple, inexpensive visit could save the health-care system tens of thousands of dollars (not to mention saving me a great deal of heartbreak). The focus on moral hazard suggests that the changes we make in our behavior when we have insurance are nearly always wasteful. Yet, when it comes to health care, many of the things we do only because we have insurance — like getting our moles checked, or getting our teeth cleaned regularly, or getting a mammogram or engaging in other routine preventive care — are anything but wasteful and inefficient. In fact, they are behaviors that could end up saving the health-care system a good deal of money.

Sered and Fernandopulle tell the story of Steve, a factory worker from northern Idaho, with a "grotesque-looking left hand — what looks like a bone sticks out the side." When he was younger, he broke his hand. "The doctor wanted to operate on it," he recalls. "And because I didn't have insurance, well, I was like 'I ain't gonna have it operated on.' The doctor said, 'Well, I can wrap it for you with an Ace bandage.' I said, 'Ahh, let's do that, then.'" Steve uses less health care than he would if he had insurance, but that's not because he has defeated the scourge of moral hazard. It's because instead of getting a broken bone fixed he put a bandage on it.

3

At the center of the Bush Administration's plan to address the health-insurance mess are Health Savings Accounts, and Health Savings Accounts are exactly what you would come up with if you were concerned, above all else, with minimizing moral hazard. The logic behind them was laid out in the 2004 Economic Report of the President. Americans, the report argues, have too much health insurance: typical plans cover things that they shouldn't, creating the problem of overconsumption. Several paragraphs are then devoted to explaining the theory of moral hazard. The report turns to the subject of the uninsured, concluding that they fall into several groups. Some are foreigners who may be covered by their countries of origin. Some are people who could be covered by Medicaid but aren't or aren't admitting that they are. Finally, a large number "remain uninsured as a matter of choice." The report continues, "Researchers believe that as many as one-quarter of those without health insurance had coverage available through an employer but declined the coverage. . . . Still others may remain uninsured because they are young and healthy and do not see the need for insurance." In other words, those with health insurance are overinsured and their behavior is distorted by moral hazard. Those without health insurance use their own money to make decisions about insurance based on an assessment of their needs. The insured are wasteful. The uninsured are prudent. So what's the solution? Make the insured a little bit more like the uninsured.

Under the Health Savings Accounts system, consumers are asked to pay   15
for routine health care with their own money — several thousand dollars of which can be put into a tax-free account. To handle their catastrophic expenses, they then purchase a basic health-insurance package with, say, a thousand-dollar annual deductible. As President Bush explained recently, "Health Savings Accounts all aim at empowering people to make decisions for themselves, owning their own health-care plan, and at the same time bringing some demand control into the cost of health care."

The country described in the President's report is a very different place from the country described in *Uninsured in America*. Sered and Fernandopulle look at the billions we spend on medical care and wonder why Americans have so little insurance. The President's report considers the same situation and worries that we have too much. Sered and Fernandopulle see the lack of insurance as a problem of poverty; a third of the uninsured, after all, have incomes below the federal poverty line. In the section on the uninsured in the President's report, the word "poverty" is never used. In the Administration's view, people are offered insurance but "decline the coverage" as "a matter of choice." The uninsured in Sered and Fernandopulle's book decline coverage, but only because they can't afford it. Gina, for instance, works for a beauty salon that offers her a bare-bones health-insurance plan with a thousand-dollar deductible for two hundred dollars a month. What's her total income? Nine hundred dollars a month. She could "choose" to accept health insurance, but only if she chose to stop buying food or paying the rent.

The biggest difference between the two accounts, though, has to do with how each views the function of insurance. Gina, Steve, and Loretta are ill, and need insurance to cover the costs of getting better. In their eyes, insurance is meant to help equalize financial risk between the healthy and the sick. In the insurance business, this model of coverage is known as "social insurance," and historically it was the way health coverage was conceived. If you were sixty and had heart disease and diabetes, you didn't pay substantially more for coverage than a perfectly healthy twenty-five-year-old. Under social insurance, the twenty-five-year-old agrees to pay thousands of dollars in premiums even though he didn't go to the doctor at all in the previous year, because he wants to make sure that someone else will subsidize his health care if he ever comes down with heart disease or diabetes. Canada and Germany and Japan and all the other industrialized nations with universal health care follow the social-insurance model. Medicare, too, is based on the social-insurance model, and, when Americans with Medicare report themselves to be happier with virtually every aspect of their insurance coverage than people with private insurance (as they do, repeatedly and overwhelmingly), they are referring to the social aspect of their insurance. They aren't getting better care. But they are getting something just as valuable: the security of being insulated against the financial shock of serious illness.

There is another way to organize insurance, however, and that is to make it actuarial. Car insurance, for instance, is actuarial. How much you pay is in large part a function of your individual situation and history: someone who drives a sports car and has received twenty speeding tickets in the past two years pays a much higher annual premium than a soccer mom with a minivan. In recent years, the private insurance industry in the United States has been moving toward the actuarial model, with profound consequences. The triumph of the actuarial model over the social-insurance model is the reason that companies unlucky enough to employ older, high-cost employees — like United Airlines — have run into such financial difficulty. It's the reason that automakers are increasingly moving their operations to Canada. It's the reason that small businesses that have one or two employees with serious illnesses suddenly face unmanageably high health-insurance premiums, and it's the reason that, in many states, people suffering from a potentially high-cost medical condition can't get anyone to insure them at all.

Health Savings Accounts represent the final, irrevocable step in the actuarial direction. If you are preoccupied with moral hazard, then you want people to pay for care with their own money, and, when you do that, the sick inevitably end up paying more than the healthy. And when you make people choose an insurance plan that fits their individual needs, those with significant medical problems will choose expensive health plans that cover lots of things, while those with few health problems will choose cheaper, bare-bones plans. The more expensive the comprehensive plans become, and the less expensive the bare-bones plans become, the more the very sick will cluster together at one end of the insurance spectrum, and the more the well will cluster together at the low-cost end. The days when the healthy twenty-five-year-old subsidizes the sixty-year-old with heart disease or diabetes are coming to an end. "The main effect of putting more of it on the consumer is to reduce the social redistributive element of insurance," the Stanford economist Victor Fuchs says. Health Savings Accounts are not a variant of universal health care. In their governing assumptions, they are the antithesis of universal health care.

The issue about what to do with the health-care system is sometimes pre-   20
sented as a technical argument about the merits of one kind of coverage over
another or as an ideological argument about socialized versus private medicine.
It is, instead, about a few very simple questions. Do you think that this kind of
redistribution of risk is a good idea? Do you think that people whose genes
predispose them to depression or cancer, or whose poverty complicates asthma
or diabetes, or who get hit by a drunk driver, or who have to keep their mouths
closed because their teeth are rotting, ought to bear a greater share of the costs
of their health care than those of us who are lucky enough to escape such mis-
fortunes? In the rest of the industrialized world, it is assumed that the more
equally and widely the burdens of illness are shared, the better off the population as a whole is likely to be. The reason the United States has forty-five million people without coverage is that its health-care policy is in the hands of
people who disagree, and who regard health insurance not as the solution but
as the problem.

Reading across Disciplines
RUSSELL KIRBY, Public Health

In this piece on the American health-care system, Malcolm Gladwell
first defines the "moral hazard" theory of health care cost containment,
then argues that the theory is based on the false assumption that health
care is analogous to other consumer goods. In so doing, Gladwell exposes
fundamental flaws in our current system for delivering and financing
health-care services in the United States.

At the beginning of the essay, Gladwell seems to be using descriptions of the biophysiological process of tooth decay and of the way dental problems affect the lives of the uninsured to illustrate the seemingly
innate inability of America's health-care system to integrate comprehensive dental coverage into most health-care financing strategies. Yet
the health-care financing strategies themselves are the primary focus of
Gladwell's article. In contrast to all other industrialized nations, the
United States defines health care not as a guaranteed benefit for all
participants in American society, but as a commodity to be bought and
sold like any other goods or professional services. Americans differ from
other Western societies in that for most of us, our health-care choices are
defined not by the government but by our employers, and health-care
coverage is used — or not — as an enticement in payroll and benefits
packages for prospective employees. While the elderly and the poor can
participate in federally mandated health-insurance plans, most of the rest

of us must choose the plan or plans offered by our employers (if any) and share an ever-increasing proportion of the monthly premiums, co-payments, and other costs associated with the use of health-care services.

The "moral hazard" argument posits that when consumers must pay a portion of the cost for each health-care encounter, they will use health-care less frivolously, thereby reducing overall costs of delivery of care. While this argument may have a certain logic on its face — and someday perhaps form the basis for the Nobel Prize in economics — several flaws in the design of most employer-funded health-care plans make this a poor theoretical foundation for a national health plan. First and foremost, proponents of the moral hazard argument implicitly presume that all Americans have innate knowledge of which pains, twinges, or injuries warrant a visit to the clinic or emergency room and which do not. As the father of three daughters now grown, I found on numerous occasions that ear infections and other maladies that seemed relatively benign to me turned out to require significant intervention. I'm a health researcher with direct access to the latest research and to medical colleagues. How knowledgeable is the average health consumer? Second, most employer-based health plans give lip service at best to the concept of preventive care. While a few screening services have been routinized and written into most health plans, these plans remain based on the concept of illness and its treatment, rather than the concept of wellness and its maintenance.

Given this situation, health financing arrangements employing the moral hazard argument seem unlikely to reduce the overall costs of health-care services. What is postponed can be a short-sighted reduction in expenditures that increases costs of treatment in the long run.

Russell Kirby is a professor in the Department of Maternal and Child Health at the University of Alabama at Birmingham.

QUESTIONING THE TEXT

1. Look for examples where Gladwell offers anecdotes to support his argument, especially the anecdotes about Gina, Steve, and Loretta. How effective do you find these stories? Which narratives work best in his article? How do the anecdotes about ordinary citizens compare to the quotations from economists as evidence to support Gladwell's claims?

2. What assumptions about American culture does Gladwell seem to think that his audience holds? Pay special attention to paragraph 5. How do these statistics evoke a set of values in the reader? Why do you think Gladwell chooses these particular statistics?

MAKING CONNECTIONS

3. Compare Gladwell's use of statistics and research to Roland Fryer's "Acting White" (p. 143). Who communicates statistical information more clearly? What are some of the challenges of reporting numerical information? Would Gladwell's argument benefit from more graphs such as the ones Fryer's piece includes? Why or why not?

4. In "An Animal's Place," Michael Pollan (p. 204) talks about the debate over animal rights and the belief of some thinkers, such as J. M. Coetzee, that speciesism will one day be considered "a crime of stupefying proportions" (paragraph 19). Gladwell's article, though it details human suffering to illustrate the importance of health insurance, does not make such large claims about how current generations will be judged for their handling of health care in the United States. Do you think that his article might benefit from such claims or from other emotional appeals? Why or why not?

JOINING THE CONVERSATION

5. Interview a family member or coworker and find out what his or her health insurance covers and how much it costs. Then interview someone without health insurance about health care issues and expenses. Reflect on these interviews to come to your own conclusions about appropriate goals for health care in the United States. Write an essay that details these goals and uses your interviews as evidence.

6. Gladwell focuses more on the practical side of the health care debate than he does on the philosophical basis. Explore some of the ideas underpinning the health care debate, particularly the question of whether health care is a right. Seek out position papers on the question of health care — easily available via Internet searches — and then write an essay expressing your own opinion.

DAVID GRATZER
Where Would You Rather Be Sick?

WHO DO YOU THINK will provide better advice about health care, the authors of government surveys or a doctor like David Gratzer, author of "Where Would You Rather Be Sick?" In his brief reply to a survey purportedly showing that Canadians under socialized medicine are healthier and happier than Americans under their more free-market (yet still highly regulated) system of health care, Gratzer's trump card is what rhetoricians describe as an argument from ethos — that is, from character and credibility. Gratzer is a physician who has practiced medicine in both countries and so can testify from personal experience that the centralized planning of health-care systems such as Canada's inevitably leads to rationing, bureaucracy, and sometimes-fatal waits for critical procedures and surgeries.

But personal experience alone usually won't get you a column in the Wall Street Journal, *where Gratzer's opinion piece appeared on June 15, 2006. Trained in Canada, Gratzer earned his right to speak on this issue on the basis of several books about health care, including a Donner-prize-winning critique of the Canadian system,* Code Blue: Reviving Canada's Health Care System *(1999). Practicing by choice now in the United States, Donner — a senior fellow at the conservative Manhattan Institute — is also the author of* The Cure: How Capitalism Can Save American Health Care *(2006). On a subject upon which amateurs are eager to float opinions, Gratzer offers an authoritative voice.* —J.R.

Is socialized medicine the prescription for better health? A recent study comparing Americans and Canadians, widely reported in the press, seems to suggest just that. But there is much less here than meets the eye.

The study, based on a telephone survey of 3,500 Canadians and 5,200 Americans (conducted by Statistics Canada and the U.S. National Center for Health Statistics), was released by the *American Journal of Public Health*. According to it, Canadians are healthier and have better access to health care than Americans, and at lower overall cost. So is the Canadian system, where the government pays for and manages the health-care system, superior? "Our study," says coauthor Dr. Steffie Woolhandler, "is a terrible indictment of the U.S. health-care system. Universal coverage under a national health insurance system is key to improving health."

It is not so clear that the survey data back up these claims. Consider access. According to the survey, Canadians are more likely to have a regular physician, to have seen a doctor in the past year, and to be able to afford medications. But the data are ambiguous; Americans are more likely to have received a pap test and mammogram, as well as treatment for high blood pressure. Moreover, Americans are generally more satisfied with their health care. (The survey did not ask about access to specialist care or diagnostic imaging.)

The survey's most trumpeted conclusion was that Canadians are health-ier than Americans. According to coauthor Dr. David Himmelstein, "We pay almost twice what Canada does for care, more than $6,000 for every American, yet Canadians are healthier, and live two to three years longer." The survey says Americans have higher rates of diabetes (6.7% vs. 4.7%), arthritis (17.9% vs. 16.0%) and high blood pressure (18.3% vs. 13.9%). Americans are also more likely to be obese and lead a sedentary lifestyle. It's damning stuff. But we shouldn't confuse problems in public health with flaws in health-care systems. Americans may be heavier than Canadians, but this speaks more to genetics, diet, exercise and culture than to the accessibility or inaccessibility of health services. The remedy for obese Americans will be found in less fast food and more gym memberships.

So how does American health care actually measure up? If we look at how well it serves its sick citizens, American medicine excels. Prostate cancer is a case in point. The mortality rate from prostate cancer among American men is 19%. In contrast, mortality rates are somewhat higher in Canada (25%) and much higher in Europe (up to 57% in the U.K.). And comparisons in cardiac care — such as the recent Heart and Stroke Foundation of Canada study on post-heart-attack quality of life — find that American patients fare far better in morbidity. Say what you want about the problems of American health care: For those stricken with serious disease, there's no better place to be than in the U.S. 5

Socialized health-care systems fall short in these critical cases because governments strictly ration care in order to reduce the explosive growth of health spending. As a result, patients have less access to specialists, diagnostic equipment and pharmaceuticals. Economist David Henderson, who grew up in Canada, once remarked that it has the best health-care system in the world — if you have only a cold and you're willing to wait in your family doctor's office for three hours. But some patients have more than a simple cold — and the long waits they must endure before they get access to various diagnostic tests and medical procedures have been documented for years. Montreal business-man George Zeliotis, for example, faced a year-long wait for a hip replacement. He sued and, as the co-plaintiff in a recent, landmark case, got the Supreme Court of Canada to strike down two major Quebec laws that banned private health insurance.

Dr. Karen Lasser, the study's third author, says that "Based on our find-ings, if I had to choose between the two systems for my patients, I would choose the Canadian system hands down." Perhaps she would. But as a physi-cian licensed in both countries, I'd disagree.

QUESTIONING THE TEXT

1. Gratzer ends his article by implying his answer to the question that ap-pears in his title. What about you? Does Gratzer persuade you to side

with him, or would you choose the Canadian system, as Dr. Lasser would? Do you base that choice on outside knowledge or what you read in this article? Inside this article, what do you find most and least persuasive?

2. Note that the Canadian health care system is described using various terms. In the first line, for example, Gratzer suggests that the Canadian system is "socialized medicine." In the second paragraph, Dr. Steffie Woolhandler recommends that the U.S. adopt "universal coverage under a national health insurance system." Can you find other terms that describe the Canadian system inside this article? Research some of these terms on the Internet or by talking to others to see what connotations they carry, and then examine how Gratzer uses terms to influence readers' reactions.

MAKING CONNECTIONS

3. Both Malcolm Gladwell in "The Moral Hazard Myth" (p. 238) and Gratzer could be said to boil their arguments down to a question. For Gratzer, the question appears in the title — "Where would you rather be sick?" For Gladwell, the question appears in the last paragraph of his article — "Do you think that this kind of redistribution of risk is a good idea?" How do these two questions appeal to different values? Which do you think is the more important question?

JOINING THE CONVERSATION

4. If you have had any major experiences with the health care system — surgery or a hospitalization, for example — reflect on those experiences, making notes about your most significant memories. (Alternatively, interview a friend or family member who has had a significant medical experience.) Based on your reflections or those of your interviewee, what do you feel are the most important aspects of good medical care? Write a narrative or an essay that illustrates your understanding of what constitutes good medical care.

5. One of Gratzer's persuasive tactics is to ask his readers to make a choice between two options even though in the context of health care, other options would surely exist. Choose an issue that you feel strongly about — it doesn't have to be a large political issue; choosing something specific to your school or specific to an organization you belong to will work just as well — and write a persuasive essay that sets up a clear choice for your readers and guides them to agree with your position.

JANE MAYER
Whatever It Takes

DO YOU APPROVE OF *the use of torture to extract information from people suspected of being terrorists? Are you an avid viewer of the hit TV show* 24? *Jane Mayer (b. 1955) finds that answers to these questions can involve a strong contradiction: some who heartily disapprove of torture (including Barbra Streisand and Bill Clinton) can't seem to get enough of* 24, *the Fox drama on counterterrorism starring Kiefer Sutherland as mega-heroic counter-terrorist agent Jack Bauer. In fact, Sutherland, who in real life is against torture—* "*Torture is not a way of procuring information,*" *he says—and describes himself as* "*leaning toward the left,*" *excuses* 24 *as* "*a fantastical show*" *in which torture* "*is a dramatic device.*" *But not all viewers are thus conflicted, and many believe the show, which won the 2006 Emmy Award for Outstanding Drama Series, is right for the post 9/11 times.*

Mayer's essay, published in February 2007, stirred up the brew of controversy already surrounding this television show. In "*Whatever It Takes,*" *Mayer surveys a number of episodes of* 24 *and doesn't like what she sees: a glorification of torture as a means of solving each episode's* "*ticking time bomb*" *plot. She's not the only person making such an assessment. In fact, as she reports, the dean of the U.S. Military Academy at West Point, along with three military interrogators, flew to California to voice their concerns to the team responsible for* 24. *The dean, who teaches a course on the law of war, told the assembled group (that pointedly did not include Joel Sarnow, executive producer of* 24*) that the show is having an impact on Academy cadets:* "*The kids see it, and say, 'If torture is wrong, what about* 24*?' " Particularly distressing is the fact that on* 24 *torture* "*is always the patriotic thing to do*" *since it inevitably yields good results. As Mayer notes, the relationship between torture and good information is not a strong one; most interrogators agree that torture is ineffective.*

Whether the critics or the supporters of 24 *are right, however, may be less important in the long run than the issue Mayer's essay raises about the relationship between life on TV and life in the real world: how much does the first affect the second?*

Mayer, who has been a staff writer at the New Yorker *since 1995, doesn't answer that question, though her essay inspired me to think and re-think my own position on it. Mayer often leads me to do some hard thinking. As the first woman to cover a presidential campaign and become White House correspondent for the* Wall Street Journal, *Mayer's credentials are impressive. Twice nominated for the Pulitzer Prize, she is the author, with Jill Abramson, of* Strange Justice: The Selling of Clarence Thomas *(1994), a finalist for the National Book Award that year, and with Doyle McManus, of* Landslide: The Unmaking of the President, 1984–1988, *an analysis of the Reagan administration's involvement in the Iran-Contra affair. As for* 24, *my guess is she is much more interested in the show's effects than in the show itself. And as for me, I haven't been able to make it through a single episode.* —A.L.

*This opening cap-
tures my attention
with its vivid de-
scription; it makes
me want to read on.*
—A.L.

The office desk of Joel Surnow — the co-
creator and executive producer of *24*, the popular
counterterrorism drama of Fox — faces a wall dominated by an American flag in a glass case. A small
label reveals that the flag once flew over Baghdad,
after the American invasion of Iraq, in 2003. A few
years ago, Surnow received it as a gift from an Army
regiment stationed in Iraq; the soldiers had shared a
collection of *24* DVDs, he told me, until it was destroyed by an enemy bomb. "The military loves our
show," he said recently. Surnow is fifty-two, and has
the gangly, coiled energy of an athlete; his hair is
close-cropped, and he has a "soul patch" — a
smidgen of beard beneath his lower lip. When he
was young, he worked as a carpet salesman with his
father. The trick to selling anything, he learned, is to
carry yourself with confidence and get the customer
to like you within the first five minutes. He's got it
down. "People in the administration love the series,
too," he said. "It's a patriotic show. They should
love it."

Surnow's production company, Real Time
Entertainment, is in the San Fernando Valley, and
occupies a former pencil factory: a bland, two-story
industrial building on an abject strip of parking lots
and fast-food restaurants. Surnow, a cigar enthusiast,
has converted a room down the hall from his office
into a salon with burled-wood humidors and a full
bar; his friend Rush Limbaugh, the conservative
talk-radio host, sometimes joins him there for a
smoke. (Not long ago, Surnow threw Limbaugh
a party and presented him with a custom-made
24 smoking jacket.) The ground floor of the factory
has a large soundstage on which many of *24*'s interior scenes are shot, including those set at the perpetually tense Los Angeles bureau of the Counter
Terrorist Unit, or C.T.U. — a fictional federal
agency that pursues America's enemies with steely
resourcefulness.

Each season of *24*, which has been airing on
Fox since 2001, depicts a single, panic-laced day in
which Jack Bauer — a heroic C.T.U. agent, played
by Kiefer Sutherland — must unravel and undermine a conspiracy that imperils the nation. Terrorists

*She uses description
and images to draw
her reader in —
very effective in
journalism such as
this — and she
never brings in the
"I" to show herself
doing all of this
reporting and inter-
viewing.* —L.S.

*Mayer links
Surnow to the mili-
tary and to patrio-
tism. What impres-
sion will this leave
on the left-leaning
readers of the New
Yorker?* —J.R.

*Surnow smoking
cigars with Rush
Limbaugh — is
this relevant?
Mayer's only point
seems to be to give
us information cal-
culated to irritate
liberals.* —J.R.

*Already, I don't
like Surnow and so
am suspicious of
24. How is Mayer
leading me to that
dislike?* —A.L.

Joel Surnow, executive producer of *24*.

are poised to set off nuclear bombs or bioweapons, or in some other way annihilate entire cities. The twisting story line forces Bauer and his colleagues to make a series of grim choices that pit liberty against security. Frequently, the dilemma is stark: a resistant suspect can either be accorded due process — allowing a terrorist plot to proceed — or be tortured in pursuit of a lead. Bauer invariably chooses coercion. With unnerving efficiency, suspects are beaten, suffocated, electrocuted, drugged, assaulted with knives, or more exotically abused; almost without fail, these suspects divulge critical secrets.

The show's appeal, however, lies less in its violence than in its giddily literal rendering of a classic thriller trope: the "ticking time bomb" plot. Each hour-long episode represents an hour in the life of the characters, and every minute that passes onscreen brings the United States a minute closer to doomsday. (Surnow came up with this concept, which he

Does 24 depict these situations to convince Americans that these kinds of treatments are acceptable when secrets are at stake?
—J.E.M.

Many of my colleagues watch this show: they either love or hate it — no in-betweens.
—A.L.

Mayer describes a show that differs from innumerable film and TV thrillers chiefly in its treatment of time, an innovation that has won it many loyal fans.
—J.R.

calls the show's "trick.") As many as half a dozen interlocking stories unfold simultaneously — frequently on a split screen — and a digital clock appears before and after every commercial break, marking each second with an ominous clang. The result is a riveting sensation of narrative velocity.

Bob Cochran, who created the show with Surnow, admitted, "Most terrorism experts will tell you that the 'ticking time bomb' situation never occurs in real life, or very rarely. But on our show it happens every week." According to Darius Rejali, a professor of political science at Reed College and the author of the forthcoming book *Torture and Democracy*, the conceit of the ticking time bomb first appeared in Jean Lartéguy's 1960 novel *Les Centurions*, written during the brutal French occupation of Algeria. The book's hero, after beating a female Arab dissident into submission, uncovers an imminent plot to explode bombs all over Algeria and must race against the clock to stop it. Rejali, who has examined the available records of the conflict, told me that the story has no basis in fact. In his view, the story line of *Les Centurions* provided French liberals a more palatable rationale for torture than the racist explanations supplied by others (such as the notion that the Algerians, inherently simpleminded, understood only brute force). Lartéguy's scenario exploited an insecurity shared by many liberal societies — that their enlightened legal systems had made them vulnerable to security threats.

24, which last year won an Emmy Award for Outstanding Drama Series, packs an improbable amount of intrigue into twenty-four hours, and its outlandishness marks it clearly as a fantasy, an heir to the baroque potboilers of Tom Clancy and Vince Flynn. Nevertheless, the show obviously plays off the anxieties that have beset the country since September 11th, and it sends a political message. The series, Surnow told me, is "ripped out of the Zeitgeist of what people's fears are — their paranoia that we're going to be attacked," and it "makes people look at what we're dealing with" in terms of threats to national security. "There are not a lot of measures short of extreme measures that will get it done," he said,

5

Most dramatic entertainments rely on devices that rarely occur in life, from the coincidences in Shakespeare's comedies to the environmental catastrophes in various global-warming and nuclear winter films. So why does Mayer want to hold 24 to a different standard of reality? —J.R.

Wouldn't it be more peculiar if art did not reflect the political events and concerns of its era? And after 9/11, is it really paranoid to fear terrorists? The attacks on that day were designed to kill as many as 40,000 people and collapse the American economic system. That's pretty serious. —J.R.

Is Mayer implying that Surnow believes Americans should combat terrorism with the same "unnerving efficiency" she describes above? —J.E.M.

This really makes
the show sound like
right-wing propa-
ganda. I certainly
don't want the war
on terror to be
fought by Bauer!
—L.S.

adding, "America wants the war on terror fought by
Jack Bauer. He's a patriot."

For all its fictional liberties, *24* depicts the fight
against Islamist extremism much as the Bush Administration has defined it: as an all-consuming struggle
for America's survival that demands the toughest of
tactics. Not long after September 11th, Vice President Dick Cheney alluded vaguely to the fact that
America must begin working through the "dark
side" in countering terrorism. On *24*, the dark side is
on full view. Surnow, who has jokingly called himself a "right-wing nut job," shares his show's hard-
line perspective. Speaking of torture, he said, "Isn't it
obvious that if there was a nuke in New York City
that was about to blow — or any other city in this
country — that, even if you were going to go to jail,
it would be the right thing to do?"

Torture might seem
"the right thing" to
Surnow, but as
critics point out, it
rarely if ever works.
—A.L.

I am curious as to
what Mayer might
consider the "bright
side" in countering
terrorism.   —J.R.

Since September 11th, depictions of torture
have become much more common on American
television. Before the attacks, fewer than four acts of
torture appeared on prime-time television each year,
according to Human Rights First, a nonprofit organization. Now there are more than a hundred, and, as
David Danzig, a project director at Human Rights
First, noted, "the torturers have changed. It used to
be almost exclusively the villains who tortured.
Today, torture is often perpetrated by the heroes."
The Parents' Television Council, a nonpartisan
watchdog group, has counted what it says are sixty-
seven torture scenes during the first five seasons of
24— more than one every other show. Melissa
Caldwell, the council's senior director of programs,
said, "*24* is the worst offender on television: the
most frequent, most graphic, and the leader in the
trend of showing the protagonists using torture."

Is it so odd that
torture might get
attention in an era
when terrorists are
routinely blowing
up civilians, be-
heading journalists,
assaulting build-
ings, bombing sub-
ways, and kidnap-
ping dissenting
politicians? Mayer's
citation of statistics
here from "non-
profit organiza-
tions" reveals her
agenda.   —J.R.

This is all too rem-
iniscent to me of
the horrors of Abu
Ghraib.   —A.L.

The show's villains usually inflict the more
gruesome tortures: their victims are hung on hooks,
like carcasses in a butcher shop; poked with smoking-
hot scalpels; or abraded with sanding machines. In
many episodes, however, heroic American officials
act as tormentors, even though torture is illegal
under U.S. law. (The United Nations Convention
against Torture, which took on the force of federal
law when it was ratified by the Senate in 1994,

specifies that "no exceptional circumstances, whatso-ever, whether a state of war or a threat of war, inter-nal political instability or any other public emer-gency, may be invoked as a justification of torture.") In one episode, a fictional president commands a member of his Secret Service to torture a suspected traitor: his national-security adviser. The victim is jolted with defibrillator paddles while his feet are submerged in a tub filled with water. As the voltage is turned up, the president, who is depicted as a scrupulous leader, watches the suspect suffer on a video feed. The viewer, who knows that the adviser is guilty and harbors secrets, becomes complicit in hoping that the torture works. A few minutes before the suspect gives in, the president utters the show's credo, "Everyone breaks eventually." (Virtually the sole exception to this rule is Jack Bauer. The current season begins with Bauer being released from a Chinese prison, after two years of ceaseless torture; his back is scarred and his hands are burnt, but a Communist official who transfers Bauer to U.S. custody says that he "never broke his silence.")

C.T.U. agents have used some of the same con-troversial interrogation methods that the U.S. has employed on some Al Qaeda suspects. In one in-stance, Bauer denies painkillers to a female terrorist who is suffering from a bullet wound, just as Ameri-can officials have acknowledged doing in the case of Abu Zubaydah — one of the highest-ranking Al Qaeda operatives in U.S. custody. "I need to use every advantage I've got," Bauer explains to the victim's distressed sister.

The show sometimes toys with the audience's discomfort about abusive interrogations. In Season Two, Bauer threatens to murder a terrorist's wife and children, one by one, before the prisoner's eyes. The suspect watches, on closed-circuit television, what appears to be an execution-style slaying of his son. Threatened with the murder of additional family members, the father gives up vital information — but Bauer appears to have gone too far. It turns out, though, that the killing of the child was staged. Bauer, the show implies, hasn't crossed the line after all. Yet, under U.S. and international law, a mock

But doesn't a TV drama have license to push the enve-lope in exactly this way as a work of fiction? It is ex-amining the moral consequences of engaging in torture. Would Mayer pre-fer fiction not depict situations that might justify trans-gressions of law? That principle would have ex-cluded, for example, sympathetic depic-tions of a woman's right to choose in fiction prior to Roe v. Wade.
—J.R.

10

What does this say about our govern-ment's ethics if the show being de-scribed as the most violent and graphic on television is es-sentially mirroring the evening news?
—L.S.

Who's to say they're uncomfort-able? After all, the viewers are choosing to watch this.
—L.S.

execution is considered psychological torture, and is illegal.

On one occasion, Bauer loses his nerve about inflicting torture, but the show implicitly rebukes his qualms. In the episode, Bauer attempts to break a suspected terrorist by plunging a knife in his shoulder; the victim's screams clearly disquiet him. Bauer says to an associate, unconvincingly, that he has looked into the victim's eyes and knows that "he's not going to tell us anything." The other man takes over, fiercely gouging the suspect's knee — at which point the suspect yells out details of a plot to explode a suitcase nuke in Los Angeles.

I cannot imagine playing Bauer and being this brutal week after week: what a weird sense of "entertainment."
—A.L.

Throughout the series, secondary characters raise moral objections to abusive interrogation tactics. Yet the show never engages in a serious dialogue on the subject. Nobody argues that torture doesn't work, or that it undermines America's foreign-policy strategy. Instead, the doubters tend to be softhearted dupes. A tremulous liberal, who defends a Middle Eastern neighbor from vigilantism, is killed when the neighbor turns out to be a terrorist. When a civil-liberties-minded lawyer makes a high-toned argument to a presidential aide against unwarranted detentions — "You continue to arrest innocent people, you're giving the terrorists exactly what they want," she says — the aide sarcastically responds, "Well! You've got the makings of a splendid law-review article here. I'll pass it on to the president."

Mayer is offended that 24 *does not present her point of view adequately. I wonder how often conservatives felt the same way watching left-wing programming such as* The West Wing, Boston Legal, All in the Family, Murphy Brown. . . .
—J.R.

In another episode, a human-rights lawyer from a fictional organization called Amnesty Global tells Bauer, who wants to rough up an uncharged terror suspect, that he will violate the Constitution. Bauer responds, "I don't wanna bypass the Constitution, but these are extraordinary circumstances." He appeals to the president, arguing that any interrogation permitted by the law won't be sufficiently harsh. "If we want to procure any information from this suspect, we're going to have to do it behind closed doors," he says.

"You're talking about torturing this man?" the president says.

"I'm talking about doing what's necessary to stop this warhead from being used against us," Bauer answers.

15

Mayer has been piling up example after example, and each one makes me dislike the show more. She is showing her own hand here.   —A.L.

When the president wavers, Bauer temporarily quits his job so that he can avoid defying the chain of command, and breaks the suspect's fingers. The suspect still won't talk, so Bauer puts a knife to his throat; this elicits the desired information. He then knocks the suspect out with a punch, telling him, "This will help you with the pain."

Howard Gordon, who is the series' "show runner," or lead writer, told me that he concocts many of the torture scenes himself. "Honest to God, I'd call them improvisations in sadism," he said. Several copies of the C.I.A.'s 1963 KUBARK interrogation manual can be found at the *24* offices, but Gordon said that, "for the most part, our imaginations are the source. Sometimes these ideas are inspired by a scene's location or come from props — what's on the set." He explained that much of the horror is conjured by the viewer. "To see a scalpel and see it move below the frame of the screen is a lot scarier than watching the whole thing. When you get a camera moving fast, and someone screaming, it really works." In recent years, he said, "we've resorted a lot to a pharmacological sort of thing." A character named Burke — a federal employee of the C.T.U. who carries a briefcase filled with elephantine hypodermic needles — has proved indispensable. "He'll inject chemicals that cause horrible pain that can knock down your defenses — a sort of sodium pentothal plus," Gordon said. "When we're stuck, we say, 'Call Burke!'" He added, "The truth is, there's a certain amount of fatigue. It's getting hard not to repeat the same torture techniques over and over."

Gordon, who is a "moderate Democrat," said that it worries him when "critics say that we've enabled and reflected the public's appetite for torture. Nobody wants to be the handmaid to a relaxed policy that accepts torture as a legitimate means of interrogation." He went on, "But the premise of *24* is the ticking time bomb. It takes an unusual situation and turns it into the meat and potatoes of the show." He paused. "I think people can differentiate between a television show and reality."

This past November, U.S. Army Brigadier General Patrick Finnegan, the dean of the United States

The question in this case is whether there is really all that much difference between television and reality where torture is concerned.   —A.L.

Can viewers differentiate between television and reality? Today, "reality" is a kind of TV show.   —L.S.

20

Military Academy at West Point, flew to Southern California to meet with the creative team behind *24*. Finnegan, who was accompanied by three of the most experienced military and F.B.I. interrogators in the country, arrived on the set as the crew was filming. At first, Finnegan — wearing an immaculate Army uniform, his chest covered in ribbons and medals — aroused confusion: he was taken for an actor and was asked by someone what time his "call" was.

In fact, Finnegan and the others had come to voice their concern that the show's central political premise — that the letter of American law must be sacrificed for the country's security — was having a toxic effect. In their view, the show promoted unethical and illegal behavior and had adversely affected the training and performance of real American soldiers. "I'd like them to stop," Finnegan said of the show's producers. "They should do a show where torture backfires."

The meeting, which lasted a couple of hours, had been arranged by David Danzig, the Human Rights First official. Several top producers of *24* were present, but Surnow was conspicuously absent. Surnow explained to me, "I just can't sit in a room that long. I'm too A.D.D. — I can't sit still." He told the group that the meeting conflicted with a planned conference call with Roger Ailes, the chairman of the Fox News Channel. (Another participant in the conference call attended the meeting.) Ailes wanted to discuss a project that Surnow has been planning for months: the début, on February 18th, of *The Half Hour News Hour*, a conservative satirical treatment of the week's news; Surnow sees the show as offering a counterpoint to the liberal slant of *The Daily Show with Jon Stewart*.

Before the meeting, Stuart Herrington, one of the three veteran interrogators, had prepared a list of seventeen effective techniques, none of which were abusive. He and the others described various tactics, such as giving suspects a postcard to send home, thereby learning the name and address of their next of kin. After Howard Gordon, the lead writer, listened to some of Herrington's suggestions, he slammed his fist on the table and joked, "You're

Imagine the reaction to the military or police voicing concern about violence in an Oliver Stone or Quentin Tarantino film.
—J.R.

hired!" He also excitedly asked the West Point delegation if they knew of any effective truth serums.

At other moments, the discussion was more strained. Finnegan told the producers that *24*, by suggesting that the U.S. government perpetrates myriad forms of torture, hurts the country's image internationally. Finnegan, who is a lawyer, has for a number of years taught a course on the laws of war to West Point seniors — cadets who would soon be commanders in the battlefields of Iraq and Afghanistan. He always tries, he said, to get his students to sort out not just what is legal but what is right. However, it had become increasingly hard to convince some cadets that America had to respect the rule of law and human rights, even when terrorists did not. One reason for the growing resistance, he suggested, was misperceptions spread by *24*, which was exceptionally popular with his students. As he told me, "The kids see it, any say, 'If torture is wrong, what about *24*?'" He continued, "The disturbing thing is that although torture may cause Jack Bauer some angst, it is always the patriotic thing to do."

Gary Solis, a retired law professor who designed and taught the Law of War for Commanders curriculum at West Point, told me that he had similar arguments with his students. He said that, under both U.S. and international law, "Jack Bauer is a criminal. In real life, he would be prosecuted." Yet the motto of many of his students was identical to Jack Bauer's: "Whatever it takes." His students were particularly impressed by a scene in which Bauer barges into a room where a stubborn suspect is being held, shoots him in one leg, and threatens to shoot the other if he doesn't talk. In less than ten seconds, the suspect reveals that his associates plan to assassinate the secretary of defense. Solis told me, "I tried to impress on them that this technique would open the wrong doors, but it was like trying to stomp out an anthill."

The *24* producers told the military and law-enforcement experts that they were careful not to glamorize torture; they noted that Bauer never enjoys inflicting pain, and that it had clearly exacted a psychological toll on the character. (As Gordon put it to me, "Jack is basically damned.") Finnegan and

The fact that military leaders object to 24 is a persuasive argument to me. —A.L.

Everyone seems to keep forgetting that 24 is fiction. —J.R.

25

"Whatever it takes" is chilling to me: does the end always justify the means? Clearly Jack Bauer thinks so. —A.L.

the others disagreed, pointing out that Bauer remains coolly rational after committing barbarous acts, including the decapitation of a state's witness with a hacksaw. Joe Navarro, one of the F.B.I.'s top experts in questioning techniques, attended the meeting; he told me, "Only a psychopath can torture and be unaffected. You don't want people like that in your organization. They are untrustworthy, and tend to have grotesque other problems."

Cochran, who has a law degree, listened politely to the delegation's complaints. He told me that he supports the use of torture "in narrow circumstances" and believes that it can be justified under the Constitution. "The Doctrine of Necessity says you can occasionally break the law to prevent greater harm," he said. "I think that could supersede the Convention against Torture." (Few legal scholars agree with this argument.) At the meeting, Cochran demanded to know what the interrogators would do if they faced the imminent threat of a nuclear blast in New York City, and had custody of a suspect who knew how to stop it. One interrogator said that he would apply physical coercion only if he received a personal directive from the president. But Navarro, who estimates that he has conducted some twelve thousand interrogations, replied that torture was not an effective response. "These are very determined people, and they won't turn just because you pull a fingernail out," he told me. And Finnegan argued that torturing fanatical Islamist terrorists is particularly pointless. "They almost welcome torture," he said. "They expect it. They want to be martyred." A ticking time bomb, he pointed out, would make a suspect only more unwilling to talk. "They know if they can simply hold out several hours, all the more glory — the ticking time bomb will go off!"

The notion that physical coercion in interrogations is unreliable, although widespread among military intelligence officers and F.B.I. agents, has been firmly rejected by the Bush Administration. Last September, President Bush defended the C.I.A.'s use of "an alternative set of procedures." In order to "save innocent lives," he said, the agency needed to be able to use "enhanced" measures to extract "vital

Her many quotes here give a good sense of action and show us she has really done her research. —L.S.

Mayer may be correct that "Few legal scholars agree," but since she does not cite any sources, the reader cannot be sure. —J.E.M.

Here, her use of quotes out of context seems odd. What did the President really say? —L.S.

information" from "dangerous" detainees who were aware of "terrorist plans we could not get anywhere else."

Although reports of abuses by U.S. troops in Iraq and Afghanistan and at Guantánamo Bay, Cuba, have angered much of the world, the response of Americans has been more tepid. Finnegan attributes the fact that "we are generally more comfortable and more accepting of this," in part, to the popularity of *24*, which has a weekly audience of 15 million viewers, and has reached millions more through DVD sales. The third expert at the meeting was Tony Lagouranis, a former Army interrogator in the war in Iraq. He told the show's staff that DVDs of shows such as *24* circulate widely among soldiers stationed in Iraq. Lagouranis said to me, "People watch the shows, and then walk into the interrogation booths and do the same things they've just seen." He recalled that some men he had worked with in Iraq watched a television program in which a suspect was forced to hear tortured screams from a neighboring cell; the men later tried to persuade their Iraqi translator to act the part of a torture "victim," in a similar intimidation ploy. Lagouranis intervened: such scenarios constitute psychological torture.

"In Iraq, I never saw pain produce intelligence," Lagouranis told me. "I worked with someone who used waterboarding" — an interrogation method involving the repeated near-drowning of a suspect. "I used severe hypothermia, dogs, and sleep deprivation. I saw suspects after soldiers had gone into their homes and broken their bones, or made them sit on a Humvee's hot exhaust pipes until they got third-degree burns. Nothing happened." Some people, he said, "gave confessions. But they just told us what we already knew. It never opened up a stream of new information." If anything, he said, "physical pain can strengthen the resolve to clam up."

Last December, the Intelligence Science Board, an advisory panel to the U.S. intelligence community, released a report declaring that "most observers, even those within professional circles, have unfortunately been influenced by the media's

So here are some who apparently cannot differentiate between TV and reality! —A.L.

I have been expecting Mayer to produce critics who argue that torture doesn't work, and here they are. —A.L.

The Hollywood left never can seem to make up its mind about its influence. When peddling drugs, sex, and pointless violence, they say films merely reflect the mores of society and so can't be blamed for its ills. But let the entertainment have a right-wing agenda, and suddenly a single TV program makes all the difference in the world. —J.R.

30

colorful (and artificial) view of interrogation as almost always involving hostility." In a clear reference to *24*, the report noted:

> Prime-time television increasingly offers up plot lines involving the incineration of metropolitan Los Angeles by an atomic weapon or its depopulation by an aerosol nerve toxin. The characters do not have the time to reflect upon, much less to utilize, what real professionals know to be the "science and art" of "educing information." They want results. Now. The public thinks the same way. They want, and rightly expect, precisely the kind of "protection" that only a skilled intelligence professional can provide. Unfortunately, they have no idea how such a person is supposed to act "in real life."

Lagouranis told the *24* team what the U.S. military and the F.B.I. teach real intelligence professionals: "rapport-building," the slow process of winning over informants, is the method that generally works best. There are also nonviolent ruses, he explained, and ways to take suspects by surprise. The *24* staff seemed interested in the narrative possibilities of such techniques; Lagouranis recalled, "They told us that they'd love to incorporate ruses and rapport-building." At the same time, he said, Cochran and the others from *24* worried that such approaches would "take too much time" on an hour-long television show.

The delegation of interrogators left the meeting with the feeling that the story lines on *24* would be changed little, if at all. "It shows they have a social conscience that they'd even meet with us at all," Navarro said. "They were receptive. But they have a format that works. They have won a lot of awards. Why would they want to play with a No. 1 show?" Lagouranis said of the *24* team, "They were a bit prickly. They have this money-making machine, and we were telling them it's immoral."

Afterward, Danzig and Finnegan had an on-set exchange with Kiefer Sutherland, who is reportedly paid $10 million a year to play Jack Bauer. Sutherland, the grandson of Tommy Douglas, a former socialist leader in Canada, has described his own political

Speaking of making money, Lagouranis is selling a book about his experiences as an army interrogator, Fear Up Harsh *(2007).*
—J.R.

views as anti-torture, and "leaning toward the left."
According to Danzig, Sutherland was "really upset,
really intense" and stressed that he tries to tell people
that the show "is just entertainment." But Sutherland,
who claimed to be bored with playing torture scenes,
admitted that he worried about the "unintended consequences of the show." Danzing proposed that
Sutherland participate in a panel at West Point or
appear in a training film in which he made clear that
the show's torture scenes are not to be emulated.
(Surnow, when asked whether he would participate
in the video, responded, "No way." Gordon, however,
agreed to be filmed.) Sutherland declined to answer
questions for this article, but, in a recent television interview with Charlie Rose, his ambivalence about his
character's methods was palpable. He condemned the
abuse of U.S.-held detainees at Abu Ghraib prison, in
Iraq, as "absolutely criminal," particularly for a country that tells others that "democracy and freedom" are
the "way to go." He also said, "You can torture someone and they'll basically tell you exactly what you
want to hear. . . . Torture is not a way of procuring
information." But things operate differently, he said,
on television: *24*, he said, is "a fantastical show. . . .
Torture is a dramatic device."

The creators of *24* deny that the show presents
only a conservative viewpoint. They mention its
many prominent Democratic fans — including
Barbra Streisand and Bill Clinton — and the diversity of political views among its writers and producers. Indeed, the story lines sometimes have a liberal
tilt. The conspiracy plot of Season Five, for example,
turns on oligarchic businessmen who go to despica-
ble lengths to protect their oil interests; the same
theme anchors liberal-paranoia thrillers such as
Syriana. This season, a White House directive that
flags all federal employees of Middle Eastern descent
as potential traitors has been presented as a gross
overreaction, and a White House official who favors
police-state tactics has come off as scheming and
ignoble. Yet David Nevins, the former Fox Television network official who, in 2000, bought the pilot
on the spot after hearing a pitch from Surnow and
Cochran, and who maintains an executive role in *24*,

$10 million to play a torturer: not a job I'd want, and Sutherland seems conflicted about it too. His rational- ization in the last sentence of this paragraph is pretty lame. —A.L.

Do viewers like TV shows that mirror their beliefs, or just shows that are entertaining? —L.S.

35

is candid about the show's core message. "There's definitely a political attitude of the show, which is that extreme measures are sometimes necessary for the greater good," he says. "The show doesn't have much patience for the niceties of civil liberties or due process. It's clearly coming from somewhere. Joel's politics suffuse the whole show."

Surnow, for his part, revels in his minority status inside the left-leaning entertainment industry. "Conservatives are the new oppressed class," he joked in his office. "Isn't it bizarre that in Hollywood it's easier to come out as gay than as conservative?" His success with *24*, he said, has protected him from the more righteous elements of the Hollywood establishment. "Right now, they have to be nice to me," he said. "But if the show tanks I'm sure they'll kill me." He spoke of his new conservative comedy show as an even bigger risk than *24*. "I'll be front and center on the new show," he said, then joked, "I'm ruining my chances of ever working again in Hollywood."

At least Mayer acknowledges that the entertainment industry leans left. —J.R.

Although he was raised in Beverly Hills — he graduated in 1972 from Beverly Hills High — Surnow said that he has always felt like an outsider. His classmates were mostly wealthy, but his father was an itinerant carpet salesman who came to California from Detroit. He cold-called potential customers, most of whom lived in Compton and Watts. Surnow was much younger than his two brothers, and he grew up virtually as an only child, living in a one-bedroom apartment in an unfashionable area south of Olympic Boulevard, where he slept on a foldout cot. If his father made a sale, he'd come home and give him the thumbs-up. But Surnow said that nine out of ten nights ended in failure. "If he made three sales a month, we could stay where we lived," he recalled. His mother, who worked as a saleswoman in a clothing store, "fought depression her whole life." Surnow, who describes his parents as "wonderful people," said, "I was a latchkey kid. . . . I raised myself." He played tennis on his high-school team but gave it up after repeatedly losing to players who could afford private lessons.

I was expecting a profile of Surnow earlier in the essay, but here it is over halfway through: I wonder why Mayer chose to put it here? —A.L.

Roger Director, a television producer and longtime friend, said that he "loves" Surnow. But, he went on, "He feels looked down upon by the world, and that kind of emotional dynamic underpins a lot of things. It's kind of 'Joel against the world.' It's as if he feels, I had to fight and claw for everything I got. It's a tough world, and no one's looking out for you." As a result, Director said, "Joel's not sentimental. He has a hard-hearted thing."

Surnow's parents were FDR Democrats. He recalled, "It was just assumed, especially in the Jewish community" — to which his family belonged. "But when you grow up you start to challenge your parents' assumptions. 'Am I Jewish? Am I a Democrat?'" Many of his peers at the University of California at Berkeley, where he attended college, were liberals or radicals. "They were all socialists and Marxists, but living off their family money," he recalled. "It seemed to me there was some obvious hypocrisy here. It was absurd." Although he wasn't consciously political, he said, "I felt like I wasn't like these people." In 1985, he divorced his wife, a medical student, who was Jewish, and with whom he has two daughters. (His relationships with them are strained.) Four years later, he remarried. His wife, who used to work in film development, is Catholic; they have three daughters, whom they send to Catholic schools. He likes to bring his girls to the set and rushes home for his wife's pork-chop dinners. "I got to know who I was and who I wasn't," he said. "I wasn't the perfect Jewish kid who is married, with a Jewish family." Instead, he said, "I decided I like Catholics. They're so grounded. I sort of reoriented myself."

Surnow is a more complex thinker than his more strident statements would suggest.
—A.L.

While studying at Berkeley, Surnow worked as an usher at the Pacific Film Archive, where he saw at least five hundred movies. A fan of crime dramas such as *Mean Streets* and *The Godfather*, he discovered foreign films as well. "That was my awakening," he said. In 1975, Surnow enrolled at the U.C.L.A. film school. Soon after graduation, he began writing for film; he then switched to television. He was only modestly successful, and had many "lost years," when he considered giving up and taking over his father's carpet business. His breakthrough came when he began writing for *Miami Vice*, in 1984. "It just clicked — I just got it!" he recalled. "It was just like

40

when you don't know how to speak a language and suddenly you do. I knew how to tell a story." By the end of the year, Universal, which owned the show, put Surnow in charge of his own series, *The Equalizer*, about a C.I.A. agent turned vigilante. The series was a success, but, Surnow told me, "I was way too arrogant. I sort of pissed off the network." Battles for creative control have followed Surnow to *24*, where, Nevins said admiringly, he continues to push for "unconventional and dangerous choices."

Surnow's tough stretches in Hollywood, he said, taught him that there were "two kinds of people" in entertainment: "those who want to be geniuses, and those who want to work." At first, he said, "I wanted to be a genius. But at a certain point I realized I just desperately wanted to work." Brian Grazer, an executive producer of *24*, who has primarily produced films, said that "TV guys either get broken by the system, or they get so tough that they have no warmth at all." Surnow, he said, is "a devoted family man" and "a really close friend." But when Grazer first met Surnow, he recalled, "I nearly walked out. He was really glib and insulting. I was shocked. He's a tough guy. He's a meat-eating alpha male. He's a monster!" He observed, "Maybe Jack Bauer has some parts of him."

With such a turn to the personal here, the article really shifts gears. Does it work? —L.S.

During three decades as a journeyman screenwriter, Surnow grew increasingly conservative. He "hated welfare," which he saw as government handouts. Liberal courts also angered him. He loved Ronald Reagan's "strength" and disdained Jimmy Carter's "belief that people would be nice to us just because we were humane. That never works." He said of Reagan, "I can hardly think of him without breaking into tears. I just felt Ronald Reagan was the father that this country needed. . . . He made me feel good that I was in his family."

Mayer co-authored a book attacking Reagan's second term. Note her inclusion of quotations about how the supposed tough guy tears up over the Gipper. —J.R.

Surnow said that he found the Clinton years obnoxious. "Hollywood under Clinton — it was like he was their guy," he said. "He was the yuppie, baby-boomer narcissist that all of Hollywood related to." During those years, Surnow recalled, he had countless arguments with liberal colleagues, some of whom stopped speaking to him. "My feeling is that the liberals' ideas are wrong," he said. "But they think I'm evil." Last year, he contributed two thousand dollars to the losing campaign of Pennsylvania's hard-line Republican senator Rick Santorum, because he "liked his position on immigration." His favorite bumper sticker, he said, is "Except for Ending Slavery, Fascism, Nazism & Communism, War Has Never Solved Anything."

Although he is a supporter of President Bush — he told me that "America is in its glory days" — Surnow is critical of the way the war in Iraq has been conducted. An "isolationist" with "no faith in nation-building," he thinks that "we could have been out of this thing three years ago." After deposing Saddam Hussein, he argued, America should have "just handed it to the Baathists and . . . put in some other monster who's going to keep these people in line but who's not going to be aggressive to us." In his view, America "is sort of the parent of the world, so we have to be stern but fair to people who are rebellious to us. We don't spoil them. That's not to say you abuse them, either. But you have to know who the adult in the room is."

Surnow's rightward turn was encouraged by one of his best friends, Cyrus Nowrasteh, a hard-core conservative who, in 2006, wrote and produced *The Path to 9/11*, a controversial ABC miniseries that presented President Clinton as having largely ignored the threat posed by Al Qaeda. (The show was denounced as defamatory by Democrats and by members of the 9/11 Commission; their complaints led ABC to call the program a "dramatization," not a "documentary.") Surnow and Nowrasteh met in 1985, when they worked together on *The Equalizer.* Nowrasteh, the son of a deposed adviser to the Shah of Iran, grew up in Madison, Wisconsin, where, like Surnow, he was alienated by the radicalism around him. He told me that he and Surnow, in addition to sharing an admiration for Reagan, found "L.A. a stultifying, stifling place because everyone thinks alike." Nowrasteh said that he and Surnow regard *24* as a kind of wish fulfillment for America. "Every American wishes we had someone out there quietly taking care of business," he said. "It's a deep, dark

To Mayer's credit, she quotes Surnow describing the professional relationship of liberals and conservatives.
—J.R.

45

ugly world out there. Maybe this is what Ollie North was trying to do. It would be nice to have a secret government that can get the answers and take care of business — even kill people. Jack Bauer fulfills that fantasy."

Does the success of 24 *prove that Americans hold this belief?* —J.E.M.

In recent years, Surnow and Nowrasteh have participated in the Liberty Film Festival, a group dedicated to promoting conservatism through mass entertainment. Surnow told me that he would like to counter the prevailing image of Senator Joseph McCarthy as a demagogue and a liar. Surnow and his friend Ann Coulter — the conservative pundit, and author of the pro-McCarthy book *Treason* — talked about creating a conservative response to George Clooney's recent film *Good Night, and Good Luck*. Surnow said, "I thought it would really provoke people to do a movie that depicted Joe McCarthy as an American hero or, maybe, someone with a good cause who maybe went too far." He likened the Communist sympathizers of the nineteen-fifties to terrorists: "The State Department in the fifties was infiltrated by people who were like Al Queda." But, he said, he shelved the project. "The blacklist is Hollywood's orthodoxy," he said. "It's not a movie I could get done now."

What effect does Mayer create by linking Surnow with figures such as McCarthy and Coulter? —A.L.

A year and a half ago, Surnow and Manny Coto, a *24* writer with similar political views, talked about starting a conservative television network. "There's a gay network, a black network — there should be a conservative network," Surnow told me. But as he and Coto explored the idea they realized that "we weren't distribution guys — we were content guys." Instead, the men developed *The Half Hour News Hour*, the conservative satire show. "*The Daily Show* tips left," Surnow said. "So we thought, let's do one that tips right." Jon Stewart's program appears on Comedy Central, an entertainment channel. But, after Surnow got Rush Limbaugh to introduce him to Roger Ailes, Fox News agreed to air two episodes. The program, which will follow the fake-news format popularized by *Saturday Night Live*, will be written by conservative humorists, including Sandy Frank and Ned Rice. Surnow said of the show, "There are so many targets, from global warming to banning tag on the playground. There's a lot of low-hanging fruit."

Last March, Supreme Court Justice Clarence Thomas and his wife, Virginia, joined Surnow and Howard Gordon for a private dinner at Rush Limbaugh's Florida home. The gathering inspired Virginia Thomas — who works at the Heritage Foundation, a conservative think tank — to organize a panel discussion on *24*. The symposium, sponsored by the foundation and held in June, was entitled "*24* and America's Image in Fighting Terrorism: Fact, Fiction, or Does It Matter?" Homeland Security Secretary Michael Chertoff, who participated in the discussion, praised the show's depiction of the war on terrorism as "trying to make the best choice with a series of bad options." He went on, "Frankly, it reflects real life." Chertoff, who is a devoted viewer of *24*, subsequently began an email correspondence with Gordon, and the two have since socialized in Los Angeles. "It's been very heady," Gordon said of Washington's enthusiasm for the show. Roger Director, Surnow's friend, joked that the conservative writers at *24* have become "like a Hollywood television annex to the White House. It's like an auxiliary wing."

The same day as the Heritage Foundation event, a private luncheon was held in the Wardrobe Room of the White House for Surnow and several others from the show. (The event was not publicized.) Among the attendees were Karl Rove, the deputy chief of staff; Tony Snow, the White House spokesman; Mary Cheney, the vice-president's daughter; and Lynn Cheney, the vice-president's wife, who, Surnow said, is "an extreme *24* fan." After the meal, Surnow recalled, he and his colleagues spent more than an hour visiting with Rove in his office. "People have this image of him as this snake-oil-dirty, secretive guy, but in his soul he's a history professor," Surnow said. He was less impressed with the Situation Room, which, unlike the sleek high-tech version at C.T.U., "looked like some old tea-room in a Victorian house."

The Heritage Foundation panel was moderated by Limbaugh. At one point, he praised the show's creators, dropped his voice to a stage whisper,

Is Mayer including this cast of characters to suggest a right-wing conspiracy? (Incidentally, she co-authored a book highly critical of Justice Thomas.)
—J.R.

So Chertoff doesn't differentiate between TV and reality either, seeing 24 *as reflecting real life: now* that *is a scary proposition!*
—A.L.

50

and added, to the audience's applause, "And most of them are conservative." When I spoke with Limbaugh, though, he reinforced the show's public posture of neutrality. "People think that they've got a bunch of right-wing writers and producers at *24*, and they're subtly sending out a message," he said. "I don't think that's happening. They're businessmen, and they don't have an agenda." Asked about the show's treatment of torture, he responded, "Torture? It's just a television show! Get a grip."

In fact, many prominent conservatives speak of *24* as if it were real. John Yoo, the former Justice Department lawyer who helped frame the Bush Administration's "torture memo" — which, in 2002, authorized the abusive treatment of detainees — invokes the show in his book *War by Other Means*. He asks, "What if, as the popular Fox television program *24* recently portrayed, a high-level terrorist leader is caught who knows the location of a nuclear weapon?" Laura Ingraham, the talk-radio host, has cited the show's popularity as proof that Americans favor brutality. "They love Jack Bauer," she noted on Fox News. "In my mind, that's as close to a national referendum that it's O.K. to use tough tactics against high-level Al Qaeda operatives as we're going to get." Surnow once appeared as a guest on Ingraham's show; she told him that, while she was undergoing chemotherapy for breast cancer, "it was soothing to see Jack Bauer torture these terrorists, and I felt better." Surnow joked, "We love to torture terrorists — it's good for you!"

As a foe of political correctness, Surnow seems to be unburdened by the controversy his show has stirred. *24*, he acknowledged, has been criticized as racially insensitive, because it frequently depicts Arab-Americans as terrorists. He said in response, "Our only politics are that terrorists are bad. In some circles, that's political." As he led me through the Situation Room set on the Real Time soundstage, I asked him if *24* has plans to use the waterboarding interrogation method, which has been defended by Vice President Cheney but is considered torture by the U.S. military. Surnow laughed and said, "Yes! But only with bottled water — it's Hollywood!"

Now I'm really worried — our Justice Department looking at 24 as "real" — good grief! —A.L.

A piece by John Yoo appears after Mayer's in this anthology. —J.R.

I'm glad that she returns to 24 in the end, after focusing for so long on Surnow. —L.S.

Do artists on the left feel burdened by the controversial nature of their art? To the contrary, provocative works are routinely celebrated and awarded. —J.R.

In a more sober tone, he said, "We've had all of these torture experts come by recently, and they say, 'You don't realize how many people are affected by this. Be careful.' They say torture doesn't work. But I don't believe that. I don't think it's honest to say that if someone you love was being held, and you had five minutes to save them, you wouldn't do it. Tell me, what would you do? If someone had one of my children, or my wife, I would hope I'd do it. There is nothing — nothing — I wouldn't do." He went on, "Young interrogators don't need our show. What the human mind can imagine is so much greater than what we show on TV. No one needs us to tell them what to do. It's not like somebody goes, 'Oh, look what they're doing, I'll do that.' Is it?"

I agree that the human imagination is powerful. I just wish Surnow would put his to better use. —A.L.

QUESTIONING THE TEXT

1. To what degree do you think that Jane Mayer's opinions appear in this article? Are there moments in the text where you can see her choices of what to include as shaping the reader's response in a certain way?

2. As is typical of a profile that appears in the *New Yorker*, this article includes abundant description that doesn't always seem necessary; for example, consider that in the second paragraph we learn that Joel Surnow is a "cigar enthusiast," even though this is not a piece about cigars. Collect several more examples of details that do not seem to be directly related to the main point of the article, and see if you can explain how these details contribute to the overall effect of the piece. Are some details more important than others? Are any easily expendable?

MAKING CONNECTIONS

3. In the next article, John Yoo defends torture in certain circumstances, just as Mayer quotes the creators of *24* doing. Yoo writes as someone involved in public policy decisions, while Surnow and others in this piece are responsible for creating a television show. Which persona do you find more persuasive in the defense of torture under extreme circumstances?

4. In "The Making of a Divorce Culture," Barbara Dafoe Whitehead (p. 224) cites the presence of divorce in television, film, and children's books as taking part in the creation of a culture of divorce (paragraph 26). How does Mayer develop a similar idea in "Whatever It Takes"? To what

degree do you think that artistic creations such as literature and television create the beliefs of a culture? To what degree do they reflect beliefs that are already present?

JOINING THE CONVERSATION

5. One fascinating aspect of this article is the importance attributed to the show by instructors at West Point, who believe that *24* shapes how their students and the general public view torture (see paragraph 25, for example). Are there other television programs that you think advance a harmful or a particularly valuable set of ideas? Write an essay in which you analyze how a television program or other media production such as a video game can be read as contributing to our sense of ethics.

6. Write a dramatic scene — perhaps one that could be included in the show *24*, if you're familiar with the program — that illustrates and then resolves an ethical dilemma. How difficult is it to try to send a particular message through a dramatic medium?

JOHN YOO
With "All Necessary and Appropriate Force"

IT'S EASY ENOUGH to offer emotional arguments against the mistreatment of detainees in wartime. The widespread publication of images of Abu Ghraib prisoners abused and humiliated by their American captors provoked outrage and may have marked a turning point in public support for the Second Gulf War — which was intended to overthrow a regime itself renowned for its abuse of human rights. Even if what the prisoners suffered differed in kind from the rape, murder, and physical abuse by which Saddam Hussein's regime controlled its citizens, Americans nonetheless expected their troops — occupiers, after all, in someone else's country — to maintain higher standards of behavior, even in the fog of war. So the images from Abu Ghraib, as well as subsequent media reports of prisoner abuse and perhaps torture at a Guantánamo Bay facility housing suspected terrorists, made the general public feel angry, ashamed, and uncertain about the entire mission. In some quarters, these places became visual symbols for that argument that all detainees, even terrorists, deserved to be treated according to the established rules of war.

In "With 'All Necessary and Appropriate Force,'" John Yoo (b. 1967) explains why that may not be the case, laying out his argument cleanly and with a distinct lack of emotion. He takes care to spell out the definitions of key terms in the Geneva Convention (which establishes rules of warfare for its signatories) and in congressional resolutions that speak to the circumstances under which prisoners may be interrogated. Yoo, a professor of law at Berkeley and one of the architects of the Patriot Act and of the Bush administration's policies in the War on Terror, certainly has his opponents and even enemies. Perhaps part of what angers them is the lawyerly way he parses issues of human rights, offering justifications for behaviors that that some fear will inevitably slide into abuse.

Yoo is the author of The Power of War and Peace: Foreign Affairs and the Constitution after 9/11 *(2005). "With 'All Necessary and Appropriate Force'" originally appeared in the* Los Angeles Times *on June 11, 2004.* —J.R.

Official Washington has been struck by a paroxysm of leaking. It involves classified memos analyzing how the Geneva Convention, the 1994 Torture Convention and a federal law banning torture apply to captured Al Qaeda and Taliban fighters. Critics suggest that the Bush administration sought to undermine or evade these laws. Sen. Dianne Feinstein (D-Calif.) claimed this week that the analyses appeared "to be an effort to redefine torture and narrow prohibitions against it."

This is mistaken. As a matter of policy, our nation has established a standard of treatment for captured terrorists. In February 2002, President Bush declared that the detainees held at Guantánamo Bay, Cuba, would be treated "humanely and, to the extend appropriate and consistent with military necessity, consistent with the principles" of the Geneva Convention. Detainees receive shelter, food, clothing, health care and the right to worship.

This policy is more generous than required. The Geneva Convention does not apply to the war on terrorism. It applies only to conflicts between its signatory nations. Al Qaeda is not a nation; it has not signed the convention; it shows no desire to obey the rules. Its very purpose — inflicting civilian casualties through surprise attack — violates the core principle of laws of war to spare innocent civilians and limit fighting to armed forces. Although the Convention applies to the Afghanistan conflict, the Taliban militia lost its right to prisoner-of-war status because it did not wear uniforms, did not operate under responsible commanders and systematically violated the laws of war.

It is true that the definition of torture in the memos is narrow, but that follows the choice of Congress. When the Senate approved the international Torture Convention, it defined torture as an act "specifically intended to inflict severe physical or mental pain or suffering." It defined mental pain or suffering as "prolonged mental harm" caused by threats of physical harm or death to a detainee or a third person, the administration of mind-altering drugs or other procedures "calculated to disrupt profoundly the senses or the personality." Congress adopted that narrow definition in the 1994 law against torture committed abroad, but it refused to implement another prohibition in the Convention — against "cruel, inhuman or degrading treatment or punishment" — because it was thought to be vague and undefined.

Physical and mental abuse is clearly illegal. But would limiting a captured   5
terrorist to six hours' sleep, isolating him, interrogating him for several hours or requiring him to do physical labor constitute "severe physical or mental pain or suffering"? Federal law commands that Al Qaeda and Taliban operatives not be tortured, and the president has ordered that they be treated humanely, but the U.S. is not required to treat captured terrorists as if they were guest at a hotel or suspects held at an American police station.

Finally, critics allege that the administration wants to evade these laws by relying on the president's commander-in-chief power. But the 1994 statute isn't being evaded, because the president's policy is to treat the detainees humanely. Besides, that statue does not explicitly regulate the president or the military. General criminal laws are usually not interpreted to apply to either, because otherwise they could interfere with the president's constitutional responsibility to manage wartime operations. If laws against murder or property destruction applied to the military in wartime, for instance, it could not engage in the violence that is a necessary part of war.

But suppose Congress did specifically intend to restrict the president's authority to interrogate captured terrorists. As commander in chief, the president still bears the responsibility to wage war. To this day, presidents from both political parties have refused to acknowledge the legality of the War Powers Resolution, which requires congressional approval for hostilities of more than 60 days. (President Clinton ignored it during Kosovo.) And in the war on terrorism, Congress has authorized the president to use "all necessary and appropriate force."

By exploring the boundaries of what is lawful, the administration's analyses identified how a decision maker could act in an extraordinary situation. For example, suppose that the United States captures a high-level Al Qaeda leader who knows the location of a nuclear weapon in an American city. Congress should not prevent the president from taking necessary measures to elicit its location, just as it should not prohibit him from making other strategic or tactical choices in war. In hearings this week, Sen. Charles E. Schumer (D-N. Y.) recognized that "very few people in this room or in America . . . would say that torture should never, ever be used, particularly if thousands of lives are at stake."

Ultimately, the administration's policy is consistent with the law. If the American people disagree with that policy, they have options: Congress can Change the law, or the electorate can change the administration.

QUESTIONING THE TEXT

1. In his discussion of ethics, John Yoo takes a more directly argumentative approach than Jane Mayer does. Summarize Yoo's thesis in your own words. How does he handle potential objections to his thesis?

2. Because Yoo is writing an op-ed, a genre that usually limits writers to about 750 words, he does not have a great deal of space to expand on his argument. Given more space, what do you think he should focus on to strengthen his argument?

MAKING CONNECTIONS

3. Compare John Yoo's and Jane Mayer's (p. 252) articles about torture. Which one do you find to be a more compelling exploration of the debate over torture? How does the publication in which each article originally appeared — the *New Yorker* for Mayer, the *Los Angeles Times* for Yoo — affect the content of that article? You may need to research those two publications to discover what kind of audience each writer has in mind.

4. Reread the third paragraph in Yoo's article, on why the Geneva Convention does not apply to Al Qaeda, and then compare Yoo's position to Stephen Carter's discussion of integrity — particularly the line that Carter says stuck in his mind: "You don't know if he was breaking the rules until you know what the rules are about following the rules" (p. 188, paragraph 37). How does this line apply to Yoo? Do his arguments about "all necessary and appropriate force" display integrity? Defend your answer.

JOINING THE CONVERSATION

5. Limiting yourself to 750 words, write a thesis-driven op-ed that stakes out a position on whether — and if so, when — torture might be appropriate.

NORA NARANJO-MORSE
Ta

NORA NARANJO-MORSE *(b. 1953), a Tewa Indian from Santa Clara Pueblo, is a story-teller, potter, sculptor, poet, video producer, and a brilliant reader of her own and others' work. Best known for* Mud Woman: Poems from the Clay *(1992), a gorgeous book that combines photographs of her Mud Woman pottery with her poems, Naranjo-Morse is also the author of* A First Clay Gathering *(1993) and of several films, including* What Was Taken and What We Sell *(1994) and* I've Been Bingo'ed by My Baby *(1996), a biting and often hilarious short video on casino culture. Through a grant, she brought together seven Pueblo, Navajo, and Hopi artists to create a large Storyteller figure; her* Clay Beings, *another brief (28-minute) film, documents the making of this remarkable piece of pottery.*

I had the great pleasure of hearing Naranjo-Morse speak at a screening of Clay Beings, *and a few days later I went to the Indian Arts Research Center in Santa Fe where the storyteller figure, "Moon Coming at Evening," was on display. The size of the piece astonished me, since I know how hard it is to fire a piece of pottery that big. But what most impressed me was Naranjo-Morse's vision: creating a Storyteller out of clays from seven different traditions and weaving them together into one unforgettable figure. It is an afternoon I won't soon forget, and I take every opportunity I get to introduce students to the work of this important artist and cultural critic.*

"Ta" appears in Mud Woman, *accompanying the photograph of a sculpture of the same name. As you read this poem about Naranjo-Morse's father, think about the criteria for success that it establishes and about your own sense of what it means to be successful.*
                                                                    —A.L.

I asked about success
        how was I to measure it,
        struggling in
        two worlds,
        between Pueblo tradition
        and modern values.
    Keeping on course,
        a balance
        of who I am
            and wish to become.

Ta took his time answering.
        I thought maybe
            he hadn't heard,
            or worse,
            not listened.

278

Waiting
>I noticed,
>how time
>had tailored my father
>into an old man
>wrinkled
>>and halting.

Finally,
>with clear
>thoughtful words,
>my father spoke:
>"Navi a yu,
>hi wu na mang,
>uvi aa yaa,
>uvi seng,
>da hihchan po o.
>Navi a yu,
>hi wodi kwee un muu
>oe to jan be,
>hi wo na mang,
>sa wo na mang."
>"My daughter,
>it is going well,
>your children,
>your husband,
>are happy.
>My daughter,
>you are a good woman,
>listen,
>it is going well,
>it goes in beauty."

Simple
>words,
>>reminding me,
>>success
>>is not only
>>respecting tradition
>>or balancing
>>modern values.
>>It is the appreciation
>>of life's basic gifts,
>>weaving
>>into the whole

of who you are
and who you can become.
Ta sat under the Elm,
drifting to sleep,
his hand in mine.

IN RESPONSE

1. The father's words in Naranjo-Morse's poem appear first in the Tewa language, then translated into English. What effect does the inclusion of the
Tewa language have on your reading and understanding of the poem?
Why do you think Naranjo-Morse chose to include the original
language?

2. It may not be obvious just how this poem addresses the main concern of
this chapter, ethics. What would you consider the ethical dimension of
this poem? Does it present an argument about ethics? What ideas about
ethical living does it imply?

3. Consider an experience you have had where you felt that you were torn
between two different cultures, groups, or loyalties. Did you manage to
balance competing claims as successfully as Naranjo-Morse seems to in
this poem? Write an essay in which you describe your experience or a
poem that re-creates the experience.

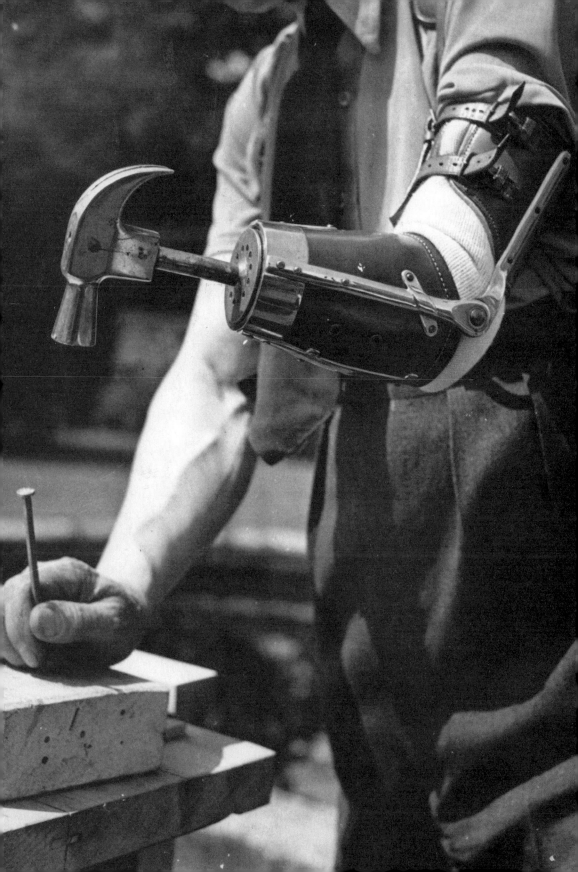

The photo on the preceding page shows a British World War II veteran using his prosthetic arm (with an attachment) to hammer nails. The veteran, Captain Maxwell, received the prosthesis from the British Ministry of Pensions, which supplied limbs to both military personnel and civilians after the war.

■ What do you notice first about this photograph?

■ What associations does it call up? ■ Do you see the photo as implying that science and technology are mainly positive, mainly negative, or both positive and negative? Why?

Science and Technology   5

TIME AND AGAIN throughout the twentieth century, we found that scientists and engineers — like the hero of Mary Shelley's *Frankenstein* (1818) — have created technologies that drive our society to the limits of what it can grasp legally and ethically. Indeed, there seems to be no boundary to what the human imagination can first contemplate and then achieve. Scientists have already mapped out the genes that control life, performed surgery in the womb, extracted the secrets of the atom, and etched the pathways of human knowledge onto tiny silicon chips. Occasionally, experiments escape our control, and we watch them poison our landscapes or explode before our eyes. But the quest for knowledge continues.

Julius Caesar, a military genius and a shrewd politician, observed once that "it is better to have expanded the frontiers of the mind than to have pushed back the boundaries of the empire." As Caesar doubtless understood, the two achievements often amount to the same thing, the powers of mind enabling one people or nation to dominate others, to cast itself in the role of a god and its neighbors as servants or slaves.

This chapter is designed to explore the resonances of *Frankenstein*, the many questions it raises, and the ways it leads us to think about science, progress, and alienation. In our mythologies, ancient and modern, we show a fondness for rebels like Victor Frankenstein, who would steal the fire of the gods and, with their new knowledge, shake the foundations of empires. Yet we cannot entirely identify with such figures either. They remain a threat to us too, a reminder that humanity finally lacks the wisdom to play God.

Your own thinking about these issues may be stimulated by considering the following questions:

- Why do contemporary readers and moviegoers continue to find *Frankenstein* fascinating? What makes the intellectual dreamer or the rebel an attractive figure?

- Why does a society usually react with suspicion toward people who, like Victor Frankenstein's monster, seem different? How do we define the outsider? How does the outsider act as a result?

- How do we deal with new technologies or learn to assess the impact of older technologies we now take for granted?
- Does scientific or technological progress always entail some loss or disruptive change? You might want to discuss this issue with a group of classmates.

• • •

MARY SHELLEY
Frankenstein

*W*ITH FRANKENSTEIN, *Mary Shelley (1797–1851) created a myth as powerful, complex, and frightening as the monster in the novel itself. The book intrigues us today as a narrative with many dimensions and interpretations. It works as the story of a scientist whose ambitions exceed his understanding, as an account of a scientific project that begins with great promise but leads to disaster, as the lament of an alien creature spurned by his maker, as the tract of an outsider besieged by his sense of difference, as the protest of a rebel striking out against a conventional and restrictive society.*

The daughter of early feminist Mary Wollstonecraft and political theorist William Godwin, and the wife of Percy Bysshe Shelley, Mary Shelley began Frankenstein; or, The Modern Prometheus, *to use its full title, in the summer of 1816 after the poet Byron invited his friends at a lake resort in Switzerland to "each write a ghost story." The short piece she composed eventually grew through several revisions (1818, 1823, 1831) into the novel we know today.*

The protagonist of her work, Victor Frankenstein, is an ambitious young scholar who discovers how to bestow "animation upon lifeless matter." He uses this knowledge to assemble a grotesque manlike creature, and then, horrified by what he has done, abandons it the moment he brings it to life. The following selection from the novel is Victor's account of those events. —J.R.

I see by your eagerness, and the wonder and hope which your eyes express, my friend, that you expect to be informed of the secret with which I am acquainted; that cannot be: listen patiently until the end of my story, and you will easily perceive why I am reserved upon that subject. I will not lead you on, unguarded and ardent as I then was, to your destruction and infallible misery. Learn from me, if not by my precepts, at least by my example, how dangerous is the acquirement of knowledge, and how much happier that man is who believes his native town to be the world, than he who aspires to become greater than his nature will allow.

When I found so astonishing a power placed within my hands, I hesitated a long time concerning the manner in which I should employ it. Although I possessed the capacity of bestowing animation, yet to prepare a frame for the reception of it, with all its intricacies of fibers, muscles, and veins, still remained a work of inconceivable difficulty and labor. I doubted at first whether I should attempt the creation of a being like myself, or one of simpler organization; but my imagination was too much exalted by my first success to permit me to doubt of my ability to give life to an animal as complex and wonderful as man.

The materials at present within my command hardly appeared adequate to so arduous an undertaking; but I doubted not that I should ultimately succeed. I prepared myself for a multitude of reverses; my operations might be incessantly baffled, and at last my work be imperfect: yet, when I considered the improvement which every day takes place in science and mechanics, I was encouraged to hope my present attempts would at least lay the foundations of future success. Nor could I consider the magnitude and complexity of my plan as any argument of its impracticability. It was with these feelings that I began the creation of a human being. As the minuteness of the parts formed a great hindrance to my speed, I resolved, contrary to my first intention, to make the being of a gigantic stature; that is to say, about eight feet in height, and proportionably large. After having formed this determination, and having spent some months in successfully collecting and arranging my materials, I began.

No one can conceive the variety of feelings which bore me onwards, like a hurricane, in the first enthusiasm of success. Life and death appeared to me ideal bounds, which I should first break through, and pour a torrent of light into our dark world. A new species would bless me as its creator and source; many happy and excellent natures would owe their being to me. No father could claim the gratitude of his child so completely as I should deserve theirs. Pursuing these reflections, I thought, that if I could bestow animation upon lifeless matter, I might in process of time (although I now found it impossible) renew life where death had apparently devoted the body to corruption.

These thoughts supported my spirits, while I pursued my undertaking with unremitting ardour. My cheek had grown pale with study, and my person had become emaciated with confinement. Sometimes, on the very brink of certainty, I failed; yet still I clung to the hope which the next day or the next hour might realize. One secret which I alone possessed was the hope to which I had dedicated myself; and the moon gazed on my midnight labors, while, with unrelaxed and breathless eagerness, I pursued nature to her hiding-places. Who shall conceive the horrors of my secret toil, as I dabbled among the unhallowed damps of the grave, or tortured the living animal to animate the lifeless clay? My limbs now tremble, and my eyes swim with the remembrance; but then a resistless, and almost frantic, impulse, urged me forward; I seemed to have lost all soul or sensation but for this one pursuit. It was indeed but a passing trance, that only made me feel with renewed acuteness so soon as, the unnatural stimulus ceasing to operate, I had returned to my old habits. I collected bones from charnel-houses; and disturbed, with profane fingers, the tremendous secrets of the human frame. In a solitary chamber, or rather cell, at the top of the house, and separated from all the other apartments by a gallery and staircase, I kept my workshop of filthy creation: my eye-balls were starting from their sockets in attending to the details of my employment. The dissecting room and the slaughter-house furnished many of my materials; and often did my human nature turn with loathing from my occupation, whilst, still urged on by an eagerness which perpetually increased, I brought my work near to a conclusion.

The summer months passed while I was thus engaged, heart and soul, in   5
one pursuit. It was a most beautiful season; never did the fields bestow a more
plentiful harvest, or the vines yield a more luxuriant vintage: but my eyes were
insensible to the charms of nature. And the same feelings which made me
neglect the scenes around me caused me also to forget those friends who were
so many miles absent, and whom I had not seen for so long a time. I knew my
silence disquieted them; and I well remembered the words of my father:
"I know that while you are pleased with yourself, you will think of us with
affection, and we shall hear regularly from you. You must pardon me if I regard
any interruption in your correspondence as a proof that your other duties are
equally neglected."

I knew well therefore what would be my father's feelings; but I could not
tear my thoughts from my employment, loathsome in itself, but which had
taken an irresistible hold of my imagination. I wished, as it were, to procrasti-
nate all that related to my feelings of affection until the great object, which
swallowed up every habit of my nature, should be completed.

I then thought that my father would be unjust if he ascribed my neglect to
vice, or faultiness on my part; but I am now convinced that he was justified in
conceiving that I should not be altogether free from blame. A human being in
perfection ought always to preserve a calm and peaceful mind, and never to allow
passion or a transitory desire to disturb his tranquility. I do not think that the
pursuit of knowledge is an exception to this rule. If the study to which you
apply yourself has a tendency to weaken your affections, and to destroy your taste
for those simple pleasures in which no alloy can possibly mix, then that study is
certainly unlawful, that is to say, not befitting the human mind. If this rule were
always observed; if no man allowed any pursuit whatsoever to interfere with the
tranquility of his domestic affections, Greece had not been enslaved; Caesar
would have spared his country; America would have been discovered more gradually; and the empires of Mexico and Peru had not been destroyed.

But I forgot that I am moralizing in the most interesting part of my tale;
and your looks remind me to proceed.

My father made no reproach in his letters, and only took notice of my
silence by enquiring into my occupations more particularly than before.
Winter, spring, and summer passed away during my labors; but I did not watch
the blossom or the expanding leaves — sights which before always yielded me
supreme delight — so deeply was I engrossed in my occupation. The leaves of
that year had withered before my work drew near to a close; and now every day
showed me more plainly how well I had succeeded. But my enthusiasm was
checked by my anxiety, and I appeared rather like one doomed by slavery to toil
in the mines, or any other unwholesome trade, than an artist occupied by his
favorite employment. Every night I was oppressed by a slow fever, and I became
nervous to a most painful degree; the fall of a leaf startled me, and I shunned my
fellow-creatures as if I had been guilty of a crime. Sometimes I grew alarmed
at the wreck I perceived that I had become; the energy of my purpose alone

sustained me: my labors would soon end, and I believed that exercise and amusement would then drive away incipient disease; and I promised myself both of these when my creation should be complete.

It was on a dreary night of November, that I beheld the accomplishment   10
of my toils. With an anxiety that almost amounted to agony, I collected the instruments of life around me, that I might infuse a spark of being into the life-less thing that lay at my feet. It was already one in the morning; the rain pat-tered dismally against the panes, and my candle was nearly burnt out, when, by the glimmer of the half-extinguished light, I saw the dull yellow eye of the creature open; it breathed hard, and a convulsive motion agitated its limbs.

How can I describe my emotions at this catastrophe, or how delineate the wretch whom with such infinite pains and care I had endeavored to form? His limbs were in proportion, and I had selected his features as beautiful. Beautiful! — Great God! His yellow skin scarcely covered the work of muscles and arteries beneath; his hair was of lustrous black, and flowing; his teeth of a pearly whiteness; but these luxuriances only formed a more horrid contrast with his watery eyes, that seemed almost of the same color as the dun white sockets in which they were set, his shriveled complexion and straight black lips.

The different accidents of life are not so changeable as the feelings of human nature. I had worked hard for nearly two years, for the sole purpose of infusing life into an inanimate body. For this I had deprived myself of rest and health. I had desired it with an ardor that far exceeded moderation; but now that I had finished, the beauty of the dream vanished, and breathless horror and disgust filled my heart. Unable to endure the aspect of the being I had created, I rushed out of the room, and continued a long time traversing my bedcham-ber, unable to compose my mind to sleep. At length lassitude succeeded to the tumult I had before endured; and I threw myself on the bed in my clothes, endeavoring to seek a few moments of forgetfulness. But it was in vain; I slept, indeed, but I was disturbed by the wildest dreams. I thought I saw Elizabeth,* in the bloom of health, walking in the streets of Ingolstadt. Delighted and surprised, I embraced her; but as I imprinted the first kiss on her lips, they became livid with the hue of death; her features appeared to change, and I thought that I held the corpse of my dead mother in my arms; a shroud enveloped her form, and I saw the graveworms crawling in the folds of the flan-nel. I started from my sleep with horror; a cold dew covered my forehead, my teeth chattered, and every limb became convulsed; when, by the dim and yellow light of the moon, as it forced its way through the window shutters, I beheld the wretch — the miserable monster whom I had created. He held up the curtain of the bed; and his eyes, if eyes they may be called, were fixed on me. His jaws opened, and he muttered some inarticulate sounds, while a grin wrinkled his cheeks. He might have spoken, but I did not hear; one hand was

---

Elizabeth: adopted sister of Victor Frankenstein

stretched out, seemingly to detain me, but I escaped, and rushed down stairs. I took refuge in the courtyard belonging to the house which I inhabited; where I remained during the rest of the night, walking up and down in the greatest agitation, listening attentively, catching and fearing each sound as if it were to announce the approach of the demoniacal corpse to which I had so miserably given life.

Oh! no mortal could support the horror of that countenance. A mummy again endued with animation could not be so hideous as that wretch. I had gazed on him while unfinished; he was ugly then; but when those muscles and joints were rendered capable of motion, it became a thing such as even Dante* could not have conceived.

I passed the night wretchedly. Sometimes my pulse beat so quickly and hardly, that I felt the palpitation of every artery; at others I nearly sank to the ground through languor and extreme weakness. Mingled with this horror, I felt the bitterness of disappointment; dreams that had been my food and pleasant rest for so long a space were now become a hell to me; and the change was so rapid, the overthrow so complete!

Morning, dismal and wet, at length dawned, and discovered to my sleepless and aching eyes the church of Ingolstadt, its white steeple and clock, which indicated the sixth hour. The porter opened the gates of the court, which had that night been my asylum, and I issued into the streets, pacing them with quick steps, as if I sought to avoid the wretch whom I feared every turning of the street would present to my view. I did not dare return to the apartment which I inhabited, but felt impelled to hurry on, although drenched by the rain which poured from a black and comfortless sky.

15

QUESTIONING THE TEXT

1. How does Victor Frankenstein explain his drive to work hard to bring a nonliving entity to life? Annotate the margins of the *Frankenstein* selection to highlight places where Frankenstein explains his motives. Do you think any of these motives account for the continuing development of science and technology today? Explore this issue with classmates.

2. To create his monster, what does Victor Frankenstein have to do to himself and to other creatures? Have you ever been so single-minded in the pursuit of a goal or passion? Explain.

3. What precisely about the creature disappoints Frankenstein? In a group, discuss Frankenstein's rejection of his monster, exploring its meanings and implications.

Dante (1265–1321): Italian poet, author of *Divine Comedy*

4. J.R.'s introduction suggests that the Frankenstein story has become a modern myth. How many versions of Shelley's tale can you think of? List them.

MAKING CONNECTIONS

5. Victor Frankenstein warns that knowledge is dangerous: "how much happier that man is who believes his native town to be the world, than he who aspires to become greater than his nature will allow" (paragraph 1). Freewrite on this idea, taking into account the essay in this chapter by J. Michael Bishop (p. 304). Is it likely that men and women will ever live contentedly in their native towns? Why, or why not?

6. Can you think of ways in which the anthologized passage from the novel differs from film versions of the Frankenstein tale you may have seen? Brainstorm a list of differences and jot them down.

JOINING THE CONVERSATION

7. Write a parody of this selection from *Frankenstein*, perhaps detailing the creation and consequences of some similar but more recent "monster," understanding that term broadly or metaphorically. You might even read Dave Barry's "Guys vs. Men" (p. 405) in Chapter 6 for a perspective on the desire to build "neat stuff."

8. Working with a group, discuss the monster as a creature who is similar to but also different from a human being. Can you compare his situation to that of other individuals or groups considered "different" in society? Write a brief position paper about Frankenstein's monster as a symbol of what it means to be different. Is the comparison convincing? Why, or why not?

9. Some critics suggest that *Frankenstein* reflects an early view of industrialization as a monstrous creation out of control. Use the library to learn what changes the industrial revolution was imposing on the landscape of England during the nineteenth century. Try also to determine how favorably people regarded changes such as the building of factories, industrial plants, and railroads. This subject is complex enough to support a full-scale research paper. Give it a try.

MICHAEL CHOROST
My Bionic Quest for Boléro

*M*AYBE YOU CAUGHT *12-year-old Kyle Krichbaum on* The Tonight Show *showing off his collection of vintage vacuum cleaners? His oddball obsession with these household appliances — their history, mechanics, and uses — is the sort of behavior that leads some parents to wonder whether their child needs Ritalin.*

But the computer age has made us think twice about fanatical, know-it-all geeks who grow up to invent things like personal computers, Web browsers, and brilliant search engines. Their passion for detail and relentless tinkering have inspired much scientific and technological innovation.

In "My Bionic Quest for Boléro," *which appeared in* Wired *(November 2005), self-confessed nerd Michael Chorost (b. 1964) explains how his own passion for a compulsive piece of music, Ravel's highly repetitive but mesmerizing* Boléro, *drove him to motivate equally obsessive software engineers to push the envelope on a cochlear implant already inserted into his brain to restore his lost hearing. Though the device had made it possible for Chorost once again to understand speech, its sixteen-channel connection to his auditory nerves seemed too frail to restore the richness of sound in the music Chorost remembered. But he persisted, finding scientists and engineers equally determined to trick circuits and software into mimicking the subtleties of human hearing. By narrating the not-always-linear or predictable ways that technology and science advance, "My Bionic Quest for* Boléro" *may help us appreciate the people behind its accomplishments.*

Chorost tells the full story of the loss and recovery of his hearing in a remarkable memoir, Rebuilt: How Becoming Part Computer Made Me More Human *(2005).* —J.R.

I still remember the first time I heard Boléro, *in a music class in college. It has stayed in my head ever since.* —A.L.

With one listen, I was hooked. I was a 15-year-old suburban New Jersey nerd, racked with teenage lust but too timid to ask for a date. When I came across *Boléro* among the LPs in my parents' record collection, I put it on the turntable. It hit me like a neural thunderstorm, titanic and glorious, each cycle building to a climax and waiting but a beat before launching into the next.

I had no idea back then of *Boléro's* reputation as one of the most famous orchestral recordings in the world. When it was first performed at the Paris Opera in 1928, the 15-minute composition stunned

Some may recall Boléro *from the 1979 film* 10, *starring Dudley Moore and Bo Derek.* —J.R.

Music often elicits such extreme reactions. Why? —A.L.

the audience. Of the French composer, Maurice Ravel, a woman in attendance reportedly cried out, "He's mad . . . he's mad!" One critic wrote that *Boléro* "departs from a thousand years of tradition."

I sat in my living room alone, listening. *Boléro* starts simply enough, a single flute accompanied by a snare drum: da-da-da-dum, da-da-da-dum, dum-dum, da-da-da-dum. The same musical clause repeats 17 more times, each cycle adding instruments, growing louder and more insistent, until the entire orchestra roars in an overpowering finale of rhythm and sound. Musically, it was perfect for my ear. It had a structure that I could easily grasp and enough variation to hold my interest.

It took a lot to hold my interest; I was nearly deaf at the time. In 1964, my mother contracted rubella while pregnant with me. Hearing aids allowed me to understand speech well enough, but most music was lost on me. *Boléro* was one of the few pieces I actually enjoyed. A few years later, I bought the CD and played it so much it eventually grew pitted and scratched. It became my touchstone. Every time I tried out a new hearing aid, I'd check to see if *Boléro* sounded OK. If it didn't, the hearing aid went back.

Note how well Chorost describes the music of Boléro *here. Later in the piece he handles the intricacies of technology with equal clarity.* —J.R.

I'm trying to imagine the sensation Chorost describes here. That his description is so matter-of-fact makes it more powerful to me. —A.L.

And then, on July 7, 2001, at 10:30 am, I lost my ability to hear *Boléro* — and everything else. While I was waiting to pick up a rental car in Reno, I suddenly thought the battery in my hearing aid had died. I replaced it. No luck. I switched hearing aids. Nothing.

I got into my rental car and drove to the nearest emergency room. For reasons that are still unknown, my only functioning ear had suffered "sudden-onset deafness." I was reeling, trying to navigate in a world where the volume had been turned down to zero.

Chorost's book, 5 Rebuilt: How Becoming Part Computer Made Me More Human *(2005), begins at this moment, when he thinks just his hearing aids have failed.* —J.R.

According to my research, approximately 100,000 people worldwide have received the implant. So we can estimate that five billion dollars have changed hands. I hope it's going to research! —J.E.M.

But there was a solution, a surgeon at Stanford Hospital told me a week later, speaking slowly so I could read his lips. I could have a computer surgically installed in my skull. A cochlear implant, as it is known, would trigger my auditory nerves with 16 electrodes that snaked inside my inner ear. It seemed drastic, and the $50,000 price tag was a dozen times more expensive than a high-end hearing aid. I went home and cried. Then I said yes.

I wonder if some would have said no — and if so, why? —A.L.

Great metaphor. His inclusion of poetic language allows us to comprehend his experience.   —L.S.

For the next two months, while awaiting surgery, I was totally deaf except for a thin trickle of sound from my right ear. I had long since become accustomed to not hearing my own voice when I spoke. It happened whenever I removed my hearing aid. But that sensation was as temporary as waking up without my glasses. Now, suddenly, the silence wasn't optional. At my job as a technical writer in Silicon Valley, I struggled at meetings. Using the phone was out of the question.

In early September, the surgeon drilled a tunnel through an inch and a half of bone behind my left ear and inserted the 16 electrodes along the auditory nerve fibers in my cochlea. He hollowed a well in my skull about the size of three stacked quarters and snapped in the implant.

When the device was turned on a month after surgery, the first sentence I heard sounded like "Zzzzzz szz szvizzz ur brfzzzzzz?" My brain gradually learned how to interpret the alien signal. Before long, "Zzzzzz szz szvizzz ur brfzzzzzz?" became "What did you have for breakfast?" After months of practice, I could use the telephone again, even converse in loud bars and cafeterias. In many ways, my hearing was better than it had ever been. Except when I listened to music.

I could hear the drums of *Boléro* just fine. But the other instruments were flat and dull. The flutes and soprano saxophones sounded as though someone had clapped pillows over them. The oboes and violins had become groans. It was like walking colorblind through a Paul Klee exhibit. I played *Boléro* again and again, hoping that practice would bring it, too, back to life. It didn't.

The implant was embedded in my head; it wasn't some flawed hearing aid I could just send back. But it was a computer. Which meant that, at least in theory, its effectiveness was limited only by the ingenuity of software engineers. As researchers learn more about how the ear works, they continually revise cochlear implant software. Users await new releases with all the anticipation of Apple zealots lining up for the latest Mac OS.

10

This paragraph helps readers to understand the essential difference between a hearing aid and Chorost's implant: Chorost and the engineers can interact with his auditory nerves, creating software better adapted to the ways ears work.
—J.R.

Good analogy — and not just for techno-geeks!
—J.E.M.

About a year after I received the implant, I asked one implant engineer how much of the device's hardware capacity was being used. "Five percent, maybe." He shrugged. "Ten, tops."

I was determined to use that other 90 percent. I set out on a crusade to explore the edges of auditory science. For two years tugging on the sleeves of scientists and engineers around the country, offering myself as a guinea pig for their experiments. I wanted to here *Boléro* again.

15

Helen Keller famously said that if she had to choose between being deaf and being blind, she'd be blind, because while blindness cut her off from things, deafness cut her off from people. For centuries, the best available hearing aid was a horn, or ear trumpet, which people held to their ears to funnel in sound. In 1952, the first electronic hearing aid was developed. It worked by blasting amplified sound into a damaged ear. However it (and the more advanced models that followed) could help only if the user had some residual hearing ability, just as glasses can help only those who still have some vision. Cochlear implants, on the other hand, bypass most of the ear's natural hearing mechanisms. The device's electrodes directly stimulate nerve endings in the ear, which transmit sound information to the brain. Since the surgery can eliminate any remaining hearing, implants are approved for use only in people who can't be helped by hearing aids. The first modern cochlear implants went on the market in Australia in 1982, and by 2004 approximately 82,500 people worldwide had been fitted with one.

Interesting background and evidence that work to support his personal story.
—L.S.

When technicians activated my cochlear implant in October 2001, they gave me a pager-sized processor that decoded sound and sent it to a headpiece that clung magnetically to the implant underneath my skin. The headpiece contained a radio transmitter, which sent the processor's data to the implant at roughly 1 megabit per second. Sixteen electrodes curled up inside my cochlea strobed on and off to stimulate my auditory nerves. The processor's software gave me eight channels of auditory resolution, each representing a frequency range. The more channels the software delivers, the better the user can distinguish between sounds of different pitches.

Some advocates of Deaf culture are critical of cochlear implants and the extreme measures medicine has used (since the European Renaissance) to make people hear. I wonder what Chorost would have to say to them? —A.L.

I often skip the technical details in science writing, but these sections are remarkably lucid. I think I actually understand how Chorost's implant works. —J.R.

Eight channels isn't much compared with the capacity of a normal ear, which has the equivalent of 3,500 channels. Still, eight works well enough for speech, which doesn't have much pitch variation. Music is another story. The lowest of my eight channels captured everything from 250 hertz (about middle C on the piano) to 494 hertz (close to the B above middle C), making it nearly impossible for me to distinguish among the 11 notes in that range. Every note that fell into a particular channel sounded the same to me.

So in mid-2002, nine months after activation, I upgraded to a program called Hi-Res, which gave me 16 channels — double the resolution! An audiologist plugged my processor into her laptop and uploaded the new code. I suddenly had a better ear, without surgery. In theory, I would now be able to distinguish among tones five notes apart instead of 11.

I eagerly plugged my Walkman into my processor and turned it on. *Boléro* did sound better. But after a day or two, I realized that "better" still wasn't good enough. The improvement was small, like being in that art gallery again and seeing only a gleam of pink here, a bit of blue there. I wasn't hearing the *Boléro* I remembered.

It's worth noting how often Chorost assists readers by using comparisons and analogies. —J.R.

At a cochlear implant conference in 2003, I heard Jay Rubinstein, a surgeon and researcher at the University of Washington, say that it took at least 100 channels of auditory information to make music pleasurable. My jaw dropped. No wonder. I wasn't even close.

20

A year later, I met Rubinstein at another conference, and he mentioned that there might be ways to bring music back to me. He told me about something called stochastic resonance; studies suggested that my music perception might be aided by deliberately adding noise to what I hear. He took a moment to give me a lesson in neural physiology. After a neuron fires, it goes dormant for a fraction of a second while it resets. During that phase, it misses any information that comes along. When an electrode zaps thousands of neurons at once, it forces them all to go dormant, making it impossible for them to receive pulses until they reset. That synchrony means I miss bits and pieces of information.

Chorost is very, very good at explaining complex technical issues, the mark of a fine science writer. —A.L.

Desynchronizing the neurons, Rubinstein explained, would guarantee that they're never all dormant simultaneously. And the best way to get them out of sync is to beam random electrical noise at them. A few months later, Rubinstein arranged a demonstration.

An audiologist at the University of Iowa working with Rubenstein handed me a processor loaded with the stochastic-resonance software. The first thing I heard was a loud whoosh — the random noise. It sounded like a cranked-up electric fan. But in about 30 seconds, the noise went away. I was puzzled. "You've adapted to it," the technician told me. The nervous system can habituate to any kind of everyday sound, but it adjusts especially quickly to noise with no variation. Stochastic-resonance noise is so content-free that the brain tunes it out in seconds.

In theory, the noise would add just enough energy to incoming sound to make faint details audible. In practice, everything I heard became rough and gritty. My own voice sounded vibrato, mechanical, and husky — even a little querulous, as if I were perpetually whining.

What we're seeing here is the kind of relentless tinkering and trial-and-error experimentation that leads to technological progress. Seen up close, it's not glamorous, but Chorost uses the details to build a compelling narrative.

— J.R.

We tried some quick tests to take my newly programmed ear out for a spin. It performed slightly better in some ways, slightly worse in others — but there was no dramatic improvement. The audiologist wasn't surprised. She told me that, in most cases, a test subject's brain will take weeks or even months to make sense of the additional information. Furthermore, the settings she chose were only an educated guess at what might work for my particular physiology. Everyone is different. Finding the right setting is like fishing for one particular cod in the Atlantic.

The university loaned me the processor to test for a few months. As soon as I was back in the hotel, I tried my preferred version of *Boléro*, a 1982 recording conducted by Charles Dutoit with the Montreal Symphony Orchestra. It sounded different, but not better. Sitting at my keyboard, I sighed a little and tapped out an email thanking Rubinstein and encouraging him to keep working on it.

Music depends on low frequencies for its richness and mellowness. The lowest-pitched string on a

25

guitar vibrates at 83 hertz, but my Hi-Res software, like the eight-channel model, bottoms out at 250 hertz. I do hear something when I pluck a string, but it's not actually an 83-hertz sound. Even though the string is vibrating at 83 times per second, portions of it are vibrating faster, giving rise to higher-frequency notes called harmonics. The harmonics are what I hear.

The engineers haven't gone below 250 hertz because the world's low-pitched sounds — air conditioners, engine rumbles — interfere with speech perception. Furthermore, increasing the total frequency range means decreasing resolution, because each channel has to accommodate more frequencies. Since speech perception has been the main goal during decades of research, the engineers haven't given much thought to representing low frequencies. Until Philip Loizou came along.

Loizou and his team of postdocs at the University of Texas at Dallas are trying to figure out ways to give cochlear implant users access to more low frequencies. A week after my frustratingly inconclusive encounter with stochastic resonance, I traveled to Dallas and asked Loizou why the government would give him a grant to develop software that increases musical appreciation. "Music lifts up people's spirits, helps them forget things," he told me in his mild Greek accent. "The goal is to have the patient live a normal life, not to be deprived of anything."

Loizou is trying to negotiate a trade-off: narrowing low-frequency channels while widening higher-frequency channels. But his theories only hinted at what specific configurations might work best, so Loizou was systematically trying a range of settings to see which ones got the better results.

The team's software ran only on a desktop computer, so on my visit to Dallas I had to be plugged directly into the machine. After a round of testing, a postdoc assured me, they would run *Boléro* through their software and pipe it into my processor via Windows Media Player.

I spent two and a half days hooked up to the computer, listening to endless sequences of tones — none of it music — in a windowless cubicle. Which of two tones sounded lower? Which of two versions

Chorost's explanations allow readers with little training in sciences to understand and keep reading.   —L.S.

30

of "Twinkle, Twinkle, Little Star" was more recognizable? Did this string of notes sound like a march or a waltz? It was exacting, high-concentration work — like taking an eye exam that lasted for two days. My responses produced reams of data that they would spend hours analyzing.

Another great analogy. —J.E.M.

Forty minutes before my cab back to the airport was due, we finished the last test and the postdoc fired up the programs he needed to play *Boléro*. Some of the lower pitches I'd heard in the previous two days had sounded rich and mellow, and I began thinking wistfully about those bassoons and oboes. I felt a rising sense of anticipation and hope.

I waited while the postdoc tinkered with the computer. And waited. Then I noticed the frustrated look of a man trying to get Windows to behave. "I do this all the time," he said, half to himself. Windows Media Player wouldn't play the file.

The great novelist Vladimir Nabokov famously said that music "assaulted" his ears. I doubt Chorost would have gone to such lengths if he had felt that way about music. —A.L.

I suggested rebooting and sampling *Boléro* through a microphone. But the postdoc told me he couldn't do that in time for my plane. A later flight wasn't an option; I had to be back in the Bay Area. I was crushed. I walked out of the building with my shoulders slumped. Scientifically, the visit was a great success. But for me, it was a failure. On the flight home, I plugged myself into my laptop and listened sadly to *Boléro* with Hi-Res. It was like eating cardboard.

Failures like this remind readers of the human side of science — that people's lives and well-being may be at stake in a quest for knowledge. —J.R.

35

It's June 2005, a few weeks after my visit to Dallas, and I'm ready to try again. A team of engineers at Advanced Bionics, one of three companies in the world that makes bionic ears, is working on a new software algorithm for so-called virtual channels. I hop on a flight to their Los Angeles headquarters, my CD player in hand.

Here he switches tenses, giving us a sense that much time has passed. —L.S.

My implant has 16 electrodes, but the virtual-channels software will make my hardware act like there are actually 121. Manipulating the flow of electricity to target neurons between each electrode creates the illusion of seven new electrodes between each actual pair, similar to the way an audio engineer can make a sound appear to emanate from between two speakers. Jay Rubinstein had told me two years ago that it would take at least 100 channels to create good music perception. I'm about to find out if he's right.

I'm sitting across a desk from Gulam Emadi, an Advanced Bionics researcher. He and an audiologist are about to fit me with the new software. Leo Litvak, who has spent three years developing the program, comes in to say hello. He's one of those people of whom others often say, "If Leo can't do it, it probably can't be done." And yet it would be hard to find a more modest person. Were it not for his clothes, which mark him as an Orthodox Jew, he would simply disappear in a roomful of people. Litvak tilts his head and smiles hello, shyly glances at Emadi's laptop, and sidles out.

At this point, I'm rationing my emotions like Spock. Hi-Res was a disappointment. Stochastic resonance remains a big if. The low-frequency experiment in Dallas was a bust. Emadi dinks with his computer and hands me my processor with the new software in it. I plug it into myself, plug my CD player into it, and press Play.

Boléro starts off softly and slowly, meandering like a breeze through the trees. Da-da-da-dum, da-da-da-dum, dum-dum, da-da-da-dum. I close my eyes to focus, switching between Hi-Res and the new software every 20 or 30 seconds by thumbing a blue dial on my processor.

My God, the oboes d'amore do sound richer and warmer. I let out a long, slow breath, coasting down a river of sound, waiting for the soprano saxophones and the piccolos. They'll come in around six minutes into the piece — and it's only then that I'll know if I've truly got it back.

As it turns out, I couldn't have chosen a better piece of music for testing new implant software. Some biographers have suggested that *Boléro*'s obsessive repetition is rooted in the neurological problems Ravel had started to exhibit in 1927, a year before he composed the piece. It's still up for debate whether he had early-onset Alzheimer's, a left-hemisphere brain lesion, or something else.

But *Boléro*'s obsessiveness, whatever its cause, is just right for my deafness. Over and over the theme repeats, allowing me to listen for specific details in each cycle.

Chorost is doing a great job of recalling and including vivid details.   —J.E.M.

40

What an amazingly fortuitous coincidence. I wonder how Ravel would respond to the story Chorost tells here?   —A.L.

*Slowing the narra-
tive to describe
seconds here makes
the reader really feel
the impact this
moment had on
him.*   —L.S.

At 5:59, the soprano saxophones leap out bright and clear, arcing above the snare drum. I hold my breath.

At 6:39, I hear the piccolos. For me, the stretch between 6:39 and 7:22 is the most *Boléro* of *Boléro*, the part I wait for each time. I concentrate. It sounds . . . right.

Hold on. Don't jump to conclusions. I backtrack to 5:59 and switch to Hi-Res. That heart-stopping leap has become an asthmatic whine. I backtrack again and switch to the new software. And there it is again, that exultant ascent. I can hear *Boléro*'s force, its intensity and passion. My chin starts to tremble.

I open my eyes, blinking back tears. "Congratulations," I say to Emadi. "You have done it." And I reach across the desk with absurd formality and shake his hand.

There's more technical work to do, more progress to be made, but I'm completely shattered. I keep zoning out and asking Emadi to repeat things. He passes me a box of tissues. I'm overtaken by a vast sensation of surprise. I did it. For years I pestered researchers and asked questions. Now I'm running 121 channels and I can hear music again.

That evening, in the airport, sitting numbly at the gate, I listen to *Boléro* again. I'd never made it through more than three or four minutes of the piece on Hi-Res before getting bored and turning it off. Now, I listen to the end, following the narrative, hearing again its holy madness.

I pull out the Advanced Bionics T-shirt that the team gave me and dab at my eyes.

During the next few days I walk around in a haze of disbelief, listening to *Boléro* over and over to prove to myself that I really am hearing it again. But *Boléro* is just one piece of music. Jonathan Berger, head of Standford's music department, tells me in an email, "There's not much of interest in terms of structure — it's a continuous crescendo, no surprises, no subtle interplay between development and contrast."

"In fact," he continues, "Ravel was not particularly happy that this study in orchestration became

*Reading this sec-
tion, we retrace the
moments during
which Chorost
recovered his expe-
rience of* Boléro. *I
wonder if I'll listen
to the music differ-
ently the next time
I hear it.*   —J.R.

45

*I'm close to tears
myself reading this,
and I've pulled out
an old CD with*
Boléro *on it. . . .*
—A.L.

50

his big hit. It pales in comparison to any of his other music in terms of sophistication, innovation, grace, and depth."

So now it's time to try out music with sophistication, innovation, grace, and depth. But I don't know where to begin. I need an expert with first-rate equipment, a huge music collection, and the ability to pick just the right pieces for my newly reprogrammed ear. I put the question to craigslist — "Looking for a music geek." Within hours, I hear from Tom Rettig, a San Francisco music producer.

In his studio, Rettig plays me Ravel's *String Quartet in F Major* and Philip Glass' *String Quartet no. 5*. I listen carefully, switching between the old software and the new. Both compositions sound enormously better on 121 channels. But when Rettig plays music with vocals, I discover that having 121 channels hasn't solved all my problems. While the crescendos in Dulce Pontes' *Canção do Mar* sound louder and clearer, I here only white noise when her voice comes in. Rettig figures that relatively simple instrumentals are my best bet — pieces where the instruments don't overlap too much — and that flutes and clarinets work well for me. Cavalcades of brass tend to overwhelm me and confuse my ear.

And some music just leaves me cold: I can't even get through Kraftwerk's *Tour de France*. I wave impatiently to Rettig to move on. (Later, a friend tells me it's not the software — Kraftwerk is just dull. It makes me think that for the first time in my life I might be developing a taste in music.)

Listening to *Boléro* more carefully in Rettig's studio reveals other bugs. The drums sound squeaky — how can drums squeak? — and in the frenetic second half of the piece, I still have trouble separating the instruments.

After I get over the initial awe of hearing music again, I discover that it's harder for me to understand ordinary speech than it was before I went to virtual channels. I report this to Advanced Bionics, and my complaint is met by a rueful shaking of heads. I'm not the first person to say that, they tell me. The idea of virtual channels is a breakthrough, but the technology is still in the early stages of development.

55

Two steps forward, one step back . . . but that is often the nature of change.
—J.R.

Chorost doesn't mention the cost of the devices after his first reference to their high price. While I am thrilled at what technology has been able to do for him, I wonder about the millions of people with disabilities and about what technology can — and can't — do for them at a cost they can afford.

—A.L.

But I no longer doubt that incredible things can be done with that unused 90 percent of my implant's hardware capacity. Tests conducted a month after my visit to Advanced Bionics show that my ability to discriminate among notes has improved considerably. With Hi-Res, I was able to identify notes only when they were at least 70 hertz apart. Now, I can hear notes that are only 30 hertz apart. It's like going from being able to tell the difference between red and blue to being able to distinguish between aquamarine and cobalt.

My hearing is no longer limited by the physical circumstances of my body. While my friends' ears will inevitably decline with age, mine will only get better. ☺   —J.E.M.

QUESTIONING THE TEXT

1. In the second sentence of this article, Chorost identifies a younger version of himself as a "nerd, racked with teenage lust but too timid to ask for a date." How does this opening help create the persona that he maintains for the rest of the article? Do you find that persona sympathetic? Cite specific textual evidence as you explain why or why not.

2. Chorost's article sometimes becomes very detailed in discussing the technology of his cochlear implant. Highlight or underline some particular moments when Chorost writes about technical details. Are these sections accessible to a general audience? Identify some specific tactics that Chorost uses to make these parts more readable or rewrite sentences to make them more intelligible for a nontechnical audience.

MAKING CONNECTIONS

3. Both Chorost and Denise Grady (p. 331) write articles that explore how technology and the body interact, particularly in terms of disability. What differences do you see in how the articles relate technology to disability? What similarities can you detect?

4. Compare Chorost's attitude toward modern technology to Christine Rosen's attitude toward the same subject in "The Image Culture" (p. 353). Whose attitude is more like your own?

JOINING THE CONVERSATION

5. Though few of us have had an interaction with technology that makes as big a difference as Chorost's cochlear implant does, there might be certain pieces of technology that you feel have changed your life — for better or for worse. Write an essay reflecting on a piece of technology that you feel has changed the way you live.

6. Chorost's article details the process of learning to listen to music. For example, after finding the music of Kraftwerk boring and having a friend agree, he writes "It makes me think for the first time in my life I might be developing a taste in music" (paragraph 56). Think about a time when you can remember the process of developing taste or judgment — the first time that you realized you had particular tastes in music or movies or when you learned to appreciate the differences in quality between, for example, two athletes in the same sport. Write an essay that reflects on this aspect of your education.

J. MICHAEL BISHOP
Enemies of Promise

NOT LONG AGO *I discovered that the onboard diagnostic system of my new vehicle will let me know via a "Check Engine" light when I haven't screwed the gas cap on tight enough to prevent fumes from polluting the atmosphere. The computer discovers the problem not by monitoring a crude switch on the gas cap itself but by checking the entire combustion process and searching for irregularities. Anomalies — even momentary ones — detected this way are stored in the computer's memory so a technician can fix them later. The technology in my car is almost as wondrous as that of the Internet, which enables me to converse with people anywhere in the world; or consider the science that produced an asthma medication that enables me to play racquetball without carrying an inhaler. As you might suspect, I'm not in the camp of those who denigrate science or criticize technological change.*

I do understand the fears of the Luddites, who yearn for a world less chemically reprocessed and technologically demanding. But I also think that many who criticize science today have either short memories or little historical sense, which is why I wanted to share "Enemies of Promise" by J. Michael Bishop (b. 1936), a professor of microbiology and Chancellor at the University of California, San Francisco, and winner of the Nobel Prize. He warns that the misperceptions many people have about science could have serious consequences for all Americans. The piece is also a fine example of an expert writing clearly to an audience of nonspecialists — something scientists will have to do more often if faith in science is to be restored.

"Enemies of Promise" appeared originally in my favorite magazine, the Wilson Quarterly *(Summer 1995), a publication of the Woodrow Wilson International Center for Scholars.* —J.R.

We live in an age of scientific triumph. Science has solved many of nature's puzzles and greatly enlarged human knowledge. And the fruits of scientific inquiry have vastly improved human welfare. Yet despite these proud achievements, science today is increasingly mistrusted and under attack.

Some of the opposition to science comes from familiar sources, including religious zealots who relentlessly press for the mandatory teaching of creationism in the public schools. It is discouraging to think that more than a century after the publication of Charles Darwin's *Origin of Species* (1859), and seventy years after the Scopes trial dramatized the issue, the same battles must still be fought. But fight them we must.

Other antagonists of science are less familiar. Strange though it may seem, there is within academe a school of thought that considers science to be wholly fraudulent as a way of knowing. According to these "postmodernists," the supposedly objective truths of science are in reality all "socially constructed fictions," no more than "useful myths," and science itself is "politics by other means." Anyone with a working knowledge of science, anyone who looks at the natural world with an honest eye, should recognize all of this for what it is: arrant nonsense.

Science, of course, is not the exclusive source of knowledge about human existence. Literature, art, philosophy, history, and religion all have their insights to offer into the human condition. To deny that is scientism — the belief that the methods of the natural sciences are the only means of obtaining knowledge. And to the extent that scientists have at times indulged in that belief, they must shoulder some of the blame for the misapprehensions that some people have about science.

But science does have something inimitable to offer humankind: it is, in   5
the words of physician-author Lewis Thomas, "the best way to learn how the world works." A postmodernist poet of my acquaintance complains that it is in the nature of science to break things apart, thereby destroying the "mysterious whole." But we scientists take things apart in order to understand the whole, to solve the mystery — an enterprise that we regard as one of the great, ennobling tasks of humankind.

In the academic medical center where I work, the efficacy and benefits of science are a daily reality. So when I first encountered the postmodernist view of science some years ago, I dismissed it as either a strategy for advancement in parochial precincts of the academy or a display of ignorance. But now I am alarmed because the postmodernist cry has been joined, outside the academy, by other strong voices raised against science.

Consider these lines from Václav Havel, the widely admired Czech writer and statesman, who has vigorously expressed his disenchantment with the ethos of science: "Modern rationalism and modern science . . . now systematically leave [the natural world] behind, deny it, degrade and defame it — and, of course, at the same time, colonize it."

Those are angry words, even if their precise meaning is elusive. And anger is evident, too, in Havel's main conclusion: "This era [of science and rationalism] has reached the end of its potential, the point beyond which the abyss begins."

Even some influential men who know science well and who have been good friends to it in the past have joined in the chorus of criticism and doubt. Thanks in part to Havel's ruminations, Representative George E. Brown, Jr. (D.-Calif.), who was trained as a physicist, reports that his faith in science has been shaken. He complains of what he calls a "knowledge paradox": an expansion of fundamental knowledge accompanied by an increase in social problems. He implies that it shouldn't be that way, that as science progresses, the problems of society should diminish. And he suggests that Congress and the "consumers" of scientific research may have to take more of a hand in determining how science is conducted, in what research gets funded.

A similar critique has been made by former Colorado governor Richard   10
Lamm. He claims no longer to believe that biomedical research contributes to the

improvement of human health — a truly astonishing stance. To validate his skepticism, he presents the example of the University of Colorado Medical Center. It has done "little or nothing," he complains, about increasing primary care, expanding medical coverage to the uninsured, dealing with various addictions and dietary excesses, and controlling violence. As if biomedical research, or even academic medical centers, had either the resources or the capabilities to do what Lamm desires!

The source of these dissatisfactions appears to be an exaggerated view of what science can do. For example, agitation within Congress may induce the National Science Foundation to establish a center for research on violence, but only the naive would expect a quick fix for that momentous problem. Three-quarters of a century after the death of the great German sociologist Max Weber (1864–1920), the social and behavioral sciences have yet to produce an antidote for even one of the common social pathologies. The genesis of human behavior entails complexities that still lie beyond the grasp of human reason.

Critics such as Brown and Lamm blame science for what are actually the failures of individuals or society to use the knowledge that science has provided. The blame is misplaced. Science has produced the vaccines required to control many childhood infections in the United States, but our nation has failed to deploy properly those vaccines. Science has sounded the alarm about acid rain and its principal origins in automobile emissions, but our society has not found the political will to bridle the internal combustion engine. Science has documented the medical risks of addiction to tobacco, yet our federal government still spends large amounts of money subsidizing the tobacco industry.

These critics also fail to understand that success in science cannot be dictated. The progress of science is ultimately driven by feasibility. Science is the art of the possible, of the soluble, to recall a phrase from the late British immunologist and Nobel laureate Sir Peter Medawar. We seldom can force nature's hand; usually, she must tip it for us.

Nor is it possible, especially in the early stages of research, to anticipate what benefits are likely to result. My own experience is a case in point. In 1911, Peyton Rous at the Rockefeller Institute in New York City discovered a virus that causes cancer in chickens, a seemingly obscure observation. Yet 65 years later, that chicken virus was the vehicle by which Harold Varmus and I, and our colleagues, were able to uncover genes that are involved in the genesis of human cancer. The lesson of history is clear: the lines of inquiry that may prove most fruitful to science are generally unpredictable.

Biologist John Tyler Bonner has whimsically recalled an exchange he had   15
some decades ago with the National Science Foundation, which had given him a grant for a research project. "After the first year, I wrote that things had not worked out very well — had tried this, that, and the other thing, and nothing had really happened. [The foundation] wrote back, saying, 'Don't worry about it — that is the way research goes sometimes. Maybe next year you will have better luck.'" Alas, no scientist today would think of writing such a report, and no scientist today could imagine receiving such a reply.

The great successes of science have helped to create the exaggerated expectations about what science can accomplish. Why has malaria not been eradicated by now? Why is there still no cure for AIDS? Why is there not a more effective vaccine for influenza? When will there be a final remedy for the common cold? When will we be able to produce energy without waste? When will alchemy at last convert quartz to gold?

When scientists fail to meet unrealistic expectations, they are condemned by critics who do not recognize the limits of science. Thus, playwright and AIDS activist Larry Kramer bitterly complains that science has yet to produce a remedy for AIDS, placing much of the blame on the National Institutes of Health (NIH) — "a research system that by law demands compromise, rewards mediocrity and actually punishes initiative and originality."

I cannot imagine what law Kramer has in mind, and I cannot agree with his description of what the NIH expects from its sponsored research. I have assisted the NIH with peer review for more than twenty years. Its standards have always been the same: it seeks work of the highest originality and demands rigor as well. I, for one, have never knowingly punished initiative or originality, and I have never seen the agencies of the NIH do so. I realize with sorrow that Mr. Kramer is unlikely to believe me.

Biomedical research is one of the great triumphs of human endeavor. It has unearthed usable knowledge at a remarkable rate. It has brought us international leadership in the battle against disease and the search for understanding. I wonder how all this could have been accomplished if we scientists did business in the way that Kramer and critics like him claim that we do.

The bitter outcry from AIDS activists over the past decade was echoed in   20 the 1992 film *Lorenzo's Oil*, which portrays medical scientists as insensitive, close-minded, and self-serving, and dismisses controlled studies of potential remedies as a waste of precious time. The film is based on a true story, the case of Lorenzo Odone, a child who suffers from a rare hereditary disease that cripples many neurological functions and leads at an agonizing pace to death.

Offered no hope by conventional medical science, Lorenzo's desperate parents scoured the medical literature and turned up a possible remedy: the administration of two natural oils known as erucic and oleic acid. In the face of the skepticism of physicians and research specialists, Lorenzo was given the oils and, in the estimation of his parents, ceased to decline — perhaps even improved marginally. It was a courageous, determined, and even reasoned effort by the parents. (Mr. Odone has since received an honorary degree from at least one university.) Whether it was effective is another matter.

The movie portrays the treatment of Lorenzo as a success, with the heroic parents triumphant over the obstructionism of medical scientists. The film ends with a collage of parents testifying that the oils had been used successfully to treat Lorenzo's disease in their children. But it fails to present any of the parents who have tried the oils with bitter disappointment. And, of course, all of this is only anecdotal information. Properly controlled studies are still in progress. To date, they have not given much cause for hope.

Meanwhile, as if on cue, medical scientists have since succeeded in isolating the damaged gene responsible for the rare disease. Thus, the stage is set for the development of decisive clinical testing and effective therapy (although the latter may be long in coming).

If misapprehensions abound about what science can and cannot do, so do misplaced fears of its hazards. For more than five years now, my employer, the University of California, San Francisco, has waged a costly battle for the right to perform biomedical research in a residential area. For all intents and purposes, the university has lost. The opponents were our neighbors, who argued that we are dangerous beyond tolerance; that we exude toxic wastes, infectious pathogens, and radioactivity; that we put at risk the lives and limbs of all who come within reach — our own lives and limbs included, I suppose, a nuance that seems lost on the opposition. One agitated citizen suggested in a public forum that the manipulation of recombinant DNA at the university had engendered the AIDS virus; another declared on television her outrage that "those people are bringing DNA into my neighborhood."

Resistance to science is born of fear. Fear, in turn, is bred by ignorance.   25
And it is ignorance that is our deepest malady. The late literary critic Lionel Trilling described the difficulty well, in words that are even more apposite now than when he wrote them: "Science in our day lies beyond the intellectual grasp of most [people]. . . . This exclusion . . . from the mode of thought which is habitually said to be the characteristic achievement of the modern age . . . is a wound . . . to our intellectual self-esteem . . . a diminution of national possibility . . . a lessening of the social hope."

The mass ignorance of science confronts us daily. In recent international testing, U.S. high school students finished ninth in physics among the top twelve nations, eleventh in chemistry, and dead last in biology. Science is poorly taught in most of our elementary and secondary schools, when it is taught at all. Surveys of adult Americans indicate that only a minority accepts evolution as an explanation for the origin of the human species. Many do not even know that the Earth circles the Sun. In a recent committee hearing, a prominent member of Congress betrayed his ignorance of how the prostate gland differs from the testes. Accountants, laborers, lawyers, poets, politicians, and even many physicians look upon science with bewilderment.

Do even we scientists understand one another? A few years ago, I read of a Russian satellite that gathers solar light to provide constant illumination of large areas of Siberia. "They are taking away the night," I thought. "They are taking away the last moments of mystery. Is nothing sacred?" But then I wondered what physicists must think of biologists' hopes to decipher the entire human genome and perhaps recraft it, ostensibly for the better.

Writing an article about cancer genes for *Scientific American* some years ago, I labored mightily to make the text universally accessible. I consulted students, journalists, laity of every stripe. When these consultants all had approved, I sent the manuscript to a solid-state physicist of considerable merit. A week later, the manuscript came back with this comment: "I have read your paper and shown it around the staff here. No one understands much of it. What exactly is a gene?"

Robert M. Hazen and James Trefil, authors of *The Sciences: An Integrated Approach* (1994), tell of twenty-three geophysicists who could not distinguish between DNA and RNA, and of a Nobel Prize-winning chemist who had never heard of plate tectonics. I have encountered biologists who thought string theory had something to do with pasta. We may be amused by these examples; we should also be troubled. If science is no longer a common culture, what can we rightfully expect of the laity by way of understanding?

Lionel Trilling knew where the problem lay in his time: "No successful method of instruction has been found . . . which can give a comprehension of sciences . . . to those students who are not professionally committed to its mastery and especially endowed to achieve it." And there the problem lies today: perplexing to our educators, ignored by all but the most public-minded of scientists, bewildering and vaguely disquieting to the general public. 30

We scientists can no longer leave the problem to others. Indeed, it has always been ours to solve, and all of society is now paying for our neglect. As physicist and historian of science Gerald Holton has said, modern men and women "who do not know the basic facts that determine their very existence, functioning, and surroundings are living in a dream world . . . are, in a very real sense, not sane. We [scientists] . . . should do what we can, or we shall be pushed out of the common culture. The lab remains our workplace, but it must not become our hiding place."

The enterprise of science embodies a great adventure: the quest for understanding in a universe that the mathematician Freeman Dyson once characterized as "infinite in all directions, not only above us in the large but also below us in the small." We of science have begun the quest well, by building a method of ever-increasing power, a method that can illuminate all that is in the natural world. In consequence, we are admired but also feared, mistrusted, even despised. We offer hope for the future but also moral conflict and ambiguous choice. The price of science seems large, but to reject science is to deny the future.

QUESTIONING THE TEXT

1. Have you ever encountered the attitude toward science that Bishop describes as *postmodern*? If so, explain this notion of science as a set of "socially constructed fictions" (paragraph 3). Share your work with classmates, and explore the difference between science as a useful fiction and science as an ennobling fact.

2. Are there any words, concepts, or examples in "Enemies of Promise" that you don't understand? Based on Bishop's text, how would you characterize his intended readership?

3. What is J.R.'s attitude toward scientific progress as demonstrated in his introduction? How does the introduction influence your reading of "Enemies of Promise"?

MAKING CONNECTIONS

4. Research a contemporary medical science debate, such as stem cell research or the efficacy of vaccination or acupuncture, paying special attention to the arguments put forward by those writers who are not scientists. How do they attempt to persuade others to accept their views? How do they establish their own authority? Can you find any authors that you find especially persuasive or any that you think fit the label of "enemies of promise"? Present your findings in class.

5. Victor Frankenstein, in Mary Shelley's selection from *Frankenstein* (p. 285), describes this way his rejection of the monster that he had created: "I felt the bitterness of disappointment; dreams that had been my food and pleasant rest for so long a space were now become a hell to me; and the change was so rapid, the overthrow so complete!" (paragraph 14). Does the rejection of science in our time as described by Bishop reflect disappointment and bitterness that we have not created the technological Utopia that once seemed just over the horizon? Freewrite on this subject, and then write a position paper on this question: has science today become Dr. Frankenstein's monster?

JOINING THE CONVERSATION

6. Write a 200-word summary or abstract of "Enemies of Promise" for readers who might not have time to study the entire piece.

7. Choose an example of a scientific or technological change that has occurred in the last hundred years; read about it in the library, using at least three different sources, and then write an evaluation of that change.

8. Examine a technology that you believe has caused more problems than it has solved, and write an essay in which you propose a solution to at least one of those problems. Trace the cause of the problem in the technology — is it a problem in the science, in social attitudes, in politics, or something else?

JEREMY RIFKIN
Biotech Century: Playing Ecological Roulette with Mother Nature's Designs

Jeremy Rifkin (b. 1945) is well known as a social activist. Organizer of the 1968 March on the Pentagon, Rifkin helped draw public attention to alleged U.S. war crimes in Vietnam. By the late 1970s, he was focusing his efforts on biotechnology, concentrating, for example, on the dangers of genetic engineering in the beef industry and in many everyday food substances. As president of the nonprofit Foundation on Economic Trends, Rifkin has gained a wide audience that includes both devoted admirers and scornful opponents: the National Milk Producers call him a "food terrorist," while reviewer and journalist Scott Landon concludes that he is a "fine synthesizer of cutting-edge issues." His most recent books are The Hydrogen Economy: The Creation of the World-Wide Energy Web and the Redistribution of Power on Earth *(2002) and* The European Dream: How Europe's Vision of the Future Is Quietly Eclipsing the American Dream *(2004).*

Rifkin himself does not take well to being labeled an antitechnology zealot, saying over and over again that he supports the use of biotechnology for making pharmaceuticals and for applying new knowledge of genetics to preventive medicine. How you respond to Rifkin's concerns in "Biotech Century" will probably be closely connected to your own value system as well as to the evidence provided for or against Rifkin's thesis.

The essay reprinted here, published in the May–June 1998 issue of E/The Environmental Magazine, *is adapted from Rifkin's book* The Biotech Century: Harnessing the Gene and Remaking the World *(1998). I chose this piece because Rifkin's trademark use of overstatement makes his claims very clear — and hard to ignore. In addition, while I am generally an advocate and admirer of science and scientific discovery, I have my own fears about human attempts to master — and effectively change — the natural world.* —A.L.

We're in the midst of a great historic transition into the Biotech Age. The ability to isolate, identify and recombine genes is making the gene pool available, for the first time, as the primary raw resource for future economic activity on Earth. After thousands of years of fusing, melting, soldering, forging and burning inanimate matter to create useful things, we are now splicing, recombining inserting and stitching living material for our own economic interests. Lord Ritchie-Calder, the British science writer, cast the biological revolution in the proper historical perspective when he observed that "just as we have manipulated plastics and metals, we are now manufacturing living materials."

The Nobel Prize-winning chemist Robert F. Curl of Rice University spoke for many of his colleagues in science when he proclaimed that the 20th century was "the century of physics and chemistry. But it is clear that the next century will be the century of biology."

Global "life-science" companies promise an economic renaissance in the coming Biotech Century — they offer a door to a new era of history where the genetic blueprints of evolution itself become subject to human authorship. Critics worry that the reseeding of the Earth with a laboratory-conceived second Genesis could lead to a far different future — a biological Tower of Babel and the spread of chaos throughout the biological world, drowning out the ancient language of creation.

A SECOND GENESIS

Human beings have been remaking the Earth for as long as we have had a history. Up to now, however, our ability to create our own second Genesis has been tempered by the restraints imposed by species boundaries. We have been forced to work narrowly, continually crossing close relatives in the plant or animal kingdoms to create new varieties, strains and breeds. Through a long, historical process of tinkering and trial and error, we have redrawn the biological map, creating new agricultural products, new sources of energy, more durable building materials, and life-saving pharmaceuticals. Still, in all this time, nature dictated the terms of engagement.

But the new technologies of the Genetic Age allow scientists, corporations and governments to manipulate the natural world at the most fundamental level — the genetic one. Imagine the wholesale transfer of genes between totally unrelated species and across all biological boundaries — plant, animal and human — creating thousands of novel life forms in a brief moment of evolutionary time. Then, with clonal propagation, mass-producing countless replicas of these new creations, releasing them into the biosphere to propagate, mutate, proliferate and migrate. This is, in fact, the radical scientific and commercial experiment now underway.

GLOBAL POWERS AT PLAY

Typical of new biotech trends is the bold decision by the Monsanto Corporation, long a world leader in chemical products, to sell off its entire chemical division in 1997 and anchor its research, development and marketing in biotech-based technologies and products. Global conglomerates are rapidly buying up biotech start-up companies, seed companies, agribusiness and agrochemical concerns, pharmaceutical, medical and health businesses, and food and drink companies, creating giant life-science complexes from which to fashion a bio-industrial world. The concentration of power is impressive. The top 10 agrochemical companies control 81 percent of the $29 billion per year global agrochemical market. Ten life-science companies control 37 percent of the $15 billion per year global seed market. Meanwhile, pharmaceutical companies spent more than $3.5 billion in 1995 buying up biotech firms. Novartis, a giant new firm resulting from the \$27 billion merger of Sandoz and Ciba-Geigy, is now the world's largest agrochemical company, the second-largest seed company and the second-largest pharmaceutical company.

Global life-science companies are expected to introduce thousands of new genetically engineered organisms into the environment in the coming century. In just the past 18 months, genetically engineered corn, soy and cotton have been planted over millions of acres of U.S. farmland. Genetically engineered insects, fish and domesticated animals have also been introduced, like the sheep/goat hybrid "geep."

Virtually every genetically engineered organism released into the environment poses a potential threat to the ecosystem. To appreciate why this is so, we need to understand why the pollution generated by genetically modified organisms is so different from the pollution resulting from the release of petrochemical products into the environment.

Because they are alive, genetically engineered organisms are inherently more unpredictable than petrochemicals in the way they interact with other living things in the environment. Consequently, it is much more difficult to assess all of the potential impacts that a genetically engineered organism might have on the Earth's ecosystems.

Genetically engineered products also reproduce. They grow and they   10 migrate. Unlike petrochemical products, it is difficult to constrain them within a given geographical locale. Finally, once released, it is virtually impossible to recall genetically engineered organisms back to the laboratory, especially those organisms that are microscopic in nature.

The risks in releasing novel, genetically engineered organisms into the biosphere are similar to those we've encountered in introducing exotic organisms into the North American habitat. Over the past several hundred years, thousands of non-native organisms have been brought to America from other regions of the world. While many of these creatures have adapted to the North American ecosystems without severe dislocations, a small percentage of them have run wild, wreaking havoc on the flora and fauna of the continent. Gypsy moth, Kudzu vine, Dutch elm disease, chestnut blight, starlings and Mediterranean fruit flies come easily to mind.

Whenever a genetically engineered organism is released, there is always a small chance that it, too, will run amok because, like nonindigenous species, it has been artificially introduced into a complex environment that has developed a web of highly integrated relationships over long periods of evolutionary history. Each new synthetic introduction is tantamount to playing ecological roulette. That is, while there is only a small chance of it triggering an environmental explosion, if it does, the consequences could be significant and irreversible.

SPREADING GENETIC POLLUTION

Nowhere are the alarm bells going off faster than in agricultural biotechnology. The life-science companies are introducing biotech crops containing newly discovered genetic traits from other plants, viruses, bacteria and animals.

The new genetically engineered crops are designed to perform in ways that have eluded scientists working with classical breeding techniques. Many of the new gene-spliced crops emanating from laboratories seem more like creations from the world of science fiction. Scientists have inserted "antifreeze" protein genes from flounder into the genetic code of tomatoes to protect the fruit from frost damage. Chicken genes have been inserted into potatoes to increase disease resistance. Fire-fly genes have been injected into the biological code of corn plants. Chinese hamster genes have been inserted into the genome of tobacco plants to increase sterol production.

Ecologists are unsure of the impacts of bypassing natural species boundaries by introducing genes into crops from wholly unrelated plant and animal species. The fact is, there is no precedent in history for this kind of "shotgun" experimentation. For more than 10,000 years, classical breeding techniques have been limited to the transference of genes between closely related plants or animals that can sexually interbreed, limiting the number of possible genetic combinations. Natural evolution appears to be similarly circumscribed. By contrast, the new gene-splicing technologies allow us to bypass all previous biological boundaries in nature, creating life forms that have never before existed. For example, consider the ambitious plans to engineer transgenic plants to serve as pharmaceutical factories for the production of chemicals and drugs. Foraging animals, seed-eating birds and soil insects will be exposed to a range of genetically engineered drugs, vaccines, industrial enzymes, plastics and hundreds of other foreign substances for the first time, with untold consequences. The notion of large numbers of species consuming plants and plant debris containing a wide assortment of chemicals that they would normally never be exposed to is an unsettling prospect.

Much of the current effort in agricultural biotechnology is centered on the creation of herbicide-tolerant, pest-resistant and virus-resistant plants. Herbicide-tolerant crops are a favorite of companies like Monsanto and Novartis that are anxious to corner the lucrative worldwide market for their herbicide products. More than 600 million pounds of poisonous herbicides are dumped on U.S. farm land each year, most sprayed on corn, cotton and soybean crops. Chemical companies gross more than $4 billion per year in U.S. herbicide sales alone. 15

To increase their share of the growing global market for herbicides, life-science companies have created transgenic crops that tolerate their own herbicides (see "Say It Ain't Soy," *In Brief* March/April, 1997). The idea is to sell farmers patented seeds that are resistant to a particular brand of herbicide in the hope of increasing a company's share of both the seed and herbicide markets. Monsanto's new "Roundup Ready" patented seeds, for example, are resistant to its best-selling chemical herbicide, Roundup.

The chemical companies hope to convince farmers that the new herbicide-tolerant crops will allow for a more efficient eradication of weeds. Farmers will be able to spray at any time during the growing season, killing weeds without killing their crops. Critics warn that with new herbicide-tolerant crops planted in the fields, farmers are likely to use even greater quantities of herbicides to control weeds, as there will be less fear of damaging their crops in the process of spraying. The increased use of herbicides, in turn, raises the possibility of weeds developing resistance, forcing an even greater use of herbicides to control the more resistant strains.

The potential deleterious impacts on soil fertility, water quality and beneficial insects that result from the increased use of poisonous herbicides, like Monsanto's Roundup, are a disquieting reminder of the escalating environmental bill that is likely to accompany the introduction of herbicide-tolerant crops.

The new pest-resistant transgenic crops pose similar environmental problems. Life-science companies are readying transgenic crops that produce insecticide in every cell of each plant. Several crops, including Ciba Geigy's pest-resistant "maximizer corn" and Rohm and Haas's pest-resistant tobacco are already available on the commercial market. A growing body of scientific evidence points to the likelihood of creating "super bugs" resistant to the effects of the new pesticide-producing genetic crops.

The new generation of virus-resistant transgenic crops pose the equally dangerous possibility of creating new viruses that have never before existed in nature. Concerns are surfacing among scientists and in scientific literature over the possibility that the protein genes could recombine with genes in related viruses that find their way naturally into the transgenic plant, creating a recombinant virus with novel features.

A growing number of ecologists warn that the biggest danger might lie in what is called "gene flow" — the transfer of genes from altered crops to weedy relatives by way of cross-pollination. Researchers are concerned that manufactured genes for herbicide tolerance, and pest and viral resistance might escape and, through cross pollination, insert themselves into the genetic makeup of weedy relatives, creating weeds that are resistant to herbicides, pests and viruses. Fears over the possibility of transgenic genes jumping to wild weedy relatives heightened in 1996 when a Danish research team, working under the auspices of Denmark's Environmental Science and Technology Department, observed the transfer of just such a gene — something critics of deliberate-release experiments have warned of for years and biotech companies have dismissed as a remote or nonexistent possibility.

Transnational life-science companies project that within 10 to 15 years, all of the major crops grown in the world will be genetically engineered to include herbicide-, pest-, virus-, bacteria-, fungus- and stress-resistant genes. Millions of acres of agricultural land and commercial forest will be transformed in the most daring experiment ever undertaken to remake the biological world. Proponents of the new science, armed with powerful gene-splicing tools and precious little data on potential impacts, are charging into this new world of agricultural biotechnology, giddy over the potential benefits and confident that the risks are minimum or non-existent. They may be right. But, what if they are wrong?

INSURING DISASTER

The insurance industry quietly let it be known several years ago that it would not insure the release of genetically engineered organisms into the environment against the possibility of catastrophic environmental damage, because the industry lacks a risk-assessment science — a predictive ecology — with which to judge the risk of any given introduction. In short, the insurance industry clearly understands the Kafka-esque implications of a government regime claiming to regulate a technology in the absence of clear scientific knowledge.

Increasingly nervous over the insurance question, one of the biotech trade associations attempted early on to raise an insurance pool among its member organizations, but gave up when it failed to raise sufficient funds to make the pool operable. Some observers worried, at the time, and continue to worry — albeit privately — over what might happen to the biotech industry if a large-scale commercial release of a genetically altered organism were to result in a catastrophic environmental event. For example, the introduction and spread of a new weed or pest comparable to Kudzu vine, Dutch elm disease or gypsy moth, might inflict costly damage to flora and fauna over extended ranges.

Corporate assurances aside, one or more significant environmental mishaps are an inevitability in the years ahead. When that happens, every nation is going to be forced to address the issue of liability. Farmers, landowners, consumers and the public at large are going to demand to know how it could have happened and who is liable for the damages inflicted. When the day arrives — and it's likely to come sooner rather than later — "genetic pollution" will take its place alongside petrochemical and nuclear pollution as a grave threat to the Earth's already beleaguered environment.

ALLERGIC TO TECHNOLOGY?

The introduction of new genetically engineered organisms also raises a number of serious human health issues that have yet to be resolved. Health professionals and consumer organizations are most concerned about the potential allergenic effects of genetically engineered foods. The Food and Drug Administration (FDA) announced in 1992 that special labeling for genetically engineered foods would not be required, touching off protest among food professionals, including the nation's leading chefs and many wholesalers and retailers.

With two percent of adults and eight percent of children having allergic responses to commonly eaten foods, consumer advocates argue that all gene-spliced foods need to be properly labeled so that consumers can avoid health risks. Their concerns were heightened in 1996 when *The New England Journal of Medicine* published a study showing genetically engineered soybeans containing a gene from a Brazil nut could create an allergic reaction in people who were allergic to the nuts. The test result was unwelcome news for Pioneer Hi-Bred

International, the Iowa-based seed company that hoped to market the new genetically engineered soy. Though the FDA said it would label any genetically engineered foods containing genes from common allergenic organisms, the agency fell well short of requiring across-the-board labeling, leaving *The New England Journal of Medicine* editors to ask what protection consumers would have against genes from organisms that have never before been part of the human diet and that might be potential allergens. Concerned over the agency's seeming disregard for human health, the *Journal* editors concluded that FDA policy "would appear to favor industry over consumer protection."

Depleting the Gene Pool

Ironically, all of the many efforts to reseed the biosphere with a laboratory-conceived second Genesis may eventually come to naught because of a massive catch-22 that lies at the heart of the new technology revolution. On the one hand, the success of the biotech revolution is wholly dependent on access to a rich reservoir of genes to create new characteristics and properties in crops and animals grown for food, fiber and energy, and products used for pharmaceutical and medical purposes. Genes containing beneficial traits that can be manipulated, transformed and inserted into organisms destined for the commercial market come from either the wild or from traditional crops and animal breeds. Notwithstanding its awesome ability to transform nature into commercially marketable commodities, the biotech industry still remains utterly dependent upon nature's seed stock — germplasm — for its raw resources. At present, it is impossible to create a "useful" new gene in the laboratory. In this sense, biotechnology remains an extractive industry. It can rearrange genetic material, but cannot create it. On the other hand, the very practice of biotechnology — including cloning, tissue culturing and gene splicing — is likely to result in increasing genetic uniformity, a narrowing of the gene pool, and loss of the very genetic diversity that is so essential to guaranteeing the success of the biotech industry in the future.

In his book *The Last Harvest*, Paul Raeburn, the science editor for *Business Week*, penetrates to the heart of the problem. He writes, "Scientists can accomplish remarkable feats in manipulating molecules and cells, but they are utterly incapable of re-creating even the simplest forms of life in test tubes. Germplasm provides our lifeline into the future. No breakthrough in fundamental research can compensate for the loss of the genetic material crop breeders depend upon."

Agricultural biotechnology greatly increases the uniformity of agricultural practices, as did the Green Revolution when it was introduced more than 30 years ago. Like its predecessor, the goal is to create superior varieties that can be planted as monocultures in agricultural regions all over the world. A handful of life-science companies are staking out the new biotech turf, each aggressively marketing their own patented brands of "super seeds" — and soon "super" farm animals as well. The new transgenic crops and animals are designed to grow faster, produce greater yields, and withstand more varied environmental and weather-related stresses. Their cost effectiveness, in the short run, is likely to guarantee them a robust market. In an industry where profit margins are notoriously low, farmers will likely jump at the opportunity of saving a few dollars per acre and a few cents per pound by shifting quickly to the new transgenic crops and animals.

However, the switch to a handful of patented transgenic seeds and livestock animals will likely further erode the genetic pool as farmers abandon the growing of traditional varieties and breeds in favor of the commercially more competitive patented products. By focusing on short-term market priorities, the biotech industry threatens to destroy the very genetic heirlooms that might one day be worth their weight in gold as a line of defense against new resistant diseases or superbugs.

Most molecular biologists and the biotechnology industry at large have all but dismissed the growing criticism of ecologists, whose recent studies suggest that the biotech revolution will likely be accompanied by the proliferation and spread of genetic pollution and the wholesale loss of genetic diversity. Nonetheless, the uncontrollable spread of super weeds, the buildup of resistant strains of bacteria and new super insects, the creation of novel viruses, the destabilization of whole ecosystems, the genetic contamination of food, and the steady depletion of the gene pool are no longer minor considerations, the mere grumbling of a few disgruntled critics. To ignore the warnings is to place the biosphere and civilization in harm's way in the coming years. Pestilence, famine, and the spread of new kinds of diseases throughout the world might yet turn out to be the final act in the script being prepared for the biotech century.

QUESTIONING THE TEXT

1. Rifkin uses an analogy to help support his argument: "The risks in releasing novel, genetically engineered organisms into the biosphere are similar to those we've encountered in introducing exotic organisms into the North American habitat" (paragraph 11). He goes on to mention some "severe dislocations" that have resulted — Dutch elm disease, for example. Working with two classmates, explore Rifkin's analogy, beginning perhaps by brainstorming about movies or TV shows you have seen that illustrate the analogy — *28 Days Later*, for instance. Then try to think of counterexamples to Rifkin's argument, genetically altered things that have been introduced but that have not been disastrous (such as disease-resistant corn). Prepare a brief report for your class that either supports or challenges Rifkin's analogical argument.

2. Reread Rifkin's essay, noting his use of metaphors ("synthetic introduction is . . . ecological roulette"; a "biological Tower of Babel") and similes ("new gene-spliced crops . . . [are] like creations from the world of

science fiction"). Then write a critical response to Rifkin's essay based on your understanding of how he uses metaphors, similes, and other figures of speech to help make his case.

MAKING CONNECTIONS

3. Rifkin has a number of worries similar to those of Victor Frankenstein. If Mary Shelley were writing *Frankenstein* (p. 285) in the twenty-first century, what might be the characteristics of the "monster" the doctor wishes to create? Where would the major pitfalls lie in accomplishing his goals? Make a list of characteristics and pitfalls, and bring it to class for discussion.

JOINING THE CONVERSATION

4. Try your hand at writing a letter of response to Rifkin. In it, make sure that you demonstrate your understanding of his argument; then give your response to that argument, and conclude with a series of questions about the "Biotech Century" you would most like to have answered. Bring your letter to class for discussion.

5. Working with two classmates, do some research on the claims Rifkin makes in his essay. One person might interview a senior professor in biology or biotechnology; one might search the Web for the latest research on genetic engineering in agriculture; another might seek out reviews of Rifkin's book and track down the reviews of several proponents and critics. After gathering as much material as you can, meet to share information and to decide what conclusions you can draw from it. Then prepare a 15- to 20-minute presentation for your class on "Rifkin's Claims: An Expanded View."

JAMES Q. WILSON
Cars and Their Enemies

Mention the word technology *and most people today think of silicon chips, iPods, high-definition TVs, and visual cell phones — not the vehicles they drive. Yet even the highest-tech computers haven't had the impact on our lives (at least, not yet) of gasoline-powered motor vehicles, a form of technology now a century old. From sea to sea, the American landscape has been bulldozed and paved to serve our national desire to move at will from one place to another. Fast cars and burly trucks have shaped our national character, changing how we live, where we live, how we court, and maybe even how we think.*

Yet the car represents a technological direction by no means inevitable. James Q. Wilson opens "Cars and Their Enemies" by suggesting how deep and determined opposition to this technology would be if it had been invented today rather than at the end of the nineteenth century. But Wilson rejects any notion of the car as a Frankenstein monster, describing it instead as a rational choice, one that makes the lives of most people freer and more pleasurable. In defending this claim, he challenges the growing number of academic and social critics made uneasy by the prospect of more and more Americans driving alone to work in 5,000-pound Suburbans and Hummers, wasting fuel, clogging streets, and avoiding public transportation.

Wilson (b. 1931), a professor emeritus at UCLA and recipient of the Presidential Medal of Freedom (2003), is one of America's most respected social critics and conservative thinkers, writing widely on crime, ethics, and character. Among his recent books are The Moral Sense *(1993),* Moral Judgment *(1997), and* The Marriage Problem *(2002). "Cars and Their Enemies" originally appeared in the July 1997 volume of* Commentary, *a journal of neoconservative opinion.* —J.R.

Imagine the country we now inhabit — big, urban, prosperous — with one exception: the automobile has not been invented. We have trains and bicycles, and some kind of self-powered buses and trucks, but no private cars driven by their owners for business or pleasure. Of late, let us suppose, someone has come forward with the idea of creating the personal automobile. Consider how we would react to such news.

Libertarians might support the idea, but hardly anyone else. Engineers would point out that such cars, if produced in any significant number, would zip along roads just a few feet — perhaps even a few inches — from one another; the chance of accidents would not simply be high, it would be certain. Public-health specialists would estimate that many of these accidents would lead to serious injuries and deaths. No one could say in advance how common they would be, but the best experts might guess that the number of people killed by cars would easily exceed the number killed by murderers. Psychologists would point out that if any young person were allowed to operate a car, the death rate would be even higher, as youngsters — those between the ages of sixteen and twenty-four — are much more likely than older persons to be impulsive risk-takers who find pleasure in reckless bravado. Educators would explain that, though they might try by training to reduce this youthful death rate, they could not be optimistic they would succeed.

Environmentalists would react in horror to the idea of automobiles powered by the internal combustion engine, apparently the most inexpensive method. Such devices, because they burn fuel incompletely, would eject large amounts of unpleasant gases into the air, such as carbon monoxide, nitrogen oxide, and sulfur dioxide. Other organic compounds, as well as clouds of particles, would also enter the atmosphere to produce unknown but probably harmful effects. Joining in this objection would be people who would not want their view spoiled by the creation of a network of roads.

Big-city mayors would add their own objections, though these would reflect their self-interest as much as their wisdom. If people could drive anywhere from anywhere, they would be able to live wherever they wished. This would produce a vast exodus from the large cities, led in all likelihood by the most prosperous — and thus the most tax-productive — citizens. Behind would remain people who, being poorer, were less mobile. Money would depart but problems remain.

Governors, pressed to keep taxes down and still fund costly health, welfare, educational, and criminal-justice programs, would wonder who would pay for the vast networks of roads that would be needed to carry automobiles. Their skepticism would be reinforced by the worries of police officials fearful of motorized thieves evading apprehension, and by the opposition of railroad executives foreseeing the collapse of their passenger business as people abandoned trains for cars. 5

Energy experts would react in horror at the prospect of supplying the gasoline stations and the vast quantities of petroleum necessary to fuel automobiles which, unlike buses and trucks, would be stored at home and not at a central depot and would burn much more fuel per person carried than some of their mass-transit alternatives.

In short, the automobile, the device on which most Americans rely for not only transportation but mobility, privacy, and fun would not exist if it had to be created today. Of course, the car does exist, and has powerfully affected the living, working, and social spaces of America. But the argument against it persists. That argument dominates the thinking of academic experts on urban transportation and much of city planning. It can be found in countless books complaining of dreary suburban architecture, endless trips to and from work, the social isolation produced by solo auto trips, and the harmful effects of the car on air quality, noise levels, petroleum consumption, and road congestion.

In her recent book, *Asphalt Nation: How the Automobile Took Over America and How We Can Take It Back*, Jane Holtz Kay, the architecture critic for the

Nation, assails the car unmercifully. It has, she writes "strangled" our lives and landscape, imposing on us "the costs of sprawl, of pollution, of congestion, of commuting." For this damage to be undone, the massively subsidized automobile will have to be sharply curtailed, by investing heavily in public transportation and imposing European-like taxes on gasoline. (According to Kay, if we cut highway spending by a mere $10 million, we could buy bicycles for all 93,000 residents of Eugene, Oregon, over the age of eleven.) What is more, people ought to live in cities with high population densities, since "for mass transit," as Kay notes, "you need mass." Housing should be built within a short walk of the corner store, and industries moved back downtown.

In Kay's book, hostility to the car is linked inextricably to hostility to the low-density suburb. Her view is by no means one that is confined to the political Left. Thus, Karl Zinsmeister, a conservative, has argued in the *American Enterprise* that we have become "slaves to our cars" and that, by using them to live in suburbs, we have created "inhospitable places for individualism and community life." Suburbs, says Zinsmeister, encourage "rootlessness," and are the enemy of the "traditional neighborhood" with its "easy daily interactions."

The same theme has been taken up by Mark Gauvreau Judge in the   10 *Weekly Standard*. Emerging from his home after a heavy snowfall, Judge, realizing that the nearest tavern was four miles away, concluded that he had to leave the suburbs. He repeats Zinsmeister's global complaint. Suburbanization, he writes, has fed, and sometimes caused,

> hurried life, the disappearance of family time, the weakening of generational links, our ignorance of history, our lack of local ties, an exaggerated focus on money, the anonymity of community life, the rise of radical feminism, the decline of civic action, the tyrannical dominance of TV and pop culture over leisure time.

Wow.

These people must live in or near very odd suburbs. The one in which I lived while my children were growing up, and the different ones in which my married daughter and married son now live, are not inhospitable, rootless, isolated, untraditional, or lacking in daily interactions. The towns are small. Life is organized around the family, for which there is a lot of time. Money goes farther for us than for Manhattanites struggling to get their children into the nursery school with the best link to Harvard. Television is less important than in big cities, where the streets are far less safe and TV becomes a major indoor activity. In most cases you can walk to a store. You know your neighbors. There is a Memorial Day parade. People care passionately and argue intensely about school policies and land-use controls. Of course, these are only my personal experiences — but unlike the critics, I find it hard to convert personal beliefs into cosmic generalizations.

Now I live in a suburb more remote from a big city than the one where my children were raised. Because population density is much lower, my wife and I walk less and drive more. But as I write this, my wife is at a neighborhood meeting where she will be joined by a travel agent, a retired firefighter, a hospital manager, and two housewives who are trying to decide how best to get the city to fix up a road intersection, prevent a nearby land development, and induce our neighbors to prepare for the fire season. On the way back, she will stop at the neighborhood mail station where she may talk to other friends, and then go on to the market where she will deal with people she has known for many years. She will do so by car.

And so back to our theme. Despite the criticisms of Kay and others, the use of the automobile has grown. In 1960, one-fifth of all households owned no car and only one-fifth owned two; by 1990, only one-tenth owned no car and over one-third owned two. In 1969, 80 percent of all urban trips involved a car and only one-twentieth involved public transport; by 1990, car use had risen to 84 percent and public transit had fallen to less than 3 percent. In 1990, three-fourths or more of the trips to and from work in nineteen out of our twenty largest metropolitan areas were by a single person in an automobile. The exception was the New York metropolitan region, but even there — with an elaborate mass-transit system and a residential concentration high enough to make it possible for some people to walk to work — solo car use made up over half of all trips to work.

Some critics explain this American fascination with the car as the unhappy consequence of public policies that make auto use more attractive than the alternatives. To Jane Holtz Kay, if only we taxed gasoline at a high enough rate to repay society for the social costs of automobiles, if only we had an elaborate mass-transit system that linked our cities, if only we placed major restraints on building suburbs on open land, if only we placed heavy restrictions on downtown parking, then things would be better.

Would they? Charles Lave, an economist at the University of California   15
at Irvine, has pointed out that most of Western Europe has long had just these sorts of anti-auto policies in effect. The result? Between 1965 and 1987, the growth in the number of autos per capita has been three times faster in Western Europe than in the United States. Part of the reason for the discrepancy is that the American auto market is approaching saturation: we now have roughly one car in existence for every person of driving age. But if this fact helps explain why the car market here is not growing rapidly, it does not explain the growth in Europe, which is the real story. Despite policies that penalize car use, make travel very expensive, and restrict parking spaces, Europeans, once they can afford to do so, buy cars, and drive them; according to Lave, the average European car is driven about two-thirds as many miles per year as the average American car. One result is obvious: the heavily subsidized trains in Europe are losing business to cars, and governments there must pay an even larger share of the running cost to keep the trains moving.

In fact, the United States *has* tried to copy the European investment in mass transit. Relentlessly, transportation planners have struggled to find ways of getting people out of their cars and into buses, trains, and subways (and car pools). Relentlessly, and unsuccessfully. Despite spending about $100 billion, Washington has yet to figure out how to do it.

New subway systems have been built, such as the BART system in San Francisco and the Metro system in Washington, D.C. But BART, in the words of the transportation economist Charles L. Wright, "connects almost nothing to little else." The Metro is still growing, and provides a fine (albeit expensive) route for people moving about the city; but only 7 percent of all residential land area in Washington is within a mile of a Metro station, which means that people must either walk a long way to get to a stop or continue to travel by car. Between 1980 and 1990, while the Washington Metrorail system grew from 30 to 73 miles of line and opened an additional 30 stations, the number of people driving to work increased from 980,000 to 1,394,000, and the transit share of all commutes declined.

The European experience should explain why this is so: if people can afford it, they will want to purchase convenience, flexibility, and privacy. These facts are as close to a Law of Nature as one can get in the transportation business. When the industrial world became prosperous, people bought cars. It is unstoppable.

Suppose, however, that the anti-car writers were to win over the vastly more numerous pro-car drivers. Let us imagine what life would be like in a carless nation. People would have to live very close together so they could walk or, for healthy people living in sunny climes, bicycle to mass-transit stops. Living in close quarters would mean life as it is now lived in Manhattan. There would be few freestanding homes, many row houses, and lots of apartment buildings. There would be few private gardens except for flowerpots on balconies. The streets would be congested by pedestrians, trucks, and buses, as they were at the turn of the century before automobiles became common.

Moving about outside the larger cities would be difficult. People would   20
be able to take trains to distant sites, but when they arrived at some attractive locale it would turn out to be another city. They could visit the beach, but only (of necessity) crowded parts of it. They could go to a national park, but only the built-up section of it. They could see the countryside, but (mostly) through a train window. More isolated or remote locations would be accessible, but since public transit would provide the only way of getting there, the departures would be infrequent and the transfers frequent.

In other words, you could see the United States much as most Europeans saw their countryside before the automobile became an important means of locomotion. A train from London or Paris would take you to "the country" by way of a long journey through ugly industrial areas to those rural parts where either you had a home (and the means to ferry yourself to it) or there was a resort (that would be crowded enough to support a nearby train stop).

All this is a way of saying that the debate between car defenders and car haters is a debate between private benefits and public goods. List the characteristics of travel that impose few costs on society and, in general, walk-ing, cycling, and some forms of public transit will be seen to be superior. Non-car methods generate less pollution, use energy a bit more efficiently, produce less noise, and (with some exceptions) are safer. But list the characteristics of travel that are desired by individuals, and (with some exceptions) the car is clearly superior. The automobile is more flexible, more punctual, supplies greater comfort, provides for carrying more parcels, creates more privacy, enables one to select fellow passengers, and, for distances over a mile or more, requires less travel time.

As a practical matter, of course, the debate between those who value pri-vate benefits and those who insist on their social costs is no real debate at all, since people select modes of travel based on individual, not social, preferences. That is why in almost every country in the world, the automobile has triumphed, and much of public policy has been devoted to the somewhat inconsistent task of subsidizing individual choices while attempting to reduce the costs attached to them. In the case of the automobile, governments have attempted to reduce ex-haust pollution, make roadways safer, and restrict use (by tolls, speed bumps, pedestrian-only streets, and parking restrictions) in neighborhoods that attach a high value to pedestrian passage. Yet none of these efforts can alter the central fact that people have found cars to be the best means for getting about.

Take traffic congestion. Television loves to focus on grim scenes of grid-locked highways and angry motorists, but in fact people still get to work faster by car than by public transit. And the reason is not that car drivers live close to work and transit users travel a greater distance. According to the best estimates, cars outperform public transit in getting people quickly from their front doors to their work places. This fact is sometimes lost on car critics. Kay, for example, writes that "the same number of people who spend an hour driving sixteen lanes of high-way can travel on a two-track train line." Wrong. Train travel is efficient *over a fixed, permanent route*, but people have to find some way to get to where the train starts and get to their final destination after the train stops. The *full* cost of mov-ing people from home to work and back to the home is lower for cars than for trains. Moreover, cars are not subject to union strikes. The Long Island railroad or the bus system may shut down when workers walk off the job; cars do not.

The transportation argument rarely seems to take cognizance of the 25 superiority of cars with respect to individual wants. Whenever there is a discus-sion about how best to move people about, mass-transit supporters typically overestimate, usually by a wide margin, how many people will leave their cars and happily hop onto trains or buses. According to one study, by Don Pickerell, the vast majority of American rail-transportation proposals greatly exaggerate the number of riders to be attracted; the actual ridership turns out to be about a third of the predicted level. For this reason, urban public transport almost never recovers from the fare box more than a fraction of the actual cost of moving people. Osaka, Japan, seems to be the only large city in the world that gets back from passengers what it spends; in Atlanta, Detroit, and Houston, public transit gets from passengers no more than a third of their cost.

So the real debate ought not be one between car enthusiasts and mass-transit advocates, but about ways of moderating the inevitable use of cars in order to minimize their deleterious effects.

One such discussion has already had substantial effects. Auto-exhaust pollution has been dramatically reduced in this country by redesigning engines, changing fuels (largely by removing lead), and imposing inspection requirements.

Since the mid-1960s, auto emissions have been reduced by about 95 percent. Just since 1982, ten years after the Clean Air Act was passed, carbon-monoxide levels have fallen by 40 percent and nitrogen-oxide levels by 25 percent. I live in the Los Angeles area and know from personal experience how irritating smog was in the 1950s. I also know that smog has decreased dramatically for most (but not all) of the region. The number of "smog alert" days called by the South Coast Air Quality Management District (AQMD) declined from 121 in the mid-1970s to seven in 1996. AQMD now predicts that by the year 2000 the number may fall to zero.

Nationally, very little of this improvement has come about from moving people from solo cars into car pools or onto mass transit. What experts call "Transportation Control Measures" (TCM's) — the combined effect of mass transit, car pools, telecommuting, and the like — have produced small reductions in smog levels. Transit expansion has decreased carbon monoxide by six-tenths of 1 percent and car pools by another seven-tenths of 1 percent. Adding BART to San Francisco has had only trivial effects on pollution. The Environmental Protection Agency (in the Clinton administration) has issued a report that puts it bluntly: "Efforts to reduce emissions through traditional TCM's have not generated significant air-quality benefits." The methods that *have* reduced pollution significantly are based on markets, not capital investments, and include smog fees, congestion pricing, gas taxes, and higher parking charges.

There is still more pollution to eliminate, but the anti-car enthusiasts   30
rarely approach the task rationally. General Motors now leases electric cars, but they are very expensive and require frequent recharging from scarce power outlets. The electric car is an impressive engineering achievement, but not if you want to travel very far.

We could pass laws that would drive down even further the pollution output of cars, but this would impose huge costs on manufacturers and buyers without addressing the real source of auto pollution — a small percentage of older or modified cars that generate huge amounts of exhaust. Devices now exist for measuring the pollution of cars as they move on highways and then ticketing the offenders, but only recently has there been a large-scale trial of this method, and the results are not yet in. The method has the virtue of targeting enforcement on real culprits, but the defect (for car critics) of not requiring a "tough new law" aimed at every auto owner.

As for traffic congestion, that has indeed become worse — because highway construction has not kept pace with the growth of automobile use. But it is not as bad as some imagine — the average commuting time was the same in 1990 as in 1980 — and it is not bad where it is often assumed to be bad. A road is officially called "congested" if its traffic volume exceeds 80 percent of its designed capacity. By this measure, the most congested highways are in and around Washington, D.C., and San Francisco. But if you drive these roads during rush hour, as I have, you will acquire a very different sense of things. The highways into Washington and San Francisco do produce blockages, usually at familiar intersections, bridges, or merges. They rarely last very long and, on most days, one can plan around them.

Indeed, the fact and consequences of auto congestion are greatly exaggerated in most large cities. During rush hour, I have driven into and out of Dallas, Kansas City, Phoenix, St. Louis, and San Diego without much more than an occasional slowdown. Moreover, despite the massive reliance on cars and a short-term decline in the economic vitality of their downtown areas, most of these cities have restored their central areas. Kansas City is bleak in the old downtown, but the shopping area (built 75 years ago!) called Country Club Plaza is filled with people, stores, and restaurants. San Diego and San Francisco have lively downtowns. Los Angeles even managed to acquire a downtown (actually, several downtowns) after it grew up without much of one — and this in a city allegedly "built around the car." Phoenix is restoring its downtown and San Diego never really lost its center.

Real congestion, by contrast, is found in New York City, Chicago, and Boston, where almost any movement on any downtown street is extremely difficult. From the moment you enter a car or taxi, you are in a traffic jam. Getting to the airport by car from Manhattan or Boston is vastly more difficult than getting there from San Francisco, Los Angeles, or Washington.

But the lesson in this should be disturbing to car critics: *car travel is most* 35 *congested in cities that have the oldest and most highly developed rail-based transit systems.* One reason is historical: having subways from their early days, these cities built up to high levels of residential and commercial concentration. A car added to this mix has to navigate through streets surrounded by high office buildings and tall apartment towers. When many people in those buildings take cars or taxis, the congestion can be phenomenal.

But there is another reason as well. Even where rail transportation exists, people will not use it enough to relieve congestion. There is, for example, an excellent rail line from O'Hare Airport to downtown Chicago, and some people use it. But it has done little or nothing to alleviate congestion on the parallel highway. People do not like dragging suitcases on and off trains. And the train does not stop where people want to go — namely, where they live. It stops at busy street corners, sometimes in dangerous neighborhoods. If you take the train, you still must shift to a car at the end, and finding one is not always easy. This is why taking a car from the Los Angeles airport, though it will place you in a few pockets of congestion, gets you to your home faster (and with all of your belongings) than taking a train and taxi a comparable distance from O'Hare.

A great deal can still be done to moderate the social costs of automobile traffic. More toll roads can be built with variable rates that will allow people to drive — at different prices, depending on the level of congestion — to and from cities. Bridges into cities can charge tolls to ensure that only highly motivated people consume scarce downtown road space. (A friend of mine, a distinguished economist, was once asked, in derision, whether he would buy the Brooklyn Bridge. "I would if I could charge tolls on it," he replied.) Cars can be banned from streets that are capable of being pedestrian malls — though there are not many such places. (A number of such malls were created for the purpose of keeping people downtown who did not want to be downtown, and were doomed to failure from the start.)

Other measures are also possible. More bicycle pathways can be created, though these are rarely alternatives to auto transportation; some people do ride a bike to work, but few do so often. Street patterns in residential areas can be arranged to minimize the amount of through road traffic they must endure. Gasoline taxes can be set high enough to recover more of the social costs of operating automobiles. (This will not happen in a society as democratic as ours, but it is a good idea, and maybe someday a crisis will create an opportunity.)

Portland, Oregon, has become well-known among American cities for having adopted a law — the Urban Growth Boundary — that denies people the right to build almost any new structure in a green belt starting about twenty minutes from downtown. This means that new subdivisions to which one must travel by car cannot be created outside the line. The nice result is that outside the city, you can drive through unspoiled farm land.

The mayor and downtown business leaders like what they have created. So do environmentalists, social-service organizations, and many ordinary citizens. The policy, described in a recent issue of *Governing* magazine, is called the New Urbanism, and has attracted interest from all over the country. But the policy also has its costs. As the city's population grows, more people must be squeezed into less space. Housing density is up. Before the Urban Growth Boundary, the average Portland house was built on a lot about 13,000 square feet and row houses made up only 3 percent of all dwelling units. Now, the average lot size has fallen to 8,700 square feet and row houses make up 12 percent of the total. And housing prices are also up. Six years ago, Portland was the nation's 55th most affordable city; today, it is the 165th. 40

As density goes up in Portland, so will the problems associated with density, such as crime. Reserving land out of a city for scenic value is an important goal, but it must be balanced with supplying affordable housing. Portland will work out the balance, once people begin to yearn for lower density.

But even if we do all the things that can be done to limit the social costs of cars, the campaign against them will not stop. It will not stop because so many of the critics dislike everything the car stands for and everything that society constructs to serve the needs of its occupants.

Cars are about privacy; critics say privacy is bad and prefer group effort. (Of course, one rarely meets these critics in groups. They seem to be too busy rushing about being critics.) Cars are about autonomy; critics say that the pursuit of autonomy destroys community. (Actually, cars allow people to select the kind of community in which they want to live.) Cars are about speed; critics abhor the fatalities they think speed causes. (In fact, auto fatalities have been declining for decades, including after the 55-mile-per-hour national speed limit was repealed. Charles Lave suggests that this is because higher speed limits reduce the variance among cars in their rates of travel, thereby producing less passing and overtaking, two dangerous highway maneuvers.) Cars are about the joyous sensation of driving on beautiful country roads; critics take their joy from politics. (A great failing of the intellectual life of this country is that so much of it is centered in Manhattan, where one finds the highest concentration of nondrivers in the country.) Cars make possible Wal-Mart, Home Depot, the Price Club, and other ways of allowing people to shop for rock-bottom prices; critics want people to spend their time gathering food at downtown shops (and paying the much higher prices that small stores occupying expensive land must charge). Cars make California possible; critics loathe California. (But they loathe it for the wrong reason. The state is not the car capital of the nation; 36 states have more cars per capita, and their residents drive more miles.)

Life in California would be very difficult without cars. This is not because the commute to work is so long; in Los Angeles, according to Charles Lave, the average trip to work in 1994 was 26 minutes, five minutes *shorter* than in New York City. Rather, a carless state could not be enjoyed. You could not see the vast areas of farm land, the huge tracts of empty mountains and deserts, the miles of deserted beaches and forests.

No one who visits Los Angeles or San Francisco can imagine how much of   45
California is, in effect, empty, unsettled. It is an empire of lightly used roads, splendid vistas, and small towns, intersected by a highway system that, should you be busy or foolish enough to use it, will speed you from San Francisco to Los Angeles or San Diego. Off the interstate, it is a kaleidoscope of charming places to be alone.

Getting there in order to be alone is best done in one of the remarkably engineered, breathtakingly fast, modern cars that give to the driver the deepest sense of what the road can offer: the beauty of its views, the excitement of command, the passion of engagement.

I know the way. If you are a friend, you need only ask.

QUESTIONING THE TEXT

1. Review "Cars and Their Enemies," looking for places where Wilson characterizes the critics of automobiles. What terms or names does he give to these critics? Where do they live, and in Wilson's opinion, how do they typically behave? How does Wilson's treatment of "car haters" enhance or detract from his argument?

2. Does "Cars and Their Enemies" have a thesis you could state in one sentence? Reread the essay carefully, highlighting sentences you think make major points or summarize Wilson's thinking. Then review these major claims, and write a summary of Wilson's case in favor of the automobile.

3. Wilson, a sociologist by profession, uses both statistics and personal experiences to make his argument. Evaluate his use of these different kinds of evidence. Where does he cite statistics? Where does he rely on personal experience? How do you react to the highly personal last paragraph of the piece: "I know the way. If you are a friend, you need only ask"?

MAKING CONNECTIONS

4. Wilson opens by asking readers to envision a world without cars, and he proposes that very few people would support the introduction of such technology now. How does Denise Grady's "Struggling Back from War's Once-Deadly Wounds" (p. 331) imply similar questions about the introduction of new technologies? What technologies might we decline to introduce if we could do so? Are technologies to which we might object inevitable, or do we have the opportunity to control technology's advance?

5. Reread paragraph 43 of Wilson's essay. How does Wilson engage the objections of others? Compare his style of considering alternative arguments to that of Christina Hoff Sommers in "The War against Boys" (p. 133). Which writer do you think uses alternative claims more fairly and effectively? Discuss the reasoning behind your answer.

JOINING THE CONVERSATION

6. Write an editorial for your campus newspaper in response to Wilson's piece, examining the issue of local transportation or, perhaps, traffic and parking at your school. In your argument, you need not simply agree or disagree with Wilson — just begin with his reflection on the automobile in American culture. Consider other possibilities for addressing the issue.

7. Write a brief essay exploring whether another older technology (besides the gasoline-powered car) might or might not be built if it were invented today rather than in the past. Use the first seven paragraphs of "Cars and Their Enemies" as a model for your piece.

8. Use both research materials and personal experience to write an essay on "_____ and Their Enemies," filling in the blank with a subject you can explore in depth. Present both your point of view on the topic and the ideas of those with whom you might disagree. Review Wilson's piece for ideas about organization and tone.

DENISE GRADY
Struggling Back from War's Once-Deadly Wounds

In early March of 2007, as the failure of Walter Reed Army Medical Center to provide adequate housing and care for soldiers returning from Iraq became known, I kept thinking of Denise Grady's "Struggling Back from War's Once-Deadly Wounds," which appeared in the New York Times *some six weeks earlier. I skim the* Times *every day, but on that particular day I read every word of this essay with care, and then I reread Grady's profile of Jason Poole, a 23-year-old Marine who suffered multiple injuries in Iraq. I marched against this war at its inception, but in all my thinking about its catastrophic effects I could not have imagined the fate of Jason Poole — much less his courage and fortitude in facing it.*

Grady (b. 1952), a New York Times *reporter since 1998, introduces readers to Corporal Poole as one way of demonstrating a great irony of the Iraq War: advancements in medicine have allowed doctors to keep more wounded soldiers alive ("seven to eight survivors for every death, compared with just two per death in World War II"), but these survivors return home with almost unimaginable injuries. Yet Poole's story is one of amazing resilience, persistence, and sheer determination. As of the writing of this essay, he was out of the hospital and trying hard to create a new life for himself. "I think something really good is going to happen to me," he says.*

Grady has been recognized with a number of awards, including a commendation from the Newspaper Guild for "excellence of crusading journalistic contributions in the areas of science in medicine" (1986). A staff writer for Time *and* Discover *magazine, she is also the author of* New York Times Deadly Invaders: Virus Outbreaks around the World *(2006) and coeditor of* New York Times Guide to Alternative Health *(2001). In an interview after her keynote address (April 20, 2006) at the Stanford Medical School's annual Medicine and the Muse Symposium, Grady spoke of the challenges facing science and health reporters today as they try to "keep up with enormous advances in genetics and molecular biology and drug development so we know what we're talking about. I think a lot of us are running like rats in wheels trying to do that." She may be running to keep up, but it definitely doesn't show in this article. As you read it, think about the research Grady had to do to write it and about all the sources she draws on. And think about others you have read about or know who fought in Iraq. Think hard.* —A.L.

It has taken hundreds of hours of therapy, but Jason Poole, a 23-year old Marine corporal, has learned all over again to speak and to walk. At times, though, words still elude him. He can read barely 16 words a minute. His memory can be fickle, his thinking delayed. Injured by a roadside bomb in Iraq, he is blind in his left eye, deaf in his left ear, weak on his right side and still getting used to his new face, which was rebuilt with skin and bone grafts and 75 to 100 titanium screws and plates.

Even so, those who know Corporal Poole say his personality — gregarious, kind and funny — has remained intact. Wounded on patrol near the Syrian border on June 30, 2004, he considers himself lucky to be alive. So do his doctors. "Basically I want to get my life back," he said. "I'm really trying."

But he knows the life ahead of him is unlikely to match the one he had planned, in which he was going to attend college and become a teacher, get married and have children. Now, he hopes to volunteer in a school. His girlfriend from before he went to war is now just a friend. Before he left, they had agreed they might talk about getting married when he got back.

"But I didn't come back," he said.

Men and women like Corporal Poole, with multiple devastating injuries,   5 are the new face of the wounded, a singular legacy of the war in Iraq. Many suffered wounds that would have been fatal in earlier wars but were saved by helmets, body armor, advances in battlefield medicine and swift evacuation to hospitals. As a result, the survival rate among Americans hurt in Iraq is higher than in any previous war — seven to eight survivors for every death, compared with just two per death in World War II.

But that triumph is also an enduring hardship of the war. Survivors are coming home with grave injuries, often from roadside bombs, that will transform their lives: combinations of damaged brains and spinal cords, vision and hearing loss, disfigured faces, burns, amputations, mangled limbs, and psychological ills like depression and post-traumatic stress.

Dr. Alexander Stojadinovic, the vice chairman of surgery at Walter Reed Army Medical Center, said, "The wounding patterns we see are similar to, say, what Israel will see with terrorist bombings — multiple complex woundings, not just a single body site."

So many who survive explosions — more than half — sustain head injuries that doctors say anyone exposed to a blast should be checked for neurological problems. Brain damage, sometimes caused by skull-penetrating fragments, sometimes by shock waves or blows to the head, is a recurring theme.

More than 1,700 of those wounded in Iraq are known to have brain injuries, half of which are severe enough that they may permanently impair thinking, memory, mood, behavior and the ability to work.

Medical treatment for brain injuries from the Iraq war will cost the   10 government at least $14 billion over the next 20 years, according to a recent study by researchers at Harvard and Columbia.

Jill Gandolfi, a co-director of the Brain Injury Rehabilitation Unit of the Veterans Affairs Palo Alto Health Care System, where Corporal Poole is being treated, said, "We are looking at an epidemic of brain injuries."

The consequences of brain injury are enormous. Penetrating injuries can knock out specific functions like vision and speech, and may eventually cause epilepsy and increase the risk of dementia. What doctors call "closed-head injuries," from blows to the head or blasts, are more likely to have diffuse effects throughout the brain, particularly on the frontal lobes, which control the ability to pay attention, make plans, manage time and solve problems.

Because of their problems with memory, emotion and thinking, brain-injured patients run a high risk of falling through the cracks in the health care system, particularly when they leave structured environments like the military, said Dr. Deborah Warden, national director of the Defense and Veterans Brain Injury Center, a government program created in 1992 to develop treatment standards for the military and veterans.

So many military men and women are returning with head injuries combined with other wounds that the government has designated four Veterans Affairs hospitals as "polytrauma rehabilitation centers" to take care of them. The Palo Alto hospital where Corporal Poole is being treated is one.

"In Vietnam, they'd bring in a soldier with two legs blown off by a mine, but he wouldn't have the head injuries," said Dr. Thomas E. Bowen, a retired Army general who was a surgeon in the Vietnam War and who is now chief of staff at the veterans hospital in Tampa, Florida, another polytrauma center. "Some of the patients we have here now, they can't swallow, they can't talk, they're paralyzed and blind," he said.   15

Other soldiers have been sent home unconscious with such hopeless brain injuries that their families have made the anguished decision to take them off life support, said Dr. Andrew Shorr, who saw several such patients at Walter Reed.

Amputations are a feature of war, but the number from Iraq — 345 as of Jan. 3, including 59 who had lost more than one limb — led the Army to open a new amputation center at Brooke Army Medical Center in San Antonio in addition to the existing center at Walter Reed. Amputees get the latest technology, including $50,000 prosthetic limbs with microchips.

Dr. Mark R. Bagg, head of orthopedic surgery at Brooke, said, "The complexity of the injuries has been challenging — horrific blast injuries to extremities, with tremendous bone loss and joint, bone, nerve, arterial and soft tissue injuries."

It is common for wounded men and women to need months of rehabilitation in the hospital. Some, like Corporal Poole, need well over a year, and will require continuing help as outpatients. Because many of these veterans are in their 20's or 30's, they will live with their disabilities for decades. "They have to reinvent who they are," said Dr. Harriet Zeiner, a neuropsychologist at the Palo Alto veterans center.

No Memory of the Blast

Corporal Poole has no memory of the explosion or even the days before   20 it, although he has had a recurring dream of being in Iraq and seeing the sky suddenly turn red.

Other marines have told him he was on a foot patrol when the bomb went off. Three others in the patrol — two Iraqi soldiers and an interpreter — were killed. Shrapnel tore into the left side of Corporal Poole's face and flew out from under his right eye. Metal fragments and the force of the blast fractured his skull in multiple places and injured his brain, one of its major arteries, and his left eye and ear. Every bone in his face was broken. Some, including his nose and portions of his eye sockets, were shattered. Part of his jawbone was pulverized.

"He could easily have died," said Dr. Henry L. Lew, an expert on brain injury and the medical director of the rehabilitation center at the Palo Alto veterans hospital. Bleeding, infection, swelling of the brain — any or all could have killed someone with such a severe head injury, Dr. Lew said.

Corporal Poole was taken by helicopter to a military hospital in Iraq and then flown to one in Germany, where surgeons cut a plug of fat from his abdomen and mixed it with other materials to seal an opening in the floor of his skull.

He was then taken to the National Naval Medical Center in Bethesda, Maryland. His parents, who are divorced, were flown there to meet him — his father, Stephen, from San Jose, California, and his mother, Trudie, from Bristol, England, where Jason was born. Jason, his twin sister, Lisa, and a younger brother, David, moved to Cupertino, California, with their father when Jason was 12.

His interest in the Marine Corps started in high school, where he was an 25 athlete and an actor, a popular young man with lots of friends. He played football and won gold medals in track, and had parts in school plays. When Marine recruiters came to the school and offered weekend outings with a chance to play sports, Corporal Poole happily took part. He enlisted after graduating in 2000.

"We talked about the possibility of war, but none of us thought it was really going to happen," said his father, who had to sign the enlistment papers because his son was only 17. Jason Poole hoped the Marines would help pay for college.

His unit was among the first to invade Iraq. He was on his third tour of duty there, just 10 days from coming home and leaving the Marines, when he was wounded in the explosion.

A week later, he was transferred to Bethesda, still in a coma, and his parents were told he might never wake up.

"I was unconscious for two months," Corporal Poole said in a recent interview at the V.A. center in Palo Alto. "One month and 23 days, really. Then I woke up and came here."

He has been a patient at the center since September 2004, mostly in the 30 brain injury rehabilitation unit. He arrived unable to speak or walk, drooling, with the left side of his face caved in, his left eye blind and sunken, a feeding tube in his stomach and an opening in his neck to help him breathe.

"He was very hard of hearing, and sometimes he didn't even know you were in the room," said Debbie Pitsch, his physical therapist.

Damage to the left side of his brain had left him weak on the right, and he tended not to notice things to his right, even though his vision in that eye was good. He had lost his sense of smell. The left side of the brain is also the home of language, and it was hard for him to talk or comprehend speech. "He would shake his head no when he meant yes," said Dr. Zeiner, the neuropsychologist. But he could communicate by pointing. His mind was working, but the thoughts were trapped inside his head.

An array of therapists — speech, physical, occupational and others — began working with him for hours every day. He needed an ankle brace and a walker just to stand at first. His balance was way off and, because of the brain injury, he could not tell where his right foot was unless he could see it. He often would just drag it behind him. His right arm would fall from the walker and hang by his side, and he would not even notice. He would bump into things to his right. Nonetheless, on his second day in Palo Alto, he managed to walk a few steps.

"He was extremely motivated, and he pushed himself to the limit, being a marine," Ms. Pitsch said. He was so driven, in fact, that at first his therapists had to strap him into a wheelchair to keep him from trying to get up and walk without help.

By the last week of September, he was beginning to climb stairs. He graduated from a walker to a cane to walking on his own. By January he was running and lifting weights.

"It's not his physical recovery that's amazing," his father said. "It's not his mental recovery. It's his attitude. He's always positive. He very rarely gets low. If it was me I'd fall apart. We think of how he was and what he's had taken from him."

Corporal Poole is philosophical. "Even when I do get low it's just for 5 or 10 minutes," he said. "I'm just a happy guy. I mean, like, it sucks, basically, but it happened to me and I'm still alive."

A NEW FACE

"Jason was definitely a ladies' man," said Zillah Hodgkins, who has been a friend for nine years.

In pictures from before he was hurt, he had a strikingly handsome face and a powerful build. Even in still photographs he seems animated, and people around him — other marines, Iraqi civilians — are always grinning, apparently at his antics.

But the explosion shattered the face in the pictures and left him with another one. In his first weeks at Palo Alto, he hid behind sunglasses and, even though the weather was hot, ski caps and high turtlenecks.

"We said, 'Jason, you're sweating. You have to get used to how you look,'" Dr. Zeiner said.

"He was an incredibly handsome guy," she said. "His twin sister is a beautiful woman. He was the life of the party. He was funny. He could have had any woman, and he comes back and feels like now he's a monster."

Gradually, he came out of wraps and tried to make peace with the image in the mirror. But his real hope was that somehow his face could be repaired.

Reconstructive surgery should have been done soon after the explosion, before broken bones could knit improperly. But the blast had caused an artery in Corporal Poole's skull to balloon into an aneurysm, and an operation could have ruptured it and killed him. By November 2004, however, the aneurysm had gone away.

Dr. H. Peter Lorenz, a plastic surgeon at Stanford University Medical   45
Center, planned several operations to repair the damage after studying pictures of Corporal Poole before he was injured. "You could say every bone in his face was fractured," Dr. Lorenz said.

The first operation took 14 hours. Dr. Lorenz started by making a cut in Corporal Poole's scalp, across the top of his head from ear to ear, and peeling the flesh down over his nose to expose the bones. To get at more bone, he made another slit inside Corporal Poole's mouth, between his upper lip and his teeth, and slipped in tools to lift the tissue.

Many bones had healed incorrectly and had to be sawed apart, repositioned and then joined with titanium pins and plates. Parts of his eye sockets had to be replaced with bone carved from the back of his skull. Bone grafts helped to reposition Corporal Poole's eyes, which had sunk in the damaged sockets.

Operations in March and July repaired his broken and dislocated jaw, his nose and damaged eyelids and tear ducts. He could not see for a week after one of the operations because his right eye had been sewn shut, and he spent several weeks unable to eat because his jaws had been wired together.

Dr. Lorenz also repaired Corporal Poole's caved-in left cheek and forehead by implanting a protein made from human skin that would act as a scaffolding and be filled in by Corporal Poole's own cells.

Later, he was fitted with a false eye to fill out the socket where his left eye   50
had shriveled.

Some facial scars remain, the false eye sometimes looks slightly larger than the real one, and because of a damaged tear duct, Corporal Poole's right eye is often watery. But his smile is still brilliant.

In a recent conversation, he acknowledged that the results of the surgery were a big improvement. When asked how he felt about his appearance, he shrugged and said, "I'm not good-looking but I'm still Jason Poole, so let's go."

But he catches people looking at him as if he is a "weird freak," he said, mimicking their reactions: a wide eyed stare, then the eyes averted. It makes him angry.

"I wish they would ask me what happened," he said. "I would tell them."

LEARNING TO SPEAK

Evi Klein, a speech therapist in Palo Alto, said that when they met in   55
September 2004 Corporal Poole could name only about half the objects in his room.

Corporal Poole works with Evi Klein, left, and Karen Kopolnek, speech pathologists, at the Veterans Affairs Palo Alto Health Care System.

"He had words, but he couldn't pull together language to express his thoughts," Ms. Klein said. "To answer a question with more than one or two words was beyond his capabilities."

Ms. Klein began with basics. She would point to items in the room. What's this called? What's that? She would show him a picture, have him say the word and write it. He would have to name five types of transportation. She would read a paragraph or play a phone message and ask him questions about it. Very gradually, he began to speak. But it was not until February that he could string together enough words for anyone to hear that he still had traces of an English accent.

Today, he is fluent enough that most people would not guess how impaired he was. When he has trouble finding the right word or loses the thread of a conversation, he collects himself and starts again. More than most people, he fills in the gaps with expressions like "basically" and "blah, blah, blah."

"I thought he would do well," Ms. Klein said. "I didn't think he'd do as well as he is doing. I expect measurable gains over the next year or so."

With months of therapy, his reading ability has gone from zero to a level   60
somewhere between second and third grade. He has to focus on one word at a time, he said. A page of print almost overwhelms him. His auditory comprehension is slow as well.

"It will take a bit of time," Corporal Poole said, "but basically I'm going to get there."

One evening over dinner, he said: "I feel so old." Not physically, he said, but mentally and emotionally.

On a recent morning, Ms. Gandolfi of the brain injury unit conducted an exercise in thinking and verbal skills with a group of patients. She handed Corporal Poole a sheet of paper that said, "Dogs can be taught how to talk." A series of questions followed. What would be the benefits? Why could it be a problem? What would you do about it?

Corporal Poole hunched over the paper, pen in hand. He looked up. "I have no clue," he said softly.

"Let's ask this one another way," Ms. Gandolfi said. "What would be cool   65 about it?"

He began to write with a ballpoint pen, slowly forming faint letters. "I would talk to him and listen to him," he wrote.

In another space, he wrote: "lonely the dog happy." But what he had actually said to Ms. Gandolfi was: "I could be really lonely and this dog would talk to me."

Some of his responses were illegible. He left one question blank. But he was performing much better than he did a year ago.

He hopes to be able to work with children, maybe those with disabilities. But, Dr. Zeiner said, "He is not competitively employable."

His memory, verbal ability and reading are too impaired. He may eventu-   70 ally read well enough to take courses at a community college, but, she said, "It's years away."

Someday, he might be able to become a teacher's aide, she said. But he may have to work just as a volunteer and get by on his military benefits of about $2,400 a month. He will also receive a $100,000 insurance payment from the government.

"People whose brains are shattered, it's incredible how resilient they are," Dr. Zeiner said. "They keep trying. They don't collapse in despair."

BACK IN THE WORLD

In mid-December, Corporal Poole was finally well enough to leave the hospital. With a roommate, he moved into a two-bedroom apartment in Cupertino, the town where Corporal Poole grew up. His share of the rent is $800 a month. But he had not lived outside a hospital in 18 months, and it was unclear how he would fare on his own.

"If he's not able to cope with the outside world, is there anywhere for him to go, anyone there to support him if it doesn't go well?" asked his mother, who still lives in Bristol, where she is raising her three younger children. "I think of people from Vietnam who wound up on the streets, or mental patients, or in prison."

He still needs therapy — speech and other types — several times a week   75
at Palo Alto and that requires taking three city buses twice a day. The trip takes
more than an hour, and he has to decipher schedules and cross hair-raising
intersections on boulevards with few pedestrians. It is an enormous step, not
without risk: people with a brain injury have increased odds of sustaining
another one, from a fall or an accident brought about by impaired judgment,
balance or senses.

In December, Corporal Poole practiced riding the buses to the hospital
with Paul Johnson, a co-director of the brain injury unit. As they crossed a busy
street, Mr. Johnson gently reminded him, several times, to turn and look back
over his left shoulder — the side on which he is blind — for cars turning right.

After Corporal Poole and Mr. Johnson had waited for a few minutes at
the stop, a bus zoomed up, and Corporal Poole ambled toward the door.

"Come on!" the driver snapped.

Corporal Poole watched intently for buildings and gas stations he had
picked as landmarks so he would know when to signal for his stop.

"I'm a little nervous, but I'll get the hang of it," he said.   80

He was delighted to move into his new apartment, pick a paint color, buy
a couch, a bed and a set of dishes, and eat something besides hospital food. With
help from his therapists in Palo Alto, he hopes to take a class at a nearby community college, not an actual course, but a class to help him to learn to study

Cpl. Jason Poole, recovering from war wounds, practiced riding buses.

and prepare for real academic work. Teaching, art therapy, children's theater and social work all appeal to him, even if he can only volunteer.

Awaiting his formal release from the military, Corporal Poole still hopes to get married and have children.

That hope is not unrealistic, Dr. Zeiner said. Brain injuries can cause people to lose their ability to empathize, she said, and that kills relationships. But Corporal Poole has not lost empathy, she said. "That's why I think he will find a partner."

Corporal Poole said: "I think something really good is going to happen to me."

Reading across Professions
MICHELLE GITTLER, Physician

Traumatic brain injury, which disrupts normal functioning of the brain, is caused by penetrating head injury or by shock waves or blows to the head. According to the Centers for Disease Control, over 1.4 million people in the United States sustain a traumatic brain injury each year; 1.1 million of these are treated in an emergency department and released, 235,000 are hospitalized, and more than 50,000 die.

The consequences of brain injury for survivors can be enormous. Many of the injured, like Jason Poole, experience weakness or partial paralysis on one side of the body; loss of some or all vision, hearing, and speech; and, as Grady notes, loss of the ability "to pay attention, make plans, manage time, and solve problems." However, as a patient at the Veterans' Administration Brain Injury Center in Palo Alto, California, from September 2004 through December 2005, Corporal Poole was one of the lucky ones. He was fortunate not just because of the tremendous physical and functional return he has achieved, but also because he was able to receive over fourteen months of intensive therapy. Most patients in the United States who sustain a traumatic brain injury are moved to a nursing home or, if they are lucky, to a rehabilitation facility where they will stay for four to eight weeks. Fourteen months of rehabilitation certainly improves the likelihood that an individual will return to independence in self-care tasks, such as bathing, eating, dressing, and toileting, and in mobility skills, such as walking, getting in and out of bed, and getting in and out of a car.

Some of Corporal Poole's injuries are apparent to observers, but many individuals with brain injury have disabilities that are not as immediately evident. Such people may look fine but have difficulty finding and keeping sustainable employment because of poor decision-making skills or an inability to interact appropriately with other people. What Corporal Poole does have in common with other Americans who have suffered traumatic brain injury is that all face a lack of community resources to help them readjust to life after the injury. For many patients, post-acute rehabilitation services are limited for a number of reasons, most having to do with cost. People without good insurance often rely on public aid — state funding — to pay medical bills. These resources are limited, the payment for services rendered is low (in my state, Illinois, physicians get paid eleven cents on the dollar), and many professionals simply cannot afford to provide care. Public aid also doesn't cover vocational services in many states, including mine. Furthermore, in my experience, traumatically injured patients find a dearth of accessible living options — and caregivers for these patients are compensated very poorly when their services are covered at all.

Like many of the soldiers wounded in Iraq, Corporal Poole is young and can expect to live for another fifty or more years. The United States needs to make a greater effort to keep people like him engaged in the community and meaningfully employed to compensate his own hard work and the efforts others have made on his behalf. In addition to providing post-acute rehabilitation services, both for the war wounded and for others who have sustained a traumatic brain injury, we need to focus on long-term community reintegration services, long-term job opportunity services (including counseling), and community service programs and mentorship that will allow people like Corporal Poole to remain in the community as independently as possible.

Michelle Gittler, M.D., is medical director of the Spinal Cord Injury Program at Schwab Rehabilitation Hospital in Chicago.

QUESTIONING THE TEXT

1. What do you think the purpose of this article is? What do you think are the characteristics of Grady's *New York Times* audience? Do you think that she expects that audience to think, feel, or act in particular ways after reading this article? Point to specific sections of the text to explain your understanding of how you think the audience would respond and how you think Grady tries to shape that response.

2. The last line of this article from Corporal Poole — "I think something really good is going to happen to me" — might be the most moving of the piece. Why do you think that Grady places this quotation here? Does the article leave you feeling optimistic or pessimistic? Identify particular passages that lead you to feel as you do.

MAKING CONNECTIONS

3. Choose a piece that presents a relatively short, straightforward argument, such as Gregg Easterbrook's "The New Fundamentalism" (p. 343) or John Yoo's "With 'All Necessary and Appropriate Force'" (p. 275). Compare that reading to Grady's piece of reporting from the *New York Times* and make a list of features that separate the two kinds of writing. What are the characteristics of a writing opportunity that would benefit from the op-ed approach? What sorts of issues benefit from the less opinion-driven feature writing that Grady offers?

4. Compare the image that opens this chapter (p. 281) with the images of Corporal Poole that accompany Grady's writing. What does the comparison tell you about how the medical technology used to help wounded soldiers has changed? Do you get a similar impression from all of the photographs, or is the effect of the older image different from the effect of the newer photos? Why?

JOINING THE CONVERSATION

5. Grady's article is about, in part, the unintended consequences of new technology that leads to fewer deaths but a large increase in severe injuries with long-term effects. What other examples can you think of in which a technological achievement produced unintended consequences? Discuss an example of unintended consequences in a personal narrative or an essay.

6. One of the recurring ideas in Grady's article is Poole's identity and how much he has or has not changed since being wounded. Poole himself says, "But I didn't come back" (paragraph 4), referring to the great physical and mental changes that resulted from the injuries. What constitutes your identity? To what degree do changes to one's body affect who one is? In a reflective essay, explore what makes you uniquely you, and be sure to include at least some commentary on whether your body is an essential part of your identity.

GREGG EASTERBROOK
The New Fundamentalism

ANDREA LUNSFORD AND I are also the authors of a textbook entitled Everything's an Argument. *But lately it seems that lots of people don't want to argue anymore. Preferring their truth straight up, they'd be happier if dissenters would just stifle, especially when scientists weigh in on their side. From embryonic stem cell research, to climate change, to teaching evolution in schools, we expect scientists to settle controversies or determine what constitutes acceptable dissent and what is beyond the pale of discussion.*

But I remember a time not so long ago when it was trendy for humanists to argue that scientists really weren't much more reliable or objective than scholars in other fields. After all, wasn't the history of science itself just a tale of one big idea (described as a paradigm*) toppling another? So it only made sense, they claimed, to treat any scientific theory as just that —* a theory *almost certain to change over time.*

The argument about global warming, however, seems to have restored faith in science throughout much of the academic community. At least, fewer of the people criticizing objective science a decade ago express concern that the researchers in lab coats might have their theories of human-induced climate change wrong this time.

*But skepticism may still be warranted when the claims of scientists are extended to areas beyond their ken. So argues journalist and author Gregg Easterbrook (b. 1953) in "The New Fundamentalism" (*Wall Street Journal, *August 8, 2000) in seeming to defend the indefensible: a much-maligned attempt by a Kansas State Board of Education to ban the teaching of evolution in favor of creationism. But, looking closer, Easterbrook discovers that the Kansas proposal, flawed though it might have been, was more sophisticated in its definition of science than the media were willing to acknowledge. His call for "teaching the controversy" has a certain appeal, at least as it might be applied to the question of the origins of life, an issue Easterbrook rightly distinguishes from evolutionary theory.*

Still I am skeptical of Easterbrook's endorsement of intelligent design as a scientific theory worthy of consideration alongside evolution. If the winds of science shift, it's in the face of convincing evidence for a better hypothesis. But intelligent design seems built upon untestable and immutable assumptions and claims, its proponents far better at nit-picking evolutionary science than at offering hard evidence for their own propositions. Precisely because science shifts its paradigms in the face of compelling evidence, it has license to exclude from debate those who don't abide by the same rules. So let's teach ethical controversies, but not bad science.   —J.R.

If John Scopes were alive today, he might be arrested for speaking against evolution in a public school, rather than in favor of it.

Scopes stood trial in Dayton, Tennessee, 75 years ago this summer for using *Hunter's Civic Biology*, a textbook containing a paragraph on Charles Darwin,   **343** in violation of a state law prohibiting the teaching of natural selection. The Tennessee law was embarrassingly wrong-headed. Evolution unquestionably occurs and is essential to understanding biology.

But today the pendulum has swung in the opposite direction, with everyone from the Supreme Court to establishment media holding that students should hear only Darwin's side of the debate. This situation is just as preposterous as the situation in Tennessee in 1925 — and just as bad for freedom of thought. Once you weren't supposed to question God. Now you're not supposed to question the head of the biology department.

DOGMATIC SCIENCE

Consider the reporting on the actions of the Kansas Board of Education. Last year, when the board voted to delete some requirements for the teaching of evolution from the state's nonbinding guidelines, the reaction was as if Galileo had been hauled back before the Inquisition. Headlines proclaimed Kansas had "banned" the teaching of Darwin, when the board's action was strictly advisory. Local school districts were free to ignore the guidelines, and almost all did.

Last week, when the board members who had voted for the new guidelines were defeated in the state primary, assuring that pro-evolution guidelines will be restored, news accounts treated this as a last-second victory over the forces of darkness. They didn't add that because of a copyright snafu, the 1999 guidelines were never actually promulgated. Not only had darkness not fallen over Kansas, from the standpoint of the classroom nothing had happened at all. 5

The 1999 guidelines did not endorse or even mention creationism. In 1986, the Supreme Court correctly ruled that public schools must not teach creationism because it is effectively a religious doctrine. The version of creationism that supposes that Earth was formed a relatively short time ago, and that man has no evolutionary antecedent, is a Biblical contention without any scientific support.

What Kansas's board did do was suggest schools teach only part of natural selection theory. It advised that children be taught that living things evolve in response to changes in their environments. The evidence on this point, as Harvard's Stephen Jay Gould has noted, is as strong as the evidence that Earth orbits the sun. But the board advised against teaching that life began through a totally natural, undirected process. The board was wrong to try to edit contemporary biology in this way. Even if a wholly spontaneous origin of life turns out to be incorrect, it is today's mainstream science and children need to learn it.

More objectionable, perhaps, was the board's advice against teaching Big Bang theory. Big Bang theory enjoys almost unanimous support among cosmologists and even has moderate theological backing, for instance from the Vatican Observatory. This theory may or may not stand the test of time — all previous theories of the origin of the cosmos are now thought wrong, so don't hold your breath for the Big Bang — but kids cannot understand astronomy without knowing the ideas behind it.

Yet though the Kansas board was wrong on some points, those who denounced it skipped the valid substance behind its thinking. There is a lively scientific debate these days on the absence of explanations for the origin of life. Evolutionary theory is commonly misunderstood to explain the origin of life; actually, it applies only to how organisms that already exist respond to their environments. All theories on origins, most recently the "RNA world" hypothesis (that life began with a chemical relative of DNA), are extremely conjectural. Darwin himself said he had no clue how life began, and considered creation an impenetrable mystery.

Inability to explain how life began hardly disproves natural selection. The   10 question is simply outside the theory's perimeter. But because today's dogma assumes science can already explain everything, most of those who denounced the Kansas board didn't seem to know that the origin of life and how life evolves are two entirely separate issues. The Kansas board was right to suggest that the origin of life is a huge unknown, and to be skeptical of applying what Mr. Gould has called evolutionary "fundamentalism."

One small bit of editing by the Kansas board has been overlooked. The board changed the definition of science from "the search for natural explanations" — the wording preferred by the National Academy of Sciences — to the search for logical explanations. When it comes to intellectual rigidity, there's little difference between the national academy declaring that only natural forces may be considered, and the church declaring that only divine explanations may be considered. The quest for logical explanations for the world is a much richer and more engaging goal.

These concerns intersect at the evolving new theory of "intelligent design." Unlike creationism, intelligent-design theory acknowledges that the universe is immensely old and that all living things are descended from earlier forms. But the theory goes on to contend that organic biology is so phenomenally complex that it is illogical to assume that life created itself. There must have been some force providing guidance.

Intelligent design is a sophisticated theory now being argued out in the nation's top universities. And though this idea assumes existence must have some higher component, it is not religious doctrine under the 1986 Supreme Court definition. Intelligent-design thinking does not propound any specific faith or even say that the higher power is divine. It simply holds that there must be an unseen intellect imbedded in the cosmos.

The intelligent design theory may or may not be correct, but it's a rich, absorbing hypothesis — the sort of thing that is fascinating to debate, and might get students excited about biology class to boot. But most kids won't know the idea unless they are taught it, and in the aftermath of the Kansas votes, pro-evolution dogma continues to suggest that any alternative to natural selection must be kept quiet.

But then, just as in 1925, opposition to natural selection was not really 15 about the theory but about sustaining a status quo in which people were not supposed to question clergy, so today's evolutionary fundamentalism is not so much about the theory but about sustaining a new status quo in which people are not supposed to question scientists. Yet this discourages students from engaging in one of the most fascinating — if not the most fascinating — of questions: Why are we here?

TEACH THE CONTROVERSY

The obvious solution is to teach the controversy. Present students with the arguments for and against natural and supernatural explanations of life, and then let them enter into this engaging, fertile debate. Yet many school systems are steering away from teaching intelligent design, believing it to be an impermissible idea under the Supreme Court ruling. Editorials and columnists prefer not to mention the new theory, hoping to tar all non-Darwinian ideas as mere creationism. This isn't freedom of thought — it's the reverse. Where is the new Scopes who will expose the new dogma as being just as bad as the old?

QUESTIONING THE TEXT

1. Easterbrook identifies "teach[ing] the controversy" as the "obvious solution" to the problem schools have in addressing the origin of life (paragraph 16). To what degree is this obvious solution a reasonable solution? Do you think that Easterbrook's solution would work? How do you think this strategy would have worked in your own high school biology class?

2. One of Easterbrook's primary tactics to get readers to agree with him is to appeal to the example of the trial of John Scopes in 1925. Do you think that his comparison — not questioning God and not questioning the head of the biology department — is fair (paragraph 3)? Drawing on both evidence in the text and your own reasoning, list the reasons that you agree or disagree with Easterbrook's framing of the debate, and defend your ideas in a discussion with your classmates.

MAKING CONNECTIONS

3. Imagine Easterbrook's response to "Church of the Flying Spaghetti Monster's Open Letter to the Kansas School Board" (p. 348) and Bobby Henderson's response to "The New Fundamentalism" (p. 343). Write a two-page dialogue between the two authors where they defend their different responses to the controversy over intelligent design in Kansas.

4. Both Easterbrook and Mary Shelley (*Frankenstein*, p. 285) critique the claims and authority of science, but the nature of their critiques is quite different. What similarities do you see between the two? What differences?

JOINING THE CONVERSATION

5. Easterbrook suggests that the argument against teaching intelligent design is a threat to students' freedom to think for themselves. Think about your own education. Was there ever a time when you felt that you were not allowed freedom of thought? Was there ever a time when a teacher gave you a notable degree of freedom or somehow helped you realize your intellectual freedom? Write an essay that reflects on your education and the freedom, or lack thereof, that you have felt as a student.

6. Come up with a lesson plan that a teacher could use to "teach the controversy" over a different issue that concerns you. Don't simply state the two sides of an issue; instead, think about how you could make both of the opposing sides sound reasonable, giving students an opportunity to think for themselves without being heavily guided.

BOBBY HENDERSON
Church of the Flying Spaghetti Monster's Open Letter to the Kansas School Board

*W*HEN *I* WAS *A* TEENAGER *in the late 1950s, a well-known British television show, Panorama, reported on the great spaghetti harvest then occurring in Switzerland, including pictures of Swiss folks gathering spaghetti from trees and putting armfuls of it into baskets. The date was April 1st, but that didn't stop people from phoning in and asking for more information about upcoming spaghetti harvests; some even wanted to know how they could grow a spaghetti tree of their own.*

Fifty years later, spaghetti was again in the news, this time in the form of the Church of the Flying Spaghetti Monster (www.venganza.org). This "church" was founded by Bobby Henderson, a physics graduate from Oregon State University, who wrote the letter we've reprinted below to the Kansas State Board of Education after they ruled in 2005 that intelligent design must be taught in Kansas schools as an alternative to evolution. On his Web site, Henderson gives the following explanation:

> *I wrote the* Open Letter *sometime around January of 2005 and posted it online several months later after receiving no reply from the Kansas School Board. Within days of posting it online, the letter became an internet phenomenon, generating tens of thousands of visits each day, as well as personal responses from the school board members themselves. To date (August 2006), the venganza website has received upwards of 350 million hits, and somewhere in the proximity of 15 million unique visits. . . . I've received over 15,000 emails in response to the letter.*

Check the site for yourself and you'll find hundreds of responses to Henderson's letter, from "instant conversions" to Flying Spaghetti Monsterism (who call themselves Pastafarians) to fierce opponents; there's even a link to hate mail. You can also buy gear — FSM T-shirts, greeting cards, even iPod covers — or you can order The Gospel of the Flying Spaghetti Monster, *published in 2006.*

In a 2005 interview with Wired, *Henderson remarks on his parody, saying that "Our theory is as much science — in fact much more so — than what the intelligent design guys are proposing. And, if you're going to redefine science to include supernatural explanations, you have to allow them all in." Do you agree with Henderson's assessment? And how effective do you find his open letter? Judging by the response he's gotten, it did have an impact. And in February 2007, the Kansas State Board of Education revised its standards to remove references to the teaching of intelligent design in science courses.* —A.L.

I am writing you with much concern after having read of your hearing to decide whether the alternative theory of Intelligent Design should be taught along with the theory of Evolution. I think we can all agree that it is important for students to hear multiple viewpoints so they can choose for themselves the theory that makes the most sense to them. I am concerned, however, that students will only hear one theory of Intelligent Design.

Let us remember that there are multiple theories of Intelligent Design. I and many others around the world are of the strong belief that the universe was created by a Flying Spaghetti Monster. It was He who created all that we see and all that we feel. We feel strongly that the overwhelming scientific evidence pointing towards evolutionary processes is nothing but a coincidence, put in place by Him.

It is for this reason that I'm writing you today, to formally request that this alternative theory be taught in your schools, along with the other two theories. In fact, I will go so far as to say, if you do not agree to do this, we will be forced to proceed with legal action. I'm sure you see where we are coming from. If the Intelligent Design theory is not based on faith, but instead another scientific theory, as is claimed, then you must also allow our theory to be taught, as it is also based on science, not on faith.

Some find that hard to believe, so it may be helpful to tell you a little more about our beliefs. We have evidence that a Flying Spaghetti Monster created the universe. None of us, of course, were around to see it, but we have written accounts of it. We have several lengthy volumes explaining all details of His power. Also, you may be surprised to hear that there are over 10 million of us, and growing. We tend to be very secretive, as many people claim our beliefs are not substantiated by observable evidence. What these people don't understand is that He built the world to make us think the earth is older than it really is. For example, a scientist may perform a carbon-dating process on an artifact. He finds that approximately 75% of the Carbon-14 has decayed by electron emission to Nitrogen-14, and infers that this artifact is approximately 10,000 years old, as the half-life of Carbon-14 appears to be 5,730 years. But what our scientist does not realize is that every time he makes a measurement, the Flying Spaghetti Monster is there changing the results with His Noodly Appendage. We have numerous texts that describe in detail how this can be possible and the reasons why He does this. He is of course invisible and can pass through normal matter with ease.

I'm sure you now realize how important it is that your students are taught this alternate theory. It is absolutely imperative that they realize that observable evidence is at the discretion of a Flying Spaghetti Monster. Furthermore, it is disrespectful to teach our beliefs without wearing His chosen outfit, which of course is full pirate regalia. I cannot stress the importance of this enough, and unfortunately cannot describe in detail why this must be done as I fear this letter is already becoming too long. The concise explanation is that He becomes angry if we don't.

You may be interested to know that global warming, earthquakes, hurricanes, and other natural disasters are a direct effect of the shrinking numbers of

Global Average Temperature vs. Number of Pirates

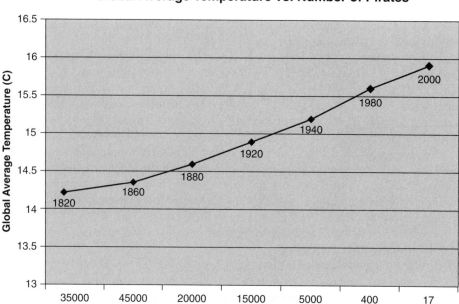

Pirates since the 1800s. For your interest, I have included a graph of the approximate number of pirates versus the average global temperature over the last 200 years. As you can see, there is a statistically significant inverse relationship between pirates and global temperature.

In conclusion, thank you for taking the time to hear our views and beliefs. I hope I was able to convey the importance of teaching this theory to your students. We will of course be able to train the teachers in this alternate theory. I am eagerly awaiting your response, and hope dearly that no legal action will need to be taken. I think we can all look forward to the time when these three theories are given equal time in our science classrooms across the country, and eventually the world: one third time for Intelligent Design, one third time for Flying Spaghetti Monsterism, and one third time for logical conjecture based on overwhelming observable evidence.

Sincerely Yours,

Bobby Henderson, concerned citizen.

P.S. I have included an artistic drawing of Him creating a mountain, trees, and a midget. Remember, we are all His creatures.

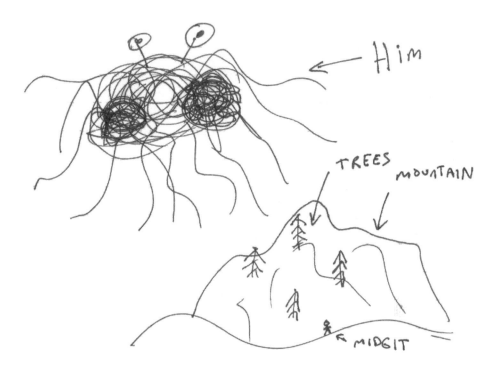

QUESTIONING THE TEXT

1. Study carefully the graph and drawing that appear with this letter. Explain how they work with the text to create the argument that Henderson is putting forward. Would Henderson's argument be more or less convincing if he had produced more professional visual aids? Why?

2. At what point did you realize that Henderson was making a satiric point? Do you think that the humorous approach works well, or do you consider this a shallow response to the controversy? Defend your response with evidence derived from the text.

MAKING CONNECTIONS

3. Compare Henderson's use of humor to Dave Barry's "Guys vs. Men" (p. 405). Which article do you think is funnier? Which one do you think more effectively makes a point?

4. Who do you think would be the ideal audience to be persuaded by Henderson's article? How would that audience compare to the ideal audience for Gregg Easterbrook's "The New Fundamentalism" (p. 343)?

JOINING THE CONVERSATION

5. Read Henderson's letter again carefully, and then rewrite it as a straight-forward essay that states his claims directly.

6. Using your best imitation of Henderson's style and humor, write an open letter about an issue that matters to you, and include at least one visual component in your argument.

CHRISTINE ROSEN
The Image Culture

*I*N THE EARLY 1960S, *it was always the cool uncle who brought the Polaroid Land camera to family gatherings, snapping shots of nieces and nephews, and then dazzling them sixty seconds later by peeling finished photographs from the back of the device. Though black-and-white and grainy, those instant photographs seemed like magic.*

Today, Dr. Land's invention seems quaint compared to the hundreds of devices that leave us awash in images, both still and moving: digital SLRs, streaming media, flat screen high-definition TVs, cell phone cameras, gaming consoles, social networking sites (MySpace, YouTube, Flickr), and so on. But his camera tapped into the same desire for graphic display and instant gratification that drives our media culture today.

In the last few decades, there can be little doubt that Western societies have shifted dramatically from print-based to image-dominated cultures. It began with film, accelerated with the development of television, and then hit warp speed when computers went graphic in the 1980s. Kids today probably don't remember a time when people didn't have instant access to films, pictures, video games, and news or couldn't create complex images themselves with the click of a few buttons.

In "The Image Culture," Christine Rosen (b. 1976), a critic of the uses we sometimes make of technology, nonetheless attempts to place our enthusiasm for visual technologies into contexts meaningful to different generations, both those who grew up with the new media and those who see them as frightening and disruptive, a decline from a world ruled by the subtlety and thoughtfulness of words on paper. In an interview for Image: A Journal of the Arts & Religion *(October 17, 2005), Rosen noted that she is "struck by the transformation of social space in recent years and how technologies such as cell phones, iPods, portable DVD players, and the like have allowed us to create little digital cocoons. . . . I think we're seeing a concomitant erosion of civility in public space." If that is the case, we will need to deal with the consequences and, perhaps, kick back against technologies that undermine our civility. Or perhaps we'll need to imagine public spaces in entirely new ways — as we already have with social networking software. Whatever option we choose, "The Image Culture" maps the terrain of visual literacy in exceptional detail and unusual clarity: here are the questions we face.*

"The Image Culture" originally appeared in The New Atlantis *in the fall of 2005.* —J.R.

When Hurricane Katrina struck the Gulf Coast of Mississippi, Alabama, and Louisiana in late August, images of the immense devastation were immediately available to anyone with a television set or an Internet connection. Although images of both natural and manmade disasters have long been displayed in newspapers and on television, the number and variety of images in the aftermath of Katrina reveals the sophistication, speed, and power of images in contemporary American culture. Satellite photographs from space offered us miniature before and after images of downtown New Orleans and the damaged coast of Biloxi; video footage from an array of news outlets tracked rescue operations and recorded the thoughts of survivors; wire photos captured the grief of victims; amateur pictures, taken with camera-enabled cell phones or digital cameras and posted to personal blogs, tracked the disaster's toll on countless individuals. The world was offered, in a negligible space of time, both God's-eye and man's-eye views of a devastated region. Within days, as pictures of the squalor at the Louisiana Superdome and photographs of dead bodies abandoned in downtown streets emerged, we confronted our inability to cope with the immediate chaos, destruction, and desperation the storm had caused. These images brutally drove home the realization of just how unprepared the U.S. was to cope with such a disaster.

But how did this saturation of images influence our understanding of what happened in New Orleans and elsewhere? How did the speed with which the images were disseminated alter the humanitarian and political response to the disaster? And how, in time, will these images influence our cultural memory of the devastation caused by Hurricane Katrina?

Such questions could be asked of any contemporary disaster — and often have been, especially in the wake of the September 2001 terrorist attacks in New York and Washington, D.C., which forever etched in public memory the image of the burning Twin Towers. But the average person sees tens of thousands of images in the course of a day. One sees images on television, in newspapers and magazines, on websites, and on the sides of buses. Images grace soda cans and T-shirts and billboards. "In our world we sleep and eat the image and pray to it and wear it too," novelist Don DeLillo observed. Internet search engines can instantly procure images for practically any word you type. On flickr.com, a photo-sharing website, you can type in a word such as "love" and find amateur digital photos of couples in steamy embrace or parents hugging their children. Type in "terror" and among the results is a photograph of the World Trade Center towers burning. "Remember when this was a shocking image?" asks the person who posted the picture.

The question is not merely rhetorical. It points to something important about images in our culture: They have, by their sheer number and ease of replication, become less magical and less shocking — a situation unknown until fairly recently in human history. Until the development of mass reproduction, images carried more power and evoked more fear. The second of the Ten Commandments listed in Exodus 20 warns against idolizing, or even making, graven images: "Thou shalt not make unto thee any graven image, or any likeness of any thing that is in heaven above, or that is in the earth beneath, or that is in the water under the earth." During the English Reformation, Henry VIII's advisor Thomas Cromwell led the effort to destroy religious images and icons in the country's churches and monasteries, and was successful enough that few survive to this day. The 2001 decision by the Taliban government in Afghanistan to destroy images throughout the country — including the two towering stone Buddhas carved into the cliffs of Bamiyan — is only the most recent example of this impulse. Political leaders have long feared images and taken extreme measures to control and manipulate them. The anonymous minions of manipulators who sanitized photographs at the behest of Stalin (a man who seemingly never met an enemy he didn't murder and then airbrush from history) are perhaps the best known example. Control of images has long been a preoccupation of the powerful.

It is understandable why so many have been so jealous of the image's   5 influence. Sight is our most powerful sense, much more dominant in translating experience than taste, touch, or hearing. And images appeal to emotion — often viscerally so. They claim our attention without uttering a word. They can persuade, repel, or charm us. They can be absorbed instantly and easily by anyone who can see. They seem to speak for themselves.

Today, anyone with a digital camera and a personal computer can produce and alter an image. As a result, the power of the image has been diluted in one sense, but strengthened in another. It has been diluted by the ubiquity of images and the many populist technologies (like inexpensive cameras and picture-editing software) that give almost everyone the power to create, distort, and transmit images. But it has been strengthened by the gradual capitulation of the printed word to pictures, particularly moving pictures — the ceding of text to image, which might be likened not to a defeated political candidate ceding to his opponent, but to an articulate person being rendered mute, forced to communicate via gesture and expression rather than language.

Americans love images. We love the democratizing power of technologies — such as digital cameras, video cameras, Photoshop, and Power-Point — that give us the capability to make and manipulate images. What we are less eager to consider are the broader cultural effects of a society devoted to the image. Historians and anthropologists have explored the story of mankind's movement from an oral-based culture to a written culture, and later to a printed one. But it is only in the past several decades that we have begun to assimilate the effects of the move from a culture based on the printed word to one based largely on images. In making images rather than texts our guide, are we opening up new vistas for understanding and expression, creating a form of communication that is "better than print," as New York University communications professor Mitchell Stephens has argued? Or are we merely making a peculiar and unwelcome return to forms of communication once ascendant in preliterate societies — perhaps creating a world of hieroglyphics and ideograms (albeit technologically sophisticated ones) — and in the process becoming, as the late Daniel Boorstin argued, slavishly devoted to the enchanting and superficial image at the expense of the deeper truths that the written word alone can convey?

Two things in particular are at stake in our contemporary confrontation with an image-based culture: First, technology has considerably undermined our ability to trust what we see, yet we have not adequately grappled with the effects of this on our notions of truth. Second, if we are indeed moving from the era of the printed word to an era dominated by the image, what impact will this have on culture, broadly speaking, and its institutions? What will art, literature, and music look like in the age of the image? And will we, in the age of the image, become too easily accustomed to verisimilar rather than true things, preferring appearance to reality and in the process rejecting the demands of discipline and patience that true things often require of us if we are to understand their meaning and describe it with precision? The potential costs of moving from the printed word to the image are immense. We may find ourselves in a world where our ability to communicate is stunted, our understanding and acceptance of what we see questionable, and our desire to transmit culture from one generation to the next seriously compromised.

THE MIRROR WITH A MEMORY

The creator of one of the earliest technologies of the image named his invention, appropriately enough, for himself. Louis-Jacques-Mandé Daguerre, a Frenchman known for his elaborate and whimsical stage design in the Paris theater, began building on the work of Joseph Nicéphore Niepce to try to produce a fixed image. Daguerre called the image he created in 1837 the "daguerreotype" (acquiring a patent from the French government for the process in 1839). He made extravagant claims for his device. It is "not merely an instrument which serves to draw nature," he wrote in 1838, it "gives her the power to reproduce herself."

Despite its technological crudeness and often-spectral images, the   10
daguerreotype was eerily effective at capturing glimmers of personality in its fixed portraits. The extant daguerreotypes of well-known Americans in the nineteenth century include a young and serious Abraham Lincoln, sans beard; an affable Horace Greeley in stovepipe hat; and a dour picture of the suffragist Lucy Stone. A daguerreotype of Edgar Allen Poe, taken in 1848, depicts the writer with a baleful expression and crossed arms, and was taken not long before Poe was found delirious and near death on the streets of Baltimore.

But the daguerreotype did more than capture the posture of a poised citizenry. It also changed artists' perceptions of human nature. Nathaniel Hawthorne's 1851 Gothic romance, *The House of the Seven Gables*, has an ancient moral ("the wrong-doing of one generation lives into the successive ones") but made use of a modern technology, daguerreotyping, to unspool its story about the unmasking of festering, latent evil. In the story, Holgrave, the strange lodger living in the gabled house, is a daguerreotypist (as well as a political radical) who says of his art: "While we give it credit only for depicting the merest surface, it actually brings out the secret character with a truth no painter would ever venture upon, even could he detect it." It is Holgrave's silvery daguerreotypes that eventually reveal the nefarious motives of Judge Pyncheon — and in so doing suggest that the camera could expose human character more acutely than the eye.

Oliver Wendell Holmes called the photo the "mirror with a memory," and in 1859 predicted that the "image would become more important than the object itself and would in fact make the object disposable." But praise for the photograph was not universal. "A revengeful God has given ear to the prayers of this multitude. Daguerre was his Messiah," said the French poet Charles Baudelaire in an essay written in 1859. "Our squalid society rushed, Narcissus to a man, to gaze at its trivial image on a scrap of metal." As a result, Baudelaire worried, "artistic genius" was being impoverished.

Contemporary critiques of photography have at times echoed Baudelaire's fear. In her elegant extended essay, *On Photography*, the late Susan Sontag argues that images — particularly photographs — carry the risk of undermining true things and genuine experiences, as well as the danger of upending our understanding of art. "Knowing a great deal about what is in the world (art, catastrophe, the beauties of nature) through photographic images," Sontag notes, "people are frequently disappointed, surprised, unmoved when they see the real thing." This is not a new problem, of course; it plagued the art world when the printing process allowed the mass reproduction of great works of art, and its effects can still be seen whenever one overhears a museum-goer express disappointment that the Van Gogh he sees hanging on the wall is nowhere near as vibrant as the one on his coffee mug.

But Sontag's point is broader, and suggests that photography has forced us to consider that exposure to images does not necessarily create understanding of the things themselves. Images do not necessarily lead to meaning; the information they convey does not always lead to knowledge. This is due in part to the fact that photographic images must constantly be refreshed if one's attention is to continue to be drawn to them. "Photographs shock insofar as they show something novel," Sontag argues. "Unfortunately, the ante keeps getting raised — partly through the very proliferation of such images of horror." Images, Sontag concludes, have turned the world "into a department store or museum-without-walls," a place where people "become customers or tourists of reality."

Other contemporary critics, such as Roger Scruton, have also lamented   15
this diversionary danger and worried about our potential dependence on images. "Photographic images, with their capacity for realization of fantasies, have a distracting character which requires masterly control if it is not to get out of hand," Scruton writes. "People raised on such images . . . inevitably require a need for them." Marshall McLuhan, the Sixties media guru, offered perhaps the most blunt and apt metaphor for photography: he called it "the brothel-without-walls." After all, he noted, the images of celebrities whose behavior we so avidly track "can be bought and hugged and thumbed more easily than public prostitutes" — and all for a greatly reduced price.

Nevertheless, photographs still retain some of the magical allure that the earliest daguerreotypes inspired. As W. J .T. Mitchell observes in *What Do Pictures Want?*, "When students scoff at the idea of a magical relation between a picture and what it represents, ask them to take a photograph of their mother and cut out the eyes." As objects, our photographs have changed; they have become physically flimsier as they have become more technologically sophisticated. Daguerre produced pictures on copper plates; today many of our photographs never become tangible things, but instead remain filed away on computers and cameras, part of the digital ether that envelops the modern world. At the same time, our patience for the creation of images has also eroded. Children today are used to being tracked from birth by digital cameras and video recorders and they expect to see the results of their poses and performances instantly. "Let me see," a child says, when you take her picture with a digital camera. And she does, immediately. The space between life as it is being lived and life as it is being displayed shrinks to a mere second. Yet, despite these technical developments, photographs remain powerful because they are reminders of the people and things we care about. They are surrogates carried into battle by a soldier or by a traveler on holiday. They exist to remind us of the absent, the beloved, and the dead. But in the new era of the digital image, they also have a greater potential for fostering falsehood and trickery, perpetuating fictions that seem so real we cannot tell the difference.

VANISHING COMMISSARS AND BLOODTHIRSTY PRESIDENTS

Human nature being what it is, little time passed after photography's invention before a means for altering and falsifying photographs was developed. A German photographer in the 1840s discovered a way to retouch negatives, Susan Sontag recounts, and, perversely if not unpredictably, "the news that the camera could lie made getting photographed much more popular."

One of the most successful mass manipulators of the photographic image was Stalin. As David King recounts in his riveting book, *The Commissar Vanishes: The Falsification of Photographs and Art in Stalin's Russia*, image manipulation was the extension of Stalin's paranoiac megalomania. "The physical eradication of Stalin's political opponents at the hands of the secret police was swiftly followed by their obliteration from all forms of pictorial existence," King writes. Airbrush, India ink, and scalpel were all marshaled to remove enemies such as Trotsky from photographs. "There is hardly a publication from the Stalinist period that does not bear the scars of this political vandalism," King concludes.

Even in non-authoritarian societies, early photo falsification was commonly used to dupe the masses. A new exhibit at the Metropolitan Museum of Art in New York, "The Perfect Medium: Photography and the Occult," displays a range of photographs from the late-nineteenth- and early-twentieth-century United States and Europe that purport to show ghosts, levitating mediums, and a motley array of other emanations that were proffered as evidence of the spirit world by devotees of the spiritualism movement popular at the time. The pictures, which include images of tiny heads shrouded in smoke and hovering over the furrowed brows of mediums, and ghosts in diaphanous robes walking through gardens, are "by turns spooky, beautiful, disturbing, and hilarious," notes the *New York Times*. They create "visual records of decades of fraud, cons, flimflams and gullibility."

Stalin and the spiritualists were not the only people to manipulate images   20 in the service of reconstructing the past — many an angry ex-lover has taken shears to photos of a once-beloved in the hope that excising the images might also excise the bad memories the images prompt. But it was the debut of a computer program called Photoshop in 1990 that allowed the masses, inexpensively and easily, to begin rewriting visual history. Photoshop and the many copycat programs that have followed in its wake allow users to manipulate digital images with great ease — resizing, changing scale, and airbrushing flaws, among other things — and they have been both denounced for facilitating the death of the old-fashioned darkroom and hailed as democratic tools for free expression. "It's the inevitable consequence of the democratization of technology," John Knoll, the inventor of Photoshop, told Salon.com. "You give people a tool, but you can't really control what they do with it."

For some people, of course, offering Photoshop as a tool is akin to giving a stick of dynamite to a toddler. Last year, *The Nation* published an advertisement that used Photoshop to superimpose President Bush's head over the image of a brutal and disturbing Richard Serra sculpture (which itself borrows from Goya's painting, *Saturn Devouring One of His Children*) so that Bush appeared to be enthusiastically devouring a naked human torso. In contrast to the sickening image, the accompanying text appears prim: www.pleasevote.com. As this and other images suggest, Photoshop has introduced a new fecklessness into our relationship with the image. We tend to lose respect for things we can manipulate. And when we can so readily manipulate images — even images of presidents or loved ones — we contribute to the decline of respect for what the image represents.

Photoshop is popular not only because it allows us visually to settle scores, but also because it appeals to our desire for the incongruous (and the ribald). "Photoshop contests" such as those found on the website Fark.com offer people the opportunity to create wacky and fantastic images that are then judged by others in cyberspace. This is an impulse that predates software and whose most enthusiastic American purveyor was, perhaps, P. T. Barnum. In the nineteenth century, Barnum barkered an infamous "mermaid woman" that was actually the moldering head of a monkey stitched onto the body of a fish. Photoshop allows us to employ pixels rather than taxidermy to achieve such fantasies, but the motivation for creating them is the same — they are a form of wish fulfillment and, at times, a vehicle for reinforcing our existing prejudices.

Of course, Photoshop meddling is not the only tactic available for producing misleading images. Magazines routinely airbrushed and retouched photographs long before picture-editing software was invented. And of course even "authentic" pictures can be staged, like the 1960s *Life* magazine pictures of Muhammad Ali that showed him training underwater; in fact, Ali couldn't even swim, and he hadn't done any underwater training for his prizefights before stepping into the pool for that photo opportunity. More recently, in July 2005, the *New York Times Magazine* raised eyebrows when it failed to disclose that the Andres Serrano photographs accompanying a cover story about prisoner interrogation were in fact staged images rather than straightforward photojournalism. (Serrano was already infamous for his controversial 1989 photograph, "Piss Christ.") The *Times* public editor chastised the magazine for violating the paper's guidelines that "images in our pages that purport to depict reality must be genuine in every way."

But while Photoshop did not invent image fraud, it has made us all potential practitioners. It enables the average computer user to become a digital prankster whose merrymaking with photographs can create more than silly images — it can spawn political and social controversy. In a well-reported article published in Salon.com in 2004, Farhad Manjoo explored in depth one such controversy: an image that purportedly showed an American Marine reservist in Iraq standing next to two young boys. One boy held a cardboard sign that read, "Lcpl Boudreaux killed my Dad then he knocked up my sister!" When the image found its way to the Council on American-Islamic Relations (CAIR), Manjoo reports, it seemed to prove the group's worst fears about the behavior of American soldiers in Iraq. An angry press release soon followed. But then another image surfaced on various websites, identical to the first except for the text written on the cardboard sign, which now read, "Lcpl Boudreaux saved my Dad then he rescued my sister!" The authenticity of both photos was never satisfactorily proven, and, as Manjoo notes, the episode serves as a reminder that in today's Photoshop world, "pictures are endlessly pliable." (Interestingly, CAIR found itself at the center of a recent Photoshop scandal, the *Weekly Standard* reported, when it was shown that the organization had Photoshopped a hijab, or headscarf, onto several women in a picture taken at a CAIR event and then posted the doctored image on the organization's website.)

Just as political campaigns in the past produced vituperative pamphlets   25
and slogans, today Photoshop helps produce misleading images. The Bush-Cheney campaign was pilloried for using a Photoshopped image of a crowd of soldiers in the recent presidential election; the photo duplicated groups of soldiers to make the crowd appear larger than it actually was. The replicated faces of the soldiers recalled an earlier and cruder montaged crowd scene, "Stalin and the Masses," produced in 1930, which purported to show the glowering dictator, in overcoat and cap, standing before a throng of loyal communists. (Other political campaigns — and university publicity departments — have also reportedly resorted to using Photoshop on pictures to make them seem more racially diverse.) Similarly, a Seventies-era image of Jane Fonda addressing an anti-war crowd with a young and raptly admiring John Kerry looking on was

also created with Photoshop sorcery but circulated widely on the Internet during the last presidential election as evidence of Kerry's extreme views. The doctored image fooled several news outlets before its questionable provenance was revealed. (Another image of Kerry and Fonda, showing them both sitting in the audience in a 1970 anti-war rally, was authentic.)

Photoshop, in effect, democratizes the ability to commit fraud. As a result, a few computer programmers are creating new digital detection techniques to uncover forgeries and manipulations. The Inspector Javert of digital fraud is Dartmouth computer science professor Hany Farid, who developed a software program that analyzes the pattern of pixels in digital images. Since all digital pictures are, in essence, a collection of codes, Farid's program ferrets out "abnormal patterns of information that, while invisible to the eye, are detectable by computer" and that represent possible tampering, according to the *New York Times*. "It used to be that you had a photograph, and that was the end of it — that was truth," Farid said last July. "We're trying to bring some of that back. To put some measure of guarantee back in photography."

But the digital manipulation of images can also be employed for far more enlightened purposes than removing models' blemishes and attacking political opponents. Some artists use Photoshop merely to enhance photographs they take; others have made digital editing a central part of their art. The expansive images of the German photographer Andreas Gursky, whose photos of Montparnasse, the Tokyo Stock Exchange, and a 99-cent store make use of digital alteration, prompt us to look at familiar spaces in unfamiliar ways. The portraits taken and Photoshopped by artist Loretta Lux are "mesmerizing images of children who seem trapped between the nineteenth and twenty-first centuries, who don't exist except in the magical realm of art," according to a *New York Times* critic. Here the manipulation of the image does not intrude. It illuminates. In these pictures, the manipulation of the image at least serves an authentic artistic vision, a vision that relies on genuine aesthetic and critical standards. Ironically, it is these very standards that a culture devoted to the image risks compromising.

THE MTV EFFECT

The still images of daguerreotyping and photography laid the groundwork for the moving image in film and video; as photography did before them, these technologies prompted wonder and sweeping claims about the merits of this new way of seeing. In 1915, after a screening of filmmaker D. W. Griffith's *The Birth of a Nation*, Woodrow Wilson declared that it was "like writing history with lightning" (a judgment Griffith promptly began using in his promotional efforts for the film). Moving images are as powerful as photos, if not more so. Like photographs, they appeal to emotion and can be read in competing ways. Yet moving images change so rapidly and so often that they arrest our attention and task the brain's ability to absorb what we are seeing. They are becoming a ubiquitous presence in public and private life — so much so that Camille Paglia, an astute critic of images, has called our world "a media starscape of explosive but evanescent images."

The moving image, like the photograph, can also be marshaled to prove or disprove competing claims. During the legal and political debate surrounding the case of Terri Schiavo, for example, videotape of her movements and apparent responsiveness to loved ones became central in this family dispute-turned-national drama. Those who argued for keeping Schiavo alive used the footage as evidence that she did indeed have feelings and thoughts that rendered attempts to remove her feeding tube barbaric and immoral. Those who believed that she should be left to die (including her husband) thought the tape "grossly deceptive," because it represented a misleading portrait of Schiavo's real condition. Most of the time, her husband and others argued, Terri did not demonstrate awareness; she was "immobile, expressionless." In the Schiavo case, the moving image was both alibi and accuser.

Most Americans consume moving images through the media of televi- 30 sion and movies (and, to a lesser degree, through the Internet and video games). In recent years, in what many observers have called "the MTV effect," those moving images have become more nimble and less demanding of our attention. Jumping quickly from image to image in hastily edited segments (in some cases as quickly as one image every one-thirtieth of a second), television and, to a lesser extent, movies offer us a constant stream of visual candy. Former Vice President Al Gore's new for-profit public access television channel, Current TV, is the latest expression of this trend. The network's website lists its upcoming programming in tiny time increments: "In 1 min," "In 3 min," "In 10 min," and so on. Reviewing the channel's first few broadcasts, *New York Times* television critic Alessandra Stanley noted the many techniques "designed to hold short attention spans," including a "progress bar" at the bottom of the screen that counts down how much time is left for each of the segments — some of which last as little as 15 seconds.

According to enthusiasts of television, the speed and sophistication of moving images allows new and improved forms of oral storytelling that can and should replace staler vehicles like the novel. Video game and television apologist Steven Johnson, author of *Everything Bad is Good for You*, dreams of a world of "DVD cases lining living room shelves like so many triple-decker novels." If television is our new form of narrative, then our storytelling skills have declined, as anyone who has watched the new raft of sitcoms and dramas that premiere (and then quickly disappear) each fall on the major networks can attest. (Shows like *The Sopranos* are perhaps the rare exception.) In fact, television doesn't really "tell stories." It constructs fantasy worlds through a combination of images and words, relying more on our visual and aural senses and leaving less to the imagination than oral storytelling does. Writing some years ago in the journal *Media & Values*, J. Francis Davis noted that although television is in one sense a form of storytelling, the most important messages that emanate from the screen "are those not verbalized — the stories and myths hidden in its constant flow of images."

It is precisely those hidden stories in the moving image that excite critics like NYU professor Mitchell Stephens. In *The Rise of the Image, The Fall of the Word*, Stephens argues that the moving image offers a potential cure for the "crisis of the spirit" that afflicts our society, and he is enthusiastic about the fact that "the image is replacing the word as the predominant means of mental transport." Stephens envisions a future of learning through synecdoche, using vivid and condensed images: "A half second of the Capitol may be enough to indicate the federal government, a quick shot of a white-haired woman may represent age. The part, in other words, will be substituted for the whole so that in a given period of time it will be possible to consider a larger number of wholes." He quotes approvingly the prediction of movie director Ridley Scott, who declares: "Film is twentieth-century theater, and it will become twenty-first-century writing."

Perhaps it will. But Stephens, like other boosters of the image, fails to acknowledge what we will lose as well as gain if this revolution succeeds. He says, for example, "our descendants undoubtedly will still learn to read and write, but they undoubtedly will read and write less often and, therefore, less well." Language, too, will be "less precise, less subtle," and books "will maintain a small, elite audience." This, then, is the future that prompts celebration: a world where, after a century's effort to make literacy as broadly accessible as possible — to make it a tool for the masses — the ability to read and write is once again returned to the elite. Reading and writing either become what they were before widespread education — a mark of privilege — or else antiquarian preoccupations or mere hobbies, like coin collecting.

Stephens also assumes that the people who will be absorbing these images will have a store of knowledge at their disposal with which to interpret them. A quick shot of a white-haired woman might effectively be absorbed as symbolizing "age" to one person, as Stephens says, but it could also reasonably prompt ideas such as "hair dye," "feebleness," or "Social Security" to another. As Camille Paglia observes of her own students, "young people today are flooded with disconnected images but lack a sympathetic instrument to analyze them as well as a historical frame of reference in which to situate them." They lack, in other words, a shared language or lexicon that would allow them to interpret images and then communicate an understanding of what they are seeing.

Such a deficit will pose a unique challenge for cultural transmission from   35
one generation to the next. How, in Stephens's future world of the moving image, will history, literature, and art be passed down to the next generation? He might envision classrooms where children watch the History Channel rather than pore over dull textbooks. But no matter how much one might enjoy the BBC's televised version of *Pride and Prejudice*, it is no substitute for actually reading Austen's prose, nor is a documentary about the American Constitutional Convention as effective at distilling the political ideals of the early

American republic as reading *The Federalist Papers*. Moving images are a rich aid to learning and understanding but their victory as the best means of forming rigorous habits of mind is by no means assured.

In addition, Stephens accepts uncritically the claim that the "old days" of written and printed culture are gone (or nearly so) and assumes that video is the language that has emerged, like some species evolving through a process of natural selection, to take its place in the culture. He does not entertain the possibility that the reason the moving image is replacing the written word is not because it is, in fact, a superior form for the communication of ideas, but because the moving image — more so than the written word — crudely but intoxicatingly satisfies our desire for stimulation and immediate gratification.

Like any good techno-enthusiast, Stephens takes the choices that we have made en masse as a culture (such as watching television rather than reading), accepts them without challenge, and then declares them inevitable. This is a form of reasoning that techno-enthusiasts often employ when they attempt to engage the concerns of skeptics. Although rhetorically useful in the short term, this strategy avoids the real questions: Did things have to happen this way rather than that way? Does every cultural trend make a culture genuinely better? By neglecting to ask these questions, the enthusiast becomes nearly Panglossian in his hymns to his new world.

There is, of course, a long and thorough literature critical of television and the moving image, most notably the work of Neil Postman, Jerry Mander, and Marie Winn. And as with photography, from its earliest days there have been those who worried that television might undermine our appreciation for true things. "Television hangs on the questionable theory that whatever happens anywhere should be sensed everywhere," E. B. White wrote in the *New Yorker* in 1948. "If everyone is going to be able to see everything, in the long run all sights may lose whatever rarity value they once possessed, and it may well turn out that people, being able to see and hear practically everything, will be specially interested in almost nothing." Others are even blunter. As Roger Scruton writes, "Observing the products of the video culture you come to see why the Greeks insisted that actors wear masks, and that all violence take place behind the scenes." It is possible, in other words, to see too much, and in the seeing lose our grasp on what is real. Television is the perfect vehicle for this experience, since it bombards us with shocking, stimulating, and pleasant images, all the while keeping us at a safe remove from what we are seeing.

But the power the moving image now exercises over modern American life has grown considerably in recent years. It is as if the Jumbotron television screen that looms over Times Square in New York has replicated and installed itself permanently in public space. Large screens broadcasting any number of images and advertisements can be found in most sports arenas, restaurants, and shopping malls; they even appear in a growing number of larger churches. The dentist's and doctor's office are no longer safe havens from a barrage of images and sounds. A walk through an airport terminal is now a gauntlet of moving images, as televisions bolted into ceilings or walls blare vacuous segments from

CNN's dedicated "airport programming"; once on board a plane, we're treated to nonstop displays of movies and TV options like "NBC In Flight." The ubiquity of television sets in public space is often explained as an attempt to entertain and distract, but in fact it seems more successful at annoyance or anesthetization. For people who wish to travel, eat, or pray in silence, there are few options beyond the deliciously subversive "TV-B-Gone" device, a universal remote control the size of a key chain that allows users to turn off televisions in public places. Considering the number of televisions currently in use, however, it would take an army of TV-B-Gone users to restore peace and quiet in public space.

One of the more startling developments in recent years is the moving   40
image's interjection into the classical concert hall. In 2004, the New York Philharmonic experimented with a 15-by-20-foot screen that projected enormous images of the musicians and conductor to the audience during performances of Wagner and Brahms. The orchestra trustee who encouraged the project was blunt about his motivation: "We want to increase attendance at concerts, change the demographics," he told the *New York Times*. "And the younger generation is more responsive to visual stimuli." A classical music industry consultant echoed the sentiment. "We have to recognize that this is a visual generation," he said. "They are used to seeing things more than they are used to hearing things." Symphonies in Vancouver, San Diego, Omaha, Atlanta, and Philadelphia have all tried using moving images during concerts, and some orchestras are resorting to gimmicks such as projecting works of art during performances of Mussorgsky's "Pictures at an Exhibition," or broadcasting images of space during Holst's "The Planets."

Among those less than pleased with the triumph of the moving image in the concert hall are the musicians themselves, who are haplessly being transformed into video stars. "I found it very distracting," a violinist with the New York Philharmonic said. "People might as well stay home with their big-screen TVs," said another resignedly. "It's going the route of MTV, and I'm not sure it's the way to go." What these musicians are expressing is a concern for the eclipse of their music, which often requires discipline and concentration to appreciate, by imagery. The images, flashing across a large screen above their heads, demand far less of their audience's active attention than the complicated notes and chords, rhythms and patterns, coming from their instruments. The capitulation of the concert hall to the moving image suggests that in an image-based culture, art will only be valuable insofar as it can be marketed as entertainment. The moving image redefines all other forms of expression in its image, often leaving us impoverished in the process.

BRAIN CANDY

Concern about the long-term effects of being saturated by moving images is not merely the expression of quasi-Luddite angst or cultural conservatism. It has a basis in what the neurosciences are teaching us about the brain and how it processes images. Images can have a profound physiological impact on those who view them. Dr. Steven Most, a postdoctoral fellow at Yale University, recently found that graphic images can "blind" us by briefly impairing the brain, often for as long as one-fifth of a second. As his fellow researcher explained to *Discovery News*: "Brain mechanisms that help us to attend to things become tied up by the provocative image, unable to orient to other stimuli."

Another study by researchers at the Center for Cognitive Science at Ohio State University found that, for young children, sound was actually more riveting than images — overwhelmingly so, in some cases. The research findings, which were published in *Child Development*, showed that "children seem to be able to process only one type of stimuli at a time" and that "for infants, sounds are preferred almost exclusively," a preference that continues up until at least age four. In their book *Imagination and Play in the Electronic Age*, Dorothy and Jerome Singer argue that "the electronic media of television, film and video games now may contribute to the child's development of an autonomous ongoing consciousness but with particular constraints. Looking and listening alone without other sensory inducements," they write, "can be misleading guides to action."

Research into the function of the primary visual cortex region of the brain suggests that it is not alarmist to assume that constant visual stimulation of the sort broadcast on television might have profound effects on the brains of children, whose neurological function continues to develop throughout childhood and adolescence. One study conducted at the University of Rochester and published in the journal *Nature* in 2004, involved, weirdly enough, tracking the visual processing patterns of ferrets that were forced to watch the movie *The Matrix*. The researchers found some surprising things: The adult ferrets "had neural patterns in their visual cortex that correlated very well with images they viewed," according to a summary of the research, "but that correlation didn't exist at all in very young ferrets, suggesting the very basis of comprehending vision may be a very different task for young brains versus old brains." The younger ferrets were "taking in and processing visual stimuli" just like the adult ferrets, but they were "not processing the stimuli in a way that reflects reality."

These kinds of findings have led to warnings about the long-term nega-   45
tive impact of moving images on young minds. A study published in 2004 in the journal *Pediatrics*, for example, found a clear link between early television viewing and later problems such as attention deficit/hyperactivity disorder, and recent research has suggested troubling, near-term effects on behavior for young players of violent video games. In short: moving images — ubiquitous in homes and public spaces — pose challenges to healthy development when they become the primary object of children's attention. Inculcating the young into the image culture may be bad for their brains.

THE CLOSING OF THE POWERPOINT MIND

A culture that raises its children on the milk of the moving image should not be surprised when they prove unwilling to wean themselves from it as adults. Nowhere is the evidence of this more apparent than in the business world, which has become enamored of and obedient to a particular image technology: the computer software program PowerPoint.

PowerPoint, a program included in the popular Microsoft Office suite of software, allows users to create visual presentations using slide templates and graphics that can be projected from a computer onto a larger screen for an audience's benefit. The addition of an "AutoContent Wizard," which is less a magician than an electronic duenna, helpfully ushers the user through an array of existing templates, suggesting bullet points and summaries and images. Its ease of use has made PowerPoint a reliable and ubiquitous presence at board meetings and conferences worldwide.

In recent years, however, PowerPoint's reach has extended beyond the business office. People have used PowerPoint slides at their wedding receptions to depict their courtship as a series of "priority points" and pictures. Elementary-school children are using the software to craft bullet-point-riddled book reports and class presentations. As a 2001 story in the *New York Times* reported, "69 percent of teachers who use Microsoft software use PowerPoint in their classrooms."

Despite its widespread use, PowerPoint has spawned criticism almost from its inception, and has been called everything from a disaster to a virus. Some claim the program aids sophistry. As a chief scientist at Sun Microsystems put it: "It gives you a persuasive sheen of authenticity that can cover a complete lack of honesty." Others have argued that it deadens discussion and allows presenters with little to say to cover up their ignorance with constantly flashing images and bullet points. Frustration with PowerPoint has grown so widespread that in 2003, the *New Yorker* published a cartoon that illustrated a typical job interview in hell. In it, the devil asks his applicant: "I need someone well versed in the art of torture — do you know PowerPoint?"

People subjected endlessly to PowerPoint presentations complain about   50 its oddly chilling effect on thought and discussion and the way the constantly changing slides easily distract attention from the substance of a speaker's presentation. These concerns prompted Scott McNealy, the chairman of Sun Microsystems, to forbid his employees from using PowerPoint in the late 1990s. But it was the exegesis of the PowerPoint mindset published by Yale emeritus professor Edward Tufte in 2003 that remains the most thorough challenge to this image-heavy, analytically weak technology. In a slim pamphlet titled *The Cognitive Style of PowerPoint*, Tufte argued that PowerPoint's dizzying array of templates and slides "weaken verbal and spatial reasoning, and almost always corrupt statistical analysis." Because PowerPoint is "presenter-oriented" rather than content or audience-oriented, Tufte wrote, it fosters a "cognitive style" characterized by "foreshortening of evidence and thought, low spatial reasoning . . . rapid temporal sequencing of thin information . . . conspicuous decoration . . . a preoccupation with format not content, [and] an attitude of commercialism that turns everything into a sales pitch." PowerPoint, Tufte concluded, is "faux-analytical."

Tufte's criticism of PowerPoint made use of a tragic but effective example: the space shuttle Columbia disaster. When NASA engineers evaluated the safety of the shuttle, which had reached orbit but faced risks upon reentry due to tiles that had been damaged by loose foam during launch, they used PowerPoint slides to illustrate their reasoning — an unfortunate decision that led to very poor technical communication. The Columbia Accident Investigation Board later cited "the endemic use of PowerPoint briefing slides instead of technical papers as an illustration of the problematic methods of technical communication at NASA." Rather than simply a tool that aids thought, PowerPoint changes the way we think, forcing us to express ourselves in terms of its own functionalities and protocols. As a result, only that which can be said using PowerPoint is worth saying at all.

PSEUDO-EVENTS AND PSEUDO-CULTURE

Although PowerPoint had not yet been created when he published his book, *The Image*, in 1961, historian Daniel Boorstin was nevertheless prescient in his warnings about the dangers of a culture that entrusted its rational decision-making to the image. By elevating image over substance and form over content, Boorstin argued that society was at risk of substituting "pseudo-events" for real life and personal image-making for real virtue. (He described in detail new efforts to create public images for the famous and not-so-famous, a process well illustrated by a Canon Camera commercial of several years ago that featured tennis star Andre Agassi insouciantly stating, "Image is everything.")

"The pseudo-events which flood our consciousness are neither true nor false in the old familiar senses," Boorstin wrote, but they have created a world "where fantasy is more real than reality, where the image has more dignity than its original." The result was a culture of "synthetic heroes, prefabricated tourist attractions, [and] homogenized interchangeable forms of art and literature." Images were wildly popular, Boorstin conceded, but they were, in fact, little different from illusions. "We risk being the first people in history to have been able to make their illusions so vivid, so persuasive, so 'realistic' that they can live in them," he wrote.

Other critics followed Boorstin. In *The Disappearance of Childhood*, Neil Postman wrote about the way the "electronic and graphic revolutions" launched an "uncoordinated but powerful assault on language and literacy, a recasting of the world of ideas into speed-of-light icons and images." Images, Postman worried, "ask us to feel, not to think." French critic Roland Barthes fretted that "the image no longer illustrates the words; it is now the words which, structurally, are parasitic on the image." In a more recent iteration of the same idea, technology critic Paul Virilio identified a "great threat to the word" in the "evocative power of the screen." "It is real time that threatens writing," he noted, "once the image is live, there is a conflict between deferred time and real time, and in this there is a serious threat to writing and to the author."

Real events are now compared to those of sitcom characters; real tra-   55
gedies or accidents are described as being "just like a movie" (a practice Susan Sontag first noticed in the 1970s). Even the imagination is often crippled by our image-based culture. For every creative artists (like Gursky) using Photoshop there is a plethora of posturing and shallow artists like Damien Hirst, who once proudly told an interviewer that he spent more time "watching TV than ever I did in the galleries."

Is it possible to find a balance between naïve techno-enthusiasm for the image culture and the "spirit of bulldog opacity," as McLuhan described it, which fueled undue skepticism about new technologies in the past? Perhaps devotees of the written word will eventually form a dwindling guild, pensioned off by universities and governments and think tanks to live out their days in quiet obscurity as the purveyors of the image culture expand their reach. But concern about a culture of the image has a rich history, and neither side can yet claim victory. In the preface to his book, *The Essence of Christianity*, published in 1843, Feuerbach complained that his own era "prefers the image to the thing, the copy to the original, the representation to the reality, appearance to being."

Techno-enthusiasts are fond of reminding us, as if relating a quaint tale of reason's triumph over superstition, that new technologies have always stirred controversy. The printing press unnerved the scholastic philosophers and religious scribes whose lives were paced to the tempo of the manuscript; later, the telephone was indicted by a cadre fearful of its threat to conviviality and face-to-face communication, and so on. The laborious copiers of manuscripts did indeed fear the printing press, and some traditionalists did vigorously resist the intrusions of the telephone. But at a time of great social hierarchy, much of this was driven by an elite disdain for the democratizing influence of these technologies and their potential for overturning social conventions (which indeed many of them did). Contemporary criticism of our image-saturated culture is not criticism of the means by which we create images (cameras, television, video). No one would seriously argue for the elimination of such technologies, as those who feared Gutenberg's invention did when they destroyed printing presses. The critique is an expression of concern about the ends of an image-based culture, and our unwillingness as yet to consider whether those ends might be what we truly want for our society.

Nor is concern about the image culture merely a fear of losing our grip on what is familiar — that known world with its long history of reliance on the printed word. Those copyists who feared the printing press were not wrong to believe that it would render them obsolete. It did. But contemporary critics who question the proliferation of images in culture and who fear that the sheer number of images will undermine the sensibility that creates readers of the written word (replacing them with clever but shallow interpreters of the image) aren't worried about being usurped by image-makers. They are motivated largely by the hope of preserving what is left of their craft. They are more like the conservationist who has made the forest his home only to discover, to his surprise, that the animals with which he shares it are rapidly dwindling in number. What he wants to know, in his perplexed state, is not "how do I retreat deeper into the forest?" but "how might I preserve the few survivors before all record of them is lost?"

So it is with those who resist an image-based culture. As its boosters suggest, it is here to stay, and likely to grow more powerful as time goes on, making all of us virtual flâneurs* strolling down boulevards filled with digital images and moving pictures. We will, of course, be enormously entertained by these images, and many of them will tell us stories in new and exciting ways. At the same time, however, we will have lost something profound: the ability to marshal words to describe the ambiguities of life and the sources of our ideas; the possibility of conveying to others, with the subtlety, precision, and poetry of the written word, why particular events or people affect us as they do; and the capacity, through language, to distill the deeper meaning of common experience. We will become a society of a million pictures without much memory, a society that looks forward every second to an immediate replication of what it has just done, but one that does not sustain the difficult labor of transmitting culture from one generation to the next.

Reading across Disciplines
TREENA CROCHET, Art History

Throughout history, images have wielded enormous power over those who created them, collected them, interpreted them, and rebuked them. But that doesn't mean that images have always allowed viewers to trust what they see. As Christine Rosen notes, art of the past was often believed to have magical properties or other great powers. Examples range from early cave paintings, expected not just to depict but to ensure a successful hunt, to colossal statues of ancient Egyptian pharaohs, created as a reminder to subjects of the pharaohs' authority, and also to the European Renaissance's use of oversized portraits and sculptures of

---

flâneur: an aimless loafer

royalty and church leaders, placed in town plazas and church entrances where they would be seen daily, to provide a constant reminder to ordinary people of who was in control.

In more recent centuries, images have continued to serve as useful tools for arousing emotional responses in viewers. Francisco Goya's painting *The Third of May, 1808* (1814) and Pablo Picasso's *Guernica* (1937) used imagery as propaganda against the invasions of Napoleon and Hitler, respectively. Goya's depiction of unarmed Spaniards being shot down by a firing squad of French soldiers evoked sympathy for the resistance and outrage against Napoleon's army. Picasso included dismembered human body parts — abstracted forms, but nevertheless identifiable — and other horrifying images in *Guernica* to denounce Hitler's bombing campaigns. And of course, propaganda films, cartoons, posters, and other print and digital images were widely used on all sides to influence public opinion in twentieth-century wars.

We are indeed always surrounded by images as we go about our daily lives, but this is not so different from the experiences of those in centuries past. The manipulation of images is nothing new, either. Those who lived in ancient Rome were not deceived by sculptures of aging Emperors who were always depicted in their youthful prime. And Joseph Stalin, who removed the evidence of his enemies through photographic retouching, followed in the footsteps of the many new ruling pharaohs of Egypt who eradicated images of their predecessors.

Rosen expresses concern that an increasingly image-based culture may lose "something profound: the ability to marshal words to describe the ambiguities of life and the sources of our ideas; the possibility of conveying to others, with the subtlety, precision, and poetry of the written word, why particular events or people affect us as they do; and the capacity, through language, to distill the deeper meaning of common experience." However, the presence of images — whether truthful or manipulated — in many cultures has inspired verbal communication rather than repressed it. The eighteenth-century philosopher Denis Diderot wrote essays about his views of art and society. Those of us living in the twenty-first century may be less likely to write essays, but writing is not lost to us. We are simply more likely to address the constant barrage of visual experience in other kinds of writing, such as email and blogs.

Treena Crochet, a historian of art and architecture and the author of many books on architecture and interior design, has taught for twenty years in colleges in the United States and the Middle East.

QUESTIONING THE TEXT

1. In the last paragraph of her article, Rosen details the decline of the power of language and suggests that an image-based culture will become "one that does not sustain the difficult labor of transmitting culture from one generation to the next." Indeed, concern about how cultural transmission will take place seems to form the heart of her argument. How valid are her concerns? How accurately does she describe your experience? Are you at risk of not understanding the culture that you are part of? Why or why not?

2. Reread paragraphs 31–37, where Rosen discusses the ideas of Steven Johnson and Mitchell Stephens. Why does Rosen engage with these arguments that are different from hers? Do you think that she effectively addresses these differing ideas? Or do their claims risk overpowering her claims? Be prepared to defend your reasoning in a discussion with your classmates.

MAKING CONNECTIONS

3. Rosen writes, "Sight is our most powerful sense, much more dominant in translating experience than taste, touch, or hearing" (paragraph 5). In "My Bionic Quest for *Boléro*," Michael Chorost quotes Helen Keller saying that if forced to choose between blindness and deafness, she'd choose blindness "because while blindness cut her off from things, deafness cut her off from people" (p. 294). Which claim about the power of the senses do you find more compelling? Why?

4. Compare Rosen's article to the selection from Mary Shelley's *Frankenstein* (p. 285). How does each piece express reservations about knowledge and technology? What differences and similarities do you see in their approaches?

JOINING THE CONVERSATION

5. Rosen brings up the software program PowerPoint as especially dangerous to how people think (paragraphs 46–51). If you have ever created a PowerPoint presentation, look over that document; if not, download one that a professor has prepared for a course, either at your school or at another college or university (a few minutes of Web searching will quickly turn up an example). Study the presentation carefully. Can you see ways that it inhibits thinking, or do you think that it effectively

condenses information for presentation? Write an essay that analyzes the presentation and either defends or attacks the usefulness of PowerPoint.

6. Put Rosen's claims to the test and create a PowerPoint presentation that summarizes her argument in "The Image Culture." At the end of the summary, include a few slides that consider what was lost and what was gained by translating her text into the new format.

The photo on the preceding page shows a pair of identical twins who seem to share a similar "thrift-store chic" taste in clothing, hair, and makeup. What do you think might motivate these women to dress in ways that stand out a bit from the crowd? What reasons might they have for nevertheless choosing to look so much like each other? ■ In which situations do you find being very much like others enjoyable? In which situations do you want to stand apart from the group? Can you draw any conclusions from your responses? ■ How can being part of a group help — and hinder — the creation of a person's unique identity? ■ What does *identity* mean to you? Does it mean one thing or many things? Does the meaning of *identity* vary from situation to situation? Explain your views.

"AND WHO ARE YOU?" a talkative snail asks Alice, the heroine of *Alice in Wonderland*, who replies, "I — I hardly know, sir, just at present — at least I know who I was when I got up this morning, but I think I must have been changed several times since then." Little wonder that Marshall McLuhan concludes his *The Medium Is the Massage* with this exchange, since in that book he argues that "electronic technology . . . is forcing us to reconsider and reevaluate practically every thought, every action, and every institution formerly taken for granted. Everything is changing — you, your family, your neighborhood, your education, your job, your government, your relation to 'the others.' And they're changing dramatically." Most of all, McLuhan insists, our ideas about who we are — our very identities — are changing.

What may be surprising to you is that McLuhan published those words in 1967, four decades before you take them up in this text. And those forty years have seen many of McLuhan's claims borne out, particularly in the threat of electronic surveillance and a concomitant loss of privacy. Would McLuhan be surprised by the kinds of "identity theft" taking place today — such as online trickery or in warring countries, where people evicted from their homes for political and religious reasons are often stripped of all papers and thus left with no official identity? We don't think so.

But have our very ideas of identity changed? Many believe that they have — or that they are doing so right now. The view of self as autonomous, coherent, and unifying, a view associated with both eighteenth-century rationalism and Romanticism, for example, has been challenged on many fronts. In place of this singular, solitary self (celebrated in dramatic and unforgettable terms in Walt Whitman's "Song of Myself" and many other works of literature), multiple alternatives have emerged: a socially constructed self that grows up through a series of negotiations with others and with the environment; a self fashioned by forces beyond the control of the individual; and, most recently, a "virtual" self or selves that may (or may not) coalesce into one individual. In turn, these theoretical debates have left many wondering just how identity *is* constituted.

The selections in this chapter all circle around questions of identity formation. Is it related primarily to a genetic base? To gender, sexuality, and religion? To nation-state and politics? To race and ethnicity? To marketing? To language — or to any number of other crucially important sources of influence in individuals' lives, such as work, physical abilities, and so on? Looking back over our own lives, we can see ways in which our sense of identity has shifted over the decades; we can identify as well periods of tension in terms of identity, particularly during moments of great change or loss. Yet on most days, we'd probably respond to the question "Who are you?" not as Alice did but with the simple statement of our names. What's in a name? And what's in an identity?

We believe you have already thought quite a lot about these issues. To add to that thinking, consider the following questions:

- What things in your surroundings do you most closely identify with — family, friends, church, team, some other group — and why?

- Can you recall a time when someone identified you in some way that seemed completely surprising or foreign to you? If so, describe that time.

- How would you define your identity? Where do your identifying characteristics or features come from? How many "selves" can you identify in yourself?

•   •   •

SOJOURNER TRUTH
Ain't I a Woman?

*S*OJOURNER *T*RUTH *(1797–1883) took her name from mystical visions that urged her, after her escape from slavery, to sojourn and speak the truth. Although she never learned to write on paper, the words of her speeches often wrote on her listeners' souls. The following speech was written down by Elizabeth Cady Stanton (whose account differs from other renditions of the famous speech), an early proponent of women's rights, and printed in* The History of Woman Suffrage. *Truth delivered it at the Women's Rights Convention in Akron, Ohio, in 1851. On that occasion she spoke to an almost all-white audience, since African Americans were, ironically, not welcome at such events. In "Ain't I a Woman?" Truth claims her identity as a woman — and as equal to men. In doing so, she speaks not just for women but for many who are oppressed, combining her devotion to abolitionism and to women's suffrage. With vigor and humor, she argues for basic human rights as one feature of identity among "all God's children."*

This brief speech always reminds me of the power of the spoken word — and of the difference one voice can sometimes make. I love Truth's use of some of the colloquialisms I grew up with (like "out of kilter"), her familiar references to those in her audience as "honey" and "children," and other aspects of her speaking style that help me feel as though she is right here in front of me talking. I chose this speech for these reasons and because Truth counters perfectly all those voices down through the ages that have dismissed people such as her as "just" women. To hear her rebuttal, and to get at some of this speech's rhythmic power, try reading it aloud. —A.L.

Well, children, where there is so much racket there must be something out of kilter. I think that 'twixt the negroes of the South and the women of the North, all talking about rights, the white men will be in a fix pretty soon. But what's all this here talking about?

That man over there says that women need to be helped into carriages, and lifted over ditches, and to have the best place everywhere. Nobody ever helps me into carriages, or over mud-puddles, or gives me any best place! And ain't I a woman? Look at me! Look at my arm! I have ploughed and planted, and gathered into barns, and no man could head me! And ain't I a woman? I could work as much and eat as much as a man — when I could get it — and bear the lash as well! And ain't I a woman? I have borne thirteen children, and seen them most all sold off to slavery, and when I cried out with my mother's grief, none but Jesus heard me! And ain't I a woman?

Then they talk about this thing in the head; what's this they call it? [Intellect, someone whispers.] That's it, honey. What's that got to do with women's rights or negro's rights? If my cup won't hold but a pint, and yours holds a quart, wouldn't you be mean not to let me have my little half-measure full?

Then that little man in black there, he says women can't have as much rights as men, 'cause Christ wasn't a woman! Where did your Christ come from? Where did your Christ come from? From God and a woman! Man had nothing to do with Him.

If the first woman God ever made was strong enough to turn the world   5 upside down all alone, these women together ought to be able to turn it back, and get it right side up again! And now they is asking to do it, the men better let them.

Obliged to you for hearing me, and now old Sojourner ain't got nothing more to say.

QUESTIONING THE TEXT

1. Truth punctuates her speech with a rhetorical question — "And ain't I a woman?" What effect does the repetition of this question have on you as a reader? What answer does Truth invoke?

2. A.L.'s introduction reveals that she is a fan of Sojourner Truth. What criticisms *could* A.L. have leveled at Truth's argument?

MAKING CONNECTIONS

3. How might Sojourner Truth respond to Dave Barry's "Guys vs. Men" (p. 405)? Read that selection. Then, using Truth's humorous and conversational tone, write a brief speech in which she responds to "Guys vs. Men."

4. Several other selections in this chapter deal with the ways in which part of one's identity brings forth discrimination, bias, oppression. Choose one of these other selections, and read it carefully after rereading Truth's speech. What arguments can you find in common between Truth and the other author you chose? What differences in evidence and in argumentative strategy do you detect?

JOINING THE CONVERSATION

5. List as many reasons as you can to support the belief that men and women should or should not have the same rights and responsibilities. Explain from your own experiences *why* you believe as you do.

6. Try your hand at writing your own manifesto of identity, using a repeated question (such as "And ain't I a _____?") to organize your brief piece of writing.

ANDREW SULLIVAN
The End of Gay Culture

LIKE LOTS OF BRIGHT PEOPLE, *writer and editor Andrew Sullivan (b. 1963) spins out ideas almost faster than he can think them and does so with jaw-dropping style and clarity. Jonah Goldberg, poking fun at Sullivan's blog, once complained that "the intervals between self-contradictory statements by Sullivan has fallen to a mere 22 minutes. Pretty soon the ends of his sentences will contradict the beginnings." Perhaps that's one consequence of writing so prolifically on issues from across the cultural and political spectrum.*

But when Sullivan, a former editor of The New Republic *whose essays and op-eds have also appeared in the* Wall Street Journal, *the* New York Times Book Review, *the* Sunday Times *of London, and* Slate, *is hitting on all cylinders, as is the case in "The End of Gay Culture" (Atlantic Monthly, October 24, 2005), few political writers are more lucid or formidable.*

As the title of his essay suggests, Sullivan examines the transformations gay culture has experienced during the thirty years in which it has had a public identity in the United States. Originally centered on "baths and bars," the culture transformed itself radically at the beginning of the AIDs epidemic, when, contrary to most expectations, gay men and women realized that their survival required them to go public with their politics and identity. Since then, Sullivan notes with wonder, a whole new generation of gay people has grown up "in a world where homosexuality was no longer a taboo subject." And so, having succeeded in persuading most straight Americans that homosexuality is, to echo the title of an earlier Sullivan book, "virtually normal," gay men and women now face a future in which their sexual choices might become a mere aspect of their lives rather than the defining element. And, ironically, this cultural mainstreaming, at least in some regions of the United States, will likely wear away the traditional elements of gay culture, leaving in place a more diverse and yet more conventional gay civil society. For example, Sullivan argues that gay and straight teenagers are already routinely indistinguishable.

In describing gay culture, however, Sullivan is also exposing the way other minority groups constitute their identities within a world alternately welcoming and hostile to their differences. Indeed, Sullivan points to the irony that among the groups still most reluctant to grant gays a place at the national table are other groups that have been routinely marginalized: Blacks, Latinos, and Catholics. And, of course, there are many gay men and women within these groups not enjoying the social transformations he describes in his vivid portrait of Provincetown.

"The End of Gay Culture" itself crosses all sorts of boundaries as a piece of writing — it is part memoir, report, argument, and manifesto, filled with claims and evidence that pull readers along. It is rich enough to be occasionally paradoxical. But that's not the same thing as contradictory. —J.R.   **381**

For the better part of two decades, I have spent much of every summer in the small resort of Provincetown, at the tip of Cape Cod. It has long attracted artists, writers, the offbeat, and the bohemian; and, for many years now, it has been to gay America what Oak Bluffs in Martha's Vineyard is to black America: a place where a separate identity essentially defines a separate place. No one bats an eye if two men walk down the street holding hands, or if a lesbian couple pecks each other on the cheek, or if a drag queen dressed as Cher careens down the main strip on a motor scooter. It's a place, in that respect, that is sui generis. Except that it isn't anymore. As gay America has changed, so, too, has Provincetown. In a microcosm of what is happening across this country, its culture is changing.

Some of these changes are obvious. A real-estate boom has made Provincetown far more expensive than it ever was, slowly excluding poorer and younger visitors and residents. Where, once, gayness trumped class, now the reverse is true. Beautiful, renovated houses are slowly outnumbering beach shacks, once crammed with twenty-something, hand-to-mouth misfits or artists. The role of lesbians in the town's civic and cultural life has grown dramatically, as it has in the broader gay world. The faces of people dying from or struggling with AIDS have dwindled to an unlucky few. The number of children of gay couples has soared, and, some weeks, strollers clog the sidewalks. Bar life is not nearly as central to socializing as it once was. Men and women gather on the beach, drink coffee on the front porch of a store, or meet at the Film Festival or Spiritus Pizza.

And, of course, week after week this summer, couple after couple got married — well over a thousand in the year and a half since gay marriage has been legal in Massachusetts. Outside my window on a patch of beach that somehow became impromptu hallowed ground, I watched dozens get hitched — under a chuppah or with a priest, in formalwear or beach clothes, some with New Age drums and horns, even one associated with a full-bore Mass. Two friends lit the town monument in purple to celebrate; a tuxedoed male couple slipping onto the beach was suddenly greeted with a huge cheer from the crowd; an elderly lesbian couple attached cans to the back of their Volkswagen and honked their horn as they drove up the high street. The heterosexuals in the crowd knew exactly what to do. They waved and cheered and smiled. Then, suddenly, as if learning the habits of a new era, gay bystanders joined in. In an instant, the difference between gay and straight receded again a little.

But here's the strange thing: These changes did not feel like a revolution. They felt merely like small, if critical, steps in an inexorable evolution toward the end of a distinctive gay culture. For what has happened to Provincetown this past decade, as with gay America as a whole, has been less like a political revolution from above than a social transformation from below. There is no single gay identity anymore, let alone a single look or style or culture. Memorial Day sees the younger generation of lesbians, looking like lost members of a boy band, with their baseball caps, preppy shirts, short hair, and earrings. Independence Day brings the partiers: the "circuit boys," with perfect torsos, a thirst for nightlife, designer drugs, and countless bottles of water. For a week in mid-July, the town is dominated by "bears" — chubby, hairy, unkempt men with an affinity for beer and pizza. Family Week heralds an influx of children and harried gay parents. Film Festival Week brings in the artsy crowd. Women's Week brings the more familiar images of older lesbians: a landlocked flotilla of windbreakers and sensible shoes. East Village bohemians drift in throughout the summer; quiet male couples spend more time browsing gourmet groceries and realtors than cruising nightspots; the predictable population of artists and writers — Michael Cunningham and John Waters are fixtures — mix with openly gay lawyers and cops and teachers and shrinks.

Slowly but unmistakably, gay culture is ending. You see it beyond the   5
poignant transformation of P-town: on the streets of the big cities, on university campuses, in the suburbs where gay couples have settled, and in the entrails of the Internet. In fact, it is beginning to dawn on many that the very concept of gay culture may one day disappear altogether. By that, I do not mean that homosexual men and lesbians will not exist — or that they won't create a community of sorts and a culture that sets them in some ways apart. I mean simply that what encompasses gay culture itself will expand into such a diverse set of subcultures that "gayness" alone will cease to tell you very much about any individual. The distinction between gay and straight culture will become so blurred, so fractured, and so intermingled that it may become more helpful not to examine them separately at all.

For many in the gay world, this is both a triumph and a threat. It is a triumph because it is what we always dreamed of: a world in which being gay is a nonissue among our families, friends, and neighbors. But it is a threat in the way that all loss is a threat. For many of us who grew up fighting a world of now-inconceivable silence and shame, distinctive gayness became an integral part of who we are. It helped define us not only to the world but also to ourselves. Letting that go is as hard as it is liberating, as saddening as it is invigorating. And, while social advance allows many of us to contemplate this gift of a problem, we are also aware that in other parts of the country and the world, the reverse may be happening. With the growth of fundamentalism across the religious world — from Pope Benedict XVI's Vatican to Islamic fatwas and American evangelicalism — gayness is under attack in many places, even as it wrests free from repression in others. In fact, the two phenomena are related. The new anti-gay fervor is a response to the growing probability that the world will one day treat gay and straight as interchangeable humans and citizens rather than as estranged others. It is the end of gay culture — not its endurance — that threatens the old order. It is the fact that, across the state of Massachusetts, "gay marriage" has just been abolished. The marriage licenses gay couples receive are indistinguishable from those given to straight couples. On paper, the difference is now history. In the real world, the consequences of that are still unfolding.

Quite how this has happened (and why) are questions that historians will fight over someday, but certain influences seem clear even now — chief among them the HIV epidemic. Before AIDS hit, a fragile but nascent gay world had formed in a handful of major U.S. cities. The gay culture that exploded from it in the 1970s had the force of something long suppressed, and it coincided with a more general relaxation of social norms. This was the era of the post-Stonewall New Left, of the Castro and the West Village, an era where sexuality forged a new meaning for gayness: of sexual adventure, political radicalism, and cultural revolution.

The fact that openly gay communities were still relatively small and geographically concentrated in a handful of urban areas created a distinctive gay culture. The central institutions for gay men were baths and bars, places where men met each other in highly sexualized contexts and where sex provided the commonality. Gay resorts had their heyday — from Provincetown to Key West. The gay press grew quickly and was centered around classified personal ads or bar and bath advertising. Popular culture was suffused with stunning displays of homosexual burlesque: the music of Queen, the costumes of the Village People, the flamboyance of Elton John's debut; the advertising of Calvin Klein; and the intoxication of disco itself, a gay creation that became emblematic of an entire heterosexual era. When this cultural explosion was acknowledged, when it explicitly penetrated the mainstream, the results, however, were highly unstable: Harvey Milk was assassinated in San Francisco and Anita Bryant led an anti-gay crusade. But the emergence of an openly gay culture, however vulnerable, was still real.

And then, of course, catastrophe. The history of gay America as an openly gay culture is not only extremely short — a mere 30 years or so — but also engulfed and defined by a plague that struck almost poignantly at the headiest moment of liberation. The entire structure of emergent gay culture — sexual, radical, subversive — met a virus that killed almost everyone it touched. Virtually the entire generation that pioneered gay culture was wiped out — quickly. Even now, it is hard to find a solid phalanx of gay men in their fifties, sixties, or seventies — men who fought from Stonewall or before for public recognition and cultural change. And those who survived the nightmare of the 1980s to mid-'90s were often overwhelmed merely with coping with plague; or fearing it themselves; or fighting for research or awareness or more effective prevention.

This astonishing story might not be believed in fiction. And, in fiction, it   10
might have led to the collapse of such a new, fragile subculture. AIDS could have been widely perceived as a salutary retribution for the gay revolution; it could have led to quarantining or the collapse of nascent gay institutions. Instead, it had the opposite effect. The tens of thousands of deaths of men from every part of the country established homosexuality as a legitimate topic more swiftly than any political manifesto could possibly have done. The images of gay male lives were recorded on quilts and in countless obituaries; men whose homosexuality might have been euphemized into nonexistence were immediately identifiable and gone. And those gay men and lesbians who witnessed this entire event became altered forever, not only emotionally, but also politically — whether through the theatrical activism of Act-Up or the furious

organization of political gays among the Democrats and some Republicans. More crucially, gay men and lesbians built civil institutions to counter the disease; they forged new ties to scientists and politicians; they found themselves forced into more intense relations with their own natural families and the families of loved ones. Where bath houses once brought gay men together, now it was memorial services. The emotional and psychic bonding became the core of a new identity. The plague provided a unifying social and cultural focus.

But it also presaged a new direction. That direction was unmistakably outward and integrative. To borrow a useful distinction deployed by the writer Bruce Bawer, integration did not necessarily mean assimilation. It was not a wholesale rejection of the gay past, as some feared and others hoped. Gay men wanted to be fully part of the world, but not at the expense of their own sexual freedom (and safer sex became a means not to renounce that freedom but to save it). What the epidemic revealed was how gay men — and, by inference, lesbians — could not seal themselves off from the rest of society. They needed scientific research, civic support, and political lobbying to survive, in this case literally. The lesson was not that sexual liberation was mistaken, but rather that it wasn't enough. Unless the gay population was tied into the broader society; unless it had roots in the wider world; unless it brought into its fold the heterosexual families and friends of gay men women, the gay population would remain at the mercy of others and of misfortune. A ghetto was no longer an option.

So, when the plague receded in the face of far more effective HIV treatments in the mid-'90s and gay men and women were able to catch their breath and reflect, the question of what a more integrated gay culture might actually mean reemerged. For a while, it arrived in a vacuum. Most of the older male generation was dead or exhausted; and so it was only natural, perhaps, that the next generation of leaders tended to be lesbian — running the major gay political groups and magazines. Lesbians also pioneered a new baby boom, with more lesbian couples adopting or having children. HIV-positive gay men developed different strategies for living suddenly posthumous lives. Some retreated into quiet relationships; others quit jobs or changed their careers completely; others choose the escapism of what became known as "the circuit," a series of rave parties around the country and the world where fears could be lost on the drug-enhanced dance floor; others still became lost in a suicidal vortex of crystal meth, Internet hook-ups, and sex addiction. HIV-negative men, many of whom had lost husbands and friends, were not so different. In some ways, the toll was greater. They had survived disaster with their health intact. But, unlike their HIV-positive friends, the threat of contracting the disease still existed while they battled survivors' guilt. The plague was over but not over; and, as they saw men with HIV celebrate survival, some even felt shut out of a new sub-sub-culture, suspended between fear and triumph but unable to experience either fully.

Then something predictable and yet unexpected happened. While the older generation struggled with plague and post-plague adjustment, the next generation was growing up. For the first time, a cohort of gay children and teens grew up in a world where homosexuality was no longer a taboo subject and where gay figures were regularly featured in the press. If the image of gay men for my generation was one gleaned from the movie *Cruising* or, subsequently, *Torch Song Trilogy*, the image for the next one was MTV's "Real World," Bravo's "Queer Eye," and Richard Hatch winning the first "Survivor." The new emphasis was on the interaction between gays and straights and on the diversity of gay life and lives. Movies featured and integrated gayness. Even more dramatically, gays went from having to find hidden meaning in mainstream films — somehow identifying with the aging, campy female lead in a way the rest of the culture missed — to everyone, gay and straight, recognizing and being in on the joke of a character like "Big Gay Al" from "South Park" or Jack from "Will & Grace."

There are now openly gay legislators. Ditto Olympic swimmers and gymnasts and Wimbledon champions. Mainstream entertainment figures — from George Michael, Ellen DeGeneres, and Rosie O'Donnell to edgy musicians, such as the Scissor Sisters, Rufus Wainwright, or Bob Mould — now have their sexual orientation as a central, but not defining, part of their identity. The National Lesbian and Gay Journalists Association didn't exist when I became a journalist. Now it has 1,300 dues-paying members in 24 chapters around the country. Among Fortune 500 companies, 21 provided domestic partner benefits for gay spouses in 1995. Today, 216 do. Of the top Fortune 50 companies, 49 provide nondiscrimination protections for gay employees. Since 2002, the number of corporations providing full protections for openly gay employees has increased sevenfold, according to the Human Rights Campaign (HRC). Among the leaders: the defense giant Raytheon and the energy company Chevron. These are not traditionally gay-friendly work environments. Nor is the Republican Party. But the offspring of such leading Republican lights as Dick Cheney, Alan Keyes, and Phyllis Schlafly are all openly gay. So is the spokesman for the most anti-gay senator in Congress, Rick Santorum.

This new tolerance and integration — combined, of course, with the   15
increased ability to connect with other gay people that the Internet provides — has undoubtedly encouraged more and more gay people to come out. The hard data for this are difficult to come by (since only recently have we had studies that identified large numbers of gays) and should be treated with caution. Nevertheless, the trend is clear. If you compare data from, say, the 1994 National Health and Social Life Survey with the 2002 National Survey of Family Growth, you will find that women are nearly three times more likely to report being gay, lesbian, or bisexual today than they were eight years ago, and men are about 1.5 times more likely. There are no reliable statistics on openly gay teens, but no one doubts that there has been an explosion in visibility in the last decade — around 3,000 high schools have "gay-straight" alliances. The census, for its part, recorded a threefold increase in the number of same-sex unmarried partners from 1990 to 2000. In 2000, there were close to 600,000 households headed by a same-sex couple, and a quarter of them had children. If you want

to know where the push for civil marriage rights came from, you need look no further. This was not an agenda invented by activists; it was a movement propelled by ordinary people.

So, as one generation literally disappeared and one generation found itself shocked to still be alive, a far larger and more empowered one emerged on the scene. This new generation knew very little about the gay culture of the '70s, and its members were oblivious to the psychically formative experience of plague that had shaped their elders. Most came from the heart of straight America and were more in tune with its new, mellower attitude toward gayness than the embattled, defensive urban gay culture of the pre-AIDS era. Even in evangelical circles, gay kids willing to acknowledge and struggle publicly with their own homosexuality represented a new form of openness. The speed of the change is still shocking. I'm only 42, and I grew up in a world where I literally never heard the word "homosexual" until I went to college. It is now not uncommon to meet gay men in their early twenties who took a boy as their date to the high school prom. When I figured out I was gay, there were no role models to speak of; and, in the popular culture, homosexuality was either a punch line or an embarrassed silence. Today's cultural climate could not be more different. And the psychological impact on the younger generation cannot be overstated.

After all, what separates homosexuals and lesbians from every other minority group is that they are born and raised within the bosom of the majority. Unlike Latino or Jewish or black communities, where parents and grandparents and siblings pass on cultural norms to children in their most formative stages, each generation of gay men and lesbians grows up being taught the heterosexual norms and culture of their home environments or absorbing what passes for their gay identity from the broader culture as a whole. Each shift in mainstream culture is therefore magnified exponentially in the next generation of gay children. To give the most powerful example: A gay child born today will grow up knowing that, in many parts of the world and in parts of the United States, gay couples can get married just as their parents did. From the very beginning of their gay lives, in other words, they will have internalized a sense of normality, of human potential, of self-worth — something that my generation never had and that previous generations would have found unimaginable. That shift in consciousness is as profound as it is irreversible.

To give another example: Black children come into society both uplifted and burdened by the weight of their communal past — a weight that is transferred within families or communities or cultural institutions, such as the church, that provide a context for self-understanding, even in rebellion. Gay children have no such support or burden. And so, in their most formative years, their self-consciousness is utterly different than that of their gay elders. That's why it has become increasingly difficult to distinguish between gay and straight teens today — or even young gay and straight adults. Less psychologically wounded, more self-confident, less isolated, young gay kids look and sound increasingly like young straight kids. On the dozens of college campuses I have visited over the past decade, the shift in just a few years has been astounding. At a Catholic institution like Boston College, for example, a generation ago there would have been no discussion of homosexuality. When I visited recently to talk about that very subject, the preppy, conservative student president was openly gay.

When you combine this generational plasticity with swift demographic growth, you have our current explosion of gay civil society, with a disproportionately young age distribution. I use the term "civil society" in its classic Tocquevillean and Burkean sense: the little platoons of social organization that undergird liberal democratic life. The gay organizations that erupted into being as AIDS killed thousands in the '80s — from the Gay Men's Health Crisis to the AIDS Project Los Angeles to the Whitman–Walker Clinic in Washington — struggled to adapt to the swift change in the epidemic in the mid-'90s. But the general principle of communal organization endured. If conservatives had been open-minded enough to see it, they would have witnessed a classic tale of self-help and self-empowerment.

Take, for example, religious life, an area not historically associated with gay   20
culture. One of the largest single gay organizations in the country today is the Metropolitan Community Church, with over 40,000 active members. Go to, yes, Dallas, and you'll find the Cathedral of Hope, one of the largest religious structures in the country, with close to 4,000 congregants — predominantly gay. Almost every faith now has an explicitly gay denomination associated with it — Dignity for gay Catholics, *Bet Mishpachah* for gay Jews, and so on. But, in many mainstream Protestant churches and among Reform Jews, such groups don't even exist because the integration of gay believers is now mundane. These groups bring gays together in a context where sexuality is less a feature of identity than faith, where the interaction of bodies is less central than the community of souls.

In contrast, look at bar life. For a very long time, the fundamental social institution for gay men was the gay bar. It was often secluded — a refuge, a safe zone, and a clearing-house for sexual pickups. Most bars still perform some of those functions. But the Internet dealt them a body-blow. If you are merely looking for sex or a date, the Web is now the first stop for most gay men. The result has been striking. Only a decade ago, you could wander up the West Side Highway in New York City and drop by several leather bars. Now, only one is left standing, and it is less a bar dedicated to the ornate codes of '70s leather culture than a place for men who adopt a more masculine self-presentation. My favorite old leather bar, the Spike, is now the "Spike Gallery." The newer gay bars are more social than sexual, often with restaurants, open windows onto the street, and a welcoming attitude toward others, especially the many urban straight women who find gay bars more congenial than heterosexual pickup joints.

Even gay political organizations often function more as social groups than as angry activist groups. HRC, for example, raises funds and lobbies Congress. Around 350,000 members have contributed in the last two years. It organizes itself chiefly through a series of formal fund-raising dinners in cities across the country — from Salt Lake City to Nashville. These dinners are a social venue for the openly gay bourgeoisie: In tuxedos and ball gowns, they contribute large sums and give awards to local businesses and politicians and community leaders. There are silent auctions, hired entertainers, even the occasional bake-sale. The closest heterosexual equivalent would be the Rotary Club. These dinners in themselves are evidence of the change: from outsider rebellion to bourgeois organization.

Take a look at the gay press. In its shallower forms — glossy lifestyle magazines — you are as likely to find a straight Hollywood star on the cover as any gay icon. In its more serious manifestations, such as regional papers like the *Washington Blade* or *Southern Voice*, the past emphasis on sex has been replaced with an emphasis on domesticity. A recent issue of the *Blade* had an eight-page insert for escort ads, personals, and the kind of material that, two decades ago, would have been the advertising mainstay of the main paper. But in the paper itself are 23 pages of real-estate ads and four pages of home-improvement classifieds. There are columns on cars, sports, DVDs, and local plays. The core ad base, according to its editor, Chris Crain, now comprises heterosexual-owned and operated companies seeking to reach the gay market. The editorial tone has shifted as well. Whereas the *Blade* was once ideologically rigid — with endless reports on small activist cells and a strident left-wing slant — now it's much more like a community paper that might be published for any well-heeled ethnic group. Genuine ideological differences are now aired, rather than bitterly decried as betrayal or agitprop. Editorials regularly take Democrats to task as well as Republicans. The maturation has been as swift as it now seems inevitable. After all, in 2004, one-quarter of self-identified gay voters backed a president who supported a constitutional ban on gay marriage. If the gay world is that politically diverse under the current polarized circumstances, it has obviously moved well beyond the time it was synonymous with radical left politics.

How gay men and lesbians express their identity has also changed. When openly gay identity first emerged, it tended toward extremes of gender expression. When society tells you that gay men and lesbians are not fully male or female, the response can be to overcompensate with caricatures of each gender or to rebel by blurring gender lines altogether. Effeminate "queens" were balanced by hyper-masculine bikers and muscle men; lipstick lesbians were offset by classically gruff "bull-dykes." All these sub-sub-cultures still exist. Many feel comfortable with them; and, thankfully, we see fewer attempts to marginalize them. But the polarities in the larger gay population are far less pronounced than they once were; the edges have softened. As gay men have become less defensive about their masculinity, their expression of it has become subtler. There is still a pronounced muscle and gym culture, but there are also now openly gay swimmers and artists and slobs and every body type in between. Go watch a gay rugby team compete in a regional tournament with straight teams and you will see how vast but subtle the revolution has been. And, in fact, this is the trend: gay civil associations in various ways are interacting with parallel straight associations in a way that leaves their gay identity more and more behind. They're rugby players first, gay rugby players second.

One of the newest reflections of this is what is known as "bear" culture: 25 heavy, hirsute, unkempt guys who revel in their slovenliness. Their concept of what it means to be gay is very different than that of the obsessive gym-rats with torsos shaved of every stray hair. Among many younger gay men, the grungy look of their straight peers has been adopted and tweaked to individual tastes. Even among bears, there are slimmer "otters" or younger "cubs" or "muscle-bears," who combine gym culture with a bear sensibility. The varieties keep proliferating; and, at the rate of current change, they will soon dissipate into the range of identities that straight men have to choose from. In fact, these variations of masculinity may even have diversified heterosexual male culture as well. While some gay men have proudly adopted some classically straight signifiers — beer bellies and back hair — many straight men have become "metrosexuals." Trying to define "gay culture" in this mix is an increasingly elusive task.

Among lesbians, Ellen DeGeneres's transition from closeted sitcom star to out-lesbian activist and back to appealingly middle-brow daytime talk-show host is almost a microcosm of diversifying lesbian identity in the past decade. There are still classic butch-femme lesbian partnerships, but more complex forms of self-expression are more common now. With the abatement in many places of prejudice, lesbian identity is formed less by reaction to hostility than by simple self-expression. And this, after all, is and was the point of gay liberation: the freedom not merely to be gay according to some preordained type, but to be yourself, whatever that is.

You see this even in drag, which once defined gayness in some respects but now is only one of many expressions. Old-school drag, the kind that dominated the '50s, '60s, and '70s, often consisted of female impersonators performing torch songs from various divas. The more miserable the life of the diva, the better able the performer was to channel his own anguish and drama into the show. After all, gayness was synonymous with tragedy and showmanship. Judy Garland, Marilyn Monroe, Bette Davis: these were the models. But today's drag looks and feels very different. The drag impresario of Provincetown, a twisted genius called Ryan Landry, hosts a weekly talent show for local drag performers called "Showgirls." Attending it each Monday night is P-town's equivalent of weekly Mass. A few old-school drag queens perform, but Landry sets the tone. He makes no attempt to look like a woman, puts on hideous wigs (including a horse mask and a pair of fake boobs perched on his head), throws on ill-fitting dresses, and performs scatological song parodies. Irony pervades the show. Comedy defines it. Gay drag is inching slowly toward a version of British pantomime, where dada humor and absurd, misogynist parodies of womanhood are central. This is post-drag; straight men could do it as well. This year, the longest-running old school drag show — "Legends" — finally closed down. Its audience had become mainly heterosexual and old.

This new post-gay cultural synthesis has its political counterpart. There was once a ferocious debate among gays between what might be caricatured as "separatists" and "assimilationists." That argument has fizzled. As the gay population has grown, it has become increasingly clear that the choice is not either/or but both/and. The issue of civil marriage reveals this most graphically. When I first argued for equal marriage rights, I found myself assailed by the gay left for social conservatism. I remember one signing for my 1995 book, *Virtually Normal*, the crux of which was an argument for the right to marry. I was picketed by a group called "Lesbian Avengers," who depicted my argument as patriarchal and reactionary. They crafted posters with my face portrayed within the crosshairs of a gun. Ten years later, lesbian couples make up a majority of civil marriages in Massachusetts and civil unions in Vermont; and some of the strongest voices for marriage equality have been lesbians, from the pioneering lawyer Mary Bonauto to writer E. J. Graff. To its credit, the left — gay male and lesbian — recognized that what was at stake was not so much the corralling of all gay individuals into a conformist social institution as a widening of choice for all. It is still possible to be a gay radical or rigid leftist. The difference now is that it is also possible to be a gay conservative, or traditionalist, or anything else in between.

Who can rescue a uniform gay culture? No one, it would seem. The generation most psychologically wedded to the separatist past is either dead from HIV or sidelined. But there are still enclaves of gay distinctiveness out there. Paradoxically, gay culture in its old form may have its most fertile ground in those states where homosexuality is still unmentionable and where openly gay men and women are more beleaguered: the red states. Earlier this year, I spoke at an HRC dinner in Nashville, Tennessee, where state politicians are trying to bar gay couples from marrying or receiving even basic legal protections. The younger gay generation is as psychologically evolved there as any place else. They see the same television and the same Internet as gay kids in New York. But their social space is smaller. And so I found a vibrant gay world, but one far more cohesive, homogeneous, and defensive than in Massachusetts. The strip of gay bars — crammed into one place rather than diffuse, as in many blue-state cities — was packed on a Saturday night. The mix of old and young, gay and lesbian, black, white, and everything in between reminded me of Boston in the '80s. The tired emblems of the past — the rainbow flags and leather outfits — retained their relevance there.

The same goes for black and Latino culture, where homophobia, propped up by black churches and the Catholic hierarchy respectively, is more intense than in much of white society. It's no surprise that these are the populations also most at risk for HIV. The underground "down-low" culture common in black gay life means less acknowledgment of sexual identity, let alone awareness or disclosure of HIV status. The same repression that facilitated the spread of HIV among gay white men in the '70s now devastates black gay America, where the latest data suggest a 50 percent HIV infection rate. (Compare that with largely white and more integrated San Francisco, where recent HIV infection rates are now half what they were four years ago.) The extremes of gender expression are also more pronounced among minorities, with many gay black or Latino men either adopting completely female personalities or refusing to identify as gay at all. Here the past lives on. The direction toward integration is clear, but the pace is far slower.

And, when you see the internalized defensiveness of gays still living in the shadow of social hostility, any nostalgia one might feel for the loss of gay culture dissipates. Some still echo critic Philip Larkin's jest that he worried about the American civil rights movement because it was ruining jazz. But the flipness of that remark is the point, and the mood today is less genuine regret — let alone a desire to return to those days — than a kind of wistfulness for a past that was probably less glamorous or unified than it now appears. It is indeed hard not to feel some sadness at the end of a rich, distinct culture built by pioneers who braved greater ostracism than today's generation will ever fully understand. But, if there is a real choice between a culture built on oppression and a culture built on freedom, the decision is an easy one. Gay culture was once primarily about pain and tragedy, because that is what heterosexuals imposed on gay people, and that was, in part, what gay people experienced. Gay culture was once primarily about sex, because that was how heterosexuals defined gay lives. But gay life, like straight life, is now and always has been about happiness as well as pain; it is about triumph as well as tragedy; it is about love and family as well as sex. It took generations to find the self-worth to move toward achieving this reality in all its forms — and an epidemiological catastrophe to accelerate it. If the end of gay culture means that we have a new complexity to grapple with and a new, less cramped humanity to embrace, then regret seems almost a rebuke to those countless generations who could only dream of the liberty so many now enjoy.

The tiny, rich space that gay men and women once created for themselves was, after all, the best they could do. In a metaphor coined by the philosopher Michael Walzer, they gilded a cage of exclusion with magnificent ornaments; they spoke to its isolation and pain; they described and maintained it with dignity and considerable beauty. But it was still a cage. And the thing that kept gay people together, that unified them into one homogeneous unit, and that defined the parameters of their culture and the limits of their dreams, were the bars on that cage. Past the ashes of thousands and through the courage of those who came before the plague and those who survived it, those bars are now slowly but inexorably being pried apart. The next generation may well be as free of that cage as any minority ever can be; and they will redefine gayness on its own terms and not on the terms of hostile outsiders. Nothing will stop this, since it is occurring in the psyches and souls of a new generation: a new consciousness that is immune to any law and propelled by the momentum of human freedom itself. While we should treasure the past, there is no recovering it. The futures — and they will be multiple — are just beginning.

QUESTIONING THE TEXT

1. Does this article surprise you? Or does Sullivan's argument seem obviously true? To what degree do you think that Sullivan is right that gay culture has ceased to be separate from straight culture? How assimilated is homosexuality in the culture that you come from?

2. Sullivan acknowledges that the loss of a distinctive gay culture "is a threat in the way that all loss is a threat" (paragraph 6), but for the most part he seems to prefer the end of a distinctive gay culture. Might groups whose members have been stigmatized in the past be more likely to welcome assimilation into the larger culture than groups whose members have always been able to fit in? Use examples to explain your reasoning.

MAKING CONNECTIONS

3. Compare Sullivan's ideas about the values of assimilation to those of Bich Minh Nguyen in "The Good Immigrant Student" (p. 458). Do you think that Nguyen would celebrate the loss of an Asian American or Vietnamese American culture by assimilation? Be prepared to explain your reasoning in a class discussion.

4. Toward the end of this article, Sullivan argues that the range of gender expression for homosexuals has widened significantly. Read Dave Barry's "Guys vs. Men" (p. 405) in the context of Sullivan's article. Do you think that Barry's world of "guys" has room for gay men? Write a paragraph or two considering whether Barry and Sullivan could find common ground on this issue.

JOINING THE CONVERSATION

5. Sullivan argues that until recent years gay culture had been forced to understand a large part of its identity based on the norms imposed by heterosexual culture. Describe how external forces — welcome or unwelcome — have helped shape part of your identity or helped define a part of your experience.

6. Sullivan compares gay culture to black culture, a move that might remind us that cultures can be defined according to many different factors. Can you define a group to which you belong or which you are aware of as a separate and distinct culture? In writing an essay defining a specific group as a culture, pay special attention to developing a set of criteria for what constitutes a culture as opposed to just a group.

* gay culture is opening up

MAXINE HONG KINGSTON
No Name Woman

MAXINE HONG KINGSTON was born (in 1940) and raised in California, but her roots grow deep in Chinese soil and culture, as is evidenced in her highly acclaimed books, The Woman Warrior *(1970),* China Men *(1980), and* The Fifth Book of Peace *(2003). In these and other works, Kingston explores the effects of Chinese legend and custom on her own identity as a woman and as a Chinese American. In "No Name Woman," an excerpt from* The Woman Warrior, *Kingston examines one identifying feature of most women — their ability to bear children — and she explores the consequences of that identifying mark.*

Many readers of this text may be able to identify a shadowy relative in their own past — an absent parent, a grandparent much discussed but seldom seen, a mysterious uncle or aunt or cousin — about whom older family members whispered. Few of us are likely to have written so powerfully about such a figure, however, or to have evoked in such a short space what it would be like to be "No Name Woman." I chose this selection precisely for its power. It has stayed vividly with me ever since I first read it — so vividly, in fact, that "No Name Woman" seems like someone I know personally. To me, she tells not only her own story but the story of all those whose lives are destroyed by narrow and rigid beliefs about what someone's identity must be.　　　　　—A.L.

"You must not tell anyone," my mother said, "what I am about to tell you. In China your father had a sister who killed herself. She jumped into the family well. We say that your father has all brothers because it is as if she had never been born.

"In 1924 just a few days after our village celebrated seventeen hurry-up weddings — to make sure that every young man who went 'out on the road' would responsibly come home — your father and his brothers and your grandfather and his brothers and your aunt's new husband sailed for America, the Gold Mountain. It was your grandfather's last trip. Those lucky enough to get contracts waved good-bye from the decks. They fed and guarded the stowaways and helped them off in Cuba, New York, Bali, Hawaii. 'We'll meet in California next year,' they said. All of them sent money home.

"I remember looking at your aunt one day when she and I were dressing; I had not noticed before that she had such a protruding melon of a stomach. But I did not think, 'She's pregnant,' until she began to look like other pregnant women, her shirt pulling and the white tops of her black pants showing. She could not have been pregnant, you see, because her husband had been gone for years. No one said anything. We did not discuss it. In early summer she was ready to have the child, long after the time when it could have been possible.

"The village had also been counting. On the night the baby was to be born the villagers raided our house. Some were crying. Like a great saw, teeth strung with lights, files of people walked zigzag across our land, tearing the rice. Their lanterns doubled in the disturbed black water, which drained away through the broken bunds. As the villagers closed in, we could see that some of them, probably men and women we knew well, wore white masks. The people with long hair hung it over their faces. Women with short hair made it stand up on end. Some had tied white bands around their foreheads, arms, and legs.

"At first they threw mud and rocks at the house. Then they threw eggs   5 and began slaughtering our stock. We could hear the animals scream their deaths — the roosters, the pigs, a last great roar from the ox. Familiar wild heads flared in our night windows; the villagers encircled us. Some of the faces stopped to peer at us, their eyes rushing like searchlights. The hands flattened against the panes, framed heads, and left red prints.

"The villagers broke in the front and the back doors at the same time, even though we had not locked the doors against them. Their knives dripped with the blood of our animals. They smeared blood on the doors and walls. One woman swung a chicken, whose throat she had slit, splattering blood in red arcs about her. We stood together in the middle of our house, in the family hall with the pictures and tables of the ancestors around us, and looked straight ahead.

"At that time the house had only two wings. When the men came back, we would build two more to enclose our courtyard and a third one to begin a second courtyard. The villagers pushed through both wings, even your grandparents' rooms, to find your aunt's, which was also mine until the men returned. From this room a new wing for one of the younger families would grow. They ripped up her clothes and shoes and broke her combs, grinding them underfoot. They tore her work from the loom. They scattered the cooking fire and rolled the new weaving in it. We could hear them in the kitchen breaking our bowls and banging the pots. They overturned the great waist-high earthenware jugs; duck eggs, pickled fruits, vegetables burst out and mixed in acrid torrents. The old woman from the next field swept a broom through the air and loosed the spirits-of-the-broom over our heads. 'Pig.' 'Ghost.' 'Pig,' they sobbed and scolded while they ruined our house.

"When they left, they took sugar and oranges to bless themselves. They cut pieces from the dead animals. Some of them took bowls that were not broken and clothes that were not torn. Afterward we swept up the rice and sewed it back up into sacks. But the smells from the spilled preserves lasted. Your aunt gave birth in the pigsty that night. The next morning when I went up for the water, I found her and the baby plugging up the family well.

"Don't let your father know that I told you. He denies her. Now that you have started to menstruate, what happened to her could happen to you. Don't humiliate us. You wouldn't like to be forgotten as if you had never been born. The villagers are watchful."

Whenever she had to warn us about life, my mother told stories that ran like this one, a story to grow up on. She tested our strength to establish realities. Those in the emigrant generations who could not reassert brute survival died young and far from home. Those of us in the first American generations have had to figure out how the invisible world the emigrants built around our childhoods fit in solid America.

The emigrants confused the gods by diverting their curses, misleading them with crooked streets and false names. They must try to confuse their offspring as well, who, I suppose, threaten them in similar ways — always trying to get things straight, always trying to name the unspeakable. The Chinese I know hide their names; sojourners take new names when their lives change and guard their real names with silence.

Chinese-Americans, when you try to understand what things in you are Chinese, how do you separate what is peculiar to childhood, to poverty, insanities, one family, your mother who marked your growing with stories, from what is Chinese? What is Chinese tradition and what is the movies?

If I want to learn what clothes my aunt wore, whether flashy or ordinary, I would have to begin, "Remember Father's drowned-in-the-well sister?" I cannot ask that. My mother has told me once and for all the useful parts. She will add nothing unless powered by Necessity, a riverbank that guides her life. She plants vegetable gardens rather than lawns; she carries the odd-shaped tomatoes home from the fields and eats food left for the gods.

Whenever we did frivolous things, we used up energy; we flew high kites. We children came up off the ground over the melting cones our parents brought home from work and the American movie on New Year's Day — *Oh, You Beautiful Doll* with Betty Grable one year, and *She Wore a Yellow Ribbon* with John Wayne another year. After the one carnival ride each, we paid in guilt; our tired father counted his change on the dark walk home.

Adultery is extravagance. Could people who hatch their own chicks and eat the embryos and the heads for delicacies and boil the feet in vinegar for party food, leaving only the gravel, eating even the gizzard lining — could such people engender a prodigal aunt? To be a woman, to have a daughter in starvation time was a waste enough. My aunt could not have been the lone romantic who gave up everything for sex. Women in the old China did not choose. Some man had commanded her to lie with him and be his secret evil. I wonder whether he masked himself when he joined the raid on her family.

Perhaps she encountered him in the fields or on the mountain where the daughters-in-law collected fuel. Or perhaps he first noticed her in the marketplace. He was not a stranger because the village housed no strangers. She had to have dealings with him other than sex. Perhaps he worked an adjoining field, or he sold her the cloth for the dress she sewed and wore. His demand must have surprised, then terrified her. She obeyed him; she always did as she was told.

When the family found a young man in the next village to be her husband, she stood tractably beside the best rooster, his proxy, and promised before they met that she would be his forever. She was lucky that he was her age and she would be the first wife, an advantage secure now. The night she first saw him, he had sex with her. Then he left for America. She had almost forgotten what he looked like. When she tried to envision him, she only saw the black and white face in the group photograph the men had taken before leaving.

The other man was not, after all, much different from her husband. They both gave orders: she followed. "If you tell your family, I'll beat you. I'll kill you. Be here again next week." No one talked sex, ever. And she might have separated the rapes from the rest of living if only she did not have to buy her oil from him or gather wood in the same forest. I want her fear to have lasted just as long as rape lasted so that the fear could have been contained. No drawn-out fear. But women at sex hazarded birth and hence lifetimes. The fear did not stop but permeated everywhere. She told the man, "I think I'm pregnant." He organized the raid against her.

On nights when my mother and father talked about their life back home, sometimes they mentioned an "outcast table" whose business they still seemed to be settling, their voices tight. In a commensal tradition, where food is precious, the powerful older people made wrongdoers eat alone. Instead of letting them start separate new lives like the Japanese, who could become samurais and geishas, the Chinese family, faces averted but eyes glowering sideways, hung on to the offenders and fed them leftovers. My aunt must have lived in the same house as my parents and eaten at an outcast table. My mother spoke about the raid as if she had seen it, when she and my aunt, a daughter-in-law to a different household, should not have been living together at all. Daughters-in-law lived with their husbands' parents, not their own; a synonym for marriage in Chinese is "taking a daughter-in-law." Her husband's parents could have sold her, mortgaged her, stoned her. But they had sent her back to her own mother and father, a mysterious act hinting at disgraces not told me. Perhaps they had thrown her out to deflect the avengers.

She was the only daughter; her four brothers went with her father, husband, and uncles "out on the road" and for some years became western men. When the goods were divided among the family, three of the brothers took land, and the youngest, my father, chose an education. After my grandparents gave their daughter away to her husband's family, they had dispensed all the adventure and all the property. They expected her alone to keep the traditional ways, which her brothers, now among the barbarians, could fumble without detection. The heavy, deep-rooted women were to maintain the past against the flood, safe for returning. But the rare urge west had fixed upon our family, and so my aunt crossed boundaries not delineated in space.

The work of preservation demands that the feelings playing about in one's guts not be turned into action. Just watch their passing like cherry blossoms. But perhaps my aunt, my forerunner, caught in a slow life, let dreams grow and fade and after some months or years went toward what persisted. Fear at the enormities of the forbidden kept her desires delicate, wire and bone. She looked at a man because she liked the way the hair was tucked behind his ears, or she liked the question-mark line of a long torso curving at the shoulder and straight at the hip. For warm eyes or a soft voice or a slow walk — that's all — a few hairs, a line, a brightness, a sound, a pace, she gave up family. She offered us up for a charm that vanished with tiredness, a pigtail that didn't toss when the wind died. Why, the wrong lighting could erase the dearest thing about him.

It could very well have been, however, that my aunt did not take subtle enjoyment of her friend, but, a wild woman, kept rollicking company. Imagining her free with sex doesn't fit, though. I don't know any women like that, or men either. Unless I see her life branching into mine, she gives me no ancestral help.

To sustain her being in love, she often worked at herself in the mirror, guessing at the colors and shapes that would interest him, changing them frequently in order to hit on the right combination. She wanted him to look back.

On a farm near the sea, a woman who tended her appearance reaped a reputation for eccentricity. All the married women blunt-cut their hair in flaps about their ears or pulled it back in tight buns. No nonsense. Neither style blew easily into heart-catching tangles. And at their weddings they displayed themselves in their long hair for the last time. "It brushed the backs of my knees," my mother tells me. "It was braided, and even so, it brushed the backs of my knees."

At the mirror my aunt combed individuality into her bob. A bun could   25 have been contrived to escape into black streamers blowing in the wind or in quiet wisps about her face, but only the older women in our picture album wear buns. She brushed her hair back from her forehead, tucking the flaps behind her ears. She looped a piece of thread, knotted into a circle between her index fingers and thumbs, and ran the double strand across her forehead. When she closed her fingers as if she were making a pair of shadow geese bite, the string twisted together catching the little hairs. Then she pulled the thread away from her skin, ripping the hairs out neatly, her eyes watering from the needles of pain. Opening her fingers, she cleaned the thread, then rolled it along her hairline and the tops of her eyebrows. My mother did the same to me and my sisters and herself. I used to believe that the expression "caught by the short hairs" meant a captive held with a depilatory string. It especially hurt at the temples, but my mother said we were lucky we didn't have to have our feet bound when we were seven. Sisters used to sit on their beds and cry together, she said, as their mothers or their slave removed the bandages for a few minutes each night and let the blood gush back into their veins. I hope that the man my aunt loved appreciated a smooth brow, that he wasn't just a tits-and-ass man.

Once my aunt found a freckle on her chin, at a spot that the almanac said predestined her for unhappiness. She dug it out with a hot needle and washed the wound with peroxide.

More attention to her looks than these pullings of hairs and pickings at spots would have caused gossip among the villagers. They owned work clothes and good clothes, and they wore good clothes for feasting the new seasons. But since a woman combing her hair hexes beginnings, my aunt rarely found an occasion to look her best. Women looked like great sea snails — the corded wood, babies, and laundry they carried were the whorls on their backs. The Chinese did not admire a bent back; goddesses and warriors stood straight. Still there must have been a marvelous freeing of beauty when a worker laid down her burden and stretched and arched.

Such commonplace loveliness, however, was not enough for my aunt. She dreamed of a lover for the fifteen days of New Year's, the time for families to exchange visits, money, and food. She plied her secret comb. And sure enough she cursed the year, the family, the village, and herself.

Even as her hair lured her imminent lover, many other men looked at her. Uncles, cousins, nephews, brothers would have looked, too, had they been home between journeys. Perhaps they had already been restraining their curiosity, and they left, fearful that their glances, like a field of nesting birds, might be startled and caught. Poverty hurt, and that was their first reason for leaving. But another, final reason for leaving the crowded house was the never-said.

She may have been unusually beloved, the precious only daughter, spoiled and mirror-gazing because of the affection the family lavished on her. When her husband left, they welcomed the chance to take her back from the in-laws; she could live like the little daughter for just a while longer. There are stories that my grandfather was different from other people, "crazy ever since the little Jap bayoneted him in the head." He used to put his naked penis on the dinner table, laughing. And one day he brought home a baby girl, wrapped up inside his brown western-style greatcoat. He had traded one of his sons, probably my father, the youngest, for her. My grandmother made him trade back. When he finally got a daughter of his own, he doted on her. They must have all loved her, except perhaps my father, the only brother who never went back to China, having once been traded for a girl.

Brothers and sisters, newly men and women, had to efface their sexual color and present plain miens. Disturbing hair and eyes, a smile like no other, threatened the ideal of five generations living under one roof. To focus blurs, people shouted face to face and yelled from room to room. The immigrants I know have loud voices, unmodulated to American tones even after years away from the village where they called their friendships out across the fields. I have not been able to stop my mother's screams in public libraries or over telephones. Walking erect (knees straight, toes pointed forward, not pigeon-toed, which is Chinese-feminine) and speaking in an inaudible voice, I have tried to turn myself American-feminine. Chinese communication was loud, public. Only sick people had to whisper. But at the dinner table, where the family members came nearest one another, no one could talk, not the outcasts nor any eaters. Every word that falls from the mouth is a coin lost. Silently they gave and accepted food with both hands. A preoccupied child who took his bowl with one hand got a sideways glare. A complete moment of total attention is due everyone alike. Children and lovers have no singularity here, but my aunt used a secret voice, a separate attentiveness.

She kept the man's name to herself throughout her labor and dying; she did not accuse him that he be punished with her. To save her inseminator's name she gave silent birth.

He may have been somebody in her own household, but intercourse with a man outside the family would have been no less abhorrent. All the village were kinsmen, and the titles shouted in loud country voices never let kinship be forgotten. Any man within visiting distance would have been neutralized as a lover — "brother," "younger brother," "older brother" — 115 relationship titles. Parents researched birth charts probably not so much to assure good fortune as to circumvent incest in a population that has but one hundred surnames. Everybody has eight million relatives. How useless then sexual mannerisms, how dangerous.

As if it came from an atavism deeper than fear, I used to add "brother" silently to boys' names. It hexed the boys, who would or would not ask me to dance, and made them less scary and as familiar and deserving of benevolence as girls.

But, of course, I hexed myself also — no dates. I should have stood up, both arms waving, and shouted out across libraries, "Hey, you! Love me back." I had no idea, though, how to make attraction selective, how to control its direction and magnitude. If I made myself American-pretty so that the five or six Chinese boys in the class fell in love with me, everyone else — the Caucasian, Negro, and Japanese boys — would too. Sisterliness, dignified and honorable, made much more sense. 35

Attraction eludes control so stubbornly that whole societies designed to organize relationships among people cannot keep order, not even when they bind people to one another from childhood and raise them together. Among the very poor and the wealthy, brothers married their adopted sisters, like doves. Our family allowed some romance, paying adult brides' prices and providing dowries so that their sons and daughters could marry strangers. Marriage promises to turn strangers into friendly relatives — a nation of siblings.

In the village structure, spirits shimmered among the live creatures, balanced and held in equilibrium by time and land. But one human being flaring up into violence could open up a black hole, a maelstrom that pulled in the sky. The frightened villagers, who depended on one another to maintain the real, went to my aunt to show her a personal, physical representation of the break she made in the "roundness." Misallying couples snapped off the future, which was to be embodied in true offspring. The villagers punished her for acting as if she could have a private life, secret and apart from them.

If my aunt had betrayed the family at a time of large grain yields and peace, when many boys were born, and wings were being built on many houses, perhaps she might have escaped such severe punishment. But the men — hungry, greedy, tired of planting in dry soil, cuckolded — had been forced to leave the village in order to send food-money home. There were ghost plagues, bandit plagues, wars with the Japanese, floods. My Chinese brother and sister had died of an unknown sickness. Adultery, perhaps only a mistake during good times, became a crime when the village needed food.

The round moon cakes and round doorways, the round tables of graduated size that fit one roundness inside another, round windows and rice bowls — these talismans had lost their power to warn this family of the law: a family must be whole, faithfully keeping the descent line by having sons to feed the old and the dead who in turn look after the family. The villagers came to show my aunt and lover-in-hiding a broken house. The villagers were speeding up the circling of events because she was too shortsighted to see that her infidelity had already harmed the village, that waves of consequences would return unpredictably, sometimes in disguise, as now, to hurt her. This roundness had to be made coin-sized so that she would see its circumference: punish her at the birth of her baby. Awaken her to the inexorable. People who refused fatalism because they could invent small resources insisted on culpability. Deny accidents and wrest fault from the stars.

After the villagers left, their lanterns now scattering in various directions toward home, the family broke their silence and cursed her. "Aiaa, we're going to die. Death is coming. Death is coming. Look what you've done. You've killed us. Ghost! Dead Ghost! Ghost! You've never been born." She ran out into the fields, far enough from the house so that she could no longer hear their voices, and pressed herself against the earth, her own land no more. When she felt the birth coming, she thought that she had been hurt. Her body seized together. "They've hurt me too much," she thought. "This is gall, and it will kill me." With forehead and knees against the earth, her body convulsed and then relaxed. She turned on her back, lay on the ground. The black well of sky and stars went out and out forever; her body and her complexity seemed to disappear. She was one of the stars, a bright dot in blackness, without home, without a companion, in eternal cold and silence. An agoraphobia rose in her, speeding higher and higher, bigger and bigger; she would not be able to contain it; there would be no end to fear.

Flayed, unprotected against space, she felt pain return, focusing her body. This pain chilled her — a cold, steady kind of surface pain. Inside, spasmodically, the other pain, the pain of the child, heated her. For hours she lay on the ground, alternately body and space. Sometimes a vision of normal comfort obliterated reality: she saw the family in the evening gambling at the dinner table, the young people massaging their elders' backs. She saw them congratulating one another, high joy on the mornings the rice shoots came up. When these pictures burst, the stars drew yet further apart. Black space opened.

She got to her feet to fight better and remembered that old-fashioned women gave birth in their pigsties to fool the jealous, pain-dealing gods, who do not snatch piglets. Before the next spasms could stop her, she ran to the pigsty, each step a rushing out into emptiness. She climbed over the fence and knelt in the dirt. It was good to have a fence enclosing her, a tribal person alone.

40

Laboring, this woman who had carried her child as a foreign growth that sickened her every day, expelled it at last. She reached down to touch the hot, wet, moving mass, surely smaller than anything human, and could feel that it was human after all — fingers, toes, nails, nose. She pulled it up on to her belly, and it lay curled there, butt in the air, feet precisely tucked one under the other. She opened her loose shirt and buttoned the child inside. After resting, it squirmed and thrashed and she pushed it up to her breast. It turned its head this way and that until it found her nipple. There, it made little snuffling noises. She clenched her teeth at its preciousness, lovely as a young calf, a piglet, a little dog.

She may have gone to the pigsty as a last act of responsibility: she would protect this child as she had protected its father. It would look after her soul, leaving supplies on her grave. But how would this tiny child without family find her grave when there would be no marker for her anywhere, neither in the earth nor the family hall? No one would give her a family hall name. She had taken the child with her into the wastes. At its birth the two of them had felt the same raw pain of separation, a wound that only the family pressing tight could close. A child with no descent line would not soften her life but only trail after her, ghostlike, begging her to give it purpose. At dawn the villagers on their way to the fields would stand around the fence and look.

Full of milk, the little ghost slept. When it awoke, she hardened her   45 breasts against the milk that crying loosens. Toward morning she picked up the baby and walked to the well.

Carrying the baby to the well shows loving. Otherwise abandon it. Turn its face into the mud. Mothers who love their children take them along. It was probably a girl; there is some hope of forgiveness for boys.

"Don't tell anyone you had an aunt. Your father does not want to hear her name. She has never been born." I have believed that sex was unspeakable and words so strong and fathers so frail that "aunt" would do my father mysterious harm. I have thought that my family, having settled among immigrants who had also been their neighbors in the ancestral land, needed to clean their name, and a wrong word would incite the kinspeople even here. But there is more to this silence: they want me to participate in her punishment. And I have.

In the twenty years since I heard this story I have not asked for details nor said my aunt's name; I do not know it. People who comfort the dead can also chase after them to hurt them further — a reverse ancestor worship. The real punishment was not the raid swiftly inflicted by the villagers, but the family's deliberately forgetting her. Her betrayal so maddened them, they saw to it that she would suffer forever, even after death. Always hungry, always needing, she would have to beg food from other ghosts, snatch and steal it from those whose living descendants give them gifts. She would have to fight the ghosts massed at crossroads for the buns a few thoughtful citizens leave to decoy her away from village and home so that the ancestral spirits could feast unharassed. At peace, they could act like gods, not ghosts, their descent lines providing them with paper suits and dresses, spirit money, paper houses, paper automobiles, chicken, meat, and rice into eternity — essences delivered up in smoke and flames, steam and incense rising from each rice bowl. In an attempt to make the Chinese care for people outside the family, Chairman Mao encourages us now to give our paper replicas to the spirits of outstanding soldiers and workers, no matter whose ancestors they may be. My aunt remains forever hungry. Goods are not distributed evenly among the dead.

My aunt haunts me — her ghost drawn to me because now, after fifty years of neglect, I alone devote pages of paper to her, though not origamied into houses and clothes. I do not think she always means me well. I am telling on her, and she was a spite suicide, drowning herself in the drinking water. The Chinese are always very frightened of the drowned one, whose weeping ghost, wet hair hanging and skin bloated, waits silently by the water to pull down a substitute.

QUESTIONING THE TEXT

1. The narrator of "No Name Woman" tells several different versions of her aunt's life. Which do you find most likely to be accurate, and why?

2. What is the narrator's attitude toward the villagers? What in the text reveals her attitude — and how does it compare with your own attitude toward them?

3. A.L.'s introduction sympathizes with No Name Woman. If one of the villagers had written the introduction, how might it differ from A.L.'s?

MAKING CONNECTIONS

4. "No Name Woman" powerfully describes the fate of a woman who is culturally marginalized for her out-of-wedlock pregnancy. Andrew Sullivan's "The End of Gay Culture" (p. 381) argues that homosexuality is becoming less and less culturally marginalized, as is out-of-wedlock pregnancy. What other identities are becoming more culturally acceptable? Can you think of identities or behaviors that are becoming *more* culturally marginalized? What trends in what is culturally acceptable do you see taking place right now?

JOINING THE CONVERSATION

5. Interview — or spend an hour or so talking with — one of your parents, grandparents, aunts, uncles, or another older person you know fairly well.

Ask your interviewee to describe the attitudes that governed female sexual behavior — or female identity — in his or her day. How were "good girls" supposed to act? What counted as *bad* behavior — and what were the subtle or overt social punishments for that behavior? Write a brief report of your findings, comparing the older person's description of attitudes at an earlier time with those you hold today.

6. Try rewriting one of Kingston's versions of No Name Woman's story from the point of view of the man. How might he see things differently? After you have written this man's version, jot down a few things about him. What does he value? What does he think of women? What is his relationship to women? Finally, bring your version to class to compare with those of two classmates. After studying each version, work together to make a list of what the three versions have in common and a list of how they differ.

DAVE BARRY
Guys vs. Men

ONE OF THE FIRST WORDS *I ever spoke was* truck, *and about forty-five years later I finally bought one, a fully skid-plated 4 × 4 Yukon tall enough to scrape the garage roof and designed to roll me safely over the treacherous ravines and gullies between . . . home and work. Well, I'm man enough to admit that gas-guzzling Big Blue made as much sense as a drawbridge, and I eventually traded it in for a smaller, more environmentally friendly SUV. But the guy in me still yearns for tow hooks, a robust V-8, and a subwoofer that will pop rivets.*

If you don't understand what makes grown men covet "neat stuff" or ruin their knees to conquer at touch football, reading Dave Barry's "Guys vs. Men" may help a little. Barry (b. 1947) is, of course, a guy, and that fact helps him at least diagnose the problem of guyness — if it is one. Suffice to say that a lot of men will recognize themselves in the categories he describes. And some women may identify with the "stupid behavioral patterns" that mark men as guys. In fact, when I discussed Barry's essay in a writing class recently, the women insisted on a "guy" term of their own and came up with chick.

"Guys vs. Men" is the preface to Dave Barry's Complete Guide to Guys: A Fairly Short Book *(1995). Barry is a Pulitzer Prize–winning humorist who, early in his career, lectured to business audiences on effective writing. He has published more than a dozen books and collections of humor, including* Stay Fit and Healthy until You're Dead *(1985) and* Dave Barry Hits below the Beltway *(2001). Barry's syndicated column appears in more than 500 newspapers.*   —J.R.

This is a book about guys. It's *not* a book about men. There are already way too many books about men, and most of them are *way* too serious.

Men itself is a serious word, not to mention *manhood* and *manly.* Such words make being male sound like a very important activity, as opposed to what it primarily consists of, namely, possessing a set of minor and frequently unreliable organs.

But men tend to attach great significance to Manhood. This results in certain characteristically masculine, by which I mean stupid, behavioral patterns that can produce unfortunate results such as violent crime, war, spitting, and ice hockey. These

Could a woman get away with such a trivialization of womanhood? The fact that a man can (and so successfully at that) is evidence in itself for Barry's argument.
     —J.G.R.

Who might write "Chicks vs. Women"? Whoopi Goldberg? Queen Latifah? Hillary Rodham Clinton?
     —A.L.

things have given males a bad name.[1] And the "Men's Movement," which is supposed to bring out the more positive aspects of Manliness, seems to be densely populated with loons and goobers.

So I'm saying that there's another way to look at males: not as aggressive macho dominators; not as sensitive, liberated, hugging drummers; but as *guys*.

And what, exactly, do I mean by "guys"? I don't know. I haven't thought that much about it. One of the major characteristics of guyhood is that we guys don't spend a lot of time pondering our deep innermost feelings. There is a serious question in my mind about whether guys actually *have* deep innermost feelings, unless you count, for example, loyalty to the Detroit Tigers, or fear of bridal showers.

But although I can't define exactly what it means to be a guy, I can describe certain guy characteristics, such as:

GUYS LIKE NEAT STUFF

By "neat," I mean "mechanical and unnecessarily complex." I'll give you an example. Right now I'm typing these words on an *extremely* powerful computer. It's the latest in a line of maybe ten computers I've owned, each one more powerful than the last. My computer is chock full of RAM and ROM and bytes and megahertzes and various other items that enable a computer to kick data-processing butt. It is probably capable of supervising the entire U.S. air-defense apparatus while simultaneously processing the tax return of every resident of Ohio. I use it mainly to write a newspaper column. This is an activity wherein I sit and stare at the screen for maybe ten minutes, then, using only my forefingers, slowly type something like:

Henry Kissinger looks like a big wart.

I stare at this for another ten minutes, have an inspiration, then amplify the original thought as

Aha! Barry's first slip — completely neglecting the computer's all-important functions of Solitaire and Hearts. How would we play these without a computer? —J.G.R.

He is counting on powerful stereotypes here, and with this one he seems right on target. Boys love toys, maybe? —A.L.

5

---

[1]Specifically, "asshole."

Henry Kissinger (b. 1923): foreign policy advisor to President Nixon and U.S. Secretary of State, 1973–77

follows:

Henry Kissinger looks like a big fat wart.

Then I stare at that for another ten minutes, pondering whether I should try to work in the concept of "hairy."

This is absurdly simple work for my computer. It sits there, humming impatiently, bored to death, passing the time between keystrokes via brain-teaser activities such as developing a Unified Field Theory of the universe and translating the complete works of Shakespeare into rap.[2]

10

How about dividing Shakespeare's characters into guys or men? Falstaff—now, there was a guy. —A.L.

Probably the most telltale line of this piece. —J.G.R.

In other words, this computer is absurdly overqualified to work for me, and yet soon, I guarantee, I will buy an *even more powerful* one. I won't be able to stop myself. I'm a guy.

Probably the ultimate example of the fundamental guy drive to have neat stuff is the Space Shuttle. Granted, the guys in charge of this program *claim* it has a Higher Scientific Purpose, namely to see how humans function in space. But of course we have known for years how humans function in space: They float around and say things like: "Looks real good, Houston!"

Little boys don't have to be taught to want toy cars or video games. —J.R.

No, the real reason for the existence of the Space Shuttle is that it is one humongous and spectacularly gizmo-intensive item of hardware. Guys can tinker with it practically forever, and occasionally even get it to work, and use it to place *other* complex mechanical items into orbit, where they almost immediately break, which provides a great excuse to send the Space Shuttle up *again*. It's Guy Heaven.

Less than amusing — especially in light of the space shuttle disasters. Is he implying that guys aren't interested in basic ethical questions like what results their gizmos have on people's lives? —A.L.

Other results of the guy need to have stuff are Star Wars, the recreational boating industry, monorails, nuclear weapons, and wristwatches that indicate the phase of the moon. I am not saying that women haven't been involved in the development or use of this stuff. I'm saying that, without guys, this stuff probably would not exist; just as, without women, virtually every piece of furniture in the world would still be in its original position. Guys do not have a

---

[2]To be or not? I got to *know.*
Might kill myself by the end of the *show.*

basic need to rearrange furniture. Whereas a woman who could cheerfully use the same computer for fifty-three years will rearrange her furniture on almost a weekly basis, sometimes in the dead of night. She'll be sound asleep in bed, and suddenly, at 2 a.m., she'll be awakened by the urgent thought: *The blue-green sofa needs to go perpendicular to the wall instead of parallel, and it needs to go there RIGHT NOW.* So she'll get up and move it, which of course necessitates moving other furniture, and soon she has rearranged her entire living room, shifting great big heavy pieces that ordinarily would require several burly men to lift, because there are few forces in Nature more powerful than a woman who needs to rearrange furniture. Every so often a guy will wake up to discover that, because of his wife's overnight efforts, he now lives in an entirely different house.

Another stereotype neatly deployed. And he counts on our not minding that he lumps all women into one category — it's part of what he has to do to make such portraits "funny."
—A.L.

A tongue-in-cheek nod at the politically correct. Nice.
—J.G.R.

(I realize that I'm making gender-based generalizations here, but my feeling is that if God did not want us to make gender-based generalizations, She would not have given us genders.)

15

GUYS LIKE A REALLY POINTLESS CHALLENGE

Not long ago I was sitting in my office at the *Miami Herald*'s Sunday magazine, *Tropic*, reading my fan mail,[3] when I heard several of my guy coworkers in the hallway talking about how fast they could run the forty-yard dash. These are guys in their thirties and forties who work in journalism, where the most demanding physical requirement is the ability to digest vending-machine food. In other words, these guys have absolutely no need to run the forty-yard dash.

But one of them, Mike Wilson, was writing a story about a star high-school football player who could run it in 4.38 seconds. Now if Mike had written a story about, say, a star high-school poet, none of my guy coworkers would have suddenly decided to find out how well they could write sonnets. But when Mike turned in his story, they became

---

[3]Typical fan letter: "Who cuts your hair? Beavers?"

deeply concerned about how fast they could run the forty-yard dash. They were so concerned that the magazine editor, Tom Shroder, decided that they should get a stopwatch and go out to a nearby park and find out. Which they did, a bunch of guys taking off their shoes and running around barefoot in a public park on company time.

This is what I heard them talking about, out in the hall. I heard Tom, who was thirty-eight years old, saying that his time in the forty had been 5.75 seconds. And I thought to myself: This is ridiculous. These are middle-aged guys, supposedly adults, and they're out there *bragging* about their performance in this stupid juvenile footrace. Finally I couldn't stand it anymore.

"Hey!" I shouted. "*I* could beat 5.75 seconds."

So we went out to the park and measured off forty yards, and the guys told me that I had three chances to make my best time. On the first try my time was 5.78 seconds, just three-hundredths of a second slower than Tom's, even though, at forty-five, I was seven years older than he. So I just *knew* I'd beat him on the second attempt if I ran really, really hard, which I did for a solid ten yards, at which point my left hamstring muscle, which had not yet shifted into Spring Mode from Mail-Reading Mode, went, and I quote, "pop."

I had to be helped off the field. I was in considerable pain, and I was obviously not going to be able to walk right for weeks. The other guys were very sympathetic, especially Tom, who took the time to call me at home, where I was sitting with an ice pack on my leg and twenty-three Advil in my bloodstream, so he could express his concern.

"Just remember," he said, "*you didn't beat my time.*"

There are countless other examples of guys rising to meet pointless challenges. Virtually all sports fall into this category, as well as a large part of U.S. foreign policy. ("I'll bet you can't capture Manuel Noriega!"* "Oh YEAH??")

Manuel Noriega (b. 1934): Panamanian dictator removed from power by armed U.S. intervention in 1989

Margin notes:

I may expire on the racquetball court some day. But I'll go happy — so long as I'm winning.
—J.R.

Or "Last one to the moon has to eat the Berlin Wall." (It took them over 20 years to pay up for this one.)
—J.G.R.

OK. Now I know I am not and never can be a "guy." This is the last thing I would do in response to a story about 40-yard dash times. —A.L.

20

Any guy who has ever competed in an "eat-til-you-puke" contest with 49-cent tacos can relate to this.
—J.G.R.

Who is it that proposed cutting out all militaries the world over and resolving all foreign policy crises by sending out squads to play some game? I can just imagine Barry describing such scenes. —A.L.

GUYS DO NOT HAVE A RIGID AND WELL-DEFINED MORAL CODE

This is not the same as saying that guys are bad. Guys *are* capable of doing bad things, but this generally happens when they try to be Men and start becoming manly and aggressive and stupid. When they're being just plain guys, they aren't so much actively *evil* as they are *lost*. Because guys have never really grasped the Basic Human Moral Code, which I believe was invented by women millions of years ago when all the guys were out engaging in some other activity, such as seeing who could burp the loudest. When they came back, there were certain rules that they were expected to follow unless they wanted to get into Big Trouble, and they have been trying to follow these rules ever since, with extremely irregular results. Because guys have never *internalized* these rules. Guys are similar to my small auxiliary backup dog, Zippy, a guy dog[4] who has been told numerous times that he is *not* supposed to (1) get into the kitchen garbage or (2) poop on the floor. He knows that these are the rules, but he has never really understood *why*, and sometimes he gets to thinking: Sure, I am *ordinarily* not supposed to get into the garbage, but obviously this rule is not meant to apply when there are certain extenuating[5] circumstances, such as (1) somebody just threw away some perfectly good seven-week-old Kung Pao Chicken, and (2) I am home alone.

And so when the humans come home, the kitchen floor has been transformed into GarbageFest USA, and Zippy, who usually comes rushing up, is off in a corner disguised in a wig and sunglasses, hoping to get into the Federal Bad Dog Relocation Program before the humans discover the scene of the crime.

When I yell at him, he frequently becomes so upset that he poops on the floor.

25

---

[4] I also have a female dog, Earnest, who *never* breaks the rules.

[5] I am taking some liberties here with Zippy's vocabulary. More likely, in his mind, he uses the term *mitigating*.

Morally, most guys are just like Zippy, only taller and usually less hairy. Guys are *aware* of the rules of moral behavior, but they have trouble keeping these rules in the forefronts of their minds at certain times, especially the present. This is especially true in the area of faithfulness to one's mate. I realize, of course, that there are countless examples of guys being faithful to their mates until they die, usually as a result of being eaten by their mates immediately following copulation. Guys outside of the spider community, however, do not have a terrific record of faithfulness.

I'm not saying guys are scum. I'm saying that many guys who consider themselves to be committed to their marriages will stray if they are confronted with overwhelming temptation, defined as "virtually any temptation."

Okay, so maybe I *am* saying guys are scum. But they're not *mean-spirited* scum. And few of them — even when they are out of town on business trips, far from their wives, and have a clear-cut opportunity — will poop on the floor.

GUYS ARE NOT GREAT AT COMMUNICATING THEIR INTIMATE FEELINGS, ASSUMING THEY HAVE ANY

This is an aspect of guyhood that is very frustrating to women. A guy will be reading the newspaper, and the phone will ring; he'll answer it, listen for ten minutes, hang up, and resume reading. Finally his wife will say: "Who was that?"

And he'll say: "Phil Wonkerman's mom."

(Phil is an old friend they haven't heard from in seventeen years.)

And the wife will say, "Well?"

And the guy will say, "Well what?"

And the wife will say, "What did she *say?*"

And the guy will say, "She said Phil is fine," making it clear by his tone of voice that, although he does not wish to be rude, he is trying to read the newspaper, and he happens to be right in the middle of an important panel of "Calvin and Hobbes."

But the wife, ignoring this, will say, "That's *all* she said?"

30

35

And she will not let up. She will continue to ask district-attorney-style questions, forcing the guy to recount the conversation until she's satisfied that she has the entire story, which is that Phil just got out of prison after serving a sentence for a murder he committed when he became a drug addict because of the guilt he felt when his wife died in a freak submarine accident while Phil was having an affair with a nun, but now he's all straightened out and has a good job as a trapeze artist and is almost through with the surgical part of his sex change and recently became happily engaged to marry a prominent member of the Grateful Dead, so in other words he is fine, which is *exactly* what the guy told her in the first place, but is that enough? No. She wants to hear *every single detail.*

Or let's say two couples get together after a long separation. The two women will have a conversation, lasting several days, during which they discuss virtually every significant event that has occurred in their lives and the lives of those they care about, sharing their innermost thoughts, analyzing and probing, inevitably coming to a deeper understanding of each other, and a strengthening of a cherished friendship. Whereas the guys will watch the play-offs.

This is not to say the guys won't share their feelings. Sometimes they'll get quite emotional.

"That's not a FOUL??" they'll say.

Or: "YOU'RE TELLING ME THAT'S NOT A *FOUL*???"

I have a good friend, Gene, and one time, when he was going through a major medical development in his life, we spent a weekend together. During this time Gene and I talked a lot and enjoyed each other's company immensely, but — this is true — the most intimate personal statement he made to me is that he has reached Level 24 of a video game called "Arkanoid." He had even seen the Evil Presence, although he refused to tell me what it looks like. We're very close, but there is a limit.

You may think that my friends and I are Neanderthals, and that a lot of guys are different. This is true. A lot of guys don't use words at *all*. They communicate entirely by nonverbal methods, such as sharing bait.

This section on "communication," especially this *communication between men and women, is the subject of several books by Deborah Tannen, whose studies might suggest that Barry is not far off the mark here.* —A.L.   40

I am glad to say I know some men who really are different, especially in the way they communicate their feelings. —A.L.

Example Chart

Men	Guys
Vince Lombardi	Joe Namath
Oliver North	Gilligan
Hemingway	Gary Larson
Columbus	Whichever astronaut hit the first golf ball on the Moon
Superman	Bart Simpson
Doberman pinschers	Labrador retrievers
Abbott	Costello
Captain Ahab	Captain Kangaroo
Satan	Snidely Whiplash
The pope	Willard Scott
Germany	Italy
Geraldo	Katie Couric

All kidding aside, I do think women need a better understanding of the way guys think, if that's the right verb for the process.
—J.R.

Are you starting to see what I mean by "guy-ness"? I'm basically talking about the part of the male psyche that is less serious and/or aggressive than the Manly Manhood part, but still essentially very male. My feeling is that the world would be a much better[6] place if more males would stop trying so hard to be Men and instead settle for being Guys. Think of the historical problems that could have been avoided if more males had been able to keep their genderhood in its proper perspective, both in themselves and in others. ("Hey, Adolf, just because you happen to possess a set of minor and frequently unreliable organs, that is no reason to invade Poland.") And think how much happier women would be if, instead of endlessly fretting about what the males in their lives are thinking, they could relax, secure in the knowledge that the correct answer is: *very little.*

45

C'mon, Dave . . . even you had to do some thinking to come up with this book. —A.L.

---

[6]As measured by total sales of [my] book.

Yes, what we need, on the part of both genders, is more understanding of guyness. And that is why I wrote this book. I intend to explore in detail every major facet of guyhood, including the historical facet, the sociological facet, the physiological facet, the psychosexual facet, and the facet of how come guys spit so much. Every statement of fact you will read in this book is either based on actual laboratory tests, or else I made it up. But you can trust me. I'm a guy.

Stimulus-Response Comparison Chart: Women vs. Men vs. Guys

Stimulus	Typical *Woman* Response	Typical *Man* Response	Typical *Guy* Response
An untamed river in the wilderness.	Contemplate its beauty.	Build a dam.	See who can pee the farthest off the dam.
A child who is sent home from school for being disruptive in class.	Talk to the child in an effort to determine the cause.	Threaten to send the child to a military academy.	Teach the child how to make armpit farts.
Human mortality	Religious faith	The pyramids	Bungee-jumping

QUESTIONING THE TEXT

1. Barry's humor obviously plays off of gross stereotypes about men. Underscore or annotate all the stereotypes you can find in the essay.

2. Barry employs a lengthy analogy featuring his dog Zippy to explore the moral behavior of guys (p. 410). In a group, discuss this analogy, focusing on the observations that seem especially apt.

MAKING CONNECTIONS

3. Pick any essay from this collection and give it the Dave Barry treatment. That is, try your hand at making readers see the subject from a comic perspective. You might, for example, write a short article portraying the issues in James Q. Wilson's "Cars and Their Enemies" (p. 320) as a battle between car nuts and tree-huggers, or think up some opportunities for humor after reading Kay S. Hymowitz's "Scenes from the Exhibitionists" (p. 233). Be certain your comic piece makes a point, and think carefully about audience: you will probably want to be careful not to offend.

4. Barry suggests that men love complicated gizmos that they can tinker with forever. Examine Barry's observations side by side with any of the readings on science and technology in Chapter 5. Write a serious response to Barry's humorous observations. Is science a male obsession with how things work? What evidence can you find in Chapter 5 to support your answer?

JOINING THE CONVERSATION

5. "Guys vs. Men" is almost a textbook exercise in writing an extended definition. Annotate the different techniques Barry uses to craft his definition (definition by contrast; class/characteristics; definition by example; negative definition). Then write a similar definitional piece — humorous if you like — contrasting two terms that might at first glance seem similar, such as chicks vs. women, cops vs. police officers, freshmen vs. first-year students.

6. Barry illustrates the competitiveness of men with a short anecdote about the forty-yard dash. Choose another stereotypical trait of either men or women (insensitivity, bad driving, excessive concern with appearance), and write an anecdote from your own experience that illustrates the trait. Try some of the techniques Barry uses to make his story funny: understatement, exaggeration, irony, self-deprecation, dialogue.

ZORA NEALE HURSTON
How It Feels to Be Colored Me

ZORA NEALE HURSTON *(1891–1960), born and raised in the first all-black town in the United States to be incorporated and self-governing (Eatonville, Florida), packed an astonishing number of careers and identities into her sixty-nine years. She was a "wardrobe girl" for traveling entertainers, a manicurist, an anthropologist and folklorist, a college professor, a drama coach, an editor, and — above all — a writer of great distinction. Author of numerous articles, essays, and stories as well as folklore collections, plays, and an autobiography, Hurston is today probably best known for her novels:* Their Eyes Were Watching God *(1937),* Jonah's Gourd Vine *(1934), and* Moses, Man of the Mountain *(1939).*

Hurston studied anthropology at Barnard College, where she was the only African American student, and gained a strong reputation for her academic work on folklore. But by the 1930s, she was being criticized for what were said to be caricatures of blacks, especially in her "minstrel" novels. Her growing conservatism led to further attacks from writers such as Richard Wright, and by 1950, her reputation gone, she was working in Florida as a maid. Evicted from her home in 1956, she suffered a stroke in 1959 and died, penniless, the next year. In recent years, Alice Walker sought out her unmarked grave in Fort Pierce, Florida, and erected a marker in memory of Hurston and her work, which is, today, widely read and influential.

The essay that follows, published in World Tomorrow *(May 1928), challenges the notion that American identity is connected to freedom, the "home of the brave," and the "land of the free." Hurston is deeply aware of such ironies and of the bitter struggles obscured by the happy image of an American identity forged in the melting pot. But she is not cast down or resentful; she has no time to waste on negativity. I chose "How It Feels to Be Colored Me" for its irrepressible spirit in the face of what are clear inequalities in America, for its ironic self-representation, and for the sheer delight it gives me to think that Hurston's spirit has triumphed after all.* —A.L.

I am colored but I offer nothing in the way of extenuating circumstances except the fact that I am the only Negro in the United States whose grandfather on the mother's side was *not* an Indian chief.

I remember the very day that I became colored. Up to my thirteenth year I lived in the little Negro town of Eatonville, Florida. It is exclusively a colored town. The only white people I knew passed through the town going to or coming from Orlando. The native whites rode dusty horses, the Northern tourists chugged down the sandy village road in automobiles. The town knew the Southerners and never stopped cane chewing* when they passed. But the Northerners were something else again. They were peered at cautiously from behind curtains by the timid. The more venturesome would come out on the porch to watch them go past and got just as much pleasure out of the tourists as the tourists got out of the village.

The front porch might seem a daring place for the rest of the town, but it was a gallery seat for me. My favorite place was atop the gate-post. Proscenium box for a born first-nighter. Not only did I enjoy the show, but I didn't mind the actors knowing that I liked it. I usually spoke to them in passing. I'd wave at them and when they returned my salute, I would say something like this: "Howdy-do-well-I-thank-you-where-you-goin'?" Usually automobile or the horse paused at this, and after a queer exchange of compliments, I would probably "go a piece of the way" with them, as we say in farthest Florida. If one of my family happened to come to the front in time to see me, of course negotiations would be rudely broken off. But even so, it is clear that I was the first "welcome-to-our-state" Floridian, and I hope the Miami Chamber of Commerce will please take notice.

During this period, white people differed from colored to me only in that they rode through town and never lived there. They liked to hear me "speak pieces" and sing and wanted to see me dance the parse-me-la, and gave me generously of their small silver for doing these things, which seemed strange to me for I wanted to do them so much that I needed bribing to stop. Only they didn't know it. The colored people gave no dimes. They deplored any joyful tendencies in me, but I was their Zora nevertheless. I belonged to them, to the nearby hotels, to the country — everybody's Zora.

But changes came in the family when I was thirteen, and I was sent to   5
school in Jacksonville. I left Eatonville, the town of the oleanders, as Zora. When I disembarked from the river-boat at Jacksonville, she was no more. It seemed that I had suffered a sea change. I was not Zora of Orange County any more. I was now a little colored girl. I found it out in certain ways. In my heart as well as in the mirror, I became a fast brown — warranted not to rub nor run.

But I am not tragically colored. There is no great sorrow dammed up in my soul, nor lurking behind my eyes. I do not mind at all. I do not belong to the sobbing school of Negrohood who hold that nature somehow has given them a lowdown dirty deal and whose feelings are all hurt about it. Even in the helter-skelter skirmish that is my life, I have seen that the world is to the strong* regardless of a little pigmentation more or less. No, I do not weep at the world — I am too busy sharpening my oyster knife.*

---

cane chewing: chewing sugar-cane stalks

the world is to the strong: an allusion to the biblical passage (in Ecclesiastes 9:11) that reads "The race is not to the swift, nor the battle to the strong"

sharpening my oyster knife: an allusion to the saying "The world is my oyster," which appears in Shakespeare's *The Merry Wives of Windsor*

Someone is always at my elbow reminding me that I am the grand-daughter of slaves. It fails to register depression with me. Slavery is sixty years in the past. The operation was successful and the patient is doing well, thank you. The terrible struggle* that made me an American out of a potential slave said "On the line!" The Reconstruction said "Get set!"; and the generation before said "Go!" I am off to a flying start and I must not halt in the stretch to look behind and weep. Slavery is the price I paid for civilization, and the choice was not with me. It is a bully adventure and worth all that I have paid through my ancestors for it. No one on earth ever had a greater chance for glory. The world to be won and nothing to be lost. It is thrilling to think — to know that for any act of mine, I shall get twice as much praise or twice as much blame. It is quite exciting to hold the center of the national stage, with the spectators not know-ing whether to laugh or to weep.

The position of my white neighbor is much more difficult. No brown specter pulls up a chair beside me when I sit down to eat. No dark ghost thrusts its leg against mine in bed. The game of keeping what one has is never so ex-citing as the game of getting.

I do not always feel colored. Even now I often achieve the unconscious Zora of Eatonville before the Hegira. I feel most colored when I am thrown against a sharp white background.

For instance at Barnard. "Beside the waters of the Hudson"* I feel my   10 race. Among the thousand white persons, I am a dark rock surged upon, and overswept, but through it all, I remain myself. When covered by the waters, I am; and the ebb but reveals me again.

Sometimes it is the other way around. A white person is set down in our midst, but the contrast is just as sharp for me. For instance, when I sit in the drafty basement that is The New World Cabaret with a white person, my color comes. We enter chatting about any little nothing that we have in common and are seated by the jazz waiters. In the abrupt way that jazz orchestras have, this one plunges into a number. It loses no time in circumlocutions, but gets right down to business. It constricts the thorax and splits the heart with its tempo and narcotic harmonies. This orchestra grows rambunctious, rears on its hind legs and attacks the tonal veil with primitive fury, rending it, clawing it until it breaks through to the jungle beyond. I follow those heathen — follow them exultingly. I dance wildly inside myself; I yell within, I whoop; I shake my as-segai above my head, I hurl it true to the mark *yeeeeooww!* I am in the jungle and living in the jungle way. My face is painted red and yellow and my body is

---

the terrible struggle: the Civil War
        "Beside the waters of the Hudson": Barnard College is near the Hudson River in New York City. For another account of how it felt to be a black student at Columbia University in the early twentieth century, see the poem by Langston Hughes, "Theme for English B" (p. 484).

painted blue. My pulse is throbbing like a war drum. I want to slaughter something — give pain, give death to what, I do not know. But the piece ends. The
men of the orchestra wipe their lips and rest their fingers. I creep back slowly
to the veneer we call civilization with the last tone and find the white friend
sitting motionless in his seat, smoking calmly.

"Good music they have here," he remarks, drumming the table with his
fingertips.

Music. The great blobs of purple and red emotion have not touched him.
He has only heard what I felt. He is far away and I see him but dimly across the
ocean and the continent that have fallen between us. He is so pale with his
whiteness then and I am *so* colored.

At certain times I have no race, I am *me*. When I set my hat at a certain
angle and saunter down Seventh Avenue, Harlem City, feeling as snooty as the
lions in front of the Forty-Second Street Library,* for instance. So far as my
feelings are concerned, Peggy Hopkins Joyce* on the Boule Mich* with her
gorgeous raiment, stately carriage, knees knocking together in a most aristo-
cratic manner, has nothing on me. The cosmic Zora emerges. I belong to no
race nor time. I am the eternal feminine with its string of beads.

I have no separate feeling about being an American citizen and colored.   15
I am merely a fragment of the Great Soul that surges within the boundaries.
My country, right or wrong.

Sometimes, I feel discriminated against, but it does not make me angry.
It merely astonishes me. How *can* any deny themselves the pleasure of my
company? It's beyond me.

But in the main, I feel like a brown bag of miscellany propped against a
wall. Against a wall in company with other bags, white, red and yellow. Pour
out the contents, and there is discovered a jumble of small things priceless and
worthless. A first-water diamond, an empty spool, bits of broken glass, lengths
of string, a key to a door long since crumbled away, a rusty knife-blade, old
shoes saved for a road that never was and never will be, a nail bent under the
weight of things too heavy for any nail, a dried flower or two still a little fra-
grant. In your hand is the brown bag. On the ground before you is the jumble
it held — so much like the jumble in the bags, could they be emptied, that all
might be dumped in a single heap and the bags refilled without altering the
content of any greatly. A bit of colored glass more or less would not matter.
Perhaps that is how the Great Stuffer of Bags filled them in the first place —
who knows?

---

the lions in front of the Forty-Second Street Library: two statues of lions that stand in front of
the main building of the New York Public Library, on Fifth Avenue at 42nd Street

Peggy Hopkins Joyce: a famous beauty who set fashions in the 1920s

the Boule Mich: the Boulevard Saint-Michel, a street in Paris

QUESTIONING THE TEXT

1. Color is a central theme in this brief essay. Jot down as many of the ways color appears as you can remember. Then go back and check the text. Complete your list, and compare it with the lists of others in your class. What are the different things color is attributed to?

2. In her introduction to this essay, A.L. makes absolutely clear how much she admires Hurston. How does her praise affect your evaluation of the essay?

3. Hurston exemplifies the *differences* among people in her vivid descriptions of her experience of jazz (paragraph 11). First, try to describe your experience with the kind of music that most engages and moves you. What do you find in common with or different from Hurston's experience? Does what you have discovered lead you to see "sharp" contrasts, as Hurston does, or commonalities? What do such contrasts and commonalities have to do with your race? With some other feature of your identity?

MAKING CONNECTIONS

4. Read Hurston's piece along with Langston Hughes's "Theme for English B" (p. 484). Do these writers hold different — or similar — views on commonalities among all people? Explain your answer in an informal statement (about a page or two) addressed to your class.

5. As the title of this essay suggests, Hurston attempts to capture what it feels like to be African American in the United States in the early twentieth century. Lynda Barry's "Common Scents" (p. 445) also offers personal experiences, giving readers an idea of what it might feel like to be from a family that does not blend in with the neighbors. Compare Hurston's essay to Barry's comic. Which do you think better conveys what it feels like to be in the author's shoes? What is it about the writing that enables you to empathize with the author (or prevents you from doing so)? How does your own identity inform your response?

JOINING THE CONVERSATION

6. Hurston concludes with a simile about bags. First, consider what simile or metaphor you might use to describe your own race or ethnicity and its relationship to others. Begin perhaps by completing the sentence "But in the main, I feel like . . ." Then write an extended description of your simile or metaphor, and bring it to class for discussion.

7. Working with two or three classmates, draft a composite description of the metaphors you came up with. What do these metaphors have in common? How do they differ?

TYINA L. STEPTOE
An Ode to Country Music from a Black Dixie Chick

"*WHAT IF THREE SOUTHERN BLACK WOMEN living in the frozen tundra of Wisconsin formed a Dixie Chicks cover band?*" This is the question Tyina L. Steptoe (b. 1975), currently a Ford Foundation Fellow completing her Ph.D. in history in Wisconsin, asked herself before she joined with two other graduate students to form Blixie (a combination of Black and Dixie), the band that went on not only to cover for the Dixie Chicks but to perform their own original blues, rock, and country music. A blurb about the band on MySpace calls the group "the hottest thing in underground-country-R&B-hip-hop-blues" that has bloomed into a "cross-racial, cross-gender, cross-regional musical collective that defies description and aims to rewrite the rules of American music once again."

This is not a future Tyina Steptoe would have predicted for herself when she was a teenager in Houston. There she rejected country music (even though she secretly liked some of it) because she associated it with "urban cowboys and racist white folk." Speaking on a panel in 2006, Steptoe remembered those high school days, when every morning the campus parking lot was the scene of a musical show-down: "While a crowd of white students known as 'kickers' blasted country music from their trucks while proudly waving Confederate flags, groups of black, Latino, Asian, and white students who disliked country music competed by blaring an assortment of hip, hop, rock, and tejano." So when she found herself moved to tears by listening to a Dixie Chicks song in a Madison music store, she was, to say the least, surprised. One country song led to another, however, and four years later she held her own "country coming-out party."

In "An Ode to Country Music from a Black Dixie Chick," Steptoe challenges her earlier stereotyping assumptions about country music and the people who like it, though she still wonders if the film and music industries will "ever acknowledge the existence of little black boys who want to be cowboys and little black girls who sing along with the Dixie Chicks." Steptoe says she has hope that the industries will come around and points to the fact that the Country Music Hall of Fame (finally) honored African American DeFord Bailey. Check back in a decade to see if her hope is well placed.

I chose this article because I remember my own graduate school days and the fervent desire to do almost anything rather than continue work on my dissertation, and I especially remember a group of women grad students (all white) who reveled in escaping from the library to perform parodic versions of Tammy Wynette's syrupy "Stand by Your Man." So when I read about Blixie, I was fascinated. But reading this article also led me to think more deeply about my own musical stereotypes and prejudices — and to ask where they came from and what I could learn about myself by interrogating them. You may well find yourself asking the same questions after you read about the Black Dixie Chicks.

—A.L.   **421**

Sissy wasn't a real cowgirl. She didn't own a horse and probably wouldn't have known what to do with a pair of spurs. She didn't live on the wide-open range but in a trailer in one of the largest cities in the United States. Nevertheless, at 10 p.m. every night, Sissy strode into Gilley's, a cavernous nightclub in Pasadena, Texas, just outside of Houston, where thousands of people came to two-step the night away. But what Sissy really loved was riding the bull. Once on top of the mechanical monster, she could ride it backwards and forwards, and sometimes she even rode it like a surfboard. Unfortunately, Sissy's ability to outride even the toughest of the citified cowboys caused major problems in her marriage to Bud, an oil-refinery worker she met and wed at Gilley's. Bud quickly found another cute girl in boots who wouldn't challenge his manhood and left Sissy looking for love in all the wrong places.

As a kid I knew the saga of Sissy and Bud from countless viewings of the 1980 film *Urban Cowboy*. I loved every scene of the movie, from the moment Sissy sidles up to Bud and asks, "Are you a real cowboy?" until she ultimately rides away with him in his pickup truck. I could even sing all the words to their theme song, "Lookin' for Love," by Johnny Lee.

But I never admitted it.

You see, I'm a black chick from Houston, born and bred in the shadow of pine trees and petrochemical plants. Sissy, played by Debra Winger, was a familiar archetype; I know plenty of girls who got married in cowboy boots. But although the two-stepping, longneck-swilling, parking-lot-fighting atmosphere of Gilley's (both real and fictional) remained close to home, I never considered myself part of that scene. By the time I was in high school, I understood that it was not cool for black girls to listen to country music or enter a honky tonk. You couldn't have paid me to walk around wearing Wranglers or even admit that I kind of liked Garth Brooks.

So imagine my surprise when I found myself, at age twenty-three, reduced to tears in a music store in Madison, Wisconsin, when I heard the familiar strains of "Cowboy Take Me Away" coming through the speaker system. It was my first semester of graduate school, and this song, performed by three white women from Texas, left me with the most profound sense of homesickness I'd felt since leaving the Lone Star State. That day I bought my first country CD, *Fly*. I began to seek out other reminders of home, and I eventually bought a used video of *Urban Cowboy*, which I watched repeatedly with my boyfriend. The first time we viewed it together, I pointed to the screen and said with some pride, "Look, it's where I'm from!"

That's the thing about homesickness: Sometimes you never know what home means until you leave it.

Four years later, I stood onstage in a popular nightclub in Madison, my corn-rowed hair crammed beneath a black cowboy hat. I looked out at the audience and began to sing:

> I said I wanna touch the earth
> I wanna break it in my hands
> I wanna grow something wild and unruly

5

And there it was — the first notes of my country coming-out party.

My band began as a joke. The concept grew from a conversation I'd had with two fellow grad students, Holly McGee and Kori Graves, about the Dixie Chicks' infamous Bush-bashing. I realized that Holly and Kori, both African Americans from the South, loved the Chicks as much as I did and knew the words to most of their songs, and our idea occurred almost instantly. What if three Southern black women living in the frozen tundra of Wisconsin formed a Dixie Chicks cover band? Together, we would bring the Dirty South to the cold North. We settled on the name Blixie, short for Black Dixie. Two of our classmates, Dave Gilbert and Charles Hughes, both Northern white dudes and phenomenal guitar players, rounded out the band. Our friends invited us to play at house parties, and soon we were performing at clubs across the city. We eventually evolved into more than a cover band and released an album of original tunes that included blues and soul music as well as country. Nowadays, I am a full-fledged country-music fan. In my CD changer, Julie Roberts rests comfortably next to Mary J. Blige.

After watching a Blixie performance, some people are shocked to learn   10
that I never gave country music a chance when I lived in the South. They are even more baffled when I tell them that my reasons for previously tuning it out are steeped in racial politics. After all, my boyfriend, Jerome, who is also African American, grew up listening to country music in suburban Atlanta and never felt any shame. He, however, attended a Protestant private school where everyone listened to country music, regardless of race. My high school was different. Located on the northeast side of Houston, North Shore Senior High was home to a mix of students who generally did not associate with one another outside of racially specific cliques. My best friend, though, was white, and we tried to buck the system: Through Stacy, I grew to appreciate Pearl Jam and Stone Temple Pilots. She, in turn, loved *The Chronic* by Dr. Dre, and often drove around town bumping Eightball & MJG in her car. But my prejudice against country music remained strong. I associated it, along with cowboy hats and pointed-toe boots, with a particular type of white person, the kind that painted Confederate flags on their trucks and called me "nigger." At my high school, we referred to them as shit-kickers, or "kickers" for short. To put it simply, I equated these urban cowboys with racist white folk — people I called "rednecks" in my less politically correct days. But why did I see cowboys and country music as white when black, red, and brown people have influenced both?

During the heyday of the cattle industry in the 1870s and 1880s, African American, Mexicano, Native American, and white men worked the range on horseback. But cowboy heroes have largely been portrayed as white, beginning as early as 1877 with Deadwood Dick, a fictional white cowboy who was most likely based on the African American slave Nat Love.

In the late 1970s, America's favorite hero — still white — returned in full form, but this time he rode a mechanical bull, lived in the city, and drove a pickup truck blaring country music. In 1978, Aaron Latham, a Texas-born editor at *Esquire* magazine, traveled to Houston to write a story about the rollicking nightlife at Gilley's and concluded that "country music is the city cowboy's Bible, his literature, his self-help book, his culture." Latham's article became the basis for the *Urban Cowboy* screenplay. Led by songs like "Lookin' for Love," the *Urban Cowboy* soundtrack went triple platinum, making it one of the top albums of the year.

"In these anxious days," Latham writes, "some Americans have turned for salvation to God, others have turned to fad prophets, but more and more people are turning to the cowboy hat." After Civil Rights, women's lib, and an unprecedented influx of immigrants, the nation looked entirely different than it had thirty years earlier. Between 1970 and 1980, Houston's population had nearly doubled, and the Latino presence had exploded by a hundred percent, causing some to complain that Mexicans were taking union jobs from white men.

Now, obviously, I was not deconstructing *Urban Cowboy* as a child, but what I saw in the film and around me in northeast Houston confirmed the notion that the kicker ethos is white, from cowboy boots to country music. In all my viewings of *Urban Cowboy*, I've never spotted a single black or Latino, even though Houston was one of the most diverse cities in the country. That said, placing people of color on the Gilley's dance floor would have been unrealistic because the honky tonk was, for the most part, a white, working-class space.

In order for me to fully enjoy country music and dress kicker-style for   15
Blixie performances, I had to confront my own racial bias. Not all people who idolize cowboys are white, and the white people who do aren't always bigots. That stereotype is just as wrong as when a salesclerk follows me around a store because he or she thinks that my brown skin and braided hair make me a thug. My own father, who came of age in Jim Crow Houston, wanted to be a cowboy, and in photographs from 1958 he's dressed in full cowboy attire. With his grandmother's old broomstick handle serving as a horse, the eight-year-old boy rode the wild range of Fifth Ward every afternoon. To this day, a picture of John Wayne adorns a wall in his garage.

But will the film and music industries ever acknowledge the existence of little black boys who want to be cowboys and black girls who sing along with the Dixie Chicks? I think there is hope. This past year the Country Music Hall of Fame honored African American DeFord Bailey for his contributions to the genre. And in fusing hip-hop and country, Cowboy Troy (who also plays with the band Big & Rich) gives the world a twenty-first-century version of an urban cowboy. And, of course, there's that lil' ol' country-blues band in Madison, Wisconsin.

QUESTIONING THE TEXT

1. Steptoe opens her article with a plot summary of *Urban Cowboy* and discusses the popularity of that film later in her article. How does she use

that film as a way into understanding her own life? How does she use it to comment on larger social trends?

2. This article originally appeared in the magazine *The Oxford American*, which has as its slogan "The Southern Magazine of Good Writing." Would you consider Steptoe's article to be well written? Identifying specific textual examples, explain why you do or do not consider Steptoe's article to be an example of good writing.

MAKING CONNECTIONS

3. When Steptoe hears the song "Cowboy Take Me Away" in a Madison, Wisconsin, music store, she's "reduced to tears" (paragraph 5) because the music reminds her of home. Lynda Barry (p. 445) writes in the last panel of her comic that if she could find a spray can of the smells of her childhood home, she'd buy that. What artistic or sensory experiences evoke memories of home or youth for you? Write an essay in which you describe how an experience reminded you of a different place or time.

4. Both Tyina Steptoe and Zora Neale Hurston ("How It Feels to Be Colored Me," p. 416) write about the experience of being African American women, but at very different points in American history. How do their experiences and attitudes differ? How are they similar?

JOINING THE CONVERSATION

5. In a short essay, describe a situation in which, like Steptoe, you embraced an identity that was at odds with what others expected of you. Why did the identity you embraced appeal to you? How do your various identities intersect?

6. Write an essay in which you analyze how your tastes — in music, fashion, movies, cars, or something you feel strongly about — contribute to your understanding of your identity.

ANDRE DUBUS
Witness

Andre Dubus (1937–99) was known to many as a "writer's writer." Author of eleven books and winner of numerous awards, including MacArthur and Guggenheim Fellowships and the runner-up Pulitzer Prize for 1992, Dubus has been described by reviewer Gary Kamiya as "one of the great psychological realists among contemporary writers of short fiction."

Dubus was also a powerful essayist. In "Witness," he takes readers with him on a typical Thursday — typical, that is, in the years since 1986, when he was hit by a car as he struggled to help two people whose car was disabled. That night, he lost most of his left leg; his right leg was shattered. On this particular Thursday, he spends time in his wheelchair and, while he waits to pick up his youngest daughters for dinner at his house, muses on pain and on the will to live. Read this essay, which originally appeared in the New Yorker (July 21, 1997), and revisit the night of his accident, a night that led to an identity shift for Dubus, to bouts of depression, and to a long hiatus from writing. And join Dubus and his family on the day he decided to write this essay.

In an interview with his hometown newspaper, Dubus recalled advice his daughter Nicole had given him: "keep writing essays about the wheelchair and let the wheelchair come into your stories and gradually it will leave." "Witness" is one of those essays, and I wanted to include it here because Dubus faces "sorrow and fear and rain" and still manages to make it through to the light. —A.L.

Thursday during the school year is a wheelchair day; they are all wheelchair days, but some more than others. On Thursdays I drive thirty minutes to Andover, the town where my daughters live. They are Cadence and Madeleine, fourteen and nine. I go to their school and park on the road that goes through the grounds and wait for their classes to end at three-twenty. My right leg hurts when I drive; it hurts when it is not at a ninety-degree angle, and most nights it hurts anyway. While driving I have to place my foot to the left of the brake pedal, and that angle makes my leg hurt sooner, and more. Often my back hurts. Years ago I learned that pain and wheelchair fatigue — *sitting*, and worrying about what can go wrong because I can't stand or walk — take most of my energy; I cannot live as normals do, and I must try to do only what is essential each day. So on Thursdays I neither write nor exercise. I make snacks for my daughters, wrap two ice packs around my leg, drive and wait, then take them to my house for dinner, then back to their house, and then I return to host a writers' workshop at my home. I like Thursdays.

I could leave my house at two-thirty or so, and my leg would not start hurting till after three, my back not till after four, or even later, or not at all.

But I try to leave by one-thirty. I bring lunch and a book, and drive to the school. I park and eat a sandwich, drink water, and read. There is no telephone. I have a car phone, which I would not have as a biped. It is harmless. It can ring only when the ignition is on, and no one knows its number; I don't know its number. In the car, I read. The pain starts. At home the phone rings and rings, and when I am writing I don't answer; but when I am reading I feel that I should answer it. But even with the pain, there is peace in the car. The moral torque is that by the time the girls come out of school the pain is tiring me. I have to be wary of impatience and irritation. A few days ago I read that a samurai philosophy is to refrain until you can respond instead of reacting. I must work on that.

This fall, in 1996, there is another difficulty: the girls have a dog. And on Thursdays the dog is alone in the house and by late afternoon it needs to be walked, to relieve itself, be a leashed animal outdoors. So from school we drive to the house where the girls live with their mother, and they go inside. The house has front steps, so I have never been in it. I would need a man to get me inside, probably three — depending on the men — to go upstairs to the rooms where my daughters sleep. While I wait in the car, I cannot imagine what the girls are doing in the house whose walls and ceilings and furniture and rooms do not exist as images in my mind. Inside the girls are invisible and soundless; they do not come out with the dog. I admire what I call their anarchy. I cannot make them hurry, not even to a movie or a play, which I tell them will start whether or not we are there; they remain insouciant. I am flesh enclosing tension: we have never been late for a movie or a play. In the car, my leg and back do not admire the girls' anarchy. Patience is leaving, irritation arriving. I read. Then, to my right, I glimpse motion; I look and see the girls finally coming out of the house, the brown short-haired dog ahead of them. Cadence holds the taut leash. The dog is of medium size, younger, eager, wagging her tail, sniffing the air. They cross the street behind me, I watch them in the mirror, then they go through a tree line — again they are invisible — and into a large field. When they disappear I'm briefly frightened; someone could do something to them. I read, I smoke, sometimes I grunt or moan.

I want the girls to have a dog, and I want them to be happily walking the dog in the field. But I also want my leg to stop hurting. I want to be home with my leg on the wheelchair's leg rest. I want to be there eating dinner with my daughters.

A woman who was my Eucharistic minister, bringing me Communion   5 when I could not go to Mass for more than a year after I got hit, once said to me, "Don't think about what you want; think about what you need." What do I need, sitting in this car? Courage? Patience? I can think only that I need the pain to leave me. My energy is flowing into it. And it is not bad pain. For bad pain there are good drugs. By now the ice packs are thawed. What I need, waiting for my girls, is for this part of the day to end. It does. After twenty-five minutes or so, they come through the tree line and cross the street and return the dog to their house. Time passes. Then they come out and get into the car and

I drive to my home where a woman I pay is cooking dinner. It is five o'clock. The girls go to Cadence's room and shut the door and play classical music for the potted plants. They study, I answer phone messages, throw away mail, keep what I have to answer or pay. At five-thirty we eat.

On a Thursday in late October, I drove with my girls from the school to their house. The sky was blue, the air warm, and there were yellow and red autumn leaves; and at the girls' house, to relieve the pain in my leg, I got out of the car. I do this by lowering my wheelchair from a carrier that holds it on the roof. With Joan Didion's *The Last Thing He Wanted*, I got in my chair and went to the front of my car, using it as a shield against the very few moving cars on this street with houses and trees. My leg rested in front of me. Soon it would stop hurting. Two young boys wearing helmets were on skateboards in the road. My daughters have new neighbors across the street. Out of that house came a brown-haired woman in her thirties, carrying a very young boy. She looked at me, then called to the skateboarding boys, told them they could not play in the street. They stalled, pleaded, then skated to the sidewalk. She looked at me again. The boy in her arms wore glasses, and was squirming. The woman came to me, looking down now at my face. She said. "I've been wanting to talk to you for some time, I saw your accident."

"You did?"

"I was with my friend at the call box."

Ten years, three months, and one day before this lovely October after-noon, between midnight and one in the morning, on I–93 north of Boston, I saw a car stopped on the highway. It was a four-lane highway, and the car was in the third lane. There was another car in the breakdown lane, and two women were standing at an emergency call box. Now one of those two women was here, and I felt as I might if she had told me that long ago we were classmates. We introduced ourselves, shook hands. She said she had just moved to this street and had been talking to neighbors and had realized that I was the man she saw that night. She saw two men hit; the other one died within hours.

She said, "You're an author?"   10

"Yes."

The boy, not yet three, twisted in her arms, grunted, reached for my wheelchair. His thick glasses made his eyes seem large.

"You were hit by a silver — " She named a car I know nothing about, but not the right one.

I said, "It was a Honda Prelude."

"And it paralyzed you?"   15

"No. Only my leg's useless. I'm very lucky. I had three broken vertebrae in my back. But my spine was okay. My brain." I felt that I was reciting; as I spoke I was seeing her at the call box while I drove up to the driver's side of the car that had stopped, the last one I ever walked to. "Where were you coming from?" I asked.

"Joe's American Bar and Grill. My friend and I ate there, and had some drinks."

"The one at the mall?"

After we see a play, my girls and I eat at a seafood restaurant near Joe's at a mall; I was imagining us doing that, connecting places with this woman standing beside me.

"No. In Boston."   20

"Where were you going?"

"Andover. I haven't driven the same since that night."

"Neither have I."

The boy was strong and kept turning, lunging, reaching. She said, "I have to get his stroller."

She carried him across the street and into her house, and I sat among   25
fallen leaves near the curb and looked up at yellow leaves and branches and the sky, and saw the woman and her friend at the restaurant, then at the call box. The two skateboarding boys were not ten years old; since that night she had borne three sons; and my daughter Madeleine had been born. The woman came out with her son strapped into a stroller and crossed the street. The boy reached for the leg rest of my chair. She said, "He goes to a special school. He sees a lot of kids in wheelchairs."

"What's wrong with him?"

"Probably autism. He's too young for the tests."

He was looking at a book with pictures. Then he started tearing it, its cover, too; he tore it in half, then into quarters. He was concentrating, grunting. I said, "He's very strong."

She smiled, and said "They aren't supposed to be able to tear them."

"He's got a life in there."   30

"Oh, he does. It's me who's frustrated. Because I can't talk to him. And I know he's frustrated because he can't talk."

The girls came out with their dog and looked at me and the woman, and I said, "Have you met your neighbor?" They came to the sidewalk, and I said, "She was there the night I got hit."

Madeleine looked intently at her; Cadence's mouth opened, and in her cheeks color rose, and she said, "You *were?*"

I saw in her face something that was in my soul, though I did not know it yet; I felt only the curiosity you might feel on hearing an unusual sound in the dark outside your window; Cadence looked as though she had just heard something painful, but it had not yet fully struck her. I introduced the woman and her son to my girls, then they went off with their dog. I looked up at the woman, seeing her beside the highway watching me fly over the car, land on its trunk. My blood wanted to know; it rushed. She said, "The woman in the broken-down car was running around in the highway."

"She was standing in the speed lane. I was trying to get her off the road."   35

The man who died was her brother.

For a moment I was there: a clear July night, no cars coming, everything I had to do seeming easy. I said, "I'm glad you had already called the state troopers. They saved my life. I might have bled to death."

"Someone else would have called."

"Maybe. But *after* I was hit."

The boy was trying to get out of his stroller; he reached for my leg rest, for a wheel of the chair, lunged and twisted in the straps.

"I have to take him in," she said.   40

I wanted to ask her what she saw, but I could not; it was like waiting to confess something, waiting for that moment, for the words to come. When I got hit, I did not lose consciousness, but have never remembered being hit, only flagging down a car for help, then lying on its trunk.

I watched her cross the street with her son and, at her stairs, lift him from the stroller and carry him inside. I began reading again. Soon a car turned the corner behind me and stopped at the woman's house; I watched a man go inside; he was not big, but his shoulders and chest were broad, and he walked with an energy that sometimes saddens me. When my daughters and their dog returned from the field, I moved to my car door, put the leg and arm rest into the back seat, and got in. Before I raised the wheelchair to its carrier, the man came out of the house, carrying his son, and walked to me. He reached over the wheelchair and we shook hands and exchanged names. His face did not have that serious look of some men, as though all play were gone from their lives, and there was only work, money, the future they may not be alive for. He was a man who could be joyful. I can now see his face more clearly than I see his wife's; when I try to remember her, I see her standing at the call box, a body whose face I could not see in the night.

"My wife said she talked to you."

"It's incredible. I've never met anyone who saw me get hit."

"She called me that night. What's it like for you, after ten years?"   45

"It's better. I'm used to some things. I still can't drive alone to Boston, at night on 93."

"Oh, that's a protective device."

"Really? You mean I don't have to think of myself as a wimp?"

"No, no. I believe everything we have is a gift."

We talked about his work, and his son, who was moving in his arms, and   50 he said he'd like to have a beer with me sometime; he would get me up his steps. I told him I would like that. In his face were the sorrow and tenderness of love as he strongly held his writhing son, looking at the small face that seemed feral in its isolation. We shook hands and he went inside.

I started the car, picked up the switch that's attached to a wire on the floor, and pressed it, and the carrier on the roof lowered, two chains with an elongated hook, which I inserted into a slot under the chair's seat. I flicked the switch again, this time in the other direction, and the chains pulled the chair up.

But when it reached the frame of the carrier, it stopped. The motor was silent. I released the switch, tried it again. It clicked. The chair did not move. I kept pushing the switch. Its click was disproportionately loud, a sound without promise; yet I kept doing it. The chair was too high for me to reach it and try to take it off the hook, and a thirty-inch metal frame was jutting out from my car.

This is why I have a car phone: for circumstances that require legs. My son-in-law, Tom, is a mechanic. I called him, thirty minutes away in southern New Hampshire. He said he would come. I was calm. I have never been calm when the wheelchair carrier fails, and usually I am not calm for hours after Tom has fixed it. But that day I was calm, maybe because I had started the day by going to Mass — this always helps — or maybe because my spirit was on the highway on the twenty-third of July in 1986.

I would not have the time to be rescued, then drive my daughters to my house for dinner at five-thirty. My daughters were still inside. When they came out, I told them, and we kissed goodbye, and they went back inside. I phoned the woman at my house, and said we would not need dinner. I read Didion. Tom came in his truck, looked under the hood, worked there for a while, then said it was fixed, for now, but he would have to get a part. My knowledge of things mechanical is very small: pens, manual typewriters, guns. I drove home, feeling that I was on the circumference of a broken circle whose separated ends were moving toward each other. Soon they would meet. Next time I saw her, I would ask everything.

Around seven-twenty, writers began arriving for the workshop, and some of us waited on the sundeck for those still on the road. I told them about the woman and said that next time I would ask her if she saw me get hit; when I heard myself say that, I was suddenly afraid of images I have been spared, and I said no, I would not ask her. We went to the living room, and I told the story again, to the people who had not been on the deck; this time, as I talked, curiosity and wonder left me, as though pushed out of my mouth by the dread rising from my stomach. I looked at the faces of the women and men sitting on the couch, the love seat, the window seat; we formed a rectangle. I was alone at one end. I felt faint, as if I had lost blood. I said, "I think I'll go into a little shock tonight, or tomorrow."

But I was calm that night, and Friday, and Saturday. On Sunday we had a family dinner with three of my grown children, their spouses, the older son's two small children, and Cadence and Madeleine. That morning the sky was blue, and I was on my bed, doing leg lifts. When I swung my leg and stump up for the fiftieth time, I began quietly to cry. Then I stopped. I made the bed, dressed, ate yogurt and strawberries, showered, dressed on my bed. The tears were gone and would not come back, but my soul was gray and cool, and pieces of it were tossed as by a breeze that had become a strong wind and could become a storm. I drove to the girls' house. They live on the corner of the street,

55

and when I turned onto it I saw the woman in her yard. She was doing some kind of work, her back was to me, and I looked away from her, at the girls' house, and I phoned them to say I'm here.

At my house we cooked on the grill, and I sat on the deck, my face warmed by the sun, and talked with my children and enjoyed the afternoon. I looked up at my two sons and told them of suddenly crying while doing leg lifts, of being fragile now, and as I talked to them I made a decision I never make, a decision about writing, because my decisions usually gestate for months, often more than a year, before I try to write anything: I told them I would start writing this on Monday, because meeting the woman, shaking her hand, hearing her voice, seeing her sons, especially the youngest one, and shaking her husband's hand, hearing his witness — *She called me that night* — had so possessed me that I may as well plunge into it, write it, not to rid myself of it, because writing does not rid me of anything, but just to go there, to wherever the woman had taken me, to go there and find the music for it, and see if in that place there was any light.

Next day I woke to a wind that brought sorrow and fear and rain, while beyond the glass doors in front of my desk the sky was blue, and leaves were red and yellow, and I wrote. For ten days I woke and lived with this storm, and with the rain were demons that always come on a bad wind: loneliness, mortality, legs. Then it was gone, as any storm. They stop. The healing tincture of time, a surgeon told me in the hospital. On the eleventh day, I woke with a calm soul, and said a prayer of thanks. While I wrote this, the red and yellow leaves fell, then the brown ones, and the nights became colder, and some days, too, most of them now in late November, and I did not find the music. Everything I have written here seems flat: the horns dissonant, the drums lagging, the piano choppy. Today the light came; *I'm here.*

QUESTIONING THE TEXT

1. Why do you think the author chooses to call this essay "Witness"? How does the title affect your understanding of the essay? When formulating your answers, consider that the word *witness* can be used as a noun or verb.

2. This essay is self-reflexive; in other words, it can be read as the story of its own creation. Within that story is at least one other: the author's account of the accident that changed his life profoundly. What effect do these and other aspects of the narrative structure (such as the heavy reliance on dialogue) have on your reading and understanding of the essay?

3. Dubus provides abundant description in this essay, engaging many senses. Choose several passages that you find particularly evocative. How does the description in these passages enhance your comprehension of Dubus's experiences and the meaning you think he intends to convey?

Use your insights to write a three- to four-page analysis of Dubus's use of description in the essay.

4. In the last two paragraphs, Dubus comments on his writing of this essay. He describes writing as a means of revisiting an experience, of "find[ing] the music for it" and seeking "light" in the experience, if any is to be found. It is against this expectation of writing that Dubus assesses the essay. "I did not find the music," he writes. "Everything I have written here seems flat: the horns dissonant, the drums lagging, the piano choppy. Today the light came: *I'm here.*" What do you make of this final comment? Why do you think Dubus chooses to end the essay this way? Discuss your thoughts with classmates.

MAKING CONNECTIONS

5. Dubus shares some thoughts about what it feels like to be an adult who is suddenly disabled by an accident. How does his experience compare to those of other writers, such as Zora Neale Hurston or Bich Minh Nguyen (see p. 416 and p. 458 for their respective essays), who, upon a life-changing event, found it necessary to adopt or adapt to new identities?

6. In their essays, Maxine Hong Kingston (p. 394) and Bich Minh Nguyen (p. 458) offer poignant glimpses into their relationships with their parents. Here we have a parent's perspective, in which Dubus provides glimpses into his relationships with his children. Reflect on what these essays reveal about the relationships between children and parents and about the challenges that developing and changing identities can pose to those relationships. Write two or three paragraphs, and share your reflections in a discussion with classmates.

JOINING THE CONVERSATION

7. How do you *feel* after reading Dubus's essay? Would you recommend it to someone else? Write a brief review of the essay for a teacher, and then write one for a peer — a classmate or a friend. What aspects of the essay do you mention to your instructor but not to your peer, and vice versa?

8. In what ways can you relate to this essay? Have you struggled with a disability or dealt with some other experience presented in the essay? Write a brief reflection that you would be willing to share with your classmates, describing how Dubus's essay illuminates an experience of your own.

ROBERT D. KING
Should English Be the Law?

N_O DOUBT ABOUT IT_ — *our native tongue helps shape our personal identity, giving us not only words and literature in common with people who speak the same language but perhaps even habits of mind. And what is true for individuals may be the case for nations as well: their history and heritage are often embedded in their language. American English, for example, carries in its genes the Germanic tongue of the ancient peoples of Britain, including Angles, Saxons, and Jutes; the linguistic residue of Roman domination of Europe; the French idioms of a later band of Norman conquerors; the distinctive vocabulary of Africans brought to North America as slaves; and an infusion of terms from Native Americans and from Spanish-speaking peoples. English in general has long been especially receptive to words and expressions from other tongues. As a result, a dialect that originated with obscure tribes in a backwater of Europe has grown to become, arguably, the world's common language.*

But some worry that English itself is now under assault on its turf in the United States. Despite genuine hostility to new groups of immigrants, from the Irish in the nineteenth century to the Vietnamese in the twentieth, Americans have eventually accepted wave after wave of opportunity seekers from all corners of the globe. And within a generation most immigrant families have assumed a distinctly American identity, with their children speaking English as glibly as youngsters whose ancestors booked passage on the Mayflower. At least that's the melting-pot story many of us have lived and retold. But today, and not for the first time, some immigrants, especially from Mexico and Central America, seem reluctant to give up their native language and, with it, a portion of their culture and identity. This resistance has been strong enough to provoke a nativist response in the form of "English Only" legislation.

But just how much of a country's identity is tied to its language? And is language diversity really a threat to national identity? These are some of the questions linguist Robert D. King examines in "Should English Be the Law?" an essay that appeared originally in the Atlantic Monthly *(April 1997). He puts the issue in historical and political perspective and comes up with surprising and, for many Americans, comforting answers.*

King (b. 1936) is Audre and Bernard Rapoport Chair of Jewish Studies at the University of Texas at Austin, where he also served as dean of Liberal Arts for almost a decade. Among his books is Nehru and the Language Politics of India *(1997).*

—J.R.

We have known race riots, draft riots, labor violence, secession, anti-war protests, and a whiskey rebellion, but one kind of trouble we've never had: a language riot. Language riot? It sounds like a joke. The very idea of language as a political force — as something that might threaten to split a country wide apart — is alien to our way of thinking and to our cultural traditions.

This may be changing. On August 1 of last year [1996] the U.S. House of Representatives approved a bill that would make English the official language of the United States. The vote was 259 to 169, with 223 Republicans and thirty-six Democrats voting in favor and eight Republicans, 160 Democrats, and one independent voting against. The debate was intense, acrid, and partisan. On March 25 of last year the Supreme Court agreed to review a case involving an Arizona law that would require public employees to conduct government business only in English. Arizona is one of several states that have passed "Official English" or "English Only" laws. The appeal to the Supreme Court followed a 6-to-5 ruling, in October of 1995, by a federal appeals court striking down the Arizona law. These events suggest how divisive a public issue language could become in America — even if it has until now scarcely been taken seriously.

Traditionally, the American way has been to make English the national language — but to do so quietly, locally, without fuss. The Constitution is silent on language: the Founding Fathers had no need to legislate that English be the official language of the country. It has always been taken for granted that English *is* the national language, and that one must learn English in order to make it in America.

To say that language has never been a major force in American history or politics, however, is not to say that politicians have always resisted linguistic jingoism. In 1753 Benjamin Franklin voiced his concern that German immigrants were not learning English: "Those [Germans] who come hither are generally the most ignorant Stupid Sort of their own Nation. . . . they will soon so out number us, that all the advantages we have will not, in My Opinion, be able to preserve our language, and even our government will become precarious." Theodore Roosevelt articulated the unspoken American linguistic-melting-pot theory when he boomed, "We have room for but one language here, and that is the English language, for we intend to see that the crucible turns our people out as Americans, of American nationality, and not as dwellers in a polyglot boarding house." And: "We must have but one flag. We must also have but one language. That must be the language of the Declaration of Independence, of Washington's Farewell address, of Lincoln's Gettysburg speech and second inaugural."

OFFICIAL ENGLISH

TR's linguistic tub-thumping long typified the tradition of American politics. That tradition began to change in the wake of the anything-goes attitudes and the celebration of cultural differences arising in the 1960s. A 1975   5 amendment to the Voting Rights Act of 1965 mandated the "bilingual ballot" under certain circumstances, notably when the voters of selected language groups reached five percent or more in a voting district. Bilingual education became a byword of educational thinking during the 1960s. By the 1970s linguists had demonstrated convincingly — at least to other academics — that black English (today called African American vernacular English or Ebonics) was not "bad" English but a different kind of authentic English with its own rules. Predictably, there have been scattered demands that black English be included in bilingual-education programs.

It was against this background that the movement to make English the official language of the country arose. In 1981 Senator S. I. Hayakawa, long a leading critic of bilingual education and bilingual ballots, introduced in the U.S. Senate a constitutional amendment that not only would have made English the official language but would have prohibited federal and state laws and regulations requiring the use of other languages. His English Language Amendment died in the Ninety-seventh Congress.

In 1983 the organization called U.S. English was founded by Hayakawa and John Tanton, a Michigan ophthalmologist. The primary purpose of the organization was to promote English as the official language of the United States. (The best background readings on America's "neolinguisticism" are the books *Hold Your Tongue*, by James Crawford, and *Language Loyalties*, edited by Crawford, both published in 1992.) Official English initiatives were passed by California in 1986, by Arkansas, Mississippi, North Carolina, North Dakota, and South Carolina in 1987, by Colorado, Florida, and Arizona in 1988, and by Alabama in 1990. The majorities voting for these initiatives were generally not insubstantial: California's, for example, passed by 73 percent.

It was probably inevitable that the Official English (or English Only — the two names are used almost interchangeably) movement would acquire a conservative, almost reactionary undertone in the 1990s. Official English is politically very incorrect. But its cofounder John Tanton brought with him strong liberal credentials. He had been active in the Sierra Club and Planned Parenthood, and in the 1970s served as the national president of Zero Population Growth. Early advisers of U.S. English resist ideological pigeonholing: they included Walter Annenberg, Jacques Barzun, Bruno Bettelheim, Alistair Cooke, Denton Cooley, Walter Cronkite, Angier Biddle Duke, George Gilder, Sidney Hook, Norman Podhoretz, Arnold Schwarzenegger, and Karl Shapiro. In 1987 U.S. English installed as its president Linda Chávez, a Hispanic who had been prominent in the Reagan Administration. A year later she resigned her position, citing "repugnant" and "anti-Hispanic" overtones in an internal memorandum written by Tanton. Tanton, too, resigned, and Walter Cronkite, describing the affair as "embarrassing," left the advisory board. One board member, Norman Cousins, defected in 1986, alluding to the "negative symbolic significance" of California's Official English initiative, Proposition 63.

The current chairman of the board and CEO of U.S. English is Mauro E. Mujica, who claims that the organization has 650,000 members.

The popular wisdom is that conservatives are pro and liberals are con. True, conservatives such as George Will and William F. Buckley Jr. have written columns supporting Official English. But would anyone characterize as conservatives the present and past U.S. English board members Alistair Cooke, Walter Cronkite, and Norman Cousins? One of the strongest opponents of bilingual education is the Mexican-American writer Richard Rodríguez, best known for his eloquent autobiography, *Hunger of Memory* (1982). There is a strain of American liberalism that defines itself in nostalgic devotion to the melting pot.

For several years relevant bills awaited consideration in the U.S. House of   10 Representatives. The Emerson Bill (H.R. 123), passed by the House last August, specifies English as the official language of government, and requires that the government "preserve and enhance" the official status of English. Exceptions are made for the teaching of foreign languages; for actions necessary for public health, international relations, foreign trade, and the protection of the rights of criminal defendants; and for the use of "terms of art" from languages other than English. It would, for example, stop the Internal Revenue Service from sending out income-tax forms and instructions in languages other than English, but it would not ban the use of foreign languages in census materials or documents dealing with national security. *"E Pluribus Unum"* can still appear on American money. U.S. English supports the bill.

What are the chances that some version of Official English will become federal law? Any language bill will face tough odds in the Senate, because some western senators have opposed English Only measures in the past for various reasons, among them a desire by Republicans not to alienate the growing number of Hispanic Republicans, most of whom are uncomfortable with mandated monolingualism. Texas Governor George W. Bush, too, has forthrightly said that he would oppose any English Only proposals in his state. Several of the Republican candidates for President in 1996 (an interesting exception is Phil Gramm) endorsed versions of Official English, as has Newt Gingrich. While governor of Arkansas, Bill Clinton signed into law an English Only bill. As President, he has described his earlier action as a mistake.

Many issues intersect in the controversy over Official English: immigration (above all), the rights of minorities (Spanish-speaking minorities in particular), the pros and cons of bilingual education, tolerance, how best to educate the children of immigrants, and the place of cultural diversity in school curricula and in the American society in general. The question that lies at the root of most of the uneasiness is this: Is America threatened by the preservation of languages other than English? Will America, if it continues on its traditional path of benign linguistic neglect, go the way of Belgium, Canada, and Sri Lanka — three countries among many whose unity is gravely imperiled by language and ethnic conflicts?

LANGUAGE AND NATIONALITY

Language and nationalism were not always so intimately intertwined. Never in the heyday of rule by sovereign was it a condition of employment that the King be able to speak the language of his subjects. George I spoke no English and spent much of his time away from England, attempting to use the power of his kingship to shore up his German possessions. In the Middle Ages nationalism was not even part of the picture: one owed loyalty to a lord, a prince, a ruler, a family, a tribe, a church, a piece of land, but not to a nation and least of all to a nation as a language unit. The capital city of the Austrian Hapsburg empire was Vienna, its ruler a monarch with effective control of peoples of the most varied and incompatible ethnicities, and languages, throughout Central and Eastern Europe. The official language, and the lingua franca as well, was German. While it stood — and it stood for hundreds of years — the empire was an anachronistic relic of what for most of human history had been the normal relationship between country and language: none.

The marriage of language and nationalism goes back at least to Romanticism and specifically to Rousseau, who argued in his *Essay on the Origin of Languages* that language must develop before politics is possible and that language originally distinguished nations from one another. A little-remembered aim of the French Revolution — itself the legacy of Rousseau* — was to impose a national language on France, where regional languages such as Provençal, Breton, and Basque were still strong competitors against standard French, the French of the Ile de France. As late as 1789, when the Revolution began, half the population of the south of France, which spoke Provençal, did not understand French. A century earlier the playwright Racine* said that he had had to resort to Spanish and Italian to make himself understood in the southern French town of Uzès. After the Revolution nationhood itself became aligned with language.

In 1846 Jacob Grimm, one of the Brothers Grimm of fairy-tale fame   15 but better known in the linguistic establishment as a forerunner of modern comparative and historical linguists, said that "a nation is the totality of people who speak the same language." After midcentury, language was invoked more than any other single criterion to define nationality. Language as a political force helped to bring about the unification of Italy and of Germany and the secession of Norway from its union with Sweden in 1905. Arnold Toynbee* observed — unhappily — soon after the First World War

---

Rousseau: Jean-Jacques Rousseau (1712–78), French writer, political theorist, and philosopher

Racine: Jean-Baptiste Racine (1639–99), French dramatist and historiographer, author of *Andromaque* (1667) and *Phèdre* (1677)

Arnold Toynbee (1889–1975): English historian, author of the twelve-volume *A Study of History* (1934–61)

that "the growing consciousness of Nationality had attached itself neither to traditional frontiers nor to new geographical associations but almost exclusively to mother tongues."

The crowning triumph of the new desideratum was the Treaty of Versailles, in 1919, when the allied victors of the First World War began redrawing the map of Central and Eastern Europe according to nationality as best they could. The magic word was "self-determination," and none of Woodrow Wilson's Fourteen Points* mentioned the word "language" at all. Self-determination was thought of as being related to "nationality," which today we would be more likely to call "ethnicity"; but language was simpler to identify than nationality or ethnicity. When it came to drawing the boundary lines of various countries — Czechoslovakia, Yugoslavia, Romania, Hungary, Albania, Bulgaria, Poland — it was principally language that guided the draftsman's hand. (The main exceptions were Alsace-Lorraine, South Tyrol, and the German-speaking parts of Bohemia and Moravia.) Almost by default language became the defining characteristic of nationality.

And so it remains today. In much of the world, ethnic unity and cultural identification are routinely defined by language. To be Arab is to speak Arabic. Bengali identity is based on language in spite of the division of Bengali-speakers between Hindu India and Muslim Bangladesh. When eastern Pakistan seceded from greater Pakistan in 1971, it named itself Bangladesh: *desa* means "country"; *bangla* means not the Bengali people or the Bengali territory but the Bengali language.

Scratch most nationalist movements and you find a linguistic grievance. The demands for independence of the Baltic states (Latvia, Lithuania, and Estonia) were intimately bound up with fears for the loss of their respective languages and cultures in a sea of Russianness. In Belgium the war between French and Flemish threatens an already weakly fused country. The present atmosphere of Belgium is dark and anxious, costive; the metaphor of divorce is a staple of private and public discourse. The lines of terrorism in Sri Lanka are drawn between Tamil Hindus and Sinhalese Buddhists — and also between the Tamil and Sinhalese languages. Worship of the French language fortifies the movement for an independent Quebec. Whether a united Canada will survive into the twenty-first century is a question too close to call. Much of the anxiety about language in the United States is probably fueled by the "Quebec problem": unlike Belgium, which is a small European country, or Sri Lanka, which is halfway around the world, Canada is our close neighbor.

Fourteen Points: fourteen terms for peace outlined by U.S. president Woodrow Wilson on May 18, 1918, during World War I

Language is a convenient surrogate for nonlinguistic claims that are often awkward to articulate, for they amount to a demand for more political and economic power. Militant Sikhs in India call for a state of their own: Khalistan ("Land of the Pure" in Punjabi). They frequently couch this as a demand for a linguistic state, which has a certain simplicity about it, a clarity of motive — justice, even, because states in India are normally linguistic states. But the Sikh demands blend religion, economics, language, and retribution for sins both punished and unpunished in a country where old sins cast long shadows.

Language is an explosive issue in the countries of the former Soviet   20
Union. The language conflict in Estonia has been especially bitter. Ethnic Russians make up almost a third of Estonia's population, and most of them do not speak or read Estonian, although Russians have lived in Estonia for more than a generation. Estonia has passed legislation requiring knowledge of the Estonian language as a condition of citizenship. Nationalist groups in independent Lithuania sought restrictions on the use of Polish — again, old sins, long shadows.

In 1995 protests erupted in Moldova, formerly the Moldavian Soviet Socialist Republic, over language and the teaching of Moldovan history. Was Moldovan history a part of Romanian history or of Soviet history? Was Moldova's language Romanian? Moldovan — earlier called Moldavian — *is* Romanian, just as American English and British English are both English. But in the days of the Moldavian SSR, Moscow insisted that the two languages were different, and in a piece of linguistic nonsense required Moldavian to be written in the Cyrillic alphabet to strengthen the case that it was not Romanian.

The official language of Yugoslavia was Serbo-Croatian, which was never so much a language as a political accommodation. The Serbian and Croatian languages are mutually intelligible. Serbian is written in the Cyrillic alphabet, is identified with the Eastern Orthodox branch of the Catholic Church, and borrows its high-culture words from the east — from Russian and Old Church Slavic. Croatian is written in the Roman alphabet, is identified with Roman Catholicism, and borrows its high-culture words from the west — from German, for example, and Latin. One of the first things the newly autonomous Republic of Serbia did, in 1991, was to pass a law decreeing Serbian in the Cyrillic alphabet the official language of the country. With Croatia divorced from Serbia, the Croatian and Serbian languages are diverging more and more. Serbo-Croatian has now passed into history, a language-museum relic from the brief period when Serbs and Croats called themselves Yugoslavs and pretended to like each other.

Slovakia, relieved now of the need to accommodate to Czech cosmopolitan sensibilities, has passed a law making Slovak its official language. (Czech is to Slovak pretty much as Croatian is to Serbian.) Doctors in state hospitals must speak to patients in Slovak, even if another language would aid diagnosis and treatment. Some 600,000 Slovaks — more than 10 percent of the population — are ethnically Hungarian. Even staff meetings in Hungarian-language schools must be in Slovak. (The government dropped a stipulation that church weddings be conducted in Slovak after heavy opposition from the Roman Catholic Church.) Language inspectors are told to weed out "all sins perpetrated on the regular Slovak language." Tensions between Slovaks and Hungarians, who had been getting along, have begun to arise.

The twentieth century is ending as it began — with trouble in the Balkans and with nationalist tensions flaring up in other parts of the globe. (Toward the end of his life Bismarck* predicted that "some damn fool thing in the Balkans" would ignite the next war.) Language isn't always part of the problem. But it usually is.

UNIQUE OTHERNESS

Is there no hope for language tolerance? Some countries manage to maintain their unity in the face of multilingualism. Examples are Finland, with a Swedish minority, and a number of African and Southeast Asian countries. Two others could not be more unlike as countries go: Switzerland and India.

German, French, Italian, and Romansh are the languages of Switzerland. The first three can be and are used for official purposes; all four are designated "national" languages. Switzerland is politically almost hyperstable. It has language problems (Romansh is losing ground), but they are not major, and they are never allowed to threaten national unity.

Contrary to public perception, India gets along pretty well with a host of different languages. The Indian constitution officially recognizes nineteen languages, English among them. Hindi is specified in the constitution as the national language of India, but that is a pious postcolonial fiction: outside the Hindi-speaking northern heartland of India, people don't want to learn it. English functions more nearly than Hindi as India's lingua franca.

From 1947, when India obtained its independence from the British, until the 1960s blood ran in the streets and people died because of language. Hindi absolutists wanted to force Hindi on the entire country, which would have split India between north and south and opened up other fracture lines as well. For as long as possible Jawaharlal Nehru, independent India's first Prime Minister, resisted nationalist demands to redraw the capricious state boundaries of British India according to language. By the time he capitulated, the country had gained a precious decade to prove its viability as a union.

Why is it that India preserves its unity with not just two languages to contend with, as Belgium, Canada, and Sri Lanka have, but nineteen? The answer is that India, like Switzerland, has a strong national identity. The two

25

Bismarck: Otto von Bismarck (1815–98), Prussian prime minister and chancellor of the German Empire

countries share something big and almost mystical that holds each together in a union transcending language. That something I call "unique otherness."

The Swiss have what the political scientist Karl Deutsch called "learned   30 habits, preferences, symbols, memories, and patterns of landholding": customs, cultural traditions, and political institutions that bind them closer to one another than to people of France, Germany, or Italy living just across the border and speaking the same language. There is Switzerland's traditional neutrality, its system of universal military training (the "citizen army"), its consensual allegiance to a strong Swiss franc — and fondue, yodeling, skiing, and mountains. Set against all this, the fact that Switzerland has four languages doesn't even approach the threshold of becoming a threat.

As for India, what Vincent Smith, in the *Oxford History of India*, calls its "deep underlying fundamental unity" resides in institutions and beliefs such as caste, cow worship, sacred places, and much more. Consider *dharma, karma,* and *maya,** the three root convictions of Hinduism; India's historical epics; Gandhi; *ahimsa* (nonviolence); vegetarianism; a distinctive cuisine and way of eating; marriage customs; a shared past; and what the Indologist Ainslie Embree calls "Brahmanical ideology." In other words, "We are Indian; we are different."

Belgium and Canada have never managed to forge a stable national identity; Czechoslovakia and Yugoslavia never did either. Unique otherness immunizes countries against linguistic destabilization. Even Switzerland and especially India have problems; in any country with as many different languages as India has, language will never *not* be a problem. However, it is one thing to have a major illness with a bleak prognosis; it is another to have a condition that is irritating and occasionally painful but not life-threatening.

History teaches a plain lesson about language and governments: there is almost nothing the government of a free country can do to change language usage and practice significantly, to force its citizens to use certain languages in preference to others, and to discourage people from speaking a language they wish to continue to speak. (The rebirth of Hebrew in Palestine and Israel's successful mandate that Hebrew be spoken and written by Israelis is a unique event in the annals of language history.) Quebec has since the 1970s passed an array of laws giving French a virtual monopoly in the province. One consequence — unintended, one wishes to believe — of these laws is that last year kosher products imported for Passover were kept off the shelves because the packages were not labeled in French. Wise governments keep their hands off language to the extent that it is politically possible to do so.

We like to believe that to pass a law is to change behavior; but passing laws about language, in a free society, almost never changes attitudes or behavior. Gaelic (Irish) is living out a slow, inexorable decline in Ireland despite

---

dharma, karma, and *maya:* In Hinduism, *dharma* is the moral and religious law; *karma* expresses the connection of past lives to future ones; *maya* describes the force that makes people believe that the phenomenal world is real.

enormous government support of every possible kind since Ireland gained its independence from Britain. The Welsh language, in contrast, is alive today in Wales in spite of heavy discrimination during its history. Three out of four people in the northern and western counties of Gwynedd and Dyfed speak Welsh.

I said earlier that language is a convenient surrogate for other national 35 problems. Official English obviously has a lot to do with concern about immigration, perhaps especially Hispanic immigration. America may be threatened by immigration; I don't know. But America is not threatened by language.

The usual arguments made by academics against Official English are commonsensical. Who needs a law when, according to the 1990 census, 94 percent of American residents speak English anyway? (Mauro E. Mujica, the chairman of U.S. English, cites a higher figure: 97 percent.) Not many of today's immigrants will see their first language survive into the second generation. This is in fact the common lament of first-generation immigrants: their children are not learning their language and are losing the culture of their parents. Spanish is hardly a threat to English, in spite of isolated (and easily visible) cases such as Miami, New York City, and pockets of the Southwest and southern California. The everyday language of south Texas is Spanish, and yet south Texas is not about to secede from America.

[But empirical, calm arguments don't engage the real issue: language is a symbol, an icon.]Nobody who favors a constitutional ban against flag burning will ever be persuaded by the argument that the flag is, after all, just a "piece of cloth." A draft card in the 1960s was never merely a piece of paper. Neither is a marriage license.

Language, as one linguist has said, is "not primarily a means of communication but a means of communion." Romanticism exalted language, made it mystical, sublime — a bond of national identity. At the same time, Romanticism created a monster: it made of language a means for destroying a country.

[America has that unique otherness of which I spoke.]In spite of all our racial divisions and economic unfairness, we have the frontier tradition, respect for the individual, and opportunity; we have our love affair with the automobile; we have in our history a civil war that freed the slaves and was fought with valor; and we have sports, hot dogs, hamburgers, and milk shakes — things big and small, noble and petty, important and trifling. "We are Americans; we are different."

[If I'm wrong, then the great American experiment will fail — not be- 40 cause of language but because it no longer means anything to be an American;] because we have forfeited that "willingness of the heart" that F. Scott Fitzgerald wrote was America; because we are no longer joined by Lincoln's "mystic chords of memory."

[We are not even close to the danger point. I suggest that we relax and luxuriate in our linguistic richness and our traditional tolerance of language differences. Language does not threaten American unity.]Benign neglect is a good policy for any country when it comes to language, and it's a good policy for America.

QUESTIONING THE TEXT

1. "Should English Be the Law?" is an argument — an essay that provides evidence in support of specific claims. What do you think are King's basic claims, and which pieces of evidence do you find either most convincing or most questionable? Offer your opinion in a brief critical analysis.

2. Near the end of his article (paragraph 40), King mentions Abraham Lincoln's phrase "mystic chords of memory," assuming that most of his readers will appreciate the allusion. Using the resources of your library reference room, track down the allusion if you do not recognize it, and then explore its aptness. In what context did Lincoln use that phrase? What do "mystic chords of memory" have to do with language and national identity?

MAKING CONNECTIONS

3. The problems of immigrants trying to learn English and adapt to American culture are discussed in the selection from Mike Rose's *Lives on the Boundary* (p. 90). Read the selection by Rose and then, in a short piece, describe whether King's analysis of the language problem in the United States confirms or contradicts Rose's observations. Don't hesitate to offer your own analysis.

4. What other readings in this chapter emphasize language as something that helps create identity? How important is language as a marker of identity in, for example, Lynda Barry's "Common Scents" (p. 445)?

JOINING THE CONVERSATION

5. King claims that a dispute over language often serves as a shorthand or surrogate for other national problems. For example, in some countries, conflicts over language are also about differences in religion or class status. In a small group, discuss some of the political and social issues that surround the "English Only" debate in the United States. Then write an argument on King's observation. Is the movement to make English the official language of the United States one issue or many?

6. King attempts briefly to describe the "unique otherness" of the American people, listing such traits as the frontier tradition, love of the automobile, a civil war, and even hot dogs. In an extended essay, explore the concept of "unique otherness" as King uses it in this selection — either by offering your own description of American otherness or by questioning the notion itself.

LYNDA BARRY
Common Scents

F OR THE LAST FIVE OR SIX YEARS, *I've been including at least one graphic novel in almost every course I teach. Every time I have included Lynda Barry's* One! Hundred! Demons!, *students have ranked it among their favorite works in the class. But that text, which Barry (b. 1956) calls an "autobifictionalography," is just one of her many, many works.*

Barry went to college at Washington's Evergreen State University (she was the first in her family to attend college), where she met Matt Groening, creator of The Simpsons *and* Life in Hell *comic strips. Groening was the first to publish her work — in the campus newspaper and without her knowledge. And she has been publishing ever since, with over a dozen books to her credit as well as numerous strips. But publishing has not always been easy. In an interview with* Independent Publisher, *Barry talks about being dropped by her publisher just a day before she was going to turn in a new book,* The Freddie Stories, *and about how she soon found much of her work out of print. Without a publisher, Barry began making books by hand and selling them by mail order while she tried to figure out what to do next. When another friend who was working at Sasquatch Books asked if she would like to reprint her work, she jumped at the chance and now credits Sasquatch with saving her career.*

Indeed, Sasquatch Books published the text from which we've taken a chapter to reprint here. One! Hundred! Demons! *is a collection of twenty autobiographical comic strips that appeared in Salon.com in 2000–2001. About this book, Barry says, "I had a ball putting [it] together. I worked with two great graphic designers. . . . We laid the whole thing out on my computer in the attic of my house. Sometimes I was at the computer, sometimes I was kneeling on the floor over scattered pages of the collage introductions with an Elmer's glue bottle in my hand. It took three months to do all the designing and my studio looked like a tipped-over ransacked aquarium when we were finished."*

Barry's work provides a vivid example of the possibilities for writers today: with its use of color, hand drawings, photographs, and wildly differing fonts, it draws readers into an adolescent world full of angst, wonder, and not a little cynicism. In "Common Scents," Barry — part Filipina in heritage — reflects upon ethnic differences evident in the smells of home. At the end of the book in which this excerpt appears, Barry guides readers in making a book of demons of their own, providing step-by-step instructions for using the Asian-style brushes and inkstick she used in her book. "Come on!" she says. "Don't you want to try it?" If you were going to draw a strip about one of your demons, what would you call it?

—A.L.

SOME OF THE SMELLS WERE UNCOMPLICATED, LIKE THE CAT PEE SMELL OF THE HOUSE NEXT DOOR. THE LADY HAD 14 CATS. IT WAS HARD TO STAY AND VISIT. SHE SOMETIMES BURNED INCENSE, WHICH ALSO SMELLED LIKE CAT PEE.

(BREATHING THROUGH MY MOUTH)

HAVE SOME PEANUT BRITTLE, DEAR. JUST PICK THE FUR OFF IF YOU'RE FUSSY, BUT IT WON'T HURT YOU NONE.

BUT THERE WERE BAD MYS- TERIES TOO, LIKE THE MYSTERY OF THE BLEACH PEOPLE, WHOSE HOUSE GAVE OFF FUMES YOU COULD SMELL FROM THE STREET. WE KEPT WAITING FOR THAT HOUSE TO EXPLODE. THE BUGS DIDN'T EVEN GO IN THEIR YARD.

ALSO GIVING OFF BLEACH FUMES

HEYA, JANINA.

HEYA.

'N I ASK YOU A PERSONAL THING?

POSSIBLY

HOW COME YOUR HOUSE SMELLS LIKE THAT?

SMELLS LIKE WHAT?

THE GIRL WHO SHOCKED ME WITH THE NEWS ABOUT THE SMELL OF MY HOUSE WAS THE ONE WHOSE HOUSE SMELLED LIKE THE FRESH BUS BATHROOM. HER MOTHER WAS THE MOST DISINFECTING, AIR FRESHENER SPRAYING PERSON THAT EVER LIVED.

SHE HAD THOSE CAR FRESHENER CHRISTMAS TREE THINGS HANGING EVERYWHERE. EVEN THE MARSHMALLOW TREATS SHE MADE HAD A FRESH PINE-SPRAY FLAVOR. SHE WAS FREE WITH HER OBSERVATIONS ABOUT THE SMELL OF OTHERS.

YOUR ORIENTALS HAVE AN ARRAY, WITH YOUR CHINESE SMELLING STRONGER THAN YOUR JAPANESE AND YOUR KOREANS FALLING SOMEWHERES IN THE MIDDLE AND DON'T GET ME STARTED ON YOUR FILIPINOS.

SHE DETAILED THE SMELLS OF BLACKS, MEXICANS, ITALIANS, SOME PEOPLE I NEVER HEARD OF CALLED "BO-HUNKS" AND THE DIFFERENCE IT MADE IF THEY WERE WET OR DRY, FAT OR SKINNY. NATURALLY I BROUGHT THIS INFORMATION HOME.

AIE N'AKO! WHITE LADIES SMELL BAD TOO, NAMAN! SHE NEVER WASH HER POOKIE! HER KILI-KILI ALWAYS SWEAT-SWEATING! THE OLD ONES SMELL LIKE E-HEE! THAT LADY IS TUNG-AH!

MY GRANDMA WAS A PHILOSOPHICAL SORT OF PERSON WHO ALWAYS HAD AN INTERESTING TAKE ON THINGS.

YOU KNOW, MY DARLING, GOD HAS MADE EVERY PEOPLE! AND EVERY PEOPLE MAKES TA-EE! AND EVERY TA-EE SMELLS BAD! ASK THIS LADY DOES PERFUME COME OUT OF HER PUEET? N'AKO, I DON'T THINK SO, DARLING! IT IS NOT GOD'S WAY. YOU TELL HER!

Reading across Professions
DONNA LIGHT-DONOVAN, Biology Teacher

More than a thousand genes code for a wide array of odor receptors. When these receptor proteins sense smells, they trigger messages both to the limbic system — a primitive part of the brain that regulates emotions and behavior and stores memory — and to the cortex, the center of conscious thought. The parts of the brain devoted to memory retrieval, odor identification, and emotions are all on the right side of the brain and quite close together. You may have heard that smells are famous for bringing back vivid memories (although some researchers believe that the vividness of such memories may actually be caused by misconnections in the brain). According to Rachel Herz, a Brown University psychology professor and olfaction expert, memories triggered by smell are no more accurate than those triggered by other senses — but smell memories are more emotional. So the scent of a lilac, as lovely as it is, may seem lovelier still because it calls up associated memories of gentle spring breezes, a walk in the park, and possibly an intoxicating moment of love.

Smell was perhaps the earliest of our senses to evolve. It's no surprise, therefore, that it is so heavily involved in identifying food, finding mates, and sensing both pleasure and danger. When I was in my twenties, smell's importance in these areas was made obvious to me. The most attractive guy I knew did not use deodorant — and for reasons that I didn't understand at the time, I found his smell intoxicating. I was thrilled when he finally invited me over for dinner. But as I approached his front door, a familiar, dreaded odor from my childhood wafted through the keyhole: liver! I had a longstanding feud with liver, and no matter how sweet the onion smothering it, I knew I wouldn't be having any . . . until he opened the door, and miraculously, the liver smell no longer seemed to be an issue. True, I didn't ask for seconds, but when liver was served by the man of my dreams, it didn't taste so bad after all.

What had happened to me? I had no idea. But recently, Northwestern University researchers have found that our perception of smells may depend on the circumstances in which we smell them. If people think that they are smelling fresh cucumber, they tend to find the smell pleasant, but if they are told that the same smell is mildew, they find it foul instead. And a person's perception of an odor — liver, for instance — can change when the odor is combined with another, different smell — such as the cocktail of testosterone and pheromones (chemical signals of attraction) coming from that desirable guy.

It's also true that people can experience a smell differently, partly because of cultural variations in what people tend to think smells good, and perhaps partly because of genetic differences in what people are able to smell. Lynda Barry's inability to smell her own house wasn't genetic; chalk it up to habituation, a kind of learning that decreases the response to a repeated stimulus. But years later, Barry recalls the aromas that her former neighbor found disgusting — "like grease and fish and cigs, like Jade East and pork and dogs, like all the wild food my grandma boiled and fried" — and finds in them a connection to delicious memories of home.

Donna Light-Donovan teaches biology and directs the science research program at Croton-Harmon High School in Croton-on-Hudson, New York.

QUESTIONING THE TEXT

1. In the twelfth panel Barry writes, "My grandma was a philosophical sort of person who always had an interesting take on things." Consider the short speech that the grandmother gives in this panel. Does she seem to you like a "philosophical sort of person"? Explain your reasoning.

2. Barry might be said to make an argument with this piece. What do you think her argument is? Try to summarize it in your own words in a one-sentence thesis.

3. To what degree does the narrator of the comic seem to be Barry herself? What's the evidence for your conclusion?

MAKING CONNECTIONS

4. Compare Lynda Barry's use of humor to Dave Barry's in "Guys vs. Men" (p. 405). Which selection do you find funnier? Even though it risks draining the humor out of the pieces, do your best to explain *why* you find them funny (or not funny, if that's the case). Does the humor or attempted humor make the pieces more or less successful? When might the humor employed by either of the two Barrys be inappropriate?

JOINING THE CONVERSATION

5. Try your hand at creating a graphic narrative that looks at some events from your childhood. You can draw the panels or use photographs to illustrate your version. Be sure to include dialogue between the figures (human or not) in the images.

6. When the narrator of this piece is told that her own house smells, she's surprised — she can't smell what she's grown so used to. Think of a time when you were surprised to learn something about yourself, your family, or a group that you're a part of. Write a one- or two-page dialogue in which you discover something about an aspect of your identity that only an outsider could make clear to you.

BICH MINH NGUYEN
The Good Immigrant Student

*W*HAT DOES IT MEAN TO ESTABLISH AN IDENTITY? *However else we might answer this question, much of this process gets shaped by a complex interaction among language, home, and school. Bich Minh Nguyen (b. 1974), whose first name is pronounced "Bit," reflects on these elements of identity formation as she describes growing up in Grand Rapids, Michigan, after immigrating from Vietnam with her father, sister, and grandmother in 1975, after the fall of Saigon. Unlike her sister Anh, who chose "rebellion rather than silence," Nguyen becomes the good immigrant student —shy, obedient, and quiet, always on time and always earning "the highest possible scores in every subject." But this identity, as hard earned as it was, did not reap the same rewards given liberally to the good nonimmigrant (in other words, white) students, nor did it lead to the invisibility Nguyen craved as a result of being treated, inevitably and continuously, as an outsider, a foreigner. Yet Nguyen perseveres, and in high school she begins to glimpse how it would feel to embody identity confidently, simply to be herself: "[T]here is a slipping between being good," she says, "and being unnoticed, and in that sliver of freedom I learned what it could feel like to walk in the world in plain, unself-conscious view."*

Nguyen obviously accomplished something else during her high school and college years: she established an identity as a writer. At the University of Michigan, where she received her MFA, Nguyen won major prizes for both essays and poetry; today she is an assistant professor of English at Purdue. She is coeditor of The Contemporary American Short Story: A Longman Anthology *(2003) and* I & Eye: Contemporary Creative Nonfiction *(2004). Her book* Stealing Buddha's Dinner: A Memoir *was published in 2007.*

The essay reprinted here first appeared in Tales Out of School: Contemporary Writers on Their Student Years *(2000). In it, she chronicles her Americanization, deciding that the cultures of early 1980s Grand Rapids simply did not allow her to engage in both assimilation and preservation of her Vietnamese heritage. Her account of her education also allows readers to explore with her the benefits and dangers of becoming the good immigrant student.*

I have been teaching for a long time, and I have loved almost every minute of it. Reading Bich Minh Nguyen's account leads me to look critically at my relationship with all students, particularly with students who have immigrated to the United States. I chose this essay because it speaks to the potential importance of student-teacher relationships in identity formation (on both sides) and because I aspire to be the kind of teacher Nguyen finds all too rare.

—A.L.

My stepmother, Rosa, who began dating my father when I was three years old, says that my sister and I used to watch *Police Woman* and rapturously repeat everything Angie Dickinson said. But when the show was over Anh and I would resume our Vietnamese, whispering together, giggling in accents. Rosa worried about this. She had the idea that she could teach us English and we could teach her Vietnamese. She would make us lunch or give us baths, speaking slowly and asking us how to say *water*, or *rice*, or *house*.

After she and my father married, Rosa swept us out of our falling-down house and into middle-class suburban Grand Rapids, Michigan. Our neighborhood surrounded Ken-O-Sha Elementary School and Plaster Creek, and was only a short drive away from the original Meijer's Thrifty Acres. In the early 1980s, this neighborhood of mismatching street names — Poinsettia, Van Auken, Senora, Ravanna — was home to families of Dutch heritage, and everyone was Christian Reformed, and conservative Republican. Except us. Even if my father hadn't left his rusted-through silver Mustang, the first car he ever owned, to languish in the driveway for months we would have stuck out simply because we weren't white. There was my Latina stepmother and her daughter, Cristina, my father, sister, grandmother, and I, refugees from Saigon; and my half-brother born a year after we moved to the house on Ravanna Street.

Although my family lived two blocks from Ken-O-Sha, my stepmother enrolled me and Anh at Sherwood Elementary, a bus ride away, because Sherwood had a bilingual education program. Rosa, who had a master's in education and taught ESL and community ed in the public school system, was a big supporter of bilingual education. School mornings, Anh and I would be at the bus stop at the corner of our street quite early, hustled out of the house by our grandmother who constantly feared we would miss our chance. I went off to first grade, Anh to second. At ten o'clock, we crept out of our classes, drawing glances and whispers from the other students, and convened with a group of Vietnamese kids from other grades to learn English. The teachers were Mr. Ho, who wore a lot of short-sleeved button-down shirts in neutral hues, and Miss Huong, who favored a maroon blouse with puffy shoulders and slight ruffles at the high neck and wrists, paired with a tweed skirt that hung heavily to her ankles. They passed out photocopied booklets of Vietnamese phrases and their English translations, with themes such as "In the Grocery Store." They asked us to repeat slowly after them and took turns coming around to each of us, bending close to hear our pronunciations.

Anh and I exchanged a lot of worried glances, for we had a secret that we were quite embarrassed about: we already knew English. It was the Vietnamese part that gave us trouble. When Mr. Ho and Miss Huong gave instructions, or passed out homework assignments, they did so in Vietnamese. Anh and I received praise for our English, but were reprimanded for failing to complete our assignments and failing to pay attention. After a couple of weeks of this Anh announced to Rosa that we didn't need bilingual education. Nonsense, she said. Our father just shrugged his shoulders. After that, Anh began skipping bilingual classes, urging me to do the same, and then we never went back. What was amazing was that no one, not Mrs. Eunice, my first grade teacher, or Mrs. Hankins, Anh's teacher, or even Mr. Ho or Miss Huong said anything directly to us about it. Or if they did, I have forgotten it entirely. Then one day my parents got a call from Miss Huong. When Rosa came to talk to me and Anh about it we were watching television the way kids do, sitting alarmingly close to the screen. Rosa confronted us with "Do you girls know English?" Then she suddenly said, "Do you know Vietnamese?" I can't remember what we replied to either question.

For many years, a towering old billboard over the expressway downtown   5 proudly declared Grand Rapids "An All-American City." For me, that all-American designation meant all-white. I couldn't believe (and still don't) that they meant to include the growing Mexican-American population, or the sudden influx of Vietnamese refugees in 1975. I often thought it a rather mean-spirited prank of some administrator at the INS, deciding with a flourish of a signature to send a thousand refugees to Grand Rapids, a city that boasted having more churches per square mile than other city in the United States. Did that administrator know what Grand Rapids was like? That in school, everywhere I turned, and often when I closed my eyes, I saw blond blond blond? The point of bilingual education was assimilation. To my stepmother, the point was preservation: she didn't want English to take over wholly, pushing the Vietnamese out of our heads. She was too ambitious. Anh and I were Americanized as soon as we turned on the television. Today, bilingual education is supposed to have become both a method of assimilation and a method of preservation, an effort to prove that kids can have it both ways. They can supposedly keep English for school and their friends and keep another language for home and family.

In Grand Rapids, Michigan, in the 1980s, I found that an impossible task.

I transferred to Ken-O-Sha Elementary in time for third grade, after Rosa finally admitted that taking the bus all the way to Sherwood was pointless. I was glad to transfer, eager to be part of a class that wasn't, in my mind, tainted with the knowledge of my bilingual stigma. Third grade was led by Mrs. Alexander, an imperious, middle-aged woman of many plaid skirts held safe by giant gold safety pins. She had a habit of turning her wedding ring around and around her finger while she stood at the chalkboard. Mrs. Alexander had an intricate system of rewards for good grades and good behavior, denoted by colored star stickers on a piece of poster board that loomed over us all. One glance and you could see who was behind, who was striding ahead.

I was an insufferably good student, with perfect Palmer cursive and the highest possible scores in every subject. I had learned this trick at Sherwood. That the quieter you are, the shyer and sweeter and better-at-school you are, the more the teacher will let you alone. Mrs. Alexander should have let me alone. For, in addition to my excellent marks, I was nearly silent, deadly shy, and wholly obedient. My greatest fear was being called on, or in any way standing out more than I already did in the class that was, except for me and one black student, dough-white. I got good grades because I feared the authority of the teacher; I felt that getting in good with Mrs. Alexander would protect me, that she would protect me from the frightful rest of the world. But Mrs. Alexander was not agreeable to this notion. If it was my turn to read aloud during reading circle, she'd interrupt me to snap, "You're reading too fast" or demand, "What does that word mean?" Things she did not do to the other students. Anh, when I told her about this, suggested that perhaps Mrs. Alexander liked me and wanted to help me get smarter. But neither of us believed it. You know when a teacher likes you and when she doesn't.

Secretly, I admired and envied the rebellious kids, like Robbie Andrews who came to school looking bleary-eyed and pinched, like a hungover adult; Robbie and his ilk snapped back at teachers, were routinely sent to the principal's office, were even spanked a few times with the principal's infamous red paddle (apparently no one in Grand Rapids objected to corporal punishment). Those kids made noise, possessed something I thought was confidence, self-knowledge, allowing them to marvelously question everything ordered of them. They had the ability to challenge the given world.

Toward the middle of third grade Mrs. Alexander introduced a stuffed lion to the pool of rewards: the best student of the week would earn the privilege of having the lion sit on his or her desk for the entire week. My quantity of gold stars was neck and neck with that of my two competitors, Brenda and Jennifer, both sweet-eyed blond girls with pastel-colored monogrammed sweaters and neatly tied Dock-Sides. My family did not have a lot of money and my stepmother had terrible taste. Thus I attended school in such ensembles as dark red parachute pants and a nubby pink sweater stitched with a picture of a unicorn rearing up. This only propelled me to try harder to be good, to make up for everything I felt was against me: my odd family, my race, my very face. And I craved that stuffed lion. Week after week, the lion perched on Brenda's desk or Jennifer's desk. Meanwhile, the class spelling bee approached. I didn't know I was such a good speller until I won it, earning a scalloped-edged certificate and a candy bar. That afternoon I started toward home, then remembered I'd forgotten my rain boots in my locker. I doubled back to school and overheard Mrs. Alexander in the classroom talking to another teacher. "Can you believe it?" Mrs. Alexander was saying. "A foreigner winning our spelling bee!"

I waited for the stuffed lion the rest of that year, with a kind of patience I have no patience for today. To no avail. In June, on the last day of school, Mrs. Alexander gave the stuffed lion to Brenda to keep forever.

The first time I had to read aloud something I had written — perhaps it was in fourth grade — I felt such terror, such a need not to have any attention upon me, that I convinced myself that I had become invisible, that the teacher could never call on me because she couldn't see me.

More than once, I was given the assignment of writing a report about my family history. I loathed this task, for I was dreadfully aware that my history could not be faked; it already showed on my face. When my turn came to read out loud the teacher had to ask me several times to speak louder. Some kids, a few of them older, in different classes, took to pressing back the corners of their eyes with the heels of their palms while they chanted, "Ching-chong, ching-chong!" during recess. (This continued until Anh, who was far tougher than me, threatened to beat them up.)

I have no way of telling what tortured me more: the actual snickers and remarks and watchfulness of my classmates, or my own imagination, conjuring disdain. My own sense of shame. At times I felt sickened by my obedience, my accumulation of gold stickers, my every effort to be invisible.

Yet Robbie Andrews must have felt the same kind of claustrophobia,   15
trapped in his own reputation, in his ability to be otherwise. I learned in school that changing oneself is not easy, that the world makes up its mind quickly.

I've heard that Robbie dropped out of high school, got a girl pregnant, found himself in and out of first juvenile detention, then jail.

What comes out of difference? What constitutes difference? Such questions, academic and unanswered, popped up in every other course description in college. But the idea of difference is easy to come by, especially in school; it is shame, the permutations and inversions of difference and self-loathing, that we should be worrying about.

Imagined torment, imagined scorn. When what is imagined and what is desired turn on each other.

Some kids want to rebel; other kids want to disappear. I wanted to disappear. I was not brave enough to shrug my shoulders and flaunt my difference; because I could not disappear into the crowd, I wished to disappear entirely. Anyone might have mistaken this for passivity.

Once, at the end of my career at Sherwood Elementary, I disappeared on   20
the bus home. Mine was usually the third stop, but that day the bus driver thought I wasn't there, and she sailed right by the corner of Ravanna and Senora. I said nothing. The bus wove its way downtown, and for the first time I got to see where other children lived, some of them in clean orderly neighborhoods, some near houses with sagging porches and boarded-up windows. All the while, the kid sitting across the aisle from me played the same cheerful song over and over on his portable boom box. *Pass the doochee from the left hand side, pass the doochee from the left hand side.* He and his brother turned out to be the last kids off the bus. Then the bus driver saw me through the rearview mirror. She walked back to where I was sitting and said, "How come you didn't get off at your stop?" I shook my head, don't know. She sighed and drove me home.

I was often doing that, shaking my head silently or staring up wordlessly. I realize that while I remember so much of what other people said when I was a child, I remember little of what I said. Probably because I didn't say much at all.

I recently came across in the stacks of the University of Michigan library *A Manual for Indochinese Refugee Education 1976–1977.* Some of it is silly, but much of it is a painstaking, fairly thoughtful effort to let school administrators and teachers know how to go about sensitively handling the influx of Vietnamese children in the public schools. Here is one of the most wonderful items of advice: "The Vietnamese child, even the older child, is also reported to be afraid of the dark, and more often than not, believes in ghosts. A teacher may have to be a little more solicitous of the child on gloomy, wintery days." Perhaps if Mrs. Alexander had read this, she would not have upbraided me so often for tracking mud into the classroom on rainy days. In third grade I was horrified and ashamed of my muddy shoes. I hung back, trying to duck behind this or that dark-haired boy. In spite of this, in spite of bilingual education, and shyness, and all that wordless shaking of my head, I was sent off every Monday to the Spectrum School for the Gifted and Talented. I still have no idea who selected me, who singled me out. Spectrum was (and still is) a public school program that invited students from every public elementary school to meet once a week and take specialized classes on topics such as the Middle Ages, Ellis Island, and fairy tales. Each student chose two classes, a major and minor, and for the rest of the semester worked toward final projects in both. I loved going to Spectrum. Not only did the range of students from other schools prove to be diverse, I found myself feeling more comfortable, mainly because Spectrum encouraged individual work. And the teachers seemed happy to be there. The best teacher at Spectrum was Mrs. King, whom every student adored. I still remember the soft gray sweaters she wore, her big wavy hair, her art-class handwriting, the way she'd often tell us to close our eyes when she read us a particular story or passage.

I believe that I figured out how to stop disappearing, how to talk and answer, even speak up, after several years in Spectrum. I was still deeply self-conscious, but I became able, sometimes, to maneuver around it.

Spectrum may have spoiled me a little, because it made me think about college and freedom, and thus made all the years in between disappointing and annoying.

In seventh grade I joined Anh and Cristina at the City School, a seventh through twelfth grade public school in the Grand Rapids system that served as an early charter school; admission was by interview, and each grade had about fifty students. The City School had the advantage of being downtown, perched over old cobblestone roads, and close to the main public library. Art and music history were required. There were no sports teams. And volunteering was mandatory. But kids didn't tend to stay at City School; as they got older they transferred to one of the big high schools nearby, perhaps wishing to play sports, perhaps wishing to get away from City's rather brutal academic system. Each half semester, after grades were doled out, giant dot-matrix printouts of everyone's GPAs were posted in the hallways.

I didn't stay at City, either. When my family moved to a different suburb, my stepmother promptly transferred me to Forest Hills Northern High School.

Most of the students there came from upper-middle-class or very well-to-do families; the ones who didn't stood out sharply. The rich kids were the same as they were anywhere in America: they wore a lot of Esprit and Guess, drove nice cars, and ran student council, prom, and sports. These kids strutted down the hallways; the boys sat in a row on the long windowsill near a group of lockers, whistling or calling out to girls who walked by. Girls gathered in bathrooms with their Clinique lipsticks.

High school was the least interesting part of my education, but I did accomplish something: I learned to forget myself a little. I learned the sweetness of apathy. And through apathy, how to forget my skin and body for a minute or two, almost not caring what would happen if I walked into a room late and all heads swiveled toward me. I learned the pleasure that reveals itself in the loss, no matter how slight, of self-consciousness. These things occurred because I remained the good immigrant student, without raising my hand often or showing off what I knew. Doing work was rote, and I went along to get along. I've never gotten over the terror of being called on in class, or the dread in knowing that I'm expected to contribute to class discussion. But there is a slippage between being good and being unnoticed, and in that sliver of freedom I learned what it could feel like to walk in the world in plain, unself-conscious view.

I would like to make a broad, accurate statement about immigrant children in schools. I would like to speak for them (us). I hesitate; I cannot. My own sister, for instance, was never as shy as I was. Anh disliked school from the start, choosing rebellion rather than silence. It was a good arrangement: I wrote papers for her and she paid me in money or candy; she gave me rides to school if I promised not to tell anyone about her cigarettes. Still, I think of an Indian friend of mine who told of an elementary school experience in which a blond schoolchild told the teacher, "I can't sit by her. My mom said I can't sit by anyone who's brown." And another friend, whose family immigrated around the same time mine did, whose second grade teacher used her as a vocabulary example: "Children, this is what a *foreigner* is." And sometimes I fall into thinking that kids today have the advantage of so much more wisdom, that they are so much more socially and politically aware than anyone was when I was in school. But I am wrong, of course. I know not every kid is fortunate enough to have a teacher like Mrs. King, or a program like Spectrum, or even the benefit of a manual written by a group of concerned educators; I know that some kids want to disappear and disappear until they actually do. Sometimes I think I see them, in the blurry background of a magazine photo, or in a gaggle of kids following a teacher's aide across the street. The kids with heads bent down, holding themselves in such a way that they seem to be self-conscious even of how they breathe. Small, shy, quiet kids, such good, good kids, *immigrant, foreigner,* their eyes watchful and waiting for whatever judgment will occur. I reassure myself that they will grow up fine, they will be okay. Maybe I cross the same street, then another, glancing back once in a while to see where they are going.

QUESTIONING THE TEXT

1. This essay does not present an explicit thesis, per se. Rather, the author reveals meaning to her readers by relating her own experiences. If the author might be said to make a general statement about "the good immigrant student," what would it be? Try to come up with an implied thesis that the essay might support. What experiences does Nguyen present to back up that thesis?

2. Readers must take Nguyen's word for much of the information she presents here; it would be difficult, if not impossible, to verify many of her observations. How does this aspect of the essay affect your reading? Do you find Nguyen a credible source? Using examples from the text, explain how Nguyen establishes your trust or causes you to question her at specific points in your reading.

MAKING CONNECTIONS

3. Nguyen describes how her stepmother's efforts at providing her daughters a bilingual education failed to achieve the desired results. After reading about Nguyen's experience, consider Robert King's "Should English Be the Law?" (p. 434). Discuss with classmates the extent to which you think schools ought to provide bilingual education, and how they might best accommodate the needs of students like Bich Minh Nguyen and her sister Anh.

4. Like "The Good Immigrant Student," Maxine Hong Kingston's "No Name Woman" (p. 394) presents insights into the experience of one woman whose family emigrated to the United States. Although the experiences and insights offered in these essays are very different, each addresses a felt need to hide or deny a woman's existence. In what ways are these experiences of hiding similar? In what ways are they different? Could these impulses to hide apply as well to men? To women of other ethnicities or races? In what situations? Write down your thoughts on these questions, and then discuss your ideas with classmates.

JOINING THE CONVERSATION

5. Do you identify or sympathize with some of the experiences Nguyen describes in this essay? How does your identity — however you define it — affect your ability to understand the incidents and feelings she describes?

6. Think about your own experiences in elementary and secondary school. How did they shape your development into the person you are today? Write an essay that explores and illuminates ways in which your school years were formative for you.

SHERMAN ALEXIE
What Sacagawea Means to Me

Artists who engage in politics *grow tiresome when they become predictable and shrill. Who can't guess precisely exactly what side of a political issue a Michael Moore, Susan Sarandon, or Oliver Stone will take? Maybe such people are really just performers? After all, we expect artists — the real thing, not celebrities crowned by a fawning media — to shake up conventional thinking and take us down paths that must sometimes surprise even them.*

Consider Sherman Alexie (b. 1966), a Spokane / Coeur d'Alene Indian and self-proclaimed liberal "brown guy," who makes films, writes poetry, publishes novels, and not infrequently offers his opinions in essays. Can you guess what Alexie had to say in Time Magazine *(July 1, 2002) about Native American icon Sacagawea on the 200th anniversary of the Lewis and Clark expedition? You might be surprised — if you were expecting him to depict an Indian heroine hopelessly oppressed by ruthless European-American colonialists. Instead, he uses his meditation on Sacagawea to raise a startling question: "I wonder if colonization might somehow be magical?" Then he explores why such an unanticipated, even upsetting, notion is plausible.*

But that's vintage Sherman Alexie, who manages in his films, prose, and even his interviews to present ideas that upset just about everybody. And that's a good thing. Whether it's suggesting that white authors like Larry McMurtry have no business writing about Indians or arguing that many Native Americans don't really care about the environment or taking his ground-breaking movies down paths elders of his tribe might not approve, Alexie negotiates his identity as a Native American artist in a way no one could call predictable.

—J.R.

In the future, every U.S. citizen will get to be Sacagawea for fifteen minutes. For the low price of admission, every American, regardless of race, religion, gender, and age, will climb through the portal into Sacagawea's Shoshone Indian brain. In the multicultural theme park called Sacagawea Land, you will be kidnapped as a child by the Hidatsa tribe and sold to Toussaint Charbonneau, the French-Canadian trader who will take you as one of his wives and father two of your children. Your first child, Jean-Baptiste, will be only a few months old as you carry him during your long journey with Lewis and Clark. The two captains will lead the adventure, fighting rivers, animals, weather, and diseases for thousands of miles, and you will march right beside them. But you, the aboriginal multitasker, will also breastfeed. And at the end of your Sacagawea journey, you will be shown the exit and given a souvenir T-shirt that reads, IF THE U.S. IS EDEN, THEN SACAGAWEA IS EVE.

Sacagawea is our mother. She is the first gene pair of the American DNA. In the beginning, she was the word, and the word was possibility. I revel in the wondrous possibilities of Sacagawea. It is good to be joyous in the presence of her spirit, because I hope she had moments of joy in what must have been a grueling life. This much is true: Sacagawea died of some mysterious illness when she was only in her twenties. Most illnesses were mysterious in the nineteenth century, but I suspect that Sacagawea's indigenous immune system was defenseless against an immigrant virus. Perhaps Lewis and Clark infected Sacagawea. If that is true, then certain postcolonial historians would argue that she was murdered not by germs but by colonists who carried those germs. I don't know much about the science of disease and immunities, but I know enough poetry to recognize that individual human beings are invaded and colonized by foreign bodies, just as individual civilizations are invaded and colonized by foreign bodies. In that sense, colonization might be a natural process, tragic and violent to be sure, but predictable and ordinary as well, and possibly necessary for the advance, however constructive and destructive, of all civilizations.

After all, Lewis and Clark's story has never been just the triumphant tale of two white men, no matter what the white historians might need to believe. Sacagawea was not the primary hero of this story either, no matter what the Native American historians and I might want to believe. The story of Lewis and Clark is also the story of the approximately forty-five nameless and faceless first- and second-generation European Americans who joined the journey, then left or completed it, often without monetary or historical compensation. Considering the time and place, I imagine those forty-five were illiterate, low-skilled laborers subject to managerial whims and nineteenth-century downsizing. And it is most certainly the story of the black slave York, who also cast votes during this allegedly democratic adventure. It's even the story of Seamen, the domesticated Newfoundland dog who must have been a welcome and friendly presence and who survived the risk of becoming supper during one lean time or another. The Lewis and Clark Expedition was exactly the kind of multicultural, trigenerational, bigendered, animal-friendly, government-supported, partly French-Canadian project that should rightly be celebrated by liberals and castigated by conservatives.

In the end, I wonder if colonization might somehow be magical. After all, Miles Davis is the direct descendant of slaves and slave owners. Hank Williams is the direct descendant of poor whites and poorer Indians. In 1876 Emily Dickinson was writing her poems in an Amherst attic while Crazy Horse was killing Custer on the banks of the Little Big Horn. I remain stunned by these contradictions, by the successive generations of social, political, and artistic mutations that can be so beautiful and painful. How did we get from there to here? This country somehow gave life to Maria Tallchief and Ted Bundy, to Geronimo and Joe McCarthy, to Nathan Bedford Forrest and Toni Morrison, to the Declaration of Independence and Executive Order No. 1066, to Cesar Chavez and Richard Nixon, to theme parks and national parks, to smallpox and the vaccine for smallpox.

THE SACAGAWEA DOLLAR COIN

As a Native American, I want to hate this country and its contradictions.   5
I want to believe that Sacagawea hated this country and its contradictions. But this
country exists, in whole and in part, because Sacagawea helped Lewis and Clark.
In the land that came to be called Idaho, she acted as diplomat between her long-
lost brother and the Lewis and Clark party. Why wouldn't she ask her brother and
her tribe to take revenge against the men who had enslaved her? Sacagawea is a
contradiction. Here in Seattle, I exist, in whole and in part, because a half-white
man named James Cox fell in love with a Spokane Indian woman named Etta
Adams and gave birth to my mother. I am a contradiction; I am Sacagawea.

Reading across Disciplines
TIMOTHY J. SHANNON, History

Academic historians surrendered the Lewis and Clark Expedition
to popular writers and storytellers a long time ago. This frontier epic is
so ingrained in the American imagination that no work of serious
scholarship — no matter how thorough in its research or startling in
its conclusions — could overturn what generations of Americans are

certain they know about it. It is an old saying in my profession that every generation writes its own history (and thank heavens for that, because it keeps me employed), but Lewis and Clark are an exception to the rule. The most recent bestseller on the topic, Stephen Ambrose's *Undaunted Courage: Meriwether Lewis, Thomas Jefferson, and the Opening of the American West*, would not have seemed out of place if published in 1896 instead of 1996. The title says it all: this is a story of courage and fortitude for the ages.

Sacagawea has always been one the main characters in that story, but the plot reduces her to a one-note performance. Like an actor who plays a role in a long-running television show, she has been typecast by history. She will always be the noble Indian guide, a selfless, nurturing female who served as den mother for the quintessential American male adventure. In word and image, she is the spiritual heir of Pocahontas, another native woman who helped struggling European colonizers, only to be repaid with separation from home, illness, and an early death. American folklore, literature, and drama are packed full of such characters, suffering Indian heroines too good and pure for this world and thus destined for a quick exit to the next.

The introduction of the Sacagawea dollar coin in 2000 brought her some new public fanfare, but that attention faded quickly as the coin went the way of the Susan B. Anthony dollar and the Thomas Jefferson two-dollar bill. Nevertheless, there is something noteworthy about the image of Sacagawea on the coin. Unlike the impassive presidential profiles featured on the rest of our pocket change, the Sacagawea on this coin offers a full-faced over-the-shoulder glance to the viewer. Her expression suggests regret (looking back) and consternation at the same time. Anyone who ever had to carry a small child on a long hike can certainly sympathize! Her eyes seem to be saying "What are you looking at?" but her body is moving forward, perpetually keeping time with Lewis and Clark in their trek across the continent.

Timothy J. Shannon is an associate professor of history at Gettysburg College in Gettysburg, Pennsylvania.

QUESTIONING THE TEXT

1. Alexie chooses Sacagawea not just because she assisted Lewis and Clark but also because she serves as a symbol of America for him. What aspects of American identity does Alexie argue that Sacagawea represents?

2. Do you think that Alexie admires Sacagawea? If so, why? If not, why not? Point to specific textual evidence to support your position.

MAKING CONNECTIONS

3. This essay originally appeared in a 2005 issue of *Time* magazine commemorating the expedition of Lewis and Clark, but Alexie seems to write with an eye toward making his topic relevant to a wide number of contemporary issues. One might, for example, be able to relate this essay to current debates on immigration. How might it be said to comment on immigration issues? To what other contemporary issues do you think this essay might be relevant?

4. Both Alexie and Tyina Steptoe ("An Ode to Country Music from a Black Dixie Chick," p. 421) make use of history to discuss their identities. Compare how the two writers use history and references to ancestors to explain their modern sense of themselves. Do you have a similar sense of how historical events and people have shaped who you are?

JOINING THE CONVERSATION

5. Alexie focuses on Sacagawea as a symbol of America. What historical or public figure would you choose as a representative American icon? Write an essay in which you explain your choice of one person who could be said to embody many essential aspects of American identity.

6. Write an essay in which you explain how an American public or historical figure could serve as a representative of all that you think is wrong with the United States.

KEITH BRADSHER
Reptile Dreams

MOST OF US WOULD PREFER TO BE KNOWN *for our accomplishments and our quali-*
ties as individuals. But advertisers and marketers prefer to think of us as creatures driven
by desires that might be manipulated or exploited. Sometimes they have wanted us to
think of ourselves as the Pepsi generation, and today they'd like us to identify with
Calvin Klein, or Tommy Hilfiger, or one of thousands of other brand names or products.
In short, advertisers and marketers want us to buy whatever they are selling, from tennis
shoes to hamburgers to Subarus.

There is, of course, a kind of logic to all of this. Birkenstocks and Fubu certainly are
markers of identity — simple ways of saying with whom you stand. The same is often
true of PC and Mac users and those who would buy only a Ford or only a Chevy: our
purchases are intertwined with our identity. What drives us to link ourselves to a
particular product? The following selection offers some possible answers.

Keith Bradsher (b. 1964) is the author of High and Mighty: The World's
Most Dangerous Vehicles and How They Got That Way *(2002), from which this*
piece is taken. Here, he analyzes the theory that primal urges persuade more than a mil-
lion people a year (myself included) to buy an SUV. Bradsher attributes this theory to
Clotaire Rapaille, a Frenchman turned Detroit marketing expert. As you will see,
Rapaille is convinced that people buy SUVs out of a primitive identification with lizards
and snakes, resulting in a "desire for survival." Judge for yourself whether ad campaigns
aimed at reptilian instincts are causing the popularity of overweight, gas-guzzling subur-
ban warfare vehicles. Or do people just want to haul lumber and tow boats?

Bradsher, a reporter and formerly Detroit bureau chief for the New York Times,
has been writing about SUVs since 1997. He has won the George Polk Award for his
work and, at one time, drove a leased Chevy Lumina.   —J.R.

Automakers employ thousands of people to figure out which models will
be popular next with American buyers, and thousands more to figure out how
to promote their latest models. A French medical anthropologist by training,
Clotaire Rapaille seems an unlikely person to have reshaped American automotive market research and marketing.

Tall and muscular at 60, with sandy blonde hair, Rapaille speaks with a
strong French accent, having only moved to the United States at the age of 38.
His background makes him an oddity in an industry dominated by the flat
Midwestern accents of men (seldom women) who grew up in Midwestern
cities like Cleveland, Toledo or Flint. Yet his psychological analysis of how sport
utility vehicles appeal to people's most primitive instincts has helped to legit-
imize the cynical marketing of SUVs.

During the 1990s, Rapaille worked on more than 20 projects with David Bostwick, Chrysler's market research director; François Castaing, Chrysler's chief of vehicle engineering; and Bob Lutz. Castaing says that he and Lutz believed in gut instinct more than market research in designing new models, and that they showed prototypes to Rapaille only after the initial design work, so as to double-check that their instincts were right. But providing the reality check on possible future models is a considerable responsibility. Because Chrysler was the unquestioned design and marketing leader in Detroit during this period, Rapaille's work also influenced other automakers, with Ford and GM eventually retaining him for projects as well.

Clotaire Rapaille was born in Paris on August 10, 1941, less than two months after Hitler's troops occupied the city. His father was an army officer who had just been captured by the Germans and would spend the entire war in a forced labor camp; he would emerge from the camp a broken man. His mother, fearful of the dangers of occupied Paris, sent her baby son out of the city to be raised by his grandmother in Vallée de Chevreuse, a small town halfway between Paris and the Normandy coastline.

Rapaille's earliest memory is of playing outdoors under his grandmother's   5
watchful eye when he was three, and unexpectedly seeing some German soldiers running away. "I said, 'How come the Germans are running away, the Germans never run away,' and then I saw a monster coming out of the forest, an American tank," he recalls. "A big American with a net on his helmet and flowers took me on the tank and gave me chocolates and gave me a ride."

That experience made an indelible impression. It convinced him at that early age that he wanted to become an American, because the French were losers in war while the Germans had been mean to everyone during the occupation.

Rapaille's parents and grandparents were nearly wiped out financially by the war, Rapaille put himself through college and graduate school in Paris by driving a beer delivery truck at night, then began consulting for Renault and Citroën, two big French automakers, in the early 1970s.

As he studied and then applied principles of psychological research, Rapaille became convinced that a person's first encounter with an object or idea shaped his or her emotional relationship with it for life. He would apply that conviction after moving in 1979 to America, where he became a prominent market researcher who specialized in psychoanalytic techniques.

Relying on the work of Carl Jung, the Swiss psychologist who founded analytic psychology, Rapaille divides people's reactions to a commercial product into three levels of brain activity. There is the cortex, for intellectual assessments of a product. There is the limbic, for emotional responses. And there is the reptilian, which he defines as reactions based on "survival and reproduction."

Rapaille focuses his attention on the deepest, most reptilian instincts   10
that people have about consumer products. He seeks to identify people's archetype of a product, the deepest emotional identity that the product holds

for them based on their earliest encounter with it. His research has led him to some disturbing conclusions about how to sell sport utility vehicles, which he sees as the most reptilian vehicles of all because their imposing, even menacing appearance appeals to people's deep-seated desires for "survival and reproduction."

With the detachment of a foreigner, Rapaille sees Americans as increasingly fearful of crime. He acknowledges that this fear is irrational and completely ignores statistics showing that crime rates have declined considerably. He attributes the pervasive fear of crime mainly to violent television shows, violent video games and lurid discussions and images on the Internet, which make young and middle-aged Americans more focused on threats to their physical safety than they need to be. At the same time, he argues, the aging of the population means that there are more older Americans, who may pay less attention to violence in the media but are more cautious than young people about personal safety in general.

The fear is most intense among today's teenagers, Rapaille has found, attributing the trend to the addition of video games and increasingly menacing toy action figures on top of the steady diet of murders on television that baby boomers had. "There is so much emphasis on violence — the war is every day, everywhere," he said in an interview two weeks before the terrorist attacks of September 11, 2001. The response of teens, he added, is that "They want to give the message, 'I want to be able to destroy, I want to be able to fight back, don't mess with me.'" While teens do not buy many SUVs, youth culture nonetheless tends to shape the attitudes of broad segments of American society.

For Rapaille, the archetype of a sport utility vehicle reflects the reptilian desire for survival. People buy SUVs, he tells auto executives, because they are trying to look as menacing as possible to allay their fears of crime and other violence. The Jeep has always had this image around the world because of its heavy use in war movies and frequent appearances in newsreels from the 1940s and 1950s, and newer SUVs share the image. "I usually say, 'If you put a machine gun on the top of them, you will sell them better,'" he said. "Even going to the supermarket, you have to be ready to fight."

To reach such conclusions, Rapaille has run dozens of consumer focus groups, or "discoveries," as he prefers to call them. First, he asks a group of 30 people to sit in a windowless room and take turns speaking for an hour about their rational, reasoned responses to a vehicle. "They tell me things I don't really care about, and I don't listen," he said.

Then he tells the group to spend another hour pretending to be five- 15 year-old boys from another planet. He asks them to tell him little stories about the vehicle, to get at their emotional responses to the vehicle. But he later discards the notes on these stories as well.

What really interests him is the third stage of research. He asks the consumers to lie down on mats and he turns the lights way down in the room. Then he asks each consumer lying in the near darkness to tell him about his or her earliest associations with vehicles, in an attempt to get at their "reptilian" responses to various designs.

The answers in these consumer groups have persuaded Rapaille that American culture is becoming frighteningly atavistic and obsessed with crime. He cites as further proof the spread of gated communities and office buildings protected by private security guards, together with the tiny but growing market in the United States for luxury vehicles with bulletproof armor. "I think we're going back to medieval times, and you can see that in that we live in ghettos with gates and private armies," he said. "SUVs are exactly that, they are armored cars for the battlefield."

Even Rapaille says that a few of his ideas are too extreme to be practical. SUV buyers want to be able to take on street gangs with their vehicles and run them down, he said, while hastening to add that that television commercials showing this would be inappropriate. He has unsuccessfully tried to persuade ad agency executives working for Chrysler to buy the television commercial rights to *Mad Max*, the 1979 film that launched Mel Gibson's career. The film shows heavily armed thugs in leather on motorcycles, driving around a post-Apocalyptic Australia and killing people so as to steal their gasoline. Rapaille wanted Chrysler to use computers to insert its SUVs into scenes from the movie, with the vehicle rescuing the hero or heroine from the clutches of one of the movie's nefarious villains in hockey masks. But the idea was dismissed as too controversial. And when I checked with someone in Hollywood, I learned that the rights to *Mad Max* are caught in a legal tangle that would make it nearly impossible to use the film for a commercial.

Yet the idea of being civil on the roads has disappeared and SUV design needs to reflect this, Rapaille says, "This is over, people don't care, and for some people, the message is it's *Mad Max* out there, it's a jungle out there and you're not going to kill me, if you attack me I will fight."

As a milder alternative, Rapaille admires SUV television ads like the one that showed a Jeep climbing home over a pile of rocks at the bottom of a house's driveway. "Your house has become a castle," he said.   20

When Rapaille came to work for Chrysler, one of his first projects was to define what consumers really saw in the company's Jeeps. His cynical, even brutal view of the world fit perfectly with the "gut" of Bob Lutz, who oversaw Chrysler's light-truck operations in the United States upon his arrival from Ford in 1986. Lutz's corporate empire had grown a lot bigger in 1987, when Chrysler bought American Motors, including its profitable Jeep brand.

Lutz insisted on ever more powerful engines mounted in ever taller SUVs and pickup trucks with ever more menacing-looking front ends — an approach enthusiastically recommended by Rapaille. Lutz's instructions were consistent, said David C. McKinnon, Chrysler's director of vehicle exterior design: "Get them up in the air and make them husky." Lutz gave this advice even for two-wheel-drive versions of SUVs that were unlikely ever to go off-road and therefore did not need a lot of height and ground clearance, McKinnon said. Because Chrysler was Detroit's design leader during this period, and Lutz the most influential car guy in town, Lutz's decisions shaped the way SUVs were designed around the world.

The Jeep Grand Cherokee's debut at the Detroit auto show in 1992 was a vintage Lutz moment. With a large crowd of journalists gathered, he drove a Grand Cherokee up the steps of Detroit's convention center and smashed through a plate-glass window to enter the building. A special window had been installed in advance to make this a little less dangerous than it sounds. The television footage was nonetheless great, and established the Grand Cherokee's credentials as a rough-and-tough vehicle.

The Dodge Ram full-sized pickup truck came out two years later with a front end that was designed to look as big and menacing as a Mack truck; *USA Today* described it admiringly as the kind of vehicle that would make other motorists want to get out of your way.

In his book, *Guts*, Lutz wrote that the Ram's in-your-face styling was care- 25 fully chosen even though consumer focus groups showed that most Americans would loathe it. "A whopping 80 percent of the respondents disliked the bold new drop-fendered design. A lot even hated it!" he wrote. However, he explained, "the remaining 20 percent of the clinic participants were saying that they were truly, madly, deeply in love with the design! And since the old Ram had only about 4 percent of the market at the time, we figured, what the hell, even if only half of those positive respondents actually buy, we'll more than double our share! The result? Our share of the pickup market shot up to 20 percent on the radical new design, and Ford and Chevy owners gawked in envy!"

Ford and GM did not take the loss of sales lightly. They responded by making the Ford F-series pickups and the Chevrolet Silverado and GMC Sierra pickups more menacing, too. The Ford and GM pickups were then modified to make seven full-sized SUVs: the Ford Excursion, Ford Expedition, Lincoln Navigator, Chevrolet Tahoe, GMC Yukon, Chevrolet Suburban and GMC Yukon XL. Since all of these SUVs shared a lot of the same front-end parts with the pickup trucks on which they were based, the shift led by Dodge Ram toward more menacing front ends caused the entire full-sized SUV market to become more menacing. Close to 90 percent of the parts for a Ford Excursion are the same as for the Ford Super Duty pickup on which it is based, according to Ford. By turning the Ram into a brute, Lutz indirectly fed the highway arms race among SUVs.

When it comes to specific vehicles, the Dodge Durango comes closest to fitting Rapaille's Hobbesian view of life as being nasty, brutish and short. The Durango's front end is intended to resemble the face of a savage jungle cat, said Rapaille. The vertical bars across the grille represent teeth, and the vehicle has bulging fenders over the wheels that look like clenched muscles in a savage jaw.

"A strong animal has a big jaw, that's why we put big fenders," Rapaille says.

Minivans, by contrast, evoke feelings of being in the womb, and of caring for others, he says. Stand a minivan on its rear bumper and it has the silhouette of a pregnant woman in a floor-length dress. Not surprisingly, minivans are being crowded out of the market by SUVs. Rapaille even dislikes SUVs like the Mercedes M-Class that look a little like minivans.

Convertibles are suffering in the marketplace because women worry that they might be assaulted by an intruder who climbs inside, Rapaille contends. "Women were telling me, if you drive a convertible with the top down, the message is 'Rape me.'" 30

The reptilian instinct for survival does not just involve crime fears, Rapaille says. It also shows up in the extent to which people are willing to put other drivers at risk in order to diminish the odds that they will be injured themselves in a crash. In other words, people in touch with their inner reptile are most likely to choose vehicles that look especially likely to demolish other people's cars in collisions.

"My theory is the reptilian always wins," he said. "The reptilian says, 'If there's a crash, I want the other guy to die.' Of course, I can't say that aloud."

But SUVs cannot just look macho and menacing on the outside, Rapaille believes. Inside, they must be as gentle, feminine and luxurious as possible. Rapaille's argument for this is based on the reptilian instinct for reproduction.

"Men are for outside and women are for inside, that's just life; to reproduce men have to take something outside and the women take something inside," Rapaille said. "The inside of an SUV should be the Ritz-Carlton, with a minibar. I'm going to be on the battlefield a long time, so on the outside I want to be menacing but inside I want to be warm, with food and hot coffee and communications."

Listen to other auto-market researchers try to define an SUV and you often hear an almost literal echo of Rapaille's advice. "It's aggressive on the outside and it's the Ritz-Carlton on the inside, that's part of the formula," Chrysler's Bostwick said. 35

Rapaille's emphasis on reptilian instincts reflects not only his early encounter with the tank, he says, but also his subsequent, difficult upbringing. Rapaille says that his father never recovered from the psychological damage of his imprisonment, and his parents were divorced after the war. He was then sent off to a Jesuit school in Laval, France, and grew up there. "I had to stay there all year long because no one wanted to take care of me from my family, but I was alive, the reptilian was survival," he says.

Rapaille has loved automobiles since boyhood. But while he can now afford to buy an SUV, he doesn't own one. Instead, he owns a Rolls Royce and a Porsche 911. Sport utilities are too tall, he says, and he has a terror of rolling over. He likes the Rolls Royce but loves the Porsche, because it allows him to retain control of his destiny with its nimbleness, excellent brakes and tremendous stability. Compared to an SUV, he says, "A Porsche is safer." He may have emigrated to America, but in this respect he remains a European.

Rapaille's work helped automakers begin to understand who buys SUVs and why. But their research has gone far beyond archetypes. Lavishing huge sums, the auto industry has developed year by year an ever more detailed knowledge of what SUV buyers want, and then tapped into these desires with multibillion dollar advertising campaigns that are slick but extremely cynical.

QUESTIONING THE TEXT

1. In his opening paragraph, Bradsher announces, "Clotaire Rapaille seems an unlikely person to have reshaped American automotive market research and marketing." Although Bradsher creates doubt about Rapaille in the beginning of the essay, does he succeed in dispelling that doubt later on? Defend your answer with an analysis of the support provided in the essay, using examples from the text.

2. What feelings do you have toward Clotaire Rapaille as you read this essay? Do you like, dislike, respect, or admire him? How does Bradsher characterize Clotaire Rapaille? What words and phrases does he use to describe Rapaille? What anecdotes does he use to give a sense of what Rapaille is like?

3. How does Bradsher present Clotaire Rapaille's views in this essay? Does he present them uncritically, favorably, skeptically, or in some other fashion? Quote passages in the text to support your claims.

4. What does this essay say about the influence of gender on identity? What does it say about the identity of those who choose to drive SUVs? About those who make them?

MAKING CONNECTIONS

5. Compare the views of men and women presented in this essay with those presented in Dave Barry's "Guys vs. Men" (p. 405). What similarities and differences do you find in the perspectives of the two writers? What limitations and strengths do you find in each of their arguments? Which essay is more convincing, and why?

6. Consider the extent to which Bradsher's essay captures a sense of American identity, and compare his observations with insights offered in other essays in this chapter, such as Maxine Hong Kingston's "No Name Woman" (p. 394), Bich Minh Nguyen's "The Good Immigrant Student" (p. 458),

or Sherman Alexie's "What Sacagawea Means to Me" (p. 466). How do these essays characterize Americans? Evaluate one or more of these American character traits, and write an essay on why you find such characterizations accurate or inaccurate.

JOINING THE CONVERSATION

7. Think of your own car or a car you would choose to drive if money were no object. Describe the car in terms that convey its personality. Write an essay on what your car, or your ideal car, says about you. What does the car reveal about who you are and/or who you aspire to be?

8. Do you believe that Rapaille's concept of human psychological impulses toward cars is accurate? Use library resources to find research that would further support his claims or cast doubt on their validity. Write a newspaper op-ed or magazine guest column that presents your informed opinion on the automobile marketing practices described by Bradsher.

SUSANNA ASHTON
Making Peace with the Greeks

*I*SSUES OF IDENTITY *nearly always focus on groups considered in some way marginalized. The groups may be identified by race, religion, ethnicity, gender, or sexual orientation. Or identity may be constituted by choices that separate one group of people from another, such as Trekkies, computer geeks, hipsters, punks, Goths, or Amway representatives. Even women, the factual majority, are still sometimes identified in terms of disparity and oppression.*

But can people who enjoy privilege and power, good looks, contacts, and access to the levers of power be marginalized, too, by the assumptions of identity that others use to stereotype them? Consider, for example, fraternity boys — as professor Susanna Ashton does in "Making Peace with the Greeks," an essay originally published in the Chronicle of Higher Education *(November 17, 2006). In the article, she describes her rather odd experiences teaching a composition class in which half the students were gregarious, backslapping, nickname-swapping fraternity brothers. Fearing that this boisterousness threatened the civility of her course, Professor Ashton assembles them for a serious discussion of their behavior. But something unexpected happens when, declining to chew them out for their high spirits, she takes a different approach — and discovers how easy it is to make wrong assumptions about people we don't know well.*

The Chronicle of Higher Education, *where the essay appeared, is read primarily by professionals in higher education — staff, administration, faculty, and graduate students. You may get a sense of that audience from the way Ashton, an associate professor of American literature, addresses her column. What does it say about the way faculty might think about Greeks from the fact that Ashton even thought to write a piece like this one? Have you ever been part of a group whose identity has been immediately suspect or disparaged in a similar way?*

—J.R.

Scanning the faces of my first-year composition students, I quickly saw that something was awry. Out of 22 students, 17 were men.

Clemson University, where I teach, does have more male than female students but the ratio didn't warrant that kind of discrepancy. Nor did my topic. This composition course was required across the board for undergraduates. So what had happened? I figured it was just a demographic fluke and handed out my syllabus.

After a few sessions, however, the rowdiness was more than I could handle. I like to have the occasional freewheeling moments in my class and I certainly appreciate discussion and interaction among students. But certain things in this class struck me as a little odd. Students were referring to each other by nicknames awfully early in the semester. By the third session I realized that students in one group were calling each other "JoeBob," "the Sweeeeeet" (to a student whose last name was, indeed "Sweet") and, inexplicably, "Wago-Pago."

It seemed odd that so many students in the class already felt so close and seemed to share so many inside jokes. While attendance seemed better than average and a lot of the boisterous behavior seemed to keep things in an upbeat mood, the cheers from the class every time I praised a comment became increasingly disconcerting.

> ME: "Good point, Sean. That's very thoughtful."   5
> CLASS: "WHOOP WHOOP WHOOP."
> ME: "I like the way Eddie framed his argument there. Did
>   everyone notice how Eddie termed . . ."
> CLASS (interrupting): "EddiEE! EddiEE! EddiEE!"

I tried my best to calm things down, but I was baffled. I'd had disruptive students before, but they were usually guilty of some sort of truly negative behavior. In this class, the behavior of many students (it seemed to be spreading rapidly) was certainly creating a fun atmosphere, but it was increasingly getting in the way of my course agenda.

Then I noticed that when I broke students up into groups (which   10
I always did in random configurations in order to mix up abilities and temperaments), the amount of off-task communication was more than I had ever noticed before. A couple of gentle rebukes would usually focus the groups, but I was nonetheless astounded by how frequently I had to force them to focus.

It must be gender, I decided, for the young women in my class were not participating in the rowdiness in any meaningful way. All those young men were just enabling this genial goofiness, I reasoned.

But after the first month, when I asked a struggling student to talk with me after class, I made a discovery. He claimed that he was having trouble doing the recent assignment because he hadn't bought one of the textbooks and had instead relied on borrowing it from his friends. That week, he said, the other students hadn't been willing to lend their copy. "Practically everyone in the frat was busy writing the paper and couldn't spare the book," he told me.

I interrupted him: "Everyone in your frat?"

Ah, yes. It transpired that 11 students, or half my class, hailed from the same fraternity. How they had managed to sign up for my course with all of the traumas that usually accompany online registration and lottery-assigned enrollment numbers, I haven't discovered. But there they all were. Apparently two former students of mine were in the same fraternity and had recommended my class to their younger friends and fraternity brothers.

Now, at least, all the bonhomie and backslapping made sense. And so   15
did the erratically reticent and occasionally frantic behavior of the rest of the class. But how to handle the increasing tide of friendly but disruptive behavior?

The next class session I asked "the gentlemen from Kappa Wokka Wakka" (or whatever its name was) to please stay after class. They gathered at my desk nervously, obviously expecting me to chew them out for what had been a particularly rowdy session. It was a tempting thought, I confess.

I took a deep breath, however, and decided upon different tactics.

It recently came to my attention, I said, that they were all from the same fraternity. I told them I would like their leadership help. There were several transfer students in the class, as well as two international students and a very recent immigrant to the United States. I explained that since they were clearly taking such a "leadership" role in keeping a positive atmosphere in the class, I would really like their help in reaching out of the other students.

I suggested they scatter their seating around the classroom differently so they weren't clustered together. I asked them to help me elicit participation from the other students by asking follow-up questions of one another in group discussion. I asked them to use the first names of other students in conversation — not necessarily to nickname them as they did with one another — but simply to make them feel part of the group. I asked the young men to put special effort into listening and responding to the other students in the class. Lastly, I asked them to help me keep everyone else on task. (That last appeal was especially disingenuous since they were the primary offenders on that score but I figured appealing to their sense of themselves as leaders who were skilled in group dynamics might work.)

The men of "Kappa Wokka Wakka" responded by standing up straighter and getting increasingly polite. "You can count on us, ma'am," "Yes ma'am," "No problem," they replied in deep and serious tones. Several of them even shook my hand as they filed out of the classroom.

Sure enough, it worked.

As the weeks went on and I saw "my frat boys," as I came to think of them, choose to pair off in partner exercises with the international students and transfer students, I saw a collective solidarity build in the class. I had exaggerated my sense of the situation in order to calm down the frat boys but now that I saw them purposefully including the international students and transfer students in everything, I realized that those students had indeed been marginalized. Our work became more focused and the rowdiness soon diminished significantly.

Drawing upon their fundamental good nature and genuine pride in themselves as representatives of a group made a difference. While I had almost gagged on my own cynicism for having appealed to their supposed leadership skills when I had really wanted to just chew them out, they turned the tables on me.

Given the opportunity to rise to the occasion, they pulled themselves and the class together. What I had thought of as canny manipulation (as a colleague put it, I had "sold my soul" by "sucking up" to them) turned out to be a genuinely positive and effective strategy.

I spent my own undergraduate years at Vassar College, which is different from the large university where I now teach. Like many small liberal-arts colleges, Vassar doesn't have fraternities or sororities and discourages exclusive societies of any kind.

Getting used to the role and influence that fraternity and sorority systems have on a campus is a hard task, and even after many years teaching at the University of Iowa, where I earned my Ph.D., and also now at Clemson, I still find much of the "Greek system" baffling. I am still suspicious of its positive influence on an academic mission. I still sometimes use "frat boy" as shorthand for a disinterested or rowdy baseball-cap-wearing undergraduate.

But I'm aware that my prejudices aren't entirely fair. My most obnoxious, troubled, or difficult students have tended to be loners, not joiners. And my sorority students have almost always been among the most responsible population of students I have ever encountered.

The presence of "Greek life" helps shape classroom dynamics for better or worse, and it poses particular challenges to the cultural expectations of many professors who may never have belonged to fraternities or sororities as undergraduates, much less those who attended institutions where fraternities and sororities were seen as positively antithetical to college culture.

My prejudices against frat boys led me to sarcastically invoke their supposed interest in "leadership" skills in order to manipulate their little gang. And yet those same students forced me to acknowledge my own shortcomings in having underestimated them. Their genuine attempt to create a positive and more scholarly environment shamed me into respecting them and their efforts.

I can't say I want another class like that. It exhausted me beyond words. But watching the frat boys effectively invite everyone into their group reminded me that some classroom problems are best solved by students, not teachers. And while I'm not likely to rush anytime soon, I've made my peace with the Greeks.

QUESTIONING THE TEXT

1. Ashton says that she is "disingenuous" in her appeal to the leadership of the fraternity members to help her, and one of her colleagues tells her that she is "sucking up" to the students. How do you judge Ashton's classroom management techniques? If you agree that she is "sucking up" to the fraternity members, does the end goal of classroom order justify the means that she uses to get there?

2. Take a look at the Jobs section of the *Chronicle of Higher Education*'s Web site (www.chronicle.com/jobs), where this article originally appeared. Who do you think the audience for this article is? What do you think is Ashton's intent in writing this article? How does she want that audience to react?

MAKING CONNECTIONS

3. How does Ashton's description of the fraternity members reflect the ideas in Dave Barry's "Guys vs. Men" (p. 405)? Are the fraternity members guys, men, or some combination of both? Explain your reasoning.

4. Compare Ashton's recognition of her students' identity to some of the teachers mentioned by Bich Minh Nguyen in the "The Good Immigrant Student" (p. 458). To what degree do you think teachers can or should acknowledge students' group identities in the classroom?

JOINING THE CONVERSATION

5. What do you think about Greek life? If you are a member of a Greek organization or on a campus where fraternities and/or sororities are present, write an essay discussing the effect that you think they have on campus life. If you have no experience with fraternities or sororities, write an essay that reflects on the role of other organizations on your campus, or discuss how you think about Greek life based on what you know about it from television, movies, or discussions with others who know more about it than you. Do you carry prejudices for or against Greeks?

6. How does membership in a group that you choose to be in — rather than membership in a group that you are born into — affect your identity? Is it more or less important as a means of creating your identity? Describe the importance of a group that you've chosen to belong to — a social organization, athletic team, or a religious group, for example — and explain in an essay how it has or has not helped shape who you are.

LANGSTON HUGHES
Theme for English B

As a young man in Joplin, Missouri, Langston Hughes (1902–67) worked as an assistant cook, a launderer, and a busboy — jobs similar to ones you may have held — before leaving to attend Columbia University in New York City. (He eventually graduated in 1929 from Lincoln University in Pennsylvania.) A prolific writer and part of the great artistic movement of the 1920s and 1930s known as the Harlem Renaissance, Hughes worked in many genres — novels, short stories, plays, essays, and poems. From his early collection of poems, The Weary Blues *(1926), to his posthumous volume of essays,* Black Misery *(1969), he explored numerous themes touching on the lives of African Americans, including that of higher education.*

The poem that follows, from 1926, describes one event in the speaker's college career and raises questions about relationships between instructors and students, between those "inside" the university and those "outside." It is one of my favorite poems, one of the few special ones I carry around with me and, in fact, now find that I know "by heart." With every new class I teach, I think of Hughes's "Theme for English B," for it speaks volumes to me about the necessity of respecting individual differences while at the same time valuing those bonds that link us to one another. —A.L.

The instructor said,

> Go home and write
> a page tonight.

> And let that page come out of you —
> Then, it will be true.   5

I wonder if it's that simple?
I am twenty-two, colored, born in Winston-Salem.
I went to school there, then Durham, then here
to this college on the hill above Harlem.
I am the only colored student in my class.   10
The steps from the hill lead down to Harlem,
through a park, then I cross St. Nicholas,
Eighth Avenue, Seventh, and I come to the Y,
the Harlem Branch Y, where I take the elevator
up to my room, sit down, and write this page: 15

It's not easy to know what is true for you or me
at twenty-two, my age. But I guess I'm what
I feel and see and hear. Harlem, I hear you:
hear you, hear me — we two — you, me talk on this page.
(I hear New York, too.) Me — who?   20
Well, I like to eat, sleep, drink, and be in love.
I like to work, read, learn, and understand life.
I like a pipe for a Christmas present,
or records — Bessie,* bop, or Bach.
I guess being colored doesn't make me not like   25
the same things other folks like who are other races.
So will my page be colored that I write?
Being me, it will not be white.
But it will be
a part of you, instructor.   30
You are white —
yet a part of me, as I am a part of you.
That's American.
Sometimes perhaps you don't want to be a part of me.
Nor do I often want to be a part of you.   35
But we are, that's true!
As I learn from you,
I guess you learn from me —
although you're older — and white —
and somewhat more free.   40

This is my page for English B.

IN RESPONSE

1. Near the end of the poem, the speaker says, addressing his instructor, "You are white — / yet a part of me, as I am a part of you. / That's American." What do you think Hughes means by "American"?

2. The speaker of this poem notes that given who he is, his theme will not be "white," but he goes on to say that it will still be "a part of you, instructor." What do you think he means? Can you describe a time when you've had a similar experience?

3. Zora Neale Hurston's "How It Feels to Be Colored Me" (p. 416) is roughly contemporary with Hughes's poem, but Tyina Steptoe's "An

---

Bessie: Bessie Smith (1898?–1937), a famous blues singer

Ode to Country Music from a Black Dixie Chick" (p. 421) comes several decades later. Compare the representations of African American experience, particularly concerning notions about commonalities between people of different races, in these three pieces.

4. Would Hughes — or his teacher — likely be found in John Henry Newman's ideal university (p. 51)? Why, or why not?

5. Consider what effects your own gender, race, class, or family background has had on your success in school. Then write a brief (one- or two-page) essay explaining those effects.

6. Brainstorm with two or three classmates about whether it is important for students to identify with their teachers, to have a number of things in common with them. Come to an agreement among yourselves on how to answer this question, and then write one page explaining why you answered it as you did.

The photo on the preceding page shows Superman costumes hanging on a clothesline. Superman, who appeared in DC Comics publications beginning in 1938, is usually considered the first superhero, and the character remains one of the most popular figures in comic literature (in addition to his successful incarnations on television and in films). ■ Why might this image of Superman's laundry suggest an American cultural myth? ■ Why do you think superheroes have such a strong appeal to many Americans? What is "American" about Superman? ■ What values does Superman represent, in your view? Are these "traditional American values"? Why or why not? ■ Are "traditional American values" permanent, fixed ideals, or do these values change in response to changes in American culture? Explain your answer.

American Cultural Myths

IN A NEW YORK TIMES COLUMN (March 30, 2003) critical of how President Bush has betrayed the "foundational national myth" of the American cowboy, author Susan Faludi offers a succinct description of the role shared stories play in the culture of any country or people: "Mythologies," Faludi suggests, "are essential to defining who we are and, more importantly, who we want to be." One can hardly imagine a clearer way of explaining the concept: we tell stories to bind us to one another, reinterpreting and retelling the tales with each generation so that we eventually accumulate many versions of the same defining narratives.

This chapter explores only a few of the many myths that make up the American story. Of course, all people have such mythologies. For Russians, the themes often focus on endurance and suffering, not surprising given the history and even geography of that sprawling country. For other ethnic groups, including both Jews and African Americans, the defining myths include tales of persecution and diaspora.

American mythologies are particularly important now, with the United States assuming new roles on the world stage, because many of those tales reach well beyond the nation's borders. The American dream, interpreted in numerous ways, is becoming a part of the world's consciousness. In the past, people were drawn to the United States by promises of equality, opportunity, and freedom; they wanted to go to America to become American. Now the question may be to what extent an imperial America wants to extend — or even impose — its values beyond its continental limits.

We began our work on this chapter by brainstorming a list of national myths. Here are some of the myths we came up with:

- **Myth of the American frontier.** This myth is told through stories about extending control over nature, land, and people. The first frontiers were the Appalachians, later the vast American West, and finally the moon and outer space. (We seem not to have envisioned the depths of the ocean as a new frontier — yet.)

- **Myth of America as the land of opportunity.** Tales of immigrants coming to America for political and economic opportunity give life to this powerful story. However, this narrative has never accommodated the forced immigration of African slaves or the "assimilation" of Native Americans. And the myth is spoken differently along the southern borders of the United States.

- **Myth of America as the land of freedom and equality.** This is the great political myth — the story of the Revolution, the Declaration of Independence, the Civil War, and the civil rights movement — yet it consistently collides with the counterstory of American oppressions.

- **Myth of the American as a rugged individual.** Most Americans prefer to portray themselves as masters of their own destinies. Consequently, they are fond of political and economic success stories — from Edison the inventor to Amelia Earhart the aviator to the Jimmy Stewart character in *Mr. Smith Goes to Washington*.

- **Myth of America as the "city on a hill."** This is the narrative of American moral righteousness and superiority. It is both *The Scarlet Letter* and *To Kill a Mockingbird*. In a parodic way, it is also *The Simpsons*.

- **Myth of the American as a rebel.** Think of Captain Ahab and James Dean, Thoreau and Walt Whitman, Emily Dickinson and Madonna, the Roots and OutKast.

- **Myth of the open road.** The frontier becomes personal when Americans exercise their option to pack their bags and move on, to change their lives, to seek better (or more interesting) opportunities. You might think of *Moby Dick* as a road trip of a kind — or of Jack Kerouac's *On the Road* or Callie Kouhri's *Thelma and Louise*.

This list of myths is, of course, incomplete and always evolving. We encourage you to add to it and to embroider the items we have offered with details from your own experience. We hope, however, that these initial suggestions and the readings that follow will spark your interest in the cultural myths that either bind us together or heighten our sense of separation and difference. At the outset of this chapter, you may want to ponder these questions:

- How well have Americans lived up to the mythic visions of their founding documents — including the Declaration of Independence?

- In what ways do our national myths sometimes seem crafted to exclude certain "others"? Could these myths retain their power if they evolved to accommodate more people?

- How do other nations now regard American dreams and aspirations? Are we really the "city on a hill," or have we become a threatening cultural, economic, and military colossus?
- Do conflicting myths about equality and opportunity divide the American people along political lines? Or are American dreams and aspirations more widely shared than some believe?

• • •

THOMAS JEFFERSON
Declaration of Independence

*W*HAT CAN YOU SAY ABOUT THE *Declaration of Independence (1776), the document that turned thirteen British colonies into what would become the United States of America? Surely it stands among the great political treatises of the Western world, as important as Plato's* Republic, *the Magna Carta, and* the Declaration of the Rights of Man. *It was, in its time, as radical a political manifesto as could be imagined, and yet part of its greatness is that it obliged future generations to fulfill promises its signers could not meet.*

The Declaration of Independence probably could not be written today: it is too clear, too bold, too confident. Just imagine the resistance of politicians and various special interest groups to the notion of unalienable rights endowed by a Creator. And when was the last time you heard a bureaucrat in Washington musing on "the pursuit of happiness"? The Declaration is also probably too forthright for modern tastes about the rights of people to resist governments that fail them. Stylistically, it is way too economical as well. Imagine what a committee of government officials today would do with the task given to Thomas Jefferson (1743–1826), Benjamin Franklin, and John Adams. Why, the staff alone assigned to such a committee would probably outnumber some of the armies the Continental Congress mustered.

Certainly, Americans have not always lived up to the spirit of this splendid founding document. Still, I would argue that the Declaration of Independence is revered around the world in part because the nation it created has succeeded so well. Freedom and equality are mythic in the United States not only because of what the Declaration promised but what generations of Americans subsequently achieved in its name. The dustbin of history is doubtless heavy with political documents no less noble or idealistic than the Declaration of Independence. The French alone have shuffled through five republics, and the former Soviet Union had a real genius for publishing idealistic sentiments. But the Declaration endures, I think, because, in a splendid moment, perhaps blessed by that deity it does not name, it created both a dream and a people. —J.R.

In Congress, July 4, 1776.

The Unanimous Declaration of the Thirteen United States of America,

When in the Course of human events, it becomes necessary for one people to dissolve the political bands which have connected them with another, and to assume among the powers of the earth, the separate and equal station to which the Laws of Nature and of Nature's God entitle them, a decent respect to the opinions of mankind requires that they should declare the causes which impel them to the separation.

We hold these truths to be self-evident, that all men are created equal, that they are endowed by their Creator with certain unalienable Rights, that among these are Life, Liberty and the pursuit of Happiness. — That to secure these rights, Governments are instituted among Men, deriving their just powers from the consent of the governed, — That whenever any Form of Government becomes destructive of these ends, it is the Right of the People to alter or to abolish it, and to institute new Government, laying its foundation on such principles and organizing its powers in such form, as to them shall seem most likely to effect their Safety and Happiness. Prudence, indeed, will dictate that Governments long established should not be changed for light and transient causes; and accordingly all experience hath shewn, that mankind are more disposed to suffer, while evils are sufferable, than to right themselves by abolishing the forms to which they are accustomed. But when a long train of abuses and usurpations, pursuing invariably the same Object evinces a design to reduce them under absolute Despotism, it is their right, it is their duty, to throw off such Government, and to provide new Guards for their future security. — Such has been the patient sufferance of these Colonies; and such is now the necessity which constrains them to alter their former Systems of Government. The history of the present King of Great Britain is a history of repeated injuries and usurpations, all having in direct object the establishment of an absolute Tyranny over these States. To prove this, let Facts be submitted to a candid world.

He has refused his Assent to Laws, the most wholesome and necessary for the public good.

He has forbidden his Governors to pass Laws of immediate and pressing importance, unless suspended in their operation till his Assent should be obtained; and when so suspended, he has utterly neglected to attend to them.

He has refused to pass other Laws for the accommodation of large districts   5
of people, unless those people would relinquish the right of Representation in the Legislature, a right inestimable to them and formidable to tyrants only.

He has called together legislative bodies at places unusual, uncomfortable, and distant from the depository of their public Records, for the sole purpose of fatiguing them into compliance with his measures.

He has dissolved Representative Houses repeatedly, for opposing with manly firmness his invasions on the rights of the people.

He has refused for a long time, after such dissolutions, to cause others to be elected; whereby the Legislative powers, incapable of Annihilation, have returned to the People at large for their exercise; the State remaining in the mean time exposed to all the dangers of invasion from without, and convulsions within.

He has endeavoured to prevent the population of these States; for that purpose obstructing the Laws for Naturalization of Foreigners; refusing to pass others to encourage their migrations hither, and raising the conditions of new Appropriations of Lands.

He has obstructed the Administration of Justice, by refusing his Assent   10
to Laws for establishing Judiciary powers.

He has made Judges dependent on his Will alone, for the tenure of their offices, and the amount and payment of their salaries.

He has erected a multitude of New Offices, and sent hither swarms of Officers to harrass our people, and eat out their substance.

He has kept among us, in times of peace, Standing Armies without the Consent of our legislatures.

He has affected to render the Military independent of and superior to the Civil power.

He has combined with others to subject us to a jurisdiction foreign to   15 our constitution, and unacknowledged by our laws; giving his Assent to their Acts of pretended Legislation:

For Quartering large bodies of armed troops among us:

For protecting them, by a mock Trial, from punishment for any Murders which they should commit on the Inhabitants of these States:

For cutting off our Trade with all parts of the world:

For imposing Taxes on us without our Consent:

For depriving us in many cases, of the benefits of Trial by Jury: 20

For transporting us beyond Seas to be tried for pretended offences:

For abolishing the free System of English Laws in a neighbouring Province, establishing therein an Arbitrary government, and enlarging its Boundaries so as to render it at once an example and fit instrument for introducing the same absolute rule into these Colonies:

For taking away our Charters, abolishing our most valuable Laws, and altering fundamentally the Forms of our Governments:

For suspending our own Legislatures, and declaring themselves invested with power to legislate for us in all cases whatsoever.

He has abdicated Government here, by declaring us out of his Protec-   25 tion and waging War against us.

He has plundered our seas, ravaged our Coasts, burnt our towns, and destroyed the lives of our people.

He is at this time transporting large Armies of foreign Mercenaries to compleat the works of death, desolation and tyranny, already begun with circumstances of Cruelty & perfidy scarcely paralleled in the most barbarous ages, and totally unworthy the Head of a civilized nation.

He has constrained our fellow Citizens taken Captive on the high Seas to bear Arms against their Country, to become the executioners of their friends and Brethren, or to fall themselves by their Hands.

He has excited domestic insurrections amongst us, and has endeavoured to bring on the inhabitants of our frontiers, the merciless Indian Savages, whose known rule of warfare, is an undistinguished destruction of all ages, sexes and conditions.

In every stage of these Oppressions We have Petitioned for Redress in   30 the most humble terms: Our repeated Petitions have been answered only by repeated injury. A Prince whose character is thus marked by every act which may define a Tyrant, is unfit to be the ruler of a free people.

Nor have We been wanting in attentions to our British brethren. We have warned them from time to time of attempts by their legislature to extend an unwarrantable jurisdiction over us. We have reminded them of the circumstances of our emigration and settlement here. We have appealed to their native justice and magnanimity, and we have conjured them by the ties of our common kindred to disavow these usurpations, which, would inevitably interrupt our connections and correspondence. They too have been deaf to the voice of justice and of consanguinity. We must, therefore, acquiesce in the necessity, which denounces our Separation, and hold them, as we hold the rest of mankind, Enemies in War, in Peace Friends.

We, therefore, the Representatives of the united States of America, in General Congress, Assembled, appealing to the Supreme Judge of the world for the rectitude of our intentions, do, in the Name, and by Authority of the good People of these Colonies, solemnly publish and declare, That these United Colonies are, and of Right ought to be Free and Independent States; that they are Absolved from all Allegiance to the British Crown, and that all political connection between them and the State of Great Britain, is and ought to be totally dissolved; and that as Free and Independent States, they have full Power to levy War, conclude Peace, contract Alliances, establish Commerce, and to do all other Acts and Things which Independent States may of right do. And for the support of this Declaration, with a firm reliance on the protection of divine Providence, we mutually pledge to each other our Lives, our Fortunes and our sacred Honor.

QUESTIONING THE TEXT

1. With a classmate, write a summary of the argument presented in the Declaration of Independence. Include in your summary a list of the main grievances, stated in language that is easily understandable to your classmates. What is the main claim used to justify the representatives' declaration of independence from Great Britain?

2. Who was the intended audience of the Declaration? Can you tell from the text itself? What rhetorical clues do you find that support your answer?

MAKING CONNECTIONS

3. In his essay "In the Ruins" (p. 586), Nicholas Lemann writes that the inability of any person to emerge as a reliable leader after Katrina "demonstrates an unimaginable failure at all levels" of government (paragraph 7).

How does Lemann's desire for a particular kind of leadership in a time of crisis echo some of the claims of the Declaration of Independence? How does his view of the government's responsibilities reflect a different understanding of the role of leadership? Use specific textual evidence from the Declaration of Independence to support your ideas.

4. In "What to the Slave Is the Fourth of July?" (p. 497), Frederick Douglass challenges some of the myths of the American founding, questioning how well they apply to the situation of the slave. How might Margaret Atwood, author of "A Letter to America" (p. 510), react to the claims put forth in the Declaration of Independence? What about Barbara Kingsolver, author of "And Our Flag Was Still There" (p. 548) or Stephanie Coontz, author of "The Way We Wish We Were" (p. 568)? Do you think that these authors would challenge the ideals set out in the Declaration of Independence? Would they challenge how well we live up to these ideals?

JOINING THE CONVERSATION

5. Write an essay on "What the Declaration of Independence Really Says," for submission as an op-ed to your campus or local newspaper. Read through some of the other selections in this chapter for inspiration: you might take a critical or straightforward approach, and you might try a sarcastic, humorous, or solemn tone.

6. The Declaration of Independence has served as a model for many groups seeking justice over the years. One example is the 1848 "Declaration of Sentiments and Resolutions of the Seneca Falls Convention," written by Elizabeth Cady Stanton, which argues for women's rights. Do some research to investigate how later declarations used the original to make new arguments. Analyze the ways in which the later documents drew on the 1776 declaration to appeal to traditional American values for support of controversial positions. You might also consider whether and how the later documents may be read as revisions of the Declaration of Independence. Write an argument of eight to ten pages based on your research and analysis.

FREDERICK DOUGLASS
What to the Slave Is the Fourth of July?

As a kid, I looked forward to the Fourth of July: for me, it was all about fireworks and watermelon right from my Granny's spring house, and maybe a trip to Cade's Cove where we swam in the cool, clear waters. I was as unreflective about the meanings of this national day of celebration as anyone could possibly be. Consequently, just as I remember where I was when I learned that John F. Kennedy, Martin Luther King Jr., and Bobby Kennedy were assassinated, so too do I remember where I was and what I was doing when I first read Frederick Douglass. Since that first reading, I have turned to Douglass again and again, studying his messages and especially the way that he crafts them. And I have never thought of the Fourth of July in the same way: for me, the national holiday is a time for quiet reflection on where we as a country have been — and on where we must go.

Douglass (1817–95), born a slave in Maryland, escaped in 1838 and devoted himself to the abolitionist movement. Eventually, Douglass was forced to flee to England to escape being reenslaved; he returned in 1847 after paying his "owners" for his freedom. The publication of The Narrative of the Life of Frederick Douglass: An American Slave *(1845) brought Douglass international acclaim, and he went on to write many speeches and treatises, including* My Bondage and My Freedom *(1855) and* Life of Frederick Douglass *(1881). In addition, Douglass wrote for and published the important abolitionist newspaper* The North Star *as well as* Douglass' Monthly *and* New National Era. *During the Civil War, Douglass was a consultant to President Abraham Lincoln; he later served as U.S. ambassador to Haiti.*

In his writing — and in the speeches for which he was renowned — Douglass reveals his prodigious powers of persuasion, his thorough understanding of rhetorical principles and strategies, and his grasp of audience psychology. All these attributes are apparent in "What to the Slave Is the Fourth of July?" delivered at the invitation of the Rochester Ladies' Anti-Slavery Society in Rochester, New York on July 5, 1852. The excerpt that follows comprises roughly the first half of Douglass's speech and its closing. Reading this speech more than 150 years after its delivery will undoubtedly prompt you to ask, "What to me is the Fourth of July — and why?" —A.L.

Mr. President, Friends and Fellow Citizens: He who could address this audience without a quailing sensation, has stronger nerves than I have. I do not remember ever to have appeared as a speaker before any assembly more shrinkingly, nor with greater distrust of my ability, than I do this day. A feeling has crept over me, quite unfavorable to the exercise of my limited powers of speech. The task before me is one which requires much previous thought and study for its proper performance. I know that apologies of this sort are generally considered

497

flat and unmeaning. I trust, however, that mine will not be so considered. Should I seem at ease, my appearance would much misrepresent me. The little experience I have had in addressing public meetings, in country school houses, avails me nothing on the present occasion.

The papers and placards say, that I am to deliver a 4th [of] July oration. This certainly sounds large, and out of the common way, for it is true that I have often had the privilege to speak in this beautiful Hall, and to address many who now honor me with their presence. But neither their familiar faces, nor the perfect gage I think I have of Corinthian Hall, seems to free me from embarrassment.

The fact is, ladies and gentlemen, the distance between this platform and the slave plantation, from which I escaped, is considerable — and the difficulties to be overcome in getting from the latter to the former, are by no means slight. That I am here to-day is, to me, a matter of astonishment as well as of gratitude. You will not, therefore, be surprised, if in what I have to say, I evince no elaborate preparation, nor grace my speech with any high sounding exordium. With little experience and with less learning, I have been able to throw my thoughts hastily and imperfectly together; and trusting to your patient and generous indulgence, I will proceed to lay them before you.

This, for the purpose of this celebration, is the 4th of July. It is the birthday of your National Independence, and of your political freedom. This, to you, is what the Passover was to the emancipated people of God. It carries your minds back to the day, and to the act of your great deliverance; and to the signs, and to the wonders, associated with that act, and that day. This celebration also marks the beginning of another year of your national life; and reminds you that the Republic of America is now 76 years old. I am glad, fellow-citizens, that your nation is so young. Seventy-six years, though a good old age for a man, is but a mere speck in the life of a nation. Three score years and ten is the allotted time for individual men; but nations number their years by thousands. According to this fact, you are, even now, only in the beginning of your national career, still lingering in the period of childhood. I repeat, I am glad this is so. There is hope in the thought, and hope is much needed, under the dark clouds which lower above the horizon. The eye of the reformer is met with angry flashes, portending disastrous times; but his heart may well beat lighter at the thought that America is young, and that she is still in the impressible stage of her existence. May he not hope that high lessons of wisdom, of justice and of truth, will yet give direction to her destiny? Were the nation older, the patriot's heart might be sadder, and the reformer's brow heavier. Its future might be shrouded in gloom, and the hope of its prophets go out in sorrow. There is consolation in the thought that America is young. Great streams are not easily turned from channels, worn deep in the course of ages. They may sometimes rise in quiet and stately majesty, and inundate the land, refreshing and fertilizing the earth with their mysterious properties. They may also rise in wrath and fury, and bear away, on their angry waves, the accumulated wealth of years of toil and hardship. They, however, gradually flow back to the same old channel, and flow on as serenely as ever. But, while the river may not be turned aside, it may dry up, and leave nothing behind but the withered branch, and the unsightly rock, to howl in the abyss-sweeping wind, the sad tale of departed glory. As with rivers so with nations.

Fellow-citizens, I shall not presume to dwell at length on the associations that cluster about this day. The simple story of it is that, 76 years ago, the people of this country were British subjects. The style and title of your "sovereign people" (in which you now glory) was not then born. You were under the British Crown. Your fathers esteemed the English Government as the home government; and England as the fatherland. This home government, you know, although a considerable distance from your home, did, in the exercise of its parental prerogatives, impose upon its colonial children, such restraints, burdens and limitations, as, in its mature judgement, it deemed wise, right and proper.

But, your fathers, who had not adopted the fashionable idea of this day, of the infallibility of government, and the absolute character of its acts, presumed to differ from the home government in respect to the wisdom and the justice of some of those burdens and restraints. They went so far in their excitement as to pronounce the measures of government unjust, unreasonable, and oppressive, and altogether such as ought not to be quietly submitted to. I scarcely need say, fellow-citizens, that my opinion of those measures fully accords with that of your fathers. Such a declaration of agreement on my part would not be worth much to anybody. It would, certainly, prove nothing, as to what part I might have taken, had I lived during the great controversy of 1776. To say now that America was right, and England wrong, is exceedingly easy. Everybody can say it; the dastard, not less than the noble brave, can flippantly discant on the tyranny of England towards the American Colonies. It is fashionable to do so; but there was a time when to pronounce against England, and in favor of the cause of the colonies, tried men's souls. They who did so were accounted in their day, plotters of mischief, agitators and rebels, dangerous men. To side with the right, against the wrong, with the weak against the strong, and with the oppressed against the oppressor! here lies the merit, and the one which, of all others, seems unfashionable in our day. The cause of liberty may be stabbed by the men who glory in the deeds of your fathers. But, to proceed.

Feeling themselves harshly and unjustly treated by the home government, your fathers, like men of honesty, and men of spirit, earnestly sought redress. They petitioned and remonstrated; they did so in a decorous, respectful, and loyal manner. Their conduct was wholly unexceptionable. This, however, did not answer the purpose. They saw themselves treated with sovereign indifference, coldness and scorn. Yet they persevered. They were not the men to look back.

As the sheet anchor takes a firmer hold, when the ship is tossed by the storm, so did the cause of your fathers grow stronger, as it breasted the chilling blasts of kingly displeasure. The greatest and best of British statesmen admitted its justice, and the loftiest eloquence of the British Senate came to its support. But, with that blindness which seems to be the unvarying characteristic of tyrants, since Pharaoh and his hosts were drowned in the Red Sea, the British Government persisted in the exactions complained of.

The madness of this course, we believe, is admitted now, even by England; but we fear the lesson is wholly lost on our present rulers.

Oppression makes a wise man mad. Your fathers were wise men, and if   10
they did not go mad, they became restive under this treatment. They felt themselves the victims of grievous wrongs, wholly incurable in their colonial capacity. With brave men there is always a remedy for oppression. Just here, the idea of a total separation of the colonies from the crown was born! It was a startling idea, much more so, than we, at this distance of time, regard it. The timid and the prudent (as has been intimated) of that day, were, of course, shocked and alarmed by it.

Such people lived then, had lived before, and will, probably, ever have a place on this planet; and their course, in respect to any great change (no matter how great the good to be attained, or the wrong to be redressed by it), may be calculated with as much precision as can be the course of the stars. They hate all changes, but silver, gold and copper change! Of this sort of change they are always strongly in favor.

These people were called tories in the days of your fathers; and the appellation, probably, conveyed the same idea that is meant by a more modern, though a somewhat less euphonious term, which we often find in our papers, applied to some of our old politicians.

Their opposition to the then dangerous thought was earnest and powerful; but, amid all their terror and affrighted vociferations against it, the alarming and revolutionary idea moved on, and the country with it.

On the 2d of July, 1776, the old Continental Congress, to the dismay of the lovers of ease, and the worshipers of property, clothed that dreadful idea with all the authority of national sanction. They did so in the form of a resolution; and as we seldom hit upon resolutions, drawn up in our day, whose transparency is at all equal to this, it may refresh your minds and help my story if I read it.

"Resolved, That these united colonies are, and of right, ought to be free   15
and Independent States; that they are absolved from all allegiance to the British Crown; and that all political connection between them and the State of Great Britain is, and ought to be, dissolved."

Citizens, your fathers made good that resolution. They succeeded; and to-day you reap the fruits of their success. The freedom gained is yours; and you, therefore, may properly celebrate this anniversary. The 4th of July is the first great fact in your nation's history — the very ring-bolt in the chain of your yet undeveloped destiny.

Pride and patriotism, not less than gratitude, prompt you to celebrate and to hold it in perpetual remembrance. I have said that the Declaration of Independence is the ring-bolt to the chain of your nation's destiny; so, indeed, I regard it. The principles contained in that instrument are saving principles. Stand by those principles, be true to them on all occasions, in all places, against all foes, and at whatever cost.

From the round top of your ship of state, dark and threatening clouds may be seen. Heavy billows, like mountains in the distance, disclose to the leeward huge forms of flinty rocks! That bolt drawn, that chain broken, and all is lost. Cling to this day — cling to it, and to its principles, with the grasp of a storm-tossed mariner to a spar at midnight.

The coming into being of a nation, in any circumstances, is an interesting event. But, besides general considerations, there were peculiar circumstances which make the advent of this republic an event of special attractiveness.

The whole scene, as I look back to it, was simple, dignified and sublime.   20

The population of the country, at the time, stood at the insignificant number of three millions. The country was poor in the munitions of war. The population was weak and scattered, and the country a wilderness unsubdued. There were then no means of concert and combination, such as exist now. Neither steam nor lightning had then been reduced to order and discipline. From the Potomac to the Delaware was a journey of many days. Under these, and innumerable other disadvantages, your fathers declared for liberty and independence and triumphed.

Fellow Citizens, I am not wanting in respect for the fathers of this republic. The signers of the Declaration of Independence were brave men. They were great men too — great enough to give fame to a great age. It does not often happen to a nation to raise, at one time, such a number of truly great men. The point from which I am compelled to view them is not, certainly, the most favorable; and yet I cannot contemplate their great deeds with less than admiration. They were statesmen, patriots and heroes, and for the good they did, and the principles they contended for, I will unite with you to honor their memory.

They loved their country better than their own private interests; and, though this is not the highest form of human excellence, all will concede that it is a rare virtue, and that when it is exhibited, it ought to command respect. He who will, intelligently, lay down his life for his country, is a man whom it is not in human nature to despise. Your fathers staked their lives, their fortunes, and their sacred honor, on the cause of their country. In their admiration of liberty, they lost sight of all other interests.

They were peace men; but they preferred revolution to peaceful submission to bondage. They were quiet men; but they did not shrink from agitating against oppression. They showed forbearance; but that they knew its limits. They believed in order; but not in the order of tyranny. With them, nothing was "settled" that was not right. With them, justice, liberty and humanity were "final"; not slavery and oppression. You may well cherish the memory of such men. They were great in their day and generation. Their solid manhood stands out the more as we contrast it with these degenerate times.

How circumspect, exact and proportionate were all their movements!   25 How unlike the politicians of an hour! Their statesmanship looked beyond the passing moment, and stretched away in strength into the distant future. They seized upon eternal principles, and set a glorious example in their defence. Mark them!

Fully appreciating the hardship to be encountered, firmly believing in the right of their cause, honorably inviting the scrutiny of an on-looking world, reverently appealing to heaven to attest their sincerity, soundly comprehending the solemn responsibility they were about to assume, wisely measuring the terrible odds against them, your fathers, the fathers of this republic, did, most deliberately, under the inspiration of a glorious patriotism, and with a sublime faith in the great principles of justice and freedom, lay deep the corner-stone of the national superstructure, which has risen and still rises in grandeur around you.

Of this fundamental work, this day is the anniversary. Our eyes are met with demonstrations of joyous enthusiasm. Banners and pennants wave exultingly on the breeze. The din of business, too, is hushed. Even Mammon seems to have quitted his grasp on this day. The ear-piercing fife and the stirring drum unite their accents with the ascending peal of a thousand church bells. Prayers are made, hymns are sung, and sermons are preached in honor of this day; while the quick martial tramp of a great and multitudinous nation, echoed back by all the hills, valleys and mountains of a vast continent, bespeak the occasion one of thrilling and universal interests nation's jubilee.

Friends and citizens, I need not enter further into the causes which led to this anniversary. Many of you understand them better than I do. You could instruct me in regard to them. That is a branch of knowledge in which you feel, perhaps, a much deeper interest than your speaker. The causes which led to the separation of the colonies from the British crown have never lacked for a tongue. They have all been taught in your common schools, narrated at your firesides, unfolded from your pulpits, and thundered from your legislative halls, and are as familiar to you as household words. They form the staple of your national poetry and eloquence.

I remember, also, that, as a people, Americans are remarkably familiar with all facts which make in their own favor. This is esteemed by some as a national trait — perhaps a national weakness. It is a fact, that whatever makes for the wealth or for the reputation of Americans, and can be had cheap! will be found by Americans. I shall not be charged with slandering Americans, if I say I think the American side of any question may be safely left in American hands.

I leave, therefore, the great deeds of your fathers to other gentlemen   30 whose claim to have been regularly descended will be less likely to be disputed than mine!

THE PRESENT

My business, if I have any here to-day, is with the present. The accepted time with God and his cause is the ever-living now.

> "Trust no future, however pleasant,
>   Let the dead past bury its dead;
> Act, act in the living present,
>   Heart within, and God overhead."

We have to do with the past only as we can make it useful to the present and to the future. To all inspiring motives, to noble deeds which can be gained from the past, we are welcome. But now is the time, the important time. Your fathers have lived, died, and have done their work, and have done much of it well. You live and must die, and you must do your work. You have no right to enjoy a child's share in the labor of your fathers, unless your children are to be blest by your labors. You have no right to wear out and waste the hard-earned fame of your fathers to cover your indolence. Sydney Smith* tells us that men seldom eulogize the wisdom and virtues of their fathers, but to excuse some folly or wickedness of their own. This truth is not a doubtful one. There are illustrations of it near and remote, ancient and modern. It was fashionable, hundreds of years ago, for the children of Jacob to boast, we have "Abraham to our father," when they had long lost Abraham's faith and spirit. That people contented themselves under the shadow of Abraham's great name, while they repudiated the deeds which made his name great. Need I remind you that a similar thing is being done all over this country to-day? Need I tell you that the Jews are not the only people who built the tombs of the prophets, and garnished the sepulchres of the righteous? Washington could not die till he had broken the chains of his slaves. Yet his monument is built up by the price of human blood, and the traders in the bodies and souls of men, shout — "We have Washington to our father." Alas! that it should be so; yet so it is.

> "The evil that men do, lives after them,
> The good is oft' interred with their bones."

Fellow-citizens, pardon me, allow me to ask, why am I called upon to   35
speak here to-day? What have I, or those I represent, to do with your national independence? Are the great principles of political freedom and of natural justice, embodied in that Declaration of Independence, extended to us? and am I, therefore, called upon to bring our humble offering to the national altar, and to confess the benefits and express devout gratitude for the blessings resulting from your independence to us?

Sydney Smith (1771–1845): English preacher and moral philosopher

Would to God, both for your sakes and ours, that an affirmative answer could be truthfully returned to these questions! Then would my task be light, and my burden easy and delightful. For who is there so cold, that a nation's sympathy could not warm him? Who so obdurate and dead to the claims of gratitude, that would not thankfully acknowledge such priceless benefits? Who so stolid and selfish, that would not give his voice to swell the hallelujahs of a nation's jubilee, when the chains of servitude had been torn from his limbs? I am not that man. In a case like that, the dumb might eloquently speak, and the "lame man leap as an hart."

But, such is not the state of the case. I say it with a sad sense of the disparity between us. I am not included within the pale of this glorious anniversary! Your high independence only reveals the immeasurable distance between us. The blessings in which you, this day, rejoice, are not enjoyed in common. The rich inheritance of justice, liberty, prosperity and independence, bequeathed by your fathers, is shared by you, not by me. The sunlight that brought life and healing to you, has brought stripes and death to me. This Fourth [of] July is yours, not mine. You may rejoice, I must mourn. To drag a man in fetters into the grand illuminated temple of liberty, and call upon him to join you in joyous anthems, were inhuman mockery and sacrilegious irony. Do you mean, citizens, to mock me, by asking me to speak to-day? If so, there is a parallel to your conduct. And let me warn you that it is dangerous to copy the example of a nation whose crimes, lowering up to heaven, were thrown down by the breath of the Almighty, burying that nation in irrecoverable ruin! I can to-day take up the plaintive lament of a peeled and woe-smitten people!

"By the rivers of Babylon, there we sat down. Yea! we wept when we remembered Zion. We hanged our harps upon the willows in the midst thereof. For there, they that carried us away captive, required of us a song; and they who wasted us required of us mirth, saying, Sing us one of the songs of Zion. How can we sing the Lord's song in a strange land? If I forget thee, O Jerusalem, let my right hand forget her cunning. If I do not remember thee, let my tongue cleave to the roof of my mouth."

Fellow-citizens; above your national, tumultuous joy, I hear the mournful wail of millions! whose chains, heavy and grievous yesterday, are, to-day, rendered more intolerable by the jubilee shouts that reach them. If I do forget, if I do not faithfully remember those bleeding children of sorrow this day, "may my right hand forget her cunning, and may my tongue cleave to the roof of my mouth!" To forget them, to pass lightly over their wrongs, and to chime in with the popular theme, would be treason most scandalous and shocking, and would make me a reproach before God and the world. My subject, then fellow-citizens, is AMERICAN SLAVERY. I shall see, this day, and its popular characteristics, from the slave's point of view. Standing, there, identified with the American bondman, making his wrongs mine, I do not hesitate to declare, with all my soul, that the character and conduct of this nation never looked blacker to me than on this 4th of July! Whether we turn to the declarations of the past, or to the professions of the present, the conduct of the nation seems equally hideous and revolting. America is false to the past, false to the present, and solemnly binds herself to be false to the future. Standing with God and the crushed and bleeding slave on this occasion, I will, in the name of humanity which is outraged, in the name of liberty which is fettered, in the name of the constitution and the Bible, which are disregarded and trampled upon, dare to call in question and to denounce, with all the emphasis I can command, everything that serves to perpetuate slavery — the great sin and shame of America! "I will not equivocate; I will not excuse;" I will use the severest language I can command; and yet not one word shall escape me that any man, whose judgement is not blinded by prejudice, or who is not at heart a slaveholder, shall not confess to be right and just.

But I fancy I hear some one of my audience say, it is just in this circum-   40
stance that you and your brother abolitionists fail to make a favorable impression on the public mind. Would you argue more, and denounce less, would you persuade more, and rebuke less, your cause would be much more likely to succeed. But, I submit, where all is plain there is nothing to be argued. What point in the anti-slavery creed would you have me argue? On what branch of the subject do the people of this country need light? Must I undertake to prove that the slave is a man? That point is conceded already. Nobody doubts it. The slaveholders themselves acknowledge it in the enactment of laws for their government. They acknowledge it when they punish disobedience on the part of the slave. There are seventy-two crimes in the State of Virginia, which, if committed by a black man (no matter how ignorant he be), subject him to the punishment of death; while only two of the same crimes will subject a white man to the like punishment. What is this but the acknowledgement that the slave is a moral, intellectual and responsible being? The manhood of the slave is conceded. It is admitted in the fact that Southern statute books are covered with enactments forbidding, under severe fines and penalties, the teaching of the slave to read or to write. When you can point to any such laws, in reference to the beasts of the field, then I may consent to argue the manhood of the slave. When the dogs in your streets, when the fowls of the air, when the cattle on your hills, when the fish of the sea, and the reptiles that crawl, shall be unable to distinguish the slave from a brute, there will I argue with you that the slave is a man!

For the present, it is enough to affirm the equal manhood of the negro race. Is it not astonishing that, while we are ploughing, planting and reaping, using all kinds of mechanical tools, erecting houses, constructing bridges, building ships, working in metals of brass, iron, copper, silver and gold; that, while we are reading, writing and cyphering, acting as clerks, merchants and secretaries, having among us lawyers, doctors, ministers, poets, authors, editors, orators and teachers; that, while we are engaged in all manner of enterprises common to other men, digging gold in California, capturing the whale in the Pacific, feeding sheep and cattle on the hill-side, living, moving, acting, thinking, planning, living in families as husbands, wives and children, and, above all, confessing and worshipping the Christian's God, and looking hopefully for life and immortality beyond the grave, we are called upon to prove that we are men!

Would you have me argue that man is entitled to liberty? that he is the rightful owner of his own body? You have already declared it. Must I argue the wrongfulness of slavery? Is that a question for Republicans? Is it to be settled by the rules of logic and argumentation, as a matter beset with great difficulty, involving a doubtful application of the principle of justice, hard to be understood? How should I look to-day, in the presence of Americans, dividing, and subdividing a discourse, to show that men have a natural right to freedom? speaking of it relatively, and positively, negatively, and affirmatively. To do so, would be to make myself ridiculous, and so offer an insult to your understanding. There is not a man beneath the canopy of heaven, that does not know that slavery is wrong for him.

What, am I to argue that it is wrong to make men brutes, to rob them of their liberty, to work them without wages, to keep them ignorant of their relations to their fellow men, to beat them with sticks, to flay their flesh with the lash, to load their limbs with irons, to hunt them with dogs, to sell them at auction, to sunder their families, to knock out their teeth, to burn their flesh, to starve them into obedience and submission to their masters? Must I argue that a system thus marked with blood, and stained with pollution, is wrong? No! I will not. I have better employments for my time and strength, than such arguments would imply.

What, then, remains to be argued? Is it that slavery is not divine; that God did not establish it; that our doctors of divinity are mistaken? There is blasphemy in the thought. That which is inhuman, cannot be divine! Who can reason on such a proposition? They that can, may; I cannot. The time for such argument is past.

At a time like this, scorching irony, not convincing argument, is needed.   45
O! had I the ability, and could I reach the nation's ear, I would, to-day, pour out a fiery stream of biting ridicule, blasting reproach, withering sarcasm, and stern rebuke. For it is not light that is needed, but fire; it is not the gentle shower, but thunder. We need the storm, the whirlwind, and the earthquake. The feeling of the nation must be quickened; the conscience of the nation must be roused; the propriety of the nation must be startled; the hypocrisy of the nation must be exposed; and its crimes against God and man must be proclaimed and denounced.

What, to the American slave, is your 4th of July? I answer: a day that reveals to him, more than all other days in the year, the gross injustice and cruelty to which he is the constant victim. To him, your celebration is a sham; your boasted liberty, an unholy license; your national greatness, swelling vanity; your sounds of rejoicing are empty and heartless; your denunciations of tyrants, brass fronted impudence; your shouts of liberty and equality, hollow mockery; your prayers and hymns, your sermons and thanksgivings, with all your religious parade, and solemnity, are, to him, mere bombast, fraud, deception, impiety, and hypocrisy — a thin veil to cover up crimes which would disgrace a nation of savages. There is not a nation on the earth guilty of practices, more shocking and bloody, than are the people of these United States, at this very hour.

Go where you may, search where you will, roam through all the monarchies and despotisms of the old world, travel through South America, search out every abuse, and when you have found the last, lay your facts by the side of the everyday practices of this nation, and you will say with me, that, for revolting barbarity and shameless hypocrisy, America reigns without a rival. . . .

Allow me to say, in conclusion, notwithstanding the dark picture I have   74
this day presented of the state of the nation, I do not despair of this country. There are forces in operation, which must inevitably work the downfall of slavery. "The arm of the Lord is not shortened," and the doom of slavery is certain. I, therefore, leave off where I began, with hope. While drawing encouragement from the Declaration of Independence, the great principles it contains, and the genius of American Institutions, my spirit is also cheered by the obvious tendencies of the age. Nations do not now stand in the same relation to each other that they did ages ago. No nation can now shut itself up from the surrounding world, and trot round in the same old path of its fathers without interference. The time was when such could be done. Long established customs of hurtful character could formerly fence themselves in, and do their evil work with social impunity. Knowledge was then confined and enjoyed by the privileged few, and the multitude walked on in mental darkness. But a change has now come over the affairs of mankind. Walled cities and empires have become unfashionable. The arm of commerce has borne away the gates of the strong city. Intelligence is penetrating the darkest corners of the globe. It makes its pathway over and under the sea, as well as on the earth. Wind, steam, and lightning are its chartered agents. Oceans no longer divide, but link nations together. From Boston to London is now a holiday excursion. Space is comparatively annihilated. Thoughts expressed on one side of the Atlantic are distinctly heard on the other. The far off and almost fabulous Pacific rolls in grandeur at our feet. The Celestial Empire, the mystery of ages, is being solved. The fiat of the Almighty, "Let there be Light," has not yet spent its force. No abuse, no outrage whether in taste, sport or avarice, can now hide itself from the all-pervading light. The iron shoe, and crippled foot of China must be seen, in contrast with nature. Africa must rise and put on her yet unwoven garment. "Ethiopia shall stretch out her hand unto God." In the fervent aspirations of William Lloyd Garrison, I say, and let every heart join in saying it:

> God speed the year of jubilee   75
>   The wide world o'er!
> When from their galling chains set free,
>   Th' oppress'd shall vilely bend the knee,
> And wear the yoke of tyranny
>   Like brutes no more.

That year will come, and freedom's reign,
To man his plundered rights again
 Restore.

God speed the day when human blood
 Shall cease to flow!
In every clime be understood,
The claims of human brotherhood,
And each return for evil, good,
 Not blow for blow;
That day will come all feuds to end
And change into a faithful friend
 Each foe.

God speed the hour, the glorious hour,
 When none on earth
Shall exercise a lordly power,
Nor in a tyrant's presence cower;
But all to manhood's stature tower,
 By equal birth!
THAT HOUR WILL, COME, to each, to all,
And from his prison-house, the thrall
 Go forth.

Until that year, day, hour, arrive,
With head, and heart, and hand I'll strive,
To break the rod, and rend the gyve,
The spoiler of his prey deprive —
 So witness Heaven!
And never from my chosen post,
Whate'er the peril or the cost,
 Be driven.

QUESTIONING THE TEXT

1. In her headnote, A.L. writes that Douglass presented this speech to the Rochester Ladies' Anti-Slavery Society in Rochester, New York. Even without knowing about this group, can you tell from Douglass's speech whether the audience he addressed was primarily white or black? Does he seem to address only the members of the group that invited him to speak, or a broader audience? How can you tell?

2. Working with a classmate, identify passages in which Douglass appeals to values he assumes the audience shares with him. How does he make these appeals? What metaphors and images does he use? How does he draw upon values associated with the American fight for independence to argue for the abolition of slavery?

3. In class discussion, consider Douglass's effectiveness at addressing potential counterarguments. On what points does Douglass seem to anticipate
   objections from the audience? List as many of these objections as you can
   find. How does Douglass address them?

MAKING CONNECTIONS

4. Working with one or two classmates, study the ways in which Douglass
   draws upon principles stated in the Declaration of Independence (p. 492)
   to make his argument. To which parts of the Declaration does he allude?
   What purposes do these allusions serve in Douglass's argument?

5. Douglass claims that "[his] spirit is . . . cheered by the obvious tendencies
   of the age" (paragraph 74), and he proceeds to describe a world that
   is continually shrinking. Consider his comments in relation to Philippe
   Legrain's arguments about globalization (p. 514). Do you think that
   Douglass would share Legrain's views of the current trends in cultural
   globalization? Why, or why not?

JOINING THE CONVERSATION

6. In her headnote, A.L. suggests asking yourself, "What to me is the Fourth
   of July — and why?" Write a speech or essay answering that question, or
   answer the same question about another national holiday. Think about
   how — or whether — you identify with the ideals represented by the
   holiday you choose to write on, and use vivid examples to convey your
   reasons.

7. Do some research into the occasion for Douglass's speech: find out about
   the origins and membership of the group he addressed, how his speech
   was received, what experience Douglass had as an orator before and after
   this occasion. Use your research in a speech or essay commemorating
   Douglass's address, for presentation at a campus event or publication in a
   campus or local newspaper. Choose an appropriate occasion to present
   your work: the Fourth of July, perhaps, a day during Black History
   Month, or even Labor Day, Martin Luther King's Birthday, or Memorial
   Day. Be sure to craft your opening to establish the relevance of your com-
   memoration to the day on which you choose to present it.

MARGARET ATWOOD
A Letter to America

As Americans, we surely have our myths of national identity — as the readings in this chapter demonstrate. But America — more specifically the United States — carries mythic status in many other places of the world as well. I first learned that lesson during the ten years I lived and taught in Vancouver, Canada, and I have been very grateful for the opportunity I had to see my home country through the eyes of others, whose vision was often clearer than mine. I learned this lesson again in the years that have elapsed since the September 11, 2001, terrorist bombings. Traveling in Europe and in Canada not long after those attacks, I read and heard what others sensed were America's strongest ideals: courage, endurance, hope. Still, in the aftermath of unsigned international treaties, a questionable war waged in Iraq, and other threatening actions, travel outside the United States is not always fun anymore: mythic images of America are overwhelmingly negative.

In "A Letter to America" (first published on March 28, 2003, in the Globe and Mail*), Canadian novelist Margaret Atwood (b. 1939) catalogues the myths that were America to her, from the heroes of American literature to mythic outsiders like Marlon Brando in* On the Waterfront *to the "city on the hill, a light to all nations." Today, Atwood says, she is no longer sure what America stands for. The symbol of plenty, embodied by the Jolly Green Giant in Atwood's letter, can turn into a symbol of greed and destruction. The mythic ideal of generosity — a hand held out to all in need — can too easily turn into a King Midas complex. Atwood challenges Americans to read her letter and to reflect — and then to summon the great national "spirits of the past" to bring out the best, rather than the worst, in the national psyche.*

Atwood, a fellow of the Royal Society of Canada who has served as president of the Writers' Union of Canada, is the author of dozens of books, among them The Blind Assassin, *awarded the Booker Prize in 2000, and* Alias Grace, *which won the Giller Prize in 1996. Her latest novel is* Oryx and Crake (2003), *a postapocalyptic tale set in a dry moonscape in the indeterminate future — which could, Atwood seems to be warning, be tomorrow.*

                      —A.L.

Dear America: This is a difficult letter to write, because I'm no longer sure who you are.

Some of you may be having the same trouble. I thought I knew you: We'd become well acquainted over the past 55 years. You were the Mickey Mouse and Donald Duck comic books I read in the late 1940s. You were the radio shows — *Jack Benny, Our Miss Brooks.* You were the music I sang and danced to: the Andrews Sisters, Ella Fitzgerald, the Platters, Elvis. You were a ton of fun.

510

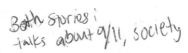

Dulce Pinzón: The Real Story of the Superheroes

Meditating on the meaning of heroism after the September 11, 2001 attacks, photographer Dulce Pinzón (b. 1974) began to think about those very visible heroes — the firefighters and police officers and bystanders who risked their lives by helping others. And then she began to think of those who are often invisible, whose heroism goes unseen and unrecognized. From this idea grew Pinzón's series of photographs of Mexican immigrants, each dressed as a popular superhero. Seeing these ordinary men and women in their workplaces wearing superhero garb shakes viewers' assumptions about who is and who is not a hero, as well as about the dependence of the American economy — and the heroes' families back home — on immigrant labor. —A.L.

The Mexican immigrant worker in New York is a perfect example of the hero who has gone unnoticed. It is common for a Mexican worker in New York to work extraordinary hours in extreme conditions for very low wages which are saved at great cost and sacrifice and sent to families and communities in Mexico who rely on them to survive.

The Mexican economy has quietly become dependent on the money sent from workers in the U.S. Conversely, the U.S. economy has quietly become dependent on the labor of Mexican immigrants. Along with the depth of their sacrifice, it is the quietness of this dependence which makes Mexican immigrant workers a subject of interest. The principal objective of this series is to pay homage to these brave and determined men and women who somehow manage, without the help of any supernatural power, to withstand extreme conditions of labor in order to help their families and communities survive and prosper.

Juventino Rosas (Aquaman), from the state of México, works in a fish market in New York. He sends $400 a week.

Minerva Valencia (Catwoman), from the state of Puebla, works as a nanny in New York. She sends $400 a week.

1. Consider the images throughout this insert in light of recent debates on immigration. What argument do they make about immigrants in America?

Adalberto Lara (El Chapulín Colorado, or the Red Grasshopper), from the state of México, works as a construction worker in New York. He sends $350 a week.

2. Research the history of the character El Chapulín Colorado, who has enjoyed enduring popularity on Spanish-language television since 1970. In what ways does this photograph draw on the history of the character?

Sergio García (Mr. Fantastic), from the state of México, works as a waiter in New York. He sends $350 a week.

3. How does the presence of other people in this photograph affect your reaction to it? How do the others' expressions and positions help create the overall effect of the picture?

Paulino Cardozo (the Incredible Hulk), from the state of Guerrero, works in a greengrocer loading trucks. He sends $300 a week.

4. Hollywood has produced a number of superhero movies in the past two decades (including one based on the Hulk), and other genres, including comic books, continue to focus on superheroes. Choose a superhero or group of superheroes that has been popular in the last several years and, in a short essay, explain why you feel this person or group has a particular appeal in our culture. What values does the hero or group represent?

Bernabe Mendez (Spiderman), from the State of Guerrero, works as a professional window cleaner in New York. He sends $500 a month.

5. Each of the subjects of Pinzón's photographs sends money back to family in Mexico. How does this knowledge affect your reaction to the images?

Maria Luisa Romero (Wonder Woman), from the state of Puebla, works in a laundromat in Brooklyn, New York. She sends $150 a week.

6. How well does Pinzón succeed in matching the power of the superhero to the work of the subject of the picture? Working with a classmate, explain which superheroes in this series best fit their jobs and which match least well. Compare your reactions with those of the rest of the class.

Noe Reyes (Superman), from the state of Puebla, works as a delivery boy in Brooklyn, New York. He sends $500 a week.

7. Superman may be the most famous of American superheroes, and his image has changed in the decades since his character was first created. What qualities do you think that a modern Superman or Superwoman should have? Do they differ by gender? Does the current age demand qualities in a superhero that past generations have not?

JOINING THE CONVERSATION

8. Part of Pinzón's goal in this series is to call attention to people who otherwise go overlooked and underappreciated. Identify someone or some group of people who you think goes underappreciated. Create a representation — verbal, visual, musical, or multimedia — to give this person or group the recognition you think is deserved. Be prepared to explain your choices and strategies in a presentation of your work.

You wrote some of my favourite books. You created Huckleberry Finn, and Hawkeye, and Beth and Jo in *Little Women*, courageous in their different ways. Later, you were my beloved Thoreau, father of environmentalism, witness to individual conscience; and Walt Whitman, singer of the great Republic; and Emily Dickinson, keeper of the private soul. You were Hammett and Chandler, heroic walkers of mean streets; even later, you were the amazing trio, Hemingway, Fitzgerald, and Faulkner, who traced the dark labyrinths of your hidden heart. You were Sinclair Lewis and Arthur Miller, who, with their own American idealism, went after the sham in you, because they thought you could do better.

You were Marlon Brando in *On The Waterfront*, you were Humphrey Bogart in *Key Largo*, you were Lillian Gish in *Night of the Hunter*. You stood up for freedom, honesty and justice; you protected the innocent. I believed most of that. I think you did, too. It seemed true at the time.

You put God on the money, though, even then. You had a way of think- 5
ing that the things of Caesar were the same as the things of God: that gave you self-confidence. You have always wanted to be a city upon a hill, a light to all nations, and for a while you were. Give me your tired, your poor, you sang, and for a while you meant it.

We've always been close, you and us. History, that old entangler, has twisted us together since the early 17th century. Some of us used to be you; some of us want to be you; some of you used to be us. You are not only our neighbours: In many cases — mine, for instance — you are also our blood relations, our colleagues, and our personal friends. But although we've had a ringside seat, we've never understood you completely, up here north of the 49th parallel.

We're like Romanized Gauls — look like Romans, dress like Romans, but aren't Romans — peering over the wall at the real Romans. What are they doing? Why? What are they doing now? (Why is the haruspex eyeballing the sheep's liver? Why is the soothsayer wholesaling the Bewares?)

Perhaps that's been my difficulty in writing you this letter: I'm not sure I know what's really going on. Anyway, you have a huge posse of experienced entrail-sifters who do nothing but analyze your every vein and lobe. What can I tell you about yourself that you don't already know?

This might be the reason for my hesitation: embarrassment, brought on by a becoming modesty. But it is more likely to be embarrassment of another sort. When my grandmother — from a New England background — was confronted with an unsavoury topic, she would change the subject and gaze out the window. And that is my own inclination: Mind your own business.

But I'll take the plunge, because your business is no longer merely your 10
business. To paraphrase Marley's Ghost, who figured it out too late, mankind is your business. And vice versa: When the Jolly Green Giant goes on the rampage, many lesser plants and animals get trampled underfoot. As for us, you're our biggest trading partner: We know perfectly well that if you go down the plug-hole, we're going with you. We have every reason to wish you well.

I won't go into the reasons why I think your recent Iraqi adventures have been — taking the long view — an ill-advised tactical error. By the time you read this, Baghdad may or may not look like the craters of the Moon, and many more sheep entrails will have been examined. Let's talk, then, not about what you're doing to other people, but about what you're doing to yourselves.

You're gutting the Constitution. Already your home can be entered without your knowledge or permission, you can be snatched away and incarcerated without cause, your mail can be spied on, your private records searched. Why isn't this a recipe for widespread business theft, political intimidation, and fraud? I know you've been told all this is for your own safety and protection, but think about it for a minute. Anyway, when did you get so scared? You didn't used to be easily frightened.

You're running up a record level of debt. Keep spending at this rate and pretty soon you won't be able to afford any big military adventures. Either that or you'll go the way of the USSR: lots of tanks, but no air conditioning. That will make folks very cross. They'll be even crosser when they can't take a shower because your short-sighted bulldozing of environmental protections has dirtied most of the water and dried up the rest. Then things will get hot and dirty indeed.

You're torching the American economy. How soon before the answer to that will be, not to produce anything yourselves, but to grab stuff other people produce, at gunboat-diplomacy prices? Is the world going to consist of a few megarich King Midases, with the rest being serfs, both inside and outside your country? Will the biggest business sector in the United States be the prison system? Let's hope not.

If you proceed much further down the slippery slope, people around the   15 world will stop admiring the good things about you. They'll decide that your city upon the hill is a slum and your democracy is a sham, and therefore you have no business trying to impose your sullied vision on them. They'll think you've abandoned the rule of law. They'll think you've fouled your own nest.

The British used to have a myth about King Arthur. He wasn't dead, but sleeping in a cave, it was said; in the country's hour of greatest peril, he would return. You, too, have great spirits of the past you may call upon: men and women of courage, of conscience, of prescience. Summon them now, to stand with you, to inspire you, to defend the best in you. You need them.

QUESTIONING THE TEXT

1. Atwood calls upon many literary and cultural figures to conjure an image of an America she says she once knew. With a classmate, find as many of these allusions as you can, and identify or describe them: where do they come from, and what do they mean? Next, consider what functions these allusions serve in the essay. What do they seem to contribute to Atwood's

purpose? Do you agree that the allusions represent the ideals she associates with them? Could they be used in other ways?

2. This essay is written in the form of a letter. Think about how it compares to a letter to the editor, a genre described on p. 30. Discuss with your class how Atwood's choice of America as her addressee opens up possibilities and also imposes limitations on her message and her means of conveying it.

3. How would you describe Atwood's tone in this essay? Does it change in the course of her letter? Cite examples from the text to support your answers.

MAKING CONNECTIONS

4. Working with a classmate, try to revise Atwood's essay to include cultural references other than those she uses. For example, try alluding to the Declaration of Independence (p. 492) or to Frederick Douglass's "What to the Slave Is the Fourth of July?" (p. 497). Share your revisions with the whole class, and discuss how the revisions change the essay.

5. Imagine a dialogue between Atwood and David Brooks, author of "One Nation, Slightly Divisible" (p. 525). How might Brooks react to Atwood's vision of an America that has lost sight of its values? What would Atwood say about Brooks's optimism about the state of the country?

JOINING THE CONVERSATION

6. Compose a letter in which you comment on one or more of the issues Atwood raises. You might address your letter to Atwood; to the editor of the *Globe and Mail*, the Canadian newspaper that originally published her essay; or to another country. When you're finished, think about how your letter compares to other pieces you have written for class. Did you use a different style or tone to appeal to your addressee?

7. List the ways in which Atwood accuses the United States of changing — or of forsaking its traditions — and consider whether some of these changes might be evidence of American myths. Share your speculations in class discussion. In your discussion, consider what makes for a national myth and how such a myth may differ from a tradition.

PHILIPPE LEGRAIN
Cultural Globalization
Is Not Americanization

PRESIDENT RONALD REAGAN *was fond of representing his vision of America as a "shining city on a hill," borrowing the image from Governor John Winthrop of the Massachusetts Bay Colony. For many people, especially in the twentieth century when totalitarian regimes darkened the political landscape, the United States often seemed to be this mythic place. Immigrants by the millions, legal and illegal, swarmed across its borders to take refuge here and to build new lives.*

With the fall of the Soviet empire, however, the United States found itself in an entirely different role. Though U.S. international power and influence had been growing for more than a century — the government had even toyed with European-style colonialism in the Philippines, Puerto Rico, and Cuba — not until after the Second World War did the nation become a permanent and deliberate player in international politics. The cold war turned the United States into a superpower, and the subsequent implosion of international communism left America as an undisputed economic, cultural, and military colossus.

Now America's ideas, corporations, and aircraft carriers reach into all corners of the globe, threatening (in the views of some) to remake every nation in the American image. The code word for this process, welcomed in some quarters but feared in others, is globalization. The shining city on a hill seems to have imperial ambitions.

In fact, American power, both economic and military, is real. Whatever Margaret Atwood may think (see "A Letter to America," p. 510), the United States is managing its affairs much better than its European allies are managing theirs, spending proportionally less on guns now than at many times in the past. The United States is able to sustain seemingly massive deficits because of the sheer size of its economy, an engine still supporting much of the world economy, even in tough times.

Yet, as Philippe Legrain demonstrates in "Cultural Globalization Is Not Americanization," the world is a bigger and more interesting place than any one nation, and much of the world's fear — or, in some quarters, envy — of American hegemony is misplaced. What has conquered the world, he argues, is not Mickey Mouse or Coca-Cola, but an attitude toward life that welcomes individual liberty, change, and diversity. As we learned on September 11, 2001, even such classic liberalism still has its enemies.

Philippe Legrain has been an advisor to the World Trade Organization, a group often associated with globalization. He is also the author of Immigrants: Your Country Needs Them *(2007). The essay reprinted here first appeared in the* Chronicle of Higher Education *(May 9, 2003).* —J.R.

"Listen man, I smoke, I snort . . . I've been begging on the street since I was just a baby. I've cleaned windshields at stoplights. I've polished shoes, I've robbed, I've killed. . . . I ain't no kid, no way. I'm a real man."

Such searing dialogue has helped make *City of God* a global hit. A chronicle of three decades of gang wars, it has proved compelling viewing for audiences worldwide. Critics compare it to Martin Scorsese's *Goodfellas*.

If you believe the cultural pessimists, Hollywood pap has driven out films like *Cidade de Deus*, as it is known in its home country. It is a Brazilian film, in Portuguese, by a little-known director, with a cast that includes no professional actors, let alone Hollywood stars. Its focus is not a person at all, but a drug-ridden, dirt-poor favela (slum) on the outskirts of Rio de Janeiro that feels as remote from the playground of the rich and famous as it does from God.

Yet *City of God* has not only made millions at the box office, it has also sparked a national debate in Brazil. It has raised awareness in the United States, Britain, and elsewhere of the terrible poverty and violence of the developing world. All that, and it makes you wince, weep, and, yes, laugh. Not bad for a film distributed by Miramax, which is owned by Disney, one of those big global companies that globaphobes compare to cultural vandals.

A lot of nonsense about the impact of globalization on culture passes   5
for conventional wisdom these days. Among the pro-globalizers, Thomas Friedman, columnist for the *New York Times* and author of *The Lexus and the Olive Tree* (Farrar, Straus & Giroux, 1999), believes that globalization is "globalizing American culture and American cultural icons." Among the antis, Naomi Klein, a Canadian journalist and author of *No Logo* (Picador, 2000), argues that "the buzzword in global marketing isn't selling America to the world, but bringing a kind of market masala to everyone in the world. . . . Despite the embrace of polyethnic imagery, market-driven globalization doesn't want diversity; quite the opposite. Its enemies are national habits, local brands and distinctive regional tastes."

Fears that globalization is imposing a deadening cultural uniformity are as ubiquitous as Coca-Cola, McDonald's, and Mickey Mouse. Europeans and Latin Americans, left-wingers and right, rich and poor — all of them dread that local cultures and national identities are dissolving into a crass all-American consumerism.

That cultural imperialism is said to impose American values as well as products, promote the commercial at the expense of the authentic, and substitute shallow gratification for deeper satisfaction.

City of God's success suggests otherwise. If critics of globalization were less obsessed with "Coca-colonization," they might notice a rich feast of cultural mixing that belies fears about Americanized uniformity. Algerians in Paris practice Thai boxing; Asian rappers in London snack on Turkish pizza; Salman Rushdie delights readers everywhere with his Anglo-Indian tales. Although — as with any change — there can be downsides to cultural globalization, this cross-fertilization is overwhelmingly a force for good.

The beauty of globalization is that it can free people from the tyranny of geography. Just because someone was born in France does not mean they can only aspire to speak French, eat French food, read French books, visit museums in France, and so on. A Frenchman — or an American, for that matter — can take holidays in Spain or Florida, eat sushi or spaghetti for dinner, drink Coke or Chilean wine, watch a Hollywood blockbuster or an Almodóvar,* listen to bhangra or rap, practice yoga or kickboxing, read *Elle* or the *Economist*, and have friends from around the world. That we are increasingly free to choose our cultural experiences enriches our lives immeasurably. We could not always enjoy the best the world has to offer.

Globalization not only increases individual freedom, but also revitalizes   10 cultures and cultural artifacts through foreign influences, technologies, and markets. Thriving cultures are not set in stone. They are forever changing from within and without. Each generation challenges the previous one; science and technology alter the way we see ourselves and the world; fashions come and go; experience and events influence our beliefs; outsiders affect us for good and ill.

Many of the best things come from cultures mixing: V. S. Naipaul's Anglo-Indo-Caribbean writing, Paul Gauguin painting in Polynesia, or the African rhythms in rock 'n' roll. Behold the great British curry. Admire the many-colored faces of France's World Cup-winning soccer team, the ferment of ideas that came from Eastern Europe's Jewish diaspora, and the cosmopolitan cities of London and New York. Western numbers are actually Arabic; zero comes most recently from India; Icelandic, French, and Sanskrit stem from a common root.

John Stuart Mill was right: "The economical benefits of commerce are surpassed in importance by those of its effects which are intellectual and moral. It is hardly possible to overrate the value, for the improvement of human beings, of things which bring them into contact with persons dissimilar to themselves, and with modes of thought and action unlike those with which they are familiar.... It is indispensable to be perpetually comparing [one's] own notions and customs with the experience and example of persons in different circumstances. . . . There is no nation which does not need to borrow from others."

It is a myth that globalization involves the imposition of Americanized uniformity, rather than an explosion of cultural exchange. For a start, many archetypal "American" products are not as all-American as they seem. Levi Strauss, a German immigrant, invented jeans by combining denim cloth (or "serge de Nîmes," because it was traditionally woven in the French town) with Genes, a style of trousers worn by Genoese sailors. So Levi's jeans are in fact an American twist on a European hybrid. Even quintessentially American exports are often tailored to local tastes. MTV in Asia promotes Thai pop stars and plays rock music sung in Mandarin. CNN en Español offers a Latin American take

---

Almodóvar: Pedro Almodóvar (b. 1951), a Spanish film director

on world news. McDonald's sells beer in France, lamb in India, and chili in Mexico.

In some ways, America is an outlier, not a global leader. Most of the world has adopted the metric system born from the French Revolution; America persists with antiquated measurements inherited from its British-colonial past. Most developed countries have become intensely secular, but many Americans burn with fundamentalist fervor — like Muslims in the Middle East. Where else in the developed world could there be a serious debate about teaching kids Bible-inspired "creationism" instead of Darwinist evolution?

America's tastes in sports are often idiosyncratic, too. Baseball and   15
American football have not traveled well, although basketball has fared rather better. Many of the world's most popular sports, notably soccer, came by way of Britain. Asian martial arts — judo, karate, kickboxing — and pastimes like yoga have also swept the world.

People are not only guzzling hamburgers and Coke. Despite Coke's ambition of displacing water as the world's drink of choice, it accounts for less than 2 of the 64 fluid ounces that the typical person drinks a day. Britain's favorite takeaway is a curry, not a burger: Indian restaurants there outnumber McDonald's six to one. For all the concerns about American fast food trashing France's culinary traditions, France imported a mere $620 million in food from the United States in 2000, while exporting to America three times that. Nor is plonk from America's Gallo displacing Europe's finest: Italy and France together account for three-fifths of global wine exports, the United States for only a 20th. Worldwide, pizzas are more popular than burgers, Chinese restaurants seem to sprout up everywhere, and sushi is spreading fast. By far the biggest purveyor of alcoholic drinks is Britain's Diageo, which sells the world's best-selling whiskey (Johnnie Walker), gin (Gordon's), vodka (Smirnoff) and liqueur (Baileys).

In fashion, the ne plus ultra* is Italian or French. Trendy Americans wear Gucci, Armani, Versace, Chanel, and Hermès. On the high street and in the mall, Sweden's Hennes & Mauritz (H&M) and Spain's Zara vie with America's Gap to dress the global masses. Nike shoes are given a run for their money by Germany's Adidas, Britain's Reebok, and Italy's Fila.

In pop music, American crooners do not have the stage to themselves. The three artists who featured most widely in national Top Ten album charts in 2000 were America's Britney Spears, closely followed by Mexico's Carlos Santana and the British Beatles. Even tiny Iceland has produced a global star: Björk. Popular opera's biggest singers are Italy's Luciano Pavarotti, Spain's José Carreras, and the Spanish-Mexican Placido Domingo. Latin American salsa, Brazilian lambada, and African music have all carved out global niches for themselves. In most countries, local artists still top the charts. According to the

---

ne plus ultra: the ultimate; the highest point

IFPI, the record-industry bible, local acts accounted for 68 percent of music sales in 2000, up from 58 percent in 1991.

One of the most famous living writers is a Colombian, Gabriel García Márquez, author of *One Hundred Years of Solitude*. Paulo Coelho, another writer who has notched up tens of millions of global sales with *The Alchemist* and other books, is Brazilian. More than 200 million Harlequin romance novels, a Canadian export, were sold in 1990; they account for two-fifths of mass-market paperback sales in the United States. The biggest publisher in the English-speaking world is Germany's Bertelsmann, which gobbled up America's largest, Random House, in 1998.

Local fare glues more eyeballs to TV screens than American programs.   20
Although nearly three-quarters of television drama exported worldwide comes from the United States, most countries' favorite shows are home-grown.

Nor are Americans the only players in the global media industry. Of the seven market leaders that have their fingers in nearly every pie, four are American (AOL Time Warner, Disney, Viacom, and News Corporation), one is German (Bertelsmann), one is French (Vivendi), and one Japanese (Sony). What they distribute comes from all quarters: Bertelsmann publishes books by American writers; News Corporation broadcasts Asian news; Sony sells Brazilian music.

The evidence is overwhelming. Fears about an Americanized uniformity are over-blown: American cultural products are not uniquely dominant; local ones are alive and well.

With one big exception: cinema. True, India produces more films (855 in 2000) than Hollywood does (762), but they are largely for a domestic audience. Japan and Hong Kong also make lots of movies, but few are seen outside Asia. France and Britain have the occasional global hit, but are still basically local players. Not only does Hollywood dominate the global movie market, but it also swamps local products in most countries. American fare accounts for more than half the market in Japan and nearly two-thirds in Europe.

Yet Hollywood's hegemony is not as worrisome as people think. Note first that Hollywood is less American than it seems. Ever since Charlie Chaplin crossed over from Britain, foreigners have flocked to California to try to become global stars: Just look at Penelope Cruz, Catherine Zeta-Jones, and Ewan McGregor. Top directors are also often from outside America: Think of Ridley Scott or the late Stanley Kubrick. Some studios are foreign-owned: Japan's Sony owns Columbia Pictures, Vivendi Universal is French. Two of AOL Time Warner's biggest recent hit franchises, *Harry Potter* and *The Lord of the Rings*, are both based on British books, have largely British casts, and, in the case of *The Lord of the Rings*, a Kiwi director. To some extent, then, Hollywood is a global industry that just happens to be in America. Rather than exporting Americana, it serves up pap to appeal to a global audience.

Hollywood's dominance is in part due to economics: Movies cost a lot   25
to make and so need a big audience to be profitable; Hollywood has used America's huge and relatively uniform domestic market as a platform to expand

overseas. So there could be a case for stuffing subsidies into a rival European film industry, just as Airbus was created to challenge Boeing's near-monopoly. But France has long pumped money into its domestic industry without persuading foreigners to flock to its films. As Tyler Cowen perceptively points out in his book *Creative Destruction: How Globalization Is Changing the World's Cultures* (Princeton University Press, 2002), "A vicious circle has been created: The more European producers fail in global markets, the more they rely on television revenue and subsidies. The more they rely on television and subsidies, the more they fail in global markets," because they serve domestic demand and the wishes of politicians and cinematic bureaucrats.

Another American export is also conquering the globe: English. Around 380 million people speak it as their first language and another 250 million or so as their second. A billion are learning it, about a third of the world's population are exposed to it, and by 2050, it is reckoned, half the world will be more or less proficient in it. A common global language would certainly be a big plus — for businessmen, scientists, and tourists — but a single one seems far less desirable. Language is often at the heart of national culture: The French would scarcely be French if they spoke English (although Belgian Walloons are not French even though they speak it). English may usurp other languages not because it is what people prefer to speak, but because, like Microsoft software, there are compelling advantages to using it if everyone else does.

But although many languages are becoming extinct, English is rarely to blame. People are learning English as well as — not instead of — their native tongue, and often many more languages besides. Some languages with few speakers, such as Icelandic, are thriving, despite Björk's choosing to sing in English. Where local languages are dying, it is typically national rivals that are stamping them out. French has all but eliminated Provençal, and German Swabian. So although, within the United States, English is displacing American Indian tongues, it is not doing away with Swahili or Norwegian.

Even though American consumer culture is widespread, its significance is often exaggerated. You can choose to drink Coke and eat at McDonald's without becoming American in any meaningful sense. One newspaper photo of Taliban fighters in Afghanistan showed them toting Kalashnikovs* — as well as a sports bag with Nike's trademark swoosh. People's culture — in the sense of their shared ideas, beliefs, knowledge, inherited traditions, and art — may scarcely be eroded by mere commercial artifacts that, despite all the furious branding, embody at best flimsy values.

The really profound cultural changes have little to do with Coca-Cola. Western ideas about liberalism and science are taking root almost everywhere, while Europe and North America are becoming multicultural societies through

---

Kalashnikovs: Soviet assault rifles. Also known as AK47s, these rifles were developed in 1947 and named *Avtomat Kalashnikova* (AK) after their designer, Mikhail Timofeyevich Kalashnikov.

immigration, mainly from developing countries. Technology is reshaping culture: Just think of the Internet. Individual choice is fragmenting the imposed uniformity of national cultures. New hybrid cultures are emerging, and regional ones reemerging. National identity is not disappearing, but the bonds of nationality are loosening.

As Tyler Cowen points out in his excellent book, cross-border cultural exchange increases diversity within societies — but at the expense of making them more alike. People everywhere have more choice, but they often choose similar things. That worries cultural pessimists, even though the right to choose to be the same is an essential part of freedom.

Cross-cultural exchange can spread greater diversity as well as greater similarity: more gourmet restaurants as well as more McDonald's. And just as a big city can support a wider spread of restaurants than a small town, so a global market for cultural products allows a wider range of artists to thrive. For sure, if all the new customers are ignorant, a wider market may drive down the quality of cultural products: Think of tourist souvenirs. But as long as some customers are well informed (or have "good taste"), a general "dumbing down" is unlikely. Hobbyists, fans, artistic pride, and professional critics also help maintain (and raise) standards. Cowen concludes that the "basic trend is of increasing variety and diversity, at all levels of quality, high and low."

A bigger worry is that greater individual freedom may come at the expense of national identity. The French fret that if they all individually choose to watch Hollywood films they might unwittingly lose their collective Frenchness. Yet such fears are overdone. Natural cultures are much stronger than people seem to think. They can embrace some foreign influences and resist others. Foreign influences can rapidly become domesticated, changing national culture, but not destroying it. Germans once objected to soccer because it was deemed English; now their soccer team is emblematic of national pride. Amartya Sen, the Nobel prize-winning economist, is quite right when he says that "the culturally fearful often take a very fragile view of each culture and tend to underestimate our ability to learn from elsewhere without being overwhelmed by that experience."

Clearly, though, there is a limit to how many foreign influences a culture can absorb before being swamped. Even when a foreign influence is largely welcomed, it can be overwhelming. Traditional cultures in the developing world that have until now evolved (or failed to evolve) in isolation may be particularly vulnerable.

In *The Silent Takeover: Global Capitalism and the Death of Democracy* (Free Press, 2001), Noreena Hertz describes the supposed spiritual Eden that was the isolated kingdom of Bhutan in the Himalayas as being defiled by such awful imports as basketball and Spice Girls T-shirts. Anthony Giddens, the director of the London School of Economics and Political Science, has told how an anthropologist who visited a remote part of Cambodia was shocked and disappointed to find that her first night's entertainment was not traditional local pastimes but watching *Basic Instinct* on video.

Is that such a bad thing? It is odd, to put it mildly, that many on the left 35 support multiculturalism in the West but advocate cultural purity in the developing world — an attitude they would be quick to tar as fascist if proposed for the United States or Britain. Hertz and the anthropologist in Cambodia appear to want people outside the industrialized West preserved in unchanging but supposedly pure poverty. Yet the Westerners who want this supposed paradise preserved in aspic rarely feel like settling there. Nor do most people in developing countries want to lead an "authentic" unspoiled life of isolated poverty.

In truth, cultural pessimists are typically not attached to diversity per se but to designated manifestations of diversity, determined by their preferences. "They often use diversity as a code word for a more particularist agenda, often of an anti-commercial or anti-American nature," Cowen argues. "They care more about the particular form that diversity takes in their favored culture, rather than about diversity more generally, freedom of choice, or a broad menu of quality options."

Cultural pessimists want to freeze things as they were. But if diversity at any point in time is desirable, why isn't diversity across time? Certainly, it is often a shame if ancient cultural traditions are lost. We should do our best to preserve them and keep them alive where possible. As Cowen points out, foreigners can often help, by providing the new customers and technologies that have enabled reggae music, Haitian art, and Persian carpet making, for instance, to thrive and reach new markets. But people cannot be made to live in a museum. We in the West are forever casting off old customs when we feel they are no longer relevant. Nobody argues that Americans should ban nightclubs to force people back to line dancing. People in poor countries have a right to change, too.

Moreover, some losses of diversity are a good thing. In 1850, some countries banned slavery, while others maintained it in various forms. Who laments that the world is now almost universally rid of it? More generally, Western ideas are reshaping the way people everywhere view themselves and the world. Like nationalism and socialism before it, liberalism — political ideas about individual liberty, the rule of law, democracy, and universal human rights, as well as economic ones about the importance of private property rights, markets, and consumer choice — is a European philosophy that has swept the world. Even people who resist liberal ideas, in the name of religion (Islamic and Christian fundamentalists), group identity (communitarians), authoritarianism (advocates of "Asian values") or tradition (cultural conservatives), now define themselves partly by their opposition to them.

Faith in science and technology is even more widespread. Even those who hate the West make use of its technologies. Osama bin Laden plots terrorism on a cellphone and crashes planes into skyscrapers. Antiglobalization

protesters organize by e-mail and over the Internet. José Bové manipulates
21st-century media in his bid to return French farming to the Middle Ages.
China no longer turns its nose up at Western technology: It tries to beat the
West at its own game.

True, many people reject Western culture. (Or, more accurately, 40
"cultures": Europeans and Americans disagree bitterly over the death penalty,
for instance; they hardly see eye to eye over the role of the state, either.) Samuel
Huntington, a professor of international politics at Harvard University, even
predicts a "clash of civilizations" that will divide the 21st-century world. Yet
Francis Fukuyama, a professor of international political economy at the Johns
Hopkins University, is nearer the mark when he talks about the "end of history." Some cultures have local appeal, but only liberalism appeals everywhere
(if not to all) — although radical environmentalism may one day challenge its
hegemony. Islamic fundamentalism poses a threat to our lives but not to our
beliefs. Unlike communism, it is not an alternative to liberal capitalism for
Westerners or other non-Muslims.

Yet for all the spread of Western ideas to the developing world, globalization is not a one-way street. Although Europe's former colonial powers have
left their stamp on much of the world, the recent flow of migration has been in
the opposite direction. There are Algerian suburbs in Paris, but not French ones
in Algiers; Pakistani parts of London, but not British ones of Lahore. Whereas
Muslims are a growing minority in Europe, Christians are a disappearing one
in the Middle East.

Foreigners are changing America even as they adopt its ways. A million
or so immigrants arrive each year (700,000 legally, 300,000 illegally), most of
them Latino or Asian. Since 1990, the number of foreign-born American residents has risen by 6 million to just over 25 million, the biggest immigration
wave since the turn of the 20th century. English may be all-conquering outside
America, but in some parts of the United States, it is now second to Spanish.
Half of the 50 million new inhabitants expected in America in the next
25 years will be immigrants or the children of immigrants.

The upshot of all this change is that national cultures are fragmenting
into a kaleidoscope of different ones. New hybrid cultures are emerging. In
"Amexica" people speak Spanglish. Regional cultures are reviving. Repressed
under Franco, Catalans, Basques, Gallegos, and others assert their identity in
Spain. The Scots and Welsh break with British monoculture. Estonia is reborn
from the Soviet Union. Voices that were silent dare to speak again.

Individuals are forming new communities, linked by shared interests and
passions, that cut across national borders. Friendships with foreigners met on
holiday. Scientists sharing ideas over the Internet. Environmentalists campaign-
ing together using e-mail. House-music lovers swapping tracks online. Greater
individualism does not spell the end of community. The new communities are
simply chosen rather than coerced, unlike the older ones that communitarians
hark back to.

Does that mean national identity is dead? Hardly. People who speak the   45
same language, were born and live near each other, face similar problems, have
a common experience, and vote in the same elections still have plenty of things
in common. For all our awareness of the world as a single place, we are not
citizens of the world but citizens of a state. But if people now wear the bonds
of nationality more loosely, is that such a bad thing? People may lament the
passing of old ways. Indeed, many of the worries about globalization echo age-
old fears about decline, a lost golden age, and so on. But by and large, people
choose the new ways because they are more relevant to their current needs and
offer new opportunities that the old ones did not.

The truth is that we increasingly define ourselves rather than let others
define us. Being British or American does not define who you are: It is part of
who you are. You can like foreign things and still have strong bonds to your fellow citizens. As Mario Vargas Llosa, the Peruvian author, has written: "Seeking
to impose a cultural identity on a people is equivalent to locking them in a
prison and denying them the most precious of liberties — that of choosing
what, how, and who they want to be."

QUESTIONING THE TEXT

1. As Legrain indicates in his title, we should not be concerned that cultural
   globalization constitutes Americanization, but does he suggest that we
   should be concerned about globalization for other reasons? Find evidence in the text to support your answer.

2. Working with a classmate, summarize Legrain's thoughts on "diversity"
   and "globalization." How are these concepts related? What contradictions does he find in others' arguments about these ideas? Do you agree
   with his views on these concepts? Why, or why not?

MAKING CONNECTIONS

3. Legrain claims that "vot[ing] in the same elections" constitutes an aspect
   of national identity (paragraph 45). Do you think David Brooks, author
   of "One Nation, Slightly Divisible" (p. 525), would agree with Legrain
   on this point? Why, or why not? Write a three- to four-page argument
   answering this question, drawing support from the two essays.

4. Legrain's argument might be said to parallel, to some degree, the argument that Virginia Postrel makes in "In Praise of Chain Stores" (p. 681).
   How do Legrain and Postrel conceive of their audiences? How do they
   anticipate alternative claims and objections to their positions? What
   differences do you see in the arguments that they make?

JOINING THE CONVERSATION

5. Think of an aspect of culture — perhaps a habit, tradition, food, or belief — that seems truly American to you, and do some research to discover its origins and history. Is this aspect of U.S. culture as American as you believed? Has it been imported into the United States from another country? Has it been transported out of the United States to other countries? Write an essay exploring the myth and truth surrounding the piece of American culture you've chosen to analyze.

6. Legrain claims that national identity still exists: "People who speak the same language, were born and live near each other, face similar problems, have a common experience, and vote in the same elections still have plenty of things in common" (paragraph 45). Pick one of these categories of identity, or another that you think of, and write an essay arguing that most (or many) Americans could be expected to identify with this aspect of experience. Support your argument with examples from your own experience, popular culture, readings in this chapter, or other sources you find.

DAVID BROOKS
One Nation, Slightly Divisible

FOLLOWING THE HARD-FOUGHT *American presidential contest of 2000, the electoral map that tallied the states going for Bush or Gore looked like a house divided. The coasts, both east and west, were awash in the blue of Democrat Gore, as were many Mid-Atlantic and Great Lakes states. Almost everything in between, with the exception of New Mexico, was red, indicating that these states had gone for Republican Bush. In the view of the pundits, Gore had won the urban enclaves and population centers — New York City, Chicago, Los Angeles, Atlanta — where the country's movers and shakers defined its policies and gave shape to its ideas; Bush had triumphed mainly in the sprawling heartland, that vast territory one flew over to get to other places. The map was certainly sobering in its suggestion that the United States had voted as two nations, a split made all the worse by the battle for Florida's decisive electoral votes.*

Of course, the United States has been divided regionally, culturally, and politically since its earliest days. At the time of the American Revolution, only a third of the colonists wanted independence from England. In the nineteenth century, the question of slavery pitted North against South. In the decades since the Civil War, America has seen fault lines emerge between immigrants and natives, men and women, haves and have-nots, even easterners and westerners.

Yet the red/blue dichotomy of the 2000 election seemed unusually ideological — a more abstract and fundamental quarrel of cultures and principles than had typically separated Americans one from another. Were the much ballyhooed "cultural wars" of the 1980s and 1990s — pitting secular, left-wing urban elites against conservative religious zealots — just the harbinger of even more bruising class conflicts on the horizon? David Brooks sets out to answer that question in "One Nation, Slightly Divisible," an essay originally published in Atlantic Monthly *(December 2001). Brooks's piece is a comparison-contrast essay that treads slowly through two counties that he chooses to represent the Red and Blue Americas. His observations are highly personal, and the validity of his conclusions rests, for the most part, on his ability to persuade readers that his observations are accurate. The story he tells is, to my mind, compelling, and his conclusion leads us to take another look at the 2000 election map. Indeed, the myth of an indivisible American nation may still be viable.*

David Brooks (b. 1961) is senior editor of the Weekly Standard, *a columnist for the* New York Times, *and a frequent contributor to* Newsweek *and* Atlantic Monthly. *He is the author of* On Paradise Drive: How We Live Now (and Always Have) in the Future Tense *(2004).* —J.R.

Sixty-five miles from where I am writing this sentence is a place with no Starbucks, no Pottery Barn, no Borders or Barnes & Noble. No blue *New York*

Times delivery bags dot the driveways on Sunday mornings. In this place people don't complain that Woody Allen isn't as funny as he used to be, because they never thought he was funny. In this place you can go to a year's worth of dinner parties without hearing anyone quote an aperçu he first heard on *Charlie Rose*. The people here don't buy those little rear-window stickers when they go to a summer-vacation spot so that they can drive around with "MV" decals the rest of the year; for the most part they don't even go to Martha's Vineyard.

The place I'm talking about goes by different names. Some call it America. Others call it Middle America. It has also come to be known as Red America, in reference to the maps that were produced on the night of the 2000 presidential election. People in Blue America, which is my part of America, tend to live around big cities on the coasts. People in Red America tend to live on farms or in small towns or small cities far away from the coasts. Things are different there.

Everything that people in my neighborhood do without motors, the people in Red America do with motors. We sail; they powerboat. We cross-country ski; they snowmobile. We hike; they drive ATVs. We have vineyard tours; they have tractor pulls. When it comes to yard work, they have rider mowers; we have illegal aliens.

Different sorts of institutions dominate life in these two places. In Red America churches are everywhere. In Blue America Thai restaurants are everywhere. In Red America they have QVC, the Pro Bowlers Tour, and hunting. In Blue America we have NPR, Doris Kearns Goodwin, and socially conscious investing. In Red America the Wal-Marts are massive, with parking lots the size of state parks. In Blue America the stores are small but the markups are big. You'll rarely see a Christmas store in Blue America, but in Red America, even in July, you'll come upon stores selling fake Christmas trees, wreath-decorated napkins, Rudolph the Red-Nosed Reindeer collectible thimbles and spoons, and little snow-covered villages.

We in the coastal metro Blue areas read more books and attend more   5
plays than the people in the Red heartland. We're more sophisticated and cosmopolitan — just ask us about our alumni trips to China or Provence, or our interest in Buddhism. But don't ask us, please, what life in Red America is like. We don't know. We don't know who Tim LaHaye and Jerry B. Jenkins are, even though the novels they have co-written have sold about 40 million copies over the past few years. We don't know what James Dobson says on his radio program, which is listened to by millions. We don't know about Reba or Travis. We don't know what happens in mega-churches on Wednesday evenings, and some of us couldn't tell you the difference between a fundamentalist and an evangelical, let alone describe what it means to be a Pentecostal. Very few of us know what goes on in Branson, Missouri, even though it has seven million visitors a year, or could name even five NASCAR drivers, although stock-car races are the best-attended sporting events in the country.

We don't know how to shoot or clean a rifle. We can't tell a military officer's rank by looking at his insignia. We don't know what soy beans look like when they're growing in a field.

All we know, or all we think we know, about Red America is that millions and millions of its people live quietly underneath flight patterns, many of them are racist and homophobic, and when you see them at highway rest stops, they're often really fat and their clothes are too tight.

And apparently we don't want to know any more than that. One can barely find any books at Amazon.com about what it is like to live in small-town America — or, at least, any books written by normal people who grew up in small towns, liked them, and stayed there. The few books that do exist were written either by people who left the heartland because they hated it (Bill Bryson's *The Lost Continent,* for example) or by urbanites who moved to Red America as part of some life-simplification plan (*Moving to a Small Town: A Guidebook for Moving from Urban to Rural America*; National Geographic's *Guide to Small Town Escapes*). Apparently no publishers or members of the Blue book-buying public are curious about Red America as seen through Red America's eyes.

CROSSING THE MEATLOAF LINE

Over the past several months, my interest piqued by those stark blocks of color on the election-night maps, I have every now and then left my home in Montgomery County, Maryland, and driven sixty-five miles northwest to Franklin County, in south-central Pennsylvania. Montgomery County is one of the steaming-hot centers of the great espresso machine that is Blue America. It is just over the border from northwestern Washington, D.C., and it is full of upper-middle-class towns inhabited by lawyers, doctors, stockbrokers, and establishment journalists like me — towns like Chevy Chase, Potomac, and Bethesda (where I live). Its central artery is a burgeoning high-tech corridor with a multitude of sparkling new office parks housing technology companies such as United Information Systems and Sybase, and pioneering biotech firms such as Celera Genomics and Human Genome Sciences. When I drive to Franklin County, I take Route 270. After about forty-five minutes I pass a Cracker Barrel — Red America condensed into chain-restaurant form. I've crossed the Meatloaf Line; from here on there will be a lot fewer sun-dried-tomato concoctions on restaurant menus and a lot more meatloaf platters.

Franklin County is Red America. It's a rural county, about twenty-five miles west of Gettysburg, and it includes the towns of Waynesboro, Chambersburg, and Mercersburg. It was originally settled by the Scotch-Irish, and has plenty of Brethren and Mennonites along with a fast-growing population of evangelicals. The joke that Pennsylvanians tell about their state is that it has Philadelphia on one end, Pittsburgh on the other, and Alabama in the middle. Franklin County is in the Alabama part. It strikes me as I drive there that even though I am going north across the Mason-Dixon line, I feel as if I were going

south. The local culture owes more to Nashville, Houston, and Daytona than
to Washington, Philadelphia, or New York.

I shuttled back and forth between Franklin and Montgomery Countries   10
because the cultural differences between the two places are great, though the
geographic distance is small. The two places are not perfect microcosms of Red
and Blue America. The part of Montgomery County I am here describing is
largely the Caucasian part. Moreover, Franklin County is in a Red part of a
Blue state: overall, Pennsylvania went for Gore. And I went to Franklin County
aware that there are tremendous differences within Red America, just as there
are within Blue. Franklin County is quite different from, say, Scottsdale,
Arizona, just as Bethesda is quite different from Oakland, California.

Nonetheless, the contrasts between the two counties leap out, and they
are broadly suggestive of the sorts of contrasts that can be seen nationwide.
When Blue America talks about social changes that convulsed society, it
tends to mean the 1960s rise of the counterculture and feminism. When Red
America talks about changes that convulsed society, it tends to mean World
War II, which shook up old town establishments and led to a great surge of
industry.

Red America makes social distinctions that Blue America doesn't. For
example, in Franklin County there seems to be a distinction between those
fiercely independent people who live in the hills and people who live in the
valleys. I got a hint of the distinct and, to me, exotic hill culture when a hill
dweller asked me why I thought hunting for squirrel and rabbit had gone out
of fashion. I thought maybe it was just more fun to hunt something bigger.
But he said, "McDonald's. It's cheaper to get a hamburger at McDonald's than
to go out and get it yourself."

There also seems to be an important distinction between men who work
outdoors and men who work indoors. The outdoor guys wear faded black
T-shirts they once picked up at a Lynyrd Skynyrd concert and wrecked jeans
that appear to be washed faithfully at least once a year. They've got wraparound
NASCAR sunglasses, maybe a NAPA auto parts cap, and hair cut in a short
wedge up front but flowing down over their shoulders in the back — a cut that
is known as a mullet, which is sort of a cross between Van Halen's style and
Kenny Rogers's, and is the ugliest hairdo since every hairdo in the seventies.
The outdoor guys are heavily accessorized, and their accessories are meant to
show how hard they work, so they will often have a gigantic wad of keys hanging from a belt loop, a tape measure strapped to the belt, a pocket knife on a
string tucked into the front pants pocket, and a pager or a cell phone affixed to
the hip, presumably in case some power lines go down somewhere and need
emergency repair. Outdoor guys have a thing against sleeves. They work so
hard that they've got to keep their arm muscles unencumbered and their armpit
hair fully ventilated, so they either buy their shirts sleeveless or rip the sleeves
off their T-shirts first thing, leaving bits of fringe hanging over their BAD TO
THE BONE tattoos.

The guys who work indoors can't project this rugged proletarian image. It's simply not that romantic to be a bank-loan officer or a shift manager at the local distribution center. So the indoor guys adopt a look that a smart-ass, sneering Blue American might call Bible-academy casual — maybe Haggar slacks, which they bought at a dry-goods store best known for its appliance department, and a short-sleeved white Van Heusen shirt from the Bon-Ton. Their image projects not "I work hard" but "I'm a devoted family man." A lot of indoor guys have a sensitive New Age demeanor. When they talk about the days their kids were born, their eyes take on a soft Garth Brooks expression, and they tear up. They exaggerate how sinful they were before they were born again. On Saturdays they are patio masters, barbecuing on their gas grills in full Father's Day-apron regalia.

At first I thought the indoor guys were the faithful, reliable ones: the ones   15
who did well in school, whereas the outdoor guys were druggies. But after talking with several preachers in Franklin County, I learned that it's not that simple. Sometimes the guys who look like bikers are the most devoted community-service volunteers and church attendees.

The kinds of distinctions we make in Blue America are different. In my world the easiest way to categorize people is by headroom needs. People who went to business school or law school like a lot of headroom. They buy humongous sport-utility vehicles that practically have cathedral ceilings over the front seats. They live in homes the size of country clubs, with soaring entry atriums so high that they could practically fly a kite when they come through the front door. These big-headroom people tend to be predators: their jobs have them negotiating and competing all day. They spend small fortunes on dry cleaning. They grow animated when talking about how much they love their Blackberries. They fill their enormous wall space with huge professional family portraits — Mom and Dad with their perfect kids (dressed in light-blue oxford shirts) laughing happily in an orchard somewhere.

Small-headroom people tend to have been liberal-arts majors, and they have liberal-arts jobs. They get passive-aggressive pleasure from demonstrating how modest and environmentally sensitive their living containers are. They hate people with SUVs, and feel virtuous driving around in their low-ceilinged little Hondas, which often display a RANDOM ACTS OF KINDNESS bumper sticker or one bearing an image of a fish with legs, along with the word "Darwin," just to show how intellectually superior to fundamentalist Christians they are.

Some of the biggest differences between Red and Blue America show up on statistical tables. Ethnic diversity is one. In Montgomery County 60 percent of the population is white, 15 percent is black, 12 percent is Hispanic, and 11 percent is Asian. In Franklin County 95 percent of the population is white. White people work the gas-station pumps and the 7-Eleven counters. (This is something one doesn't often see in my part of the country.) Although the nation is growing more diverse, it's doing so only in certain spots. According to an analysis of the 2000 census by Bill Frey, a demographer at the Milken Institute, well over half the counties in America are still at least 85 percent white.

Another big thing is that, according to 1990 census data, in Franklin County only 12 percent of the adults have college degrees and only 69 percent have high school diplomas. In Montgomery County 50 percent of the adults have college degrees and 91 percent have high school diplomas. The education gap extends to the children. At Walt Whitman High School, a public school in Bethesda, the average SAT scores are 601 verbal and 622 math, whereas the national average is 506 verbal and 514 math. In Franklin County, where people are quite proud of their schools, the average SAT scores at, for example, the Waynesboro area high school are 495 verbal and 480 math. More and more kids in Franklin County are going on to college, but it is hard to believe that their prospects will be as bright as those of the kids in Montgomery County and the rest of upscale Blue America.

Because the information age rewards education with money, it's not surprising that Montgomery County is much richer than Franklin County. According to some estimates, in Montgomery County 51 percent of households have annual incomes above $75,000, and the average household income is $100,365. In Franklin County only 16 percent of households have incomes above $75,000, and the average is $51,872.   20

A major employer in Montgomery County is the National Institutes of Health, which grows like a scientific boomtown in Bethesda. A major economic engine in Franklin County is the interstate highway Route 81. Trucking companies have gotten sick of fighting the congestion on Route 95, which runs up the Blue corridor along the northeast coast, so they move their stuff along 81, farther inland. Several new distribution centers have been built along 81 in Franklin County, and some of the workers who were laid off when their factories closed, several years ago, are now settling for $8.00 or $9.00 an hour loading boxes.

The two counties vote differently, of course — the differences, on a nationwide scale, were what led to those red–and–blue maps. Like upscale areas everywhere, from Silicon Valley to Chicago's North Shore to suburban Connecticut, Montgomery County supported the Democratic ticket in last year's presidential election, by a margin of 63 percent to 34 percent. Meanwhile, like almost all of rural America, Franklin County went Republican, by 67 percent to 30 percent.

However, other voting patterns sometimes obscure the Red-Blue cultural divide. For example, minority voters all over the country overwhelmingly supported the Democratic ticket last November. But — in many respects, at least — blacks and Hispanics in Red America are more traditionalist than blacks and Hispanics in Blue America, just as their white counterparts are. For example, the Pew Research Center for the People and the Press, in Washington, D.C., recently found that 45 percent of minority members in Red states agree with the statement "AIDS might be God's punishment for immoral sexual behavior," but only 31 percent of minority members in Blue states do. Similarly, 40 percent of minorities in Red states believe that school boards should have the right to fire homosexual teachers, but only 21 percent of minorities in Blue states do.

FROM CRACKS TO A CHASM?

These differences are so many and so stark that they lead to some pretty troubling questions: Are Americans any longer a common people? Do we have one national conversation and one national culture? Are we loyal to the same institutions and the same values? How do people on one side of the divide regard those on the other?

I went to Franklin County because I wanted to get a sense of how deep   25
the divide really is, to see how people there live, and to gauge how different their lives are from those in my part of America. I spoke with ministers, journalists, teachers, community leaders, and pretty much anyone I ran across. I consulted with pollsters, demographers, and market-research firms.

Toward the end of my project the World Trade Center and the Pentagon were attacked. This put a new slant on my little investigation. In the days immediately following September 11 the evidence seemed clear that despite our differences, we are still a united people. American flags flew everywhere in Franklin County and in Montgomery County. Patriotism surged. Pollsters started to measure Americans' reactions to the events. Whatever questions they asked, the replies were near unanimous. Do you support a military response against terror? More than four fifths of Americans said yes. Do you support a military response even if it means thousands of U.S. casualties? More than three fifths said yes. There were no significant variations across geographic or demographic lines.

A sweeping feeling of solidarity was noticeable in every neighborhood, school, and workplace. Headlines blared, "A NATION UNITED" and "UNITED STATE." An attack had been made on the very epicenter of Blue America — downtown Manhattan. And in a flash all the jokes about and seeming hostility toward New Yorkers vanished, to be replaced by an outpouring of respect, support, and love. The old hostility came to seem merely a sort of sibling rivalry, which means nothing when the family itself is under threat.

But very soon there were hints that the solidarity was fraying. A few stray notes of dissent were sounded in the organs of Blue America. Susan Sontag wrote a sour piece in *The New Yorker* about how depressing it was to see what she considered to be a simplistically pro-American reaction to the attacks. At rallies on college campuses across the country speakers pointed out that America had been bombing other countries for years, and turnabout was fair play. On one NPR talk show I heard numerous callers express unease about what they saw as a crude us-versus-them mentality behind President Bush's rhetoric. Katha Pollitt wrote in *The Nation* that she would not permit her daughter to hang the American flag from the living-room window, because, she felt, it "stands for jingoism and vengeance and war." And there was evidence that among those with less-strident voices, too, differences were beginning to show. Polls revealed that people without a college education were far more confident than people with a college education that the military could defeat the terrorists.

People in the South were far more eager than people in the rest of the country for an American counterattack to begin.

It started to seem likely that these cracks would widen once the American response got under way, when the focus would be not on firemen and rescue workers but on the Marines, the CIA, and the special-operations forces. If the war was protracted, the cracks could widen into a chasm, as they did during Vietnam. Red America, the home of patriotism and military service (there's a big military-recruitment center in downtown Chambersburg), would undoubtedly support the war effort, but would Blue America (there's a big gourmet dog bakery in downtown Bethesda) decide that a crude military response would only deepen animosities and make things worse?

So toward the end of my project I investigated Franklin County with a   30
heightened sense of gravity and with much more urgency. If America was not firmly united in the early days of the conflict, we would certainly not be united later, when the going got tough.

"THE PEOPLE VERSUS THE POWERFUL"

There are a couple of long-standing theories about why America is divided. One of the main ones holds that the division is along class lines, between the haves and the have-nots. This theory is popular chiefly on the left, and can be found in the pages of *The American Prospect* and other liberal magazines; in news reports by liberal journalists such as Donald L. Barlett and James B. Steele, of *Time*; and in books such as *Middle Class Dreams* (1995), by the Clinton and Gore pollster Stanley Greenberg, and *America's Forgotten Majority: Why the White Working Class Still Matters* (2000), by the demographer Ruy Teixeira and the social scientist Joel Rogers.

According to this theory, during most of the twentieth century gaps in income between the rich and the poor in America gradually shrank. Then came the information age. The rich started getting spectacularly richer, the poor started getting poorer, and wages for the middle class stagnated, at best. Over the previous decade, these writers emphasized, remuneration for top-level executives had skyrocketed: now the average CEO made 116 times as much as the average rank-and-file worker. Assembly-line workers found themselves competing for jobs against Third World workers who earned less than a dollar an hour. Those who had once labored at well-paying blue-collar jobs were forced to settle for poorly paying service-economy jobs without benefits.

People with graduate degrees have done well over the past couple of decades: their real hourly wages climbed by 13 percent from 1979 to 1997, according to Teixeira and Rogers. But those with only some college education saw their wages fall by nine percent, while those with only high school diplomas saw their wages fall by 12 percent, and high school dropouts saw a stunning 26 percent decline in their pay.

Such trends have created a new working class, these writers argue — not a traditional factory-and-mill working class but a suburban and small-town working class, made up largely of service workers and low-level white-collar employees. Teixeira and Rogers estimate that the average household income for this group, which accounts for about 55 percent of American adults, is roughly $42,000. "It is not hard to imagine how [recent economic trends] must have felt to the forgotten majority man," they write.

> As at least part of America was becoming ever more affluent, an affluence that was well covered on television and in the evening news, he did not seem to be making much progress. What could he be doing wrong to be faring so poorly? Why couldn't he afford what others could? And why were they moving ahead while he was standing still?

Stanley Greenberg tailored Al Gore's presidential campaign to appeal to   35
such voters. Gore's most significant slogan was "The People versus the Powerful," which was meant to rally members of the middle class who felt threatened by "powerful forces" beyond their control, such as HMOs, tobacco companies, big corporations, and globalization, and to channel their resentment against the upper class. Gore dressed down throughout his campaign in the hope that these middle-class workers would identify with him.

Driving from Bethesda to Franklin County, one can see that the theory of a divide between the classes has a certain plausibility. In Montgomery County we have Saks Fifth Avenue, Cartier, Anthropologie, Brooks Brothers. In Franklin County they have Dollar General and Value City, along with a plethora of secondhand stores. It's as if Franklin County has only forty-five coffee tables, which are sold again and again.

When the locals are asked about their economy, they tell a story very similar to the one that Greenberg, Teixeira, Rogers, and the rest of the wage-stagnation liberals recount. There used to be plenty of good factory jobs in Franklin County, and people could work at those factories for life. But some of the businesses, including the textile company J. Schoeneman, once Franklin County's largest manufacturer, have closed. Others have moved off-shore. The remaining manufacturers, such as Grove Worldwide and JLG Industries, which both make cranes and aerial platforms, have laid off workers. The local Army depot, Letterkenny, has radically shrunk its work force. The new jobs are in distribution centers or nursing homes. People tend to repeat the same phrase: "We've taken some hits."

And yet when they are asked about the broader theory, whether there is class conflict between the educated affluents and the stagnant middles, they stare blankly as if suddenly the interview were being conducted in Aramaic. I kept asking, Do you feel that the highly educated people around, say, New York and Washington are getting all the goodies? Do you think there is resentment toward all the latte sippers who shop at Nieman Marcus? Do you see a gulf between high-income people in the big cities and middle-income people here?

I got only polite, fumbling answers as people tried to figure out what the hell I was talking about.

When I rephrased the question in more-general terms, as Do you believe the country is divided between the haves and the have-nots?, everyone responded decisively: yes. But as the conversation continued, it became clear that the people saying yes did not consider themselves to be among the have-nots. Even people with incomes well below the median thought of themselves as haves.

What I found was entirely consistent with the election returns from   40
November of last year. Gore's pitch failed miserably among the voters it was intended to target: nationally he lost among non-college-educated white voters by 17 points and among non-college-educated white men by 29 points. But it worked beautifully on the affluent, educated class: for example, Gore won among women with graduate degrees by 22 points. The lesson seems to be that if you run a campaign under the slogan "The People versus the Powerful," you will not do well in the places where "the people" live, but you will do fantastically well in the places where "the powerful" live. This phenomenon mirrors, on a larger scale, one I noted a couple of years ago, when I traveled the country for a year talking about *Bobos in Paradise*, a book I had written on upscale America. The richer the community, the more likely I was to be asked about wage inequality. In middle-class communities the subject almost never came up.

Hanging around Franklin County, one begins to understand some of the reasons that people there don't spend much time worrying about economic class lines. The first and most obvious one is that although the incomes in Franklin County are lower than those in Montgomery County, living expenses are also lower — very much so. Driving from Montgomery County to Franklin County is like driving through an invisible deflation machine. Gas is thirty, forty, or even fifty cents a gallon cheaper in Franklin County. I parked at meters that accepted only pennies and nickels. When I got a parking ticket in Chambersburg, the fine was $3.00. At the department store in Greencastle there were racks and racks of blouses for $9.99.

The biggest difference is in real-estate prices. In Franklin County one can buy a nice four-bedroom split-level house with about 2,200 square feet of living space for $150,000 to $180,000. In Bethesda that same house would cost about $450,000. (According to the Coldwell Banker Real Estate Corporation, that house would sell for $784,000 in Greenwich, Connecticut; for $812,000 in Manhattan Beach, California; and for about $1.23 million in Palo Alto, California.)

Some of the people I met in Franklin County were just getting by. Some were in debt and couldn't afford to buy their kids the Christmas presents they wanted to. But I didn't find many who assessed their own place in society according to their income. Rather, the people I met commonly told me that although those in affluent places like Manhattan and Bethesda might make more money and have more-exciting jobs, they are the unlucky ones, because they don't get to live in Franklin County. They don't get to enjoy the beautiful green hillsides, the friendly people, the wonderful church groups and volunteer organizations. They may be nice people and all, but they are certainly not as happy as we are.

Another thing I found is that most people don't think sociologically. They don't compare themselves with faraway millionaires who appear on their TV screens. They compare themselves with their neighbors. "One of the challenges we face is that it is hard to get people to look beyond the four-state region," Lynne Woehrle, a sociologist at Wilson College, in Chambersburg, told me, referring to the cultural zone composed of the nearby rural areas in Pennsylvania, West Virginia, Maryland, and Virginia. Many of the people in Franklin County view the lifestyles of the upper class in California or Seattle much the way we in Blue America might view the lifestyle of someone in Eritrea or Mongolia — or, for that matter, Butte, Montana. Such ways of life are distant and basically irrelevant, except as a source of academic interest or titillation. One man in Mercersburg, Pennsylvania, told me about a friend who had recently bought a car. "He paid twenty-five thousand dollars for that car!" he exclaimed, his eyes wide with amazement. "He got it fully loaded." I didn't tell him that in Bethesda almost no one but a college kid pays as little as $25,000 for a car.

Franklin County is a world in which there is little obvious inequality, and   45
the standard of living is reasonably comfortable. Youth-soccer teams are able to raise money for a summer trip to England; the Lowe's hardware superstore carries Laura Ashley carpets; many people have pools, although they are almost always above ground; the planning commission has to cope with an increasing number of cars in the county every year, even though the population is growing only gradually. But the sort of high-end experiences that are everywhere in Montgomery County are entirely missing here.

On my journeys to Franklin County, I set a goal: I was going to spend $20 on a restaurant meal. But although I ordered the most expensive thing on the menu — steak au jus, "slippery beef pot pie," or whatever — I always failed. I began asking people to direct me to the most-expensive places in town. They would send me to Red Lobster or Applebee's. I'd go into a restaurant that looked from the outside as if it had some pretensions — may be a "Les Desserts" glass cooler for the key-lime pie and the tapioca pudding. I'd scan the menu and realize that I'd been beaten once again. I went through great vats of chipped beef and "seafood delight" trying to drop twenty dollars. I waded through enough surf-and-turfs and enough creamed corn to last a lifetime. I could not do it.

No wonder people in Franklin County have no class resentment or class consciousness; where they live, they can afford just about anything that is for sale. (In Montgomery County, however — and this is one of the most striking contrasts between the two counties — almost nobody can say that. In Blue America, unless you are very, very rich, there is always, all around you, stuff for sale that you cannot afford.) And if they sought to improve their situation, they would look only to themselves. If a person wants to make more money, the feeling goes, he or she had better work hard and think like an entrepreneur.

I could barely get fifteen minutes into an interview before the local work ethic came up. Karen Jewell, who helps to oversee the continuing-education program for the local Penn State branch campus, told me, "People are very vested in what they do. There's an awareness of where they fit in the organization. They feel empowered to be agents of change."

People do work extremely hard in Franklin County — even people in supposedly dead-end jobs. You can see it in little things, such as drugstore shelves. The drugstores in Bethesda look the way Rome must have looked after a visit from the Visigoths. But in Franklin County the boxes are in perfect little rows. Shelves are fully stocked, and cans are evenly spaced. The floors are less dusty than those in a microchip-processing plant. The nail clippers on a rack by the cash register are arranged with a precision that would put the Swiss to shame.

There are few unions in Franklin County. People abhor the thought of   50
depending on welfare; they consider themselves masters of their own economic fate. "People are really into the free market here," Bill Pukmel, formerly the editor of the weekly paper in Chambersburg, told me.

In sum, I found absolutely no evidence that a Stanley Greenberg-prompted Democratic Party (or a Pat Buchanan-led Republican Party) could mobilize white middle-class Americans on the basis of class consciousness. I found no evidence that economic differences explain much of anything about the divide between Red and Blue America.

Ted Hale, a Presbyterian minister in the western part of the county, spoke of the matter this way: "There's nowhere near as much resentment as you would expect. People have come to understand that they will struggle financially. It's part of their identity. But the economy is not their god. That's the thing some others don't understand. People value a sense of community far more than they do their portfolio." Hale, who worked at a church in East Hampton, New York, before coming to Franklin County, said that he saw a lot more economic resentment in New York.

Hale's observations are supported by nationwide polling data. Pew has conducted a broad survey of the differences between Red and Blue states. The survey found that views on economic issues do not explain the different voting habits in the two regions. There simply isn't much of the sort of economic dissatisfaction that could drive a class-based political movement. Eighty-five percent of Americans with an annual household income between $30,000 and $50,000 are satisfied with their housing. Nearly 70 percent are satisfied with the kind of car they can afford. Roughly two thirds are satisfied with their furniture and their ability to afford a night out. These levels of satisfaction are not very different from those found in upper-middle-class America.

The Pew researchers found this sort of trend in question after question. Part of the draft of their report is titled "Economic Divide Dissolves."

A LOT OF RELIGION BUT FEW CRUSADERS

This leaves us with the second major hypothesis about the nature of the   55
divide between Red and Blue America, which comes mainly from conservatives: America is divided between two moral systems. Red America is
traditional, religious, self-disciplined, and patriotic. Blue America is modern,
secular, self-expressive, and discomfited by blatant displays of patriotism. Proponents of this hypothesis in its most radical form contend that America is in
the midst of a culture war, with two opposing armies fighting on behalf of
their views. The historian Gertrude Himmelfarb offered a more moderate
picture in *One Nation, Two Cultures* (1999), in which she argued that although
America is not fatally split, it is deeply divided, between a heartland conservative population that adheres to a strict morality and a liberal population that
lives by a loose one. The political journalist Michael Barone put it this way in
a recent essay in *National Journal*: "The two Americas apparent in the 48 percent to 48 percent 2000 election are two nations of different faiths. One is
observant, tradition-minded, moralistic. The other is unobservant, liberation-
minded, relativistic."

The values-divide school has a fair bit of statistical evidence on its side.
Whereas income is a poor predictor of voting patterns, church attendance — as
Barone points out — is a pretty good one. Of those who attend religious
services weekly (42 percent of the electorate), 59 percent voted for Bush,
39 percent for Gore. Of those who seldom or never attend religious services
(another 42 percent), 56 percent voted for Gore, 39 percent for Bush.

The Pew data reveal significant divides on at least a few values issues.
Take, for example, the statement "We will all be called before God on Judgment
Day to answer for our sins." In Red states 70 percent of the people believe that
statement. In Blue states only 50 percent do.

One can feel the religiosity in Franklin County after a single day's visit.
It's on the bumper stickers: WARNING: IN CASE OF RAPTURE THIS VEHICLE
WILL BE UNMANNED. REAL TRUCKERS TALK ABOUT JESUS ON CHANNEL 10.
It's on the radio. The airwaves are filled not with the usual mixture of hit
tunes but with evangelicals preaching the gospel. The book section of
Wal-Mart features titles such as *The Beginner's Guide to Fasting, Deepen Your
Conversation with God*, and *Are We Living in the End Times?* Some general
stores carry the "Heroes of the Faith" series, which consists of small biographies of William Carey, George Müller, and other notable missionaries,
ministers, and theologians — notable in Red America, that is, but largely
unknown where I live.

Chambersburg and its vicinity have eighty-five churches and one syna-
gogue. The Bethesda-Chevy Chase area, which has a vastly greater population,
has forty-five churches and five synagogues. Professors at the local college in
Chambersburg have learned not to schedule public lectures on Wednesday
nights, because everybody is at prayer meetings.

Events that are part of daily life in Franklin County are unheard of in   60
most of Blue America. One United Brethren minister told me that he is asked
to talk about morals in the public school as part of the health and sex-
education curriculum, and nobody raises a fuss. A number of schools have a
"Bible release program," whereby elementary school students are allowed to
leave school for an hour a week to attend Bible-study meetings. At an elementary school in Waynesboro the Gideons used to distribute Bibles to any
students who wanted them. (That ended after the village agnostic threatened
to simultaneously distribute a booklet called *God Is Just Pretend*.)

There are healing ministries all throughout Franklin County, and even
mainstream denominations have healing teams on hand after Sunday services. As
in most places where evangelism is strong, the locals are fervently pro-Israel.
Almost every minister I visited has mementos in his study from visits to Jerusalem.
A few had lived in Israel for extended periods and spoke Hebrew. One delivered a
tirade against CNN for its bias against the Jewish state. One or two pointed out
(without quite bragging) that whereas some Jewish groups had canceled trips to
Israel since the upsurge in intifada violence, evangelical groups were still going.

David Rawley, a United Brethren minister in Greencastle, spoke for many of
the social conservatives I met when he said that looking at the mainstream Hollywood culture made him feel that he was "walking against the current." "The
tremendous force of culture means we can either float or fight," Rawley said.
"Should you drift or stand on a rock? I tell people there is a rock we can hang on
— the word of God. That rock will never give way. That rock's never going to
move." When I asked Rawley what he thought of big-city culture, he said, "The
individual is swallowed up by the largeness of the city. I see a world that doesn't
want to take responsibility for itself. They have the babies but they decide they're
not going to be the daddies. I'd really have to cling to the rock if I lived there."

I met with Rawley at the height of the scandal involving Representative
Gary Condit and the missing intern Chandra Levy. Levy's mother was quoted
in *The Washington Times* as calling herself a "Heinz 57 mutt" when it came to
religion. "All religions tie to similar beliefs," she said. "I believe in spirituality
and God. I'm Jewish. I think we have a wonderful religion. I'm also Christian.
I do believe in Jesus, too." The contrast between her New Age approach to spirituality and Rawley's Red America one could not have been greater.

Life is complicated, however. Yes, there are a lot of churches in Franklin
County; there are also a lot of tattoo parlors. And despite all the churches and
bumper stickers, Franklin County doesn't seem much different from anywhere
else. People go to a few local bars to hang out after softball games. Teenagers
drive recklessly along fast-food strips. Young women in halter tops sometimes
prowl in the pool halls. The local college has a gay-and-lesbian group. One
conservative clergyman I spoke with estimated that 10 percent of his congregants are gay. He believes that church is the place where one should be able to
leave the controversy surrounding this sort of issue behind. Another described
how his congregation united behind a young man who was dying of AIDS.

Sex seems to be on people's minds almost as much as it is anywhere else. 65
Conservative evangelical circles have their own sex manuals (Tim LaHaye
wrote one of them before he moved on to the "Left Behind" series), which
appear to have had some effect: according to a 1994 study conducted by
researchers at the University of Chicago, conservative Protestant women have
more orgasms than any other group.

Franklin County is probably a bit more wholesome than most suburbs in
Blue America. (The notion that deviance and corruption lie underneath the
seeming conformism of suburban middle-class life, popular in Hollywood and
in creative-writing workshops, is largely nonsense.) But it has most of the problems that afflict other parts of the country: heroin addiction, teen pregnancy,
and so on. Nobody I spoke to felt part of a pristine culture that is exempt from
the problems of the big cities. There are even enough spectacular crimes in
Franklin County to make a devoted *New York Post* reader happy. During one of
my visits the front pages of the local papers were ablaze with the tale of a young
woman arrested for assault and homicide after shooting her way through a
Veterans of the Vietnam War post. It was reported that she had intended to rob
the post for money to run away with her lesbian girlfriend.

If the problems are the same as in the rest of America, so are many of the
solutions. Franklin County residents who find themselves in trouble go to their
clergy first, but they are often referred to psychologists and therapists as part of
their recovery process. Prozac is a part of life.

Almost nobody I spoke with understood, let alone embraced, the concept
of a culture war. Few could see themselves as fighting such a war, in part
because few have any idea where the boundary between the two sides lies. People in Franklin County may have a clear sense of what constitutes good or evil
(many people in Blue America have trouble with the very concept of evil), but
they will say that good and evil are in all neighborhoods, as they are in all of us.
People take the Scriptures seriously but have no interest in imposing them on
others. One finds little crusader zeal in Franklin County. For one thing, people
in small towns don't want to offend people whom they'll be encountering on
the street for the next fifty years. Potentially controversial subjects are often
played down. "We would never take a stance on gun control or abortion," Sue
Hadden, the editor of the Waynesboro paper, told me. Whenever I asked what
the local view of abortion was, I got the same response: "We don't talk about it
much," or "We try to avoid that subject." Bill Pukmel, the former Chambersburg newspaper editor, says, "A majority would be opposed to abortion around
here, but it wouldn't be a big majority." It would simply be uncivil to thrust
such a raw disagreement in people's faces.

William Harter, a Presbyterian minister in Chambersburg, spans the divide between Red and Blue America. Harter was raised on a farm near Buffalo.
He went to the prestigious Deerfield Academy, in Massachusetts, before getting
a bachelor's degree in history from Williams College, a master's in education
from Harvard, and, after serving for a while in the military, a Ph.D. in Judaism
and Christian origins from the Union Theological Seminary, in Manhattan. He

has lived in Chambersburg for the past twenty-four years, and he says that the range of opinion in Franklin County is much wider than it was in Cambridge or New York. "We're more authentically pluralistic here," he told me.

I found Harter and the other preachers in Franklin County especially   70
interesting to talk with. That was in part because the ones I met were fiercely intelligent and extremely well read, but also because I could see them wrestling with the problem of how to live according to the Scriptures while being inclusive and respectful of others' freedoms. For example, many of them struggle over whether it is right to marry a couple who are already living together. This would not be a consideration in most of Blue America.

"Some of the evangelicals won't marry [such couples]," Harter told me. "Others will insist that they live apart for six months before they'll marry them. But that's not the real world. These couples often don't understand the theological basis for not living together. Even if you don't condone their situations, you have to start where they are — help them have loyal marriages."

Divorce is tolerated much more than it used to be. And none of the ministers I spoke with said that they would condemn a parishioner who was having an affair. They would confront the parishioner, but with the goal of gently bringing that person back to Jesus Christ. "How could I love that person if I didn't?" Patrick Jones, of the United Brethren's King Street Church, in Chambersburg, asked. People in Franklin County are contemptuous of Bill Clinton and his serial infidelities, but they are not necessarily fans of Kenneth Starr — at least not the Kenneth Starr the media portrayed. They don't like public scolds.

Roger Murray, a Pentecostal minister in Mercersburg, whose father was also a Pentecostal minister, exemplifies the way in which many church authorities are torn by the sometimes conflicting desires to uphold authority and respect personal freedom. "My father would preach about what you could do and what you couldn't do," Murray recalls. "He would preach about smoking, about TV, about ladies who dress provocatively, against divorce." As a boy, Murray used to go visit his uncle, and he would sit in another room when his uncle's family watched television. "I was sure they were going to hell," he told me. But now he would never dream of telling people how to live. For one thing, his congregants wouldn't defer. And he is in no rush to condemn others. "I don't think preaching against homosexuality is what you should do," he told me. "A positive message works better."

Like most of the people I met in Franklin County, Murray regards such culture warriors as Jerry Falwell and Pat Robertson as loose cannons, and televangelists as being far too interested in raising money. "I get pretty disgusted with Christian TV," he said. And that was before Falwell and Robertson made their notorious comments about the attacks of September 11 being a judgment from God. When I asked locals about those remarks, they answered with words like "disgusting," "horrendous," and "horrible." Almost no one in the county voted for Pat Buchanan; he was simply too contentious.

Certainly Red and Blue America disagree strongly on some issues, such as homosexuality and abortion. But for the most part the disagreements are not large. For example, the Pew researchers asked Americans to respond to the statement "There are clear guidelines about what's good or evil that apply to everyone regardless of their situation." Forty-three percent of people in Blue states and 49 percent of people in Red states agreed. Forty-seven percent of Blue America and 55 percent of Red America agreed with the statement "I have old-fashioned values about family and marriage." Seventy percent of the people in Blue states and 77 percent of the people in Red states agreed that "too many children are being raised in day-care centers these days." These are small gaps. And, the Pew researchers found, there is no culture gap at all among suburban voters. In a Red state like Arizona suburban voters' opinions are not much different from those in a Blue state like Connecticut. The starkest differences that exist are between people in cities and people in rural areas, especially rural areas in the South.

The conservatism I found in Franklin County is not an ideological or a reactionary conservatism. It is a temperamental conservatism. People place tremendous value on being agreeable, civil, and kind. They are happy to sit quietly with one another. They are hesitant to stir one another's passions. They appreciate what they have. They value continuity and revere the past. They work hard to reinforce community bonds. Their newspapers are filled with items about fundraising drives, car washes, bake sales, penny-collection efforts, and auxiliary thrift shops. Their streets are lined with lodges: VFW, Rotarians, Elks, Moose. Luncheons go on everywhere. Retired federal employees will be holding their weekly luncheon at one restaurant, Harley riders at another. I became fascinated by a group called the Tuscarora Longbeards, a local chapter of something called the National Wild Turkey Federation. The Longbeards go around to schools distributing Wild About Turkey Education boxes, which contain posters, lesson plans, and CD-ROMs on turkey preservation.

These are the sorts of things that really mobilize people in Franklin County. Building community and preserving local ways are far more important to them than any culture war.

THE EGO CURTAIN

The best explanation of the differences between people in Montgomery and Franklin Counties has to do with sensibility, not class or culture. If I had to describe the differences between the two sensibilities in a single phrase, it would be conception of the self. In Red America the self is small. People declare in a million ways, "I am normal. Nobody is better, nobody is worse. I am humble before God." In Blue America the self is more commonly large. People say in a million ways, "I am special. I have carved out my own unique way of life. I am independent. I make up my own mind."

In Red America there is very little one-upmanship. Nobody tries to be avant-garde in choosing a wardrobe. The chocolate-brown suits and baggy denim dresses hanging in local department stores aren't there by accident; people conspicuously want to be seen as not trying to dress to impress.

For a person in Blue America the blandness in Red America can be a little oppressive. But it's hard not to be struck by the enormous social pressure not to put on airs. If a Franklin County resident drove up to church one day in a shiny new Lexus, he would face huge waves of disapproval. If one hired a nanny, people would wonder who died and made her queen.   80

In Franklin County people don't go looking for obscure beers to demonstrate their connoisseurship. They wear T-shirts and caps with big-brand names on them — Coke, McDonald's, Chevrolet. In Bethesda people prefer cognoscenti brands — the Black Dog restaurant, or the independent bookstore Politics and Prose. In Franklin County it would be an affront to the egalitarian ethos to put a Princeton sticker on the rear window of one's car. In Montgomery County some proud parents can barely see through their back windows for all the Ivy League stickers. People in Franklin County say they felt comfortable voting for Bush, because if he came to town he wouldn't act superior to anybody else; he could settle into a barber's chair and fit right in. They couldn't stand Al Gore, because they thought he'd always be trying to awe everyone with his accomplishments. People in Montgomery County tended to admire Gore's accomplishments. They were leery of Bush, because for most of his life he seemed not to have achieved anything.

I sometimes think that Franklin County takes its unpretentiousness a little too far. I wouldn't care to live there, because I'd find it too unchanging. I prefer the subtle and not-so-subtle status climbing on my side of the Ego Curtain — it's more entertaining. Still, I can't help respecting the genuine modesty of Franklin County people. It shows up strikingly in data collected by Mediamark Research. In survey after survey, residents of conservative Red America come across as humbler than residents of liberal Blue America. About half of those who describe themselves as "very conservative" agree with the statement "I have more ability than most people," but nearly two thirds of those who describe themselves as "very liberal" agree. Only 53 percent of conservatives agree with the statement "I consider myself an intellectual," but 75 percent of liberals do. Only 23 percent of conservatives agree with the statement "I must admit that I like to show off," whereas 43 percent of liberals do.

A Cafeteria Nation

These differences in sensibility don't in themselves mean that America has become a fundamentally divided nation. As the sociologist Seymour Martin Lipset pointed out in *The First New Nation* (1963), achievement and equality are the two rival themes running throughout American history. Most people, most places, and most epochs have tried to intertwine them in some way.

Moreover, after bouncing between Montgomery and Franklin Counties, I became convinced that a lot of our fear that America is split into rival camps arises from mistaken notions of how society is shaped. Some of us still carry the old Marxist categories in our heads. We think that society is like a layer cake, with the upper class on top. And, like Marx, we tend to assume that wherever there is class division there is conflict. Or else we have a sort of *Crossfire* model in our heads: where would people we meet sit if they were guests on that show?

But traveling back and forth between the two counties was not like cross- 85 ing from one rival camp to another. It was like crossing a high school cafeteria. Remember high school? There were nerds, jocks, punks, bikers, techies, druggies, God Squadders, drama geeks, poets, and Dungeons & Dragons weirdoes. All these cliques were part of the same school: they had different sensibilities; sometimes they knew very little about the people in the other cliques; but the jocks knew there would always be nerds, and the nerds knew there would always be jocks. That's just the way life is.

And that's the way America is. We are not a divided nation. We are a cafeteria nation. We form cliques (call them communities, or market segments, or whatever), and when they get too big, we form subcliques. Some people even get together in churches that are "nondenominational" or in political groups that are "independent." These are cliques built around the supposed rejection of cliques.

We live our lives by migrating through the many different cliques associated with the activities we enjoy and the goals we have set for ourselves. Our freedom comes in the interstices; we can choose which set of standards to live by, and when.

We should remember that there is generally some distance between cliques — a buffer zone that separates one set of aspirations from another. People who are happy within their cliques feel no great compulsion to go out and reform other cliques. The jocks don't try to change the nerds. David Rawley, the Greencastle minister who felt he was clinging to a rock, has been to New York City only once in his life. "I was happy to get back home," he told me. "It's a planet I'm a little scared of. I have no desire to go back."

What unites the two Americas, then, is our mutual commitment to this way of life — to the idea that a person is not bound by his class, or by the religion of his fathers, but is free to build a plurality of connections for himself. We are participants in the same striving process, the same experimental journey.

Never has this been more apparent than in the weeks following the 90 September 11 attacks. Before then Montgomery County people and Franklin County people gave little thought to one another: an attitude of benign neglect toward other parts of the country generally prevailed. But the events of that day generated what one of my lunch mates in Franklin County called a primal response. Our homeland was under attack. Suddenly there was a positive sense that we Americans are all bound together — a sense that, despite some little fissures here and there, has endured.

On September 11 people in Franklin County flocked to the institutions that are so strong there — the churches and the American Legion and the VFW posts. Houses of worship held spontaneous prayer services and large ecumenical services. In the weeks since, firemen, veterans, and Scouts have held rallies. There have been blood drives. Just about every service organization in the county — and there are apparently thousands — has mobilized to raise funds or ship teddy bears. The rescue squad and the Salvation Army branch went to New York to help.

Early every morning Ted Hale, the Presbyterian minister who once worked in East Hampton, goes to one of the local restaurants and sits as the regulars cycle through. One of the things that has struck him since the attacks is how little partisan feeling is left. "I expected to hear a certain amount of Clinton bashing, for creating the mess in which this could take place," he told me in October. "But there's been absolutely none of that." Instead Hale has been deluged with questions — about Islam, about why God restrains himself in the face of evil, about how people could commit such acts.

The area's churches have not been monolithic in their responses. Many of the most conservative churches — the Mennonites and the Brethren, for example — have pacifist traditions. Bill Harter, in contrast, told his congregation during a recent sermon that the pacifist course is not the right one. "We must face the fact that there is a power of evil loose in the universe, which is dedicated to attacking all that is good, all that comes from God," he said. This evil, Harter continued, has cloaked itself in a perverted form of one of the world's major faiths. Citing the Protestant theologian Reinhold Niebuhr, he reminded his congregants that there is no sinless way to defend ourselves against this hostile ideology. But defend we must. "We must humbly make our choice while recognizing that we must constantly turn to God for forgiveness," he told them.

The churches and synagogues in Bethesda, too, have been struggling. Over the Jewish High Holy Days, I heard of three synagogues in which the sermon was interrupted by a member of the congregation. In one instance the rabbi had said that it is always impossible to know where good and evil lie. A man rose up angrily to declare that in this case that sentiment was nonsense.

Most people in my part of Blue America know few who will be called on to fight in the war. In Franklin County military service is common. Many families have an enlisted son or daughter, and many more have a relative in the reserves or the National Guard. Franklin County is engaged in an urgent discussion, largely absent where I live, about how to fill in for the reservists called up for active duty.

Still, there's an attitude of determination in both places. If I had to boil down all the conversations I have had in Franklin and Montgomery Counties since September 11, the essence would be this: A horrible thing happened. We're going to deal with it. We're going to restore order. We got through Pearl Harbor. We're going to get through this. "There is no flaccidity," Harter observed, in words that apply to both communities.

If the September 11 attacks rallied people in both Red and Blue America, they also neutralized the political and cultural leaders who tend to exploit the differences between the two. Americans are in no mood for a class struggle or a culture war. The aftermath of the attacks has been a bit like a national Sabbath, taking us out of our usual pleasures and distractions and reminding us what is really important. Over time the shock will dissipate. But in important ways the psychological effects will linger, just as the effects of John F. Kennedy's assassination have lingered. The early evidence still holds: although there are some real differences between Red and Blue America, there is no fundamental conflict. There may be cracks, but there is no chasm. Rather, there is a common love for this nation — one nation in the end.

Reading across Disciplines
ROBERT C. BULMAN, Sociology

For a political journalist, David Brooks has a pretty good sociological imagination. That is, he seeks to explain phenomena not simply by looking at the attitudes and behaviors of individuals, but by looking at how those attitudes and behaviors are often patterned by individuals' membership in different social groups. Brooks is correct to think that a sociological analysis might reveal something about the ways we make sense of the world and the ways in which we act within it.

In this article, Brooks is largely concerned with understanding the so-called cultural divide between residents of "red" and "blue" states. It is true that in the 2000 presidential election (and again in 2004) there was an apparent divide between residents of urban and coastal areas (the "blue" Democrats) and residents of the rural interior of the country (the "red" Republicans). Just what explains these differences, and do they signal a dangerous cultural divide in the United States?

Brooks does what any good sociologist would do — he seeks to explain the differences between the "red" and "blue" states by looking at the different social characteristics of the different areas. While a sociologist would approach the investigation more systematically and scientifically with a carefully designed research project, representative samples, and statistical controls (as opposed to Brooks's anecdotal methods), most sociologists would look at many of the same variables that Brooks does.

For instance, Brooks looks at how the variables of social class and religion might help to explain the key difference between the "red" and the "blue" states. He dismisses the argument that social-class inequality explains the difference since he finds no support for class resentment among the working-class folks he talked to. However, as a sociologist,

I would fault Brooks for conceiving of social class too narrowly. It is not enough to measure class by looking at income statistics. Class is also measured by wealth (net assets), educational attainment, occupational status, and what sociologists call "cultural capital." In other words, styles of life (an interest in NASCAR rather than in yacht racing, for instance) may be expressions of important class differences that Brooks overlooks.

Brooks finds more support for the argument that the differences between the "red" and "blue" states are influenced by moral concerns. Active membership in a religious community does seem to explain some of the electoral differences between people in "red" and "blue" states. However, I agree with Brooks that this should not be overstated. While there are some significant moral issues that divide the country, there are perhaps many more issues upon which we share a moral perspective.

I agree with Brooks's conclusion that there is no fundamental "culture war" in the United States. We are, as he argues, a diverse and pluralistic nation (much like cliques in a high school cafeteria). However, I also think that Brooks ended his investigation too soon. There are many more important sociological variables besides class and religion that I wish he had explored. For instance, what about race? Non-whites voted overwhelmingly for Gore. What about gender? Women voted for Gore. What about age? Young people voted for Gore. There are more social cleavages in the United States than class, religion, and the urban/rural divide. Perhaps we have made too much of the difference between the so-called "red" and "blue" states. After all, the "red" states of Missouri, Nevada, and Ohio voted for Bush by majorities of only 51 percent, 49 percent, and 50 percent, respectively. Furthermore, while urban centers voted in favor of Gore and rural areas tended to vote in favor of Bush, the suburbs were very evenly divided. Perhaps we aren't so much "red" and "blue" as we are purple.

Robert C. Bulman is an associate professor of sociology at St. Mary's College of California.

QUESTIONING THE TEXT

1. Whom do you envision as Brooks's primary audience? Do you think he writes mainly to people in Red or Blue America? What evidence in the essay supports your speculation about his audience?

2. With a classmate, locate and count the assertions Brooks makes about Red and Blue America. How many of each do you find? What do these numbers tell you about the focus of the essay? For each of the assertions, what kind of support does Brooks offer? Do you find his characterizations of Red and Blue America convincing? Why or why not?

3. Reread Brooks's essay, tracing his reasoning from the images he presents of the divided America shown on the map of 2000 election results (see p. 9) to his conclusion that the United States is "one nation in the end" (paragraph 97). Does he persuade you that this conclusion is true? Write a response to his essay in which you support or challenge his view, providing reasons for your claims.

MAKING CONNECTIONS

4. Read the Declaration of Independence (p. 492), and consider the common principles and values espoused by the signers of that document. Compare those principles or values with the ones that Brooks identifies as uniting Americans today. What similarities and differences do you find? Use this comparison to discuss in class how you think American ideals may have changed, or how they may have endured, from 1776 until now.

5. How might Brooks's description of Red and Blue America make sense of New Orleans, a place that Nicholas Lemann argues in "In the Ruins" (p. 586) has long suffered from a "deep civic weakness" and that has been largely destroyed by the ravages of Hurricane Katrina? How does post-Katrina New Orleans fit into Brooks's description of American culture?

JOINING THE CONVERSATION

6. Think of a cultural divide that you might examine in the way Brooks did. Is there a rival school or college, or a neighborhood that on the surface appears very different from your own, which you might visit for a day and report on? Write an essay in which you illuminate the differences you perceive between the two cultures. Try to assess the extent to which these differences are sustained by myths — by beliefs passed on from one generation to another through narratives.

7. For class discussion, think about whether you identify with Brooks's characterizations of Blue or Red America — or Franklin or Montgomery counties. Do you see yourself on either side of the divide, or perhaps "span[ning] the divide" as Brooks describes William Harter (paragraph 69)? Jot down the ways in which you identify with some of his descriptions, or ways in which they seem foreign to you. Bring your notes, to share your response with classmates. Consider using your ideas as the basis for an op-ed for a newspaper or guest column for a magazine.

BARBARA KINGSOLVER
And Our Flag Was Still There

THE FLAG IS ONE OF THE OLDEST and most enduring elements of American mythology, a supreme symbol of patriotism. As Barbara Kingsolver (b. 1955) points out in the essay that follows, the flag and other American icons "grew out of war," a fact she alludes to in her title with its evocations of the "rockets' red glare" in the national anthem. For Kingsolver, this original association goes a long way toward explaining why, in the debate over what patriotic should mean, those linking patriotism and war have a strong upper hand.

In the aftermath of September 11, 2001, and the wars that followed, Kingsolver argues that it is time to "retire the rockets' red glare and the bloody bandage as obsolete symbols of Old Glory." Kingsolver knows such a goal is daunting, given the hate crimes and hate speech directed against many of those who stand up for peace rather than war or question the righteousness of making war. Yet this peaceful kind of patriotism has its place in America too, says Kingsolver: the flag belongs to all of us, she says, and she insists on waving it over "a few things I believe in," including our nation's commitment to protecting dissenting points of view.

Born and raised in Kentucky, Kingsolver graduated from DePauw University and later received a master of science degree from the University of Arizona. She worked at a number of professions, including x-ray technician and freelance journalist, before turning to fiction. Her novel The Bean Trees, *published in 1988, was followed by* Animal Dreams *(1990);* Pigs in Heaven *(1993);* The Poisonwood Bible *(1998), which was a finalist for the Pulitzer Prize for fiction; and* Prodigal Summer *(2000).*

Kingsolver says that reading Doris Lessing led her to "understand how a person could write about the problems of the world in a compelling and beautiful way. And it seemed to me that was the most important thing I could ever do. . . ." In her fiction and in her essays, including the one reprinted here, Kingsolver does write about the problems of our world, and she does so compellingly. As you read this essay, which comes from her collection Small Wonder *(2002), you may want to consider your own definitions of patriotism and the associations the American flag holds for you. How do they compare to those described in "And Our Flag Was Still There"?* —A.L.

My daughter came home from kindergarten and announced, "Tomorrow we all have to wear red, white, and blue."

"Why?" I asked, trying not to sound anxious.

"For all the people that died when the airplanes hit the buildings."

I said quietly, "Why not wear black, then? Why the colors of the flag, what does that mean?"

"It means we're a country. Just all people together."

I love my country dearly. Not long after the September 11 attacks, as I stood in a high school cafeteria listening to my older daughter and a hundred other teenagers in the orchestra play "Stars and Stripes Forever" on their earnest, vibrating strings, I burst into tears of simultaneous pride and grief. I love what we will do for one another in the name of inclusion and kindness. So I long to feel comforted and thrilled by the sight of Old Glory, as so many others seem to feel when our country plunges into war or dire straits. Symbols are many things to many people. In those raw months following the September 11 attacks, I saw my flag waved over used car and truck lots, designer-label clothing sales, and the funerals of genuine heroes. In my lifetime I have seen it waved over the sound of saber-rattling too many times for my comfort. When I heard about this kindergarten red-white-and-blue plan, my first impulse was to dread that my sweet child was being dragged to the newly patriotic cause of wreaking death in the wake of death. Nevertheless, any symbol conceived in liberty deserves the benefit of the doubt. We sent her to school in its colors because it felt to my daughter like some small thing she could do to help the people who were hurting. And because my wise husband put a hand on my arm and said, "You can't let hateful people steal the flag from us."

He didn't mean foreign terrorists, he meant certain Americans. Like the man in a city near us who went on a rampage, crying "I'm an American" as he shot at foreign-born neighbors, killing a gentle Sikh man in a turban and terrifying every brown-skinned person I know. Or the talk-radio hosts who viciously bullied members of Congress and anyone else for showing sensible skepticism during the mad rush toward war. After Representative Barbara Lee cast the House's only vote against handing over virtually unlimited war powers to a man whom fully half of us — let's be honest — didn't support a year before, so many red-blooded Americans threatened to kill her that she had to be assigned additional bodyguards.

While the anthrax threats in congressional and media offices were minute-by-minute breaking news, the letters of pseudo-patriotism carrying equally deadly threats to many other citizens did not get coverage. Hate radio reaches thousands of avid listeners, and fear stalked many families in the autumn and winter of our nation's discontent, when belonging to *any* minority — including the one arguing for peaceful and diplomatic solutions to violence — was enough to put one at risk. When fear rules the day, many minds are weak enough to crack the world into nothing but "me" and "evildoers," and as long as we're proudly killing unlike minds over there, they feel emboldened to do the same over here. For minds like that, the great attraction to patriotism is, as Aldous Huxley wrote, that "it fulfills our worst wishes. In the person of our nation we are able, vicariously, to bully and cheat. Bully and cheat, what's more, with a feeling that we are profoundly virtuous."

Such cowards have surely never arrived at a majority in this country, though their power has taken the helm in such dark moments as the McCarthy persecutions and the Japanese American internments. At such times, patriotism falls to whoever claims it loudest, and the rest of us are left struggling to find a definition in a clamor of reaction. In the days and months following September 11, some bully-patriots claiming to own my flag promoted a brand of nationalism that threatened freedom of speech and religion with death, as witnessed by the Sikhs and Muslims in my own community, and U.S. Representative Barbara Lee in hers. (Several of her colleagues confessed they wanted to vote the same way she did, but were frightened by the obvious threat from vigilante patriots.) Such men were infuriated by thoughtful hesitation, constructive criticism of our leaders, and pleas for peace. They ridiculed and despised people of foreign birth (one of our congressmen actually used the hideous term "rag heads") who've spent years becoming part of our culture and contributing their labor and talents to our economy. In one stunning statement uttered by a fundamentalist religious leader, this brand of patriotism specifically blamed homosexuals, feminists, and the American Civil Liberties Union for the horrors of September 11. In other words, these hoodlum-Americans were asking me to believe that their flag stood for intimidation, censorship, violence, bigotry, sexism, homophobia, and shoving the Constitution through a paper shredder? Well, *our* flag does not, and I'm determined that it never will. Outsiders can destroy airplanes and buildings, but only we the people have the power to demolish our own ideals.

It's a fact of our culture that the loudest mouths get the most airplay, and the loudmouths are saying that in times of crisis it's treasonous to question our leaders. Nonsense. That kind of thinking allowed the seeds of a dangerous racism to grow into fascism during the international economic crisis of the 1930s. It is precisely in critical times that our leaders need *most* to be influenced by the moderating force of dissent. That is the basis of democracy, especially when national choices are difficult and carry grave consequences. The flag was never meant to be a stand-in for information and good judgment.   10

In the wake of the September 11 attacks, an amazing windfall befell our local flag-and-map store, which had heretofore been one of the sleepiest little independent businesses in the city. Suddenly it was swamped with unprecedented hordes of customers who came in to buy not maps, of course, but flags. After the stock quickly sold out, a cashier reported that customers came near to rioting as they stomped around empty-handed and the waiting list swelled to six hundred names. She said a few customers demanded to know why she personally wasn't in the back room sewing more Old Glories. Had I been in her position, I might have said, "Hey, friends and countrymen, wouldn't this be a great time to buy yourselves a map?" The sturdiest form of national pride is educated about the alternatives. And in fairness to my more polite compatriots, I was greatly heartened in that same season to see the country's best-seller lists suddenly swollen with books about Islam and relevant political history.

We're a much nobler country than our narrowest minds and loudest mouths suggest. I believe it is *my* patriotic duty to recapture my flag from the men who wave it in the name of jingoism and censorship. This is difficult, for many reasons. To begin with, when we civil libertarians on the one hand insist that every voice in the political spectrum must be heard, and the hard right on the other hand insists that our side should stuff a sock in it, the deck is stacked. And the next challenge is, I can never hope to match their nationalistic right-eousness. The last time I looked at a flag with an unambiguous thrill, I was thirteen. Right after that, Vietnam began teaching me lessons in ambiguity, and the lessons have kept coming. I've learned of things my government has done to the world that make me shudder: Covert assassinations of democratically elected leaders in Chile and the Congo; support of brutal dictators in dozens of nations because they smiled on our economic interests; training of torturers in a military camp in Georgia; secret support even of the rising Taliban in Afghanistan, until that business partnership came to a nasty end. In history books and numbers of our *Congressional Record* I've discovered many secrets that made me ashamed of how my country's proud ideology sometimes places last, after money for the win and power for the show. And yet, when I've dared to speak up about these skeletons in our closet, I've been further alienated from my flag by people who waved it at me, declaring I should love it or leave it. I always wonder, What makes them think that's their flag and not mine? Why are *they* the good Americans, and not me? I have never shrunk from sacrifice but have always faced it head on when I needed to, in order to defend the American ideals of freedom and human kindness.

I've been told the pacifists should get down on their knees and thank the men who gave their lives for our freedom, and I've thought about this, a lot. I believe absolutely that the American Revolution and the Civil War were ideolog-ical confrontations; if I had been born to a different time and gender with my present character otherwise intact, I might well have joined them, at least as a medic, or something. (Where I grew up, I'd likely have been conscripted into dying for the wrong side in the Civil War, but that's another story.) I wish I could claim to possess a nature I could honestly call pacifist, but I've had long friendships with genuine pacifists in the Quaker community and have seen in them a quality I lack. I can rarely summon the strength to pray for my enemies, as some do every day. On the rare occasions when my life has been put directly at risk by another, I've clawed like a lioness. My gut, if not my head, is a devotee of self-defense.

But my head is unconvinced by the sleight of hand and sloganeering that put the label "self-defense" on certain campaigns waged far from my bedroom win-dow, against people who have no wish to come anywhere near it. It's extremely important to note that in my lifetime our multitude of wars in Central America and the Middle East have been not so much about the freedom of humans as about the freedom of financial markets. My spiritual faith does not allow me to accept equivalence of these two values; I wonder that anyone's does.

Our entry into wars most resembling self-defense, World War II and the 2001 Afghanistan campaign, both followed direct attacks on our country. The latter, at least, remains a far more convoluted entanglement than the headlines ever suggested. In the 1990s, most of us have now learned, the United States tacitly supported the viciously sexist, violent Taliban warlords — only to then

15

bomb them out of power in 2001. I'm profoundly relieved to see any such violent men removed from command, of course. But I'm deeply uncomfortable, also, with the notion that two wrongs add up to one right, and I'm worried about the next turn of that logic. It is only prudent to ask questions, and only reasonable to discuss alternate, less violent ways to promote the general welfare. Americans who read and think have frequently seen how the much-touted "national interest" can differ drastically from their own.

And Americans who read and think are patriots of the first order — the kind who know enough to roll their eyes whenever anyone tries to claim sole custody of the flag and wield it as a blunt instrument. There are as many ways to love America as there are Americans, and our country needs us all. The rights and liberties described in our Constitution are guaranteed not just to those citizens who have the most money and power, but also to those who have the least, and yet it has taken hard struggle through every year of our history to hold our nation to that promise. Dissidents innocent of any crime greater than a belief in fair treatment of our poorest and ill-treated citizens have died right here on American soil for our freedom, as tragically as any soldier in any war: Karen Silkwood, Medgar Evars, Malcolm X, Denise McNair, Cynthia Wesley, Carole Robertson, Addie Mae Collins, Martin Luther King Jr., Albert Parsons, August Spies, Adolph Fisher, George Engel, Joe Hill, Nicola Sacco, Bartolomeo Vanzetti — the list of names stretches on endlessly and makes me tremble with gratitude. Any of us who steps up to the platform of American protest is standing on bloodstained and hallowed ground, and let no one ever dare call it un-American or uncourageous. While we peace lovers are down on our knees with gratitude, as requested, the warriors might do well to get down here with us and give thanks for Dr. King and Gandhi and a thousand other peacemakers who gave their lives to help lift humanity out of the trough of bare-toothed carnage. Where in the Bill of Rights is it written that the entitlement to bear arms — and use them — trumps any aspiration to peaceful solutions? I search my soul and find I cannot rejoice over killing, but that does not make me any less a citizen. When I look at the flag, why must I see it backlit with the rockets' red glare?

The first time I thought of it that way, I stumbled on a huge revelation. *This* is why the war supporters so easily gain the upper hand in the patriot game: Our nation was established with a fight for independence, so our iconography grew out of war. Anyone who is tempted to dismiss art as useless in matters of politics must agree that art is supremely powerful here, in connecting patriotism with war. Our national anthem celebrates it; our nationalist imagery memorializes it; our most familiar poetry of patriotism is inseparable from a battle cry. Our every military campaign is still launched with phrases about men dying for the freedoms we hold dear, even when this is impossible to square with reality. During the Gulf War [1990–91] I heard plenty of words about freedom's defense as our military rushed to the aid of Kuwait, a monarchy in which women enjoyed approximately the same rights as a nineteenth-century American slave. The values we fought for there are best understood by oil companies and the royalty of Saudi Arabia — the ones who asked us to do this work on the

Iraq-Kuwaiti border, and with whom we remain friendly. (Not incidentally, we have never confronted the Saudis about women-hating Wahhabism and vast, unending support for schools of anti-American wrath.) After a swift and celebrated U.S. victory, a nation of Iraqi civilians was left with its hospitals, its water-delivery lines, and its food-production systems devastated, its capacity for reconstruction crushed by our ongoing economic sanctions, and its fate — at the time of this writing — still in the hands of one of the vilest dictators I've ever read about. There's the reality of war for you: Freedom often *loses*.

Stating these realities is not so poetic, granted, but it is absolutely a form of patriotism. Questioning our government's actions does not violate the principles of liberty, equality, and freedom of speech; it exercises them, and by exercise we grow stronger. I have read enough of Thomas Jefferson to feel sure he would back me up on this. Our founding fathers, those vocal critics of imperialism, were among the world's first leaders to understand that to a democratic people, freedom of speech and belief are not just nice luxuries, they're as necessary as breathing. The authors of our Constitution knew, from experience with King George and company, that governments don't remain benevolent to the interests of all, including their less powerful members, without constant vigilance and reasoned criticism. And so the founding fathers guaranteed the right of reasoned criticism in our citizenship contract — for *always*. No emergency shutdowns allowed. However desperate things may get, there are to be no historical moments when beliefs can be abridged, vegetarians required to praise meat, Christians forced to pray as Muslims, or vice versa. Angry critics have said to me in stressful periods, "Don't you understand it's *wartime?*" As if this were just such a historical moment of emergency shutdown. Yes, we all know it's wartime. It's easy to speak up for peace in peacetime — anybody can do that. Now is when it gets hard. But our flag is not just a logo for wars; it's the flag of American pacifists, too. It's the flag of all of us who love our country enough to do the hard work of living up to its highest ideals.

I have two American flags. Both were gifts. One was handmade out of colored paper by my younger child; it's a few stars shy of regulation but nonetheless cherished. Each has its place in my home, so I can look up from time to time and remember. That's *mine*. Maybe this is hard for some men to understand, but that emblem wasn't handed to me by soldiers on foreign soil; it wasn't *handed* to me by men at all — they withheld it from women for our nation's first century and a half. I would never have gained it if everyone's idea of patriotism had been simply to go along with the status quo. That flag protects and represents me only because of Ida B. Wells, Lucy Stone, Susan B. Anthony, and countless other women who risked everything so I could be a full citizen. Each of us who is female, or nonwhite, or without land, would have been guaranteed in 1776 the same voting rights as a horse. We owe a precious debt to courageous Americans before us who risked threats and public ridicule for an unpopular cause: ours. Now that flag is mine to carry on, promising me that I may, and that I must, continue believing in the dignity and sanctity of life, and stating that position in a public forum.

And so I would like to stand up for my flag and wave it over a few things   20
I believe in, including but not limited to the protection of dissenting points of
view. After 225 years, I vote to retire the rockets' red glare and the bloody bandage as obsolete symbols of Old Glory. We desperately need a new iconography of patriotism. I propose that we rip strips of cloth from the uniforms of the
unbelievably courageous firefighters who rescued the injured and panic-
stricken from the World Trade Center on September 11, 2001, and remained
at their posts until the buildings collapsed on them. Praise the red glare of candles held up in vigils everywhere as peace-loving people pray for the bereaved
and plead for compassionate resolutions. Honor the blood donated to the Red
Cross; respect the stars of all kinds who have used their influence to raise funds
for humanitarian assistance; glory in the generous hands of schoolchildren collecting pennies, teddy bears, and anything else they think might help the kids
who've lost their moms and dads. Let me sing praise to the ballot box and the
jury box, and to the unyielding protest marches of my foremothers who fought
for those rights so I could be fully human under our Constitution. What could
be a more honorable symbol of American freedom than the suffragist's banner,
the striker's picket, the abolitionist's drinking gourd, the placards of humane
protest from every decade of our forward-marching history? Let me propose
aloud that the dove is at least as honorable a creature as the carnivorous eagle.
And give me liberty, now, with signs of life.

Shortly after the September attacks, my town became famous for a simple gesture in which some eight thousand people wearing red, white, or blue
T-shirts assembled themselves in the shape of a flag on a baseball field and had
their photograph taken from above. That picture soon began to turn up everywhere, but we saw it first on our newspaper's front page. Our family stood in
silence for a minute looking at that stunningly beautiful photograph of a
human flag, trying to know what to make of it. Then my teenager, who has a
quick mind for numbers and a sensitive heart, did an interesting thing. She laid
her hand over part of the picture, leaving visible more or less five thousand
people, and said, "In New York, that many might be dead." We stared at what
that looked like — that many innocent souls, particolored and packed into a
conjoined destiny — and shuddered at the one simple truth behind all the
noise, which was that so many beloved, fragile lives were suddenly gone from
us. That is my flag, and that's what it means: We're all just people, together.

QUESTIONING THE TEXT

1. Briefly summarize Kingsolver's argument. What is her main claim? How
   does she support that claim?

2. In personal anecdotes, Kingsolver provides glimpses into her life, describing scenes with her family and neighbors. She also alludes to a wide range
   of historical and political personages and events. With a classmate, examine

some of these people and narratives, and discuss the rhetorical purposes you think they may serve in this essay. Which of the allusions and illustrations do you find most compelling, and why? Do you think the diverse range of characters and events that populate Kingsolver's essay help make it more persuasive? Why or why not?

3. Kingsolver presents a list of people she describes as "[d]issidents innocent of any crime greater than a belief in fair treatment of our poorest and ill-treated citizens" — dissidents who "have died right here on American soil for our freedom" (paragraph 16). How many of the people on this list have you heard of? Divide up the list among classmates, and do some research on these individuals — where and when they lived, the causes they championed, how they died. Present your findings in class, and discuss why Kingsolver believes these people are worthy of admiration for their struggles. Do you agree with Kingsolver's judgment about them? Why or why not?

MAKING CONNECTIONS

4. With a classmate, compare Kingsolver's essay to Frederick Douglass's speech, "What to the Slave Is the Fourth of July?" (p. 497). Both writers argue for their right to be included in national practices of patriotism. How do their arguments differ, and how are they similar? Share your observations in a discussion with the whole class.

5. Toward the end of her essay, Kingsolver lists "a few things I believe in" (paragraph 20). Note her list of people who she thinks should be considered heroic. How does her idea of heroism compare to Dulce Pinzón's in her photo essay of immigrant workers dressed as superheroes (see color insert)? Whose notion of heroism do you find more compelling?

JOINING THE CONVERSATION

6. As Kingsolver uses a line from the national anthem for the title of her essay, choose a line from a patriotic text — perhaps the Declaration of Independence (p. 492) or the Preamble to the Constitution — and imagine it as a title for a brief essay that you might publish online or in a periodical. In your essay, try to convey anew the significance of the line you've chosen as your title, illuminating its meaning for you and your readers, here and now.

7. As A.L. suggests in her headnote, consider your own definitions of *patriotism* and the associations the American flag holds for you. How do they compare to those described in "And Our Flag Was Still There"? Freewrite on this topic, and be prepared to share your thoughts in class discussion.

MIM UDOVITCH
A Secret Society of the Starving

I HAVE BEEN TEACHING *for over thirty years now, and during those three decades I have watched with growing alarm as students, almost all of them women, struggled with eating disorders. Over the years, I learned to identify the signs, to watch for them and then to worry myself into a conversation — sometimes a confrontation — with the student. Very rarely have I been wrong in my assessment. But just as rarely have I been able to be of much help.*

In "A Secret Society of the Starving," pop culture critic Mim Udovitch helps me understand why, as she reports on interviews with three young women — Clairegirl, Chaos, and Futurebird — who talk of their experience with anorexia and bulimia. These women, who all crave control and use eating (and not eating) as one way of exerting it, often see their eating problem as a matter of choice, as a lifestyle rather than a "disorder." And like my students with similar issues, these women have a lot going for them; one of them has a job and is a double major in college; she also plays a musical instrument and is an accomplished photographer. Yet she is obsessive-compulsive and a severe bulimic who, as Udovitch points out, "stands a very real chance of dying any time."

Along with her discussions with the young women, Udovitch explores the many blogs and Web sites associated with eating disorders. Particularly troubling are the "pro-ana" sites that glorify thinness and tout the power of self-control: the "Ana creed" on one site says "I believe in Control, the only force mighty enough to bring order into the chaos that is my world." This same creed continues with "I believe that I am the most vile, worthless and useless person ever to have existed on this planet." And how to become less vile? Purify, purify, fast, fast, fast. As one girl says, pro-ana "is a virtue, almost. Like if you do wrong and you eat, then you sin."

According to Udovitch, "one in two hundred American women suffers from anorexia; two or three in one hundred suffer from bulimia." The results of such numbers are grim indeed, with eating disorders leading to suicide and to high fatality rates. Yet for the women Udovitch talks with, eating disorders represent a "coping mechanism," and the pro-ana sites are a way to belong to a community, to make connections with others. But, as the director of an eating disorder clinic says, such connection may be illusory at best: " . . . they become very isolated. Women with eating disorders really thrive in a lot of ways on being disconnected. At the same time, of course, they have a yearning to be connected."

Udovitch's essay appeared in the New York Times *in 2002, and as I read it I determined to keep watching for students who may be in trouble. I wonder if Mim Udovitch, a contributing editor at* Rolling Stone *who has also written about popular culture for* Slate, Esquire, *and* New York Magazine, *came away from writing this essay with any conclusions about how to respond to friends, family members, or others with eating disorders. If so, she doesn't disclose them here — and doing so was clearly not her intent. Yet I wonder if you are like me in knowing people — and people about whom you care a great deal — who are anorexic or bulimic. In such cases, where do our responsibilities lie?*

—A.L.

Claire is 18. She is a pretty teenager, with long strawberry-blond hair, and she is almost abnormally self-possessed for a girl from a small town who has suddenly been descended upon by a big-city reporter who is there to talk to her, in secret, about her secret life. She is sitting on the track that runs around the field of her high school's football stadium, wearing running shorts and a T-shirt and shivering a little because even through we are in Florida — in the kind of town where, according to Claire, during "season" when you see yet another car with New York plates, you just feel like running it down — there's an evening chill.

Claire's is also the kind of town where how the local high school does in sports matters. Claire herself plays two sports. Practice and team fund-raisers are a regular part of her life, along with the typical small-town-Florida teenage occupations — going to "some hick party," hanging out with friends in the parking lot of the Taco Bell, bowling, going to the beach.

Another regular part of her life, also a common teenage occupation, is anorexia — refusal to eat enough to maintain a minimally healthy weight. So she is possibly shivering because she hasn't consumed enough calories for her body to keep itself warm. Claire first got into eating disorders when she was 14 or 15 and a bulimic friend introduced her to them. But she was already kind of on the lookout for something: "I was gonna do it on my own, basically. Just because, like, exercise can only take you so far, you know? And I don't know, I just started to wonder if there was another way. Because they made it seem like, 'You do drugs, you die; be anorexic and you're gonna die in a year.' I knew that they kind of overplayed it and tried to frighten you away. So I always thought it can't be that bad for you."

Bulimia — binge eating followed by purging through vomiting or laxatives — didn't suit her, however, so after a little while she moved onto anorexia. But she is not, by her own lights, anorexic. And her name isn't Claire. She is, in her terms, "an ana" or "pro-ana" (shortened from pro-anorexia), and Claire is a variation of Clairegirl, the name she uses on the Web sites that are the fulcrum of the pro-ana community, which also includes people who are pro-mia (for bulimia) or simply pro-E.D., for eating disorder.

About one in 200 American women suffers from anorexia; two or three   5
in 100 suffer from bulimia. Arguably, these disorders have the highest fatality rates of any mental illness, through suicide as well as the obvious health problems. But because they are not threatening to the passer-by, as psychotic disorders are, or likely to render people unemployable or criminal, as alcoholism and addiction are, and perhaps also because they are disorders that primarily afflict girls and women, they are not a proportionately imperative social priority.

They have been, however, topics of almost prurient media fascination for more than 20 years — regularly the subject of articles in magazines that have a sizable young female readership. In these forums, eating disorders are generally depicted as fundamentally body-image disorders, very extreme versions of the non-eating-disordered woman's desire to be thin, which just happen, rivetingly, to carry the risk of the ultimate consequence. "So many women who don't have the disorder say to me: 'Well, what's the big deal? It's like a diet gone bad,'" says Ellen Davis, the clinical director of the Renfrew Center of Philadelphia, an eating-disorder treatment facility. "And it is so different from that. Women with the vulnerability, they really fall into an abyss, and they can't get out. And it's not about, 'O.K., I want to lose the 10 pounds and go on with my life.' It's, 'This has consumed my entire existence.'"

And now there's pro-ana, in many ways an almost too lucid clarification of what it really feels like to be eating disordered. "Pain of mind is worse than pain of body" reads the legend on one Web site's live-journal page, above a picture of the Web mistress's arm, so heavily scored with what look like razor cuts that there is more open wound than flesh. "I'm already disturbed," reads the home page of another. "Please don't come in." The wish to conform to a certain external ideal for the external ideal's sake is certainly a component of anorexia and bulimia. But as they are experienced by the people who suffer from them, it is just that: a component, a stepping-off point into the abyss.

As the girls (and in smaller numbers, boys) who frequent the pro-E.D. sites know, being an ana is a state of mind — part addiction, part obsession and part seesawing sense of self-worth, not necessarily correlating to what you actually weigh. "Body image is a major deal, but it's about not being good enough," says Jill M. Pollack, the executive director of the Center for the Study of Anorexia and Bulimia, "and they're trying to fix everything from the outside." Clairegirl, like many of the girls who include their stats — height, weight and goal weight — when posting on such sites, would not receive a diagnosis of anorexia, because she is not 15 percent under normal weight for her height and age.

But she does not have self-devised rules and restrictions regarding eating, which, if she does not meet them, make her feel that she has erred — "I kind of believe it is a virtue, almost," she says of pro-ana. "Like if you do wrong and you eat, then you sin." If she does not meet her goals, it makes her dislike herself, makes her feel anxiety and a sense of danger. If she does meet them, she feels "clean." She has a goal weight, lower than the weight she is now. She plays sports for two hours a day after school and tries to exercise at least another hour after she gets home. She also has a touch of obsessive-compulsive disorder regarding non-food-related things — cleaning, laundry, the numeral three. ("Both anorexia and bulimia are highly O.C.D.," says Pollack, "Highly.")

And she does spend between one and three hours a day online, in the   10 world of pro-ana. Asked what she likes best about the sites, Claire says: "Just really, like at the end of the day, it would be really nice if you could share with the whole world how you felt, you know? Because truthfully, you just don't feel comfortable, you can't tell the truth. Then, like, if I don't eat lunch or something, people will get on my case about it, and I can't just come out and tell them I don't eat, or something like that. But at the end of the day, I can go online and talk to them there, and they know exactly what I'm going through and how I feel. And I don't have to worry about them judging me for how I feel."

Pro-ana, the basic premise of which is that an eating disorder is not a disorder but a lifestyle choice, is very much an ideology of the early 21st century, one that could not exist absent the anonymity and accessibility of the Internet, without which the only place large numbers of anorexics and bulimics would find themselves together would be at inpatient treatment. "Primarily, the sites reinforce the secretiveness and the 'specialness' of the disorder," Davis says. "When young women get into the grips of this disease, their thoughts become very distorted, and part of it is they believe they're unique and special. The sites are a way for them to connect with other girls and to basically talk about how special they are. And they become very isolated. Women with eating disorders really thrive in a lot of ways on being very disconnected. At the same time, of course, they have a yearning to be connected."

Perfectionism, attention to detail and a sense of superiority combine to make the pro-ana sites the most meticulous and clinically fluent self-representations of a mental disorder you could hope to find, almost checklists of diagnostic criteria expressed in poignantly human terms. Starving yourself, just on the basis of its sheer difficulty, is a high-dedication ailment — to choose to be an ana, if choice it is, is to choose a way of life, a hobby and a credo. And on the Web, which is both very public and completely faceless, the aspects of the disorder that are about attention-getting and secret-keeping are a resolved paradox. "I kind of want people to understand," Clairegirl says, "but I also like having this little hidden thing that only I know about, like — this little secret that's all yours."

Pro-ana has its roots in various newsgroups and lists deep inside various Internet service providers. Now there are numerous well-known-to-those-who-know sites, plus who knows how many dozens more that are just the lone teenager's Web page, with names that put them beyond the scope of search engines. And based on the two-week sign-up of 973 members to a recent message-board adjunct to one of the older and more established sites, the pro-ana community probably numbers in the thousands, with girls using names like Wannabeboney, Neverthinenuf, DiETpEpSiUhHuh! and Afraidtolookin-themirror posting things like: "I can't take it anymore! I'm fasting! I'm going out, getting all diet soda, sugar-free gum, sugar-free candy and having myself a 14-day fast. Then we'll see who is the skinny girl in the family!"

That ana and mia are childlike nicknames, names that might be the names of friends (one Web site that is now defunct was even called, with girlish fondness, "My Friend Ana"), is indicative. The pro-ana community is largely made up of girls or young women, most of whom are between the ages of 13 and 25. And it is a close community, close in the manner of close friendships of girls and young women. The members of a few sites send each other bracelets, like friendship bracelets, as symbols of solidarity and support. And like any ideology subscribed to by many individuals, pro-ana is not a monolithic system of belief.

At its most militant, the ideology is something along the lines of, as the opening page of one site puts it: "Volitional, proactive anorexia is not a disease   15 or a disorder. . . . There are no victims here. It is a lifestyle that begins and ends with a particular faculty human beings seem in drastically short supply of today: the will. . . . Contrary to popular misconception, anorectics possess the most iron-cored, indomitable wills of all. Our way is not that of the weak. . . . if we ever completely tapped that potential in our midst . . . we could change the world. Completely. Maybe we could even rule it."

Mostly, though, the philosophical underpinnings of pro-ana thought are not quite so Nietzschean. The "Thin Commandments" on one site, which appear under a picture of Bugs Bunny smiling his toothy open-mouthed smile, leaning against a mailbox and holding a carrot with one bite taken out of it, include: "If thou aren't thin, thou aren't attractive"; "Being thin is more important than being healthy"; "Thou shall not eat without feeling guilty"; "Thou shall not eat fattening food without punishing thyself afterward"; and "Being thin and not eating are signs of true willpower and success."

The "Ana Creed" from the same site begins: "I believe in Control, the only force mighty enough to bring order into the chaos that is my world. I believe that I am the most vile, worthless and useless person ever to have existed on this planet."

In fact, to those truly "in the disorder" — a phrase one anonymous ana used to describe it, just as an anonymous alcoholic might describe being in A.A. as being "in the rooms" — pro-ana is something of a misnomer. It suggests the promotion of something, rather than its defense, for reasons either sad or militant. That it is generally understood otherwise and even exploited ("Anorexia: Not just for suicidal teenage white girls anymore" read the home page of Anorexic Nation, now a disabled site, the real purpose of which was to push diet drugs) is a source of both resentment and secret satisfaction to the true pro-ana community. Its adherents might be vile and worthless, but they are the elite.

The usual elements of most sites are pretty much the same, although the presentation is variable enough to suggest Web mistresses ranging from young women with a fair amount of programming know-how and editorial judgment to angry little girls who want to assert their right to protect an unhealthy behavior in the face of parental opposition and who happen to know a little HTML. But there are usually "tips" and "techniques" — on the face of it, the scariest aspect of pro-ana, but in reality, pretty much the same things that both dieters and anorexics have been figuring out on their own for decades. There are "thinspirational" quotes — You can never be too rich or too thin"; "Hunger hurts but starving works"; "Nothing tastes as good as thin feels"; "The thinner, the winner!" There are "thinspirational" photo galleries, usually pretty much the same group of very thin models, actresses and singers — Jodie Kidd, Kate Moss, Calista Flockhart, Fiona Apple. And at pro-ana's saddest extreme, balancing the militance on the scales of the double-digit goal weight, there are warnings of such severity that they might as well be the beginning of the third canto of Dante's "Inferno": "I am the way into the city of woe. I am the way to a forsaken people. I am the way into eternal sorrow." The pro-ana version of which, from one site, is:

> Please Note: anorexia is not a diet. Bulimia is not a weight-loss plan. These are dangerous, potentially life-threatening disorders that you cannot choose, catch or learn. If you do not already have an eating disorder, that's wonderful! If you're looking for a new diet, if you want to drop a few pounds to be slimmer or more popular or whatever, if you're generally content with yourself and just want to look a bit better in a bikini, go away. Find a Weight Watchers meeting. Better yet, eat moderate portions of healthy food and go for a walk.
>
> However.
>
> If you are half as emotionally scarred as I am, if you look in the mirror and truly loathe what you see, if your relationships with food and your body are already beyond "normal" parameters no matter what you weigh, then come inside. If you're already too far into this to quit, come in and have a look around. I won't tell you to give up what I need to keep hold of myself.

Most of the pro-ana sites also explicitly discourage people under 18 from   20
entering, partly for moral and partly for self-interested reasons. Under pressure from the National Eating Disorders Association, a number of servers shut down the pro-ana sites they were hosting last fall. But obviously, pretty much anyone who wanted to find her way to these sites and into them could do so, irrespective of age. And could find there, as Clairegirl did, a kind of perverse support group, a place where a group of for the most part very unhappy and in some part very angry girls and women come together to support each other in sickness rather than in health.

Then there's Chaos — also her Web name — who like her friend Futurebird (ditto) runs an established and well-respected pro-E.D. site. Chaos, whom I met in Manhattan although that's not where she lives, is a very smart, very winning, very attractive 23-year-old who has been either bulimic or anorexic since she was 10. Recently she's been bingeing and purging somewhere between 4 and 10 times a week. But when not bingeing, she also practices "restricting" — she doesn't eat in front of people, or in public, or food that isn't sealed, or food that she hasn't prepared herself, or food that isn't one of her "safe" foods, which since they are a certain kind of candy and a certain kind of sugar-free gum, is practically all food. ("You're catching on quickly," she says, laughing, when this is remarked on.) Also recently, she has been having trouble making herself throw up. "I think my body's just not wanting to do it right now," she says. "You have the toothbrush trick, and usually I can just hit my stomach in the right spot, or my fingernails will gag me in the right spot. It just depends on what I've eaten. And if that doesn't work, laxis always do."

Chaos, like Clairegirl, is obsessive-compulsive about a certain number (which it would freak her out to see printed), and when she takes laxatives she either has to take that number of them, which is no longer enough to work, or that number plus 10, or that number plus 20, and so forth. The most she has ever taken is that number plus 60, and the total number she takes depends on the total number of calories she has consumed.

While it hardly needs to be pointed out that starving yourself is not good for you, bulimia is in its own inexorable if less direct way also a deadly disorder. Because of the severity of Chaos's bulimia, its longstanding nature and the other things she does — taking ephedra or Xenadrine, two forms of, as she says, "legal speed," available at any health food or vitamin store; exercising in excess; fasting — she stands a very real chance of dying any time.

As it is, she has been to the emergency room more than half a dozen times with "heart things." It would freak her out to see the details of her heart things in print. But the kinds of heart things a severe bulimic might experience range from palpitations to cardiac arrest. And although Chaos hasn't had her kidney function tested in the recent past, it probably isn't great. Her spleen might also be near the point of rupturing.

Chaos is by no means a young woman with nothing going for her. She   25 has a full-time job and is a full-time college student, a double major. She can play a musical instrument and take good photographs. She writes beautifully, well enough to have won competitions.

But despite her many positive attributes, Chaos punishes herself physically on a regular basis, not only through bulimia but also through cutting — hers is the live-journal page with the picture of the sliced-up arm. To be beheld is, to Chaos, so painful that after meeting me in person, she was still vomiting and crying with fear over the possible consequences of cooperating with this story a week later. "Some days," she says of her bulimia, "it's all I have."

One thing that she does not have is health insurance, so her treatment options are both limited and inadequate. So with everything she has going for her, with all her real-world dreams and aspirations, the palpitating heart of her emotional life is in the pro-E.D. community. As another girl I spoke with described herself as telling her doctors: "Show me a coping mechanism that works as well as this and I'll trade my eating disorder for it in a minute."

And while in some moods Chaos says she would do anything to be free of her eating disorders, in others she has more excuses not to be than the mere lack of health insurance: she has a job, she is in school, she doesn't deserve help. And what she has, on all days, is her Web site, a place where people who have only their eating disorders can congregate, along with the people who aspire to having eating disorders — who for unknowable reasons of neurochemistry and personal experience identify with the self-lacerating worlds of anorexia and bulimia.

Futurebird, whom I also met in Manhattan, says that she has noticed a trend, repeating itself in new member after new member, of people who don't think they're anorexic enough to get treatment. And it's true, very much a function of the Internet — its accessibility, its anonymity — that the pro-ana sites seem to have amplified an almost-diagnostic category: the subclinical eating disorder, for the girl who's anorexic on the inside, the girl who hates herself so much that she forms a virtual attachment to a highly traumatized body of women, in a place where through posts and the adoption of certain behaviors, she can make her internal state external.

Futurebird and Chaos are sitting in a little plaza just to the south of   30 Washington Square Park, with the sun behind them. Futurebird is a small African American woman. As she notes, and as she has experienced when being taken to the hospital, it is a big help being African American if you don't want people to think you have anorexia, which is generally and inaccurately considered to be solely an affliction of the white middle class. Futurebird has had an eating disorder since she was in junior high school and is now, at 22, looking for a way to become what you might call a maintenance anorexic — eating a little bit more healthily, restricting to foods like fruits and whole-grain cereal and compensating for the extra calories with excessive exercising.

Like Chaos, she is opposed, in principle, to eating disorders in general and says that she hates anorexia with a blind and burning hatred. Although she also says she thinks she's fat, which she so emphatically is not that in the interest of not sounding illogical and irrational, she almost immediately amends this to: she'd not as thin as she'd like to be.

Both she and Chaos would vigorously dispute the assertion that the sites can give anyone an eating disorder. You certainly can't give anyone without the vulnerability to it an eating disorder. But many adolescent girls teeter on the edge of vulnerability. And the sites certainly might give those girls the suggestion to . . . hey, what the hell, give it a try.

"What I'd like people to understand," Futurebird says, "is that it is very difficult for people who have an eating disorder to ask for help. What a lot of people are able to do is to say, well, I can't go to a recovery site and ask for help. I can't go to a doctor or a friend and ask for help. I can't tell anyone. But I can go to this site because it's going to quote-unquote make me worse. And instead what I hope they find is people who share their experience and that they're able to just simply talk. And I've actually tested this. I've posted the same thing that I've posted on my site on some recovery sites, and I've read the reactions, and in a lot of ways it's more helpful."

In what ways?

"The main difference is that if you post — if someone's feeling really bad,   35 like, I'm so fat, et cetera, on a recovery site, they'll say, that's not recovery talk. You have to speak recovery-speak."

"Fat is not a feeling," Chaos says, in tones that indicate she is echoing a recovery truism.

"And they'll use this language of recovery," Futurebird continues. "Which does work at some point in the negative thinking patterns that you have. But one tiny thing that I wish they would do is validate that the feeling does exist. To say, yes, I understand that you might feel that way. And you get not as much of that. A lot of times people just need to know that they aren't reacting in a completely crazy way."

The problem is that by and large, the people posting on these sites are reacting in a completely crazy way. There are many, many more discussions answering questions like, "What do you guys do about starvation headaches?" than there are questions like, "I am feeling really down; can you help me?" And in no case, in answering the former question, does anyone say, "Um . . . stop starving yourself." A site like Futurebird's, or like the message board of Chaos's, are designed with the best intentions. But as everybody knows, that is what the way into the city of woe, the way to a forsaken people and the way into eternal sorrow are paved with.

What Clairegirl, sitting shivering on the running track, would say today is that when she reaches her current goal weight, she will stay there. But she can't ever really see herself giving ana up altogether. "I don't think I could ever stop, like, wanting to not eat. Like, I could keep myself from eating below 300 calories a day. But I could never see myself eating more than 1,000," she says, wrapping her arms around her knees. "I consider myself to be one of the extreme dieters. Like, I could never want to be — I mean, it would be so awesome to be able to say a double-digit number as your weight, but it would look sick, you know?" (Clairegirl is 5 feet 7 inches.)

And what about the people on the pro-ana sites who are not so happy,   40 who describe the disorder as a living hell, who are in very bad shape? "Those girls have been going at it a lot longer than me. But you can't ever really say that ana isn't a form of self-hatred, even though I try to say that. If I was truthfully happy with myself, then I would allow myself to eat. But I don't. And it's kind of like a strive for perfection, and for making myself better. So I can't honestly say there's no. . . ."

She trails off, and gazes up, as if the answer were written in the night sky, waiting to be decoded. "Like, you can't say that every ana loves herself and that she doesn't think anything is wrong with her at all," she says. "Or else she wouldn't be ana in the first place."

Reading across Professions
LISA D. GALYNKER, Psychologist

As a psychologist, it is my job to understand why people do what they do. One of the most valuable tools in this work is my own reaction. While reading "A Secret Society of the Starving," I was somewhat surprised by what I saw as Udovitch's dispassionate descriptions of the girls and the "pro-ana" Web sites. Of course, Udovitch is a reporter, so perhaps she needs to keep a distance from her subjects. But what was my excuse?

It was uncomfortable for me to admit to myself that I found it hard to feel compassion — the bread and butter of my work — for the girls in the article. The more I thought about it, though, the more I realized that these girls aren't asking for compassion. They are asking to be heard as they speak an uncomfortable truth. Raised with many mixed messages about how physical appearance and weight determine their status in the world, these girls are turning to the "pro-ana" movement as a provocative way to express their reactions. I found myself thinking that the extremity of their behavior marked the extent to which they felt misunderstood. Maybe it is time to listen.

Theories about family dynamics include a concept known as "the identified patient" or "scapegoat." This is the person in a family, usually a child, who responds to the stress of family conflict by taking the blame. The child then behaves in increasingly dysfunctional ways in an unknow- ing attempt to draw attention to the family's problems. As I see it, the girls in Udovitch's piece are the "identified patients" of our societal family. These patients have seen and heard much to convince them that our culture values extreme thinness as a symbol of beauty. As they absorb information about the multimillion-dollar diet industry or about how disgusting imperfect bodies are, they respond dysfunctionally by becom- ing eating disordered.

Perhaps eating disorders are not seen as a high-priority problem in our culture because we are ambivalent about them. The article calls Claire a "pretty teenager" who is "almost abnormally self-possessed" and says that Chaos is "very smart, very winning, very attractive." Udovitch describes the pro-ana sites as "the most meticulous and clinically fluent self-representations of a mental disorder you could hope to find, almost checklists of diagnostic criteria expressed in poignantly human terms." These descriptions seem to embody the mixed messages that anorexic girls experience every day: "We hate what you're doing; stop doing it, you beautiful, articulate, special little angels!"

Udovitch describes her subjects as feeling "both resentment and secret satisfaction" at the ways they are viewed by the culture at large and as acting on the view that they are "vile and worthless, but . . . elite." The girls want to conform to an externally imposed ideal of thinness, but they simultaneously want to be seen as "unique and special." Clairegirl de- scribes anorexia as "a form of self-hatred" and almost in the same breath as "a striv[ing] for perfection, and for making myself better." The clinical name for this paradoxical behavior is "passive-aggression," and what it means is that Clairegirl has found an indirect way to express feelings of anger, hurt, and shame that ends up becoming self-destructive and destructive to those around her. She is the "identified patient" desperately trying to find a way to draw attention to feelings she sees as unacceptable or invalidated by others.

The pro-ana girls in "A Secret Society of the Starving" are physical manifestations of our cultural hypocrisy. Of course these girls need psychological help, but I believe our approach to them should go beyond the pathology. We need to listen to what they are saying and, more importantly, as a culture, we need to take responsibility for how confusing messages about the importance of thinness are affecting them. Addressing the societal component of eating disorders would, I feel, significantly decrease both the number of girls who develop eating disorders and the number of pro-ana sites.

Lisa D. Galynker is a psychologist specializing in cognitive-behavior therapy.

QUESTIONING THE TEXT

1. Udovitch describes eating disorders as "topics of almost prurient media fascination" but not an "imperative social priority" (paragraphs 5 and 6). What is the distinction between these two descriptions? What role do media have in shaping social priorities?

2. What do you think the purpose of Udovitch's article is? Why does she want to bring attention to this "secret society"? Are there any suggested or implied solutions in her article? Is her article another example of the "prurient media fascination" mentioned in the previous question? If not, what prevents it from being prurient fascination?

MAKING CONNECTIONS

3. In paragraph 32 Udovitch writes that Futurebird and Chaos "vigorously dispute the assertion that the [pro-ana] sites can give anyone an eating disorder," but at the end of that paragraph Udovitch suggests that perhaps the sites are dangerous. In paragraph 38, Udovitch claims that most people posting on pro-ana sites "are reacting in a completely crazy way." To what degree does this kind of speech pose a threat to the safety of those who might visit the sites? Read John Leo's "Free Inquiry? Not on Campus" (p. 592). Do you think it would be acceptable to limit the speech on pro-ana sites? What do you think Leo's position would be?

4. What does Udovitch's article suggest about the desire of her subjects for a particular identity? Compare her essay to Tyina Steptoe's "An Ode to

Country Music from a Black Dixie Chick" (p. 421) or Bich Minh Nguyen's "The Good Immigrant Student" (p. 458). Though these essays are all very different, what ideas about identity formation might be seen to be common to all of them?

JOINING THE CONVERSATION

5. Udovitch speculates that eating disorders are nonthreatening to others because they do not render those who suffer from them unemployable and because they afflict primarily women and girls. What other issue, problem, or concern do you think does not receive appropriate attention from the media or culture? In a few paragraphs, explain the issue and suggest reasons why it might be little noticed.

STEPHANIE COONTZ
The Way We Wish We Were

AMERICANS PAY A HIGH PRICE *for their nostalgia about "traditional" families and homes, argues Stephanie Coontz in* The Way We Never Were: American Families and the Nostalgia Trap *(1992). In Coontz's view, as her title suggests, the good old days so many people long for never actually existed, and the futile effort to restore them keeps Americans from seeking realistic ways to enhance family life in the twenty-first century.*

In the following chapter from her book, Coontz (b. 1944), a professor of history and family studies at Evergreen State College in Washington, traces changes in American family life and values from colonial times to the present, in each case emphasizing the complexity of family relationships; the shifting influence of social, political, and economic changes on families; and the often careless use of statistical data to make shaky claims about families. The impact of Coontz's work has been substantial: she has served as a consultant for many government and community agencies interested in children and families. Her books The Way We Really Are: Coming to Terms with America's Changing Families *(1997) and* American Families: A Multicultural Reader *(1998) continue to provide rich and complex explorations of the meaning of family life in the United States.*

I chose this selection in part because recent discussions in my classes tend to support Coontz's claim that students' key images of the "traditional family" are often related to television representations of family life. In addition, I quite like the title of her chapter: "The Way We Wish We Were." Where home and family are concerned, my guess is that such wishes are widely divergent — and that they will be fascinating to discuss. —A.L.

When I begin teaching a course on family history, I often ask my students to write down ideas that spring to mind when they think of the "traditional family." Their lists always include several images. One is of extended families in which all members worked together, grandparents were an integral part of family life, children learned responsibility and the work ethic from their elders, and there were clear lines of authority based on respect for age. Another is of nuclear families in which nurturing mothers sheltered children from premature exposure to sex, financial worries, or other adult concerns, while fathers taught adolescents not to sacrifice their education by going to work too early. Still another image gives pride of place to the couple relationship. In traditional families, my students write — half derisively, half wistfully — men and women remained chaste until marriage, at which time they extricated themselves from competing obligations to kin and neighbors and committed themselves wholly to the marital relationship, experiencing an all-encompassing intimacy that our more crowded modern life seems to preclude. As one freshman wrote: "They truly respected the marriage vowels"; I assume she meant *I-O-U.*

Such visions of past family life exert a powerful emotional pull on most Americans, and with good reason, given the fragility of many modern commitments. The problem is not only that these visions bear a suspicious resemblance to reruns of old television series, but also that the scripts of different shows have been mixed up: June Cleaver suddenly has a Grandpa Walton dispensing advice in her kitchen; Donna Stone, vacuuming the living room in her inevitable pearls and high heels, is no longer married to a busy modern pediatrician but to a small-town sheriff who, like Andy Taylor* of *The Andy Griffith Show*, solves community problems through informal, old-fashioned common sense.

Like most visions of a "golden age," the "traditional family" my students describe evaporates on closer examination. It is an ahistorical amalgam of structures, values, and behaviors that never coexisted in the same time and place. The notion that traditional families fostered intense intimacy between husbands and wives while creating mothers who were totally available to their children, for example, is an idea that combines some characteristics of the white, middle-class family in the mid-nineteenth century and some of a rival family ideal first articulated in the 1920s. The first family revolved emotionally around the mother-child axis, leaving the husband-wife relationship stilted and formal. The second focused on an eroticized couple relationship, demanding that mothers curb emotional "overinvestment" in their children. The hybrid idea that a woman can be fully absorbed with her youngsters while simultaneously maintaining passionate sexual excitement with her husband was a 1950s invention that drove thousands of women to therapists, tranquilizers, or alcohol when they actually tried to live up to it.

Similarly, an extended family in which all members work together under the top-down authority of the household elder operates very differently from a nuclear family in which husband and wife are envisioned as friends who patiently devise ways to let the children learn by trial and error. Children who worked in family enterprises seldom had time for the extracurricular activities that Wally and the Beaver* recounted to their parents over the dinner table; often, they did not even go to school full-time. Mothers who did home production generally relegated child care to older children or servants; they did not suspend work to savor a baby's first steps or discuss with their husband how to facilitate a grade-schooler's "self-esteem." Such families emphasized formality, obedience to authority, and "the way it's always been" in their childrearing.

Nuclear families, by contrast, have tended to pride themselves on the   5
"modernity" of parent-child relations, diluting the authority of grandparents, denigrating "old-fashioned" ideas about childraising, and resisting the

---

June Cleaver . . . Andy Taylor: Characters in various family-oriented television series. June Cleaver played a housewife in *Leave It to Beaver*; Donna Stone was a housewife in *The Donna Reed Show*; Andy Taylor was the sheriff of Mayberry in *The Andy Griffith Show*.
Wally and the Beaver: brothers in the television sitcom *Leave It to Beaver*

"interference" of relatives. It is difficult to imagine the Cleavers or the college-educated title figure of *Father Knows Best* letting grandparents, maiden aunts, or in-laws have a major voice in childrearing decisions. Indeed, the kind of family exemplified by the Cleavers ... represented a conscious *rejection* of the Waltons' model.

THE ELUSIVE TRADITIONAL FAMILY

Whenever people propose that we go back to the traditional family, I always suggest that they pick a ballpark date for the family they have in mind. Once pinned down, they are invariably unwilling to accept the package deal that comes with their chosen model. Some people, for example, admire the discipline of colonial families, which were certainly not much troubled by divorce or fragmenting individualism. But colonial families were hardly stable: High mortality rates meant that the average length of marriage was less than a dozen years. One-third to one-half of all children lost at least one parent before the age of twenty-one; in the South, more than half of all children aged thirteen or under had lost at least one parent.[1]

While there are a few modern Americans who would like to return to the strict patriarchal authority of colonial days, in which disobedience by women and children was considered a small form of treason, these individuals would doubtless be horrified by other aspects of colonial families, such as their failure to protect children from knowledge of sexuality. Eighteenth-century spelling and grammar books routinely used *fornication* as an example of a four-syllable word, and preachers detailed sexual offenses in astonishingly explicit terms. Sexual conversations between men and women, even in front of children, were remarkably frank. It is worth contrasting this colonial candor to the climate in 1991, when the Department of Health and Human Services was forced to cancel a proposed survey of teenagers' sexual practices after some groups charged that such knowledge might "inadvertently" encourage more sex.[2]

Other people searching for an ideal traditional family might pick the more sentimental and gentle Victorian family, which arose in the 1830s and 1840s as household production gave way to wage work and professional

---

[1] Philip Greven, *Four Generations: Population, Land, and Family in Colonial Andover, Massachusetts* (Ithaca, N.Y.: Cornell University Press, 1970); Vivian Fox and Martin Quit, *Loving, Parenting, and Dying: The Family Cycle in England and America, Past and Present* (New York: Psychohistory Press, 1980), p. 401.

[2] John Demos, *A Little Commonwealth: Family Life in Plymouth Colony* (New York: Oxford University Press, 1970), p. 108; Mary Ryan, *Cradle of the Middle Class: The Family in Oneida County, New York, 1790–1865* (New York: Cambridge University Press, 1981), pp. 33, 38–39; Carroll Smith-Rosenberg, *Disorderly Conduct: Visions of Gender in Victorian America* (New York: Oxford University Press, 1985), p. 24.

occupations outside the home. A new division of labor by age and sex emerged among the middle class. Women's roles were redefined in terms of domesticity rather than production, men were labeled "breadwinners" (a masculine identity unheard of in colonial days), children were said to need time to play, and gentle maternal guidance supplanted the patriarchal authoritarianism of the past.

But the middle-class Victorian family depended for its existence on the multiplication of other families who were too poor and powerless to retreat into their own little oases and who therefore had to provision the oases of others. Childhood was prolonged for the nineteenth-century middle class only because it was drastically foreshortened for other sectors of the population. The spread of textile mills, for example, freed middle-class women from the most time-consuming of their former chores, making cloth. But the raw materials for these mills were produced by slave labor. Slave children were not exempt from field labor unless they were infants, and even then their mothers were not allowed time off to nurture them. Frederick Douglass* could not remember seeing his mother until he was seven.[3]

Domesticity was also not an option for the white families who worked   10 twelve hours a day in Northern factories and workshops transforming slave-picked cotton into ready-made clothing. By 1820, "half the workers in many factories were boys and girls who had not reached their eleventh birthday." Rhode Island investigators found "little half-clothed children" making their way to the textile mills before dawn. In 1845, shoemaking families and makers of artificial flowers worked fifteen to eighteen hours a day, according to the New York *Daily Tribune*.[4]

Within the home, prior to the diffusion of household technology at the end of the century, house cleaning and food preparation remained mammoth tasks. Middle-class women were able to shift more time into childrearing in this period only by hiring domestic help. Between 1800 and 1850, the proportion of servants to white households doubled, to about one in nine. Some servants were poverty-stricken mothers who had to board or bind out their own children. Employers found such workers tended to be "distracted," however; they usually preferred young girls. In his study of Buffalo, New York, in the 1850s,

---

Frederick Douglass (1817–95): Son of a slave mother and white father, Douglass became an abolitionist leader and eloquent advocate for human rights.

[3]Frederick Douglass, *My Bondage and My Freedom* (New York: Dover, 1968), p. 48.

[4]David Roediger and Philip Foner, *Our Own Time: A History of American Labor and the Working Day* (London: Greenwood, 1989), p. 9; Norman Ware, *The Industrial Worker, 1840–1860* (New York: Quadrangle, 1964), p. 5; Barbara Wertheimer, *We Were There: The Story of Working Women in America* (New York: Pantheon, 1977), p. 91; Sean Wilentz, *Chants Democratic: New York City and the Rise of the Working Class, 1788–1850* (New York: Oxford University Press, 1984), p. 126.

historian Lawrence Glasco found that Irish and German girls often went into service at the age of eleven or twelve.[5]

For every nineteenth-century middle-class family that protected its wife and child within the family circle, then, there was an Irish or a German girl scrubbing floors in that middle-class home, a Welsh boy mining coal to keep the home-baked goodies warm, a black girl doing the family laundry, a black mother and child picking cotton to be made into clothes for the family, and a Jewish or an Italian daughter in a sweatshop making "ladies" dresses or artificial flowers for the family to purchase.

Furthermore, people who lived in these periods were seldom as enamored of their family arrangements as modern nostalgia might suggest. Colonial Americans lamented "the great neglect in many parents and masters in training up their children" and expressed the "greatest trouble and grief about the rising generation." No sooner did Victorian middle-class families begin to withdraw their children from the work world than observers began to worry that children were becoming *too* sheltered. By 1851, the Reverend Horace Bushnell spoke for many in bemoaning the passing of the traditional days of household production, when the whole family was "harnessed, all together, into the producing process, young and old, male and female, from the boy who rode the plough-horse to the grandmother knitting under her spectacles."[6]

The late nineteenth century saw a modest but significant growth of extended families and a substantial increase in the number of families who were "harnessed" together in household production. Extended families have never been the norm in America; the highest figure for extended-family households ever recorded in American history is 20 percent. Contrary to the popular myth that industrialization destroyed "traditional" extended families, this high point occurred between 1850 and 1885, during the most intensive period of early industrialization. Many of these extended families, and most "producing" families of the time, depended on the labor of children; they were held together by dire necessity and sometimes by brute force.[7]

---

[5]Faye Dudden, *Serving Women: Household Service in Nineteenth-Century America* (Middletown, Conn.: Wesleyan University Press, 1983), p. 206; Susan Strasser, *Never Done: A History of American Housework* (New York: Pantheon, 1982); Lawrence Glasco, "The Life Cycles and Household Structure of American Ethnic Groups, in *A Heritage of Her Own: Toward a New Social History of American Women*, ed. Nancy Cott and Elizabeth Pleck (New York: Simon & Schuster, 1979), pp. 281, 285.

[6]Robert Bremner et al., eds., *Children and Youth in America: A Documentary History* (Cambridge: Harvard University Press, 1970), vol. 1, p. 39; Barbara Cross, *Horace Bushnell: Minister to a Changing America* (Chicago: University of Chicago Press, 1958); Ann Douglas, *The Feminization of American Culture* (New York: Knopf, 1977), p. 52.

[7]Peter Laslett, "Characteristics of the Western Family over Time," in *Family Life and Illicit Love in Earlier Generations*, ed. Peter Laslett (New York: Cambridge University Press, 1977); William Goode, *World Revolution and Family Patterns* (New York: Free Press, 1963); Michael Anderson, *Family Structure in Nineteenth-Century Lancashire* (Cambridge, England: Cambridge University Press, 1971); Tamara Hareven, ed., *Transitions: The Family and the Life Course in Historical Perspective*

There was a significant increase in child labor during the last third of the   15
nineteenth century. Some children worked at home in crowded tenement
sweatshops that produced cigars or women's clothing. Reformer Helen Campbell found one house where "nearly thirty children of all ages and sizes, babies
predominating, rolled in the tobacco which covered the floor and was piled in
every direction."[8] Many producing households resembled the one described by
Mary Van Kleeck of the Russell Sage Foundation in 1913:

> In a tenement on MacDougal Street lives a family of seven — grandmother,
> father, mother and four children aged four years, three years, two years and
> one month respectively. All excepting the father and the two babies make
> violets. The three year old girl picks apart the petals; her sister, aged four
> years, separates the stems, dipping an end of each into paste spread on a
> piece of board on the kitchen table; and the mother and grandmother slip
> the petals up the stems.[9]

Where children worked outside the home, conditions were no better. In
1900, 120,000 children worked in Pennsylvania mines and factories; most of
them had started work by age eleven. In Scranton, a third of the girls between
the ages of thirteen and sixteen worked in the silk mills in 1904. In New York,
Boston, and Chicago, teenagers worked long hours in textile factories and frequently died in fires or industrial accidents. Children made up 23.7 percent of
the 36,415 workers in southern textile mills around the turn of the century.
When reformer Marie Van Vorse took a job at one in 1903, she found children
as young as six or seven working twelve-hour shifts. At the end of the day, she
reported: "They are usually beyond speech. They fall asleep at the tables, on the
stairs; they are carried to bed and there laid down as they are, unwashed, un-
dressed; and the inanimate bundles of rags so lie until the mill summons them
with its imperious cry before sunrise."[10]

(New York: Academic Press, 1978); Tamara Hareven, "The Dynamics of Kin in an Industrial
Community," in *Turning Points: Historical and Sociological Essays on the Family,* ed. John Demos and
S. S. Boocock (Chicago: University of Chicago Press, 1978); Linda Gordon, *Heroes of Their Own
Lives: The Politics and History of Family Violence, 1800–1960* (New York, Viking, 1988).

[8]Helen Campbell, *Prisoners of Poverty: Women Wage Workers, Their Trades and Their Lives*
(Westport, Conn.: Greenwood Press, 1970), p. 206.

[9]Rosalyn Baxandall, Linda Gordon, and Susan Reverby, eds., *America's Working Women*
(New York: Random House, 1976), p. 162.

[10]Rose Schneiderman, *All For One* (New York: P. S. Eriksson, 1967); John Bodnar,
"Socialization and Adaptation: Immigrant Families in Scranton," in *Growing Up in America: His-
torical Experiences,* ed. Harvey Graff (Detroit: Wayne State Press, 1987), pp. 391–92; Robert and
Helen Lynd, *Middletown: A Study in Modern American Culture* (New York: Harcourt Brace
Jovanovich, 1956), p. 31; Barbara Wertheimer, *We Were There: The Story of Working Women in
America* (New York: Pantheon, 1977), pp. 336–43; Francesco Cordasco, *Jacob Riis Revisited: Poverty
and the Slum in Another Era* (Garden City, N.Y.: Doubleday, 1968); Campbell, *Prisoners of Poverty:
Women Wage-Earners* (Boston: Arnoff, 1893); Lynn Weiner, *From Working Girl to Working Mother:
The Female Labor Force in the United States, 1829–1980* (Chapel Hill: University of North
Carolina Press, 1985), p. 92.

By the end of the nineteenth century, shocked by the conditions in urban tenements and by the sight of young children working full-time at home or earning money out on the streets, middle-class reformers put aside nostalgia for "harnessed" family production and elevated the antebellum model once more, blaming immigrants for introducing such "un-American" family values as child labor. Reformers advocated adoption of a "true American" family — a restricted, exclusive nuclear unit in which women and children were divorced from the world of work.

In the late 1920s and early 1930s, however, the wheel turned yet again, as social theorists noted the independence and isolation of the nuclear family with renewed anxiety. The influential Chicago School of sociology believed that immigration and urbanization had weakened the traditional family by destroying kinship and community networks. Although sociologists welcomed the increased democracy of "companionate marriage," they worried about the rootlessness of nuclear families and the breakdown of older solidarities. By the time of the Great Depression, some observers even saw a silver lining in economic hardship, since it revived the economic functions and social importance of kin and family ties. With housing starts down by more than 90 percent, approximately one-sixth of urban families had to "double up" in apartments. The incidence of three-generation households increased, while recreational interactions outside the home were cut back or confined to the kinship network. One newspaper opined: "Many a family that has lost its car has found its soul."[11]

Depression families evoke nostalgia in some contemporary observers, because they tended to create "dependability and domestic inclination" among girls and "maturity in the management of money" among boys. But, in many cases, such responsibility was inseparable from "a corrosive and disabling poverty that shattered the hopes and dreams of . . . young parents and twisted the lives of those who were 'stuck together' in it." Men withdrew from family life or turned violent; women exhausted themselves trying to "take up the slack" both financially and emotionally, or they belittled their husbands as failures; and children gave up their dreams of education to work at dead-end jobs.[12]

---

[11]For examples of the analysis of the Chicago School, see Ernest Burgess and Harvey Locke, *The Family: From Institution to Companionship* (New York: American Book Company, 1945); Ernest Mowrer, *The Family: Its Organization and Disorganization* (Chicago: University of Chicago Press, 1932); W. I. Thomas and F. Znaniecki, *The Polish Peasant in Europe and America*, 5 vols. (Boston: Dover Publications, 1918–20). On families in the Depression, see Steven Mintz and Susan Kellogg, *Domestic Revolutions: A Social History of American Family Life* (New York: Free Press, 1988), pp. 133–49, quote on p. 136.
[12]Glen Elder, Jr., *Children of the Great Depression: Social Change in Life Experience* (Chicago: University of Chicago Press, 1974), pp. 64–82; Lillian Rubin, *Worlds of Pain: Life in the Working-Class Family* (New York: Basic Books, 1976), p. 23; Edward Robb Ellis, *A Nation in Torment: The Great American Depression, 1929–1939* (New York: Coward McCann, 1970); Ruth Milkman, "Women's Work and the Economic Crisis," in *A Heritage of Her Own: Toward a New Social History of American Women*, ed. Nancy Cott and Elizabeth Pleck (New York: Simon & Schuster, 1979), pp. 507–41.

From the hardships of the Great Depression and the Second World   20
War and the euphoria of the postwar economic recovery came a new kind of
family ideal that still enters our homes in *Leave It to Beaver* and *Donna Reed*
reruns. . . . [T]he 1950s were no more a "golden age" of the family than any
other period in American history. . . . I will argue that our recurring search for
a traditional family model denies the diversity of family life, both past and
present, and leads to false generalizations about the past as well as wildly exaggerated claims about the present and the future.

THE COMPLEXITIES OF ASSESSING FAMILY TRENDS

If it is hard to find a satisfactory model of the traditional family, it is also
hard to make global judgments about how families have changed and whether
they are getting better or worse. Some generalizations about the past are pure
myth. Whatever the merit of recurring complaints about the "rootlessness" of
modern life, for instance, families are *not* more mobile and transient than they
used to be. In most nineteenth-century cities, both large and small, more than
50 percent — and often up to 75 percent — of the residents in any given year
were no longer there ten years later. People born in the twentieth century are
much more likely to live near their birthplace than were people born in the
nineteenth century.[13]

This is not to say, of course, that mobility did not have different effects
then than it does now. In the nineteenth century, claims historian Thomas
Bender, people moved from community to community, taking advantage . . . of
nonfamilial networks and institutions that integrated them into new work and
social relations. In the late twentieth century, people move from job to job,
following a career path that shuffles them from one single-family home to
another and does not link them to neighborly networks beyond the family. But
this change is in our community ties, not in our family ones.[14]

A related myth is that modern Americans have lost touch with extended-
kinship networks or have let parent-child bonds lapse. In fact, more Americans
than ever before have grandparents alive, and there is good evidence that ties
between grandparents and grandchildren have become stronger over the past
fifty years. In the late 1970s, researchers returned to the "Middletown" studied
by sociologists Robert and Helen Lynd in the 1920s and found that most

---

[13]Rudy Ray Seward, *The American Family: A Demographic History* (Beverly Hills: Sage,
1978); Kenneth Winkle, *The Politics of Community: Migration and Politics in Antebellum Ohio* (New
York: Cambridge University Press, 1988); Michael Weber, *Social Change in an Industrial Town:
Patterns of Progress in Warren, Pennsylvania, from the Civil War to World War I* (University Park: Penn-
sylvania State University Press, 1976), pp. 138–48; Stephen Thernstrom, *Poverty and Progress*
(Cambridge: Harvard University Press, 1964).

[14]Thomas Bender, *Community and Social Change in America* (New Brunswick: Rutgers
University Press, 1978).

people there maintained closer extended-family networks than in earlier times. There had been some decline in the family's control over the daily lives of youth, especially females, but "the expressive/emotional function of the family" was "more important for Middletown students of 1977 than it was in 1924." More recent research shows that visits with relatives did *not* decline between the 1950s and the late 1980s.[15]

Today 54 percent of adults see a parent, and 68 percent talk on the phone with a parent, at least once a week. Fully 90 percent of Americans describe their relationship with their mother as close, and 78 percent say their relationship with their grandparents is close. And for all the family disruption of divorce, most modern children live with at least *one* parent. As late as 1940, 10 percent of American children did not live with either parent, compared to only one in twenty-five today.[16]

What about the supposed eclipse of marriage? Neither the rising age of   25
those who marry nor the frequency of divorce necessarily means that marriage is becoming a less prominent institution than it was in earlier days. Ninety percent of men and women eventually marry, more than 70 percent of divorced men and women remarry, and fewer people remain single for their entire lives today than at the turn of the century. One author even suggests that the availability of divorce in the second half of the twentieth century has allowed some women to try marriage who would formerly have remained single all their lives. Others argue that the rate of hidden marital separation in the late nineteenth century was not much less than the rate of visible separation today.[17]

Studies of marital satisfaction reveal that more couples reported their marriages to be happy in the late 1970s than did so in 1957, while couples in their second marriages believe them to be much happier than their first ones. Some commentators conclude that marriage is becoming less permanent but more satisfying. Others wonder, however, whether there is a vicious circle in our country, where no one even tries to sustain a relationship. Between the late 1970s and late 1980s, moreover, reported marital happiness did decline slightly

---

[15]Edward Kain, *The Myth of Family Decline: Understanding Families in a World of Rapid Social Change* (Lexington, Mass.: D. C. Heath, 1990), pp. 10, 37; Theodore Caplow, "The Sociological Myth of Family Decline," *The Tocqueville Review* 3 (1981): 366; Howard Bahr, "Changes in Family Life in Middletown, 1924–77," *Public Opinion Quarterly* 44 (1980): 51.

[16]*American Demographics,* February 1990; Dennis Orthner, "The Family in Transition," in *Rebuilding the Nest: A New Commitment to the American Family*, ed. David Blankenhorn, Steven Bayme, and Jean Bethke Elshtain (Milwaukee: Family Service America, 1990), pp. 95–97; Sar Levitan and Richard Belous, *What's Happening to the American Family?* (Baltimore: Johns Hopkins University Press, 1981), p. 63.

[17]Daniel Kallgren, "Women out of Marriage: Work and Residence Patterns of Never Married American Women, 1900–1980" (Paper presented at Social Science History Association Conference, Minneapolis, Minn., October 1990), p. 8; Richard Sennett, *Families against the City: Middle Class Homes in Industrial Chicago, 1872–1890* (Cambridge: Harvard University Press, 1984), pp. 114–15.

in the United States. Some authors see this as reflecting our decreasing appreciation of marriage, although others suggest that it reflects unrealistically high expectations of love in a culture that denies people safe, culturally approved ways of getting used to marriage or cultivating other relationships to meet some of the needs that we currently load onto the couple alone.[18]

Part of the problem in making simple generalizations about what is happening to marriage is that there has been a polarization of experiences. Marriages are much more likely to be ended by divorce today, but marriages that do last are described by their participants as happier than those in the past and are far more likely to confer such happiness over many years. It is important to remember that the 50 percent divorce rate estimates are calculated in terms of a forty-year period and that many marriages in the past were terminated well before that date by the death of one partner. Historian Lawrence Stone suggests that divorce has become "a functional substitute for death" in the modern world. At the end of the 1970s, the rise in divorce rates seemed to overtake the fall in death rates, but the slight decline in divorce rates since then means that "a couple marrying today is more likely to celebrate a fortieth wedding anniversary than were couples around the turn of the century."[19]

A similar polarization allows some observers to argue that fathers are deserting their children, while others celebrate the new commitment of fathers to child-rearing. Both viewpoints are right. Sociologist Frank Furstenberg comments on the emergence of a "good dad–bad dad complex": Many fathers spend more time with their children than ever before and feel more free to be affectionate with them; others, however, feel more free simply to walk out on their families. According to 1981 statistics, 42 percent of the children whose father had left the marriage had not seen him in the past year. Yet studies show steadily increasing involvement of fathers with their children as long as they are in the home.[20]

---

[18]Mary Jo Bane, *Here to Stay: American Families in the Twentieth Century* (New York: Basic Books, 1976); Stephen Nock, *Sociology of the Family* (Englewood Cliffs, N.J.: Prentice Hall, 1987); Kain, *Myth of Family Decline*, pp. 71, 74–75; Joseph Veroff, Elizabeth Douvan, and Richard Kulka, *The Inner American: A Self Portrait from 1957 to 1976* (New York: Basic Books, 1981); Norval Glenn, "The Recent Trend in Marital Success in the United States," *Journal of Marriage and the Family* 53 (1991); Tracy Cabot, *Marrying Later, Marrying Smarter* (New York: McGraw-Hill, 1990); Judith Brown, *Sanctions and Sanctuary: Cultural Perspectives on the Beating of Wives* (Boulder, Colo.: Westview Press, 1991); Maxine Baca Zinn and Stanley Eitzen, *Diversity in American Families* (New York: Harper & Row, 1987).

[19]Dorrian Apple Sweetser, "Broken Homes: Stable Risk, Changing Reason, Changing Forms," *Journal of Marriage and the Family* (August 1985); Lawrence Stone, "The Road to Polygamy," *New York Review of Books*, 2 March 1989, p. 13; Arlene Skolnick, *Embattled Paradise: The American Family in an Age of Uncertainty* (New York: Basic Books, 1991), p. 156.

[20]Frank Furstenberg Jr., "Good Dads–Bad Dads: Two Faces of Fatherhood," in *The Changing American Family and Public Policy*, ed. Andrew Cherlin (Washington, D.C.: Urban Institute Press, 1988); Joseph Pleck, "The Contemporary Man," in *Handbook of Counseling and Psychotherapy*, ed. Murray Scher et al. (Beverly Hills: Sage, 1987).

These kinds of ambiguities should make us leery of hard-and-fast pronouncements about what's happening to the American family. In many cases, we simply don't know precisely what our figures actually mean. For example, the proportion of youngsters receiving psychological assistance rose by 80 percent between 1981 and 1988. Does that mean they are getting more sick or receiving more help, or is it some complex combination of the two? Child abuse reports increased by 225 percent between 1976 and 1987. Does this represent an actual increase in rates of abuse or a heightened consciousness about the problem? During the same period, parents' self-reports about very severe violence toward their children declined 47 percent. Does this represent a real improvement in their behavior or a decreasing willingness to admit to such acts?[21]

Assessing the direction of family change is further complicated because many contemporary trends represent a reversal of developments that were themselves rather recent. The expectation that the family should be the main source of personal fulfillment, for example, was not traditional in the eighteenth and nineteenth centuries. . . . Prior to the 1900s, the family festivities that now fill us with such nostalgia for "the good old days" (and cause such heartbreak when they go poorly) were "relatively undeveloped." Civic festivals and Fourth of July parades were more important occasions for celebration and strong emotion than family holidays, such as Thanksgiving. Christmas "seems to have been more a time for attending parties and dances than for celebrating family solidarity." Only in the twentieth century did the family come to be the center of festive attention and emotional intensity.[22]

Today, such emotional investment in the family may be waning again. This could be interpreted as a reestablishment of balance between family life and other social ties; on the other hand, such a trend may have different results today than in earlier times, because in many cases the extrafamilial institutions and customs that used to socialize individuals and provide them with a range of emotional alternatives to family life no longer exist.

In other cases, close analysis of statistics showing a deterioration in family well-being supposedly caused by abandonment of tradition suggests a more complicated train of events. Children's health, for example, improved dramatically in the 1960s and 1970s, a period of extensive family transformation. It ceased to improve, and even slid backward, in the 1980s, when innovative social programs designed to relieve families of some "traditional" responsibilities were

---

[21]National Commission on Children, *Beyond Rhetoric: A New Agenda for Children and Families* (Washington, D.C.: GPO, 1991), p. 34; Richard Gelles and Jon Conte, "Domestic Violence and Sexual Abuse of Children," in *Contemporary Families: Looking Forward, Looking Back*, ed. Alan Booth (Minneapolis: National Council on Family Relations, 1991), p. 328.

[22]Arlene Skolnick, "The American Family: The Paradox of Perfection," *The Wilson Quarterly* (Summer 1980); Barbara Laslett, "Family Membership: Past and Present," *Social Problems* 25 (1978); Theodore Caplow et al., *Middletown Families: Fifty Years of Change and Continuity* (Minneapolis: University of Minnesota Press, 1982), p. 225.

repealed. While infant mortality rates fell by 4.7 percent a year during the 1970s, the rate of decline decreased in the 1980s, and in both 1988 and 1989, infant mortality rates did not show a statistically significant decline. Similarly, the proportion of low-birth-weight babies fell during the 1970s but stayed steady during the 1980s, and had even increased slightly as of 1988. Child poverty is lower today than it was in the "traditional" 1950s but much higher than it was in the nontraditional late 1960s.[23]

WILD CLAIMS AND PHONY FORECASTS

Lack of perspective on where families have come from and how their evolution connects to other social trends tends to encourage contradictory claims and wild exaggerations about where families are going. One category of generalizations seems to be a product of wishful thinking. As of 1988, nearly half of all families with children had both parents in the work force. The two-parent family in which only the father worked for wages represented just 25 percent of all families with children, down from 44 percent in 1975. For people overwhelmed by the difficulties of adjusting work and schools to the realities of working moms, it has been tempting to discern a "return to tradition" and hope the problems will go away. Thus in 1991, we saw a flurry of media reports that the number of women in the work force was headed down: "More Choose to Stay Home with Children" proclaimed the headlines; "More Women Opting for Chance to Watch Their Children Grow."[24]

The cause of all this commotion? The percentage of women aged twenty-five to thirty-four who were employed dropped from 74 percent to 72.8 percent between January 1990 and January 1991. However, there was an exactly equal decline in the percentage of men in the work force during the same period, and for both sexes the explanation was the same. "The dip is the recession," explained Judy Waldrop, research editor at *American Demographics* magazine, to anyone who bothered to listen. In fact, the proportion of *mothers* who worked increased slightly during the same period.[25]

This is not to say that parents, especially mothers, are happy with the pressures of balancing work and family life. Poll after poll reveals that both men and women feel starved for time. The percentage of women who say they would

35

---

[23]*The State of America's Children, 1991* (Washington, D.C.: Children's Defense Fund, 1991), pp. 55–63; *Seattle Post-Intelligencer,* 19 April 1991; National Commission on Children, *Beyond Rhetoric,* p. 32; *Washington Post National Weekly Edition,* 13–19 May 1991; James Wetzel, *American Youth: A Statistical Snapshot* (Washington, D.C.: William T. Grant Foundation, August 1989), pp. 12–14.

[24]*USA Today,* 12 May 1991, p. 1A; Richard Morin, "Myth of the Drop out Mom," *Washington Post,* 14 July 1991; Christine Reinhardt, "Trend Check," *Working Woman,* October 1991, p. 34; Howard Hayghe, "Family Members in the Work Force," *Monthly Labor Review* 113 (1990).

[25]Morin, "Myth of the Drop out Mom"; Reinhardt, "Trend Check," p. 34.

prefer to stay home with their children if they could afford to do so rose from 33 percent in 1986 to 56 percent in 1990. Other polls show that even larger majorities of women would trade a day's pay for an extra day off. But, above all, what these polls reveal is women's growing dissatisfaction with the failure of employers, schools, and government to pioneer arrangements that make it possible to combine work and family life. They do not suggest that women are actually going to stop working, or that this would be women's preferred solution to their stresses. The polls did not ask, for example, how *long* women would like to take off work, and failed to take account of the large majority of mothers who report that they would miss their work if they did manage to take time off. Working mothers are here to stay, and we will not meet the challenge this poses for family life by inventing an imaginary trend to define the problem out of existence.

At another extreme is the kind of generalization that taps into our worst fears. One example of this is found in the almost daily reporting of cases of child molestation or kidnapping by sexual predators. The highlighting of such cases, drawn from every corner of the country, helps disguise how rare these cases actually are when compared to crimes committed within the family.

A well-publicized instance of the cataclysmic predictions that get made when family trends are taken out of historical context is the famous *Newsweek* contention that a single woman of forty has a better chance of being killed by a terrorist than of finding a husband. It is true that the proportion of never-married women under age forty has increased substantially since the 1950s, but it is also true that the proportion has *decreased* dramatically among women over that age. A woman over thirty-five has a *better* chance to marry today than she did in the 1950s. In the past twelve years, first-time marriages have increased almost 40 percent for women aged thirty-five to thirty-nine. A single woman aged forty to forty-four still has a 24 percent probability of marriage, while 15 percent of women in their late forties will marry. These figures would undoubtedly be higher if many women over forty did not simply pass up opportunities that a more desperate generation might have snatched.[26]

Yet another example of the exaggeration that pervades many analyses of modern families is the widely quoted contention that "parents today spend 40 percent less time with their children than did parents in 1965." Again, of course, part of the problem is where researchers are measuring from. A comparative study of Muncie, Indiana, for example, found that parents spent much more

---

[26]"Too Late for Prince Charming," *Newsweek*, 2 June 1986, p. 55; John Modell, *Into One's Own: From Youth to Adulthood in the United States, 1920–1975* (Berkeley: University of California Press, 1989), p. 249; Barbara Lovenheim, *Beating the Marriage Odds: When You Are Smart, Single, and Over 35* (New York: William Morrow, 1990), pp. 26–27; *U.S. News & World Report*, 29 January 1990, p. 50; *New York Times*, 7 June 1991.

time with their children in the mid-1970s than did parents in the mid-1920s. But another problem is keeping the categories consistent. Trying to track down the source of the 40 percent decline figure, I called demographer John P. Robinson, whose studies on time formed the basis of this claim. Robinson's data, however, show that parents today spend about the same amount of time caring for children as they did in 1965. If the total amount of time devoted to children is less, he suggested, I might want to check how many fewer children there are today. In 1970, the average family had 1.34 children under the age of eighteen; in 1990, the average family had only .96 children under age eighteen — a decrease of 28.4 percent. In other words, most of the decline in the total amount of time parents spend with children is because of the decline in the number of children they have to spend time with![27]

Now I am not trying to say that the residual amount of decrease is not serious, or that it may not become worse, given the trends in women's employment. Robinson's data show that working mothers spend substantially less time in primary child-care activities than do nonemployed mothers (though they also tend to have fewer children); more than 40 percent of working mothers report feeling "trapped" by their daily routines; many routinely sacrifice sleep in order to meet the demands of work and family. Even so, a majority believe they are *not* giving enough time to their children. It is also true that children may benefit merely from having their parents available, even though the parents may not be spending time with them.

But there is no reason to assume the worst. Americans have actually gained   40
free time since 1965, despite an increase in work hours, largely as a result of a decline in housework and an increasing tendency to fit some personal requirements and errands into the work day. And according to a recent Gallup poll, most modern mothers think they are doing a better job of communicating with their children (though a worse job of house cleaning) than did their own mothers and that they put a higher value on spending time with their family than did their mothers.[28]

[27]William Mattox Jr., "The Parent Trap," *Policy Review* (Winter 1991): 6, 8; Sylvia Ann Hewlett, "Running Hard Just to Keep Up," *Time* (Fall 1990), and *When the Bough Breaks: The Cost of Neglecting Our Children* (New York: Basic Books, 1991), p. 73; Richard Whitmore, "Education Decline Linked with Erosion of Family," *The Olympian*, 1 October 1991; John Robinson, "Caring for Kids," *American Demographics*, July 1989, p. 52; "Household and Family Characteristics: March 1990 and 1989," *Current Population Reports*, series P-20, no. 447, table A-1. I am indebted to George Hough, Executive Policy Analyst, Office of Financial Management, Washington State, for finding these figures and helping me with the calculations.

[28]John Robinson, "Time for Work," *American Demographics*, April 1989, p. 68, and "Time's Up," *American Demographics*, July 1989, p. 34; Trish Hall, "Time on Your Hands? You May Have More Than You Think," *New York Times*, 3 July 1991, pp. C1, C7; Gannett News Service Wire Report, 27 August 1991.

NEGOTIATING THROUGH THE EXTREMES

Most people react to these conflicting claims and contradictory trends with understandable confusion. They know that family ties remain central to their own lives, but they are constantly hearing about people who seem to have *no* family feeling. Thus, at the same time as Americans report high levels of satisfaction with their *own* families, they express a pervasive fear that other people's families are falling apart. In a typical recent poll, for example, 71 percent of respondents said they were "very satisfied" with their own family life, but more than half rated the overall quality of family life as negative: "I'm okay; you're not."[29]

This seemingly schizophrenic approach does not reflect an essentially intolerant attitude. People worry about families, and to the extent that they associate modern social ills with changes in family life, they are ambivalent about innovations. Voters often defeat measures to grant unmarried couples, whether heterosexual or homosexual, the same rights as married ones. In polls, however, most Americans support tolerance for gay and lesbian relationships. Although two-thirds of respondents to one national poll said they wanted "more traditional standards of family life," the same percentage rejected the idea that "women should return to their traditional role." Still larger majorities support women's right to work, including their right to use child care, even when they worry about relying on day-care centers too much. In a 1990 *Newsweek* poll, 42 percent predicted that the family would be worse in ten years and exactly the same percentage predicted that it would be better. Although 87 percent of people polled in 1987 said they had "old-fashioned ideas about family and marriage," only 22 percent of the people polled in 1989 defined a family solely in terms of blood, marriage, or adoption. Seventy-four percent declared, instead, that family is any group whose members love and care for one another.[30]

These conflicted responses do not mean that people are hopelessly confused. Instead, they reflect people's gut-level understanding that the "crisis of the family" is more complex than is often asserted by political demagogues or others with an ax to grind. In popular commentary, the received wisdom is to "keep it simple." I know one television reporter who refuses to air an interview with anyone who uses the phrase "on the other hand." But my experience in discussing these issues with both the general public and specialists in the field is that people are hungry to get beyond oversimplifications. They don't want to be told that everything is fine in families or that if the economy improved and the government mandated parental leave, everything would be fine. But they don't believe that every

---

[29] *New York Times*, 10 October 1989, p. A18.

[30] E. J. Dionne Jr., *Why Americans Hate Politics* (New York: Simon & Schuster, 1991), pp. 110, 115, 325; *The Olympian*, 11 October 1989; *New York Times*, 10 October 1989; *Time*, 20 November 1989; *Seattle Post-Intelligencer*, 12 October 1990; Jerold Footlick, "What Happened to the Family?" *Newsweek Special Issue*, Winter/Spring 1990, p. 18.

hard-won victory for women's rights and personal liberty has been destructive of social bonds and that the only way to find a sense of community is to go back to some sketchily defined "traditional" family that clearly involves denying the validity of any alternative familial and personal choices.

Americans understand that along with welcome changes have come difficult new problems; uneasy with simplistic answers, they are willing to consider more nuanced analyses of family gains and losses during the past few decades. Indeed, argues political reporter E. J. Dionne, they are *desperate* to engage in such analyses.[31] Few Americans are satisfied with liberal and feminist accounts that blame all modern family dilemmas on structural inequalities, ignoring the moral crisis of commitment and obligation in our society. Yet neither are they convinced that "in the final analysis," as David Blankenhorn of the Institute for American Values puts it, "the problem is not the system. The problem is us."[32]

Despite humane intentions, an overemphasis on personal responsibility   45 for strengthening family values encourages a way of thinking that leads to moralizing rather than mobilizing for concrete reforms. While values are important to Americans, most do not support the sort of scapegoating that occurs when all family problems are blamed on "bad values." Most of us are painfully aware that there is no clear way of separating "family values" from "the system." Our values may make a difference in the way we respond to the challenges posed by economic and political institutions, but those institutions also reinforce certain values and extinguish others. The problem is not to berate people for abandoning past family values, nor to exhort them to adopt better values in the future — the problem is to build the institutions and social support networks that allow people to act on their best values rather than on their worst ones. We need to get past abstract nostalgia for traditional family values and develop a clearer sense of how past families actually worked and what the different consequences of various family behaviors and values have been. Good history and responsible social policy should help people incorporate the full complexity and the tradeoffs of family change into their analyses and thus into action. Mythmaking does not accomplish this end.

QUESTIONING THE TEXT

1. Coontz is highly critical of some researchers' careless or deceptive use of statistics to make "wild claims and phony forecasts" about families. Look closely at the author's use of statistical evidence. Does Coontz use statistics in a fully explained and evenhanded way? Explain the reasons for your answer.

---

[31]Dionne, *Why Americans Hate Politics.*
[32]David Blankenhorn, "Does Grandmother Know Best?" *Family Affairs* 3 (1990): 13, 16.

2. How might Coontz describe the way *she* wishes families were defined? Discuss this question with a classmate and then reread the selection, taking notes on the underlying assumptions Coontz makes about families — traditional or otherwise. Bring your notes to class for a discussion of "where the author is coming from" in this selection.

3. Working with a classmate, do some research into current statistics on birth rates, infant mortality rates, low-birth-weight babies, or child poverty. How do the current numbers compare to those Coontz cites?

MAKING CONNECTIONS

4. Read Barbara Dafoe Whitehead's "The Making of a Divorce Culture" (p. 224), keeping Coontz's views on divorce in mind. Then write a two- to three-page essay comparing and contrasting the two writers' positions on divorce, and explaining which one you find more persuasive.

5. Compare Andre Dubus's description of his experience of family in "Witness" (p. 426) with the "elusive traditional family" discussed by Coontz. In what ways does Dubus's family resemble the traditional patriarchal family? Does his essay help support any of Coontz's claims, or does it challenge her argument in some way? Explain you reasoning.

JOINING THE CONVERSATION

6. Coontz says her students' visions of traditional family life "bear a suspicious resemblance to reruns of old television series" except that "the scripts of different shows have been mixed up" (paragraph 2). Working with a classmate, choose a television series, either current or rerun, that features a family/home, and watch and tape as many episodes as you can within a week or so. Take notes during and after the episodes, jotting down the family members' characteristics, the roles they play, the values they represent, the kind of home they live in, and any other observations you make about the TV family. Compare your notes with your classmate's, noting any discrepancies and resolving them, if possible. Then, with your partner, prepare a 15-minute presentation (about six pages of double-spaced text with accompanying video clips) on "The American Family as Represented in [name of TV series]."

7. After freewriting or brainstorming about your own family experience, write a journal entry exploring how your experience matches up with or differs from any of the family paradigms Coontz describes. If you keep a reading log, write the entry there.

8. Imagine that you are asked to prepare a one- to two-page description of "a typical American family" to be placed in a time capsule marked for opening in 2150. Write the description; then ask several classmates to read and respond to it. With their feedback in mind, write a brief analysis of your description of the typical family, noting where you overgeneralize, leave out counterexamples, or use terms that may be unfamiliar to readers of the twenty-second century, for example. Bring your description and your analysis of it to class for discussion.

NICHOLAS LEMANN
In the Ruins

*E*ARLY IN THE MORNING *of August 29, 2005, the costliest hurricane in U.S. history barreled into New Orleans, breaching the levees, flooding the city, and leaving far more death and destruction in its wake than the city had been prepared for. Even though warnings had been coming for days about the force and deadliness of Katrina, lack of planning and preparation as well as a kind of paralysis of will led to devastating failures at every level of government. People in New Orleans and along the Gulf Coast waited in vain for help. And waited. And waited.*

In the years since Katrina struck, many have struggled to understand just what went wrong and why. Nicholas Lemann (b. 1954), who was born and raised in New Orleans and is now dean of Columbia University's Graduate School of Journalism, is one such writer. His "In the Ruins," a piece written for the New Yorker's *"Talk of the Town" column a couple of weeks after the hurricane hit, offers a meditation on his home city, where "Nature has the upper hand." Taking an historical view, Lemann describes the attitudes and (lack of) policies that led to the slow deterioration of the wetlands that had been part of the city's protection and the series of hurricanes and floods that lashed the city in 1888, 1927, and 1965. He connects the violence of these natural disasters with the periodic breakdowns of social order in New Orleans, from the time of Reconstruction through Huey Long's governorship to the post-Katrina nightmarish collapse of all institutions that should have been there to help. "The dramatic weather alone is not sufficient to explain the thinness of the veneer of civilization in the Gulf South," Lemann concludes; "A society that doesn't deliver for its many poor people, most of whom are black, doesn't generate a lot of trust and cohesion. The Biblical weather events reveal a deep civic weakness that makes violence a constant possibility."*

Lemann, widely recognized as a major voice in the field of journalism, has written for many major publications and is the author of The Promised Land: The Great Black Migration and How It Changed America *(which won the* Los Angeles Times *Book Award for History in 1991); and* The Big Test: The Secret History of the American Meritocracy *(1999), which led to major reforms in the SAT exam. His most recent book is* Redemption: The Last Battle of the Civil War *(2006), a horrifying account of post-Civil War Mississippi. Lemann has clearly studied the South, especially during and after Reconstruction, and he brings that background as well as a deep personal understanding of New Orleans to this essay, one that allows him to view this deeply flawed city ("New Orleans is an affront to nature," he says) with affection and a sense of longing. As I read "In the Ruins," I thought of the many hurricanes I weathered during the twenty years I lived in Florida; though I never had to evacuate, I have seen firsthand the fury of such storms and felt the utter helplessness any person feels in the face of nature's wrath.* —A.L.

New Orleans is an affront to nature, and nature isn't shy about reminding New Orleans of it. Lots of other places are affronts to nature, too, but, if they are in the United States, they usually have the hermetically sealed feeling of high-rise beachfront condominiums and desert suburbs and houses perched on mountaintops. New Orleans is too scruffy ever to achieve that. Tendrils of vines poke up through the floorboards. Paint flakes, wood rots, stamps self-adhere, and chunks of concrete must fly out of the roadbeds in the middle of the night (how else could they have disappeared?). The air is wet and heavy enough to slice into chunks and carry out of town in shopping bags. Streams lose their coherence and turn into swamps. Rats and roaches and snakes sashay through the gutters. Southern Louisiana is the site of many environmental depredations, but one of them will never be a feeling of locked-down sterility as an appurtenance of human habitation. Nature has the upper hand.

Natural disasters are always lurking somewhere close to the front of the New Orleans mind — especially aquatic disasters, and most especially hurricanes. Hurricanes are an eternal theme in the literature of New Orleans, for reasons having more to do with New Orleans than with literature. Lafcadio Hearn's story "Chita," about the famous hurricane of 1856, before hurricanes had official names, got down the rhythm that never changes: the palpable gathering of the storm, the largely unheeded advice to flee, the howling climax, the debris and the looting afterward. His description of the storm itself still works, too: "So the hurricane passed, — tearing off the heads of the prodigious waves, to hurl them a hundred feet in the air, — heaping up the ocean against the land, — upturning the woods. Bays and passes were swollen to abysses; rivers regorged; the sea-marshes were changed to raging wastes of water."

"Chita" was first published in 1888. Five years later, there was another devastating hurricane, which returned the barrier island next to the one described in "Chita" to the possession of the Gulf of Mexico. In the twentieth century, the highest-impact aquatic disaster was the Mississippi River flood of 1927 (the subject of a lovely 1939 novella, "Old Man," by William Faulkner), but New Orleans also got a direct hit from Hurricane Betsy, in 1965, and had many near-misses. The late-summer hurricane season entails an annual alteration of consciousness and a distinct set of rituals: laying in supplies, taping windows, deciding how much to trust official admonitions. It feels almost like a sacramental activity, consecrating the vulnerability that defines the place. But there's a peril in that, as is now obvious, when one year it's the farthest thing from just a ritual.

I like to tease my father, a New Orleanian, and a man whose idea of a good time would not include "dealing with his issues," that he has never fully explored the implications of having been sent away from his parents for six months, at the age of one, to live with relatives in Chicago in the pestilential aftermath of the 1927 flood. Maybe that explains why he prefers to spend hurricane season hunkered down at home. In 1965, I cowered happily in my parents' bed while Betsy beat against our windows. Three seasons ago, my stepmother persuaded my father to evacuate — unnecessarily, it turned out. This year, the two of them actually flew back to New Orleans from a vacation the night before Katrina hit, just when you were supposed to be getting out. On Monday afternoon, they were gloating; on Tuesday, they formed a small caravan of neighbors, bearing arms, and managed to escape by car. So for my father evacuations — the first at the age of one, the other at a few months short of eighty — form a set of bookends for his life, which, like many New Orleanians, he has lived entirely in one neighborhood.

When, after Katrina passed, the levees broke and the pumps failed, an-   5 other essential part of at least this New Orleanian's mind was activated: the part devoted to doubt about our competence to operate the purely human aspects of our society. New Orleans is, and for a long time has been, the opposite of a city that works. It perennially ranks near the bottom on practically every basic measure of civic health. It's true that the Bush Administration has repeatedly proposed cutting the budget of the Army Corps of Engineers, and that for years there has been a list of widely agreed-upon hurricane-protection measures that the federal government has chosen not to fund, with now horrific conse-quences. But it's also true that, after the levees broke, we watched every single system associated with the life of a city fail: the electric grid, the water system, the sewer system, the transportation system, the telephone system, the police force, the fire department, the hospitals, even the system for disposing of corpses. Perhaps it is all the fault of the force of the storm; I suspect that, as we move into the yearned-for realm of reliable information, we will find out that society and nature were co-conspirators in the tragedy. And the societal fault won't all have been the federal government's.

The wetlands that protected the city on the south and west have been deteriorating from commercial exploitation for years, thanks to inaction by Louisiana as well as by the United States. It isn't Washington that decided it's O.K. to let retail establishments in New Orleans sell firearms — which are now being extensively stolen and turned to the service of increasing the chaos in the city. It seems like a million years ago that President Bush had admirers who saw in him a Churchillian ability to rally a nation in crisis; last week, as both the President and Michael Brown, the director of the Federal Emergency Manage-ment Agency, offered bland, undignified, and ill-timed restatements of the obvious about the direness of the situation, you could practically see them thinking, I'm not getting blamed for this! But they were positively helpful next to Louisiana's governor, who cried and said that we should all pray, and New Orleans' mayor, who told citizens they should evacuate but didn't say how, predicted a second major flood, which didn't materialize, sniped at the federal authorities, and kept reminding everyone that the situation was desperate.

Because the feeling of a crisis fades so quickly, it's worth recalling that for the whole week of the hurricane most people in the city had no access to offi-cial help. The emergency numbers didn't work. There was no obvious person in charge, and no obvious plan being carried out. If you were lucky enough to have Internet access, you were more likely to find useful information — about, for example, which parts of the city were dry, or where drinking water was available — on blogs than on any government site. People who could find their way to institutional protection seemed almost worse off than people individually trapped, subjected as they were to violence, disease, starvation, overcrowding, and lies. It was unbelievable that it could take so long to get supplies in and people out, and to restore public safety, and to fix the levees. Even to have a person who could project calm and hope, and who could offer useful, reliable counsel would have been a gift from above — but that the emergence of such a person seemed so completely out of the question demonstrates an unimaginable failure at all levels. If national officials are incapable of rising to the occasion, the responsibility and duty of local officials goes beyond simply pointing that out.

There is a final, even deeper recess of the New Orleans mind, where a constant awareness of the possibility of the breakdown of the social order resides. The televised scenes of civil collapse that have so horrified the country have registered with New Orleanians as the awful realization of an ever-present set of fears. It isn't just that New Orleans has one of the highest murder rates in the country; the city has repeatedly been the scene of armed conflict, most notably during Reconstruction and the governorship of Huey Long. Walker Percy's 1971 novel *Love in the Ruins*, set on the Gulf Coast outside New Orleans, imagined a scene not too far from (though not nearly as bad as) what we've seen for the past week, with armed bands roaming the countryside, columns of smoke rising on the horizon, and people hiding out in half-destroyed buildings. Thirty years earlier, in a memoir called *Lanterns on the Levee*, Percy's cousin William Alexander Percy proudly conjured up the echt-Bourbon picture of himself facing down unruly homeless African Americans in the wake of the 1927 flood. The dramatic weather alone is not sufficient to explain the thinness of the veneer of civilization in the Gulf South. A society that doesn't deliver for its many poor people, most of whom are black, doesn't generate a lot of trust and cohesion. The Biblical weather events reveal a deep civic weakness that makes violence a constant possibility.

We're all wondering now what will become of New Orleans. A big American city has never before been entirely emptied of people, and had most of its housing rendered useless, and had all its basic systems fail at once. While the city is being cleared and drained and given an infrastructure, there will be no economic activity there at all. That will be the case for weeks (remember how devastating just a few days of inactivity in just a few industries and neighborhoods was after September 11th), so how will people live? How many will wait until they can move back and repossess their ruined homes and pray for the restoration of their jobs? Over the years, New Orleans has moved from being a top-ranked port toward becoming an economically optional city. Traditionally, it has had the kind of developing economy that runs on plantation agriculture, mineral extraction, and an intentionally impoverished, unempowered, and uneducated populace; its transformation into a tourist mecca was a form of going to ground, and it means that the city will be especially difficult to re-start. Every convention can always be held somewhere else. All one can do is hope that the city will be rebuilt with a much more solid social compact, as well as better hurricane protection.

You don't really think about the situation rationally at such an over-   10 whelming time, of course. If it's home, elegiac competes with angry for emotional first place. With information so frustratingly scarce, you can scan the citizen posts on the Internet for a scrap of news about a familiar place, or find yourself thinking in peculiarly specific terms about an acquaintance's face, or a tree on a particular corner, or a long-ago meal in a place where, chances are, nobody will ever be able to go again. My family's conversations seesaw between the tragedy in its full dimension — how many dead and how much destroyed, and, worse, what proportion was needless — and the quotidian minor resonances that the mind can't help offering up. My oldest son called demanding to know what had become of a particular rock in Audubon Park where I used to perch him as a toddler. I've been preoccupied with our family burial plot in Metairie Cemetery, where we laid my mother to rest six summers ago. The suddenly famous Seventeenth Street Canal runs perilously nearby. I've always assumed that I would be buried there — but I guess not.

QUESTIONING THE TEXT

1. What do you think is Lemann's attitude toward New Orleans? Does it shift in the essay? In thinking about your response, consider how "New Orleans" might mean different things — the physical place, the people, or an idea of a city, for example.

2. In the second paragraph and again in the eighth paragraph, Lemann refers to how literary works have presented the history of New Orleans, and particularly to disasters that have struck the area. Working with a classmate, make notes on how the inclusion of literary evidence affects readers of the essay. Why do you think that Lemann includes these examples? Bring your notes to class for discussion.

MAKING CONNECTIONS

3. What creates the character of New Orleans for Lemann? Compare his description of what constitutes the character of the place to Virginia Postrel's discussion of place in "In Praise of Chain Stores" (p. 681). To what extent do they agree on what makes a place unique?

4. In paragraphs 39 through 47 of "What to the Slave Is the Fourth of July?" (p. 497), Frederick Douglass acknowledges his anger toward some of his audience. In talking about the shortcomings of leadership in the

wake of Katrina in paragraphs 6 and 7, Lemann might be said to at least imply his anger. Which strategy — a direct expression of anger or a more muted one — do you find more effective? Do you think that the effectiveness of either article would be enhanced by a different approach?

JOINING THE CONVERSATION

5. Lemann suggests that political leadership after Hurricane Katrina was a failure at the national, state, and local levels. In a short essay, discuss an example of a time when you have seen effective leadership help people cope with or solve a problem, or when a failure of leadership has exacerbated a problem.

6. In the last paragraph of the essay, Lemann writes that his family discusses both "the tragedy in its full dimension . . . and the quotidian minor resonances that the mind can't help offering up." Think back to your own childhood or to more recent years. Are there any small memories, such as the Audubon Park rock that Lemann mentions, that are especially vivid for you? In a short essay, reflect on a memory of the quotidian that seems especially powerful to you.

JOHN LEO
Free Inquiry? Not on Campus

Recently, at a public university on the West Coast, students from an international socialist organization were brought before a disciplinary panel for trampling on American and British flags in a protest against the Iraq War. The group was charged with "attempts to incite violence and create a hostile environment." Stepping on the British flag, you see, can be construed as offensive to Christians since it carries the Cross of St. George as one of its emblems.

Absurd, you think? And you'd be right: the incident didn't actually happen. Surely, university administrators would not restrict the right of socialists to express their opinions or prosecute students at an anti-war rally on a charge of religious incivility. After all, freedom of speech is among the most cherished of ideals, a hallmark of American democracy that differentiates it even from other Western governments.

No, the group actually hauled before the disciplinary panel was the College Republicans, for staging an anti-terrorism rally, where some people did step on butcher-paper versions of the banners of Hamas and Hezbollah — which, like the British flag, carry religious characters. Does the university's judicial action make more sense now?

The College Republicans were predictably exonerated — given the legal precedents in these situations, the First Amendment and all. But bringing the conservative group before a university tribunal was likely intended simply to chill its political activities, a strong signal to the group that the powers-that-be on campus had them under scrutiny and could make lives difficult. I doubt that the Republicans were surprised. Most college and universities — committed to diversity in everything but ideas — have dozens of techniques for signaling to students exactly which opinions on campus are preferred.

Just walk down the corridors of any English, history, education, or sociology department and you'll get the message from the posters on the wall or the lists of required reading. The faculty member who hangs a liberal political screed on her door sends a not-so-covert signal to conservative students that they aren't welcome. And the strategy works, not only discouraging students on the right from majoring in many disciplines, but assuring people already in those fields that their pools of graduate students and future faculty hires will always sing from the same songbook. In other contexts, techniques like those used to constrain the range of acceptable opinion on college campuses — from choice of campus speakers to near-total faculty discretion in hiring practices to institutional support for agenda-driven offices, centers, special initiatives, and departments — have been described as institutional racism. But when it comes to students and faculty not on the political left, it's business as usual.

John Leo (b. 1935), a former contributing editor and columnist for U.S. News & World Report who has long been concerned about the politicized state of higher education in America, offers his take on the issue in "Free Inquiry? Not on Campus," which originally appeared in City Journal (Winter 2007), a magazine that focuses on subjects *relating to urban policy. Documenting the political left's growing enthusiasm for censorship, Leo — who once had a lecture at Columbia University cancelled because of protesters — suggests that the repression of ideas already customary on college campuses is in danger of spreading, through legislation and litigation, to other areas of our political life. Perhaps our cherished notion of freedom of speech may indeed, one day, become just another cultural myth.* —J.R.

And the college speech police threaten the liberty of us all.

Remember when the Right had a near-monopoly on censorship? If so, you must be in your sixties, or older. Now the champions of censorship are mostly on the left. And they are thickest on the ground in our colleges and universities. Since the late 1980s, what should be the most open, debate-driven, and tolerant sector of society has been in thrall to the diversity and political correctness that now form the aggressive secular religion of America's elites.

The censors have only grown in power, elevating antidiscrimination rules above "absolutist" free-speech principles, silencing dissent with anti-harassment policies, and looking away when students bar or disrupt conservative speakers or steal conservative newspapers. Operating under the tacit principle that "error has no rights," an ancient Catholic theological rule, the new censors aren't interested in debates or open forums. They want to shut up dissenters.

In October, for instance, a student mob stormed a Columbia University stage, shutting down speeches by two members of the Minutemen, an anti-illegal-immigration group. The students shouted: "They have no right to speak!" Campus opponents of Congressman Tom Tancredo, an illegal-immigration foe, set off fire alarms at Georgetown to disrupt his planned speech, and their counterparts at Michigan State roughed up his student backers. Conservative activist David Horowitz, black conservative columnist Star Parker, and Daniel Pipes, an outspoken critic of Islamism, frequently find themselves shouted down or disrupted on campus.

In my experience, there are plenty of advocates for censorship on the right as well as on the left. —A.L.

On my campus, students also "disappear" the only really left-wing journal. —A.L.

While I don't approve of students' shutting down discourse, remember that they too have a right to speak. —A.L.

He immediately establishes colleges and universities as the enemy, alienating me from his argument. —L.S.

Conservative speakers cannot assume they'll be able to speak on my campus. They must always anticipate hostile demonstrators whose primary aim is to disrupt the exchange of ideas. Left-wing speakers rarely face such prior restraints on their speech. —J.R.

After months of investigation, Columbia's response to the protesters' violation of free speech was mild "disciplinary warning." —J.R.

Why is he focusing on Columbia? I could give examples and counterexamples from a number of other schools. —A.L.

School officials seem to have little more inter-est in free speech. At Columbia this fall, officials turned away most of a large crowd gathered to hear former PLO terrorist-turned-anti-jihadist Walid Shoebat, citing security worries. Only Columbia students and 20 guests got in. Colleges often cite the danger of violence as they cancel controversial speeches — a new form of heckler's veto: shrinking an audience so that an event will seem unimportant is itself a way to cave to critics. In 2003, Columbia, facing leftist fury at the scheduled speeches of several conservatives (myself included), banned scores of in-vited nonstudents who had agreed to attend. Though some schools cancel left-wing speakers, too — including Ward Churchill and Michael Moore, or abortion-supporters Anna Quindlen and Christie Whitman at Catholic universities — right-of-center speakers are the campus speech cop's normal targets.

5

He addresses the other side of the argument a bit here, but too briefly to convince me that his stance is not thoroughly one-sided. A good writer always takes other views into account! —L.S.

Leo adds credibility to his arraignment by this concession. —J.R.

Official censorship — now renamed speech codes and antiharassment codes — pervades the campuses. The Foundation for Individual Rights in Education (FIRE) recently surveyed more than 300 schools, including the top universities and liberal arts colleges, and found that over 68 percent explicitly prohibit speech that the First Amendment would protect if uttered off campus. At 229 schools, FIRE found clear and substantial restriction of speech, while 91 more had policies that one could interpret as restricting speech. Only eight permitted genuine free expression.

What were the questions FIRE asked, and what was their agenda? —A.L.

Note Leo's strategic move to cast policies native to most cam-puses (speech and anti-harassment codes) in a different light as "official censorship." —J.R.

A 2002 New York Times article reported that today's college kids seem more guarded in their views than previous generations of students. The writer suggested several possible explanations — disgust with partisan politics and uncivil debates on cable news shows, perhaps, or simple politeness. A more likely reason is that universities have made honest disagreement dangerous, making students fearful of saying what they think.

I have seen a lot of "honest disagreement." —L.S.

Much campus censorship rests on philosophi-cal underpinnings that go back to social theorist Herbert Marcuse, a hero to sixties radicals. Marcuse argued that traditional tolerance is repressive — it wards off reform by making the status quo . . . well,

Students are not afraid, as Leo sug-gests, but are voicing their opinions in new ways. Possibly students don't feel as compelled to speak out on cam-pus today because there are now so many ways to speak out on the Web, where the potential to be heard is great. —J.E.M.

tolerable. Marcuse favored intolerance of established and conservative views, with tolerance offered only to the opinions of the oppressed, radicals, subversives, and other outsiders. Indoctrination of students and "deeply pervasive" censorship of others would be necessary, starting on the campuses and fanning out from there.

By the late 1980s, many of the double standards that Marcuse called for were in place in academe. Marcuse's candor was missing, but everyone knew that speakers, student newspapers, and professors on the right could (make that should) receive different treatment from those on the left. The officially oppressed — designated race and gender groups — knew that they weren't subject to the standards and rules set for other students.

Marcuse's thinking has influenced a generation of influential radical scholars. They included Mari Matsuda, who followed Marcuse by arguing that complete free speech should belong mainly to the powerless; and Catharine MacKinnon, a pioneer of modern sexual harassment and "hostile environment" doctrine. In MacKinnon's hands, sexual harassment became a form of gender-based class discrimination and inegalitarian speech a kind of harmful action.

Confusing speech and action has a long pedigree on the PC campus. At the time of the first wave of speech codes 20 years ago, Kenneth Lasson, a law professor at the University of Baltimore, argued that "racial defamation does not merely 'preach hate'; it is the practice of hatred by the speaker" — and is thus punishable as a form of assault. Indeed, the Left has evolved a whole new vocabulary to blur the line between acts and speech: "verbal conduct" and "expressive behavior" (speech), "non-traditional violence" (Lani Guinier's term for strong criticism), and "anti-feminist intellectual harassment" (rolling one's eyeballs over feminist dogma).

Campus censors frequently emulate the Marcusian double standard by combining effusive praise for free speech with an eagerness to suppress unwelcome views. "I often have to struggle with right and wrong because I am a strong believer in free speech," said Ronni Santo, a gay student activist at UCLA in the late nineties. "Opinions are protected under the First Amendment, but when negative opinions come out of a person's fist, mouth, or pen to intentionally hurt others, that's when their opinions should no longer be protected."

In their 1993 book, *The Shadow University*, Alan Charles Kors and Harvey Silverglate turned some of the early speech codes into national laughingstocks. Among the banned comments and action they listed: "intentionally producing psychological discomfort" (University of North Dakota), "insensitivity to the experience of women" (University of Minnesota), and "inconsiderate jokes" (University of Connecticut). Serious nonverbal offenses included "inappropriate laughter" (Sarah Lawrence College), "eye contact or the lack of it" (Michigan State University), and "subtle discrimination," such as "licking lips or teeth; holding food provocatively" (University of Maryland). Later gems, added well after the courts struck down campus codes as overly broad, included bans on "inappropriate non-verbals" (Macalester College), "communication with sexual overtones" (Lincoln University), and "discussing sexual activities" (State University of New York–Brockport). Other codes bar any comment or gesture that "annoys," "offends," or otherwise makes someone feel bad. Tufts ruled that attributing harassment complaints to the "hypersensitivity of others who feel hurt" is itself harassment.

Brockport, which banned "cartoons that depict religious figures in compromising situations," "jokes making fun of any protected group," and "calling someone an old hag," helpfully described for students what does not constitute sexual harassment: "non-coercive interaction(s) . . . that are acceptable to both parties." Commented Greg Lukianoff of FIRE: "The wonder is that anyone would risk speaking at all at SUNY Brockport."

Despite numerous court decisions overturning these codes, they have proliferated. College officials point to the hurt feelings of women or minorities as evidence that a violation must have occurred, in part because they want to avoid charges of racism, sexism,

It appalls me when people — especially political activists who should know better — allow petty feelings to corrupt hard-won rights. It suggests how poorly we are educating students about basic principles of American democracy. (And I suppose Leo cites the example to generate just such outrage.)   —J.R.

These particular bits of evidence seem more rooted in claims of sexual harassment than simple free speech.   —L.S.

Think of the uproar over the Danish cartoons depicting Muhammad.   —A.L.

15

and homophobia — an overriding fear in today's academe, where diversity offices can swarm with 40 or 50 administrators. The Clinton administration's commissioner of civil rights in the Department of Education, Norma Cantú reinforced this trend by interpreting racial and sexual harassment broadly, with an implied threat to withhold federal funds if universities didn't vigorously counter it. In 2003, the DOE office of civil rights issued a weary clarification, explaining to universities that harassment doesn't mean merely feeling offended. The letter has had little effect on the censoring fervor of the campuses, however. Occidental College officials soon found a student radio shock jock guilty of sexual harassment for using various crude terms on the air, calling one student a "bearded feminist" and another "half man, half vagina." On many a campus, tastelessness equals harassment.

Georgia Tech went so far as to ban "denigrating" comments on "beliefs," which would make almost any passionate argument over ideas a violation. Needless to say, the targets here are usually conservative. Ohio State University at Mansfield launched a sexual harassment investigation of a research librarian, Scott Savage, for recommending the inclusion of four conservative books, including popular works by David Horowitz and ex-senator Rick Santorum, on a freshman reading list. Two professors had complained that one of the books, *The Marketing of Evil*, by journalist David Kupelian, was "homophobic tripe" and "hate literature." This may have been the first time that a campus charged that a book recommendation qualified as sexual harassment. After a burst of publicity and a threat to sue, the university dropped the investigation.

Student censors regularly spirit away whole print runs of conservative student newspapers, almost always without reproof from administrators. Over the years, campus officials, including a few university presidents, have even encouraged such stealing. After repeated thefts of the *Dartmouth Review*, an official egged on the thieves by calling the paper "litter" and "abandoned property." In a commencement speech, former Cornell president

Hunter Rawlings III praised students who seized and burned copies of the conservative *Cornell Review* in retaliation for printing a gross parody of Ebonics.

Once in a blue moon, a college president vigorously defends free speech. At Northern Kentucky University, president James Votruba rebuked and suspended a tenured feminist professor, Sally Jacobsen, who led a group that demolished a campus-approved right-to-life display. Jacobsen cited two justifications: her deep feelings and her alleged free-speech right to tear down displays that offend her. "I did invite students to express their freedom of speech rights to destroy the display if they wished," she said. "Any violence perpetrated against that silly display was minor compared to how I felt when I saw it."

But far more typical than Votruba was Washington State University president V. Lane Rawlins, who hailed the disruption — and subsequent cancellation — of an intentionally offensive student play that irritated blacks, Christians, Jews, gays, and others. Rawlins defended the disrupters, saying that they had "exercised their rights of free speech in a very responsible manner." Later documents showed that the university had actually organized and financed them. In the real world, such a revelation would have cost Rawlins his job. But on today's campus, it passes without comment, in part because students can point out, with perfect moral justification, that forcing the cancellation of speeches and stealing newspapers are just logical extensions of campus speech codes.

Leo lets the accumulation of examples have its effect on readers. —J.R.

Leo's long list of examples does little to sway me — I'd like a little more acknowledgement of the other side of this issue and a little more about what this all means to the author. —L.S.

Nothing makes the campus censors angrier than someone who dares to question race and gender preferences, especially if he uses satire to do it. That's why the anti-affirmative-action bake sales that conservative students have sponsored at many schools — white male customers can buy cookies for $1, with lower prices for women and various minorities — have provoked such ferocious responses from campus authorities.

20

Grand Valley State University in Allendale, Michigan, provides a typical example. A Republican club there staged a bake sale, and several students then said that they felt offended. This amounted to a

This bake sale strikes me as silly, but note that women still earn less on the dollar than men — so they can use a break on cookies! —A.L.

powerful argument, since hurt feelings are trump cards in the contemporary campus culture. (At the University of Wisconsin, for example, a black student testified in defense of the faculty speech code, complaining bitterly that a professor had used the word "niggardly" while teaching Chaucer. "I was in tears," she said. "It's not up to the rest of the class to decide whether my feelings are valid.")

Next came the usual administrative scramble to suppress free speech while expressing great respect for it. The university charged the club with a violation of the student code and threatened sanctions. The students folded under administrative pressure and apologized. When the Republican club president refused to back down, club members asked him to resign, and he did. The students' retreat was understandable, if not very courageous. The university in effect was trying them for bias, with the likelihood that a notation of racism would become part of their academic record and follow them to post-college job interviews.

The College Republicans at Northeastern Illinois University canceled an announced affirmative-action bake sale after the administration threatened punishment. Dean of students Michael Kelly announced that the cookie sellers would be violating university rules and that "any disruption of university activities that would be caused by this event is also actionable." This principle — politically incorrect speakers are responsible for attacks on them by students who resent their speech — is dear to campus censors' hearts. The university didn't view itself as engaging in censorship — and double-standard censorship at that, since it freely allowed a satirical wage-gap bake sale run by feminists. Absurdly, Kelly said that the affirmative-action sale would be fine — if cookie prices were the same for whites, minorities, and women. Other administrators complained that differential pricing of baked goods is unfair, thus unwittingly proving the whole point of the parody.

Schools will use almost any tactic to shut the bake sales down. At the University of Washington, the administration said that the sponsor had failed to get a food permit. At Grand Valley, the university

What would be the consequences of allowing individual feelings to dictate rights of expression? No one would be free. People who think this way — faculty included — need more course work in history, law, and government. —J.R.

The bake sales seem like a red herring here: what's Leo really arguing for? —A.L.

counsel argued that the sale of a single cupcake would convert political commentary into forbidden campus commerce. At Texas A&M, the athletics director argued that a satirical bake sale would damage the sports teams by making it harder to recruit minorities.

It's clever that Leo uses Texas A&M, traditionally a conservative school, as an example.
—J.E.M.

One of the PC campus's worst excesses in suppressing unwanted speech is the drive by gays and their allies to banish or break Christian groups for their traditional beliefs on sexuality. Some 20 campuses have acted to de-recognize or de-fund religious groups that oppose homosexuality (as well as nonmarital sex), often accusing them of violating antidiscrimination rules — that is, refusing to let gays be members, or allowing them to belong but not serve as officers. The language of many policies would require a Democratic club to accept a Republican president, a Jewish group to allow a Holocaust-denying member, or a Muslim organization to accept a leader who practices voodoo.

25

About half of the attempts to move against Christian clubs have failed. The University of North Carolina–Chapel Hill dropped its move against a Christian club three days after getting a friendly warning letter from FIRE. "UNC couldn't defend in public what it was willing to do in private," said FIRE president Alan Charles Kors. "If an evangelical Christian who believed homosexuality to be a sin tried to become president of a university's Bisexual, Gay and Lesbian Alliance, the administration would have led candlelight vigils on behalf of diversity and free association."

The real issue here is the need for mutual respect, which coexists easily with the right to speak when speakers take full responsibility for what they say.
—A.L.

Such Marcusian double standards — freedom for me, but not for thee — now have a beachhead in the law, thanks to the legendarily left-wing Ninth Circuit. In response to a "Day of Silence" sponsored by the Gay-Straight Alliance at his Poway, California, high school, Tyler Harper wore a shirt that proclaimed, on the front, "Be Ashamed, Our School Embraced What God Has Condemned," and on the back, "Homosexuality Is Shameful/Romans 1:27." The school principal ordered Harper to take off the shirt. Harper refused, and sued. He argued that the purpose of the "Day of Silence" was to "endorse, promote and encourage homosexual activity" and that he had a First Amendment right to use his T-shirt message as a rebuttal.

When the Poway case reached the Ninth Circuit, Judge Stephen Reinhardt and his colleague Judge Sidney R. Thomas argued in a two-to-one decision that it is permissible to exclude T-shirt messages from First Amendment protection if they strike at a "core identifying characteristic of students on the basis of their membership as a minority group" — with minority status conveyed by categories "such as race, religion, and sexual orientation." This ruling, unless the Supreme Court takes it up and overturns it, creates a large new category of viewpoints that the First Amendment doesn't safeguard, at least within the Ninth Circuit. Based on the loose language — "such as" could apply to numerous groups — criticism of illegal aliens might now lack First Amendment protection, says UCLA law prof Eugene Volokh. Presumably, too, one can no longer criticize any minority religious opinion, such as the Islamic view that cartoons mocking Mohammed are out-of-bounds. But pictures of Christ in urine would be perfectly fine, since Christianity remains America's majority faith.

Some on the left applaud such Marcusian hairsplitting, arguing that First Amendment "absolutists" must learn to "balance" free speech and special protections for vulnerable groups. But in dissent, Judge Alex Kozinski expressed "considerable difficulty understanding the source and sweep of the novel doctrine the majority announces today" — nothing in state, federal, or common law supports it, he noted.

To understand the rising disrespect for free expression in the U.S., Kozinski might have been better off looking to Canada and Europe, both a bit ahead of us — if that's the right phrase — in embracing PC censorship.

Despite stated respect for free speech in its national constitution, Canada now has a national speech code and judges and elites eager to expand it. The Canadian Supreme Court has issued a series of rulings stating that the government may limit speech in the name of worthwhile goals, such as ending

Note how Leo now draws out the consequences of the Marcusian principles he introduced earlier. They justify the application of double standards. —J.R.

By this time, I am completely alienated by Leo's slanted and highly selective examples, constant repetition, and overgeneralizations. He certainly seems to have an ax to grind. —A.L.

Most students assume that the First Amendment is a universal principle. They'd be surprised how routinely people elsewhere are prosecuted for their ideas. This long section puts the principle of free speech into an important context. Some societies maintain civility with a little repression. —J.R. 30

I lived in Canada for ten years and found it a very civil society, one that had a healthy respect for free speech — and for the rights of all.

—A.L.

discrimination, ensuring social harmony, or promoting sexual equality. The state may now seize published material judged to "degrade" or "dehumanize" any group.

What free-speech supporters would regard as horrendous abuses have become commonplace. In 1997, for instance, the mayor of London, Ontario, ran afoul of Canada's Human Rights Code for refusing to declare a Gay Pride day, citing her Christian beliefs. The British Columbia College of Teachers refuses to certify teacher education programs at Christian universities if they urge students to abstain from premarital sex, adultery, or homosexual sex. The province's hate-speech laws use extremely broad language, criminalizing statements that "indicate" discrimination or that "likely" will expose a group or one of its members to hatred or contempt.

Ted Byfield, editor of the now-defunct *Alberta Report*, violated that province's human rights law by publishing an article noting that some children were grateful for the education they received at the government's residential schools for Indians, much despised by multiculturalists and admittedly abuse-plagued. An injunction against the *Alberta Report* forbade stories on partial-birth abortions after Byfield ran a story quoting unnamed nurses and official documents saying that some babies subject to the procedure at a Calgary hospital were born alive and deliberately allowed to starve to death.

Canada has become "a pleasantly authoritarian country," observes Alan Borovoy, general counsel of the Canadian Civil Liberties Association. Robert Martin, a constitutional law prof at the University of Western Ontario, is harsher: Canada is now "a totalitarian theocracy," he says, devoted to the secular state religion of political correctness.

Things are no freer across the pond. The Irish Council for Civil Liberties announced that it would prosecute any priests found distributing or quoting the pope's words forbidding gay marriage. In England, author Lynette Burrows drew a police investigation for saying on a talk show that she opposes homosexual adoption. An Oxford student fared worse after a night out to celebrate the end of exams.

Would "pleasantly authoritarian" also describe the atmosphere at many American institutions of higher learning?   —J.R.

35

Stopped by a mounted policeman, he drunkenly quipped, "Excuse me, do you realize your horse is gay?" Unfortunately, the humor-free local constabulary arrested the young man under the Public Order Act for making homophobic remarks.

By law, 11 European nations can punish anyone who publicly denies the Holocaust. That's why the discredited Holocaust-denying British historian David Irving went to prison in Austria. Ken Livingstone, London's madcap mayor, drew a monthlong suspension for calling a Jewish reporter a Nazi. A Swedish pastor went through a long and harrowing prosecution for a sermon criticizing homosexuality, finally beating the rap in Sweden's supreme court.

Naturally enough, Muslims want to play the same victim game as other aggrieved groups. The French Council of Muslims says that it's considering taking *France Soir*, which reprinted the Danish cartoons, to court for provocation. When French novelist Michel Houellebecq said some derogatory things about the Koran, Muslim groups hauled him into court, which eventually exonerated him. The late Italian journalist Oriana Fallaci wrote an angry anti-Muslim book, meant to waken the West to the gravity of the threat posed by Islam. Her prosecution in Italy for writing the book was pending when she died in October.

Much of Europe has painted itself into a corner on Muslim-driven censorship. What can Norway say to pro-censorship Muslims when it already has a hate-speech law forbidding, among other things, "publicly stirring up one part of the population against another," or any utterance that "threatens, insults or subjects to hatred, persecution, or contempt any person or group of persons because of their creed, race, color, or national or ethnic origin . . . or homosexual bent"? No insulting utterances at all? Since most strong opinions can seem insulting to someone — can hurt someone's feelings — no insults means no free speech.

Chafing under First Amendment restrictions, many censorship-prone American leftists look longingly toward successful speech control up north or overseas. That's what they want right here.

I genuinely hope that Leo is wrong here. The left should know from its own experiences that repressive regimes eventually silence all people — even the controllers of speech. —J.R.

I believe that everyone, including conservatives, should be able to express their beliefs freely. But minority groups' voices also deserve to be heard, and such groups often lack the power to speak out against more mainstream views. The examples in this essay fail to convince me that conservatives on campus are in danger of being silenced.   —L.S.

We are very lucky to have the First Amendment. Without it, our chattering classes would be falling all over themselves to ban speech that offends sensitive groups, just as Canadian- and Euro-chatterers are doing now. We know this because our campus speech codes, the models for the disastrous hate-speech laws elsewhere, were the inventions of our own elites. Without a First Amendment, the distortions and suppressions of campus life would likely have gone national. Mel Gibson, Michael Richards, and many rap artists would be in jail, or at least facing charges.

The cause of free speech can no longer expect much help from the American Civil Liberties Union, more concerned today with civil rights and multicultural issues than with civil liberties and free speech. True, the ACLU still takes some censorship cases — it led the fight against the first wave of campus speech codes circa 1990, for instance. But the rise of the ACLU's internal lobbies or "projects," such as the Lesbian and Gay Project and the Immigrants' Rights Project, has made the organization look more and more like a traditional left-wing pressure group, with little passion for the First Amendment. The ACLU is also following the money: funds flow in because the group responds to concerns of feminists, gays, and other identity groups, not because of its historical defense of free speech and civil liberties.

These days, the ACLU visibly stands aloof from obvious First Amendment cases — such as the college speech and harassment codes — and even comes down on the anti-free-speech side. Consider the group's stance in Aguilar v. Avis Rent-A-Car System, a case involving ethnic epithets aimed by supervisors at Latino employees of Avis in San Francisco. A California court ruled that Avis had permitted a hostile environment. The California Supreme Court, abetted by both the northern Californian and the national ACLU, agreed, and upheld the lower court's startling speech restriction: prior restraint on workers' speech, forbidding a judge-made list of specific words. These words, not yet revealed or promulgated, will soon be taboo in every California workplace, even outside the earshot of Latino

40

employees, and even if they are welcome. As civil libertarian Nat Hentoff wrote: "This may be the broadest and vaguest restriction of speech in American legal history."

Even with the ACLU, the mainstream media, school officials, and much of the professorate AWOL, the speech police haven't gone unopposed. Just ask former Clinton official Donna Shalala. As chancellor of the University of Wisconsin in the late eighties, she proved a fervent early advocate of campus speech restrictions. Though Shalala occasionally praised free speech, she and her team imposed not only a full-fledged student speech code, later struck down in federal court, but also a faculty code that provoked the first (and so far, only) pro-free-speech campus campaign strong enough to repeal such repressive restrictions. The Wisconsin faculty code was a primitive, totalitarian horror. Professors found themselves under investigation, sometimes for months, without a chance to defend themselves or even to know about the secret proceedings. One female professor said: "It was like being put in prison for no reason. I had no idea what it was that I was supposed to have done."

A small group of free-speech-minded faculty formed the Committee for Academic Freedom and Rights (CAFR). The group asked for help from the Wisconsin chapter of the pro-free-speech National Association of Scholars, which enlisted as speakers such celebrated allies as Alan Dershowitz and *National Journal* columnist Jonathan Rauch.

The first Amendment forces got a lucky break when the university signed a foolish contract with Reebok, in which it received millions of dollars in exchange for the use of the company's footwear by campus sports teams. The contract included a clause forbidding negative comments on Reebok products by any "University employee, agent or representative." The clause greatly irritated the anticorporate campus Left, which had usually been lukewarm or indifferent to free-speech concerns, helping convert some of its members to the anti-speech-code side. Later, a strong defense of free speech by a homosexual professor, called a traitor to his identity group for his

Sounds like the sixties all over again, and, once again, the enemy is us. —J.R.

45

"Traitor to his identity group"? This intolerant and profoundly hateful concept should be antithetical to all higher education stands for. —J.R.

courage, brought in other campus leftist allies. CAFR was amazed at how quickly many would-be censors backed down when confronted with controversy and threatened lawsuits. Wisconsin rescinded its faculty code — the first university to do so without a court order.

New national groups have joined the fight for free speech on campus (and off), among them the Center for Individual Rights, the Alliance Defense Fund, and FIRE, the most relentless of the newcomers. FIRE usually starts a campaign with a polite letter to a university president, noting that some policy is either unconstitutional or a clear violation of civil liberties. If it doesn't get the change it wants, it will then write to trustees, parents, and alumni, and take its case to the media.

FIRE now has an extensive network of campus free-speech "spies," as its cofounder, Harvey Silverglate, jauntily calls them (Alan Charles Kors, the other cofounder, prefers "concerned members of the community"). The organization is seeking new ways to open up closed campus systems, too, such as suing administrators as individuals, which FIRE believes will get their full attention. Another new tactic is to publicize what colleges spend on fighting for unconstitutional speech codes. Most of all, FIRE is trying to show stubborn administrators that the era of hiding gross civil liberties violations behind a PC wall of silence is over: the group wins more than 95 percent of its cases.

Political correctness took hold when there were 40 radio talk shows, three networks, and no bloggers. Today, the cross-referencing of PC outrages among bloggers, radio talkers, and rights groups makes it hard to run an old-fashioned repressive campus. University presidents now understand that their reputations do not rest entirely with the PC platoons. Donna Shalala escaped Wisconsin with her reputation intact. Sheldon Hackney, former president of Penn, did not. (I named my own annual award for the worst college president, the "Sheldon," in his honor.) When he stepped down from the Penn presidency, he didn't become the head of a major

Because most campus speech codes violate the First Amendment, FIRE has knocked down one after another, usually without litigation. But why have some college administrators allowed such repressive policies to stand for years? —J.R.

Incredible. —J.E.M.

There's nothing like the bright light of truth to expose corruption and folly. —J.R.

Without saying so directly, Leo keeps trying to leave the impression that only conservatives oppose restrictive campus speech codes. But many on the left have been passionate defenders of free speech and civil liberties. Admitting this wouldn't suit his agenda, though! —A.L.

foundation, as many expected; instead, he wound up returning to Penn as a professor. Other reputations hang in the balance. Lee Bollinger, a First Amendment expert (and affirmative-action advocate), was invisible during the free-speech debates at Michigan and is almost as recessive today as president of Columbia. But it is getting harder for the Hackneys and Bollingers to waffle.

Perhaps the battle to release the campuses from the iron grasp of PC will take decades, but the struggle for free speech is being fought — and won — now.

I wonder what prompted this tirade! Is Leo equally concerned when conservatives denounce speech on the left as un-American or treasonous?

—A.L.

If in fact our speech is becoming increasingly censored on campus — and I am not yet convinced — I am confident that much student dialogue has been not muted, but merely shifted online. Is speech restricted there? —J.E.M.

QUESTIONING THE TEXT

1. How well do you think that Leo builds his case? Analyze the evidence that Leo provides. What moments do you find most persuasive? Where is his evidence least persuasive? Based on your reactions to this reading, outline some general principles that help define good evidence.

2. Why do you think that Leo turns to a consideration of free speech in Europe beginning in paragraph 35? Does it enhance or detract from his argument about the state of free speech on American campuses? Explain your reasoning.

MAKING CONNECTIONS

3. How does your experience of campus life compare to Leo's descriptions of college as a place where speech is restricted? Does your school have a speech code? Do you feel social pressures not to speak out for fear of retribution? Describe your experience with freedom of speech, or a lack thereof, at your school.

4. Consider the ideals of the United States as expressed in the Declaration of Independence (p. 492), particularly in the famous second paragraph. To what degree do you think that Leo's position, which of course focuses more on the First Amendment than it does the Declaration, upholds those ideals? Do you think that any of the policies that he criticizes might pursue the ideals outlined in the Declaration more truly or effectively than Leo does?

JOINING THE CONVERSATION

5. Most people would defend at least some restrictions on free speech; one famous example is the prohibition against yelling "Fire!" in a crowded theater in which there is no fire; another example is laws against threatening others with harm. Think of an example of speech that you or others might wish to ban and explain why this kind of speech should or should not be tolerated.

6. Research the history of a free speech debate at a college campus, using one of Leo's examples or discovering one that he does not mention. You might research how the debate was covered by a student or local newspaper in addition to any national coverage. Next, prepare a report for class on your findings, focusing especially on how complex the case was. Do you feel that the debate was as straightforward as Leo suggests most are, or were there good arguments on both sides of the issue?

The photo on the preceding page shows a woman in business clothing photocopying her face. What impression do you take from the details of this photograph? If you were the young woman's employer, how would you react to this image? ■ What does this image suggest about business and labor, the subject of this chapter? What differences do you see between *business* and *labor*? Explain how you define these terms. ■ What makes people deliberately waste time or play pranks at work? Is such behavior wrong, in your view? Why or why not?

Business and Labor 8

THE UNITED STATES OF AMERICA declared its independence from Great Britain in 1776, the same year that the Scottish philosopher Adam Smith (1723–90) published what would become the classic work on capitalism, *The Wealth of Nations.* The conjunction of events proved to be auspicious: nowhere on earth would the principles of free market capitalism be more enthusiastically applied than in the nation assembled from Britain's thirteen rebellious colonies. The revolutionaries in New York, Virginia, and Massachusetts fought not only for political liberty but also for the freedom to buy and sell in competitive world markets. At the time of the War of Independence, American entrepreneurs, schooled in the economic wisdom of Benjamin Franklin's Poor Richard, had already set into motion economic forces that would make the United States affluent and powerful.

The American Revolution also coincided with the dawn of the industrial revolution. Within a century after the shots fired at Lexington and Concord, powerful new machines capable of doing many times the work of manual laborers had transformed the economic structure of the nation. Processes as different as weaving, mining, and reaping would be successfully mechanized, reducing the cost of goods and making them available to more people. And the new industries would generate yet more capital, leading to still more entrepreneurship, investment, and development. It seemed that a formula for enduring prosperity had been discovered.

But the convergence of industrialism and capitalism also brought suffering. Human labor became a commodity measurable by the hour and subject to market forces. People looking for employment abandoned the countryside to crowd into urban slums with high levels of crime and poor sanitation. Disease was rampant. Workers, many of them mere children, faced grueling days in dangerous factories and mines, earning meager wages that they then often had to spend in company stores. Mills and foundries brutalized the landscape, darkening the skies and fouling the rivers.

In England, conditions like these moved Karl Marx to write *Das Kapital* (vol. 1, 1867), in which he condemned laissez-faire capitalism, predicted its demise, and imagined a utopian socialist alternative: communism. For more than a century afterward, capitalists and communists struggled worldwide for economic and military supremacy — the United States and western Europe as the major proponents of free markets and entrepreneurship, and the Soviet Union, China, and eastern Europe as the advocates of socialism.

Socialism lost. Today, serious arguments for Marxist economics are still being made only perhaps in China, in Cuba, and in American universities. Overcoming industrialism's initial ills, capitalist countries offered their citizens vastly greater wealth and liberty than authoritarian Marxist regimes could. Labor unions and numerous reform movements in the West also helped quash monopolies and increase membership in the dominant middle class. Yet all is not perfect. Far from it.

In this chapter, we explore some of the economic problems and opportunities that Americans still face today — a subject both vast and complicated. Some of our selections examine the nature of American economic thinking; others look at the ways Americans actually work in or are excluded from the economic mainstream. At times, we can only point to areas for more reading and exploration. This is one chapter we know will raise many questions and provoke lengthy debates.

Following are some questions that you may want to think about as you read this chapter:

- How do Americans feel about work?
- Have the economic values of Americans changed? What major questions of economics divide people or political parties in the United States?
- What rights do workers have to a job? For what reasons may employers exclude someone from employment?
- Does the United States manage prosperity well?
- What is the mission of business?
- Do we put too much emphasis on work? Do Americans fear leisure?

• • •

MERIDEL LESUEUR
Women and Work

*M*ERIDEL L*E*S*UEUR (1900–96) wrote all her life in the service of those too-often-invisible Americans who do the work of our world. LeSueur — a writer who held many other jobs, including actress, stuntwoman, and labor organizer — was a fascinating figure. From her earliest essays in the 1920s, her writings offer an unromanticized and vivid picture of twentieth-century work and workers (especially women), and she was well known as an author during the 1930s and 1940s. Her association with labor organizations and with communism, however, brought down the wrath of Senator Joseph McCarthy and his cohorts. Blacklisted in the 1950s, LeSueur had great difficulty publishing her work during the next thirty years, although the last two decades of her life were kinder to her. LeSueur reported doing the "best writing" of her life at ninety-four and rejoiced at the new audience she found among the American Indian, Chicano/a, and women's movements.*

LeSueur's books and essays speak to all people who know what it is to work, and especially to those who do the work of writing. In the brief autobiographical essay that follows, she reflects on what work meant in her life, on the work she was allowed (and not allowed) to do, and on the 140 notebooks of writing she accumulated over the years — one hard-working woman's "letter to the world." I chose this selection because LeSueur's work and life demonstrate how one can live through the worst deprivations, the worst economic depressions, and still find meaningful work. I also chose this piece because it's inspirational to see someone writing and thinking and publishing right to the end of a long and truly remarkable life. "Women and Work" originally appeared in a 1994 collection of essays by the same title edited by Maureen R. Michelson. —A.L.

When I was 10 years old in 1910 I knew my two brothers could be anything they wanted. I knew I could be a wife and mother, a teacher, a nurse or a whore. And without an education, I could not be a nurse or teacher and we were very poor. Women could be china painters, quiltmakers, embroiderers. They often wrote secretly. Even read certain books secretly. My mother tried to go to college and women could not take math or history, only the domestic sciences.

I began to write down what I heard, sitting under the quilting frames. I tried to listen to these imprisoned and silenced women. I had a passion to be witness and recorder of the hidden, submerged, and silent women. I did not want to be a writer; I did not know a woman writer; I did not read a woman writer. It was a thick, heavy silence and I began to take down what I heard.

My Gramma hated my writing. "We have tried to hide what has happened to us," she said, "and now you are going to tell it." "I am. I am going to tell it," I cried, and I began a long howl and cry that finally found its voice in the women's movement, as it is called. A book I wrote in 1930, cruelly criticized by male editors, was not published until 1975. My audience was women, who now wanted to talk, bear witness.

I made my living working in factories, writing for the labor movement. A good thing for a writer to keep close to life, to the happening, and I have lived in the most brutal century of two world wars, millions killed and exploited, and now the atom bomb and the global struggle.

I went to the International Women's Conference in Nairobi at 85 years old to see the thousands of women now bearing their own witness and I read my poem *Solidarity*, which I wrote for the Vietnamese Women's Union, and it was translated at once into Swahili as I read it. A great climax to my life. I believe this is the most enlightened moment I have seen in history and rooted in my life's passion to bear witness to the common struggle, the heroic people rising out of the violence, all becoming visible and alive.

My struggle was never alone, always with others. This makes my life bright with comradeship, marches with banners, tribal courage, and warmth. Remember, I didn't vote 'til I was 19 in 1919. Women only came into the offices after the first World War. Every young man I knew in high school never returned. The fathers and husbands had been killed. A terrible reaction set in after that bloody war to consolidate patriarchal money and power. The twenties were a terrible sinking into the Depression.

My mother, wanting to be an actress, sent me to dramatic school. I tried to fulfill her desires. The theater then was developing actresses who exploited the sexist feminine, and males who had to be John Waynes. The plays were also made for this image of sexism. Coming from the prairies, I played *Lady Windermere's Fan* by Oscar Wilde, learning to walk and use a fan and speak British. I didn't cotton to that at all. I went to Hollywood where again, your career was based on sexism, the female stereotypes. You had to go every morning to the hiring hall and show your legs and teeth and get a job for the day signing a contract that if you were killed or injured the company would not be responsible. Many extras were killed. You were a dime a dozen and the studios were flooded with the beautiful prairie girls from the Midwest. It was a meat market and developed one of the greatest prostitute rings in Los Angeles, San Francisco, Seattle, and Las Vegas.

My first job was to jump off a burning ship into salt water with dangerous tides. I lived. You could make $25 a day, an enormous sum, and I could save it and hole in and write for a few months. So I began to write about the open market on women; cheap labor of women, oppression and silencing and bartering of women. Also, fighting in the unions and housing. In the Depression, women were not on any list. There were no soup kitchens for women. Also, there was the danger of sterilization. Groups of women were netted and taken to women's prisons and might be sterilized by morning. There was a theory that the only solution to the Depression was sterilization of the workers. It began to be known Hitler had the same idea.

In desperation, I think, I boldly had two children at the beginning of the Depression. You couldn't get any other kind of life, and you might give birth to friends and allies. I had two girls, who all my life, have been just that.

I became a correspondent from the Middle West, reporting on the farm- 10 ers' struggles, the third party, all that was happening. I wrote for several national magazines and began to have stories in *American Mercury*, and university quarterlies, and writings about my children were sold to the women's magazines. So I began to make a modest living at writing, which was wonderful. I became known as a witness, as I wanted to be. I became well known for two pieces: *Corn Village*, about the small town; and, *I Was Marching*, about the '34 teamsters' strike.

I feel we must be deeply rooted in the tribal family and in the social community. This is becoming a strong and beautiful force now in our societies. Women speaking out boldly, going to jail for peace and sanctuary, defending the children against hunger. We still get half of what men get. But as I saw in Nairobi the struggle of women is now global. My Gramma and mother are not any more silenced and alone. Writing has become with women not a concealment, but an illumination. We are not alone. The hundreds of women writers now who speak for us to a large audience.

This makes me write more than I ever did. I have 140 notebooks, my letter to the world, published some day for a new woman I dreamed of. I have 24 great grandchildren who have freedoms I could only dream of. One granddaughter is raising five children herself. Another has two sons. They are not alone; that's the point. They live in collectives and work in social fields with women and children. They have an independence I never had, a boldness and a communal life and support.

I am writing as I never wrote before. I have three books, besides my notebooks, to "finish." I call it getting in my crop before the frost! It is my best writing, I believe . . . I have learned to bear witness with love and compassion and warm readers to whom I am truthful. And they return my witness, so women rise from the darkness singing together, not the small and tortured chorus of my grandmothers, but millions becoming visible and singing.

QUESTIONING THE TEXT

1. LeSueur speaks of "female stereotypes." Reread her essay, highlighting every example of such stereotypes. How much evidence does LeSueur marshal to illustrate these stereotypes? Discuss these examples.

2. LeSueur calls Hollywood and the film industry a "meat market" (paragraph 7). What evidence does she give to support this analogy? Does the analogy still hold today? What evidence can you offer to support or refute it?

MAKING CONNECTIONS

3. Look through all the selections in this chapter, and decide which writer LeSueur has the most in common with as well as which writer she would probably disagree with most strongly. In an entry in your journal or reading log, explore these similarities and differences, and weigh in with your own ideas as well. Which of these writers do you have most in common with, and why?

4. One of LeSueur's principles is stated at the beginning of paragraph 11: "I feel we must be deeply rooted in the tribal family and in the social community." To what degree do Dagoberto Gilb in "Work Union" (p. 650) and Eric Schlosser in "The Most Dangerous Job" (p. 654) express similar sentiments in their essays on work? How do they differ?

JOINING THE CONVERSATION

5. Working with two or three classmates, draw up some questions you would like to ask people who are now in their eighties or nineties about their experiences with work. Start with your own grandparents or great-grandparents, or those of your friends. If possible, find three or four additional men and women to interview, perhaps through the American Association of Retired Persons or an assisted-living group in your community. Together, write a brief report for your class on your interviewees' experiences with work.

6. Spend some time thinking about the kind of work you most want to do. Then write an exploration of your knowledge and feelings about such work, including an examination of both positive and negative points. If you keep a reading log, explore this issue there.

NAOMI BARKO
The Other Gender Gap: Why Women Still Fail to Receive Comparable Wages for Comparable Work

*A*MONG PROPOSALS AIMED AT THE WORKPLACE, *few have raised the tempers of more folks than "comparable worth," which proposes that people who have "comparable skills, education, and experience be paid comparable amounts." Sounds simple, right? But the struggles and fights that have grown up around this concept are anything but simple. Into this fray comes freelance journalist Naomi Barko, who argues that "the other gender gap" is all about inequality of pay, and she uses several vivid and dramatic examples to support the efficacy of "comparable worth." Others were quick to respond: reviewing Barko's work, conservative American Enterprise Institute fellow Diana Furchgott-Roth attacks Barko and her argument, countering that "Comparable-worth systems are wreaking havoc in Canada, which has had some forms of comparable worth since the Canadian Human Rights Act was passed in the mid 1970s."*

When so much heat and light surround an issue, we can be pretty sure it is worth considering carefully. You may want, in fact, to do some research in your own community: How do pay scales compare for men and women? Can you detect evidence of a gender gap in pay? What other inequalities may be at work? Where I teach, students have been very active in monitoring pay issues for campus workers — and very successful in helping bring about change. In fact, students have been at the forefront of those responsible for increasing wages on my campus — for all workers. What's going on with such issues where you go to school? Barko's essay originally appeared in The American Prospect, *June 19–July 3, 2000.* —A.L.

Hazel Dews is slightly embarrassed when you ask about her salary. She pauses and then confesses that after twenty-five years cleaning the Russell Senate Office Building in Washington five nights a week, she makes barely $22,000 a year. That's not what really bothers her, though. What irks her is that men who do the same job earn $30,000.

The men, she explains, are called "laborers." They can progress five grades. The women, however, are called "custodial workers," which means they can only advance two grades. "But," she protests, "they scrub with a mop and bucket. We scrub with a mop and bucket. They vacuum. We vacuum. They push a trash truck. We push a trash truck. The only thing they do that we don't is run a scrub machine. But that's on wheels, so we could do it too."

Thirty-seven years after the Equal Pay Act of 1963, American women working full time still earn an average of 74 cents for each dollar earned by men, according to a new report published jointly by the AFL-CIO and the Institute for Women's Policy Research (IWPR) in Washington, D.C. This affects all economic classes, but its impact is strongest on lower-income workers: If men and women were paid equally, more than 50 percent of low-income households across the country — dual-earner as well as single-mother — would rise above the poverty line.

New figures challenge the long-heard arguments that women's lower pay results from fewer years in the workforce or time out for childbearing and rearing. The Women's Bureau of the Department of Labor cites a study by the president's Council of Economic Advisers showing that even in light of the vicissitudes of motherhood, 43 percent of the wage gap remains "unexplained," evidently due in large part to discrimination.

The Overview of Salary Surveys, published in 1999 by the National Committee on Pay Equity (NCPE) — a coalition of thirty women's, civil rights, and religious groups — summarized twenty-three surveys of specific salary titles conducted by professional associations and trade magazines. It reported that, for instance, among women engineers — where the salary gap averages 26 percent — women with the same qualifications continue to earn less than men even after they've been in the field for many years (20.4 percent less among women with a B.S. degree and twenty to twenty-four years of experience; 19.2 percent less among women with an M.S. degree and twenty to twenty-four years experience). Yet another study found that women physicians earned less than men in forty-four of forty-five specialties, including obstetrics-gynecology (14 percent less) and pediatrics (15.8 percent less), with lower compensation only partly explainable by hours worked or time spent in the field. And a 1999 report by the American Association of University Professors found that though women had grown from 23 to 34 percent of faculty since 1975, the salary gap had actually widened in that time period.

But the biggest reason for the pay gap is not discrimination against individual women but rather discrimination against women's occupations. As the percentage of women in an occupation rises, wages tend to fall. More than 55 percent of employed women work in traditional "women's jobs" — librarians, clerical workers, nurses, teachers, and child-care workers. If these women are compared not to male workers but to women with similar education and experience in more gender-balanced occupations, they would earn about 18 percent — or $3,446 — more per year, according to the IWPR. (The 8.5 percent of men in these jobs earn an average of $6,259 less per year than men of comparable backgrounds working in "men's" fields.)

Why are "women's jobs" less lucrative? Is a truck driver — who earns an average annual wage of $25,030 — really 45 percent more valuable than a child-care worker who may have a four-year degree in early childhood education? Is a beginning engineer really worth between 30 and 70 percent more

5

than a beginning teacher? Rarely, in the almost daily reports of teacher short-ages, is it mentioned that the market alone cannot account for the striking dis-parity between teachers' and other professionals' salaries. No one ever suggests that it might have something to do with the fact that 75 percent of elementary and secondary schoolteachers are women.

In response to these disparities, women are beginning to mobilize. Three years ago, for example, Hazel Dews and 300 of her fellow women custodians joined the American Federation of State, County and Municipal Employees (AFSCME), which, after several futile attempts to negotiate, is now suing Dews's employer, the Architect of the Capitol, for equal pay. Since 1997, as women's membership in the labor movement has mushroomed to 40 percent, the AFL-CIO has conducted two surveys to discover the chief concerns of both union and nonunion working women. "And the runaway answer was equal pay," reports Karen Nussbaum, the director of the AFL-CIO's working women's department. Ninety-four percent of women in both surveys said equal pay was a top concern, and one-third — one-half of African American women — said they did not have equal pay in their own jobs.

In 1999, calling pay equity a "family issue," the labor movement helped launch equal-pay bills in both houses of Congress and twenty-seven state leg-islatures. Also last year, as Dews and her co-workers were demonstrating at the Capitol, the Eastman Kodak Company was agreeing to pay $13 million in pre-sent and retroactive wages to employees underpaid on the basis of either race or gender. The Massachusetts Institute of Technology, after protests by women faculty, made an unprecedented admission that it had discriminated against women "in salaries, space, awards, resources and response to outside offers."

Moreover, since 1997, the Office of Federal Contract Compliance Pro-grams (OFCCP) has collected $10 million in equal-pay settlements from such corporations as Texaco, US Airways, Pepsi-Cola, the computer manufacturer Gateway, and health insurer Highmark, Inc. At the same time, two major na-tional chains, Home Depot and Publix Supermarkets, agreed to pay more than $80 million each to settle lawsuits based on sex discrimination.

Recently, advocates have arrived at what they believe to be an effective means of generating pay equity — the concept of "comparable worth," which, as the name suggests, requires two people with comparable skills, education, and experience to be paid comparable amounts, even when they're working at two very different jobs. The Xerox Corporation, for example, uses comparable-worth analysis, weighing such factors as education, experience, skill, responsibility, deci-sion making, and discomfort or danger in working conditions, to set salary levels within the country. During the 1980s, some twenty state governments studied the comparable worth of their own employees and made adjustments totaling almost $750 million in increased pay to women. Minnesota, the leader in the field, has made pay-equity adjustments in 1,544 counties and localities.

Perhaps the most dramatic argument for comparable worth, however, was made by a man. In the class-action suit *AFSCME v. Washington State* in 1982, one of the nine named plaintiffs was Milt Tedrow, a licensed practical nurse at Eastern State Hospital in Spokane. Approaching retirement and realizing that his "woman's" job wouldn't give him much of a pension, Tedrow switched to carpentry at the same hospital. To qualify as an LPN, he had needed at least four years of experience, four quarters of schooling, and a license. As a carpenter, he was self-taught, had no paid work experience, and had no need of a license. And yet, when he transferred from the top of the LPN wage scale to the bottom of the carpenter's, his salary jumped more than $200 a month — from $1,614 to $1,826. Why, Tedrow wondered at the time, does the state resent "paying people decently who are taking care of people's bodies, when they'd pay a lot for someone fixing cars or plumbing"?

Since then, the courts have ruled that evidence of unfair salaries is not enough to prove violation of the Equal Pay Act. Plaintiffs must prove that employers intentionally discriminated by lowering women's wages in comparison to men's. But some unions have prevailed on comparable-worth questions by way of negotiations.

For example, Service Employees International Union Local 715, in Santa Clara County, just south of San Francisco, won nearly $30 million for 4,500 county employees, from secretaries to mental-health counselors. A study of some 150 job titles, performed by a consulting firm chosen jointly by the county and the union, showed that underpayment was common in job classes with more than 50 percent minorities, such as licensed vocational nurses and beginning social workers, and that 70 percent of such positions were filled by women. "We worked for at least three years to bring our male members along on this," says Kristy Sermersheim, Local 715's executive secretary. "When the county argued that in order to raise women's wages they'd have to lower men's, we refused to even discuss it. We kept regular pay negotiations completely separate."

Another key to the local's success was the staunch support of allies   15
among local women's groups. "We had fifty-four women's community groups on our side," reports Sermersheim. "The National Organization for Women, the American Association of University Women, the League of Women Voters, the Silicon Valley women engineers. . . ." On the day the county board of supervisors voted on whether to proceed with the study, the local delivered 1,000 pink balloons — symbolizing the pink-collar ghetto — to workplaces around the city. "We had balloons everywhere," recalls Sermersheim. "We had Unitarian women out there singing 'Union Maid.'"

It is this kind of coalition that pay-equity advocates are counting on to push through the equal-pay bills now before state legislatures. Many of the new bills, unlike those passed in the 1980s, would extend comparable worth to private as well as public employees and would specifically extend benefits to minorities. Most are based on the Fair Pay Act designed in consultation with the NCPE — and introduced in Congress in 1999 by two Democrats, Senator Tom Harkin of Iowa and Representative Eleanor Holmes Norton of the

District of Columbia. (A more modest Paycheck Fairness Act, backed by the Clinton administration, would toughen the Equal Pay Act of 1963 by removing present caps on damages and making it easier to bring class-action suits.)

So far, the new state bills have met with only modest success. The New Jersey and New Mexico legislatures have voted to study pay equity in both public and private employment, and Vermont's legislature voted to study just state employment. In Maine, where the new welfare laws gave rise to a commission to study poverty among working parents, it was discovered that the state already had a 1965 law on the books that mandated equal pay for both public and private employees and that specifically mentioned comparable worth. The state is now studying ways to put the law into effect.

Efforts like these have raised opposition from business and conservative groups. Economist Diana Furchgott-Roth, a resident fellow at the American Enterprise Institute who recently represented business at an NCPE forum, supports "equal pay for equal work" but claims that comparable worth causes labor shortages because men refuse to take jobs where their wages will be tied to women's. "How can a government bureaucrat calculate if a secretary is worth the same as a truck driver, or a nurse as an oil driller?"

In Ontario, Canada, where the practice of comparable worth is more common, day-care centers are actually closing down because parents can't afford to pay for the higher salaries, says Furchgott-Roth. But these charges turn out to be only partially true. Child-care centers in Ontario were threatened when a Progressive Conservative government succeeded the liberal New Democrats and slashed funding. But the centers have not closed down. After a court challenge and an enormous public outcry, the provincial government is still subsidizing pay equity for child-care workers (who, even with subsidies, earn an average of only $16,000 a year).

State employment officials in Minnesota and Wisconsin, two states with   20
comparable-worth laws, say that any labor shortages have far more to do with the tight labor market than with comparable worth. "There's a lot of flexibility in the law," says Faith Zwemke, Minnesota's pay-equity coordinator. "For information technology people, for instance, we can give them signing bonuses and let them advance faster within the parameters of the policy."

Some male workers inevitably do resent women getting increases. "But many men can see pay equity as a family issue," says Karen Nussbaum of the AFL-CIO. A recent poll by Democratic pollster Celinda Lake showed that six out of ten voters, both men and women, said equal pay was good for families.

Pay-equity advocates had better be patient and persistent. The market has been biased against women at least since it was written in the Old Testament that when a vow offering is made to God, it should be based on the value of the person, and "[if] a male, from the age of twenty years up to the age of sixty years, your assessment shall be fifty silver shekels . . . and if it is a female, your assessment shall be thirty shekels." At this rate, winning equal pay may take a long time.

QUESTIONING THE TEXT

1. Briefly summarize the problem Barko poses in this essay and the solution she recommends. Do you think she adequately argues for each? Is her description of the problem convincing? Do you find the solution feasible? Be prepared to discuss these questions in class, using examples from the text to support your answers.

2. Throughout this essay, Barko cites studies and statistics to support her claims. Working with a group of classmates, examine those pieces of evidence to see if they hold up under close scrutiny. What questions do the figures Barko uses raise? Do you need more information to assess how Barko has used statistical evidence? Use library or Internet resources to search for the sources of studies she cites. Who did the research, under what auspices, and using what methods?

MAKING CONNECTIONS

3. According to one study, Barko writes, "even in light of the vicissitudes of motherhood, 43 percent of the wage gap remains 'unexplained,' evidently due in large part to discrimination" (paragraph 4). That last explanatory phrase — "evidently due in large part to discrimination" — is one that Steven Pinker challenges in the excerpt from the "Gender" chapter in his book *The Blank Slate*. Read Pinker's excerpt (p. 624), and note the ways in which he refutes the argument Barko makes here. How might Barko respond? Discuss the two authors' views in class, being careful to assess their claims using the evidence they offer. Can your class come to a consensus on the value of using "comparable-worth" assessments to achieve pay equity?

4. Meridel LeSueur draws from her experience in writing about "Women and Work" (p. 613). How does her essay inform your thoughts on the issues raised by Barko in this essay and by Steven Pinker in the excerpt from "Gender" (p. 624)?

JOINING THE CONVERSATION

5. A.L. remarks in her headnote to this essay that the amount of controversy surrounding the issue of pay equity between men and women suggests it is "worth considering carefully." Following her cue, work with a team of classmates to investigate how fairly men and women are paid for comparable work in your own community — perhaps in your town or county,

or on your campus. You might choose a particular institution or profession and compare wage and salary scales among men and women. Search Internet databases for articles on the topic, and look for other sources in the library. You might also then conduct interviews with workers in the fields you have chosen to study. Your research findings could serve as the basis for an article that you might submit to a local newspaper or magazine, offer to a labor organization, or publish on a class Web site.

6. Barko identifies Hazel Dews, whose experience opens this essay, as one of three hundred women who took union action to press their suit for comparable pay. Do you know someone who has participated in a similar labor action, or are you familiar with one through the news? Find out the details of the protest, including the outcome. Was the issue fairly resolved, or is it ongoing? Does the case serve as a good or bad example of labor or management actions? Write an op-ed piece that presents your opinion on the case and the issues it illuminates; depending on the circumstances and what you wish to say, you might make an argument of value, or you might propose an action or policy. Consider submitting your article to a newspaper for publication.

STEVEN PINKER
Gender

IN THE PAST SEVERAL DECADES, few statistics have wielded more political power than the familiar comparison of male and female earnings in the United States. Here's Betty Friedan's version, as relayed by Steven Pinker: "women still earn no more than 72 cents for every dollar that men earn."

This kind of comparison works because it distills a complex mixture of political, cultural, and social relationships into a single malt of economic disparity. As long as the gap between male and female wages persists, the struggle for gender equity must continue.

Convincing as the argument seems, however, it has its critics, Steven Pinker (b. 1954) among them. Pinker, an evolutionary psychologist at Harvard and the author of several best-selling books on language, risks the ire of some fellow scientists and most feminist activists to suggest that the wage disparity may be due, in part, to biological differences between men and women. He dares to suggest that no amount of social engineering is going to convince large numbers of women to become engineers or mathematicians, nor are men ever likely to flock into developmental psycholinguistics or teaching.

This controversial thesis is just part of more sweeping claims Pinker asserts for the biological basis of human nature throughout The Blank Slate *(2002), the book from which our selection is taken. In it, Pinker challenges the notion that society alone shapes human character and behavior, arguing instead that a preponderance of scientific evidence now suggests that biology and evolution play a substantial part in determining who we are and what we choose to do. There is, Pinker believes, a human nature that exists prior to culture, prior to nurture. Few theses in the intellectual world provoke more combustive reactions or have deeper implications than this one.*

Whether you agree with Pinker or not, this selection will give you some sense of him as a thinker and writer. Pinker also writes with great verve and erudition on language and cognition in such books as The Language Instinct *(1994),* How the Mind Works *(1997), and* Words and Rules *(1999).* —J.R.

By now many people are happy to say what was unsayable in polite company a few years ago: that males and females do not have interchangeable minds. Even the comic pages have commented on the shift in the debate, as we see in this dialogue

I know enough about Pinker's work to predict that he will be making an argument for genetic causes of difference: let's see where this leads. —A.L.

---

*The original notes accompanying this excerpt required cross-referencing with the bibliography at the end of Pinker's book. We have therefore reformatted the notes to include the most complete publication data. —EDS.

This cartoon is one of several Pinker reprints in his 400+-page book, usually to show that an issue he is raising actually resonates with the public. —J.R.

There's an awkward transition at this point from the biological claim that men and women are wired differently to the political claim that they should be paid comparably. —J.R.

Friedan also mentions how educated women felt restless in their homes, taking care of children and feeding husbands. They wanted to explore their interests in the work field. This is important to keep in mind later in Pinker's argument. —B.K.

between the free-associating, junkfood-loving Zippy and the cartoonist's alter ego Griffy:

But among many professional women the existence of sex differences is still a source of discomfort. As one colleague said to me, "Look, I know that males and females are not identical. I see it in my kids, I see it in myself, I know about the research. I can't explain it, but when I read claims about sex differences, *steam comes out of my ears.*" The most likely cause of her disquiet is captured in a recent editorial by Betty Friedan, the cofounder of the National Organization for Women and the author of the 1963 book *The Feminine Mystique*:

> Though the women's movement has begun to achieve equality for women on many economic and political measures, the victory remains incomplete. To take two of the simplest and most obvious indicators: women still earn no more than 72 cents for every dollar that men earn, and we are nowhere near equality in numbers at the very top of decision making in business, government, or the professions.[1]

Like Friedan, many people believe that the gender gap in wages and a "glass ceiling" that keeps women from rising to the uppermost levels of power are the two main injustices facing women in the West today. In his 1999 State of the Union address,

Is this supposed to be funny?? —A.L.

Of course women feel uncomfortable: those "sex differences" are always equated to "men are superior" and "women are inferior." —B.K.

Well, the most likely cause of disquiet has got to be the long history of inequity based on gender. —A.L.

---

[1]B. Friedan, "The Future of Feminism," *Free Inquiry*, Summer 1999.

Bill Clinton said, "We can be proud of this progress, but 75 cents on the dollar is still only three-quarters of the way there, and Americans can't be satisfied until we're all the way there." The gender gap and the glass ceiling have inspired lawsuits against companies that have too few women in the top positions, pressure on the government to regulate all salaries so men and women are paid according to the "comparable worth" of their jobs, and aggressive measures to change girls' attitudes to the professions, such as the annual Take Our Daughters to Work Day.

Scientists and engineers face the issue in the form of the "leaky pipeline." Though women make up almost 60 percent of university students and about half of the students majoring in many fields of science, the proportion advancing to the next career stage diminishes as they go from being undergraduates to graduate students to postdoctoral fellows to junior professors to tenured professors. Women make up less than 20 percent of the workforce in science, engineering, and technology development, and only 9 percent of the workforce in engineering.[2] Readers of the flagship journals *Science* and *Nature* have seen two decades of headlines such as "Diversity: Easier Said Than Done" and "Efforts to Boost Diversity Face Persistent Problems."[3] A typical story, commenting on the many national commissions set up to investigate the problem, said, "These activities are meant to continue chipping away at a problem that, experts say, begins with negative messages in elementary school, continues through undergraduate and graduate programs that erect barriers — financial, academic, and cultural — to all but the best

Why is that?
—B.K.

My own school encourages women (now a majority on campus) to become engineers and scientists but supports no programs to move more men into fields in which they are underrepresented, such as English or education. —J.R.

"Leaky pipeline" is a new metaphor for me, though its connotations are as odd as the one I am more familiar with: that few women make it into good positions in certain scientific fields because the "pool is too shallow." Both metaphors carry powerful and largely unexamined assumptions. —A.L.

---

[2]"Land of Plenty: Diversity as America's Competitive Edge in Science, Engineering, and Technology," Report of the Congressional Commission on the Advancement of Women and Minorities in Science, Engineering, and Technology Development, September 2000.

[3]J. Alper, "The Pipeline Is Leaking Women All the Way Along," *Science, 260*, April 16, 1993; J. Mervis, "Efforts to boost diversity face persistent problems," *Science, 284*, June 11, 1999; J. Mervis, "Diversity: Easier Said than Done," *Science, 289*, March 16, 2000; J. Mervis, "NSF searches for right way to help women," *Science, 289*, July 21, 2000; J. Mervis, "Gender Equity: NSF Program Targets Institutional Change," *Science, 291*, July 21, 2001.

candidates, and persists into the workplace.[4] A meeting in 2001 of the presidents of nine elite American universities called for "significant changes," such as setting aside grants and fellowships for women faculty, giving them the best parking spaces on campus, and ensuring that the percentage of women faculty equals the percentage of women students.[5]

> *Whoa. The president of my university attended this meeting: I've never heard anything at all about giving women the best parking spaces. What's the effect of Pinker's adding this detail?*   —A.L.

But there is something odd in these stories about negative messages, hidden barriers, and gender prejudices. The way of science is to lay out every hypothesis that could account for a phenomenon and to eliminate all but the correct one. Scientists prize the ability to think up alternative explanations, and proponents of a hypothesis are expected to refute even the unlikely ones, Nonetheless, discussions of the leaky pipeline in science rarely even *mention* an alternative to the theory of barriers and bias. One of the rare exceptions was a sidebar to a 2000 story in *Science*, which quoted from a presentation at the National Academy of Engineering by the social scientist Patti Hausman:

> *How would giving women "the best parking spaces" fill the gender gap? Preferential treatment such as this, along with the concept of "ladies first" or opening doors for women, is another form of sexism that makes the gap larger.*   —B.K.

> *But this begs the question of why women don't want to choose some careers.*   —A.L.

> The question of why more women don't choose careers in engineering has a rather obvious answer: Because they don't want to. Wherever you go, you will find females far less likely than males to see what is so fascinating about ohms, carburetors, or quarks. Reinventing the curriculum will not make me more interested in learning how my dishwasher works.[6]

An eminent woman engineer in the audience immediately denounced her analysis as "pseudoscience." But Linda Gottfredson, an expert in the literature on vocational preferences, pointed out that Hausman had the data on her side: "On average, women are more interested in dealing with people and men with things." Vocational tests also show that boys are more interested in "realistic," "theoretical,"

---

[4]J. Mervis, "Efforts to Boost Diversity," p. 1757.
[5]P. Healy, "Faculty Shortage: Women in Sciences," *Boston Globe,* January 31, 2001.
[6]C. Holden, "Parity as a Goal Sparks Bitter Battle," *Science, 289,* July 21, 2000, p. 380.

and "investigative" pursuits, and girls more interested in "artistic" and "social" pursuits.

Hausman and Gottfredson are lonely voices, because the gender gap is almost always analyzed in the following way. Any imbalance between men and women in their occupations or earnings is direct proof of gender bias — if not in the form of overt discrimination, then in the form of discouraging messages and hidden barriers. The possibility that men and women might differ from each other in ways that affect what jobs they hold or how much they get paid may never be mentioned in public, because it will set back the cause of equity in the workplace and harm the interests of women. It is this conviction that led Friedan and Clinton, for example, to say that we will not have attained gender equity until earnings and representation in the professions are identical for men and women. In a 1998 television interview, Gloria Steinem and the congresswoman Bella Abzug called the very idea of sex differences "poppycock" and "anti-American crazy thinking," and when Abzug was asked whether gender equality meant equal numbers in every field, she replied, "Fifty-fifty — absolutely."[7] This analysis of the gender gap has also become the official position of universities. That the presidents of the nation's elite universities are happy to accuse their colleagues of shameful prejudice without even considering alternative explanations (whether or not they would end up accepting them) shows how deeply rooted the taboo is.

The problem with this analysis is that inequality of *outcome* cannot be used as proof of inequality of *opportunity* unless the groups being compared are identical in all of their psychological traits, which is likely to be true only if we are blank slates. But the suggestion that the gender gap may arise, even in part, from differences between the sexes can be fightin' words. Anyone bringing it up is certain to be *accused* of "wanting to keep women in their place"

Pinker is overstating here; most arguments for gender equity I am familiar with do not make such direct causal claims. Pinker is carefully choosing sources that hold the extreme view he wants to pit his argument against. —A.L.

Most societies and institutions have many "official stories" like that on the gender gap that can't be challenged easily. But falsehoods erode over time. As John Adams put it, "Facts are stubborn things." —J.R.

It is clear Pinker does not agree with Abzug's "fifty-fifty" argument. I'm interested to see his argument against it. —B.K.

So here's the blank slate argument I've been expecting. Pinker is well known for taking the "nature" side in the old debate between "nature" and "nurture." —A.L.

---

[7]Quoted in C. Young, *Ceasefire! Why Women and Men Must Join Forces to Achieve True Equality* (New York: Free Press, 1999), pp. 22, 34–35.

or "justifying the status quo." This makes about as much sense as saying that a scientist who studies why women live longer than men "wants old men to die." And far from being a ploy by self-serving men, analyses exposing the flaws of the glass-ceiling theory have largely come from women, including Hausman, Gottfredson, Judith Kleinfeld, Karen Lehrman, Cathy Young, and Camille Benbow, the economists Jennifer Roback, Felice Schwartz, Diana Furchtgott-Roth, and Christine Stolba, the legal scholar Jennifer Braceras, and, more guardedly, the economist Claudia Goldin and the legal scholar Susan Estrich.[8]

A neat rhetorical touch here. Pinker bolsters his credibility on this touchy issue of gender by appealing to experts who are women. —J.R.

I believe these writers have given us a better understanding of the gender gap than the standard one, for a number of reasons. Their analysis is not afraid of the possibility that the sexes might differ, and therefore does not force us to choose between scientific findings on human nature and the fair treatment of women. If offers a more sophisticated understanding of the causes of the gender gap, one that is consistent with our best social science. It takes a more respectful view of women and their choices. And ultimately it promises more humane and effective remedies for gender inequities in the workplace.

At last, a more nuanced analysis: of course we don't have to choose between "human nature" and the "fair treatment of women." —A.L.

Before presenting the new analysis of the gender gap from equity feminists, let me reiterate three points that are not in dispute. First, discouraging women from pursuing their ambitions, and

10

---

[8]S. Estrich, *Sex and Power* (New York: Riverhead Press, 2000); D. Furchtgott-Roth and C. Stolba, *Women's Figures: An Illustrated Guide to the Economic Progress of Women in America* (Washington, D.C.: American Enterprise Institute Press, 1999); C. Goldin, *Understanding the Gender Gap: An Economic History of American Workers* (New York: Oxford University Press, 1990); L. S. Gottfredson, "Reconsidering Fairness: A Matter of Social and Ethical Priorities, *Journal of Vocational Behavior, 29,* 1988, pp. 379–410; P. Hausman, *On the Rarity of Mathematically and Mechanically Gifted Females* (Santa Barbara, CA: The Fielding Institute, 1999); J. Kleinfeld, *MIT Tarnishes Its Reputation with Gender Junk Science,* Special Report (Arlington, VA: Independent Women's Forum, 1999), www.uaf.edu/northern/mitstudy; K. Lehrman, *The Lipstick Proviso: Women, Sex, and Power in the Real World* (New York: Doubleday, 1997); D. Lubinski and C. Benbow, "Gender Differences in Abilities and Preferences among the Gifted: Implications for the Math-science Pipeline, *Current Directions in Psychological Science, 1,* 1992, pp. 61–66; J. Roback, "Beyond Equality," *Georgetown Law Journal, 82,* 1993, pp. 121–133; F. N. Schwartz, *Breaking with Tradition: Women and Work, the New Facts of Life* (New York: Warner Books, 1992); Young, *Ceasefire!*

Another skillful, if conventional, rhetorical move: Pinker qualifies his argument about gender difference to reduce any suspicion that he opposes equal opportunity for women. I doubt that it's enough, however, to satisfy those who prefer the "official position."
—J.R.

So Pinker recognizes the factuality of inequity and discrimination based on gender. I'm still not ready to accept his claim that inequity in wages is based on genetic difference, however.
—A.L.

discriminating against them on the basis of their sex, are injustices that should be stopped wherever they are discovered.

Second, there is no doubt that women faced widespread discrimination in the past and continue to face it in some sectors today. This cannot be proven by showing that men earn more than women or that the sex ratio departs from fifty-fifty, but it can be proven in other ways. Experimenters can send out fake résumés or grant proposals that are identical in all ways except the sex of the applicant and see whether they are treated differently. Economists can do a regression analysis that takes measures of people's qualifications and interests and determines whether the men and the women earn different amounts, or are promoted at different rates, *when their qualifications and interests are statistically held constant.* The point that differences in outcome don't show discrimination unless one has equated for other relevant traits is elementary social science (not to mention common sense), and is accepted by all economists when they analyze data sets looking for evidence of wage discrimination.[9]

Third, there is no question of whether women are "qualified" to be scientists, CEOs, leaders of nations, or elite professionals of any other kind. That was decisively answered years ago: some are and some aren't, just as some men are qualified and some aren't. The only question is whether the proportions of qualified men and women must be identical.

As in many other topics related to human nature, people's unwillingness to think in statistical terms has led to pointless false dichotomies. Here is how to think about gender distributions in the professions without having to choose between the extremes of "women are unqualified" and "fifty-fifty absolutely," or between "there is no discrimination" and "there is nothing but discrimination."

Although I can appreciate Pinker's disclaimer, it doesn't do anything to obliterate present discriminations.
—B.K.

Yes, we all agree discrimination exists. However, I feel all this argument does is set us up for a solution that Pinker is not giving.
—B.K.

Pinker has himself set up a dichotomy between claims for the influence of "human nature" and the concept of a blank slate. I agree that such dichotomies are almost always destructive, so why does he keep referring to them?
—A.L.

---

[9]K. Browne, *Divided Labors: An Evolutionary View of Women at Work* (London: Weidenfeld and Nicholson, 1998); Furchtgott-Roth and Stolba; Goldin.

In a free and unprejudiced labor market, people will be hired and paid according to the match between their traits and the demands of the job. A given job requires some mixture of cognitive talents (such as mathematical or linguistic skill), personality traits (such as risk taking or cooperation), and tolerance of lifestyle demands (rigid schedules, relocations, updating job skills). And it offers some mixture of personal rewards: people, gadgets, ideas, the outdoors, pride in workmanship. The salary is influenced, among other things, by supply and demand: how many people want the job, how many can do it, and how many the employer can pay to do it. Readily filled jobs may pay less; difficult-to-fill jobs may pay more.

People vary in the traits relevant to employment. Most people can think logically, work with people, tolerate conflict or unpleasant surroundings, and so on, but not to an identical extent; everyone has a unique profile of strengths and tastes. Given all the evidence for sex differences (some biological, some cultural, some both), the statistical distributions for men and women in these strengths and tastes are unlikely to be identical. If one now matches the distribution of traits for men and for women with the distribution of the demands of the jobs in the economy, the chance that the proportion of men and of women in each profession will be identical, or that the mean salary of men and of women will be identical, is very close to zero — even if there were no barriers or discrimination.

None of this implies that women will end up with the short end of the stick. It depends on the menu of opportunities that a given society makes available. If there are more high-paying jobs that call for typical male strengths (say, willingness to put oneself in physical danger, or an interest in machines), men may do better on average; if there are more that call for typical female strengths (say, a proficiency with language, or an interest in people), women may do better on average. In either case, members of both sexes will be found in both kinds of jobs, just in different numbers. That is why some relatively prestigious professions are dominated by

15

This paragraph is crucial to Pinker's argument. It presents the logical and material facts weighing against the political claim that a wage gap between men and women must be due to prejudice. —J.R.

But in the past and now, women have ended up with the "short end of the stick." —B.K.

Unfortunately, jobs that call for "typical male strengths" are almost always more valued — and better paid — than those that call for typical female attributes. —A.L.

women. An example is my own field, the study of language development in children, in which women outnumber men by a large margin.[10] In her book *The First Sex: The Natural Talents of Women and How They Are Changing the World*, the anthropologist Helen Fisher speculates that the culture of business in our knowledge-driven, globalized economy will soon favor women. Women are more articulate and cooperative, are not as obsessed with rank, and are better able to negotiate win-win outcomes. The workplaces of the new century, she predicts, will increasingly demand these talents, and women may surpass men in status and earnings.

In today's world, of course, the gap favors men. Some of the gap is caused by discrimination. Employers may underestimate the skills of women, or assume that an all-male workplace is more efficient, or worry that their male employees will resent female supervisors, or fear resistance from prejudiced customers and clients. But the evidence suggests that not *all* sex differences in the professions are caused by these barriers.[11] It is unlikely, for example, that among academics the mathematicians are unusually biased against women, the developmental psycholinguists are unusually biased against men, and the evolutionary psychologists are unusually free of bias.

In a few professions, differences in ability may play some role. The fact that more men than women have exceptional abilities in mathematical reasoning and in mentally manipulating 3-D objects is enough to explain a departure from a fifty-fifty sex ratio among engineers, physicists, organic chemists, and professors in some branches of mathematics (though of course it does not mean that the proportion of women should be anywhere near zero).

[10]In a random sample of 100 members of the International Association for the Study of Child Language, I counted 75 women and 25 men. The Stanford Child Language Research Forum lists 18 past keynote speakers on its web site (csli.stanford.edu/~clrf/history.html): 15 women and 3 men.

[11]Browne; Furchtgott-Roth and Stolba; Goldin; Gottfredson; Kleinfeld; Roback; Young, *Ceasefire!*

In most professions, average differences in ability are irrelevant, but average differences in *preferences* may set the sexes on different paths. The most dramatic example comes from an analysis by David Lubinski and Camille Benbow of a sample of mathematically precocious seventh-graders selected in a nationwide talent search.[12] The teenagers were born during the second wave of feminism, were encouraged by their parents to develop their talents (all were sent to summer programs in math and science), and were fully aware of their ability to achieve. But the gifted girls told the researchers that they were more interested in people, "social values," and humanitarian and altruistic goals, whereas the gifted boys said they were more interested in things, "theoretical values," and abstract intellectual inquiry. In college, the young women chose a broad range of courses in the humanities, arts, and sciences, whereas the boys were geeks who stuck to math and science. And sure enough, fewer than 1 percent of the young women pursued doctorates in math, physical sciences, or engineering, whereas 8 percent of the young men did. The women went into medicine, law, the humanities, and biology instead.

This asymmetry is writ large in massive surveys of job-related values and career choices, another kind of study in which men and women actually say what they want rather than having activists speak for them.[13] On average, men's self-esteem is more highly tied to their status, salary, and wealth, and so is their attractiveness as a sexual partner and marriage partner, as revealed in studies of what people look for in the opposite sex.[14] Not surprisingly, men say they are more keen to work longer hours and to sacrifice

Even though the kids were nurtured in an "encouraging" environment and born during the feminist movement, the possibility that the differences in their preferences could be attributed to society, dictating what boys and girls should like, is neglected. —B.K.

It seems to me that math, physical sciences, and engineering could be seen — and taught — as having a great deal to contribute to people, "social values," and "humanitarian goals." If Pinker is right, making such changes would have no effect because women are genetically predisposed to be uninterested in these fields. Hmmmm . . . —A.L.

These differences in natural inclinations and abilities still do not explain the inequality in pay and treatment between the sexes for the same duties and jobs. —B.K.   20

---

[12]Lubinski and Benbow.

[13]See Browne and the references in note 8.

[14]D. M. Buss, "Mate preference mechanisms: Consequences for partner choice and intrasexual competition," in J. Barkow, L. Cosmides, and J. Tooby, eds., *The Adapted Mind: Evolutionary Psychology and the Generation of Culture* (New York: Oxford University Press, 1992); B. J. Ellis, "The evolution of sexual attraction: Evaluative mechanisms in women," in Barkow, Cosmides, and Tooby, eds.

Pinker is catalogu-
ing differences asso-
ciated with men; I
assume he will soon
do the same for
women. He is
clearly setting up
his readers to accept
the genetic differ-
ences argument.
—A.L.

other parts of their lives — to live in a less attractive city, or to leave friends and family when they relocate — in order to climb the corporate ladder or achieve notoriety in their fields. Men, on average, are also more willing to undergo physical discomfort and danger, and thus are more likely to be found in grungy but relatively lucrative jobs such as repairing factory equipment, working on oil rigs, and jack-hammering sludge from the inside of oil tanks. Women, on average, are more likely to choose administrative support jobs that offer lower pay in air-conditioned offices. Men are greater risk takers, and that is reflected in their career paths even when qualifications are held constant. Men prefer to work for corporations, women for government agencies and nonprofit organizations. Male doctors are more likely to specialize and to open up private practices; female doctors are more likely to be general practi-tioners on salary in hospitals and clinics. Men are more likely to be managers in factories, women more likely to be managers in human resources or corporate communications.

Mothers are more attached to their children, on average, than are fathers. That is true in societies all over the world and probably has been true of our lineage since the first mammals evolved some two hundred million years ago. As Susan Estrich puts it, "Waiting for the connection between gender and parenting to be broken is waiting for Godot." This does not mean that women in any society have ever been uninterested in work; among hunter-gatherers, women do most of the gathering and some of the hunting, especially when it involves nets rather than rocks and spears.[15] Nor does it mean that men in any society are indifferent to their children; male parental investment is a conspicuous and zoologically unusual feature of *Homo sapiens*. But it does mean that the biologically ubiquitous tradeoff between investing in a child and working to stay healthy (ultimately to

---

[15]S. B. Hrdy, *Mother Nature: A History of Mothers, Infants, and Natural Selection* (New York: Pantheon Books, 1999).

beget or invest in other children) may be balanced at different points by males and females. Not only are women the sex who nurse, but women are more attentive to their babies' well-being and, in surveys, place a higher value on spending time with their children.[16]

So even if both sexes value work and both sexes value children, the different weightings may lead women, more often than men, to make career choices that allow them to spend more time with their children — shorter or more flexible hours, fewer relocations, skills that don't become obsolete as quickly — in exchange for lower wages or prestige. As the economist Jennifer Roback points out, "Once we observe that people sacrifice money income for other pleasurable things we can infer next to nothing by comparing the income of one person with another's."[17] The economist Gary Becker has shown that marriage can magnify the effects of sex differences, even if they are small to begin with, because of what economists call the law of comparative advantage. In couples where the husband can earn a bit more than the wife, but the wife is a somewhat better parent than the husband, they might rationally decide they are both better off if she works less than he does.[18]

To repeat: none of this means that sex discrimination has vanished, or that it is justified when it occurs. The point is only that gender gaps *by themselves* say nothing about discrimination unless the slates of men and women are blank, which they are not. The only way to establish discrimination is to compare their jobs or wages when choices and qualifications are equalized. And in fact a recent study of data from the National Longitudinal Survey of Youth found that childless women between the ages of twenty-seven and thirty-three earn 98 cents to men's dollar.[19] Even to people who are cynical about

For these reasons, many women argue that careers should not be adversely affected by these decisions, as is clearly the case today. —A.L.

So gender gaps are related to discrimination only if minds are blank slates? Has Pinker supported this claim adequately? —A.L.

---

[16]Browne; Hrdy.

[17]Roback.

[18]G. S. Becker, *A Treatise on the Family,* enlarged ed. (Cambridge, MA: Harvard University Press, 1991).

[19]Furchtgott-Roth and Stolba.

the motivations of American employers, this should come as no shock. In a cutthroat market, any company stupid enough to overlook qualified women or to overpay unqualified men would be driven out of business by a more meritocratic competitor.

And yet these businesses do exist and do thrive. —B.K.

Another claim I'm suspicious of, especially since companies "stupid enough to overlook qualified women" are well documented. —A.L.

Now, there is nothing in science or social science that would rule out policies implementing a fifty-fifty distribution of wages and jobs between the sexes, if a democracy decided that this was an inherently worthy goal. What the findings do say is that such policies will come with costs as well as benefits. The obvious benefit of equality-of-outcome policies is that they might neutralize the remaining discrimination against women. But if men and women are not interchangeable, the costs have to be considered as well.

Some costs would be borne by men or by both sexes. The two most obvious are the possibility of reverse discrimination against men and of a false presumption of sexism among the men and women who make decisions about hiring and salary today. Another cost borne by both sexes is the inefficiency that could result if employment decisions were based on factors other than the best match between the demands of a job and the traits of the person.

25

This assumes that employers only look for compatibility between the person and the demands of the job without factoring in other variables, which I believe is currently untrue. —B.K.

But many of the costs of equality-of-outcome policies would be borne by *women*. Many women scientists are opposed to hard gender preferences in science, such as designated faculty positions for women, or the policy (advocated by one activist) in which federal research grants would be awarded in exact proportion to the number of men and women who apply for them. The problem with these well-meaning policies is that they can plant seeds of doubt in people's minds about the excellence of the beneficiaries. As the astronomer Lynne Hillenbrand said, "If you're given an opportunity for the reason of being female, it doesn't do anyone any favors; it makes people question why you're there."[20]

Again, this seems like a pretty big overstatement and another dichotomy set up: either give grants equally or don't give them at all. As for casting doubt on those chosen under a system of gender equality, who gains most by casting such doubt? —A.L.

This argument brings up the issue of affirmative action — an issue that could get complicated and messy. Although I feel Pinker's brief overview of this subject increases his readability, I feel he glosses over the important arguments for these policies and oversimplifies the issue altogether. —B.K.

Certainly there *are* institutional barriers to the advancement of women. People are mammals, and

---

[20]Quoted in C. Young, "Sex and Science," *Salon*, April 12, 2001.

we should think through the ethical implications of the fact that it is women who bear, nurse, and disproportionately raise children. One ought not to assume that the default human being is a man and that children are an indulgence or an accident that strikes a deviant subset. Sex differences therefore can be used to justify, rather than endanger, woman-friendly policies such as parental leave, subsidized childcare, flexible hours, and stoppages of the tenure clock or the elimination of tenure altogether (a possibility recently broached by the biologist and Princeton University president Shirley Tilghman).

Of course, there is no such thing as a free lunch, and these policies are also decisions — perhaps justifiable ones — to penalize men and women who are childless, have grown children, or choose to stay at home with their children. But even when it comes to weighing these tradeoffs, thinking about human nature can raise deep new questions that could ultimately improve the lot of working women. Which of the onerous job demands that deter women really contribute to economic efficiency, and which are obstacle courses in which men compete for alpha status? In reasoning about fairness in the workplace, should we consider people as isolated individuals, or should we consider them as members of families who probably will have children at some point in their lives and who probably will care for aging parents at some point in their lives? If we trade off some economic efficiency for more pleasant working conditions in all jobs, might there be a net increase in happiness? I don't have answers, but the questions are well worth asking.

There is one more reason that acknowledging sex differences can be more humane than denying them. It is men and women, not the male gender and the female gender, who prosper or suffer, and those men and women are endowed with brains — perhaps not identical brains — that give them values and an ability to make choices. Those choices should be respected. A regular feature of the lifestyle pages is the story about women who are made to feel ashamed about staying at home with their children. As they always say, "I thought feminism was supposed to be

I want to count the number of times Pinker has said "of course," thus suggesting that "of course" readers agree with him.
—A.L.

about choices." The same should apply to women who do choose to work but also to trade off some income in order to "have a life" (and, of course, to men who make that choice). It is not obviously progressive to insist that equal numbers of men and women work eighty-hour weeks in a corporate law firm or leave their families for months at a time to dodge steel pipes on a frigid oil platform. And it is grotesque to demand (as advocates of gender parity did in the pages of *Science*) that more young women "be conditioned to choose engineering," as if they were rats in a Skinner box.[21]

Indeed, feminism is about choice! —A.L.

No one should have to "work 80-hour weeks . . . or leave their families." Here's where choice is really important. —A.L.

Gottfredson points out, "If you insist on using gender parity as your measure of social justice, it means you will have to keep many men and women out of the work they like best and push them into work they don't like."[22] She is echoed by Kleinfeld on the leaky pipeline in science: "We should not be sending [gifted] women the messages that they are less worthy human beings, less valuable to our civilization, lazy or low in status, if they choose to be teachers rather than mathematicians, journalists rather than physicists, lawyers rather than engineers."[23] These are not hypothetical worries: a recent survey by the National Science Foundation found that many more women than men say they majored in science, mathematics, or engineering under pressure from teachers or family members rather than to pursue their own aspirations — and that many eventually switched out for that reason.[24] I will give the final word to Margaret Mead, who, despite being wrong in her early career about the malleability of gender, was surely right when she said, "If we are to achieve a richer culture, rich in contrasting values, we must recognize the whole gamut of human potentialities, and so weave a less arbitrary social fabric, one in which each diverse human gift will find a fitting place."

30

If we shouldn't send such messages, then let's pay *teachers as much as other professionals.* —A.L.

Everyone I know would agree with Mead. So where does this leave Pinker and his argument? I accept many of his premises, but I still don't get the connection he is trying to make among gender, genes, and pay. —A.L.

---

[21]Quoted in Holden.
[22]Quoted in Holden.
[23]Kleinfeld.
[24]National Science Foundation, *Women, Minorities, and Persons with Disabilities in Science and Engineering: 1998*, www.nsf.gov/sbe/srs/nsf99338.

QUESTIONING THE TEXT

1. Summarize Pinker's argument in a few sentences. What is his main claim? How does he support this claim?

2. Working with a classmate, examine the sources Pinker cites and the evidence he gathers from them. What information about these sources does Pinker provide in the essay? What useful information about the sources do you find missing? Do some library research to discover details about his sources and the organizations he cites that will help you determine whether you agree with his claims.

3. Pinker makes a crucial claim on p. 635: "[N]one of this means that sex discrimination has vanished, or that it is justified when it occurs. The point is only that gender gaps *by themselves* say nothing about discrimination unless the slates of men and women are blank, which they are not." Discuss with one or two classmates the effects of Pinker's style in this passage. What words and phrases does Pinker use to qualify his claim? How does he use sentence structure to emphasize certain elements in relationship to others? What are the effects of the words he has chosen? (How might synonyms for some words change his meaning, even slightly?) How do these stylistic choices affect your reading of this claim, and of Pinker's argument overall? Are you inclined to agree or disagree with him? Explain why.

MAKING CONNECTIONS

4. Consider Pinker's claims in light of those made by Naomi Barko in "The Other Gender Gap" (p. 617). Can the two arguments be reconciled in any way? In other words, can you agree with Barko and with Pinker on some points? Try doing so in a pair of one- or two-page essays — one presenting Barko's viewpoint and the other presenting Pinker's. Make each essay as convincing as possible; your readers should not be able to tell which argument really reflects your own opinion.

5. How might Pinker's arguments be extended to apply to race, ethnicity, sexual orientation, or other aspects of identity that have led to discrimination in employment and other arenas? Read one or two of the essays in Chapter 6 of this book in considering this question, and share your thoughts in class discussion. How does this discussion affect your view of Pinker's argument?

JOINING THE CONVERSATION

6. What subjects or careers were you most interested in as a child? Later in life? What subjects or careers were you encouraged to pursue? Do you think your gender played a role in the future your parents, teachers, friends — even you yourself — envisioned for you? Freewrite on these questions, and then share some of your thoughts with classmates. How do your experiences compare?

7. Have you ever found yourself in a situation that defied traditional expectations for your gender? How does this experience affect your response to Pinker's argument? Use your personal insight to write a short essay in the form of a letter to Pinker, responding to this excerpt on gender.

BELL HOOKS
Work Makes Life Sweet

DO PEOPLE WORK TO LIVE OR LIVE TO WORK — *or some combination of the two? In "Work Makes Life Sweet," from* Sisters of the Yam: Black Women and Self-Recovery *(1993), bell hooks (b. 1952) takes a look at the working traditions of African American women, noting that "[t]he vast majority of black women in the United States know in girlhood that [they] will be workers." She also considers the different circumstances that allow work to be "sweet" or that ensure that it will be sour — alienating and unsatisfying. In sum, she says the majority of black women she has talked with do not enjoy their work — and she goes on to offer reasons for such dissatisfaction as well as a way to "unlearn" conventional thinking about work so that it will once again have the capacity to make life sweet.*

For hooks, the work of writing seems sweet indeed, as evidenced by her publication of seventeen books in less than twenty years. Yet she often remarks on the ways in which her need to work for a living — accompanied by fears of poverty or joblessness — have interfered with her ability to live for the work of her writing. And for this work she is often criticized — for writing without extensive footnotes and bibliography, for not being "intellectual" enough, for writing about the same subjects (especially the intersection of class, race, and gender), even for writing too much. To these criticisms, hooks generally turns a deaf ear, saying "I'm playful, anybody who hangs with me knows that, but I am also a dead-serious intellectual woman who is on the job." To these criticisms, hooks also offers an outpouring of work: her recent books include Soul Sister: Women, Friendship, and Fulfillment *(2007);* We Real Cool: Black Men and Masculinity *(2003); and* Rock My Soul: Black People and Self-Esteem *(2003).*

In her Remembered Rapture: The Writer at Work *(1999), hooks offers recent ideas on the work of writing and on her passion for that work. What work, I wonder, do you have a passion for? In what ways does that work make your life sweet?*   —A.L.

"Work makes life sweet!" I often heard this phrase growing up, mainly from old black folks who did not have jobs in the traditional sense of the word. They were usually self-employed, living off the land, selling fishing worms, picking up an odd job here and there. They were people who had a passion for work. They took pride in a job done well. My Aunt Margaret took in ironing. Folks brought her clothes from miles around because she was such an expert. That was in the days when using starch was common and she knew how to do an excellent job. Watching her iron with skill and grace was like watching a ballerina dance. Like all the other black girls raised in the fifties that I knew, it was clear to me that I would be a working woman. Even though our mother stayed home, raising her seven children, we saw her constantly at work, washing, ironing, cleaning, and cooking (she is an incredible cook). And she never allowed her six girls to imagine we would not be working women. No, she let us know that we would work and be proud to work.

The vast majority of black women in the United States know in girlhood that we will be workers. Despite sexist and racist stereotypes about black women living off welfare, most black women who receive welfare have been in the workforce. In *Hard Times Cotton Mill Girls*,* one can read about black women who went to work in the cotton mills, usually leaving farm labor or domestic service. Katie Geneva Cannon* remembers: "It was always assumed that we would work. Work was a given in life, almost like breathing and sleeping. I'm always surprised when I hear people talking about somebody taking care of them, because we always knew that we were going to work." Like older generations of southern black women, we were taught not only that we would be workers, but that there was no "shame" in doing any honest job. The black women around us who worked as maids, who stripped tobacco when it was the season, were accorded dignity and respect. We learned in our black churches and in our schools that it "was not what you did, but how you did it" that mattered.

A philosophy of work that emphasizes commitment to any task was useful to black people living in a racist society that for so many years made only certain jobs (usually service work or other labor deemed "undesirable") available to us. Just as many Buddhist traditions teach that any task becomes sacred when we do it mindfully and with care, southern black work traditions taught us the importance of working with integrity irrespective of the task. Yet these attitudes towards work did not blind anyone to the reality that racism made it difficult to work for white people. It took "gumption" to work with integrity in settings where white folks were disrespectful and downright hateful. And it was obvious to me as a child that the black people who were saying "work makes life sweet" were the folks who did not work for whites, who did what they wanted to do. For example, those who sold fishing worms were usually folks who loved to fish. Clearly there was a meaningful connection between positive thinking about work and those who did the work that they had chosen.

Most of us did not enter the workforce thinking of work in terms of finding a "calling" or a vocation. Instead, we thought of work as a way to make money. Many of us started our work lives early and we worked to acquire money to buy necessities. Some of us worked to buy school books or needed or desired clothing. Despite the emphasis on "right livelihood" that was present in our life growing up, my sisters and I were more inclined to think of work in relation to doing what you needed to do to get money to buy what you wanted. In general, we have had unsatisfying work lives. Ironically, Mama entered the paid

---

Hard Times Cotton Mill Girls: an oral history of life in southern textile mills, compiled by Victoria Byerly (b. 1949), a former mill worker

Katie Geneva Cannon: The first black woman ordained a Presbyterian minister. She worked with Victoria Byerly, author of *Hard Times Cotton Mill Girls*.

workforce very late, after we were all raised, working for the school system and at times in domestic service, yet there are ways in which she has found work outside the home more rewarding than any of her children. The black women I talked with about work tended to see jobs primarily as a means to an end, as a way to make money to provide for material needs. Since so many working black women often have dependents, whether children or other relatives, they enter the workforce with the realistic conviction that they need to make money for survival purposes. This attitude coupled with the reality of a job market that remains deeply shaped by racism and sexism means that as black women we often end up working jobs that we do not like. Many of us feel that we do not have a lot of options. Of the women I interviewed, the ones who saw themselves as having options tended to have the highest levels of education. Yet nearly all the black women I spoke with agreed that they would always choose to work, even if they did not need to. It was only a very few young black females, teenagers and folks in their early twenties, who talked with me about fantasy lives where they would be taken care of by someone else.

Speaking with young black women who rely on welfare benefits to   5 survive economically, I found that overall they wanted to work. However, they are acutely aware of the difference between a job and a fulfilling vocation. Most of them felt that it would not be a sign of progress for them to "get off welfare" and work low-paying jobs, in situations that could be stressful or dehumanizing. Individuals receiving welfare who are trying to develop skills, to attend school or college, often find that they are treated with much greater hostility by social-service workers than if they were just sitting at home watching television. One woman seeking assistance was told by an angry white woman worker, "welfare is not going to pay for you to get your B.A." This young woman had been making many personal sacrifices to try and develop skills and educational resources that would enable her to be gainfully employed and she was constantly disappointed by the level of resentment toward her whenever she needed to deal with social services.

Through the years, in my own working life, I have noticed that many black women do not like or enjoy their work. The vast majority of women I talked to . . . agreed that they were not satisfied with their working lives even though they see themselves as performing well on the job. That is why I talk so much about work-related stress in [*Remembered Rapture*]. It is practically impossible to maintain a spirit of emotional well-being if one is daily doing work that is unsatisfying, that causes intense stress, and that gives little satisfaction. Again and again, I found that many black women I interviewed had far superior skills than the jobs they were performing called for but were held back because of their "lack of education," or in some cases, "necessary experience." This routinely prevented them from moving upward. While they performed their jobs well, they felt added tension generated in the work environment by supervisors who often saw them as "too uppity" or by their own struggle to maintain interest in their assigned tasks. One white-woman administrator shared that the clearly overly skilled black woman who works as an administrative assistant in her office was resented by white male "bosses" who felt that she did not have the proper attitude of a "subordinate." When I spoke to this woman she acknowledged not liking her job, stating that her lack of education and the urgent need to raise children and send them to college had prevented her from working towards a chosen career. She holds to the dream that she will return to school and someday gain the necessary education that will give her access to the career she desires and deserves. Work is so often a source of pain and frustration.

Learning how to think about work and our job choices from the standpoint of "right livelihood" enhances black female well-being. Our self-recovery is fundamentally linked to experiencing that quality of "work that makes life sweet." In one of my favorite self-help books, Marsha Sinetar's *Do What You Love, the Money Will Follow*, the author defines right livelihood as a concept initially coming from the teachings of Buddha which emphasized "work consciously chosen, done with full awareness and care, and leading to enlightenment." This is an attitude toward work that our society does not promote, and it especially does not encourage black females to think of work in this way. As Sinetar notes:

> Right Livelihood, in both its ancient and its contemporary sense, embodies self-expression, commitment, mindfulness, and conscious choice. Finding and doing work of this sort is predicated upon high self-esteem and self-trust, since only those who like themselves, who subjectively feel they are trustworthy and deserving dare to choose on behalf of what is right and true for them. When the powerful quality of conscious choice is present in our work, we can be enormously productive. When we consciously choose to do work we enjoy, not only can we get things done, we can get them done well and be intrinsically rewarded for our effort.

Black women need to learn about "right livelihood." Even though I had been raised in a world where elderly black people had this wisdom, I was more socialized by the get-ahead generation that felt how much money you were making was more important than what you did to make that money. We have difficult choices ahead.

As black females collectively develop greater self-esteem, a greater sense of entitlement, we will learn from one another's example how to practice right livelihood. Of the black women I interviewed the individuals who enjoyed their work the most felt they were realizing a particular vocation or calling. C.J. (now almost forty) recalls that generations of her family were college-educated. She was taught to choose work that would be linked with the political desire to enhance the overall well-being of black people. C. J. says, "I went to college with a mission and a passion to have my work be about African Americans. The spirit of mission came to me from my family, who taught us that you don't just work to get money, you work to create meaning for yourself and other people." With this philosophy as a guiding standpoint, she has always had a satisfying work life.

When one of my sisters, a welfare recipient, decided to return to college, I encouraged her to try and recall her childhood vocational dreams and to allow herself adult dreams, so that she would not be pushed into preparing for a job that holds no interest for her. Many of us must work hard to unlearn the socialization that teaches us that we should just be lucky to get any old job. We can begin to think about our work lives in terms of vocation and calling. One black woman I interviewed, who has worked as a housewife for many years, began to experience agoraphobia. Struggling to regain her emotional well-being, she saw a therapist, against the will of her family. In this therapeutic setting, she received affirmation for her desire to finish her undergraduate degree and continue in a graduate program. She found that finishing a master's and becoming a college teacher gave her enormous satisfaction. Yet this achievement was not fully appreciated by her husband. A worker in a factory, whose job is long and tedious, he was jealous of her newfound excitement about work. Since her work brings her in touch with the public, it yields rewards unlike any he can hope to receive from his job. Although she has encouraged him to go back to school (one of his unfulfilled goals), he is reluctant. Despite these relational tensions, she has found that "loving" her work has helped her attend to and transform previous feelings of low self-esteem.

A few of the black women I interviewed claimed to be doing work they liked but complained bitterly about their jobs, particularly where they must make decisions that affect the work lives of other people. One woman had been involved in a decision-making process that required her to take a stance that would leave another person jobless. Though many of her peers were proud of the way she handled this difficult decision, her response was to feel "victimized." Indeed, she kept referring to herself as "battered." This response troubled me for it seemed to bespeak a contradiction many women experience in positions of power. Though we may like the status of a power position and wielding power, we may still want to see ourselves as "victims" in the process, especially if we must act in ways that "good girls, dutiful daughters" have been taught are "bad." 10

I suggested to the women I interviewed that they had chosen particular careers that involved "playing hard ball" yet they seemed to be undermining the value of their choices and the excellence of their work by complaining that they had to get their hands dirty and suffer some bruises. I shared with them my sense that if you choose to play hardball then you should be prepared for the bruises and not be devastated when they occur. In some ways it seemed to me these black women wanted to be "equals" in a man's world while they simultaneously wanted to be treated like fragile "ladies." Had they been able to assume full responsibility for their career choices, they would have enjoyed their work more and been able to reward themselves for jobs well done. In some cases it seemed that the individuals were addicted to being martyrs. They wanted to control everything, to be the person "in power" but also resented the position. These individuals, like those I describe in the chapter on stress, seemed not to know when to set boundaries or that work duties could be shared. They frequently over-extended themselves. When we over-extend ourselves in work settings, pushing ourselves to the breaking point, we rarely feel positive about tasks even if we are performing them well.

Since many people rely on powerful black women in jobs (unwittingly turning us into "mammies" who will bear all the burdens — and there are certainly those among us who take pride in this role), we can easily become tragically over-extended. I noticed that a number of us (myself included) talk about starting off in careers that we really "loved" but over-working to the point of "burn-out" so that the pleasure we initially found dissipated. I remember finding a self-help book that listed twelve symptoms of "burn-out," encouraging readers to go down the list and check those that described their experience. At the end, it said, "If you checked three or more of these boxes, chances are you are probably suffering from burn-out." I found I had checked all twelve! That let me know it was time for a change. Yet changing was not easy. When you do something and you do it well, it is hard to take a break, or to confront the reality that I had to face, which was that I really didn't want to be doing the job I was doing even though I did it well. In retrospect it occurred to me that it takes a lot more energy to do a job well when you really do not want to be doing it. This work is often more tiring. And maybe that extra energy would be better spent in the search for one's true vocation or calling.

In my case, I have always wanted to be a writer. And even though I have become just that and I love this work, my obsessive fears about "not being poor" have made it difficult for me to take time away from my other career, teaching and lecturing, to "just write." Susan Jeffers' book, *Feel the Fear and Do It Anyway*, has helped me to finally reach the point in my life where I can take time to "just write." Like many black women who do not come from privileged class backgrounds, who do not have family we can rely on to help if the financial going gets rough (we in fact are usually the people who are relied on), it feels very frightening to think about letting go of financial security, even for a short time, to do work one loves but may not pay the bills. In my case, even though I had worked with a self-created financial program aimed at bringing me to a point in life when I could focus solely on writing, I still found it hard to take time away. It was then that I had to tap into my deep fears of ending up poor and counter them with messages that affirm my ability to take care of myself economically irrespective of the circumstance. These fears are not irrational (though certainly mine were a bit extreme). In the last few years, I have witnessed several family members go from working as professionals to unemployment and various degrees of homelessness. Their experiences highlighted the reality that it is risky to be without secure employment and yet they also indicated that one could survive, even start all over again if need be.

My sister V. quit a job that allowed her to use excellent skills because she had major conflicts with her immediate supervisor. She quit because the level of on-the-job stress had become hazardous to her mental well-being. She quit confident that she would find a job in a few months. When that did not happen, she was stunned. It had not occurred to her that she would find it practically impossible to find work in the area she most wanted to live in. Confronting racism, sexism, and a host of other unclear responses, months passed and she has not found another job. It has changed her whole life. While material survival has been difficult, she is learning more about what really matters to her in life. She is learning about "right livelihood." The grace and skill with which she has confronted her circumstance has been a wonderful example for me. With therapy, with the help of friends and loved ones, she is discovering the work she would really like to do and no longer feels the need to have a high-paying, high-status job. And she has learned more about what it means to take risks.

In *Do What You Love, the Money Will Follow*, Sinetar cautions those of us   15
who have not been risk-takers to go slowly, to practice, to begin by taking small risks, and to plan carefully. Because I have planned carefully, I am able to finally take a year's leave from my teaching job without pay. During this time, I want to see if I enjoy working solely as a writer and if I can support myself. I want to see if (like those old-time black folks I talk about at the start of the essay) doing solely the work I feel most "called" to do will enhance my joy in living. For the past few months, I have been "just writing" and indeed, so far, I feel it is "work that makes life sweet."

The historical legacy of black women shows that we have worked hard, long, and well, yet rarely been paid what we deserve. We rarely get the recognition we deserve. However, even in the midst of domination, individual black women have found their calling, and do the work they are best suited for. Onnie Lee Logan, the Alabama midwife who tells her story in *Motherwit*, never went to high school or college, never made a lot of money in her working life, but listened to her inner voice and found her calling. Logan shares:

> I let God work the plan on my life and I am satisfied at what has happened to me in my life. The sun wasn't shinin' every time and moon wasn't either. I was in the snow and the rain at night by my lonely self. . . . There had been many dreary nights but I didn't look at em as dreary nights. I had my mind on where I was going and what I was going for.
>
> Whatever I've done, I've done as well as I could and beyond. . . . I'm satisfied at what has happened in my life. Perfectly satisfied at what my life has done for me. I was a good midwife. One of the best as they say. This book was the last thing I had planned to do until God said well done. I consider myself — in fact if I leave tomorrow — I've lived my life and I've lived it well.

The life stories of black women like Onnie Logan remind us that "right livelihood" can be found irrespective of our class position, or the level of our education.

To know the work we are "called" to do in this world, we must know ourselves. The practice of "right livelihood" invites us to become more fully aware of our reality, of the labor we do and of the way we do it. Now that I have chosen my writing more fully than at any other moment of my life, the work itself feels more joyous. I feel my whole being affirmed in the act of writing. As black women unlearn the conventional thinking about work — which views money and/or status as more important than the work we do or the way we feel about that work — we will find our way back to those moments celebrated by our ancestors, when work was a passion. We will know again that "work makes life sweet."

QUESTIONING THE TEXT

1. hooks takes a definition of "right livelihood" (paragraph 7) from Marsha Sinetar's *Do What You Love, the Money Will Follow.* Look at the way hooks defines this term and at the passages she quotes from Sinetar's book. Then list the people mentioned in hooks's essay who successfully practice "right livelihood." What do they have in common?

2. According to hooks, under what circumstances can "work make life sweet"? Do you accept the conditions she offers? Might there be other circumstances in which work could make someone's life sweet? After thinking carefully about your responses to these questions, write a paragraph arguing for or against hooks's claims.

MAKING CONNECTIONS

3. Read hooks's essay alongside the selection by Dagoberto Gilb (p. 650). Then, working with a classmate, consider how hooks might respond to Gilb's views on work. Write up a dialogue between Gilb and hooks on the value of work and what work situations merit complaint.

4. Consider how hooks might respond to Eric Schlosser's "The Most Dangerous Job" (p. 654). To what degree can slaughterhouse workers find that work makes life sweet? What evidence can you find that some people find meaning or pleasure in the job of working at a slaughterhouse?

JOINING THE CONVERSATION

5. In paragraph 6, hooks claims "[i]t is practically impossible to maintain a spirit of emotional well-being if one is daily doing work that is unsatisfying. . . ." Does this statement reflect your firsthand experience of

work? Write a journal entry describing your work experience and explaining why it does or does not support hooks's claim. If you keep a reading log, write the entry there.

6. Imagine that you are applying for the job of your dreams, one that would indeed make your life sweet. Write a job announcement or advertisement for the position, and bring it to class for discussion. Be prepared to explain your reasons for wanting this job as well as the ways you are — and are not — currently prepared for it.

7. Working with one or two classmates, discuss this slight revision of hooks's title: "Schoolwork Makes Life Sweet." Decide what conditions would need to exist for this statement to be accurate. Then, working together, write up a catalog description of the kind of schoolwork guaranteed to make life sweet. You may decide to take a humorous approach to this topic.

DAGOBERTO GILB
Work Union

*F*ROM THE TIME I WAS ABOUT ELEVEN YEARS OLD, *I picked up some extra money with babysitting gigs, but my first real job was at the soda fountain in our local drugstore. I wore a big apron (no gloves or hairnets then) and took orders and filled them — mostly for milk shakes, ice cream sodas, and sweetish concoctions like Cherry Cokes and Brown Cows. Sometimes I got tips, and these I coveted for weeks, deciding what I would treat myself to (usually a record with the latest hits). I held this job throughout high school, and every summer during college I returned home to similar jobs, though I eventually graduated to waiting tables at a full-blown restaurant. At the time, I felt fortunate to have this work and the money it brought in; looking back, I still feel lucky: throughout my life I have always had work to do and, almost always, work I believed in. The benefit of hindsight also tells me that my jobs have brought me into contact with many other people — and that's one of the things I value most about the work experiences I have had.*

In the very brief essay that follows, Dagoberto Gilb (b. 1950) criticizes those who look upon some work as good and other work as somehow beneath them, arguing that "there is only good in work." Gilb speaks from experience. He's worked at many jobs, from construction worker to high-rise carpenter to teacher and writer. In this last role, Gilb has been highly successful, winning awards for his collection of short stories, The Magic of Blood *(1993), and for his novel,* The Last Known Residence of Mickey Acuña *(1994). "Work Union" appears in a collection of Gilb's essays,* Gritos, *published in 2003. His current work is teaching creative writing at Southwest Texas State University. As you read Gilb's essay, think about your own current work — and the value you place on it. Does your system of value for work match that of society in general?*

—A.L.

From the richest high school to the poorest high school in America, students are being told that employment in the computer industry is nothing less than salvation from the indignities of the jobs those others have to do to survive. If you don't learn your computer skills well, if by some chance you're bored sitting in front of that screen, day after day under buzzing fluorescents, pecking at a vanilla keyboard, clicking a mouse, it's your problem, and there will be no excuse for your fate in this new economy: you will be doomed to menial, manual labor. That dirty, anybody-can-do-that work. Poor income, low prestige. Pues, así va la vida, compa, that's life if you don't get your stuff right.

But if every young person did learn software programming or Web-page design, if everybody was taught to be so good at these and the rest, there simply wouldn't be enough of those jobs to go around, and the current high income associated with that employment would, as we know, fall dramatically. What is being taught is not only these skills but a justification for keeping an imbalance of power between the new high-tech workers and jobs that will always be necessary — building the offices, highways, bridges where those others do their business through modems and cell phones.

There was a time when work, a man who worked, a man who worked hard, who sweated, got dirty, even, who built things with tools in his hands, was looked upon with respect and honor. And it was the union that made for more personal dignity and real wages.

Not everybody wants to sit at a desk for a living. So many of us come from cultures where it is expected that we will move our bodies in the wind and sun, at dawn and into dusk. Many of us have been taught by family that physical work feels good and is good — when the day is over, we know what we did because we see it, we feel the efforts in our feet and hands and bones, and when we go home, when the wife puts food on the table and the family sits down and eats, there is unmistakable pride that all of it is because we have done our job.

It is human to work, to bend and grip, to lift and pull. It's never about get- 5 ting tired or dirty. There is nothing wrong with sweat and toil. It is only about conditions and decent wages that there can come complaint. This is what so many people don't understand, especially those who sit in chairs in offices. They see us tired, they see us worried. They say, Well, if you don't like your sit-uation, why don't you get a better job? Because it isn't the job, the kind of work. The job is good. Being a carpenter, an electrician, a plumber, a iron-worker, a laborer, those are all good. What isn't good is to be earning a living that can't bring in enough money to raise a healthy family, buy a home, go to a dentist and doctor, and be around comfortably for grandchildren.

A writer from Detroit who worked years for the Fisher Body Plant in Flint, Michigan, has recently been profiled in the newspapers because he won a prize for his writing. In the exultation of winning, he has been quoted often about those years he worked on the assembly line, saying, "I can't stress to you enough how much I hated it." This writer, he is certainly a good man, but like so many, he simply forgot what a joy employment is, what a job means to peo-ple and their families. There is only good in work, and the very best people are those who work hard.

QUESTIONING THE TEXT

1. To whom do you think Gilb is writing? Can you infer anything about the audience he envisions? What clues about the potential audience do you find in the text?

2. Gilb claims that those who promote computer industry work are also advancing "a justification for keeping an imbalance of power between the new high-tech workers and jobs that will always be necessary — building the offices, highways, bridges where those others do their business through modems and cell phones" (paragraph 2). With a classmate, elaborate on this claim to explain Gilb's reasoning. What support does he provide for this claim? What unstated assumptions does the claim rely on? After explicating this claim, decide whether you agree with it, and note your reasons.

MAKING CONNECTIONS

3. Read Naomi Barko's "The Other Gender Gap" (p. 617), and consider the assumptions Gilb makes about work in this essay as he conjures images of men working in traditionally male jobs. In class discussion, consider how Gilb might respond to Barko's claim that women's work is devalued, often because "women's occupations" suffer from discrimination. Do you think Gilb contributes to that discrimination with descriptions like those offered in paragraphs 3 and 4, or do you think he would readily include descriptions of nurses, teachers, and day-care workers in his lists of honorable, hard jobs? What evidence in his essay supports your answer?

4. Compare Gilb's argument with that of bell hooks in "Work Makes Life Sweet" (p. 641) or that of Marge Piercy in "To Be of Use" (p. 689). On what points do the authors agree, and on what points do they differ? Which argument do you find most convincing, and why?

5. Gilb writes that "it isn't the job, the kind of work" that deserves complaint. "There is nothing wrong with sweat and toil. It is only about conditions and decent wages that there can come complaint. . . . What isn't good is to be earning a living that can't bring in enough money to raise a healthy family, buy a home, go to a dentist and doctor, and be around comfortably for grandchildren" (paragraph 5). Given these sentiments, what position do you think Gilb would take on the issue of "comparable worth" debated by Naomi Barko and Steven Pinker in this chapter?

JOINING THE CONVERSATION

6. "Work Union" can be read as an argument of praise or blame because Gilb praises "those who work hard" and blames those who overlook the value of physical labor. Write your own short argument of praise or blame about a type of work you have done or a type of work you have been taught to respect. You might take a serious tone, as Gilb does here,

or you might try writing a humorous or satirical piece. Think of your essay as a piece that you might share with others, perhaps on your Web site or as an op-ed for a campus or local newspaper.

7. With a group of classmates, list the jobs you have performed, and state how you feel about them. Having read Gilb's essay, does anyone in your group admit to feeling differently about those jobs now? Do you think Gilb would impart greater dignity to some of your more "menial" work than you do? What issues related to "conditions and decent wages" might you complain about now?

ERIC SCHLOSSER
The Most Dangerous Job

I'M JUST OLD ENOUGH TO REMEMBER the first fast food restaurants appearing, bright and clean, at suburban crossroads in the 1950s — as well as the aptly named greasy spoons they displaced. We've since romanticized the latter, forgetting how dreadful the food in mom-and-pop operations could be and how unreliable the service usually was. You'd sit at a table waiting and waiting for a lump of meatloaf served by a waiter or waitress who expected tips but did little to earn them. In contrast, McDonald's and its imitators were the epitome of efficiency — cheery places that served up burgers and fries better than mom made (the fries especially) and did so almost faster than a customer could pay for them. It didn't take long for clever marketing to drill the virtues of fast food into the public mind.

Nevertheless, after reading Eric Schlosser's sobering critique of the all-American fast food industry, Fast Food Nation *(2001), you might never look at a* Big Mac *or* Whopper *the same way again. In this exposé, Schlosser asks his readers to ponder the real costs behind the relatively inexpensive burgers and fries Americans and, increasingly, people in the rest of the world devour in huge quantities every day. Pressure from the fast food companies to keep costs down, he argues, has lowered standards throughout the meat-packing and poultry industries and endangered or exploited workers at every level of production, from the farmers who raise chickens to the kids who peddle the patties.*

In "The Most Dangerous Job," a chapter from Fast Food Nation, *Schlosser takes readers into the slaughterhouse where, not surprisingly, animals die to become food. But by Schlosser's account the employees there also pay an extraordinarily high price, working under unremitting pressure and handling dangerous equipment that often leaves them injured or maimed. This is difficult reading that raises serious questions about the inadequate regulation of meatpacking industries — and not for the first time in American history.*

Eric Schlosser (b. 1960) is an investigative journalist and critic of corporate capitalism. A correspondent for the Atlantic, *he has written about agriculture, prisons, and pornography, and, more recently, in* Reefer Madness *(2003), about the American underground economy. Working with Richard Linklater, he co-wrote the screenplay for a film version of* Fast Food Nation *(2006).*   —J.R.

One night I visit a slaughterhouse somewhere in the High Plains. The slaughterhouse is one of the nation's largest. About five thousand head of cattle enter it every day, single file, and leave in a different form. Someone who has access to the plant, who's upset by its working conditions, offers to give me a tour. The slaughterhouse is an immense building, gray and square, about three stories high, with no windows on the front and no architectural clues to what's happening inside. My friend gives me a chain-mail apron and gloves, suggesting I try them on. Workers on the line wear about eight pounds of chain mail beneath their white coats, shiny steel armor that covers their hands, wrists, stomach, and back. The chain mail's designed to protect workers from cutting themselves and from being cut by other workers. But knives somehow manage to get past it. My host hands me some Wellingtons, the kind of knee-high rubber boots that English gentlemen wear in the countryside. "Tuck your pants into the boots," he says. "We'll be walking through some blood."

I put on a hardhat and climb a stairway. The sounds get louder, factory sounds, the noise of power tools and machinery, bursts of compressed air. We start at the end of the line, the fabricating room. Workers call it "fab." When we step inside, fab seems familiar: steel catwalks, pipes along the walls, a vast room, a maze of conveyer belts. This could be the Lamb Weston plant in Idaho, except hunks of red meat ride the belts instead of french fries. Some machines assemble cardboard boxes, others vacuum-seal subprimals of beef in clear plastic. The workers look extremely busy, but there's nothing unsettling about this part of the plant. You see meat like this all the time in the back of your local supermarket.

The fab room is cooled to about 40 degrees, and as you head up the line, the feel of the place starts to change. The pieces of meat get bigger. Workers — about half of them women, almost all of them young and Latino — slice meat with long slender knives. They stand at a table that's chest high, grab meat off a conveyer belt, trim away fat, throw meat back on the belt, toss the scraps onto a conveyer belt above them, and then grab more meat, all in a matter of seconds. I'm now struck by how many workers there are, hundreds of them, pressed close together, constantly moving, slicing. You see hardhats, white coats, flashes of steel. Nobody is smiling or chatting, they're too busy, anxiously trying not to fall behind. An old man walks past me, pushing a blue plastic barrel filled with scraps. A few workers carve the meat with Whizzards, small electric knives that have spinning round blades. The Whizzards look like the Norelco razors that Santa rides in the TV ads. I notice that a few of the women near me are sweating, even though the place is freezing cold.

Sides of beef suspended from an overhead trolley swing toward a group of men. Each worker has a large knife in one hand and a steel hook in the other. They grab the meat with their hooks and attack it fiercely with their knives. As they hack away, using all their strength, grunting, the place suddenly feels different, primordial. The machinery seems beside the point, and what's going on before me has been going on for thousands of years — the meat, the hook, the knife, men straining to cut more meat.

On the kill floor, what I see no longer unfolds in a logical manner. It's one strange image after another. A worker with a power saw slices cattle into halves as though they were two-by-fours, and then the halves swing by me into the cooler. It feels like a slaughterhouse now. Dozens of cattle, stripped of their skins, dangle on chains from their hind legs. My host stops and asks how I feel, if I want to go any further. This is where some people get sick. I feel fine, determined to see the whole process, the world that's been deliberately hidden. The kill floor is hot and humid. It stinks of manure. Cattle have a body temperature of about 101 degrees, and there are a lot of them in the room. Carcasses swing so fast along the rail that you have to keep an eye on them constantly, dodge them, watch your step, or one will slam you and throw you onto the bloody concrete floor. It happens to workers all the time.

I see: a man reach inside cattle and pull out their kidneys with his bare hands, then drop the kidneys down a metal chute, over and over again, as each animal passes by him; a stainless steel rack of tongues; Whizzards peeling meat off decapitated heads, picking them almost as clean as the white skulls painted by Georgia O'Keeffe. We wade through blood that's ankle deep and that pours down drains into huge vats below us. As we approach the start of the line, for the first time I hear the steady *pop, pop, pop* of live animals being stunned.

Now the cattle suspended above me look just like the cattle I've seen on ranches for years, but these ones are upside down swinging on hooks. For a moment, the sight seems unreal; there are so many of them, a herd of them, lifeless. And then I see a few hind legs still kicking, a final reflex action, and the reality comes hard and clear.

For eight and a half hours, a worker called a "sticker" does nothing but stand in a river of blood, being drenched in blood, slitting the neck of a steer every ten seconds or so, severing its carotid artery. He uses a long knife and must hit exactly the right spot to kill the animal humanely. He hits that spot again and again. We walk up a slippery metal stairway and reach a small platform, where the production line begins. A man turns and smiles at me. He wears safety goggles and a hardhat. His face is splattered with gray matter and blood. He is the "knocker," the man who welcomes cattle to the building. Cattle walk down a narrow chute and pause in front of him, blocked by a gate, and then he shoots them in the head with a captive bolt stunner — a compressed-air gun attached to the ceiling by a long hose — which fires a steel bolt that knocks the cattle unconscious. The animals keep strolling up, oblivious to what comes next, and he stands over them and shoots. For eight and a half hours, he just shoots. As I stand there, he misses a few times and shoots the same animal twice. As soon as the steer falls, a worker grabs one of its hind legs, shackles it to a chain, and the chain lifts the huge animal into the air.

I watch the knocker knock cattle for a couple of minutes. The animals are powerful and imposing one moment and then gone in an instant, suspended from a rail, ready for carving. A steer slips from its chain, falls to the ground, and gets its head caught in one end of a conveyer belt. The production line stops as workers struggle to free the steer, stunned but alive, from the machinery. I've seen enough.

I step out of the building into the cool night air and follow the path that   10 leads cattle into the slaughterhouse. They pass me, driven toward the building by workers with long white sticks that seem to glow in the dark. One steer, perhaps sensing instinctively what the others don't, turns and tries to run. But workers drive him back to join the rest. The cattle lazily walk single-file toward the muffled sounds, *pop, pop, pop*, coming from the open door.

The path has hairpin turns that prevent cattle from seeing what's in store and keep them relaxed. As the ramp gently slopes upward, the animals may think they're headed for another truck, another road trip — and they are, in unexpected ways. The ramp widens as it reaches ground level and then leads to a large cattle pen with wooden fences, a corral that belongs in a meadow, not here. As I walk along the fence, a group of cattle approach me, looking me straight in the eye, like dogs hoping for a treat, and follow me out of some mysterious impulse. I stop and try to absorb the whole scene: the cool breeze, the cattle and their gentle lowing, a cloudless sky, steam rising from the plant in the moonlight. And then I notice that the building does have one window, a small square of light on the second floor. It offers a glimpse of what's hidden behind this huge blank façade. Through the little window you can see bright red carcasses on hooks, going round and round.

SHARP KNIVES

Knocker, Sticker, Shackler, Rumper, First Legger, Knuckle Dropper, Navel Boner, Splitter Top/Bottom Butt, Feed Kill Chain — the names of job assignments at a modern slaughterhouse convey some of the brutality inherent in the work. Meatpacking is now the most dangerous job in the United States. The injury rate in a slaughterhouse is about three times higher than the rate in a typical American factory. Every year more than one-quarter of the meatpacking workers in this country — roughly forty thousand men and women — suffer an injury or a work-related illness that requires medical attention beyond first aid. There is strong evidence that these numbers, compiled by the Bureau of Labor Statistics, understate the number of meatpacking injuries that occur. Thousands of additional injuries and illnesses most likely go unrecorded.

Despite the use of conveyer belts, forklifts, dehiding machine, and a variety of power tools, most of the work in the nation's slaughterhouses is still performed by hand. Poultry plants can be largely mechanized, thanks to the breeding of chickens that are uniform in size. The birds in some Tyson factories are killed, plucked, gutted, beheaded, and sliced into cutlets by robots and machines. But cattle still come in all sizes and shapes, varying in weight by hundreds of pounds. The lack of a standardized steer has hindered the mechanization of beef plants. In one crucial respect meatpacking work has changed little in the past hundred years. At the dawn of the twenty-first century, amid an era of extraordinary technological advance, the most important tool in a modern slaughterhouse is a sharp knife.

Lacerations are the most common injuries suffered by meatpackers, who often stab themselves or stab someone working nearby. Tendinitis and cumulative trauma disorders are also quite common. Meatpacking workers routinely develop back problems, shoulder problems, carpal tunnel syndrome, and "trigger finger" (a syndrome in which a finger becomes frozen in a curled position). Indeed, the rate of these cumulative trauma injuries in the meatpacking industry is far higher than the rate in any other American industry. It is roughly thirty-three times higher than the national average in industry. Many slaughterhouse workers make a knife cut every two or three seconds, which adds up to about 10,000 cuts during an eight-hour shift. If the knife has become dull, additional pressure is placed on the worker's tendons, joints, and nerves. A dull knife can cause pain to extend from the cutting hand all the way down the spine.

Workers often bring their knives home and spend at least forty minutes a day keeping the edges smooth, sharp, and sanded, with no pits. One IBP worker, a small Guatemalan woman with graying hair, spoke with me in the cramped kitchen of her mobile home. As a pot of beans cooked on the stove, she sat in a wooden chair, gently rocking, telling the story of her life, of her journey north in search of work, the whole time sharpening big knives in her lap as though she were knitting a sweater.

The "IBP revolution" has been directly responsible for many of the hazards that meatpacking workers now face. One of the leading determinants of the injury rate at a slaughterhouse today is the speed of the disassembly line. The faster it runs, the more likely that workers will get hurt. The old meatpacking plants in Chicago slaughtered about 50 cattle an hour. Twenty years ago, new plants in the High Plains slaughtered about 175 cattle an hour. Today some plants slaughter up to 400 cattle an hour — about half a dozen animals every minute, sent down a single production line, carved by workers desperate not to fall behind. While trying to keep up with the flow of meat, workers often neglect resharpen their knives and thereby place more stress on their bodies. As the pace increases, so does the risk of accidental cuts and stabbings. "I could always tell the line speed," a former Monfort nurse told me, "by the number of people with lacerations coming into my office." People usually cut themselves; nevertheless, everyone on the line tries to stay alert. Meatpackers often work within inches of each other, wielding large knives. A simple mistake can cause a serious injury. A former IBP worker told me about boning knives suddenly flying out of hands and ricocheting off of machinery. "They're very flexible," she said, "and they'll spring on you . . . zwing, and they're gone."

Much like french fry factories, beef slaughterhouses often operate at profit margins as low as a few pennies a pound. The three meatpacking giants — ConAgra, IBP, and Excel — try to increase their earning by maximizing the volume of production at each plant. Once a slaughterhouse is up and running, fully staffed, the profits it will earn are directly related to the speed of the line. A faster pace means higher profits. Market pressures now exert a perverse influence on the management of beef plants: the same factors that make these slaughterhouses relatively inefficient (the lack of mechanization, the reliance on human labor) encourage companies to make them even more dangerous (by speeding up the pace).

The unrelenting pressure of trying to keep up with the line has encouraged widespread methamphetamine use among meatpackers. Workers taking "crank" feel charged and self-confident, ready for anything. Supervisors have been known to sell crank to their workers or to supply it free in return for

15

certain favors, such as working a second shift. Workers who use methamphetamine may feel energized and invincible, but are actually putting themselves at much greater risk of having an accident. For obvious reasons, a modern slaughterhouse is not a safe place to be high.

In the days when labor unions were strong, workers could complain about excessive line speeds and injury rates without fear of getting fired. Today only one-third of IBP's workers belong to a union. Most of the nonunion workers are recent immigrants; many are illegals; and they are generally employed "at will." That means they can be fired without warning, for just about any reason. Such an arrangement does not encourage them to lodge complaints. Workers who have traveled a great distance for this job, who have families to support, who are earning ten times more an hour in a meatpacking plant than they could possibly earn back home, are wary about speaking out and losing everything. The line speeds and labor costs at IBP's nonunion plants now set the standard for the rest of the industry. Every other company must try to produce beef as quickly and cheaply as IBP does; slowing the pace to protect workers can lead to a competitive disadvantage.

Again and again workers told me that they are under tremendous pressure   20
not to report injuries. The annual bonuses of plant foremen and supervisors are often based in part on the injury rate of their workers. Instead of creating a safer workplace, these bonus schemes encourage slaughterhouse managers to make sure that accidents and injuries go unreported. Missing fingers, broken bones, deep lacerations, and amputated limbs are difficult to conceal from authorities. But the dramatic and catastrophic injuries in a slaughterhouse are greatly outnumbered by less visible, though no less debilitating, ailments: torn muscles, slipped disks, pinched nerves.

If a worker agrees not to report an injury, a supervisor will usually shift him or her to an easier job for a while, providing some time to heal. If the injury seems more serious, a Mexican worker is often given the opportunity to return home for a while, to recuperate there, then come back to his or her slaughterhouse job in the United States. Workers who abide by these unwritten rules are treated respectfully; those who disobey are likely to be punished and made an example. As one former IBP worker explained, "They're trying to deter you, period, from going to the doctor."

From a purely economic point of view, injured workers are a drag on profits. They are less productive. Getting rid of them makes a good deal of financial sense, especially when new workers are readily available and inexpensive to train. Injured workers are often given some of the most unpleasant tasks in the slaughterhouse. Their hourly wages are cut. And through a wide variety of unsubtle means they are encouraged to quit.

Not all supervisors in a slaughterhouse behave like Simon Legree, shouting at workers, cursing them, belittling their injuries, always pushing them to move faster. But enough supervisors act that way to warrant the comparison. Production supervisors tend to be men in their late twenties and early thirties. Most are Anglos and don't speak Spanish, although more and more Latinos are being promoted to the job. They earn about $30,000 a year, plus bonuses and benefits. In many rural communities, being a supervisor at a meatpacking plant is one of the best jobs in town. It comes with a fair amount of pressure: a supervisor must meet production goals, keep the number of recorded injuries low, and most importantly, keep the meat flowing down the line without interruption. The job also brings enormous power. Each supervisor is like a little dictator in his or her section of the plant, largely free to boss, fire, berate, or reassign workers. That sort of power can lead to all sorts of abuses, especially when the hourly workers being supervised are women.

Many women told me stories about being fondled and grabbed on the production line, and the behavior of supervisors sets the tone for the other male workers. In February of 1999, a federal jury in Des Moines awarded $2.4 million to a female employee at an IBP slaughterhouse. According to the woman's testimony, coworkers had "screamed obscenities and rubbed their bodies against hers while supervisors laughed." Seven months later, Monfort agreed to settle a lawsuit filed by the U.S. Equal Employment Opportunity Commission on behalf of fourteen female workers in Texas. As part of the settlement, the company paid the women $900,000 and vowed to establish formal procedures for handling sexual harassment complaints. In their lawsuit the women alleged that supervisors at a Monfort plant in Cactus, Texas, pressured them for dates and sex, and that male coworkers groped them, kissed them, and used animal parts in a sexually explicit manner.

The sexual relationships between supervisors and "hourlies" are for the most part consensual. Many female workers optimistically regard sex with their supervisor as a way to gain a secure place in American society, a green card, a husband — or at the very least a transfer to an easier job at the plant. Some supervisors become meatpacking Casanovas, engaging in multiple affairs. Sex, drugs, and slaughterhouses may seem an unlikely combination, but as one former Monfort employee told me: "Inside those walls is a different world that obeys different laws." Late on the second shift, when it's dark outside, assignations take place in locker rooms, staff rooms, and parked cars, even on the catwalk over the kill floor.

The Worst

Some of the most dangerous jobs in meatpacking today are performed by the late-night cleaning crews. A large proportion of these workers are illegal immigrants. They are considered "independent contractors," employed not by the meatpacking firms but by sanitation companies. They earn hourly wages that are about one-third lower than those of regular production employees. And their work is so hard and so horrendous that words seem inadequate to describe it. The men and women who now clean the nation's slaughterhouses may arguably have the worst job in the United States. "It takes a really dedicated person," a former member of a cleaning crew told me, "or a really desperate person to get the job done."

When a sanitation crew arrives at a meatpacking plant, usually around midnight, it faces a mess of monumental proportions. Three to four thousand cattle, each weighing about a thousand pounds, have been slaughtered there that day. The place has to be clean by sunrise. Some of the workers wear water-resistant clothing; most don't. Their principal cleaning tool is a high-pressure hose that shoots a mixture of water and chlorine heated to about 180 degrees. As the water is sprayed, the plant fills with a thick, heavy fog. Visibility drops to as little as five feet. The conveyer belts and machinery are running. Workers stand on the belts, spraying them, riding them like moving sidewalks, as high as fifteen feet off the ground. Workers climb ladders with hoses and spray the catwalks. They get under tables and conveyer belts, climbing right into the bloody muck, cleaning out grease, fat, manure, leftover scraps of meat.

Glasses and safety goggles fog up. The inside of the plant heats up; temperatures soon exceed 100 degrees. "It's hot, and it's foggy, and you can't see anything," a former sanitation worker said. The crew members can't see or hear each other when the machinery's running. They routinely spray each other with burning hot, chemical-laden water. They are sickened by the fumes. Jesus, a soft-spoken employee of DCS Sanitation Management, Inc., the company that IBP uses in many of its plants, told me that every night on the job he gets terrible headaches. "You feel it in your head," he said. "You feel it in your stomach, like you want to throw up." A friend of his vomits whenever they clean the rendering area. Other workers tease the young man as he retches. Jesus says the stench in rendering is so powerful that it won't wash off; no matter how much soap you use after a shift, the smell comes home with you, seeps from your pores.

One night while Jesus was cleaning, a coworker forgot to turn off a machine, lost two fingers, and went into shock. An ambulance came and took him away, as everyone else continued to clean. He was back at work the following week. "If one hand is no good," the supervisor told him, "use the other." Another sanitation worker lost an arm in a machine. Now he folds towels in the locker room. The scariest job, according to Jesus, is cleaning the vents on the roof of the slaughterhouse. The vents become clogged with grease and dried blood. In the winter, when everything gets icy and the winds pick up, Jesus worries that a sudden gust will blow him off the roof into the darkness.

Although official statistics are not kept, the death rate among slaughterhouse sanitation crews is extraordinarily high. They are the ultimate in disposable workers: illegal, illiterate, impoverished, untrained. The nation's worst job can end in just about the worst way. Sometimes these workers are literally ground up and reduced to nothing.

A brief description of some cleaning-crew accidents over the past decade says more about the work and the danger than any set of statistics. At the Monfort plant in Grand Island, Nebraska, Richard Skala was beheaded by a dehiding machine. Carlos Vincente — an employee of T and G Service

Company, a twenty-eight-year-old Guatemalan who'd been in the United States for only a week — was pulled into the cogs of a conveyer belt at an Excel plant in Fort Morgan, Colorado, and torn apart. Lorenzo Marin, Sr., an employee of DCS Sanitation, fell from the top of a skinning machine while cleaning it with a high-pressure hose, struck his head on the concrete floor of an IBP plant in Columbus Junction, Iowa, and died. Another employee of DCS Sanitation, Salvador Hernandez-Gonzalez, had his head crushed by a port-loin processing machine at an IBP plant in Madison, Nebraska. The same machine had fatally crushed the head of another worker, Ben Barone, a few years earlier. At a National Beef plant in Liberal, Kansas, Homer Stull climbed into a blood-collection tank to clean it, a filthy tank thirty feet high. Stull was overcome by hydrogen sulfide fumes. Two coworkers climbed into the tank and tried to rescue him. All three men died. Eight years earlier, Henry Wolf had been overcome by hydrogen sulfide fumes while cleaning the very same tank; Gary Sanders had tried to rescue him; both men died; and the Occupational Safety and Health Administration (OSHA) later fined National Beef for its negligence. The fine was $480 for each man's death.

DON'T GET CAUGHT

During the same years when the working conditions at America's meatpacking plants became more dangerous — when line speeds increased and illegal immigrants replaced skilled workers — the federal government greatly reduced the enforcement of health and safety laws. OSHA had long been despised by the nation's manufacturers, who considered the agency a source of meddlesome regulations and unnecessary red tape. When Ronald Reagan was elected president in 1980, OSHA was already underfunded and understaffed: its 1,300 inspectors were responsible for the safety of more than 5 million workplaces across the country. A typical American employer could expect an OSHA inspection about once every eighty years. Nevertheless, the Reagan administration was determined to reduce OSHA's authority even further, as part of the push for deregulation. The number of OSHA inspectors was eventually cut by 20 percent, and in 1981 the agency adopted a new policy of "voluntary compliance." Instead of arriving unannounced at a factory and performing an inspection, OSHA employees were required to look at a company's injury log before setting foot inside the plant. If the records showed an injury rate at the factory lower than the national average for all manufacturers, the OSHA inspector had to turn around and leave at once — without entering the plant, examining its equipment, or talking to any of its workers. These injury logs were kept and maintained by company officials.

For most of the 1980s OSHA's relationship with the meatpacking industry was far from adversarial. While the number of serious injuries rose, the number of OSHA inspections fell. The death of a worker on the job was punished with a fine of just a few hundred dollars. At a gathering of meat company executives in October of 1987, OSHA's safety director, Barry White, promised to change federal safety standards that "appear amazingly stupid to you or over-burdening or just not useful." According to an account of the meeting later published in the *Chicago Tribune*, the safety director at OSHA — the federal official most responsible for protecting the lives of meatpacking workers — acknowledged his own lack of qualification for the job. "I know very well that you know more about safety and health in the meat industry than I do," White told the executives. "And you know more about safety and health in the meat industry than any single employee at OSHA."

OSHA's voluntary compliance policy did indeed reduce the number of recorded injuries in meatpacking plants. It did not, however, reduce the number of people getting hurt. It merely encouraged companies, in the words of a subsequent congressional investigation, "to understate injuries, to falsify records, and to cover up accidents." At the IBP beef plant in Dakota City, Nebraska, for example, the company kept two sets of injury logs: one of them recording every injury and illness at the slaughterhouse, the other provided to visiting OSHA inspectors and researchers from the Bureau of Labor Statistics. During a three-month period in 1985, the first log recorded 1,800 injuries and illnesses at the plant. The OSHA log recorded only 160 — a discrepancy of more than 1,000 percent.

At congressional hearings on meatpacking in 1987, Robert L. Peterson,   35 the chief executive of IBP, denied under oath that two sets of logs were ever kept and called IBP's safety record "the best of the best." Congressional investigators later got hold of both logs — and found that the injury rate at its Dakota City plant was as much as one-third higher than the average rate in the meatpacking industry. Congressional investigators also discovered that IBP had altered injury records at its beef plant in Emporia, Kansas. Another leading meatpacking company, John Morrell, was caught lying about injuries at its plant in Sioux Falls, South Dakota. The congressional investigation concluded that these companies had failed to report "serious injuries such as fractures, concussions, major cuts, hernias, some requiring hospitalization, surgery, even amputation."

Congressman Tom Lantos, whose subcommittee conducted the meat-packing injury, called IBP "one of the most irresponsible and reckless corpora-tions in America." A Labor Department official called the company's behavior "the worst example of underreporting injuries and illnesses to workers ever encountered in OSHA's sixteen-year history." Nevertheless, Robert L. Peterson was never charged with perjury for his misleading testimony before Congress. Investigators argued that it would be difficult to prove "conclusively" that Peterson had "willfully" lied. In 1987 IBP was fined $2.6 million by OSHA for underreporting injuries and later fined an additional $3.1 million for the high rate of cumulative trauma injuries at the Dakota City plant. After the company introduced a new safety program there, the fines were reduced to $975,000 — a sum that might have appeared large at the time, yet represented about one one-hundredth of a percent of IBP's annual revenues.

Three years after the OSHA fines, a worker named Kevin Wilson injured his back at an IBP slaughterhouse in Council Bluffs, Iowa. Wilson went to see Diane Arndt, a nurse at the plant, who sent him to a doctor selected by the company. Wilson's injury was not serious, the doctor said, later assigning him to light duty at the plant. Wilson sought a second opinion; the new doctor said that he had a disk injury that required a period of absence from work. When Wilson stopped reporting for light duty, IBP's corporate security department began to conduct surveillance of his house. Eleven days after Wilson's new doctor told IBP that back surgery might be required, Diane Arndt called the doctor and said that IBP had obtained a videotape of Wilson engaging in strenuous physical activities at home. The doctor felt deceived, met with Wilson, accused him of being a liar, refused to provide him with any more treatment, and told him to get back to work. Convinced that no such videotape existed and that IBP had fabricated the entire story in order to deny him medical treatment, Kevin Wilson sued the company for slander.

The lawsuit eventually reached the Iowa Supreme Court. In a decision that received little media attention, the Supreme Court upheld a lower court's award of $2 million to Wilson and described some of IBP's unethical practices. The court found that seriously injured workers were required to show up at the IBP plant briefly each day so that the company could avoid reporting "lost workdays" to OSHA. Some workers were compelled to show up for work on the same day as a surgery or the day after an amputation. "IBP's management was aware of, and participated in, this practice," the Iowa Supreme Court noted. IBP nurses regularly entered false information into the plant's computer system, reclassifying injuries so that they didn't have to be reported to OSHA. Injured workers who proved uncooperative were assigned to jobs "watching gauges in the rendering plant, where they were subjected to an atrocious smell while hog remains were boiled down into fertilizers and blood was drained into tanks." According to evidence introduced in court, Diane Arndt had a low opinion of the workers whose injuries she was supposed to be treating. The IBP nurse called them "idiots" and "jerks," telling doctors that "this guy's a cry-baby" and "this guy's full of shit." She later admitted that Wilson's back injury was legitimate. The Iowa Supreme Court concluded that the lies she told in his medical case, as well as in others, had been partly motivated by IBP's financial incentive program, which gave staff members bonuses and prizes when the number of lost workdays was kept low. The program, in the court's opinion, was "somewhat disingenuously called 'the safety award system.'"

IBP's attitude toward worker safety was hardly unique in the industry, according to Edward Murphy's testimony before Congress in 1992. Murphy had served as the safety director of the Monfort beef plant in Grand Island. After two workers were killed there in 1991, Monfort fired him. Murphy claimed that he had battled the company for years over safety issues and that Monfort had unfairly made him the scapegoat for its own illegal behavior. The company later paid him an undisclosed sum of money to settle a civil lawsuit over wrongful termination.

Murphy told Congress that during his tenure at the Grand Island plant, 40 Monfort maintained two sets of injury logs, routinely lied to OSHA, and shredded documents requested by OSHA. He wanted Congress to know that the safety lapses at the plant were not accidental. They stemmed directly from Monfort's corporate philosophy, which Murphy described in these terms: "The first commandment is that only production counts . . . The employee's duty is to follow orders. Period. As I was repeatedly told, 'Do what I tell you, even if it is illegal . . . Don't get caught.'"

A lawsuit filed in May of 1998 suggests that little has changed since IBP was caught keeping two sets of injury logs more than a decade ago. Michael D. Ferrell, a former vice president at IBP, contends that the real blame for the high injury rate at the company lies not with the workers, supervisors, nurses, safety directors, or plant managers, but with IBP's top executives. Ferrell had ample opportunity to observe their decision-making process. Among other duties, he was in charge of the health and safety programs at IBP.

When Ferrell accepted the job in 1991, after many years as an industrial engineer at other firms, he believed that IBP's desire to improve worker safety was sincere. According to his legal complaint, Ferrell later discovered that IBP's safety records were routinely falsified and that the company cared more about production than anything else. Ferrell was fired by IBP in 1997, not long after a series of safety problems at slaughterhouse in Palestine, Texas. The circumstances surrounding his firing are at the heart of the lawsuit. On December 4, 1996, an OSHA inspection of the Palestine plant found a number of serious violations and imposed a fine of $35,125. Less than a week later, a worker named Clarence Dupree lost an arm in a bone-crushing machine. And two days after that, another worker, Willie Morris, was killed by an ammonia gas explosion. Morris's body lay on the floor for hours, just ten feet from the door, as toxic gas filled the building. Nobody at the plant had been trained to use hazardous-materials gas masks or protective suits; the equipment sat in a locked storage room. Ferrell flew to Texas and toured the plant after the accidents. He thought the facility was in terrible shape — with a cooling system that violated OSHA standards, faulty wiring that threatened to cause a mass electrocution, and safety mechanisms that had deliberately been disabled with magnets. He wanted the slaughterhouse to be shut down immediately, and it was. Two months later, Ferrell lost his job.

In his lawsuit seeking payment for wrongful termination, Ferrell contends that he was fired for giving the order to close the Palestine plant. He claims that IBP had never before shut down a slaughterhouse purely for safety reasons and that Robert L. Peterson was enraged by the decision. IBP disputes this version of events, contending that Farrell had never fit into IBP's corporate culture, that he delegated too much authority, and that he had not, in fact, made the decision to shut down the Palestine plant. According to IBP, the decision to shut it was made after a unanimous vote by its top executives.

IBP's Palestine slaughterhouse reopened in January of 1997. It was shut down again a year later — this time by the USDA. Federal inspectors cited the plant for "inhumane slaughter" and halted production there for one week, an extremely rare penalty imposed for the mistreatment of cattle. In 1999 IBP closed the plant. As of this writing, it sits empty, awaiting a buyer.

THE VALUE OF AN ARM

When I First Visited Greeley in 1997, Javier Ramirez was president of the   45
UFCW, Local 990, the union representing employees at the Monfort beef plant. The National Labor Relations Board had ruled that Monfort committed "numerous, pervasive, and outrageous" violations of labor law after reopening the Greeley beef plant in 1982, discriminating against former union members at hiring time and intimidating new workers during a union election. Former employees who'd been treated unfairly ultimately received a $10.6 million settlement. After a long and arduous organizing drive, workers at the Monfort beef plant voted to join the UFCW in 1992. Javier Ramirez is thirty-one and knows a fair amount about beef. His father is Ruben Ramirez, the Chicago union leader. Javier grew up around slaughterhouses and watched the meatpacking industry abandon his hometown for the High Plains. Instead of finding another line of work, he followed the industry to Colorado, trying to gain better wages and working conditions for the mainly Latino workforce.

The UFCW has given workers in Greeley the ability to challenge unfair dismissals, file grievances against supervisors, and report safety lapses without fear of reprisal. But the union's power is limited by the plant's high turnover rate. Every year a new set of workers must be persuaded to support the UFCW. The plant's revolving door is not conducive to worker solidarity. At the moment some of the most pressing issues for the UFCW are related to the high injury rate at the slaughterhouse. It is a constant struggle not only to prevent workers from getting hurt, but also to gain them proper medical treatment and benefits once they've been hurt.

Colorado was one of the first states to pass a workers' compensation law. The idea behind the legislation, enacted in 1919, was to provide speedy medical care and a steady income to workers injured on the job. Workers' comp was meant to function much like no-fault insurance. In return for surrendering the right to sue employers for injuries, workers were supposed to receive immediate benefits. Similar workers' comp plans were adopted throughout the United States. In 1991, Colorado started another trend, becoming one of the first states to impose harsh restrictions on workers' comp payments. In addition to reducing the benefits afforded to injured employees, Colorado's new law granted employers the right to choose the physician who'd determine the severity of any work-related ailment. Enormous power over workers' comp claims was handed to company doctors.

Many other states subsequently followed Colorado's lead and cut back their workers' comp benefits. The Colorado bill, promoted as "workers' comp reform," was first introduced in the legislature by Tom Norton, the president of the Colorado State Senate and a conservative Republican. Norton represented Greeley, where his wife, Kay, was the vice president of legal and governmental affairs at ConAgra Red Meat.

In most businesses, a high injury rate would prompt insurance companies to demand changes in the workplace. But ConAgra, IBP, and the other large meatpacking firms are self-insured. They are under no pressure from independent underwriters and have a strong incentive to keep workers' comp payments to a bare minimum. Every penny spent on workers' comp is one less penny of corporate revenue.

Javier Ramirez began to educate Monfort workers about their legal right to get workers' comp benefits after an injury at the plant. Many workers don't realize that such insurance even exists. The workers' comp claim forms look intimidating, especially to people who don't speak any English and can't read any language. Filing a claim, challenging a powerful meatpacking company, and placing faith in the American legal system requires a good deal of courage, especially for a recent immigrant.

When a workers' comp claim involves an injury that is nearly impossible to refute (such as an on-the-job amputation), the meatpacking companies generally agree to pay. But when injuries are less visible (such as those stemming from cumulative trauma) the meatpackers often prolong the whole workers' comp process through litigation, insisting upon hearings and filing seemingly endless appeals. Some of the most painful and debilitating injuries are the hardest to prove.

Today it can take years for an injured worker to receive workers' comp benefits. During that time, he or she must pay medical bills and find a source of income. Many rely on public assistance. The ability of meatpacking firms to delay payment discourages many injured workers from ever filing workers' comp claims. It leads others to accept a reduced sum of money as part of a negotiated settlement in order to cover medical bills. The system now leaves countless unskilled and uneducated manual workers poorly compensated for injuries that will forever hamper their ability to earn a living. The few who win in court and receive full benefits are hardly set for life. Under Colorado's new law, the payment for losing an arm is $36,000. An amputated finger gets you anywhere from $2,200 to $4,500, depending on which one is lost. And "serious permanent disfigurement about the head, face, or parts of the body normally exposed to public view" entitles you to a maximum of $2,000.

As workers' comp benefits have become more difficult to obtain, the threat to workplace safety has grown more serious. During the first two years of the Clinton administration, OSHA seemed like a revitalized agency. It began to draw up the first ergonomics standards for the nation's manufacturers, aiming to reduce cumulative trauma disorders. The election of 1994, however, marked a turning point. The Republican majority in Congress that rose to power that year not only impeded the adoption of ergonomics standards but also raised questions about the future of OSHA. Working closely with the U.S. Chamber of Commerce and the National Association of Manufacturers, House Republicans have worked hard to limit OSHA's authority. Congressman Cass Ballenger, a Republican from North Carolina, introduced legislation that would require OSHA to spend at least half of its budget on "consultation" with businesses, instead of enforcement. This new budget requirement would further reduce the number of OSHA inspections, which by the late 1990s had already reached an all-time low. Ballenger has long opposed OSHA inspections, despite the fact that near his own district a fire at a poultry plant killed twenty-five workers in 1991. The plant had never been inspected by OSHA, its emergency exits had been chained shut, and the bodies of workers were found in piles near the locked doors. Congressman Joel Hefley, a Colorado Republican whose district includes Colorado Springs, has introduced a bill that makes Ballenger's seem moderate. Hefley's "OSHA Reform Act" would essentially repeal the Occupational Safety and Health Act of 1970. It would forbid OSHA from conducting any workplace inspections or imposing any fines.

KENNY

During my trips to meatpacking towns in the High Plains I met dozens of workers who'd been injured. Each of their stories was different, yet somehow familiar, linked to common elements — the same struggle to receive proper medical care, the same fear of speaking out, the same underlying corporate indifference. We are human beings, more than one person told me, but they treat us like animals. The workers I met wanted their stories to be told. They wanted people to know about what is happening right now. A young woman who'd injured her back and her right hand at the Greeley plant said to me, "I want to get on top of a rooftop and scream my lungs out so that somebody will hear." The voices and faces of these workers are indelibly with me, as is the sight of their hands, the light brown skin criss-crossed with white scars. Although I cannot tell all of their stories, a few need to be mentioned. Like all lives, they can be used as examples or serve as representative types. But ultimately they are unique, individual, impossible to define or replace — the opposite of how this system has treated them.

Raoul was born in Zapoteca, Mexico, and did construction work in   55
Anaheim before moving to Colorado. He speaks no English. After hearing a Monfort ad on a Spanish-language radio station, he applied for a job at the Greeley plant. One day Raoul reached into a processing machine to remove a piece of meat. The machine accidentally went on. Raoul's arm got stuck, and it

took workers twenty minutes to get it out. The machine had to be taken apart. An ambulance brought Raoul to the hospital, where a deep gash in his shoulder was sewn shut. A tendon had been severed. After getting stitches and a strong prescription painkiller, he was driven back to the slaughterhouse and put back on the production line. Bandaged, groggy, and in pain, one arm tied in a sling, Raoul spent the rest of the day wiping blood off cardboard boxes with his good hand.

Renaldo was another Monfort worker who spoke no English, an older man with graying hair. He developed carpal tunnel syndrome while cutting meat. The injury got so bad that sharp pain shot from his hand all the way up to his shoulder. At night it hurt so much he could not fall asleep in bed. Instead he would fall asleep sitting in a chair beside the bed where his wife lay. For three years he slept in that chair every night.

Kenny Dobbins was a Monfort employee for almost sixteen years. He was born in Keokuk, Iowa, had a tough childhood and an abusive stepfather, left home at the age of thirteen, went in and out of various schools, never learned to read, did various odd jobs, and wound up at the Monfort slaughterhouse in Grand Island, Nebraska. He started working there in 1979, right after the company bought it from Swift. He was twenty-four. He worked in the shipping department at first, hauling boxes that weighed as much as 120 pounds. Kenny could handle it, though. He was a big man, muscular and six-foot-five, and nothing in his life had ever been easy.

One day Kenny heard someone yell, "Watch out!" then turned around and saw a ninety-pound box falling from an upper level of the shipping department. Kenny caught the box with one arm, but the momentum threw him against a conveyer belt, and the metal rim of the belt pierced his lower back. The company doctor bandaged Kenny's back and said the pain was just a pulled muscle. Kenny never filed for workers' comp, stayed home for a few days, then returned to work. He had a wife and three children to support. For the next few months, he was in terrible pain. "It hurt so fucking bad you wouldn't believe it," he told me. He saw another doctor, got a second opinion. The new doctor said Kenny had a pair of severely herniated disks. Kenny had back surgery, spent a month in the hospital, got sent to a pain clinic when the operation didn't work. His marriage broke up amid the stress and financial difficulty. Fourteen months after the injury, Kenny returned to the slaughterhouse. "GIVE UP AFTER BACK SURGERY? NOT KEN DOBBINS!!" a Monfort newsletter proclaimed. "Ken has learned how to handle the rigors of working in a packing plant and is trying to help others do the same. Thanks, Ken, and keep up the good work."

Kenny felt a strong loyalty to Monfort. He could not read, possessed few skills other than his strength, and the company had still given him a job. When Monfort decided to reopen its Greeley plant with a non-union workforce, Kenny volunteered to go there and help. He did not think highly of labor unions. His supervisors told him that unions had been responsible for shutting down meatpacking plants all over the country. When the UFCW tried to organize the Greeley slaughterhouse, Kenny became an active and outspoken member of an anti-union group.

At the Grand Island facility, Kenny had been restricted to light duty after his injury. But his supervisor in Greeley said that old restrictions didn't apply in this new job. Soon Kenny was doing tough, physical labor once again, wielding a knife and grabbing forty- to fifty-pound pieces of beef off a table. When the pain became unbearable, he was transferred to ground beef, then to rendering. According to a former manager at the Greeley plant, Monfort was trying to get rid of Kenny, trying to make his work so unpleasant that he'd quit. Kenny didn't realize it. "He still believes in his heart that people are honest and good," the former manager said about Kenny. "And he's wrong."   60

As part of the job in rendering, Kenny sometimes had to climb into gigantic blood tanks and gut bins, reach to the bottom of them with his long arms, and unclog the drains. One day he was unexpectedly called to work over the weekend. There had been a problem with *Salmonella* contamination. The plant needed to be disinfected, and some of the maintenance workers had refused to do it. In his street clothes, Kenny began cleaning the place, climbing into tanks and spraying a liquid chlorine mix. Chlorine is a hazardous chemical that can be inhaled or absorbed through the skin, causing a litany of health problems. Workers who spray it need to wear protective gloves, safety goggles, a self-contained respirator, and full coveralls. Kenny's supervisor gave him a paper dust mask to wear, but it quickly dissolved. After eight hours or working with the chlorine in unventilated areas, Kenny went home and fell ill. He was rushed to the hospital and placed in an oxygen tent. His lungs had been burned by the chemicals. His body was covered in blisters. Kenny spent a month in the hospital.

Kenny eventually recovered from the overexposure to chlorine, but it left his chest feeling raw, made him susceptible to colds and sensitive to chemical aromas. He went back to work at the Greeley plant. He had remarried, didn't know what other kind of work to do, still felt loyal to the company. He was assigned to an early morning shift. He had to drive an old truck from one part of the slaughterhouse complex to another. The truck was filled with leftover scraps of meat. The headlights and the wipers didn't work. The windshield was filthy and cracked. One cold, dark morning in the middle of winter, Kenny became disoriented while driving. He stopped the truck, opened the door, got out to see where he was — and was struck by a train. It knocked his glasses off, threw him up in the air, and knocked both of his work boots off. The train was moving slowly, or he would've been killed. Kenny somehow made it back to the plant, barefoot and bleeding from deep gashes in his back and his face. He spent two weeks at the hospital, then went back to work.

One day, Kenny was in rendering and saw a worker about to stick his head into a pre-breaker machine, a device that uses hundreds of small hammers to pulverize gristle and bone into a fine powder. The worker had just turned the machine off, but Kenny knew the hammers inside were still spinning. It takes fifteen minutes for the machine to shut down completely. Kenny yelled, "Stop!" but the worker didn't hear him. And so Kenny ran across the room, grabbed the man by the seat of his pants, and pulled him away from the machine an instant before it would have pulverized him. To honor this act of bravery, Monfort gave Kenny an award for "Outstanding Achievement in CONCERN FOR FELLOW WORKERS." The award was a paper certificate, signed by his supervisor and the plant safety manager.

Kenny later broke his leg stepping into a hole in the slaughterhouse's concrete floor. On another occasion he shattered an ankle, an injury that required surgery and the insertion of five steel pins. Now Kenny had to wear a metal brace on one leg in order to walk, an elaborate, spring-loaded brace that cost $2,000. Standing for long periods caused him great pain. He was given a job recycling old knives at the plant. Despite his many injuries, the job required him to climb up and down three flights of narrow stairs carrying garbage bags filled with knives. In December of 1995 Kenny felt a sharp pain in his chest while lifting some boxes. He thought it was a heart attack. His union steward took him to see the nurse, who said it was just a pulled muscle and sent Kenny home. He was indeed having a massive heart attack. A friend rushed Kenny to a nearby hospital. A stent was inserted in his heart, and the doctors told Kenny that he was lucky to be alive.

While Kenny Dobbins was recuperating, Monfort fired him. Despite the 65 fact that Kenny had been with the company for almost sixteen years, despite the fact that he was first in seniority at the Greeley plant, that he'd cleaned blood tanks with his bare hands, fought the union, done whatever the company had asked him to do, suffered injuries that would've killed weaker men, nobody from Monfort called him with the news. Nobody even bothered to write him. Kenny learned that he'd been fired when his payments to the company health insurance plan kept being returned by the post office. He called Monfort repeatedly to find out what was going on, and a sympathetic clerk in the claims office finally told Kenny that the checks were being returned because he was no longer a Monfort employee. When I asked company spokesmen to comment on the accuracy of Kenny's story, they would neither confirm nor deny any of the details.

Today Kenny is in poor health. His heart is permanently damaged. His immune system seems shot. His back hurts, his ankle hurts, and every so often he coughs up blood. He is unable to work at any job. His wife, Clara — who's half-Latina and half-Cheyenne, and looks like a younger sister of Cher's — was working as a nursing home attendant when Kenny had the heart attack. Amid the stress of his illness, she developed a serious kidney ailment. She is unemployed and recovering from a kidney transplant.

As I sat in the living room of their Greeley home, its walls decorated with paintings of wolves, Denver Broncos memorabilia, and an American flag, Kenny and Clara told me about their financial condition. After almost sixteen years on the job, Kenny did not get any pension from Monfort. The company challenged his workers' comp claim and finally agreed — three years after the initial filing — to pay him a settlement of $35,000. Fifteen percent of that money went to Kenny's lawyer, and the rest is long gone. Some months Kenny has to hock things to get money for Clara's medicine. They have two teenage children and live on Social Security payments. Kenny's health insurance, which costs more than $600 a month, is about to run out. His anger at Monfort, his feelings of betrayal, are of truly biblical proportions.

"They used me to the point where I had no body parts left to give," Kenny said, struggling to maintain his composure. "Then they just tossed me into the trash can." Once strong and powerfully built, he now walks with difficulty, tires easily, and feels useless, as though his life were over. He is forty-six years old.

Reading across Professions
MARJORIE BUTLER, Labor Lawyer

Before I finished college and went to law school, I worked for about seven years in factories. I worked in heavy industry in an auto factory on the assembly line and in light industry making loudspeakers, tape recorders (remember those?) and projection televisions (way before their time). Reading this chapter from *Fast Food Nation* by Eric Schlosser reminded me of those days when I was an appendage to an assembly line, when I was part of the machinery.

I know about speed-up on the line. When I worked in the auto factory, production numbers were set and often we had to work overtime to make production. We made one car every 90 seconds. I worked in the soft trim department, and I had a number of things to put on each car: door locks and handles, window handles and automatic openers, inside door panels, some of the dashboard trim. I had to work so hard and fast that I was running down the line behind the cars. When I got home, I was so sore that I had to soak in a tub of hot water before I could sleep.

There was a ninety-day probation period, and I thought I would never survive. After a while, though, my body adapted. I began to read newspapers between cars and I became an avid radio baseball fan because I could do all of the work on a car while the pitcher set up. But at the end of each car model season, the model changed and each job was redone by efficiency engineers. More tasks were added to each job so that some jobs could be eliminated. If 15 seconds of work could be added to a position, every sixth job on each side of the car could be cut. Every year when the new model line started, workers' bodies would have to get used to the job all over again, running down the line, chasing the cars.

I know about immigrants on the line. I worked in an electronics factory with workers from all over the world. One woman from Costa Rica, a country with a long history of democracy, had found herself in domestic slavery at a rich professional's home outside of Boston. She had been rescued by a domestic in a nearby house who had contacted a relief organization. I met refugees from poverty and dictatorships all over the Caribbean and Latin America. I did not know who was legal and who was illegal until Immigration raided the plant and people began to hide and flee, until friends were seized and separated from their families.

I know about "accidents" on the line. Before the Occupational Safety and Health Act (OSHA) became law in 1970, I worked at the electronics plant with a young man whose face was completely disfigured. He thought that he had had a reaction to a solvent that he had used on a previous job at a factory. There was no ingredient label on the solvent, so he did not know what had caused the disfigurement. Lawyers tried to get the information, but the factory had since closed down and the manufacturer would not help. A few years later, OSHA issued a regulation requiring an MSDS (Material Safety Data Sheet) for all such materials, something that might have saved my friend considerable anguish.

I went back to college to become a labor lawyer precisely to fight for the rights of workers on the job. I never forgot the lessons from the line: that people from all over the world come here to work and feed their families, that workers deserve to be treated with dignity, that bodies can be pushed and pushed and pushed for more production until they break, and that most injuries are caused by poor safety conditions or poor training and are preventable.

OSHA's current literature states that each year, "almost 5200 Americans die from workplace injuries in the private sector," "as many as 50,000 employees die from illnesses in which workplace exposures were a contributing factor," and "nearly 4.3 million people suffer non-fatal workplace injuries and illnesses." Nothing in my experience, though, prepared me for Schlosser's description of the slaughterhouse. The conditions he depicts are gruesome, and the treatment of the workers is unconscionable. As Schlosser points out, the meatpacking industry is one of the most dangerous industries to work in, particularly when you combine speed-up, sharp knives, and blood everywhere.

In 1906, Upton Sinclair's *The Jungle*, an account of working life in the Chicago slaughterhouses, caused a great public outcry that led to the passage of the Pure Food and Drug Act of 1910. Although Sinclair focused on the work conditions, the outcry focused on ensuring safer food. Much of *Fast Food Nation* concentrates on the food we eat today, but in this excerpt, Schlosser examines the toll that brutal slaughterhouse conditions take on workers on the line. Recently, the labor movement has spotlighted conditions in Smithfield Packing's hog slaughter and pork processing plant in Tar Heel, North Carolina, because of the plant's high injury rate and work conditions similar to those described in Schlosser's piece. Perhaps Schlosser's exposé of the conditions in the slaughterhouses in *Fast Food Nation* has finally helped open eyes to the dangerous plight of the workers.

Marjorie Butler is a lawyer who works to enforce federal labor laws.

QUESTIONING THE TEXT

1. How would you describe the narrative voice that Schlosser uses in this article? Is he is a disinterested observer? Is he outraged by what he sees? Does his voice ever shift in the course of the article? Use specific textual evidence to explain your answer.

2. Schlosser's article is one that many people might read as just "telling it like it is." In paragraph 6, though, Schlosser writes that the Whizzards cut meat from cows' heads, leaving them "almost as clean as the white skulls painted by Georgia O'Keeffe." Find other examples where Schlosser uses vivid imagery or figurative language. What effect do his metaphors, similes, and imagery have on the reader? How does figurative language shape Schlosser's piece?

MAKING CONNECTIONS

3. Compare Schlosser's discussion of business ethics — particularly the section "Don't Get Caught" — to James Surowiecki's consideration of business ethics in "Don't Do the Math" (p. 676). What principles of good business ethics do you think these two authors would agree on? In what ways might they disagree?

4. Think about Kenny Dobbins's loyalty to the slaughterhouse where he worked. Is he someone who exemplifies the pride in work that Dagoberto Gilb celebrates in "Work Union" (p. 650)? How do you think that Gilb would react to the story of Kenny Dobbins? Be prepared to explain your response with textual evidence drawn from both pieces.

JOINING THE CONVERSATION

5. Schlosser's story of the life of Kenny Dobbins at the end of the selection provides a good example of a narrative argument where the details of the

story provide an argument that is not directly stated. Write a narrative argument of your own: a self-contained story that makes a point without necessarily stating that point directly in a thesis.

6. Write a brief essay about an experience you've had in the world of work. Try to capture what you learned from this job. Would you go back to that type of work? Under what circumstances might you consider doing so? Compare your essay to those by others in your class. What similarities emerge? To what degree does a particular job shape the worker's experience? To what degree is the simple fact of working itself a part of the experience?

JAMES SUROWIECKI
Don't Do the Math

Remember the $200 million in damages that went to two women who suffered extensive heart damage from taking fen-phen diet drugs? Or the $80 million awarded to the widow of a long-time smoker who died of lung cancer? Well, James Surowiecki remembers them, as well as a number of other $100 million-plus awards made since 1999.

Twice a month, financial columnist James Surowiecki (b. 1967) writes a column for the New Yorker that examines hot topics in the financial world, often bringing insights from economics, sociology, and business history to bear on them. In "Don't Do the Math," he takes a look at the growing tendency of juries to give "blockbuster awards" — those that top a hundred million dollars — to plaintiffs, thus driving some of the corporations on the other side of the lawsuit into bankruptcy. Why, he asks, are juries handing out these gigantic damage awards? In exploring the question, Surowiecki looks carefully at the case of Merck, the pharmaceutical company that developed and marketed Vioxx, a drug that treated pain (especially from arthritis) very effectively but that also was eventually linked to increased heart disease. Merck pulled Vioxx from the market, but not soon enough to avert hundreds of lawsuits brought against the company.

Surowiecki, who also writes for prestigious publications like Fortune, the Wall Street Journal, and Wired, finds that Merck had been aware of risks associated with taking Vioxx but that the company did not judge the risks sufficient to recall a drug that had such a strong benefit (as Surowiecki puts it, Vioxx "was less likely to cause the internal bleeding that aspirin and ibuprofen cause, and that kills thousands of people a year"). Weighing risks and benefits happens all the time in everyday life as well as in the corporate world, but juries react strongly against companies that engage in risk-benefit analysis. So where does Surowiecki stand? While he seems unhappy with juries who award millions — even billions — to individual plaintiffs, he sees the companies as culpable too, aggressively marketing drugs to millions of people who may not really need them.

Reading this essay reminded me what big business drugs are in this country and how much responsibility consumers need to take in learning about drugs and their side effects before taking them. For some years, I've been developing osteoarthritis, and I remember watching a late-night talk show devoted completely to Vioxx: one Hollywood star after another came on to tell before-and-after stories, each of which featured Vioxx as the hero. "Ask your doctor about Vioxx," the commercials all said. And so I did — and my doctor prescribed the drug for me. I asked only one question — would Vioxx be easier on my stomach than other painkillers — and was assured that the answer was yes. Luckily for me, I had a visible allergic reaction to the drug and stopped taking it after just a week. Next time I will be a lot more careful.   —A.L.

In the business world, bad news is usually good news — for somebody else. Ever since Merck announced, this past fall, that the pain reliever Vioxx could be linked to an increased risk of strokes or heart attacks, ads from lawyers trolling for potential plaintiffs ("Hire a Texas Vioxx lawyer," "Vioxx injury claims") have become ubiquitous on the Internet and cable television. Merck is already defending itself against almost five hundred lawsuits, and the number is expected to soar in the next few months. One Wall Street analyst has estimated that the company could face a total bill of more than fifty billion dollars. The impending parade of jury verdicts and out-of-court settlements may render a kind of rough justice. But you may not realize just how rough.

In recent years, juries have become more willing to punish corporate offenders by issuing immense damage awards. According to the Harvard law professor W. Kip Viscusi, more than half of all "blockbuster awards" — those totalling more than a hundred million dollars — have been decided since 1999. The system that produces these awards is often perplexingly arbitrary. Where a case is tried, for instance, can have an enormous effect on how much a company ends up paying. (Two states, Texas and California, have been responsible for almost half of all blockbuster awards.) Nor is the level of scientific rigor in such cases always high: litigation over silicon breast implants cost Dow Corning $2.3 billion and forced it into bankruptcy even though the implants have never been proved to cause immune disorders, as plaintiffs alleged.

Merck would seem to have one big thing in its favor: the company voluntarily withdrew Vioxx from the market. But while Merck executives may have hoped to persuade people that they were acting responsibly, plaintiffs' attorneys have taken the withdrawal as an admission of guilt. Questions about Vioxx's potential risks have been common since its introduction, six years ago, especially after a 2000 trial suggested that the drug increased the risk of heart disease. Merck did not hide these data, and beginning in 2002 the drug's label included a warning about the possible cardiovascular risks. Some critics, however, have suggested that the company soft-pedalled the dangers. Internal company documents show that Merck employees were debating the safety of the drug for years before the recall.

From a scientific perspective, this is hardly damning. The internal debates about the drug's safety were just that — debates, with different scientists arguing for and against the drug. The simple fact that Vioxx might have risks wasn't reason to recall it, since the drug also had an important benefit: it was less likely to cause the internal bleeding that aspirin and ibuprofen cause, and that kills thousands of people a year. And there's no clear evidence that Merck kept selling Vioxx after it decided that the drug's dangers outweighed its benefits.

While that kind of weighing of risk and benefit may be medically rational, in the legal arena it's poison. Nothing infuriates juries like finding out that companies knew about dangers and then "balanced" them away. In fact, any kind of risk-benefit analysis, honest or not, is likely to get you in trouble with juries. In 1999, for instance, jurors in California ordered General Motors to pay $4.8 billion

5

to people who were injured when the gas tank in their 1979 Chevrolet Malibu caught fire. The jurors made it plain that they did so because G.M. engineers had calculated how much it would cost to move the gas tank (which might have made the car safer). Viscusi has shown that people are inclined to award heftier punitive damages against a company that had performed a risk analysis before selling a product than a company that didn't bother to. Even if the company puts a very high value on each life, the fact that it has weighed costs against benefits is, in itself, reprehensible. "We're just numbers, I feel, to them" is how a juror in the G.M. case put it. "Statistics. That's something that is wrong."

In everyday life, of course, we're always making trade-offs between safety and things like cost or convenience. There's not a car on the road that couldn't be made safer, if you didn't care about looks, mileage, cost, and so on. It's just that the trade-offs we make are seldom explicit: we don't tell ourselves that a sixty-five-mile-an-hour speed limit means a certain number of extra deaths, that buying this car instead of that car will affect our life expectancy — and, as individuals, we often don't see the costs. In the courtroom, the calculations can be seen in all their cold rationality, and the costs are vividly embodied. Before a jury, then, a firm is better off being ignorant than informed.

Obviously, there's something wrong with a system that discourages the careful weighing of costs against benefits — we want companies to learn as much as they can about the downsides of their products. But companies like Merck, which spend hundreds of millions on ads targeting consumers, have themselves to blame, too. Instead of getting people to think about drugs in terms of costs and benefits, these ads encourage people to think of medicine in the same way they think of other consumer goods. It would be one thing if Merck had marketed Vioxx only to people who really needed it — people who couldn't take ibuprofen or aspirin safely. Instead, the company marketed it aggressively to everyone, so that some twenty million Americans had Vioxx prescriptions. That's why the potential damages against Merck are so vast. If juries have a hard time accepting a risk-benefit trade-off when it comes to drugs, it's in part because the drug companies have convinced them that no such trade-off has to be made.

Reading across Disciplines
ROSEMARY THOMAS CUNNINGHAM,
Economics

As the prices of pharmaceuticals rise rapidly and become an increasing proportion of the amount consumers pay for health care, pharmaceutical companies are often portrayed as evil capitalists profiting at the expense of the customers' illnesses. Many see jury awards like those discussed in

James Surowiecki's article "Don't Do the Math" as justified because a product that was supposed to help instead caused harm. However, as any economist will explain, the pharmaceutical industry is special in many ways, and it is not clear how these jury awards will ultimately affect the general public. If we take the perspective that pharmaceutical companies are developers of a high-risk product, we can understand their high prices and high profit margins. However, their aggressive marketing strategy, which aims to circumvent the cautionary judgment of medical professionals, makes us more willing to extract penalties for problems that emerge.

One of the special features of the pharmaceutical industry is that it faces large initial fixed costs in developing a drug. As Surowiecki explains, part of the high initial costs come from the expense involved in doing substantial testing aimed at trying to understand the potential risks of new drugs. Yet, as Merck discovered, firms can be penalized for investigating the potential risks. Many firms try to perform a balancing act, researching enough of the risks to justify approval by the U.S. Food and Drug Administration — but not enough to reveal potentially disastrous defects. Consumers need pharmaceutical companies to continue to research the development of potentially life-saving and life-improving drugs, but the companies may need more incentive to provide full knowledge of the risks involved. It would help if FDA approval was not seen as a barrier for pharmaceutical companies to hurdle but as an indication that all possible testing has been done and known side-effects have been identified.

After successfully bringing a drug to market, the drug company has a monopoly on that patent and a powerful incentive to market the drug aggressively: the more successful the marketing campaign, the larger the profit to the firm. The *New York Times* reported in June 2004 that "drug companies spend twice as much marketing medicines as they do researching them." When a pharmaceutical company makes aggressive efforts to market its drug, the company targets both physicians and consumers. But consumers usually turn to a physician for help in making a complex drug decision. So doctors may feel pressure to prescribe a drug both from their patients (who have seen television and magazine advertisements) and from drug-company representatives. Of course, doctors should be able to resist pressure to dispense a drug that they do not consider the best treatment for the patient, but they are, after all, human. So high jury awards may indeed be an appropriate response if they serve to discourage marketing strategies that may adversely affect consumers.

Much of the increase in the quality of life that we have experienced over the last century is due the introduction of life-saving and life-improving drugs. Jury awards may be warranted in cases where companies knew of significant health risks associated with their drugs and did little to address, or worse, hid, these negative side effects. However, we need to find ways to encourage pharmaceutical companies to develop new and better drugs while providing incentives for these companies to research and reveal any problems. Finally, the FDA must ensure that the marketing strategies of pharmaceutical companies rely more on providing accurate information and less on persuasion.

Rosemary Thomas Cunningham is a professor of economics at Agnes Scott College in Decatur, Georgia.

QUESTIONING THE TEXT

1. What would you say is Surowiecki's primary argument? Restate his major claim in one sentence, using your own words.

2. To what degree do you think that Surowiecki sympathizes with businesses that juries force to pay "blockbuster claims"? How can you determine what his sympathies are? Point to specific textual evidence that leads to your conclusions.

MAKING CONNECTIONS

3. Both Surowiecki and Jonah Goldberg, in "Global Cooling Costs Too Much" (p. 686), emphasize the importance of trade-offs and cost-benefit analysis. Which author do you think makes better use of this idea in creating a persuasive argument?

4. Surowiecki quotes a juror from the General Motors case as saying, "We're just numbers, I feel, to them" (paragraph 5). How does Eric Schlosser's "The Most Dangerous Job" (p. 654) explore similar concerns about corporate ethics? To what degree can corporations contribute to a culture in which work constitutes a central part of one's identity, as Dagoberto Gilb describes in "Work Union" (p. 650)?

JOINING THE CONVERSATION

5. As Surowiecki emphasizes, trade-offs are part of everything in our lives. Research the history of some of the "blockbuster awards" that Professor Viscusi has studied and see what trade-offs these huge lawsuits entail. For example, how much of their reward do most plaintiffs see? How do these lawsuits affect other business practices?

6. What kind of costs — beyond the price of tuition — does going to college have? What are the trade-offs in, for example, owning a car (or any other object) that you value greatly? Write an essay in which you reflect on a trade-off that you have made in your own life or in which you consider how something mostly positive still has its costs.

VIRGINIA POSTREL
In Praise of Chain Stores

Looking for a paper topic? Take an idea that everyone seems to agree on — Wal-Mart destroys small-town commerce, fast food makes kids fat, teachers are underpaid, urban sprawl is bad — and consider the case to be made for the other, often unfashionable, side of the argument. Author and columnist Virginia Postrel (b. 1960) shows how to do exactly that in "In Praise of Chain Stores," a column that challenges the knee-jerk notion that the spread of chain stores across suburban and small-town America is blighting the landscape and making America unvarying and uninteresting, "the most boring country to tour."

Postrel begins by laying out the almost ritualized charges, quoting respectable spokesmen mouthing the familiar complaints of blandness and predictability in American towns caused by shopping malls and strips dominated by the same clusters of national chains. In case we don't understand the complaint, she runs through the roster of offending stores, a list we surely all recognize — and to which we could easily contribute a dozen more names.

Then Postrel begins her demolition of the conventional wisdom, point by point. She highlights the absurdity in thinking that Chandler, Arizona, surrounded by desert landscapes, is no different from, say, frigid Ashtabula, Ohio, or ocean-lapped Naples, Florida.

And how about those much-lamented mom-and-pop enterprises supposedly overwhelmed by the chains? Were they really all they were cracked up to be? And aren't the critics of the chains, usually people living in urban centers with lots of shopping options, underestimating the services and opportunities that national stores bring to more remote American communities? And what about the way people in the towns experience their bland malls and repetitive chains? Maybe they find the shopping experiences there more satisfying than the critics of chain stores might imagine.

An inventive argument like Postrel's invites us to be skeptical about any claims we hear so often that we begin to take them on faith. But it also reminds us, perhaps, that we should be no less suspicious of clever challenges to received wisdom. A critical thinker like Postrel likely wouldn't want it any other way.

A contributor to the Atlantic Monthly *and* Forbes, *Virginia Postrel was editor of* Reason *magazine from 1989–2000 and is the author of an influential book on design,* The Substance of Style: How the Rise of Aesthetic Value Is Remaking Commerce *(2003).* —J.R.

Every well-traveled cosmopolite knows that America is mind-numbingly monotonous — "the most boring country to tour, because everywhere looks like everywhere else," as the columnist Thomas Friedman once told Charlie Rose. Boston has the same stores as Denver, which has the same stores as Charlotte or Seattle or Chicago. We live in a "Stepford world," says Rachel

Dresbeck, the author of *Insiders' Guide to Portland, Oregon*. Even Boston's historic Faneuil Hall, she complains, is "dominated by the Gap, Anthropologie, Starbucks, and all the other usual suspects. Why go anywhere? Every place looks the same." This complaint is more than the old worry, dating back to the 1920s, that the big guys are putting Mom and Pop out of business. Today's critics focus less on what isn't there — Mom and Pop — than on what is. Faneuil Hall actually has plenty of locally owned businesses, from the Geoclassics store selling minerals and jewelry, to Pizzeria Regina ("since 1926"). But you do find the same chains everywhere.

The suburbs are the worst. Take Chandler, Arizona, just south of Phoenix. At Chandler Fashion Center, the area's big shopping mall, you'll find P. F. Chang's, California Pizza Kitchen, Chipotle Mexican Grill, and the Cheesecake Factory. Drive along Chandler's straight, flat boulevards, and you'll see Bed Bath & Beyond and Linens-n-Things; Barnes & Noble and Borders; PetSmart and Petco; Circuit City and Best Buy; Lowe's and Home Depot; CVS and Walgreens. Chandler has the Apple Store and Pottery Barn, the Gap and Ann Taylor, Banana Republic and DSW, and, of course, Target and Wal-Mart, Starbucks and McDonald's. For people allergic to brands, Chandler must be hell — even without the 110-degree days.

One of the fastest-growing cities in the country, Chandler is definitely the kind of place urbanists have in mind as they intone, "When every place looks the same, there is no such thing as place anymore." Like so many towns in America, it has lost much of its historic character as a farming community. The annual Ostrich Festival still honors one traditional product, but these days Chandler raises more subdivisions and strip malls than ostrich plumes or cotton, another former staple. Yet it still refutes the common assertion that national chains are a blight on the landscape, that they've turned American towns into an indistinguishable "geography of nowhere."

The first thing you notice in Chandler is that, as a broad empirical claim, the cliché that "everywhere looks like everywhere else" is obvious nonsense. Chandler's land and air and foliage are peculiar to the desert Southwest. The people dress differently. Even the cookie-cutter housing developments, with their xeriscaping and washed-out desert palette, remind you where you are. Forget New England clapboard, Carolina columns, or yellow Texas brick. In the intense sun of Chandler, the red-tile roofs common in California turn a pale, pale pink.

Stores don't give places their character. Terrain and weather and culture do.   5 Familiar retailers may take some of the discovery out of travel — to the consternation of journalists looking for obvious local color — but by holding some of the commercial background constant, chains make it easier to discern the real differences that define a place: the way, for instance, that people in Chandler come out to enjoy the summer twilight, when the sky glows purple and the dry air cools.

Besides, the idea that America was once filled with wildly varied business establishments is largely a myth. Big cities could, and still can, support more retail niches than small towns. And in a less competitive national market, there was certainly more variation in business efficiency — in prices, service, and merchandise quality. But the range of retailing ideas in any given town was rarely that great. One deli or diner or lunch counter or cafeteria was pretty much like every other one. A hardware store was a hardware store, a pharmacy a pharmacy. Before it became a ubiquitous part of urban life, Starbucks was, in most American cities, a radically new idea.

Chains do more than bargain down prices from suppliers or divide fixed costs across a lot of units. They rapidly spread economic discovery — the scarce and costly knowledge of what retail concepts and operational innovations actually work. That knowledge can be gained only through the expensive and time-consuming process of trial and error. Expecting each town to independently invent every new business is a prescription for real monotony, at least for the locals. Chains make a large range of choices available in more places. They increase local variety, even as they reduce the differences from place to place. People who mostly stay put get to have experiences once available only to frequent travelers, and this loss of exclusivity is one reason why frequent travelers are the ones who complain. When Borders was a unique Ann Arbor institution, people in places like Chandler — or, for that matter, Philadelphia and Los Angeles — didn't have much in the way of bookstores. Back in 1986, when California Pizza Kitchen was an innovative local restaurant about to open its second location, food writers at the *L. A. Daily News* declared it "the kind of place every neighborhood should have." So what's wrong if the country has 158 neighborhood CPKs instead of one or two?

The process of multiplication is particularly important for fast-growing towns like Chandler, where rollouts of established stores allow retail variety to expand as fast as the growing population can support new businesses. I heard the same refrain in Chandler that I've heard in similar boomburgs elsewhere, and for similar reasons. "It's got all the advantages of a small town, in terms of being friendly, but it's got all the things of a big town," says Scott Stephens, who moved from Manhattan Beach, California, in 1998 to work for Motorola. Chains let people in a city of 250,000 enjoy retail amenities once available only in a huge metropolitan center. At the same time, familiar establishments make it easier for people to make a home in a new place. When Nissan recently moved its headquarters from Southern California to Tennessee, an unusually high percentage of its Los Angeles–area employees accepted the transfer. "The fact that Starbucks are everywhere helps make moving a lot easier these days," a rueful Greg Whitney, vice president of business development for the Los Angeles County Economic Development Corporation, told the *Los Angeles Times* reporter John O'Dell. Orth Hedrick, a Nissan product manager, decided he could stay with the job he loved when he turned off the interstate near Nashville and realized, "You could really be Anywhere, U.S.A. There's a great big regional shopping mall, and most of the stores and restaurants are the same ones we see in California. Yet a few miles away you're in downtown, and there's lots of local color, too."

Contrary to the rhetoric of bored cosmopolites, most cities don't exist primarily to please tourists. The children toddling through the Chandler mall hugging their soft Build-A-Bear animals are no less delighted because kids can also build a bear in Memphis or St. Louis. For them, this isn't tourism; it's life — the experiences that create the memories from which the meaning of a place arises over time. Among Chandler's most charming sights are the business-casual dads joining their wives and kids for lunch in the mall food court. The food isn't the point, let alone whether it's from Subway or Dairy Queen. The restaurants merely provide the props and setting for the family time. When those kids grow up, they'll remember the food court as happily as an older generation recalls the diners and motels of Route 66 — not because of the businesses' innate appeal but because of the memories they evoke.

The contempt for chains represents a brand-obsessed view of place, as if   10
store names were all that mattered to a city's character. For many critics, the name on the store really is all that matters. The planning consultant Robert Gibbs works with cities that want to revive their downtowns, and he also helps developers find space for retailers. To his frustration, he finds that many cities actually turn away national chains, preferring a moribund downtown that seems authentically local. But, he says, the same local activists who oppose chains "want specialty retail that sells exactly what the chains sell — the same price, the same fit, the same qualities, the same sizes, the same brands, even." You can show people pictures of a Pottery Barn with nothing but the name changed, he says, and they'll love the store. So downtown stores stay empty, or sell low-value tourist items like candles and kites, while the chains open on the edge of town. In the name of urbanism, officials and activists in cities like Ann Arbor and Fort Collins, Colorado, are driving business to the suburbs. "If people like shopping at the Banana Republic or the Gap, if that's your market — or Payless Shoes — why not?" says an exasperated Gibbs. "Why not sell the goods and services people want?"

QUESTIONING THE TEXT

1. Postrel establishes the importance of her argument by first defending chain stores against the attacks often leveled against them. Reread the article and locate Postrel's positive claims that praise chain stores. Why are chain stores more than just "not dangerous" to a community? What makes them good in Postrel's eyes?

2. What values does Postrel appeal to in this article? What does she believe that her audience finds most important in the stores that they want to go to? What does she suggest are the important things in building a life?

MAKING CONNECTIONS

3. Postrel states clearly whom she disagrees with: those she calls "well-traveled cosmopolites" and "bored cosmopolites" (paragraphs 2 and 9). Compare Postrel's characterization of those with whom she disagrees to the way that John Leo in "Free Inquiry? Not on Campus" (p. 592) and Jonah Goldberg in "Global Cooling Costs Too Much" (p. 686) treat thinkers with opposing ideas. Who is most respectful of disagreement? Whose treatment of alternative claims do you feel most effectively enhances his or her argument?

4. Postrel is the former editor of *Reason*, a magazine of libertarian ideas, and overall she strongly values capitalism. What other writers in this section do you think defend capitalism? Which authors seem to question or attack capitalist values? Discuss your opinions with a classmate and be prepared to talk about your ideas in class.

JOINING THE CONVERSATION

5. According to Postrel, "terrain and weather and culture" are what give character to a place (paragraph 5). Write an essay in which you describe the most important elements in creating the character of the place that you live in or another place that you know well.

6. What is your experience with chain stores? Have they helped or hurt a town that you live in or have visited and know well? Are there any chain stores that you particularly like or dislike? In a brief essay of praise or blame, explain what you think about a chain store that you have been to, and why you continue to go there or why you don't. If applicable, you might consider comparing a chain store to a similar locally owned store.

JONAH GOLDBERG
Global Cooling Costs Too Much

*O*NE OF THESE DAYS *at a departmental meeting I'm going to urge my mostly left-wing colleagues to take their environmental commitments seriously and agree to give up air travel to professional conferences and conventions. Why contribute to global warming by boarding yet another stratosphere-despoiling 767 or Airbus to yet another academic pow-wow in New York or San Francisco or (whoopee!) England or Spain? The fact is that everything substantive about such meetings (the lectures, professional papers, and intellectual give-and-take) can now be experienced with a much lighter carbon footprint via the Internet — except, of course, for the subsidized hotels, the four-star restaurants, the hallway gossip, the museum tours, the theater, the shopping, the bookstores. . . .*

Ay, there's the global warming rub that Jonah Goldberg (b. 1969) examines in "Global Cooling Costs Too Much," a brief exploratory essay posted to the conservative National Review Online *on February 9, 2007. Goldberg argues that Westerners are being asked to give up way too much of their hard-won pursuit of happiness for tenuous environmental benefits. Just try to tow your Jet Ski Ultra with a Prius.*

Like many op-ed pieces, Goldberg's essay chooses facts and incidents selectively to prop up broad claims that would, in other circumstances, require far more research and documentation. But the point of many an essay is to try out ideas, and Goldberg deserves credit for stirring the pot, asking readers to be honest about their environmental choices. Don't expect academics — or environmentalists, for that matter — to give up their globe-trotting anytime soon.

—J.R.

Public policy is all about trade-offs. Economists understand this better than politicians because voters want to have their cake and eat it too, and politicians think whatever is popular must also be true.

Economists understand that if we put a chicken in every pot, it might cost us an aircraft carrier or a hospital. We can build a hospital, but it might come at the expense of a little patch of forest. We can protect a wetland, but that will make a new school more expensive.

You get it already. But in the history of trade-offs, never has there been a better one than trading a tiny amount of global warming for a massive amount of global prosperity.

Earth got about 0.7 degrees Celsius warmer in the 20th century while it increased its GDP by 1,800 percent, by one estimate. How much of that 0.7 degrees can be laid at the feet of that 1,800 percent is unknowable, but let's stipulate that all of the warming was the result of our prosperity and that this warming is in fact indisputably bad (which is hardly obvious).

That's still an amazing bargain. Life expectancies in the United States   5
increased from about 47 years to about 77 years. Literacy, medicine, leisure and
even, in many respects, the environment have improved mightily over the
course of the 20th century, at least in the prosperous West.

Given the option of getting another 1,800 percent richer in exchange for
another 0.7 degrees warmer, I'd take the heat in a heartbeat. Of course, warming
might get more expensive for us (and we might get a lot richer than 1,800 percent
too). There are tipping points in every sphere of life, and what cost us little in the
20th century could cost us enormously in the 21st — at least that's what we're told.

And boy, are we told. We're (deceitfully) told polar bears are the canaries
in the global coal mine. Al Gore even hosts an apocalyptic infomercial on the
subject, complete with fancy renderings of New York City underwater.

Skeptics are heckled for calling attention to global warming scare tactics.
But the simple fact is that activists need to hype the threat, and not just because
that's what the media demand of them. Their proposed remedies cost so much
money — bidding starts at 1 percent of global GDP a year and rises quickly —
they have to ratchet up the fear factor just to get the conversation started.

The costs are just too high for too little payoff. Even if the Kyoto Proto-
col were put into effect tomorrow — a total impossibility — we'd barely affect
global warming. Jerry Mahlman of the National Center for Atmospheric
Research speculated in *Science* magazine that "it might take another 30 Kyotos
over the next century" to beat back global warming.

Thirty Kyotos! That's going to be tough considering that China alone   10
plans on building an additional 2,200 coal plants by 2030. Oh, but because
China (like India) is exempt from Kyoto as a developing country, the West will
just have to reduce its own emissions even more.

A more persuasive cost-benefit analysis hinges not on prophecies of
environmental doom but on geopolitics. We buy too much oil from places we
shouldn't, which makes us dependent on nasty regimes and makes those
regimes nastier.

Environmentalists like to claim the "energy independence" issue, but it's
not a neat fit. We could be energy independent soon enough with coal and
nuclear power. But coal contributes to global warming, and nuclear power is
icky. So, instead, we're going to massively subsidize the government-brewed
moonshine called ethanol.

Here again, the benefits barely outweigh the costs. Ethanol requires
almost as much energy to make as it provides, and the costs to the environment
and the economy may be staggering.

Frankly, I don't think the trade-off is worth it — yet. The history of
capitalism and technology tells us that what starts out expensive and arduous
becomes cheap and easy over time.

Lewis and Clark took months to do what a truck carrying Tickle-Me   15
Elmos does every week. Technology 10 years from now could solve global
warming at a fraction of today's costs. What technologies? I don't know. Maybe

fusion. Maybe hydrogen. Maybe we'll harness the perpetual motion of Sen. Joe Biden's mouth.

The fact is we can't afford to fix global warming right now, in part because poor countries want to get rich, too. And rich countries, where the global warming debate is settled, are finding even the first of 30 Kyotos too fiscally onerous. There are no solutions in the realm of the politically possible. So why throw trillions of dollars into "remedies" that even their proponents concede won't solve the problem?

QUESTIONING THE TEXT

1. How would you describe Goldberg's tone or attitude toward global warming? What about toward those who work to publicize the dangers of global warming? Point to specific passages to explain your reasoning.

2. Analyze Goldberg's use of evidence, particularly scientific and statistical evidence. What parts of his evidence do you find most persuasive? What is least persuasive? Do you trust his use of statistics? Why or why not?

MAKING CONNECTIONS

3. In paragraph 14 of his essay Goldberg writes, "The history of capitalism and technology tells us that what starts out expensive and arduous becomes cheap and easy over time." Look through the readings in Chapter 5, Science and Technology. Which authors there display a similar faith in the power of technology? Which have doubts? Which approach to the promise of technology do you find more appealing?

4. Imagine a conversation between Goldberg and Jeremy Rifkin, author of "Biotech Century: Playing Ecological Roulette with Mother Nature's Designs" (p. 311), on the dangers of global warming. How do you think that Rifkin would respond to Goldberg's idea that solutions cost too much? Write a one- or two-page dialogue between the two that illustrates how each would respond to the other's ideas.

JOINING THE CONVERSATION

5. One of the hallmarks of Goldberg's writing is the humor he builds through specific detail — consider, for example, the "truck carrying Tickle-Me Elmos" (paragraph 15). Write a short essay in which you take a humorous approach to a serious issue and use specific details to build the humor of your piece.

6. Where do you stand on global warming? Write a 750-word opinion piece, suitable for the op-ed page of a newspaper, that outlines your position.

MARGE PIERCY
To Be of Use

MARGE PIERCY (b. 1936) is remarkable by any standard: she is the author of over two dozen books of poetry (including The Moon Is Always Female *[1980] and* Mars and Her Children *[1992]) and fiction (including* Going Down Fast *[1969],* Woman on the Edge of Time *[1976],* Fly Away Home *[1984], and* He, She, and It *[1991]); a political activist (she helped organize Students for a Democratic Society in the 1960s); an ardent feminist; and a constant social critic. Piercy writes with passion and power that are hard to ignore. Often, her passion for justice and equity as well as for what she calls "work that is real" is born of hard experience. The child of often poor and working-class parents, Piercy (who is white and Jewish) grew up in a predominantly African American section of Detroit, where she learned firsthand about what she calls "the indifference of the rich, racism . . . the working-class pitted against itself." The first member of her family to attend college, she won a scholarship and graduated from the University of Michigan; she has contributed her prolific collection of manuscripts to its graduate library. Her recent books include* The Third Child: A Novel *(2003) and* Crooked Inheritance: Poems *(2006).*

Many of Piercy's poems get their power from a kind of pent-up rage that explodes on the page in front of her readers. In fact, I first got to know her work through just such poems, a number of which (like "Barbie Doll," which appeared in the first edition of this book) haunt me still. But Piercy can be hopeful, even celebratory, as well. And in the following poem from To Be of Use *(1973), she is both, defining in vivid images and rhythmic cadences "work that is real." This is one of only four poems I carry with me always.*   —A.L.

The people I love the best
jump into work head first
without dallying in the shallows
and swim off with sure strokes almost out of sight.
They seem to become natives of that element,   5
the black sleek heads of seals
bouncing like half-submerged balls.

I love people who harness themselves, an ox to a heavy cart,
who pull like water buffalo, with massive patience,
who strain in the mud and the muck to move things forward,   10
who do what has to be done, again and again.

I want to be with people who submerge
in the task, who go into the fields to harvest

and work in a row and pass the bags along,
who stand in the line and haul in their places,   15
who are not parlor generals and field deserters
but move in a common rhythm
when the food must come in or the fire be put out.

The work of the world is common as mud.
Botched, it smears the hands, crumbles to dust.   20
But the thing worth doing well done
has a shape that satisfies, clean and evident.
Greek amphoras for wine or oil,
Hopi vases that held corn, are put in museums
but you know they were made to be used.   25
The pitcher cries for water to carry
and a person for work that is real.

IN RESPONSE

1. Piercy says work that is worth doing "has a shape that satisfies, clean and evident" (line 22). Think for a while about examples you could give of such work. Reflect on them and on your relationship to and feelings about them in a journal entry. If you keep a reading log, record your responses there.

2. Try your hand at adding a stanza to this poem, after the second stanza. Begin with the words "I love people who . . . ." Bring your stanza to class to share with others.

3. Which writers in this chapter might Piercy see as doing "work that is real"? In a brief exploratory essay, give reasons for your choices.

Acknowledgments

Sherman Alexie. "What Sacagawea Means to Me." First published in *Time*, June 30, 2002. Copyright © 2002 Time, Inc. Reprinted with permission in the format Textbook by Copyright Clearance Center.

K. Anthony Appiah. "College Makeover: Learn Statistics. Go Abroad." Originally published in *Slate*, November 15, 2005. Copyright © 2005 by K. Anthony Appiah. Reprinted by permission of the author.

Susanna Ashton. "Making Peace with the Greeks." *The Chronicle of Higher Education*, November 17, 2006. Copyright © 2006, The Chronicle of Higher Education. Reprinted with permission.

Margaret Atwood. "Letter to America." Copyright © 2003, O.W. Toad Ltd. Originally published in *The Globe and Mail*. Included in the anthologies *Writing with Intent*, published in the U.S. by Carroll and Graf, and *Moving Targets*, published in Canada by House of Anansi Press. Reprinted by permission of Margaret Atwood.

Naomi Barko. Reprinted with permission from Naomi Barko, "The Other Gender Gap: Why Women Still Fail to Receive Comparable Wages for Comparable Work," *The American Prospect*, Volume 11, Number 5: June 19, 2000. The American Prospect, 2000 L Street NW, Suite 717, Washington, DC 20036. All rights reserved.

Dave Barry. Excerpts from "Guys vs. Men." The preface to Dave Barry's *Complete Guide to Guys: A Fairly Short Book* by Dave Barry. Copyright © 1995 by Dave Barry. Used by permission of Random House, Inc.

Lynda Barry. "Common Scents" from *One! Hundred! Demons!* Copyright © 2002. Reprinted with permission of Darhansoff Verrill Feldman Literary Agents.

Berea College Mission Statement. Reprinted by permission.

J. Michael Bishop. "Enemies of Promise." Originally published in the *Wilson Quarterly* (Summer 1995). Copyright © 1995 by J. Michael Bishop. Reprinted with permission.

Keith Bradsher. "Reptile Dreams." From *High and Mighty* by Keith Bradsher. Copyright © 2002 Keith Bradsher. Reprinted by permission of PUBLIC AFFAIRS, a member of Perseus Books Group.

David Brooks. "One Nation, Slightly Divisible." Reprinted from *The Atlantic*, December 2001. Reprinted by permission of David Brooks, c/o Writers Representatives, LLC. All rights reserved.

Gwendolyn Brooks. "We Real Cool" from *Blacks* (Chicago, IL: Third World Press, 1991). Reprinted by consent of Brooks Permissions.

The California State University Mission statement. © 2006 California State University. Reprinted by permission.

Stephen Carter. From *INTEGRITY* by Stephen Carter. Copyright © by Basic Books, a member of Perseus Books Group.

Michael Chorost. "My Bionic Quest for *Boléro*: He's Been Haunted by Ravel's Masterpiece Since He Lost His Hearing. A Deaf Man's Pursuit of the Perfect Audio Upgrade," *Wired*. Copyright © 2007. Reprinted by permission of the author.

Mark Clayton. "Whole Lot of Cheatin' Going On." Reproduced with permission from the January 19, 1999 issue of *The Christian Science Monitor*. Copyright © 1999 by *The Christian Science Monitor*. All rights reserved.

Index